D0142572

ITALIA
(Carta Politica)
SCALA DI CHILOMETRI
0 40 80 120 160
SCALA DI MIGLIA
0 20 40 60 80 100
SVIZZERA
AUSTRIA
UNGHERIA
SLOVENIA
CROAZIA
SERBIA
BOSNIA-ERZEGOVINA
MONTENEGRO
FRANCIA
TRENTINO-ALTO ADIGE
FRIULI-VENEZIA GIULIA
VALLE D'AOSTA
LOMBARDIA
VENETO
PIEMONTE
EMILIA-ROMAGNA
LIGURIA
REPUBBLICA DI SAN MARINO
MARCHE
TOSCANA
UMBRIA
LAZIO
ABRUZZI
MOLISE
CAMPANIA
PUGLIA
BASILICATA
CALABRIA
SICILIA
SARDEGNA
Corsica (FRANCIA)
Trento
Udine
Trieste
Como
Milano
Brescia
Mantova
Verona
Padova
Venezia
Torino
Asti
Parma
Ferrara
Bologna
Ravenna
Genova
La Spezia
San Remo
Pisa
Firenze
Arezzo
Siena
Urbino
Ancona
Perugia
Assissi
Orvieto
Elba
Roma
L'Aquila
Campobasso
Napoli
Pompei
Amalfi
Bari
Potenza
Taranto
Sassari
Cagliari
Cosenza
Isole Lipari
Messina
Reggio
Palermo
Marsala
Taormina
Catania
Agrigento
Siracusa
Tunisi
ALGERIA
TUNISIA
AFRICA
MARE LIGURE
MARE ADRIATICO
MARE TIRRENO
MARE IONIO
MARE MEDITERRANEO

EUROPA
(Carta Politica)
SCALA DI CHILOMETRI
0 100 200 400 600
SCALA DI MIGLIA
0 50 100 200 300
30°
20°
10°
0°
10°
20°
60°
Reykjavik
ISLANDA
OCEANO ATLANTICO
NORVEGIA
SVEZIA
FINLANDIA
Oslo
Stoccolma
MARE BALTICO
LETTONIA
LITUANIA
RUSSIA
DANIMARCA
Copenhagen
MARE DEL NORD
IRLANDA
Dublino

Londra
Amsterdam
PAESI BASSI
Berlino
Varsavia
Bruxelles
BELGIO
GERMANIA
POLONIA
LUSSEMBURGO
Praga
Parigi
REPUBBLICA CECA
SLOVACCHIA
OCEANO ATLANTICO
Vaduz
Vienna
Bratislava
AUSTRIA
Berna
LIECHTENSTEIN
FRANCIA
SVIZZERA
Budapest
UNGHERIA
Lubiana
SLOVENIA
Zagabria
CROAZIA
ITALIA
Belgrado
Sarajevo
BOSNIA-ERZEGOVINA
SERBIA
ANDORRA
PORTOGALLO
MARE ADRIATICO
Madrid
Roma
MONTENEGRO
Tirana
SPAGNA
ALBANIA
GRECIA
MARE MEDITERRANEO
Rabat
Algeri
Tunisi
MARE IONIO
MAROCCO
ALGERIA
TUNISIA

ITALIA
(Carta Fisica)
SCALA DI CHILOMETRI
0 40 80 120 160
SCALA DI MIGLIA
0 20 40 60 80 100
A L P I
A P P E N N I N I
SVIZZERA
AUSTRIA
UNGHERIA
SLOVENIA
CROAZIA
SERBIA
BOSNIA-ERZEGOVINA
MONTENEGRO
FRANCIA
ALGERIA
TUNISIA
A F R I C A
Monte Cervino
Monte Bianco
Lago Maggiore
Lago di Como
Lago di Garda
Cortina
Piave
Venezia
Adige
Po
Milano
Torino
Taro
Reno
Genova
Rapallo
Bologna
Viareggio
Rimini
Pisa
Firenze
Arno
Ombrone
Tevere
Roma
ELBA
Corsica (FRANCIA)
MARE LIGURE
MARE ADRIATICO
MARE TIRRENO
Volturno
Vesuvio
Napoli
Pompei
ISCHIA
CAPRI
Alberobello
Taranto
Agri
Coghinas
SARDEGNA
Tirso
Flumendosa
Mannu
Palermo
Belice
NEBRODI
Etna
Dittaino
SICILIA
MARE IONIO
M A R E M E D I T E R R A N E O

Ciao!

third edition

Ciao!

third edition

Carla Federici
PROFESSOR EMERITUS
SAN JOSE STATE UNIVERSITY

Carla Larese Riga
FOOTHILL–DE ANZA COLLEGE

HOLT, RINEHART AND WINSTON, INC.
HARCOURT BRACE COLLEGE PUBLISHERS

FORT WORTH PHILADELPHIA SAN DIEGO NEW YORK
ORLANDO AUSTIN SAN ANTONIO TORONTO MONTREAL
LONDON SIDNEY TOKYO

Publisher: Ted Buchholz
Senior Acquisitions Editor: Jim Harmon
Developmental Editor: Nancy Geilen
Production Manager: Erin Gregg
Photo Research Editor: Judy Mason
Illustrator: Susan Jones
Text Design: Vee Sawyer, Monotype Editorial Services Group
Cover Design: Jim Dodson
Project Management: Monotype Editorial Services Group
Composition and Pre-press: Monotype Composition Company

Photo and literary credits appear on page 509.

Requests for permission to make copies of any part of the work should be mailed to: Permissions Department, Harcourt Brace & Company, 8th Floor, Orlando, Florida 32887.

Address for editorial correspondence: Harcourt Brace College Publishers, 301 Commerce Street, Suite 3700, Fort Worth, Texas, 76412.

Address for orders: Harcourt Brace & Company, 6277 Sea Harbor Drive, Orlando, Florida, 32887.
Tel: 1-800-782-4479, or 1-800-443-0001.

Library of Congress Cataloging-in-Publication Data

Federici, Carla.
Ciao! / Carla Federici, Carla Larese Riga. — 3rd ed.
p. cm.
English and Italian.
Includes index.
ISBN 0-15-500645-2
1. Italian language—Textbooks for foreign speakers—English.
I. Riga, Carla Larese. II. Title.
PC1128.F43 1994
458.2'421—dc20 93-37214
CIP

ISBN: 0-15-500645-2

Printed in the United States of America.

3 4 5 6 7 8 9 0 1 2 048 9 8 7 6 5 4 3 2 1

This book is printed on acid-free paper.

TO MARIO

C.F.

TO MY DAUGHTERS,

LILIANA AND ROBERTA

C.L.R.

PREFACE

Ciao!, Third Edition, is a beginning Italian textbook that emphasizes active and practical use of the language while teaching the four language skills. The *Ciao!* program consistently provides students with opportunities for self-expression and interaction in simple, but genuine Italian. It is designed to put them in touch not only with the language but also with the daily life and culture of the Italian people.

Each chapter of *Ciao!* is easily identifiable both by its theme and its grammar content. Each chapter title announces that chapter's particular theme, which is introduced and amplified in the opening *Punti di vista* section, then reflected and expanded upon throughout the chapter. This emphasis allows students to assimilate the vocabulary gradually, proceeding from practical and limited situations to broader and more abstract ones.

A similar "crescendo" pattern distinguishes the presentation of grammatical structures. Everyone is aware of the difficulties and frustrations that beginning language students experience while trying to assimilate many new concepts in a short period of time. In the first two chapters, students are introduced gradually to basic concepts: nouns; articles; adjectives; the present of **essere** and **avere.** The pace allows students to feel comfortable while mastering the new structures and thus encourages them to express themselves with confidence from the start. This effort to grade the sequence of grammatical structures is consistent throughout the entire program. Whenever possible, the presentation of each main grammatical topic has been confined to a single chapter in order to avoid dispersion and to facilitate the student's task of reviewing a given structure.

The program's organization and content are such that they can be adapted to different teaching situations, and may be used by instructors who desire to focus on particular skills. Because of its flexibility, the program can be used successfully at the high school and college or university level.

ORGANIZATION OF THE THIRD EDITION OF *CIAO!*

The core of *Ciao!, Third Edition,* consists of 20 chapters, each comprising the following sections:

PUNTI DI VISTA

An opening dialogue presents each chapter's theme in a simple, realistic, and lively situation. The dialogue provides further practice of previously learned concepts while introducing new ones. The difficulty of the latter is minimized through judicious use of marginal glosses. The *Studio di parole* introduces related theme vocabulary, which is in turn further amplified in the *Ascoltiamo!* section, based on a second dialogue on cassette. Related exercises and activities complement the two dialogues and the *Studio di parole* and sustain and reinforce reading, speaking, and listening skills.

PUNTI GRAMMATICALI

The *Punti grammaticali* focus on the grammar topics informally introduced in the *Punti di vista.* Throughout this section, an effort is made to concentrate on the essential, and to explain grammar points in a clear, concise way. Each *punto grammaticale* is preceded by captioned drawings, which are a distinctive feature of the book. They serve as instructional devices by simplifying grammar visually and graphically and presenting it in a light vein. Abundant charts and examples also enhance the presentation. Exercises under the heading of *Pratica* are designed to develop control of new structures and self-confidence; they often involve exchanges between students.

LETTURA

This reading section recombines the chapter grammar and vocabulary. Readings deal with scenes from everyday life, and are enlivened by recurrent characters whose experiences and struggles arouse students' empathy. Comprehension and personal questions invite students' involvement with what has been read.

ATTIVITÀ SUPPLEMENTARI

These are follow-up activities, in the form of role-plays, interviews, discussion topics, directed conversations, descriptions, narrations, and translations. They provide additional structured opportunities for self-expression, creativity, and writing practice.

VOCABOLARIO

This vocabulary list contains all new words appearing in the chapter that are not covered in *Studio di parole.*

PAGINA CULTURALE

This final reading is related to the lexical theme of the chapter and offers a wealth of information on Italian life and culture. Although many words are glossed, this section is a challenge to the students because it encourages them to develop their ability to grasp ideas without relying on word-for-word translation. The instructor may use these cultural readings to prompt additional discussions about Italy's history, people, and culture.

The 20 chapters are preceded by a preliminary chapter, *Capitolo preliminare*, which deals with Italian pronunciation and cognates, and by a short section, *Introduzione*, which focuses mainly on common expressions of courtesy. The chapters are followed by appendices (*futuro anteriore*; *trapassato remoto*; verbs and expressions requiring a preposition before an infinitive; conjugation of verbs); vocabularies (Italian-English; English-Italian for translations); and an Index.

Throughout the text, an abundance of photos, drawings, and authentic Italian material provide a lively picture of Italy, its people, and its culture.

ANCILLARY MATERIALS

The combined **Workbook/Laboratory Manual** supplements the textbook. Both sections are coordinated, chapter by chapter, with *CIAO!, Third Edition* and with the **Audio Program**. The workbook section of the manual provides written exercises that review the full range of structures and vocabulary learned in each chapter of the textbook. It gives students the opportunity to work on their own and to deal further with specific problem areas. Immediate self-correction is possible through checking the **Answer Key** found at the end of the manual.

The laboratory section serves as a guide to the **Audio Program.** The exercises reinforce students' audio-oral skills, since they interact with native speakers in different activities, ranging from comprehension checks of dialogue and readings to exercises on basic forms and dictation. The lab section, like the workbook, corresponds directly to the textbook. The *Capitolo preliminare*, for instance, expands on the phonetic elements presented in the preliminary chapter of the textbook, and includes a series of pronunciation exerçises. Whenever students are expected to respond orally, the correct response is given by the speaker for immediate correction and repetition. The written dictation can be corrected by consulting the answer key found at the end of the manual.

Acknowledgments

The authors express their appreciation to Jim Harmon, Senior Acquisition's Editor, and Nancy Geilen, Foreign Language Developmental Editor, for their assistance throughout the project. They are greatly indebted to the

Developmental Editor, Barbara Lyons, for her critical supervision and for her invaluable suggestions. Their gratitude goes also to Professor Mario Federici for his constant assistance and encouragement during the preparation of this text. Special thanks are due to the staff of Monotype Composition whose creative expertise turned the manuscript into the present book. Finally, they would like to acknowledge the following reviewers who helped shape this text with their constructive comments:

Peter Alfieri, Salve Regina University; Deborah Contrada, University of Iowa; Patricia DeBellis, Muhlenberg College; Terry Edwards, The Florida State University; Richard Hilary, The Florida State University; Geremie Hoff, University of Missouri; Robin Pickering-Iazzi, University of Wisconsin–Milwaukee; Judy Raggi Moore, Emory University; Claretta Tonetti, Boston University; Roberta Waldbaum, University of Denver; James Ward, Michigan State University; Sebastian Cassarino, San José State University; Peter N. Pedroni, Miami University.

Carla Federici
Carla Larese Riga

Contents

Capitolo 1 La Città

Capitolo 2 Persone e personalità

Capitolo 3 All'università

Capitolo 4 A tavola

Capitolo 5 Attività e passatempi

Capitolo 6 La famiglia e i parenti

Capitolo 7 *Buon Viaggio*

Capitolo 8 *Tempo e denaro*

Capitolo 9 *Abiti e stagioni*

Capitolo 10 *In cucina*

Capitolo 11 Le vacanze

Capitolo 12 La politica

Capitolo 13 La casa

Capitolo 14 Mestieri e professioni

Capitolo 15 Paesi e paesaggi

Capitolo 16 Gli sport

Capitolo 17 Medici e pazienti

Capitolo 18 La macchina e l'ecologia

Capitolo 19 Mezzi di diffusione

Capitolo 20 Arte e teatro

Appendixes

Ciao!

third edition

CAPITOLO PRELIMINARE

Venezia. Basilica di Santa Maria della Salute, sul Canal Grande.

I. La pronuncia italiana

II. Parole affini per origine

I. LA PRONUNCIA ITALIANA

There are 21 letters in the Italian alphabet. The written forms and names are:

a	**a**	h	**acca**	q	**qu**
b	**bi**	i	**i**	r	**erre**
c	**ci**	l	**elle**	s	**esse**
d	**di**	m	**emme**	t	**ti**
e	**e**	n	**enne**	u	**u**
f	**effe**	o	**o**	v	**vu** (or **vi**)
g	**gi**	p	**pi**	z	**zeta**

Five additional letters appear in words of foreign origin:

j	**i lunga**	w	**doppia vu**	y	**ipsilon**
k	**cappa**	x	**ics** (or **i greca**)		

The following sections deal primarily with spelling-sound correspondences in Italian and their English equivalents. Listen carefully to your instructor and then repeat the examples. Practice the pronunciation exercises recorded on the tape which corresponds to the Preliminary Chapter; they have been devised to help you acquire good pronunciation. In describing Italian sounds, we will make use of the international phonetic symbols (given between slants). You will notice that spellings and sounds in Italian are almost always identical. This is particularly true of vowel sounds.

1. Vocali *Vowels*

In Italian, there are five basic vowel sounds that correspond to the five letters **a, e, i, o, u.** The pronunciation of **e** and **o** may vary slightly (closed or open sound)*. Contrary to English vowels, Italian vowels represent only one sound; they are never slurred or glided. When pronouncing them, lips, jaws, and tongue must be kept in the same tense position to avoid off-glide. The vowels will be presented according to their point of articulation, **i** being the first of the front vowels and **u** the last of the back vowels, as illustrated in the diagram below.

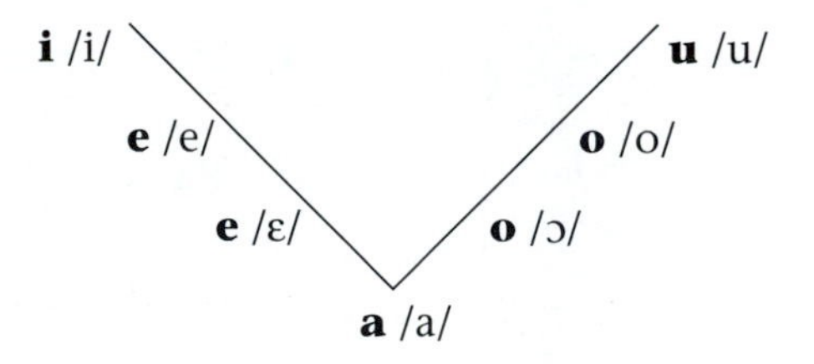

*Closed and open pronunciation of **e** and **o** are illustrated by the following words: **e** (and), **è** (is); **o** (or), **ho** (I have). The pronunciation of these two vowels often varies regionally.

i	/i/	is like *i* in *marine.*	I vini di Rịmini
e	/e/	is like *a* (without glide) in *late.*	Se Ebe vede te
e	/ɛ/	is like *e* in *let.*	Ecco sette fratelli
a	/a/	is like *a* in *father.*	La mia cara mamma
o	/ɔ/	is like *o* in *soft.*	Oggi no
o	/o/	is like *o* in *oh.*	Nome e cognome
u	/u/	is like *u* in *rule.*	Una mụsica pura

2. Dittonghi *Diphthongs*

When **i** and **u** are unstressed and precede or follow another vowel, they form with this vowel a diphthong and acquire the semivowel sounds /j/ and /w/.

i	/j/	is like *y* in *yet.*	Più piano	Lei e lui
u	/w/	is like the *u* in *wet.*	Un uomo buono	

When two semi-vowels combine with a vowel, they form a triphthong (**miei, tuoi, guai**).

The vowels that form a diphthong or a triphthong are pronounced with just one emission of voice and correspond to just one syllable.

3. Consonanti *Consonants*

Many single consonants are pronounced in Italian as they are in English. The sounds of the consonants **b**, **f**, **m**, **n**, and **v** present no difference in the two language. Several consonant sounds, however, need special attention because of the manner in which they are pronounced or the way they are spelled. In general, Italian consonants are clear-cut and without aspiration.

h is always silent:

ha hanno ahi! oh! hotel

d /d/ and **t** /t/ are similar to English but more dentalized:

due	denti	vado	grande	modo
tre	Tịvoli	alto	tempo	molto

p /p/ is as in English but less plosive:

papa Padova dopo piano parola

q /kw/ is always followed by the letter **u** and is pronounced like *qu* in *quest:*

qui quando Pasqua quale quaderno

l /l/ is produced more forward in the mouth than in English:

la lira lei libro lingua

r /r/ is trilled. It is pronounced by pointing the tip of the tongue toward the gum of the upper front teeth:

Roma caro treno amore vero

s /z/ is pronounced as in *rose* when it is between vowels or when it begins a word in combination with the voiced consonants **b**, **d**, **g**, **l**, **m**, **n**, **r**, and **v**:

rosa paese esame snob sviluppo

s is voiceless /s/ as in *sell* in all other cases:

sto stụdio destino rosso sera

z is sometimes voiced /dz/ as in *beds*, sometimes voiceless /ts/ as in *bets:*

/dz/		/ts/	
zero	romanzo	marzo	Venẹzia
zeta	mezzo	pizza	grạzie

c and **g** before **i** or **e** are soft /č/ , /ğ/ as in *chill* and *gentle:*

cento baci ciao Cẹsare cịnema
gesto gentile giorno viạggio pạgina

c and **g** in all other cases are hard /k/, /g/ as in *call* and *go:*

poco caffè caro amico cura classe scrịvere
pago guida lungo guerra gusto grosso dogma

ch and **gh** (found only before **e** or **i**) are also hard /k/, /g/:

che chi pochi perchè cuochi
aghi righe laghi ghetto paghiamo

gli /ʎ/ sounds approximately like **lli** in *million:*

gli fọglio fịglio famịglia vọglio

gn /ɲ/ sounds approximately like *ni* in *onion:*

ogni signora lavagna cognome insegnare

sc before **i** or **e** has a soft sound /š/ as in *shell:*

sciare pesce scienza scena scemo

sch before **i** or **e** sounds hard /sk/ as in *skill:*

schiavo schema dischi mosche maschio

4. Consonanti doppie *Double consonants*

Double consonants are a characteristic of Italian. The sound of a double consonant is longer then the sound of a single consonant. To pronounce it correctly, it is necessary to shorten the sound of the preceding vowel and hold the sound of the double consonant twice as long. (A similar phenomenon may also be observed in English when pronouncing pairs of words such as *miss school; met Tim.*) The reverse happens when pronouncing a single consonant. In this case one should keep the sound of the preceding vowel longer, especially if the vowel is stressed. Compare:

sono / sonno	sera / serra
casa / cassa	sano / sanno
rosa / rossa	camino / cammino
speso / spesso	lego / leggo

5. Sillabazione *Syllabication*

Phonetically, the tendency in Italian is, whenever possible, to begin the syllable with a consonant sound and to end it with a vowel sound. Grammatically, the separation of a word into syllables follows these rules:

a. A single consonant between two vowels belongs with the following vowel or diphthong.

a-ma-re	no-me	i-ta-lia-no	be-ne	le-zio-ne

b. Double consonants are always divided:

bel-lo	mez-zo	sil-la-ba	mam-ma	ra-gaz-za

c. A combination of two different consonants belongs with the following vowel, unless the first consonant is **l**, **m**, **n**, or **r**. In this case, the two consonants are divided:

pre-sto	so-pra	si-gno-ra	pri-ma	li-bro	
but: pron-to	gior-no	El-vi-ra	par-to	dor-mi	lam-po

d. In a combination of three consonants, the first goes with the preceding syllable, but **s** always goes with the following syllable:

al-tro	sem-pre	en-tra-re	im-pres-sio-ne		in-gle-se
but: fi-ne-stra	spre-mu-ta	gio-stra	sdra-io	e-sper-to	

e. Unstressed **i** and **u** are not divided from the vowel they combine with:

uó-mo	piá-no	pié-de	Gio-ván-ni		Eu-ró-pa
but: mí-o	zí-i	po-e-sí-a	pa-ú-ra		far-ma-cí-a

6. Accento tonico *Stress*

The great majority of Italian words are stressed on the next-to-the-last syllable:

signóra　　bambíno　　ragázzo　　cantáre　　veníre

Several words are stressed on the last syllable; these words have a written accent on the last vowel. Although the accent mark can be grave (`) or acute (´) , most Italians normally use the grave accent, and that practice is followed in this text.

città　　virtù　　perchè　　lunedì

A few monosyllabic words do not carry a stress mark except to distinguish two words that are spelled the same but have a different meaning:

e (*and*) vs. **è** (*is*)
da (*from*) vs. **dà** (*gives*)
te (*you*) vs. **tè** (*tea*)
si (*oneself*) vs. **sì** (*yes*)
se (*if*) vs. **sè** (*self*)
la (*the*) vs. **là** (*there*)

Some words have the stress on the third-from-the last syllable, and a few verb forms on the fourth-from-the-last syllable:

sábato　　cómpito　　távola　　diffícile　　diméticano

Note: When the stress does not fall on the next-to-the-last syllable or if the word ends in a diphthong, the stress has been indicated by a dot under the stressed syllable to help the student (Chapters 1–10):

fạcile　　spiạggia　　prạticano

7. Intonazione *Intonation*

In general, the Italian sentence follows a homogeneous rhythm. Each syllable is important in determining its tempo. Pronounce the following sentence maintaining smooth, even timing:

Sono Marcello Scotti.　　So - no - Mar - cel - lo - Scot - ti.
　　　　　　　　　　　　1　2　3　4　5　6　7

The voice normally follows a gently undulating movement, usually dropping toward the end when the meaning is completed. In a question, however, the voice rises on the last syllable:

Declarative sentence: I signori Bettini sono di Milano.

Interrogative sentence: Sono di Milano i signori Bettini?

II. PAROLE AFFINI PER ORIGINE *COGNATES*

While studying Italian, you will encounter many cognates, that is, an Italian word that looks like an English word and has a similar meaning because the words have a common origin. The following are a few tips that should help you recognize and use cognates.

1. Nouns ending in:

-ịa in Italian and *-y* in English.

biologia	*biology*	**filosofia**	*philosophy*
sociologia	*sociology*	**anatomia**	*anatomy*

-ica in Italian and *-ic(s)* in English.

mụsica	*music*	**polịtica**	*politics*
repụbblica	*republic*	**matemạtica**	*mathematics*

-tà in Italian and *-ty* in English.

città	*city*	**identità**	*identity*
società	*society*	**università**	*university*

-za in Italian and *-ce* in English.

importanza	*importance*	**eleganza**	*elegance*
violenza	*violence*	**pazienza**	*patience*

-zione in Italian and *-tion* in English.

nazione	*nation*	**attenzione**	*attention*
educazione	*education*	**situazione**	*situation*

-ore in Italian and *-or* in English.

attore	*actor*	**dottore**	*doctor*
professore	*professor*	**motore**	*motor*

-ạrio in Italian and *-ary* in English.

segretạrio	*secretary*	**vocabolạrio**	*vocabulary*
salạrio	*salary*	**funzionạrio**	*functionary*

-ista in Italian and *-ist* in English.

artista	*artist*	**violinista**	*violinist*
pianista	*pianist*	**ottimista**	*optimist*

2. Adjectives ending in:

-ale in Italian and *-al* in English.

speciale	*special*	**personale**	*personal*
originale	*original*	**sentimentale**	*sentimental*

-etto in Italian and *-ect* in English.

perfetto	*perfect*	**corretto**	*correct*
eretto	*erect*	**diretto**	*direct*

-ico in Italian and *-ical* in English.

tịpico	*typical*	**clạssico**	*classical*
polịtico	*political*	**geogrạfico**	*geographical*

-oso in Italian and *-ous* in English.

generoso	*generous*	**curioso**	*curious*
nervoso	*nervous*	**ambizioso**	*ambitious*

3. Verbs ending in:

-care in Italian and *-cate* in English.

educare	*educate*	**indicare**	*indicate*
complicare	*complicate*	**masticare**	*masticate*

-izzare in Italian and *-ize* in English.

organizzare	*organize*	**simpatizzare**	*sympathize*
analizzare	*analyze*	**minimizzare**	*minimize*

-ire in Italian and *-ish* in English.

finire	*to finish*	**abolire**	*to abolish*
punire	*to punish*	**stabilire**	*to establish*

INTRODUZIONE

Un incontro di amici.

Punti di vista
Ciao, come stai?

Studio di parole

Pagina culturale
The Italian Language and Its Dialects

PUNTI DI VISTA

Due ragazze si danno la mano.

CIAO, COME STAI?

	Filippo *incontra* Marcello. Marcello è *con* Mary, una ragazza americana.	meets/with
Marcello	Ciao Filippo, come va?	
Filippo	Bene, grazie, e tu come stai?	
Marcello	*Non c'è male*, grazie. *Ti presento* Mary Clark, un'*amica*.	Not bad/I introduce you friend
Filippo	Buon giorno, signorina.	
Mary	Buon giorno.	
Filippo	*Mi chiamo* Filippo Pini.	My name is
	(*Si danno la mano*)	They shake hands
Mary	Molto piacere.	
Filippo	Piacere mio. *Di dov'è Lei*, signorina?	Where are you from?
Mary	*Sono di* New York, e Lei?	I'm from
Filippo	Io sono di Pisa.	
Marcello	Mary è studentessa *qui* a Milano.	here
Filippo	*Anch'io* sono studente a Milano.	I also
Marcello	Scusa Filippo, *dobbiamo andare. A domani.*	we must go/I'll see you tomorrow
Filippo	Ciao Marcello. ArrivederLa, signorina.	
Mary	ArrivederLa.	

NOTE: **Tu** (*you, singular*) is the familiar form used by close friends and family members, and with children. **Lei** (*you, singular*), the formal form, is used in all other cases.

Studio di parole

ESPRESSIONI DI CORTESIA

Ciao! Hello. Good-bye.
Buon giorno, signore. Good morning (good day), Sir.
Buona sera, signora. Good evening, Madam.
Buona notte, signorina. Good night, Miss.
Arrivederci.
ArrivederLa. (*formal sing.*) } Good-bye.
A domani. I'll see you tomorrow.
Come si chiama? What is your name? (*formal*)
Come ti chiami? What is your name? (*familiar*)
Mi chiamo Marcello Scotti. My name is Marcello Scotti.
Molto piacere. Nice to meet you.
Piacere mio. My pleasure.
Per favore. Per piacere. Please.

Grạzie. Thank you.
Grạzie mille. Thanks a million.
Prego. You're welcome. That's quite all right.
Scusi. (*formal sing.*) **Scusa.** (*familiar sing.*) Excuse me.
Come stai? Come va? *(familiar sing.)*
Bene, grạzie, e tu? *(familiar sing.)*
How are you?
Fine, thank you, and you?
Come sta? (*formal sing.)*
Bene, grạzie, e Lei? *(formal sing.)*
How are you?
Fine, thank you, and you?
Molto bene. Very well.
Non c'è male. Not bad.

Come si dice...? How do you say...
Ti presento... Let me introduce ... to you. (*Lit.*, I introduce to you...)
Di dov'è Lei? (*formal sing.*)
Di dove sei? (*familiar sing.*) } Where are you from?
Sì yes
No no

Applicazione

A. Completate i dialoghi in gruppi di due studenti, scegliendo l'espressione corretta da «*Studio di parole*». (*Complete the dialogues in groups of two students, choosing the correct expression from* Studio di parole.)

1. —Buon __________, signore (signora/signorina). Come __________?
—Bene, __________, e Lei?
—__________, grazie.
—Come si __________?
—Mi chiamo __________, e Lei?
—__________ mi chiamo __________.
—Molto __________.
—Piacere __________. (Vi date la mano.) (*You shake hands*).

2. —Ciao, __________, come stai?
—Bene, grazie, e __________?
—Non c'è __________, grazie.
—Per __________, come si dice in italiano "*Excuse me*"?
—Si dice "Scusa" o "__________".
—__________.
—Prego.

B. Con gli amici. (*With friends*) *You are with friends at school; how can you respond to the following pleasantries?*

1. E tu, come stai?
2. Come ti chiami?
3. Scusa, Carlo, dobbiamo andare.
4. A domani.

C. Buon giorno. *How would you:*

1. greet and introduce yourself to another student in class?
2. ask another student how he/she is?
3. ask your professor how he/she is?
4. say good-bye to a classmate?

D. Mi chiamo... *Tell a student sitting nearby what your name is and indicate where you are from. Then ask him/her for the same information.*

E. Sono le otto di sera. (*It's eight o'clock in the evening*). *Complete the following exchange between you and one of your professors, whom you happen to run into one evening.*

— ______________, professore. Come __________?
— Bene, grazie, e tu, Paolo, __________ __________?
— Non c'è __________, __________.
— Arrivederci, Paolo.
— ______________, professore.

F. Un diạlogo. *Complete the following exchange between Filippo and Lisa Smith, who has just arrived from San Francisco for a year's study.*

Filippo	______________________ signorina.
	______________________?
Lisa	Bene, ______________________, e Lei?
Filippo	______________________, grazie.
Lisa	______________________ Lisa, e Lei?
Filippo	______________________ Filippo.
Lisa	Molto ______________________.
Filippo	______________________.
	(Si danno la mano).

G. Che cosa dịcono? *(What are they saying?). Look at the drawings in the* "Studio di parole" *and indicate what the various people might be saying to each other.*

Firenze. Monumento al poeta Dante Alighieri.

THE ITALIAN LANGUAGE AND ITS DIALECTS

The Italian language stems directly from Latin. As the authority of ancient Rome fragmented, its language, Latin, also broke apart and formed several national European idioms. In the same way, numerous linguistic varieties, or dialects, took form within the Italian peninsula. They were the expressions of different centers of civilization within the larger Italian world.

The dialect of Tuscany was assured linguistic supremacy by the political importance and geographical position of its principal city, Florence, and above all by the authority of the thirteenth-century Tuscan writers, Dante, Petrarca, and Boccaccio. Each of these men wrote works of major literary significance in their native Tuscan dialect. Eventually, the Tuscan dialect became recognized as the official Italian language.

However, for many centuries the Italian language remained a literary expression of only learned people. The different dialects continued to be spoken, a situation favored by the historical and political conditions of Italy, which remained a country divided into many separate city-states until the second half of the nineteenth century. The local dialect was often accepted as the official language of the court of that particular city-state. This was the case in Venice, a republic renowned for the skill of its diplomats. The eighteenth-century playwright, Carlo Goldoni, who has been called by critics the Italian Molière, wrote many of his plays in Venetian. For example, in his dialect we find the word *schiao,* meaning "your servant," which is derived from the Latin word for slave, *esclavum*. This is the original version of the international greeting "ciao."

Today Italy has achieved political as well as linguistic unity, and with few exceptions everyone speaks Italian. The dialects, however, remain very much alive. Indeed, Italians may be considered bilingual because, in addition to speaking Italian, they also speak or at least understand the dialect of their own region or city.

1 LA CITTÀ

Milano. In centro c'è la Galleria.

Punti di vista

In centro
In un ufficio turistico

Punti grammaticali

I *Essere* (to be)
II Il nome
III Gli articoli
IV *C'è, ci sono* e *ecco!*
V Espressioni interrogative

Lettura

Cosa c'è in una città?

Pagina culturale

Milano

PUNTI DI VISTA

Conversazione tra due amiche a un caffè.

IN CENTRO

downtown

Oggi Liliana e Lucia *s'incọntrano* in centro. — meet

Liliana	Ciao Lucia, come va?	
Lucia	Non c'è male, grạzie, e tu?	
Liliana	Oggi, *così-così*. *Domani ho* un esame di matemạtica con il professor Perfetti.	so-so/tomorrow I have
Lucia	È un professore *severo*?	strict
Liliana	Sì, molto.	
Lucia	Dov'è Marcello oggi? È a *scuola*?	school
Liliana	No, Marcello non è a scuola. È con un'amica di New York.	
Lucia	Dove sono?	
Liliana	Marcello e l'amica *vịsitano* la chiesa di Santa Maria delle Grạzie, dove *c'è* l'*affresco* di Leonardo, *L'Ụltima Cena,* e il Castello Sforzesco.	visit / there is/fresco / the Last Supper
Lucia	Come si chiama l'amica di Marcello?	
Liliana	Si chiama Mary Clark. È una studentessa *simpạtica* e intelligente. *Parla* italiano *molto bene*.	nice/she speaks/very well

Comprensione

1. Dove (*where*) s'incọntrano Liliana e Lucia? 2. Domani Liliana ha (*has*) un esame di matemạtica o un esame d'inglese? 3. Il professore di matemạtica è severo? 4. È a scuola Marcello oggi? 5. Con chi (*whom*) è Marcello oggi? 6. Di dov'è l'amica di Marcello? 7. Perchè (*why*) la chiesa di Santa Maria delle Grạzie è famosa? 8. Chi (*Who*) è la signorina Clark? 9. La signorina Clark parla bene o parla male (*badly*) l'italiano?

Studio di parole

LA CITTÀ DI MILANO

una strada* street, road
una via* street, way
una piazza square
una fontana fountain
un monumento monument
una chiesa church
un museo museum
un edifịcio building
un albergo hotel
un caffè coffee shop
un ristorante restaurant

un negọzio store, shop
un uffịcio office
un parco (*pl.* chi) park
un cịnema (tọgrafo) movie theater
un teatro theater
una banca bank
un ospedale hospital
un ạutobus bus
un tram streetcar
un'automọbile (*f.*) car

C'è un tour, per favore? Is there a tour, please?
Sì, c'è. Ecco le informazioni. Yes, there is. Here is the information.

***Strada** is a more general term; **via** is used before the name of a street: **via Mazzini, via Torino.**

A. La pianta di Milano. Guardando la pianta di Milano, uno studente domanda ad un altro le seguenti informazioni. *(Looking at the map of Milano, one student asks another for the following information).*

1. Santa Maria delle Grạzie è una chiesa o un teatro?
2. Il teatro La Scala è in via Manzoni o in via Dante?
3. Il Duomo è in un parco o in una piazza?
4. Dov'è il Castello Sforzesco?
5. Che cos'è via Dante?
6. Il Castello Sforzesco è vicino a (*near*) Piazza del Duomo?

B. Che cos'è...? Seguite l'esempio. *(What is each of the following famous places? Follow the example to create questions and answers).*

ESEMPIO l'Empire State Building
—Che cos'è l'Empire State Building?
—È un edifịcio.

1. San Pietro
2. il Louvre
3. Trafalgar Square
4. il Golden Gate Park
5. Nạpoli
6. 1a Fifth Avenue

C. Domande personali.

1. Dov'è Lei oggi, a scuola o in centro?
2. Ha (*Do you have*) un esame domani? (Sì, ho.../No, non ho...)
3. Lei ha un professore severo?
4. Come parla Lei l'italiano? Bene o male?
5. Lei ha un'amica simpạtica e intelligente?

D. Ecco le informazioni. *(Here is the information.) Imagine that your city's office of tourism offers a tour of the main points of interest downtown. Indicate what the tour includes by completing the description below.*

C'è un tour: include (*it includes*) ______________________________
____
____
____

Ascoltiamo!

In un ufficio turistico. *Anna Verri, a visitor to Milan, has stopped by the tourist office to make an inquiry. Listen to her conversation with the clerk, then answer the following questions.*

Comprensione

1. Dov'è la turista Anna Verri?
2. La turista desidera (*wishes*) visitare la città di Roma o la città di Milano?
3. Che cosa (*What*) include il tour?
4. L'impiegato (*The clerk*) ha le informazioni?
5. Che cosa dice la turista? (*What does the tourist say?*)

Dialogo

Two students play the role of a tourist and an employee in the tourist office. They greet each other. The employee asks what he/she would like. He/she would like information on a tour of Milan. The employee provides the information. They exchange polite words and say good-bye.

PUNTI GRAMMATICALI

I. Essere (*To be*)

Marcello è in classe con Gabriella.

Essere (*to be*) is an irregular verb (**verbo**). It is conjugated in the present tense (**presente**) as follows:

Person	Singular	Plural
1st	io **sono** (*I am*)	noi **siamo** (*we are*)
2nd	tu **sei** (*you are, familiar*)	voi **siete** (*you are, familiar*)
3rd	lui **è** (*he is*) lei **è** (*she is*) Lei **è** (*you are, formal*)	loro **sono** (*they are*) Loro **sono** (*you are, formal*)

Luigi **è** italiano. — *Luigi is Italian.*
Marco e io **siamo** studenti. — *Marco and I are students.*
Lisa e Gino **sono** di Roma. — *Lisa and Gino are from Rome.*
Tu e Piero **siete** buoni amici. — *You and Piero are good friends.*

1. There are many rules regarding verbs and their usage:

    a. Contrary to English verbs, Italian verbs have a different ending for each person.

    b. The negative of a verb is formed by placing non before the verb.

    Non siamo a teatro. — *We are not at the theater.*
    Filippo **non è** in classe. — *Filippo is not in class.*

    c. The interrogative of a verb is formed either by placing the subject at the end of the sentence or by leaving it at the beginning of the sentence. In both cases, there is a change in intonation, and the pitch rises at the last word:

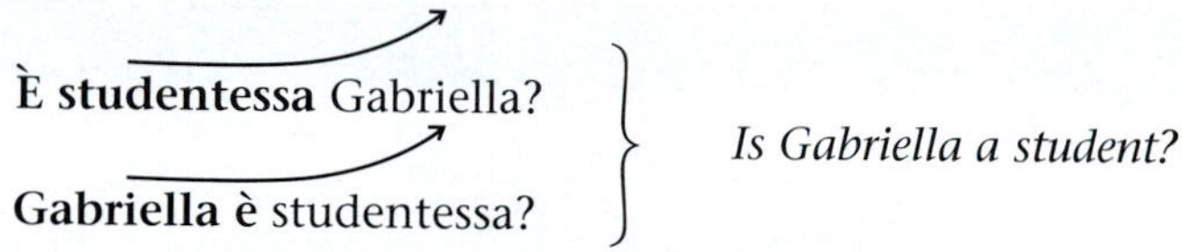

È studentessa Gabriella?
Gabriella è studentessa?
Is Gabriella a student?

2. The subject pronouns (**pronomi soggetto**) in Italian are:

io	*I*	**noi, voi**	*we*
tu	*you (familiar sing.)*	**voi**	*you (familiar pl.)*
lui, lei	*he, she*	**loro**	*they*
Lei	*you (formal sing.)*	**Loro**	*you (formal pl.)*

a. The subject pronoun *you* is expressed in Italian in several ways: **tu** (singular) and **voi** (plural) are the familiar forms. They are used to address relatives, close friends, and children; young people also use them to address each other.

Io sono di Pisa, e **tu**? — *I am from Pisa, and you?*
Siete a scuola **voi** oggi? — *Are you in school today?*

Lei (singular) and **Loro** (plural) are formal forms and are used among persons who are not well acquainted. **Lei** and **Loro** are used for both men and women. They take, respectively, the third person singular and the third person plural of the verb and are usually written with a capital L to distinguish them from **lei** (she) and **loro** (they).

Buona sera, signore. Come sta **Lei** oggi?	*Good evening, sir. How are you today?*
Maria è a casa; **lei** non sta bene.	*Maria is at home; she does not feel well.*
Sono a casa **Loro** stasera?	*Are you at home tonight?*

NOTE: In contemporary Italian the familiar plural form **voi** is used more frequently than **Loro**, particularly when addressing young people.

—Io sono di Pisa, e Lei?
—Io sono di Bagdad.

b. In Italian, the subject pronouns are often omitted since the subject of the sentence is indicated by the verb ending. However, the subject pronouns are used for emphasis and to avoid ambiguities.*

Sono Marcello.	*I am Marcello.*
Io sono Marcello.	***I** am Marcello.* (emphatic)
Pio e Lina non sono a casa: **lui** è a Nạpoli, **lei** è a Pisa.	*Pio and Lina are not at home; **he** is in Naples, **she** is in Pisa.* (for clarification)

Pratica

A. Completate con la forma corretta del presente di **ẹssere**. *(Complete with the correct present tense form of* ***ẹssere****.)*

ESEMPIO Los Angeles __________ in America.
Los Angeles è in America.

1. Giuseppe _____ con Mirella. **2.** Gabriella e io non _____ a Firenze. **3.** Madrid _____ in Spagna. **4.** Tu e lei _____ in Califọrnia; non_____ in Florida. **5.** Lui non _____ dottore; _____professore. **6.** San Francisco e Chicago _____ in Amẹrica. **7.** Piazza San Marco _____ a Venẹzia. **8.** Gabriella _____ un'amica di Marcello. **9.** Tu _____ a scuola. **10.** Io _____ studente (studentessa); non _____ professore (professoressa).

*The pronouns *it* and *they*, when referring to animals and things, are usually not expressed in Italian. For clarification, they may sometimes be expressed by **esso, essa** (*sing. m. and f.*) and **essi, esse** (*pl. m. and f.*).

B. Trasformate le seguenti affermazioni in domande. (*Transform the following statements into questions.*)

ESEMPIO Filippo è di Pisa.
È di Pisa Filippo?

1. Milano è in Lombardia. **2.** Tu sei di Venezia. **3.** Tu e Marcello siete studenti. **4.** Lei è professore di francese. **5.** Voi siete a casa oggi. **6.** Gina e Luisa sono studentesse di filosofia. **7.** Laura è americana.

C. Rispondete alle domande, scegliendo l'alternativa che preferite. *(Answer the questions, choosing the alternative you prefer).*

ESEMPIO Dove sei tu oggi? a casa/a scuola
Oggi io sono a casa. *o* **Oggi io sono a scuola.**

1. Dove sono Marcello e Liliana? a Roma/a Milano/in Califọrnia/in Itạlia **2.** Quando è a casa Lei? oggi/domani/questa (*this*) sera **3.** Dove siete tu e gli amici (*your friends*) domẹnica (*on Sunday*)? a un museo/al (*at the*) parco/a un concerto/al cinematọgrafo/a un caffè **4.** Dove siamo tu e io in questo momento? in classe/a scuola/alla (*at the*) lezione d'italiano **5.** Dove sono il papà e la mamma di Mary Clark? a casa/a Firenze/a New York/al ristorante

D. **Domanda e risposta.** *(Question and answer.) This type of exercise involves two students: one student asks and the other answers. The student who answers then asks the question that follows.*

ESEMPIO Lucia, professoressa
—È professoressa Lucia?
—No, Lucia non è professoressa. È studentessa.

1. tu, di Nạpoli **2.** Lei (*you*), in classe domani sera **3.** noi, in un ufficio turịstico **4.** *L'Ụltima Cena* di Leonardo, a Roma **5.** Gabriella e Filippo, americani

E. *Tell a classmate who you are, what you are (occupation, nationality), where you are today* (oggi), *and where you are not.*

II. Il nome

Ecco una piazza con una chiesa, un giardino e degli edifici.

1. **Gender of nouns.** A noun (**nome**) is either masculine or feminine. Usually, nouns ending in **-o** are masculine and nouns ending in **-a** are feminine. There is also a class of nouns that end in **-e**. These nouns can be *either* masculine *or* feminine.

   treno (*m.*) **casa** (*f.*)
   ristorante (*m.*) **stazione** (*f.*)

NOTE:

a. To remember the gender of a noun ending in **-e**, it is advisable to memorize it with the article.

   un ristorante *una* stazione

b. Nouns ending in **-ore** or in a *consonant* are masculine.

   fi**ore** pitt**ore** scult**ore** ạutobu**s** spor**t** ba**r**

c. Nouns ending in **-ione** are generally feminine.

   lez**ione** presentaz**ione** conversaz**ione**

2. **Plural of nouns.** In Italian, the plural is usually formed according to the final vowel of the noun. The chart below shows the most common changes.

	Singular	Plural	Examples	
Nouns ending in	-o	-i	un giardin**o**	due giardin**i**
	-a	-e	una cas**a**	due cas**e**
	-e	-i	un dottor**e** (*m.*)	due dottor**i**
			una stazion**e** (*f.*)	due stazion**i**

NOTE:

a. Some nouns are invariable and thus do not change in the plural.

- nouns ending in accented vowels

  una citt**à** due citt**à** un caff**è** due caff**è**

- nouns ending in a consonant

  un ba**r** due ba**r** un fil**m** due fil**m**

- nouns abbreviated

  un cịnem**a**(tografo) due cịnem**a** una fot**o**(grafia) due fot**o**

b. Nouns that end in **-ca** change to **-che**

   un'ami**ca** due ami**che** una ban**ca** due ban**che**

c. Most nouns ending in **-io** change to **-i**

   un negọz**io** due negoz**i** un uffịc**io** due uffic**i**

Pratica

A. **Maschile o femminile?** Indicate il gẹnere dei seguenti nomi. (*Indicate the gender of the following nouns.*)

1. bambino 2. studente 3. casa 4. amico 5. giardino 6. scultore 7. conversazione 8. piazza 9. professoressa 10. classe 11. amica 12. cịnema 13. città 14. banca 15. stụdio 16. nome 17. pittore 18. ạutobus 19. negọzio 20. sport 21. università

22. lezione

B. Formate il plurale dei nomi dell'esercizio A. (*Give the plural of the nouns listed in Exercise A.*)

C. Formate il plurale dei nomi in parentesi. (*Give the plural of the nouns in parentheses.*)

1. Leonardo da Vinci e Raffaello sono due (pittore) __________.
2. Oggi (studente) __________ e (professore) __________ sono a casa.
3. Lungo (*along*) la strada ci sono (ạutobus) __________, (automọbile) __________ e (bicicletta) __________. **4.** In Piazza del Duomo ci sono (negọzio) __________, (bar) __________, (caffè) __________, (uffịcio) __________ e (ristorante) __________. **5.** In un giardino ci sono (ạlbero [*tree*]) __________ e (fiore) __________.

III. Gli articoli

Ecco una strada con il bar, la banca, i negozi, gli ạlberi e le automọbili.

1. **Artịcolo indeterminativo.** The *indefinite article* (*a, an*) has the following forms: the masculine forms **un**, **uno** and the feminine forms **una**, **un'**, according to the first letter of the noun the article precedes. The indefinite article does not have a plural form.

		Masculine	Feminine
before	*consonant*	**un** libro	**una** casa
	vowel	**un** amico	**un'**amica
	z	**uno** zoo	**una** zebra
	s + *consonant*	**uno** studente	**una** studentessa

La Sicịlia è **un'**ịsola.	*Sicily is an island.*
Dov'è **una** banca, per favore?	*Where is a bank, please?*
Ecco **un** ristorante!	*Here is a restaurant!*
C'è **uno** zoo in questa città?	*Is there a zoo in this city?*

NOTE:
When a noun indicates a profession, the indefinite article is generally omitted.

Paolo è dottore, ed io sono professore. — *Paolo is a doctor, and I am a professor.*

2. **Articolo determinativo.** The **definite article** (*the*) agrees with the noun it precedes in gender (masculine or feminine) and in number (singular or plural). The masculine forms are **il, l', lo, i, gli,** and the feminine forms are **la, l', le,** according to the initial letter and number of the word the definite article accompanies.

	Definite article		Singular		Plural	
Masculine	*before*	*consonant*	**il**	giardino	**i**	giardini
		vowel	**l'**	albero	**gli**	alberi
		z	**lo**	zero	**gli**	zeri
		s + consonant	**lo**	studio	**gli**	studi
Feminine	*before*	*consonant*	**la**	casa	**le**	case
		vowel	**l'**	autostrada (*freeway*)	**le**	autostrade

Ecco **l'** autobus!	*Here is the bus!*
Dove sono **gli** studenti?	*Where are the students?*
Gina *è* **l'** amica di Maria.	*Gina is Maria's friend.*
Ecco **le** informazioni, signora.	*Here is the information, Madam.*

If a noun ending in **-e** is masculine, it will have the appropriate masculine article (**il, l', lo, i, gli**), depending on its initial letter. If a noun is feminine, it will have the appropriate feminine article (**la, l', le**), depending on its initial letter.

il fiore (*m.*)	**i** fiori
l'automobile (*f.*)	**le** automobili

NOTE:

a. When using a title to address someone, omit the article. When you are speaking *about* someone, use the appropriate definite article *before* the title.

Buon giorno, signor Neri.	*Good morning, Mr. Neri*
Buona sera, dottor Lisi.	*Good evening, Dr. Lisi.*
Il professor Rossi non è in casa.	*Professor Rossi is not home.*
I signori Bianchi sono a teatro.	*Mr. and Mrs. Bianchi are at the theater.*

b. Such titles as **signore, professore,** and **dottore** drop the final **-e** in front of a proper name.

—Buon giorno, dottor Lisi.
—Buon giorno, professore.

Pratica

A. **Che cos'è?** Rispondete usando la forma corretta dell'articolo indeterminativo. *(Answer the question using the correct form of the indefinite article.)*

ESEMPIO treno **È un treno.**

1. negọzio 2. piazza 3. sport 4. edifịcio 5. parco 6. scuola 7. ristorante 8. idea 9. stụdio 10. città 11. cịnema 12. stazione 13. automọbile 14. caffè 15. museo 16. lezione 17. uffịcio 18. ạlbero 19. chiesa 20. zoo 21. strada 22. autostrada

B. Leggete i seguenti nomi con la forma corretta dell'articolo determinativo. (*Read the following nouns with the correct form of the definite article.*)

1. edifịcio e giardino 2. strada e piazza 3. stazione e treno 4. automọbile e ạutobus 5. stụdio e sport 6. negọzio e banca 7. libro e pạgina 8. studente e professore 9. caffè e bar

C. Mettete al plurale i nomi dell'esercizio B. (*Give the plural of the nouns in Exercise B.*)

D. **Domanda e risposta.** (*Two people are looking at pictures.*)

ESEMPIO monumento/a Garibaldi **—È un monumento?**
—Sì, è il monumento a Garibaldi.

1. chiesa/di San Pietro 2. uffịcio/di Francesca Rovati 3. stazione/di Firenze 4. università/di Milano 5. affresco/di Leonardo 6. parco/di Gẹnova 7. caffè/«Sport» 8. zoo/di San Diego 9. automọbile/di un amico 10. stụdio/di un pittore 11. treno/Milano–Roma 12. banca/d'Itạlia 13. negọzio/«Lui e Lei»

E. **Domanda e risposta.** La domanda è al singolare, la risposta è al plurale, secondo l'esempio. (*The question is in the singular, and the answer is in the plural, according to the example.*)

ESEMPIO ragazzo/a scuola **—Dov'è il ragazzo?**
—I ragazzi sono a scuola.

1. banca/in centro 2. amica di Marisa/a casa 3. automọbile/in garage 4. treno/in stazione 5. negọzio/in via Dante 6. caffè/in Galleria 7. studente/in classe

F. **Dov'è? Domanda e risposta.**

ESEMPIO dottore, Aspirina/in uffịcio **—Per favore, dov'è il dottor Aspirina?**
—È in uffịcio.

1. signore, Giannini/a Roma 2. professore, Tommasi/a casa 3. professoressa, Manzoni/a teatro 4. dottoressa, Piccoli/in centro

G. Completate con l'articolo determinativo, dov'è necessario. (*Complete with the definite article, where necessary.*)

1. Buon giorno, _____ dottor Bianchi! Come sta? 2. Ecco _____ signor Rossi! 3. Scusi, dov'è _____ professor Marini? 4. ArrivederLa _____ dottore! 5. Per favore, c'è _____ professoressa Rovati? 6. _______ signori Verdi sono a casa.

IV. C'è, ci sono e ecco!

Ecco la stazione centrale.

1. **C'è** (*there is*) and **ci sono** (*there are*) are used to indicate the existence of someone or something (in sight or not). Their negative forms are **non c'è** and **non ci sono**, respectively.

   C'è la metropolitana a Roma? — *Is there the subway in Rome?*

   Oggi **ci sono** diciotto studenti. — *Today there are eighteen students.*
   Non ci sono fiori in giardino. — *There are no flowers in the garden.*

2. **Ecco** is invariable and is used to *point out* someone or something *in sight*. It has several meanings: *look!, here is ...!, here are ...!, there is ...!, there are ...!*

   Ecco l'autobus! — *Here (There) is the bus!*
   Ecco i signori Parini! — *There are Mr. and Mrs. Parini!*

A. **Per piacere, dove...? Domanda e risposta.** *(Using the map of Milan on page 17, one student will ask where the following places are, and another student will point them out on the map, saying* **Ecco...!***)*

1. Duomo 2. Scala 3. giardini 4. Castello Sforzesco 5. chiesa di Santa Maria delle Gr̦azie 6. Galleria 7. stazione centrale

B. Completate le frasi con **c'è** o **ci sono.** *(Complete the sentences with* **c'è** *or* **ci sono.***)*

1. _____ un ci̦nema in via Dante? 2. _____ negozi in Galleria? 3. Non _____ un a̦utobus qui (*here*). 4. In un giardino _____ a̦lberi e fiori. 5. Non _____ chiese in centro. 6. _____ un monumento in piazza. 7. Non _____ il professore oggi? 8. In una città _____ molti ristoranti. 9. In un parco _____ lo zoo. 10. In una stazione _____ i treni.

C. **C'è...? Ci sono...? Domanda e risposta.**

ESEMPIO parchi —**Ci sono parchi a...**(*your city*)?
—**Sì, ci sono.** (*o:* **No, non ci sono.**)

1. un'università 2. a̦utobus (pl.) 3. musei 4. una piazza 5. treni 6. ristoranti 7. un monumento a Garibaldi

V. Espressioni interrogative

—Che cos'è?
—È una casa.
—Dov'è? —È in Italia.

Some interrogative words and expressions are:

Chi?	*Who? Whom?*	**Chi** è Marcello?	*Who is Marcello?*
Che cosa? / **Cosa?** / **Che?**	*What?*	**Cos'**è un pronome?	*What is a pronoun?*
Come?	*How?*	**Com'**è Firenze?	*How is Florence?*
Dove?	*Where?*	**Dov'**è Palermo?	*Where is Palermo?*
Quando?	*When?*	**Quando** sei a casa?	*When are you at home?*

Cosa, come, and **dove** are elided before **è.**

Cos'è? *What is it?* or *What is he (she)?*
Dov'è? *Where is it?* or *Where is he (she)?*

Pratica

A. **Chi? o Che cosa?** Domanda e risposta tra due studenti, secondo l'esempio.

ESEMPIO Filippo/studente **—Chi è Filippo? —È uno studente.**
Venezia/città **—Che cos'è Venezia? —È una città.**

1. Michelangelo/scultore (*sculptor*) **2.** «*Il Davide*»/scultura (*sculpture*) di Michelangelo **3.** *Giulietta e Romeo*/tragedia di Shakespeare **4.** Harvard/università **5.** Leonardo da Vinci/pittore **6.** tu/studente(ssa) d'italiano **7.** Il Duomo di Milano/chiesa **8.** La Scala/teatro **9.** Marcello/ragazzo italiano **10.** Luciano Pavarotti/tenore **11.** Firenze/città

B. Formulate le domande per le seguenti risposte. *(Ask questions for the following answers by using* **chi, che (che cosa, cosa), come, dove,** *or* **quando.**)

ESEMPIO Io sono a casa questa (*this*) sera.
—Dove sei questa sera?

1. Io sono un amico di Francesca. **2.** Tokio è in Giappone. **3.** Genova è un porto in Italia. **4.** Piazza San Marco è a Venezia. **5.** Bene, grazie. **6.** Oggi Francesca Rovati è a casa. **7.** Capri è un'isola (*island*). **8.** Dante Alighieri è un poeta. **9.** Siamo a casa domani. **10.** Sono Loredana.

LETTURA

Milano. In centro c'è il duomo, di stile gotico.

COSA C'È IN UNA CITTÀ?

Ecco una conversazione *fra* due *bambini*. — between/children

Alberto	Dove *ạbiti?*	do you live?
Paolo	Ạbito a Milano, e tu?	
Alberto	Io ạbito a Rapallo. *Com'è* Milano?	What is … like?
Paolo	Milano è una grande città, con *molti* edifici, con i negozi, le banche, i ristoranti, i caffè, i cinematọgrafi, i monumenti, le chiese, i musei, le scuole e un teatro famoso, la Scala.	many
Alberto	C'è uno zoo?	
Paolo	Sì, c'è. Con gli animali feroci. C'è *anche* un *castello*, in un grande parco, con gli ạlberi, i fiori e le fontane.	also castle
Alberto	Ci sono molte automobili? Ci sono le Ferrari?	
Paolo	Sì ci sono molte automọbili e anche le Ferrari. Ci sono gli ạutobus, i tram e le stazioni *dei* treni. Com'è Rapallo?	of the
Alberto	Rapallo è una *pịccola* città. Non ci sono molte automọbili, *però* è una città *molto bella*.	small but very beautiful

Comprensione

1. Dove ạbita Paolo? **2.** Milano è una città pịccola o grande? **3.** Cosa c'è a Milano? **4.** Come si chiama il famoso teatro di Milano? **5.** C'è o non c'è uno zoo? **6.** Dov'è il castello? **7.** Cosa c'è in un parco? **8.** A Milano ci sono molte automọbili? E a Rapallo? **9.** Com'è Rapallo, secondo (*according to*) Alberto?

Domande personali

1. Dove ạbita Lei? 2. Com'è la Sua *(your)* città? È grande o pịccola? Cosa c'è in centro? C'è molto trạffico? 3. È molto bella la Sua città? 4. C'è anche un museo? 5. C'è la stazione dei treni?

ATTIVITÀ SUPPLEMENTARI

A. **Dịalogo.** Gli student, in gruppi di due, completano il dialogo. *(The students, in groups of two, will complete the dialogue).*

Studente 1 Dove ạbiti?
Studente 2 ____________________________
Studente 1 È una città grande, pịccola o mẹdia?
Studente 2 ____________________________
Studente 1 C'è molto (*a lot of*) trạffico o poco (*little*) trạffico?
Studente 2 ____________________________
Studente 1 Ci sono i tram e gli ạutobus?
Studente 2 ____________________________
Studente 1 C'è anche un teatro?
Studente 2 ____________________________

B. **Descrivete** la fotografia. *(Describe the picture).*

C. **Come si dice in italiano?**

1. Excuse me, where is the university? 2. There is the university! 3. Is professor Pini there? 4. Who? Doctor Pini? Today he is not in. (**Non c'è.**) He is at home. 5. Please, where is the Bank of Italy? 6. It is downtown. 7. Are there restaurants, too? 8. Yes. The restaurants and the shops are downtown. 9. Thank you. Good-bye. 10. You are welcome, Madam. Good-bye. 11. What's your name? 12. My name is Lisa. I'm a student of Italian.

Vocabolario

Nomi

l'affresco	*fresco*
l'ạlbero	*tree*
l'amico, l'amica	*friend*
l'animale(*m.*)	*animal*
il bambino, la bambina	*little boy, little girl*
la casa	*house, home*
il castello	*castle*
la città	*city, town*
la classe	*class*
il cognome	*last name*
la conversazione	*conversation*
il dottore, la dottoressa	*doctor, university graduate*
l'esame (*m.*)	*examination*
il fiore	*flower*
il giardino	*garden*
l'impiegato	*employee*
l'inglese (*m.*)	*English (language)*
l'Itạlia	*Italy*
l'italiano	*Italian language*
la lezione	*lesson*
il libro	*book*
il nome	*noun, name*
la pạgina	*page*
il pittore, la pittrice	*painter*
il professore, la professoressa	*professor*
il ragazzo, la ragazza	*boy, girl; boyfriend, girlfriend*
la scuola	*school*
lo studente, la studentessa	*student*
lo stụdio	*study*
il trạffico	*traffic*
il (la) turista	*tourist*
l'università	*university*
lo zoo	*zoo*

Aggettivi

americano(a)	*American*
bello(a)	*beautiful, handsome*
famoso(a)	*famous*
grande	*big, large, wide; great*
intelligente	*intelligent*
italiano(a)	*Italian*
molti, molte	*many*
pịccolo(a)	*small, little*
severo(a)	*strict*
simpạtico(a)	*nice, charming*

Verbi

ẹssere	*to be*

Altre Espressioni

a	*in, at, to*
anche	*also, too, as well*
bene	*well*
benịssimo	*very well*
c'è, ci sono	*there is, there are*
che?, che cosa?, cosa?	*what?*
chi?	*who, whom?*
come? com'è?	*how? What is … like?*
con	*with*
così-così	*so-so*
di, d'	*of, from*
di dove sei?	*where are you from?*
domani	*tomorrow*
dove?	*where?*
e, ed *(often before a vowel)*	*and*
ecco!	*here (there) is (are)!*
in	*in*
in cẹntro	*downtown*
male	*badly*
molto (*inv.*)	*very*
molto bene	*very well*
no	*no*
oggi	*today*
per	*for*
perchè	*why?; because*
quando?	*when?*

Il Castello Sforzesco (degli Sforza).

MILANO

Milano (dal latino *Mediolanum*) è la *città-capoluogo* della regione chiamata Lombardia. La prosperità di *questa* città è *dovuta* alla sua posizione al centro della fẹrtile *valle del Po. Già nel Mẹdio Evo* i *banchieri* lombardi sono famosi *quanto* i banchieri di Firenze.* Durante il *Rinascimento,* Milano *diventa* anche un centro artịstico *grạzie al* patronato delle famịglie Visconti e Sforza, e di artisti *come* Leonardo da Vinci. *Tre sẹcoli più tardi* Milano esercita con *i suoi cịrcoli* intellettuali un'influenza molto importante nell'unificazione dell'Itạlia.

place in the middle/regional capital
this/due
Po valley/Already in the Middle Ages/bankers/as much as/Renaissance/becomes/thanks to/such as
Three centuries later/its circles

Oggi Milano è il *primo* centro industriale e finanziario d'Itạlia. L'indụstria della *moda* e *la Fiera Campionạria* sono di fama internazionale.

first
fashion
Trade Show

Comprensione

1. Milano è il capoluogo...
   a. d'Itạlia. **b.** della valle del Po. **c.** della Lombardia.
2. Leonardo da Vinci è un pittore...
   a. del Medioevo. **b.** del Rinascimento. **c.** dell'Ottocento (*19th century*).
3. Oggi Milano è molto famosa per...
   a. l'indụstria della moda. **b.** i suoi (*its*) banchieri. **c.** i suoi artisti.
4. Il primo centro industriale d'Itạlia è...
   a. Firenze. **b.** il Po. **c.** Milano.

---

*Lombard Street, the famous banking street in London, England, is named after these Italian bankers.

2 PERSONE E PERSONALITÀ

Milano. Compagni di corso, studiosi o pigri, ma tutti (all) giovani.

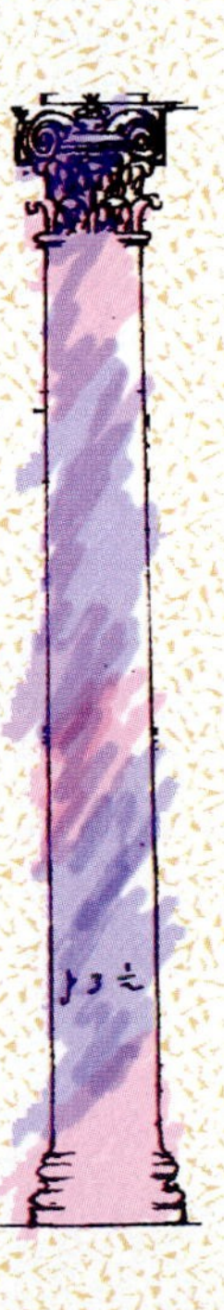

Punti di vista

Com'è il tuo compagno di stanza?
La sera della festa

Punti grammaticali

I L'aggettivo
II *Buono* e *bello*
III *Avere*
IV *Quanto?* e i numeri cardinali da 0 a 100

Lettura

Due amici differenti

Pagina culturale

Alcune regioni e città-capoluogo d'Italia

PUNTI DI VISTA

Claudio è biondo e simpatico. Com'è Luciano?

COM' È *IL TUO COMPAGNO DI STANZA?* — your roommate

Rita e Luciano sono compagni di classe. Oggi *s'incontrano dopo* le lezioni. — they meet after

Rita	Ciao, Luciano. Come va?	
Luciano	Non c'è male, e tu?	
Rita	*Abbastanza bene. Quanti* compagni di stanza hai *quest'*anno?	pretty well/how many this
Luciano	Ho *solo* un compagno di stanza. Si chiama Claudio. È romano.	only
Rita	Com'è? È un ragazzo simpatico?	
Luciano	Sì, è un ragazzo molto simpatico. È anche un bel ragazzo—alto, biondo, con gli occhi verdi.	
Rita	È un bravo studente?	
Luciano	Sì, è molto studioso e *parla* quattro lingue.	he speaks
Rita	Sono curiosa di *conoscerlo.*	to meet him
Luciano	Bene. Domani sera c'è una festa a casa di Marco. Sei *invitata.*	invited
Rita	Grazie. A domani sera.	

Comprensione

1. Chi è Rita? 2. Quando s'incọntrano Rita e Luciano? 3. Quanti compagni di stanza ha Luciano quest'anno? 4. Come si chiama? 5. Di che città è? 6. È uno studente mediocre? 7. Quante lịngue parla? 8. Che cosa c'è domani sera? 9. Chi è invitato?

Studio di parole

COME SEI TU?

biondo(a) blond
bruno(a) dark-haired
alto(a) tall
basso(a) short
magro(a) thin
snello(a) slender
giọvane young
intelligente intelligent
stụpido(a) stupid
simpạtico(a) nice, charming
antipạtico(a) unpleasant
generoso(a) generous
avaro(a) stingy
studioso(a) studious
pigro(a) lazy
interessante interesting
noioso(a) boring
bello(a) beautiful
brutto(a) ugly
contento(a) content, happy
triste sad
fortunato(a) lucky
sfortunato(a) unlucky

HAI I CAPELLI...?

neri black
biondi blond
bianchi white
castani brown
rossi red
corti short
lunghi long

HAI GLI OCCHI...?

neri black
castani brown
blu blue
azzurri light blue
verdi green
grigi grey

Applicazione

A. Domande. Rispondete alle seguenti domande scegliendo l'aggettivo appropriato. (*Answer the following questions by choosing the appropriate adjective.*)

1. È severo il professore d'italiano? (È severa la professoressa d'italiano?)
2. Come sono i capelli di Babbo Natale (*Santa Claus*)?
3. È generoso Scrooge?
4. Com'è Miss America?
5. È bruna e bassa, in genere, una ragazza svedese (*Swedish*)?
6. Ha gli occhi neri Robert Redford?
7. Com'è un topo di biblioteca (*bookworm*)?
8. È noioso o divertente (*amusing*) un film di Robin Williams?
9. Cos'è il contrario (*opposite*) di grasso? E il contrario di antipatico?
10. È brutto Kevin Costner?

B. Domande personali.

1. Ha un compagno (una compagna) di stanza? Se non ha un compagno (una compagna) di stanza parli di (*talk about*) un amico (un'amica).
2. Come si chiama?
3. Di dov'è?
4. È bruno(a) o biondo(a)? Alto(a) o basso(a)? Ha gli occhi neri o azzurri?
5. È simpatico(a)?
6. È intelligente? È studioso(a) o pigro(a)?
7. È paziente o impaziente con gli amici?
8. Quante lingue parla? Una? Due? Tre?

C. Sono curioso(a) di conoscerlo(a). Descrivete un amico (un'amica) ideale.

Ascoltiamo!

La sera della festa. *It is the evening of Marco's party. Marco is greeting Rita and introducing her to Claudio. Listen to the exchange that follows, then answer the related questions.*

Comprensione

1. Dove sono Claudio e Rita? **2.** Di dov'è Claudio? **3.** Come si chiama l'amica di Claudio? È inglese (*English*)? **4.** Di quale (*which*) città è Marilyn? **5.** Come sono i giovani americani? Sono antipatici?

Dialogo

Three students play the role of Claudio, Rita, and Marilyn. Claudio introduces Marilyn to Rita. They greet each other and ask each other questions.

PUNTI GRAMMATICALI

I. L'Aggettivo

Lucia è carina: ha i capelli corti e neri e gli occhi castani.

1. È brutta o è carina Lucia?
2. Ha i capelli lunghi o corti?
3. Ha gli occhi verdi o castani?

1. An adjective (**aggettivo**) must agree in gender and number with the noun it modifies. [When an adjective ends in **-o**, it has four endings: **-o** (*m. sing.*), **-i** (*m. pl.*), **-a** (*f. sing.*), and **-e** (*f. pl.*).]

	Singular	Plural
Masculine	il bambino biond**o**	i bambini biond**i**
Feminine	la bambina biond**a**	le bambine biond**e**

Luigi è alto e biondo. — *Luigi is tall and blond.*
Maria è bassa e bruna. — *Maria is short and brunette.*
Maria e Carlo sono generosi.* — *Maria and Carlo are generous.*

[When an adjective ends in **-e**, it has two endings: **-e** (*m. & f. sing.*) and **-i** (*m. & f. pl.*).]

	Singular	Plural
Masculine	il ragazzo intelligent**e**	i ragazzi intelligent**i**
Feminine	la ragazza intelligent**e**	le ragazze intelligent**i**

una ragazza studios**a** — *a studious girl*
due ragazze studios**e** — *two studious girls*

la lezione difficil**e** — *the difficult lesson*
le lezioni difficil**i** — *the difficult lessons*

---

*If an adjective modifies two nouns of different gender, the masculine plural ending is used: **Lisa e Paolo sono simpatici.** ***Lisa and Paolo are nice.***

2. As shown above, an adjective usually follows the noun it modifies. However, the following common adjectives generally precede the noun:

bello	*beautiful, handsome, fine*	**vẹcchio**	*old*
brutto	*ugly*	**grande**	*big, large; great*
buono	*good*	**pịccolo**	*small, short*
bravo	*good, talented*	**stesso**	*same*
cattivo	*bad, mean*	**altro**	*other*
giọvane	*young*	**caro***	*dear*
nuovo	*new*	**vero**	*true*

l'**altro** giorno	*the other day*
un **caro** amico	*a dear friend*
una **grande** casa	*a big house*
un **grande** artista	*a great artist*
gli **stessi** ragazzi	*the same boys*

When the adjective precedes the noun, the form of the article depends on the first letter of the adjective.

gli studenti BUT: **i** bravi studenti

NOTE: All adjectives follow the noun when they are modified by the adverb **molto** (*very*).

un amico **molto caro**	*a very dear friend*
una casa **molto grande**	*a very big house*

3. Adjectives denoting *nationality* or *color* always follow the noun:

italiano**	*Italian*	**americano**	*American*
giapponese	*Japanese*	**tedesco** (*pl.* ***tedeschi***)	*German*
francese	*French*	**spagnolo**	*Spanish*
irlandese	*Irish*	**russo**	*Russian*
inglese	*English*	**cinese**	*Chinese*
messicano	*Mexican*	**greco**	*Greek*
canadese	*Canadian*		

bianco (*pl.* ***bianchi***)	*white*	**blu**	*blue*
nero	*black*	**azzurro**	*light blue*
rosso	*red*	**marrone**	*brown*
verde	*green*	**rosa**	*pink*
grịgio	*grey*	**viola**	*purple*
giạllo	*yellow*		

nero
viola
blu
azzurro
verde
giallo
arancione
rosso
nero

Spettro solare

---

*caro, after the noun, means *expensive:* **un'automọbile cara**, *an expensive car.*
In Italian, adjectives denoting nationality are not capitalized, while nouns are: **gli Italiani, gli Americani, etc.

una signora **inglese**	*an English lady*
la lingua **cinese**	*the Chinese language*
una mạcchina **tedesca**	*a German car*
due belle donne **americane**	*two beautiful American women*
un fiore **giallo**	*a yellow flower*
due case **bianche**	*two white houses*

NOTE:

a. Like nouns ending in **-ca**, the adjectives ending in **-ca** change the plural to **-che**.

b. The adjectives **rosa, blu,** and **viola** are invariable.

due biciclette **blu**	*two blue bicycles*
due rose **rosa**	*two pink roses*

Pratica

A. Di che colore è (sono)...? (*What color is, are...?*) **Domanda e risposta.**

ESEMPIO gli ạlberi **—Di che colore sono gli ạlberi?**
—Sono verdi.

1. i tassì (*taxis*) di New York **2.** la bandiera (*flag*) americana **3.** la bandiera italiana **4.** la neve (*snow*) **5.** gli occhi della compagna di classe vicino a te (*near you*) **6.** i capelli del compagno di classe vicino a te **7.** il cielo (*sky*) quando piove (*it rains*) **8.** il cielo quando è sereno (*it is clear*)

B. Com'è? Come sono? Domanda e risposta.

ESEMPIO chiesa di San Pietro/grande **—Com'è la chiesa di San Pietro?**
—È grande.

1. città di Firenze/bello **2.** ragazze italiane/bruno **3.** compagne di classe/simpạtico **4.** gelati italiani/buono **5.** veri amici/caro **6.** professore(ssa) d'italiano/buono, bello, bravo **7.** occhi di.../verde, blu, castano **8.** mạcchine tedesche/caro **9.** studenti d'italiano/intelligente **10.** film di Cọppola/interessante **11.** edifici in centro/alto

C. No. Domanda e risposta.

ESEMPIO cattivo/gelato italiano/buono
—È cattivo il gelato italiano?
—No, è buono.

1. basso/edifici di Manhattan/alto **2.** americano/automọbili Toyota/giapponese **3.** diffịcile/lezioni d'italiano/fạcile **4.** spagnolo/mạcchine Fiat/italiano **5.** antipạtico/compagni di classe/simpạtico **6.** pigro/topi di biblioteca/studioso **7.** corto/Fifth Avenue (*f.*)/lungo **8.** brutto/Firenze (*f.*)/bello **9.** pọvero/signor J. Paul Getty/ricco **10.** americano/mạcchine BMW/tedesco

D. Leggete i nomi con gli aggettivi nella posizione corretta e fate i cambiamenti necessari. (*Read the nouns with the adjectives in the proper place, and make the necessary changes.*)

1. (giọvane) la signora 2. (pịccolo) un giardino 3. (giapponese) le macchine 4. (caro) gli amici 5. (nero) i capelli 6. (interessante) una cosa 7. (francese) i caffè 8. (rosa) i fiori 9. (grande) le piazze 10. (bello) le feste 11. (simpạtico) le signorine 12. (bravo) una dottoressa 13. (facile) le parole 14. (pịccolo, verde) una casa 15. (messicano, nuovo) un ristorante 16. (nero, stesso) gli occhi.

E. Rispondete usando **molto**. (*Answer using* ***molto***.)

ESEMPIO È una buona ragazza Lisa? **—Sì, è una ragazza molto buona.**

1. Siete studenti simpạtici voi? 2. È una lịngua fạcile l'italiano? 3. Ci sono buone ragazze in classe? 4. Sei un(a) ragazzo(a) studioso(a), tu? 5. È una lịngua diffịcile il cinese? 6. È una bella città Perụgia? 7. Sono due città industriali Milano e Torino? 8. Sono due bravi tenori Pavarotti e Domingo? 9. È un aẹreo veloce (*fast*) il Concord?

F. Mettete le frasi al plurale, secondo l'esempio. (*Change the sentences to the plural, according to the example.*)

ESEMPIO Lucia è una ragazza carina e molto simpạtica. (Lucia e Rita)
Lucia e Rita sono due ragazze carine e molto simpạtiche.

1. Claudio è un compagno intelligente e anche studioso. (Claudio e Luciano) 2. Antọnio è un bravo studente, ma molto pọvero. (Antọnio e Liliana) 3. Fido è un vẹcchio cane molto buono. (Fido e Lassie) 4. La Mercedes è una mạcchina elegante, ma molto cara. (La Mercedes e la Ferrari) 5. L'italiano è una lịngua un po' (*a little*) diffịcile, ma molto bella. (L'italiano e il francese)

II. Buono e bello

—Buona fortuna! Good luck!
—Buon viaggio! Have a nice trip!
—Buone vacanze Have a nice vacation!

1. When the adjective **buono** (*good*) precedes a singular noun, it has the same endings as the indefinite article **un**.

un libro, un **buon** libro	*a book, a good book*
un'amica, una **buon**'amica	*a friend, a good friend*

NOTE:
Buono in its plural forms has regular endings:

due **buoni** amici	*two good friends*
due **buone** ragazze	*two good girls*

2. When the adjective **bello** (*beautiful, handsome*) precedes a noun, it has the same endings as the definite article **il**.

il ragazzo, il **bel** ragazzo	*the boy, the handsome boy*
i fiori, i **bei** fiori	*the flowers, the beautiful flowers*
l'ạlbero, il **bell'**albero	*the tree, the beautiful tree*
la casa, la **bella** casa	*the house, the beautiful house*
l'amica, la **bell'**amica	*the friend, the beautiful friend*
gli occhi, i **begli** occhi	*the eyes, the beautiful eyes*
le parole, le **belle** parole	*the words, the beautiful words*
lo stato, il **bello** stato	*the state, the beautiful state*

Pratica

A. **Buono. Domanda e risposta.** (*You want to know what something or someone is like.*)

ESEMPIO caffè —**Com'è il caffè?**
—**È un buon caffè.**
—**Come sono i compagni?**
—**Sono buoni compagni.**

1. ristorante **2.** lezione **3.** automọbile **4.** libro **5.** idea **6.** amici **7.** dottore **8.** cane **9.** consigli (*advices*) **10.** film (*sing.*) **11.** ragazze

B. **Bello.** *(You are showing a friend some pictures, and your friend comments by using* **bello***.)*

ESEMPIO casa di Anna —**Ecco la casa di Anna.**
—**Che bella casa!**

1. fontana di Trevi **2.** negọzio Gucci **3.** uffịcio del dottor Sarzi **4.** ạlberi di rose **5.** automọbile di Marcello **6.** ragazzo di Gabriella **7.** zoo di San Diego **8.** stụdio di un pittore italiano **9.** chiesa di San Marco **10.** giardini Bọboli di Firenze

C. **No!** Rispondete usando il contrario di **cattivo** e di **brutto.** *(Answer by using the opposite of* **cattivo** *and* **brutto***.)*

1. È un brutto negọzio? **2.** È un brutto cane? **3.** Sono brutti edifici? **4.** Sono cattive amiche? **5.** È un cattivo libro? **6.** È una brutta città? **7.** Sono brutti giardini? **8.** È un cattivo gelato? **9.** È una brutta cosa? **10.** È un brutto sogno (*dream*)? **11.** È una cattiva abitụdine (*habit*)? **12.** È una cattiva idea?

III. Avere

—Che naso ha Pinocchio?
—Ha un naso lungo.

The present tense (**presente**) of **avere** is conjugated as follows:

Person	Singular	Plural
1st	io **ho** (*I have*)	noi **abbiamo** (*we have*)
2nd	tu **hai** (*you have, familiar*)	voi **avete** (*you have, familiar*)
3rd	lui **ha** (*he has*) lei **ha** (*she has*) Lei **ha** (*you have, formal*)	loro **hanno** (*they have*) Loro **hanno** (*you have, formal*)

Io **ho** un cane. E tu? — *I have a dog. And you?*
Gianni non **ha** i capelli neri. — *Gianni does not have black hair.*
Voi non **avete** il libro. — *You don't have the book.*
Ha una macchina americana Lei? — *Do you have an American car?*
I signori Scotti **hanno** una bella casa? — *Do Mr. and Mrs. Scotti have a nice home?*

Hai una bicicletta, (non è) vero? — *You have a bicycle, don't you?*
Marcello **ha** gli occhi verdi, (non è) vero? — *Marcello has green eyes, doesn't he?*

NOTE:

a. To use the verb **avere** in the negative or interrogative form, follow the general rules given in Chapter 1, pp. 14–15.

b. Another way of asking a question in Italian is by placing **(non è) vero?** at the end of a statement.

A. Completate con la forma corretta del presente di **avere**. (*Complete with the correct form of the present tense of* ***avere***.)

1. Antọnio non _____ un bel cane nero. **2.** Lui e io _____ un bel negọzio a Roma. **3.** Anche tu _____ una bicicletta blu? **4.** Io _____ un buon amico. **5.** Lui _____ i capelli castani. **6.** Non _____ una foto del Colosseo voi? **7.** Un dottore _____ una professione diffịcile. **8.** _____ un compagno di stanza tu? **9.** Tu e Lisa _____ una mạcchina americana o tedesca? **10.** Oggi noi non _____ tempo (*time*). **11.** _____ un computer tu? **12.** Quanti (*How many*) libri d'italiano _____ gli stụdenti di questa classe?

B. **...non è vero? Domanda e risposta.**

ESEMPIO tu, una mạcchina nuova
—**Tu hai una mạcchina nuova, non è vero?**
—**Sì, ho una mạcchina nuova.** *o* **No, non ho una mạcchina nuova.**)

1. voi, un esame d'italiano **2.** il tuo (*your*) amico, una motocicletta **3.** gli studenti, il week-end lịbero (*free*) **4.** noi, esami diffịcili **5.** tu, un appuntamento (*date*) domani **6.** tu ed io, un(a) professore(ssa) simpạtico(a) **7.** tu e i compagni di classe, il nụmero di telẹfono del(la) professore(ssa) **8.** gli studenti di questa classe, due lezioni d'italiano alla settimana (*per week*)

C. **No! Domanda e risposta.** Rispondete usando l'aggettivo contrario (*opposite*).

ESEMPIO Marcello, un amico stụpido
—**Ha un amico stụpido Marcello?**
—**No, ha un amico intelligente.**

1. il tuo (*your*) amico, una mạcchina nera **2.** voi, cattivi amici **3.** tu, compagni pigri **4.** i professori, una professione noiosa **5.** tu, una bicicletta nuova **6.** gli studenti, corsi fạcili **7.** un ragazzo di dọdici (12) anni, i capelli bianchi **8.** tu, un grande appartamento

IV. Quanto? (*How much?*) e i numeri cardinali da 0 a 100

—Quanti anni hai, nonno?
—Ho settant'anni, bambina.

1. **Quanto (quanta, quanti, quante)** used as an interrogative adjective must agree in gender and number with the noun it modifies.

Quante lezioni hai oggi?	*How many classes do you have today?*
Quanto tempo hai?	*How much time do you have?*

2. **Quanto** is invariable when it precedes a verb and is used as an indefinite interrogative expression.

Quanto costa la torta? **Quant'è** la torta?	*How much is the cake?*
Sette dollari.	*Seven dollars.*
Quanto fa quaranta meno sette?	*How much is forty minus seven?*
Fa trentatrè.	*It is thirty-three.*

Ecco due topi di biblioteca!

3. The cardinal numbers from *zero* to 100 are:

0	zero	10	dieci	20	venti	30	trenta
1	uno	11	ụndici	21	ventuno	31	trentuno
2	due	12	dọdici	22	ventidue	40	quaranta
3	tre	13	trẹdici	23	ventitrè	50	cinquanta
4	quattro	14	quattọrdici	24	ventiquattro	60	sessanta
5	cinque	15	quịndici	25	venticinque	70	settanta
6	sei	16	sẹdici	26	ventisei	80	ottanta
7	sette	17	diciassette	27	ventisette	90	novanta
8	otto	18	diciotto	28	ventotto	100	cento
9	nove	19	diciannove	29	ventinove		

a. All these numbers are invariable except **zero** and **uno. Uno** has the same forms (**un, uno, una, un'**) as the indefinite article **un** when it precedes a noun. (**Un amico** translates as *a friend* or *one friend.*)

C'è **una** fontana in Piazza Navona? — *Is there **one** fountain in Piazza Navona?*

No, ci sono **tre** fontane. — *No, there are **three** fountains.*

In 100 (cento), ci sono **due zeri.** — *In 100, there are **two** zeros.*

b. The numbers **venti, trenta, quaranta,** up to **novanta,** drop the final vowel before adding **uno** and **otto.**

trentụn giorni — *thirty-one days*

quarantotto minuti — *forty-eight minutes*

c. The numbers **ventuno, trentuno, quarantuno,** up to **novantuno,** drop the final **o** in front of a noun.

Lisa ha **ventụn** anni. — *Lisa is twenty-one years old.*

d. The numbers **venti, trenta, quaranta,** up to **cento,** usually drop the final vowel in front of the word **anni.**

La nonna ha **ottant'anni.** — *Grandma is eighty.*

e. Tre takes an accent when it is added to **venti, trenta,** and so on: **ventitrè, trentatrè,** etc.

NOTE:
In decimal numbers, Italian uses a comma (**vịrgola**), while English uses a period (**punto**). $3,25 = tre dọllari e venticinque centẹsimi

Pratica

A. Contate da due a venti per due. (*Count from 2 to 20 by twos.*)

B. Leggete le seguenti frasi ad alta voce. (*Read the following sentences aloud.*)

1. Domani abbiamo 3 lezioni. **2.** Oggi ho 17 dọllari (*dollars*). **3.** 13 è un brutto nụmero. **4.** La signora non ha 5 bambini; ha 7 bambini. **5.** Ho un cọmpito (*homework*) di 19 pạgine! **6.** Per piacere, non hai 20 dọllari? **7.** In giardino, ci sono 15 ạlberi di rose. **8.** 51 è un nụmero pari (*even*) o dịspari (*odd*)? **9.** Un gatto (*cat*) ha 9 vite (*lives*). **10.** Io ho 1 computer e 1 mạcchina da scrịvere.

C. Scrivete in parole i seguenti numeri. (*Write in full words the following numbers*).

15, 21, 28, 31, 43, 66, 78, 91, 100

D. **Quanto fa...? Domanda e risposta.** Uno studente domanda e l'altro completa le seguenti operazioni. (*One student asks and another completes the following equations.*)

1. 11 + (**più**) 30 = (**fa**) _____
2. 80 – (**meno**) 22 = _____
3. 10 × (**per**) 7 = _____
4. 100 : (**diviso**) 4 = _____

E. Rispondete alle seguenti domande. (*Answer the following questions.*)

1. Quanti minuti ci sono in un'ora (*hour*)? **2.** Quante ore ci sono in un giorno? **3.** Quanti giorni ci sono nel mese di aprile? **4.** Quanti anni ci sono in un secolo (*century*)? **5.** Quanti anni ha il presidente degli Stati Uniti? **6.** Quante stelle (*stars*) ci sono sulla (*on the*) bandiera americana? **7.** Quante libbre (*pounds*) ci sono, approssimativamente, in un chilogrammo? **8.** Quanti zeri ci sono in 1000 (mille) dollari? **9.** Quanti studenti ci sono nella classe d'italiano? **10.** Quante sillabe ci sono nella parola più lunga (*longest*) della lingua italiana: «precipitevolissimevolmente» (*very fast*)

F. **Quanti anni hai?** Domandate a un(a) compagno(a) quanti anni ha, e dite (*say*) quanti anni avete voi. È permesso mentire! (*You are allowed to lie!*)

LETTURA

DUE AMICI DIFFERENTI

Marcello Scotti e Antonio Catalano sono buoni amici. Marcello è giovane, alto, snello e biondo. Ha gli occhi verdi, il *naso* greco e la *bocca* regolare. È un bel ragazzo? Sì, un vero Adone! Ha anche una nuova Ferrari rossa. È un ragazzo fortunato, *un po'* superficiale, ma generoso.

E Antonio? Anche lui è giovane, ha gli stessi anni di Marcello, ma non è molto bello. È un po' basso e *grassottello*. Ha i capelli neri e il naso un po' *storto*, ma ha due begli occhi azzurri ed è molto simpatico. Non ha la macchina, ma ha la *chitarra* e Fido, un vecchio cane, basso e grasso, con le *gambe* storte.

E in classe, come sono i due amici? Be', in classe è un'altra cosa, perchè Marcello è mediocre, ma Antonio è molto bravo. Sì, Antonio è un vero *campione*.

naso nose
bocca mouth
un po' a little
grassottello chubby
storto crooked
chitarra guitar
gambe legs
campione champion

Comprensione

1. Chi sono Marcello e Antọnio? **2.** Sono vẹcchi? **3.** È vero che Marcello è un brutto ragazzo? **4.** Di che colore sono gli occhi di Marcello? **5.** Che mạcchina ha? **6.** È un amico avaro? **7.** È un bel ragazzo Antọnio? **8.** È alto? **9.** Di che colore sono gli occhi di Antọnio? **10.** Ha la mạcchina? Che cos'ha? **11.** Com'è Antọnio in classe? **12.** È un bravo studente Marcello?

Domande personali

1. Com'è Lei? È alto(a) o basso(a)? È grasso(a) o magro(a)? Di che colore sono gli occhi? E i capelli? Ha i capelli corti o lunghi? **2.** Lei è studioso(a) o pigro(a)? È avaro(a) o generoso(a) con gli amici? Quando Lei è nella (*in the*) classe d'italiano, è contento(a) o triste?

ATTIVITÀ SUPPLEMENTARI

A. *In pairs, ask each other about yourselves. Then present each other to the class, and describe each other.*

B. **Descrivete le persone nella foto.** (*Describe the people in the picture*). Chi sono, quanti sono, come si chiạmano, come sono, dove sono?

C. **Riempite la vostra carta d'identità.** *(Fill out your own identification card using the example of Antonio's card, and some imagination.)*

Cognome *Catalano*	Cognome ____________________
Nome *Antonio*	Nome ____________________
*Nato il *26-4-1974*	Nato il ____________________
a *Napoli*	a ____________________
Cittadinanza *Italiana*	Cittadinanza ____________________
Residenza *Milano*	Residenza ____________________
Via *Carducci 25*	Via ____________________
**Stato civile *Celibe*	Stato civile ____________________
Professione *Studente*	Professione ____________________
Connotati	Connotati
Statura *m.1, 62*	Statura ____________________
Capelli *neri*	Capelli ____________________
Occhi *azzurri*	Occhi ____________________
Segni particolari	Segni particolari

D. **Come si dice in italiano?**

1. Lisa and Graziella are two good friends.
2. They have brown eyes, but Lisa is blond and tall, whereas (**mentre**) Graziella is short and dark-haired.
3. They are very pretty and young.
4. Lisa is rich and has a small car.
5. Graziella has an old bicycle.
6. They have the same German professor.
7. It is a difficult class.
8. But today they have a very easy exam.

---

*born
Stato civile: sposato/a, divorziato/a, cẹlibe/nụbile (*single*)

Vocabolario

Nomi

l'anno	*year*
la bandiera	*flag*
il cane	*dog*
il chilogrammo	*kilo*
il colore	*color*
il compagno (la compagna) di stanza, di scuola	*roommate, classmate*
il corso	*class, (academic) course*
la cosa	*thing*
il dọllaro	*dollar*
la festa	*party*
il film	*movie*
il gatto	*cat*
il gelato	*ice cream*
il giorno	*day*
l'idea	*idea*
la libbra	*pound*
la lịngua	*language*
la mạcchina	*car*
il mese	*month*
il minuto	*minute*
la motocicletta	*motorcycle*
la nazionalità	*nationality*
il nụmero	*number*
l'ọcchio (*pl.* gli occhi)	*eye(s)*
l'ora	*hour*
il papà	*dad*
la parola	*word*
la professione	*profession*
la rosa	*rose*
la sera	*evening*
la settimana	*week*
la sịllaba	*syllable*
la stanza	*room*
lo stato	*state*
il tempo	*time*
lo zio, la zia	*uncle, aunt*

Aggettivi

altro	*other*
bianco (*pl.* bianchi)	*white*
blu (*inv.*)	*blue*
bravo	*good, talented*
buono	*good*
canadese	*Canadian*
carino	*pretty, cute*
caro	*dear, expensive*
castano	*brown (for eyes and hair)*
cattivo	*bad, mean*
che...?	*what...?*
cinese	*Chinese*
corto	*short (for things)*
curioso	*curious*
diffịcile	*difficult*
divertente	*amusing*
fạcile	*easy*
francese	*French*
giallo	*yellow*
giapponese	*Japanese*
greco	*Greek*
grịgio	*grey*
inglese	*English*
irlandese	*Irish*
marrone	*brown (for objects)*
messicano	*Mexican*
nero	*black*
nuovo	*new*
quale...?	*which...?*
quanti? quante?	*how many?*
regolare	*regular*
ricco (*pl.* ricchi)	*rich*
romano	*Roman*
rosa (*inv.*)	*pink*
rosso	*red*
russo	*Russian*
spagnolo	*Spanish*
stesso	*same*
tedesco (*pl.* tedeschi)	*German*
verde	*green*
vero	*true*
viola (*inv.*)	*purple*

Verbi

avere	*to have*

Altre Espressioni

Bè	*well*
Buona fortuna!	*Good luck!*
in generale	*generally*
quanti anni hai?	*how old are you?*
o	*or*
solo (*inv.*)	*only*
stasera	*tonight*
un po' (+ *adj.*)	*a little*
un topo di biblioteca	*bookworm*
vicino a	*near*

Venezia. Festa sul Canal Grande. Dietro (behind), si trova Piazza San Marco, con l'alto campanile e il Palazzo Ducale in marmo bianco e rosa.

ALCUNE REGIONI E *CITTÀ–CAPOLUOGO* D'ITALIA

some / regional capitals

Gli Italiani considerano *il loro paese* diviso geograficamente in quattro parti: Italia settentrionale (del nord), centrale (del centro), meridionale (del sud) e insulare (delle *isole*). L'Italia è anche divisa amministrativamente in venti regioni, e *ogni* regione ha la sua città–capoluogo. La più famosa è nell'Italia centrale: Roma, capoluogo del Lazio e *dal* 1870 (mille ottocento settanta) capitale d'Italia. Roma è *chiamata* «la città eterna», centro dell'antico impero romano e *sede* dei *Papi*.*

their country / islands / each / since / called / seat/Popes

Al sud *si trova* la Campania con il suo capoluogo: Napoli. *Questa* città è un porto sul *mare* Tirreno, vicino al *maestoso* Vesuvio e alle belle isole di Capri e di Ischia.

is found / this/sea / majestic

Il *primo* porto d'Italia è al nord: Genova (in Liguria), *patria* del grande navigatore Cristoforo Colombo. La città si estende sulle *colline*, di fronte al mar Ligure. La città romantica per eccellenza è Venezia, capoluogo del Veneto. È una città sull'acqua: i canali, i *ponti*, le gondole, i palazzi pittoreschi e Piazza San Marco *conferiscono* alla città un'atmosfera magica.

first / country / hills / bridges / bestow

---

*Rome will be described more extensively in **Pagina culturale**, *Chapter 8*.

Comprensione

Completate le seguenti frasi. (*Complete the following sentences.*)

1. L'Itạlia è divisa geograficamente in...
2. In Itạlia ci sono venti...
3. L'Itạlia del sud è chiamata anche l'Itạlia...
4. La capitale d'Itạlia e la città-capoluogo del Lạzio è...
5. Nạpoli è un porto sul mare...
6. Capri e Ịschia sono due....
7. Gẹnova è la pạtria del famoso navigatore...
8. Venẹzia è il capoluogo del...

Roma. Piazza Navona e la fontana di Nettuno, una delle tre fontane di questa grande piazza.

3 ALL'UNIVERSITÀ

Studenti in un'aula dell'Università di Roma.

Punti di vista

Oggi studio per gli esami
In classe

Punti grammaticali

I Verbi regolari in *-are:* il presente
II Le preposizioni
III Frasi idiomatiche con *avere*
IV *Quale?* e *che?* (Which? and what?)
V *Anche*

Lettura

La stanza di Lucia

Pagina culturale

Il sistema scolastico italiano

PUNTI DI VISTA

Gina e Pietro ripassano (review) gli appunti di un corso. Il professore spiega un punto difficile.

OGGI *STUDIO* PER GLI ESAMI — I study

Gina e Pietro pạrlano *davanti* alla biblioteca. — in front of

Gina	Pietro, quante lezioni hai oggi?	
Pietro	Ho una lezione di biologia e un'altra di fịsica. E tu?	
Gina	Io ho un esame di chịmica e *ho bisogno di* studiare perchè gli esami *del* professor Riva sono sempre diffịcili.	I need to of (the)
Pietro	Non hai gli *appunti?*	notes
Gina	No, ma Franca, *la mia* compagna di classe, è una ragazza molto studiosa e ha molte pạgine di appunti.	my
Pietro	Gina, *io ho fame,* e tu?	I am hungry
Gina	Anch'io. C'è un pịccolo caffè vicino alla biblioteca. Perchè non mangiamo *lì?*	there
Pietro	Sì, *va bene,* perchè non ho molto tempo. *Dopo* le lezioni *lavoro* in biblioteca. E ho anche molti *cọmpiti* per domani.	it's o.k./After I work homework
Gina	La vita *dei* pọveri studenti non è fạcile!	of the

Comprensione

1. Quante lezioni ha Pietro oggi? **2.** Che cosa stụdia Gina oggi? Perchè? **3.** Chi è Franca? **4.** Com'è? **5.** Perchè Gina e Pietro mạngiano vicino alla biblioteca? **6.** Dove lavora oggi Pietro? **7.** Che cos'ha per domani? **8.** Com'è la vita degli studenti?

Studio di parole

NELL'ẠULA *IN THE CLASSROOM*

la conferenza lecture
la lavagna blackboard
la scrivania desk
il gesso chalk
la matita pencil
la penna pen
la mạcchina da scrịvere typewriter
la calcolatrice calculator
gli appunti notes
il quaderno notebook
il cọmpito homework
il voto grade
il trimestre quarter
il semestre semester
la biologia biology
la chịmica chemistry
le relazioni internazionali international relations
le lịngue straniere foreign languages
la biblioteca library
presente present
assente absent
l'informạtica computer science
la fịsica physics
la matemạtica math(ematics)
l'economia economics
le scienze polịtiche political science
la stọria dell'arte art history
la mụsica music
il corso di stọria the history course (class)
la lezione di chịmica the chemistry class
l'esame (*m.*) di fịsica the physics exam
l'esame orale oral exam
l'esame scritto written exam
studiare to study
frequentare to attend
il liceo high school
l'università university
la facoltà di scienze (legge, medicina, ingegneria) school of science (law, medicine, engineering)
il diploma high school degree
la lạurea university degree

A. Domande.

1. Dove sono gli studenti nel disegno (*drawing*)?
2. La professoressa è alla (*at the*) scrivania o alla lavagna?
3. Che cosa insegna?
4. Di cosa ha bisogno (*What does she need*) per scrịvere sulla lavagna?
5. Sono distratti o attenti gli studenti?
6. Di cosa hanno bisogno per prẹndere (*to take*) appunti?

B. Domande personali.

1. Lei frequenta il liceo o l'università?
2. Quanti corsi ha Lei questo trimestre? (semestre?) Quali (*Which*) sono?
3. Quale corso è interessante?
4. Quali cọmpiti sono noiosi?
5. Ha bisogno di un computer Lei per ẹssere un bravo studente (una brava studentessa)?
6. Ha un computer Lei? Una mạcchina da scrịvere? un IBM?
7. Quante lezioni ha Lei oggi?
8. Che cosa stụdia oggi?
9. Lavora oggi? E domani? Dove lavora?
10. Com'è la Sua (*your*) vita?
11. Ha molto tempo lịbero (*free*)?
12. Lavora spesso (*often*) in biblioteca?

UNIVERSITÀ DEGLI STUDI DI PARMA

matr. n. 066940

Il Sig. ROSSI CINZIA

nato a MANTOVA il 18/06/70

è stato immatricolato studente nella Università degli studi di Parma

FACULTA' DI SCIENZE MM. FF. NN.

nell'anno accademico: 1989/90

CORSO DI LAUREA IN MATEMATICA

Parma, 02/02/90

IL SEGRETARIO
(Elia Papadini)

FIRMA DELLO STUDENTE

Rossi Cinzia

AVVERTENZE - Il presente libretto-tessera contiene 16 pagine a stampa; quello nel quale siano stati tolti o sostituiti dei fogli o che abbia cancellature e raschiature, non giustificate dal Segretario, è nullo.

Il libretto-tessera deve essere custodito gelosamente dallo studente, salvo comprovati apprezzabili motivi, non si rilasciano duplicati.

Questo libretto-tessera non è valevole nè può servire in nessun modo e sotto qualsiasi forma come documento comprovante la iscrizione.

Al termine degli Studi esso deve essere depositato in Segreteria ed acquisito definitivamente agli atti.

Tẹssera universitạria

Biblioteca Comunale di Mantova

N. ____

Nome e Cognome Marisa Vicini

Professione Studentessa

Indirizzo Via L. Einaudi, 5
46100 Mantova

N. Telefono 0376-3358

Data 24 febbraio

Entra con materiale proprio

(SI) No

In caso di risposta affermativa indicare:

libri n. 2

riviste n. —

giornali n. —

altro quaderni

Scheda necessạria per entrare in una biblioteca

Ascoltiamo!

In classe. *A teacher is greeting his students in a* **liceo** *in Rome, and asking and answering a variety of questions at the beginning of class. Listen to the exchanges, then answer the related questions.*

Comprensione

1. Che (*What*) scuola frequentano gli studenti? **2.** Hanno un esame d'informatica oggi? **3.** Sono tutti presenti? **4.** Quanti minuti hanno gli studenti per l'esame? **5.** Gli studenti hanno tre esami orali questo (*this*) trimestre? **6.** Secondo (*According to*) il professore, è difficile l'esame? **7.** Gli studenti hanno bisogno di concentrazione. Una studentessa ha bisogno di un miracolo. Secondo voi, è preparata per l'esame?

Dialogo

In groups of three, play the role of the professor and the two students. Expand on the dialogue, drawing from the vocabulary in "Studio di parole."

PUNTI GRAMMATICALI

I. Verbi regolari in *-are*: il presente

Mamma e Nino suonano; il papà canta.

I tre ragazzi giocano: a golf, a tennis, a pallone.

1. Chi suona la chitarra?
2. Anche il papà suona?
3. A che cosa giocano i tre ragazzi?

cantare (*to sing*)	
cant **o**	cant **iamo**
cant **i**	cant **ate**
cant **a**	cạnt **ano**

1. Verbs that end in **-are** are the most frequently used verbs and are identified as first conjugation verbs. With few exceptions, they are regular. The infinitive of a regular verb such as **cantare** consists of the stem **cant-** (invariable) and the ending **-are.** To conjugate the present tense (**presente**) of **cantare,** we replace **-are** with a different ending for each person: **-o, -i, -a, -iamo, -ate, -ano.**

2. The present tense in Italian is rendered in English in different ways:

   Io canto. { *I sing.* / *I am singing.* / *I do sing.* }

   Canta Maria? { *Does Maria sing?* / *Is Maria singing?* }

   Maria non canta. { *Maria does not sing.* / *Maria is not singing.* }

Aspetti un amico?	*Are you waiting for a friend?*
Desịdero guardare la TV.	*I want to watch TV.*
Giochiamo a tennis oggi?	*Are we playing tennis today?*
Quante lịngue **parli**?	*How many languages do you speak?*
(Loro) **Ạbitano** in una pịccola città.	*They live in a small city.*

3. The present tense is often used to express the future tense.

   I corsi **comịnciano** domani. — *Courses will begin tomorrow.*

4. Here is a list of some common **-are** verbs:

abitare	*to live*	**(in)cominciare**	*to begin*
ascoltare	*to listen (to)*	**insegnare**	*to teach*
aspettare	*to wait (for)*	**lavorare**	*to work*
cantare	*to sing*	**mangiare**	*to eat*
comprare	*to buy*	**parlare (a)/(di)**	*to speak (to)/(about)*
desiderare	*to wish, to want*	**pensare (a)**	*to think (about)*
domandare	*to ask*	**spiegare**	*to explain*
giocare (a)	*to play (a game)*	**studiare**	*to study*
guardare	*to look at, to watch*	**suonare**	*to play (an instrument)*
imparare	*to learn*		

   a. Verbs ending in **-iare** drop the **i** of the infinitive stem before adding the endings **-i** and **-iamo.**

      studi**are**: studi, studi**amo** — incominci**are**: incominci, incominci**amo**

b. Verbs ending in **-care** and **-gare** add an **h** before the endings **-i** and **-iamo** to preserve the hard sounds of /k/ and /g/.

gio**care**: gio**chi**, gio**chi**amo   spie**gare**: spie**ghi**, spie**ghi**amo

All these spelling changes are limited to the first conjugation verbs.

5. Contrary to their English equivalents, the verbs **ascoltare**, **aspettare**, and **guardare** take a direct object and therefore are *not* followed by a preposition.

Aspettiamo l'ạutobus.	*We are waiting* ***for*** *the bus.*
Perchè non **ascolti** la rạdio?	*Why don't you listen* ***to*** *the radio?*
Guardate le foto?	*Are you looking* ***at*** *the photographs?*

6. **Imparare**, **(in)cominciare**, and **insegnare** take the preposition **a** before an infinitive.

Incomịncio a imparare a parlare in italiano.	*I'm beginning to learn to speak Italian.*

For a list of verbs that take a preposition (**a** or **di**) before an infinitive, see Appendix 2.

7. To express purpose (*in order to*), Italian uses **per** + *infinitive.*

Stụdio **per imparare.**	*I study (in order) to learn.*

Pratica

A. Completate le risposte. (*Complete the answers with the suggested verbs*).

1. *Che cosa o chi aspẹttano?*
   Tu ______ l'ạutobus e Franco ______ il treno. Noi ______ il dottore e le bambine ______ la mamma.
2. *A chi o a cosa pẹnsano?*
   Lui ______ a Maria e tu ______ a Roberto. Noi ______ all'esame di oggi e voi ______ alla festa di domani. Anch'io ______ alla festa di domani.
3. *Di che cosa pạrlano?*
   Il dottor Negri ______ di medicina. I professori ______ di polịtica e noi ______ di altre cose.
4. *Che strumento suọnano?*
   Papà ______ il violino. Noi ______ il pianoforte. Io ______ anche la tromba. E voi, che strumento ______?

B. **No! Domanda e risposta.** *(Follow the example.)*

ESEMPIO abitare in Italia/...   **—Ạbiti in Itạlia?**
—No, non ạbito in Itạlia, ạbito in Amẹrica.

1. studiare matemạtica/... 2. desiderare un disco (*record*) di Elvis Presley/... 3. imparare la lịngua giapponese/... 4. giocare a golf/... 5. ascoltare i compagni/... 6. parlare cinque lịngue/... 7. lavorare in biblioteca/... 8. mangiare all'università/... 9. comprare un'Alfa Romeo/...

C. **Imparo a…; Incomịncio a…** *(Say in a complete sentence what the following people are learning or beginning to do.)*

ESEMPIO (imparare) io, cantare **Io imparo a cantare.**

imparare **1.** noi, giocare a tennis **2.** la mamma, suonare il piano **3.** il bambino, parlare bene **4.** voi, ẹssere generosi **5.** la signorina, cantare **6.** Pietro ed io, usare il computer **7.** gli studenti, pensare **8.** io, studiare efficientemente

ESEMPIO (incominciare) io, lavorare **Io incomịncio a lavorare.**

incominciare **1.** ragazzi, giocare a pallone (*football*) **2.** il corso, ẹssere interessante **3.** noi, parlare degli esami **4.** voi, studiare la lezione **5.** uno studente, ẹssere impaziente **6.** voi, parlare italiano **7.** io, capire (*to understand*) la grammạtica **8.** noi, ẹssere stanchi (*tired*) di questo esercizio

D. Rispondete con una frase completa. *(Answer with a complete sentence.)*

1. Studi al liceo o all'università tu? **2.** Incominci a parlare italiano? **3.** Stasera mangi a casa o al ristorante? **4.** In quale città ạbiti? **5.** Ascolti la rạdio stasera? **6.** Guardi la televisione la sera? **7.** Lavori o studi solamente (*only*) tu? **8.** Se lavori, dove lavori? **9.** Parli italiano o inglese con i compagni in classe?

II. Le preposizioni

—Oggi siamo all'università. Il professore è alla lavagna. —Nella biblioteca i libri sono sugli scaffali.

1. Dove siamo oggi? **2.** Dov'è il professore? **3.** Cosa c'è sugli scaffali?

1. **Simple prepositions.** You have already learned some simple prepositions (**preposizioni sẹmplici**): **a**, **di**, **in**, **per.** The following chart lists all the simple prepositions and their meanings.

di (d')	*of*	**con**	*with*
a	*at, to, in*	**su**	*on, over, above*
da	*from, by*	**per**	*for*
in	*in*	**tra (fra)**	*between, among*

Ecco il professore **d'**inglese. — *There is the English professor (the professor of English).*
Abitiamo **a** New York. — *We live in New York.*
Il treno arriva **da** Roma. — *The train is arriving from Rome.*
Siamo **in** America. — *We are in America.*
Giochi **con** Gino? — *Are you playing with Gino?*
Il dizionario è **su** uno scaffale. — *The dictionary is on a shelf.*
La bicicletta è **per** Lia. — *The bicycle is for Lia.*
Il quaderno è **tra** due libri. — *The notebook is between two books.*

Note that **di** is used to express:

a. **possession:**
Di chi è il dizionario? *Whose dictionary is it?*
È **di** Antonio. *It is Antonio's.*

b. **place of origin:**
Di dov'è il signor Smith? *Where is Mr. Smith from?*
È **di** Londra. *He is from London.*

2. When the prepositions **a, da, di, in,** and **su** are used with a definite article, they combine to form one word (**preposizione articolata**), as follows:

	il	lo	l' (*m.*)	la	l' (*f.*)	i	gli	le
a	al	allo	all'	alla	all'	ai	agli	alle
da	dal	dallo	dall'	dalla	dall'	dai	dagli	dalle
di	del	dello	dell'	della	dell'	dei	degli	delle
in	nel	nello	nell'	nella	nell'	nei	negli	nelle
su	sul	sullo	sull'	sulla	sull'	sui	sugli	sulle

Studiamo **all'**università. — *We are studying at the university.*
Ecco l'ufficio **del** professore. — *Here is the office of the professor.*
La penna è **sul** tavolo. — *The pen is on the table.*
Lavorano **negli** Stati Uniti. — *They work in the United States.*
Lisa aspetta **nello** studio. — *Lisa is waiting in the study.*

The preposition **con** is seldom contracted. Its most common contractions are **col** and **coi; con i (coi) bambini.**

NOTE:

The contractions with the definite article occur when nouns are preceded by the article. First names and names of cities do not have an article.

È il libro **di** Luca? — *Is it Luca's book?*
No, è il libro **della** professoressa. — *No, it is the professor's book.*
Loro abitano **a** Verona. — *They live in Verona.*

A. Fulvio stụdia. Completate la pịccola stọria con le preposizioni sẹmplici **di, a, da, in, con, su, per, tra.**

1. Oggi Fụlvio è _____ biblioteca. 2. La biblioteca è _____ due alti edifici. 3. Fụlvio stụdia _____ un compagno. 4. Stụdia _____ l'esame di biologia. 5. Incomịncia a studiare _____ pạgina 18. 6. Ma ora il libro è _____ una sedia. 7. Fụlvio pensa _____ una ragazza bruna. 8. È mezzogiorno (*noon*); Fụlvio mạngia un panino (*sandwich*) _____ un pịccolo caffè. 9. Dov'è il libro _____ biologia?

B. Di che nazionalità? Domanda e risposta. Seguite l'esẹmpio. *(Follow the example.)*

ESEMPIO una signorina, Bari **—Di che nazionalità è una signorina di Bari?**
—Una signorina di Bari è italiana.

1. i turisti, Londra 2. una professoressa, Parigi 3. una ragazza, Mosca (*Moscow*) 4. i signori, Berlino 5. un ingegnere (*engineer*), Tọkio 6. gli studenti, Guadalajara 7. un architetto, Toronto 8. una dottoressa, Atene 9. due mẹdici (*physicians*), Belfast

C. Combinate (*combine*) la preposizione con l'artịcolo, come dall'esẹmpio.

ESEMPIO È il libro (di)/(lo) studente
È il libro dello studente.

1. Il professore spiega (a)/(gli) studenti 2. Siamo (a)/(la) lezione d'italiano 3. Il dizionạrio è (su)/(il) tạvolo 4. Ho bisogno (di)/(gli) appunti di stọria 5. Oggi parliamo (a)/(l') impiegato 6. I quaderni sono (su)/(lo) scaffale 7. Ci sono molti fiori (su)/(gli) ạlberi 8. La conferenza è (in)/(l') edifịcio di lingue straniere 9. Pietro lavora (in)/(il) ristorante vicino (a)/(l') università 10. Ecco la mạcchina (di)/(il) ragazzo di Gabriella 11. Ci sono due semestri (in)/(l') anno accadẹmico 12. C'è un virus (in)/(il) computer (di)/(il) mio compagno di stanza.

D. Completate le frasi con la preposizione articolata corretta.

ESEMPIO Questa sera siamo (a) _____ cinematọgrafo.
Questa sera siamo al cinematọgrafo.

1. La mia penna nera è (su) _____ tạvolo. 2. I quaderni sono (su) _____ scrivania. 3. La bell'automọbile grịgia è (di) _____ ragazzo di Gabriella. 4. Ci sono molte persone (in) _____ negozi. 5. Gli studenti sono (in) _____ ạula di fịsica. 6. Questa sera mangiate (a) _____ ristorante? 8. La mamma e i bambini sono (a) _____ zoo. 8. La professoressa spiega la lezione (a) _____ studenti. 9. Domani è il giorno (di) _____ esami. 10. Gianpạolo stụdia (a) _____ liceo.

E. Di chi (*Whose*) è (sono)...? Domanda e risposta.

ESEMPIO pallone/bambino
—Di chi è il pallone?
—È del bambino.

1. casa con il bel giardino/signori Giusti **2.** calcolatrice sulla sẹdia/signorina Ricci **3.** edifịcio rosso/dottor Galli **4.** orolọgio sul tạvolo /Antọnio **5.** quaderno nero/studentessa di medicina **6.** due computer /ingegner Scotti **7.** belle fotografie di Venẹzia/Lucia

F. Rispondete, secondo l'esẹmpio. *(Use the proper contraction in each instance.)*

ESEMPIO Dove mangiate oggi?/ristorante
—Oggi mangiamo al ristorante.

1. A che cosa pensate?/esame di biologia **2.** Dove studiate?/università di Pạdova **3.** Dove sono i libri?/scaffali **4.** Dove giọcano i bambini?/ parco **5.** Dove ci sono molte (*many*) persone?/negozi **6.** Dove lavora Pietro?/ristorante **7.** Dove aspettate gli amici?/caffè **8.** Dove aspettate il professore (la professoressa)?/ạula **9.** Dove cọmprate le banane?/ negọzio di frutta **10.** Dove canta Antọnio/dọccia (*shower*)

III. Frasi idiomatiche con *avere*

—Cara, non hai paura, vero?

1. In Italian, the following idiomatic expressions (**espressioni idiomạtiche**) are formed by using **avere** + *noun,* while in English they are formed in most cases by using *to be* + *adjective.*

avere fame	*to be hungry*	**avere caldo**	*to be hot*
avere sete	*to be thirsty*	**avere freddo**	*to be cold*
avere sonno	*to be sleepy*	**avere ragione**	*to be right*
avere paura (di)	*to be afraid (of)*	**avere torto**	*to be wrong*
avere bisogno (di)	*to need*	**avere fretta**	*to be in a hurry*
avere voglia (di)	*to feel like*		

Hai paura di un esame diffịcile? *Are you afraid of a difficult exam?*

Ha bisogno di un quaderno?	*Do you need a notebook?*
Ho caldo e **ho** anche **sete.**	*I am hot and I am also thirsty.*
Hai ragione: è un corso interessante.	*You are right: it is an interesting course.*
Hai voglia di mangiare un buon gelato?	*Do you feel like eating a good ice cream?*

NOTE:
When referring to an object as hot or cold, use **essere**: Il caffè **è** caldo. *The coffee is hot.*

2. To express age, Italian uses **avere** + *number* + **anni.**

Gina **ha** diciannove **anni.**	*Gina is nineteen years old.*
Quanti **anni ha** Pietro?	*How old is Pietro?*
Pietro **ha sette** anni.	*Pietro is 7 (years old).*

Pratica

A. A che cosa pensi se...? Domanda e risposta. *(Use the expressions from the list below to form questions and answers.)*

ESEMPIO avere fame/lasagne, fettuccine
—A che cosa pensi se hai fame?
—Penso alle lasagne o alle fettuccine.

1. avere sete/Coca Cola, acqua (*water*) **2.** avere sonno/letto, siesta **3.** avere fame/pizza, spaghetti **4.** avere caldo/tè freddo, gelato **5.** non avere voglia di studiare/amici, cinema **6.** avere freddo/mese (*m.*) d'agosto, caffè caldo

B. Completate con le preposizioni articolate.

1. lo ho paura degli esami, e Lei? Io no, ma ho paura _____ professori severi, _____ lezioni difficili, _____ dentista (*m.*), _____ cattivi dottori, _____ cani feroci e _____ amici disonesti. **2.** Noi abbiamo bisogno del quaderno per (*in order to*) studiare, e tu? Io no, ma ho bisogno _____ libro, _____ fogli, _____ tavolo, _____ lampada, _____ penna, _____ caffè, _____ appunti di chimica. **3.** Maurizio ha vent'anni: pensa _____ cinema, _____ ragazze, _____ musica rock, _____ sport; non pensa _____ studio, _____ compiti, _____ università, _____ professori, _____ esami.

C. *Agree or disagree with the following statements using* **avere ragione** *or* **avere torto.**

ESEMPIO —Non studio per gli esami. **—Hai torto. (*o:* Hai ragione.)**

1. Non mangio perchè ho paura di ingrassare (*of getting fat*).
2. Ascolto i buoni consigli (*advices*) di un amico. **3.** Non aspetto gli amici quando sono in ritardo (*they are late*). **4.** Gli studenti giocano a tennis e non studiano per gli esami. **5.** Siamo preoccupati per l'esame d'italiano. **6.** Il mio compagno di stanza guarda la TV e non pensa ai compiti. **7.** Questa mattina (*This morning*) mangio rapidamente perchè ho fretta.

D. **Perchè? Perchè...** (*Why? Because...*) Rispondete con frasi complete alle seguenti domande.

1. È mezzogiorno e i ragazzi desiderano mangiare. Perchè? 2. Stasera Mariella non guarda la televisione. Perchè? 3. Aldo è in una cartoleria (*stationery store*). Perchè? 4. Questa mattina Piero non ha tempo di parlare con gli amici. Perchè? 5. È un giorno caldo d'agosto e Luisa ha bisogno di una Coca Cola. Perchè?

IV. Quale? e che? (*Which?* and *what?*)

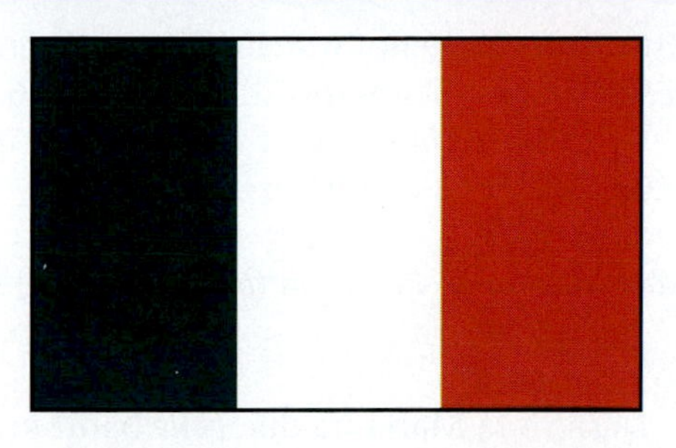

Quali sono i colori della bandiera italiana?

1. **Quale** and **che** are interrogative adjectives. **Quale** implies a choice and identification, and it usually drops the **-e** before **è**. Like the adjectives ending in **-e**, **quale** has only two forms: **quale** and **quali**.

Qual è la casa di Gino?	*Which is Gino's house?*
Quale professore hai?	*Which professor do you have?*
Quali possibilità ci sono?	*Which possibilities are there?*

Che indicates *what kind* and is an invariable adjective.

Che macchina hai?	*What (kind of) car do you have?*
Che libro è?	*What book is it?*

2. **Che** is also used in exclamations. In this case, it means *What ...!* or *What a ...!*

Che bravo studente!	*What a good student!*
Che bei bambini!	*What beautiful children!*

3. **Che** may also be a relative pronoun translating *that/which* or *who/whom* in a complex sentence. In Italian it must *always* be expressed, even if it is omitted in English.

Ecco la rivista **che** leggo.	*Here is the magazine (that/which) I am reading.*
Ecco i due ragazzi **che** abitano a Bologna.	*Here are the two boys who live in Bologna.*

Pratica

A. **Quale...? Domanda e risposta.** (*Follow the example.*)

ESEMPIO libro/Pietro
—Dov'è il libro?
—Quale libro?
—Il libro di Pietro.

1. dizionario/professore 2. quaderni/compagna di Franca 3. compiti/altro giorno 4. fotografie/bambini di Lorenzo 5. cose/Maria 6. nomi/compagne di classe 7. negozio/frutta 8. aula/conferenza 9. appunti/corso di chimica 10. biblioteca/università

B. **Che...?** (*A friend is making the following statements. Solicit more information by asking* **Che...?**)

ESEMPIO macchina/Volvo **—Oggi compro una macchina.**
—Che macchina?
—Una (macchina) Volvo.

1. cane/setter 2. orologio (*watch*)/Gucci 3. motocicletta/Honda 4. libro/di storia 5. dizionario/di spagnolo 6. penna/biro (*ballpoint pen*) nera. 7. automobile/Fiat 8. computer/Apple 9. bicicletta/Bianchi 10. macchina da scrivere/Olivetti

C. **Che...!** *(React with an exclamation to the following statements, according to the example.)*

ESEMPIO La signora Maria ha due *belle* bambine.
—Che *belle* bambine!

1. Lucia ha una stanza *disordinata.* 2. Marco non studia perchè è un ragazzo *pigro.* 3. Il (La) professore(ssa) è *paziente* quando spiega. 4. Questa pizza è molto *buona.* 5. Stefano è un ragazzo molto *generoso* con gli amici. 6. I film di...non sono interessanti, sono *stupidi.* 7. Marisa è una studentessa molto *brava* a scuola.

D. **Ecco... che...** *(Imagine that you are pointing out at people or objects. Make statements, following the example.)*

ESEMPIO _____ i ragazzi _____ giocano a tennis.
Ecco i ragazzi che giocano a tennis.

1. _____ la signorina _____ è spesso assente. 2. _____ le due bambine _____ parlano bene l'italiano. 3. _____ il professore _____ insegna scienze. 4. _____ l'autobus _____ io aspetto. 5. _____ la calcolatrice _____ desidero comprare. 6. _____ le fotografie _____ desidero guardare.

V. Anche (*Also, too, as well*)

1. This very commonly used word conveys a different meaning, according to its position in the sentence.

Anche Paolo ha una bicicletta.	*Paolo too* (not only Luciano) *has a bicycle.*
Paolo ha **anche** una bicicletta.	*Paolo has also a bicycle* (in addition to a car).

2. When **anche** modifies a subject pronoun, the pronoun must be expressed.

Io ho un computer. Hai un computer **anche** tu?	*I have a computer. Do you also have a computer?*
Sì, **anch'io** ho un computer.	*Yes, I too have a computer.*

Pratica

Rispondete alle domande e usate **anche** seguendo gli esempi. (*Answer the questions and use **anche**, following the examples.*)

ESEMPIO Io ho una bicicletta. E tu?
Anch'io ho una bicicletta.

Hai una bicicletta o una motocicletta?
Ho una bicicletta e anche una motocicletta.

1. Io ho un cane. E tu? **2.** Hai la bicicletta o l'automọbile? **3.** Ginetta ha tre corsi oggi. E voi? **4.** Luca è intelligente o solo studioso? **5.** Gli studenti d'italiano sono bravi o solo simpạtici? **6.** Io ho gli occhi azzurri, e Lei? **7.** Marcello è un ragazzo fortunato. E Rita?

LETTURA

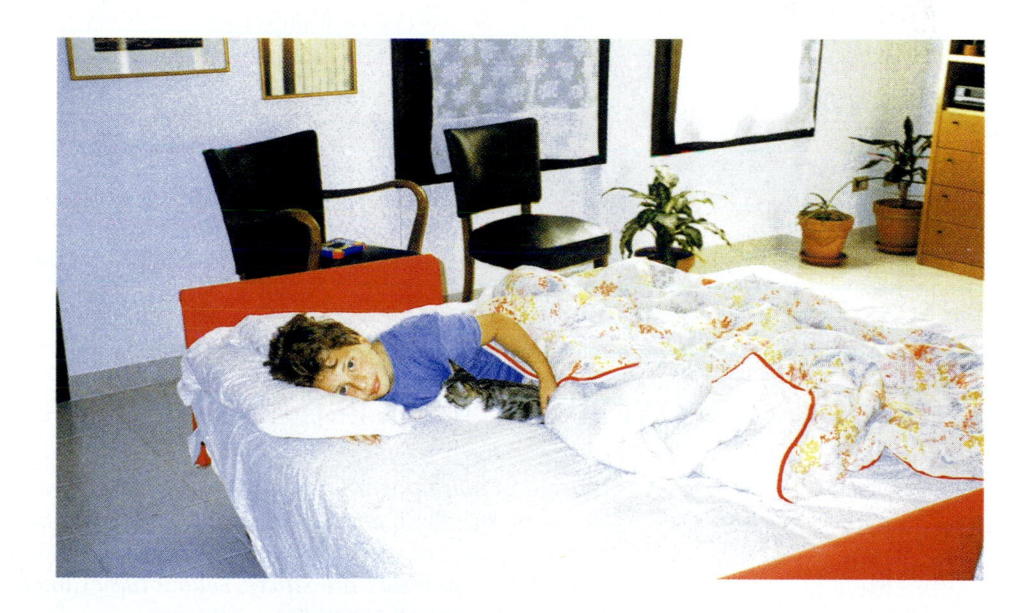

LA STANZA DI LUCIA

Lucia ạbita in un vẹcchio edifịcio in via Senato. La stanza di Lucia non è molto grande, ma ha una bella *finestra che dà sul* giardino. Nella stanza ci sono un letto, due sẹdie e un tạvolo. Sul tạvolo ci sono molti oggetti: carte, matite, libri, quaderni e una *lạmpada.* Alle pareti e sulla porta ci sono fotografie di bei

window that overlooks

lamp

paesaggi perchè Lucia ha l'hobby della fotografia. Sul pavimento ci sono molti fogli di carta. La stanza è disordinata perchè Lucia studia lingue all'università di Milano e, quando è *libera,* lavora nel negozio di un amico di famiglia.

landscapes

free

Oggi Lucia e Liliana studiano *insieme* perchè domani mattina hanno un esame difficile. Le due ragazze desiderano guardare la TV o ascoltare *della* musica, ma hanno bisogno di studiare perchè hanno paura dell'esame.

together

some

Dopo due *ore* di studio, Lucia ha fame.

after/hours

—Liliana, quando ho fame, io non imparo *anche se* studio.

even if

—Hai ragione. Perchè non mangiamo una pizza?

—Adesso *telefono* alla pizzeria e *ordino* una bella pizza *al pomodoro.*

I (will) phone/I (will) order/with tomato sauce

Comprensione

1. È in un nuovo edificio la stanza di Lucia? 2. Com'è la stanza? 3. Che mobili (*furniture*) ci sono nella stanza? 4. Quali oggetti ci sono sul tavolo? 5. Perchè Lucia ha molte foto alle pareti? 6. È ordinata la stanza? Perchè? 7. Con chi studia oggi? 8. Perchè hanno bisogno di studiare? 9. Perchè ordinano una pizza? 10. Che pizza mangiano?

Domande personali

1. Ha una grande stanza Lei? È ordinata? 2. Cosa c'è nella Sua (*in your*) stanza? 3. Ci sono poster alle pareti? Quante lampade ci sono? 4. Lei studia solo(a) o con un(a) compagno(a) di classe quando ha un esame? 5. Quando Lei è stanco(a) (*tired*) di studiare, guarda la TV o telefona (*do you call*) a un amico (un'amica)?

ATTIVITÀ SUPPLEMENTARI

A. **Dialogo.** *Team up with another student and ask each other about your classes (for example, how many you have, which classes are difficult, if you have an exam today or tomorrow, if you need to study a lot for exams, if you have many notes, if the professors are strict). Follow the example of the opening dialogue* "Oggi studio per gli esami."

B. **La stanza di una studentessa universitaria.** Descrivete la foto a pagina 69. Cosa rappresenta? Che mobili (*furniture*) e oggetti ci sono? Usate le espressioni della lettura «*La stanza di Lucia*».

C. **Cerco un(a) compagno(a) di stanza.** *(I'm looking for a roommate.) Working in pairs, one student can interview the other as a possible roommate. (You may want to ask what the other person's name is, if he/she studies at home or in the library, if he/she is neat or messy, if he/she listens to music a lot, if he/she works part-time, or if he/she has a lot of furniture.)*

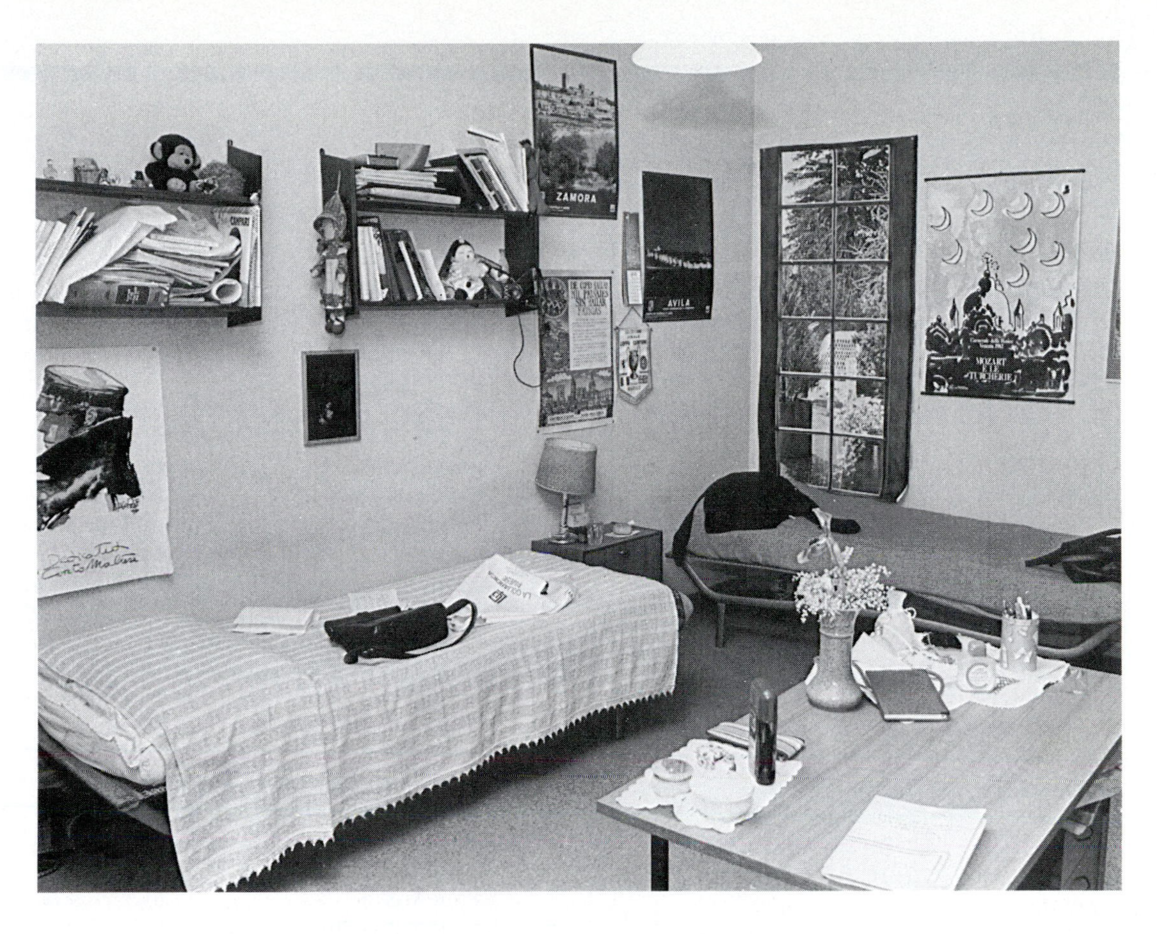

D. **Di cosa ho bisogno?** *One student is thinking of moving into his/her own room at school. He/she addresses the other students in the class, asking them what they think will be needed for the new room. Each student will offer suggestions.*

E. **Come si dice in italiano?**

1. Here is a conversation between two roommates, Nina and Lori.
2. You are very messy, Nina. You have books, paper, and other things on the floor.
3. You're right. I am afraid because Professor Riva's exams are always difficult.
4. Are you studying today?
5. Yes, in the library.
6. If you wish, we (will) study together (*insieme*).
7. Yes, but now I am hungry, and you?
8. No, I am thirsty. I need a cup (*tazza*) of coffee.
9. I do, too, because I am sleepy.

Vocabolario

Nomi

il capịtolo	*chapter*
la carta	*paper*
la cartoleria	*stationery store*
la chitarra	*guitar*
il consịglio	*advice*
il dizionạrio	*dictionary*
la finestra	*window*
il fọglio	*sheet (of paper)*
la fotografia	*photo, picture*
la frutta	*fruit*
l'ingegnere	*engineer*
la lạmpada	*lamp*
il letto	*bed*
la mattina	*morning*
il mezzogiorno	*noon*
i mọbili	*furniture*
l'oggetto	*object*
l'orolọgio	*watch, clock*
la parete	*wall*
il pavimento	*floor*
la porta	*door*
lo scaffale	*shelf*
la sẹdia	*chair*
i soldi	*money*
lo strumento	*instrument*
il tạvolo	*table*
la televisione	*television*
la tromba	*trumpet*
il violino	*violin*
la vita	*life*

Aggettivi

attento	*attentive, careful*
caldo	*warm*
disordinato	*messy*
distratto	*distracted*
freddo	*cold*
impaziente	*impatient*
lịbero	*free*
il mio, la mia	*my*
molto	*much, a lot of (pl. many)*
ordinato	*neat*
paziente	*patient*
preoccupato	*worried*
pronto	*ready*
questo	*this*
stanco (pl. stanchi)	*tired*

Verbi

abitare	*to live*
ascoltare	*to listen to*
aspettare	*to wait for*
cantare	*to sing*
comprare	*to buy*
desiderare	*to wish*
domandare	*to ask*
giocare (a)	*to play (a game)*
guardare	*to look at, to watch*
imparare	*to learn*
(in)cominciare	*to begin*
insegnare	*to teach*
lavorare	*to work*
mangiare	*to eat*
parlare (a)/(di)	*to speak (to)/(about)*
pensare (a)	*to think about*
spiegare	*to explain*
suonare	*to play (an instrument); to ring (a bell, phone, etc.)*

Altre Espressioni

adesso	*now*
avere...anni	*to be ... years old*
avere bisogno (di)	*to need*
avere caldo	*to be hot*
avere fame	*to be hungry*
avere freddo	*to be cold*
avere fretta	*to be in a hurry*
avere paura (di)	*to be afraid (of)*
avere ragione	*to be right*
avere sete	*to be thirsty*
avere sonno	*to be sleepy*
avere torto	*to be wrong*
avere voglia (di)	*to feel like; to fancy*
che...!	*What (a)...!*
che (*pronoun*)	*who/whom; that/which*
da	*from, by*
dopo	*after*
la mattina	*in the morning*
per (+ *inf.*)	*in order to*
se	*if*
sempre	*always*
solamente	*only*
spesso	*often*
su	*on, over, above*
tra (*or* fra)	*between, among*

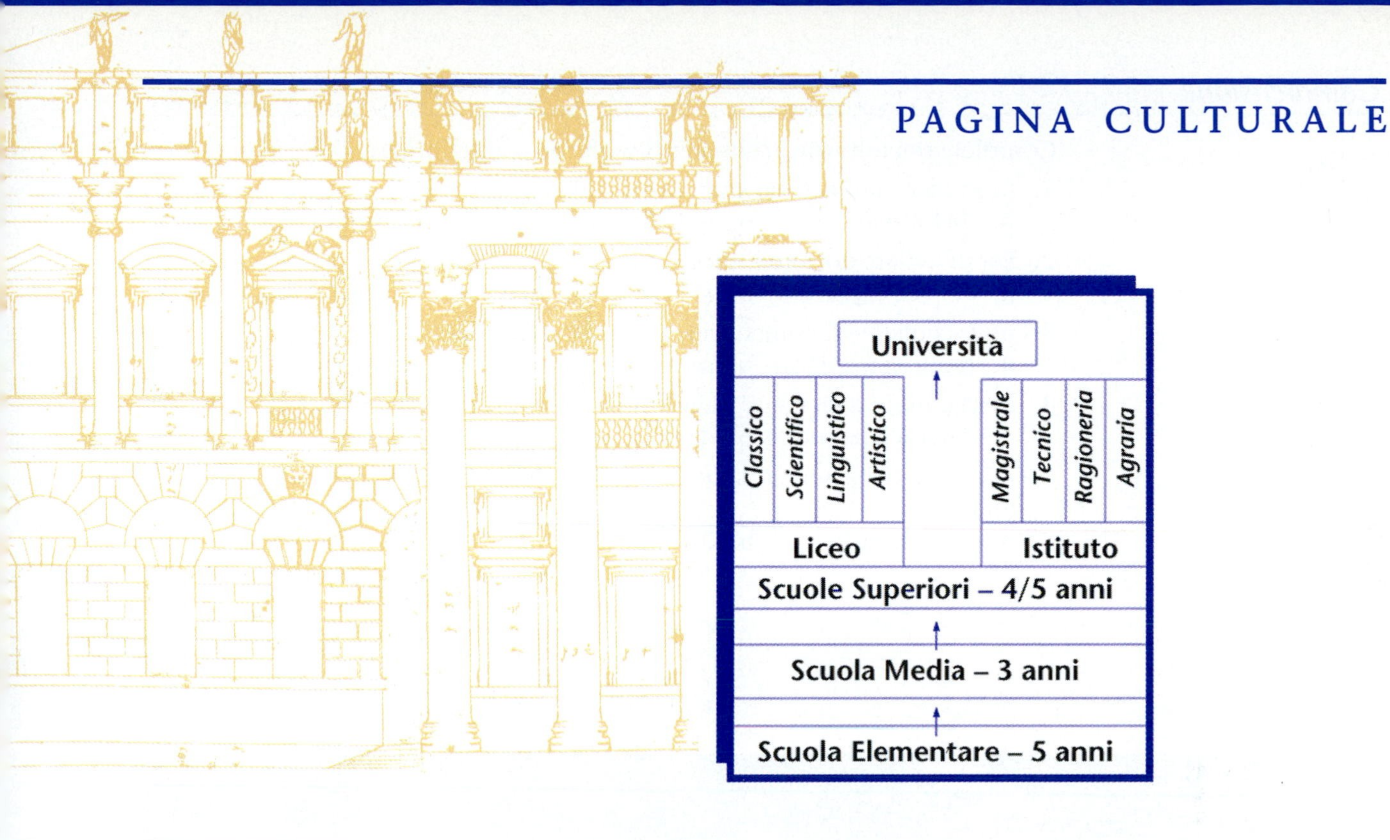

IL SISTEMA SCOLASTICO ITALIANO

In Italia la scuola è obbligatoria fino all'età di quattordici anni e include cinque anni di scuola elementare e tre di scuola media. Dopo la scuola media è necessario *decidere* a quale scuola continuare gli studi. Infatti esiste una varietà di scuole secondarie superiori: il liceo classico o scientifico, per esempio, se uno desidera *diventare* professore, *medico,* avvocato o ingegnere; il liceo artistico; l'istituto magistrale per i maestri e le maestre di scuola elementare; e altri istituti professionali.

to decide

to become/physician

Le scuole secondarie superiori durano quattro o cinque anni e hanno programmi controllati dallo Stato. Gli studenti del liceo classico, per esempio, studiano la lingua e letteratura italiana, le lingue classiche (latina e greca) e una lingua straniera; geografia, filosofia, scienze naturali, chimica, matematica, fisica, storia dell'arte, religione, educazione fisica. *Di solito* non esistono attività sociali, come club, sport e danze.

usually

Alla fine delle scuole secondarie superiori ci sono gli esami di maturità, scritti e orali. Gli studenti ricevono un diploma e sono *liberi* di continuare gli studi all'università.

free

Comprensione

Complete the following statements with the correct phrase.

1. In Italia è obbligatorio studiare fino ai...
   a. diciotto anni **b.** sedici anni **c.** quattordici anni
2. Per diventare dottore è necessario studiare...
   a. al liceo classico **b.** al liceo linguistico **c.** all'istituto magistrale
3. Alle scuole medie superiori le attività sociali sono...
   a. molto importanti **b.** poco importanti **c.** inesistenti
4. I programmi e gli esami delle scuole superiori sono controllati...
   a. dalla scuola locale **b.** dall'università **c.** dallo Stato
5. Alla fine della scuola superiore gli studenti di liceo ricevono (*receive*) il diploma...
   a. universitario **b.** di maturità **c.** di scuola media

Studenti al tavolo della biblioteca.

4 A TAVOLA

Roma. Caffè in Piazza Navona.

Punti di vista

Al ristorante
Una colazione

Punti grammaticali

I Verbi regolari in *-ere* e *-ire:* il presente
II Il partitivo (some, any)
III *Alcuni, qualche, un po' di*
IV *Molto, tanto, troppo, poco, tutto, ogni*
V Le preposizioni avverbiali

Lettura

Una festa di compleanno

Pagina culturale

Dove e cosa mangiare

PUNTI DI VISTA

Roma. Cena al ristorante "Il Tinello."

AL RISTORANTE

Linda e Gianni sono al ristorante.

Linda	È un *locale* pịccolo, ma carino, no? Io non ho molta fame, e tu?	place
Gianni	*Ho una fame da lupo.* Ma che menù pọvero! Non ci sono *nè* lasagne *nè* scaloppine!	I'm hungry as a wolf neither ... nor
Linda	Per piacere, Gianni! Non sei stanco di mangiare sempre le stesse cose? Sst! Ecco il cameriere!	
Cameriere	*Desịderano* un antipasto? Abbiamo del prosciutto *squisito*	would you like delicious
Gianni	Non per me, grạzie. *Non mi piace* il prosciutto. *Io vorrei* degli spaghetti al pomodoro. Anche tu, Linda?	I don't like I would like
Linda	*Scherzi?* Ho bisogno di vitamine, io, non di calorie. Per me, una zuppa di verdure.	are you joking?
Cameriere	E come secondo, che cosa *ọrdinano?* Oggi abbiamo arrosto di vitello, molto buono, con piselli.	are you ordering
Gianni	*D'accordo.*	o.k.
Cameriere	E Lei, signorina?	
Linda	Io vorrei una bistecca con insalata verde.	
Cameriere	Vino bianco o vino rosso?	
Gianni	Vino rosso, per favore. *Mezzo litro.*	a half liter.
Linda	Per me ạcqua minerale, per favore.	

Comprensione

1. Dove sono Linda e Gianni? **2.** Com'è il ristorante? **3.** Ha poca o molta fame Gianni? **4.** Perchè non è contento? **5.** Che cosa mạngia spesso? **6.** Che cosa c'è oggi come antipasto? **7.** Ọrdinano l'antipasto Linda e Gianni? **8.** Che cosa ọrdina Gianni? E Linda? Perchè? **9.** Che cosa mạngiano Linda e Gianni come secondo? **10.** Gianni ọrdina dell'ạcqua minerale o del vino rosso?

Studio di parole

—I signori desiderano?
—Vorrei ...

Al bar un panino al prosciutto (*ham sandwich*) o al formạggio, un panino con salame o con mozzarella e pomodoro, una pizzetta, una brioche (*croissant*), un succo di frutta, un caffè, una Coca-cola, un'aranciata, un'ạcqua minerale, un aperitivo, un gelato.

Il cameriere (*waiter*), la cameriera (*waitress*); i clienti (*customers*); il conto (*check, bill*); la mancia (*tip*)

I PASTI *MEALS*:
la colazione, il pranzo, la cena (*breakfast, lunch, dinner*).

A colazione Il caffè espresso, il caffelatte, il cappuccino, il tè, il latte (*milk*), il succo d'arạncia (*orange juice*), il succo di pompelmo (*grapefruit*); i cereali, le uova strapazzate (*scrambled eggs*), il toast, il pane (*bread*); il burro (*butter*), la marmellata (*jam*).

A pranzo o a cena L'antipasto (*hors d'oeuvre*): il prosciutto e melone (*ham and cantaloupe*), il salame, il cocktail di gamberetti (*shrimps*), avocado con olio e limone.

IL PRIMO PIATTO
FIRST COURSE

la minestra soup
la zuppa di verdure vegetable soup
la pastasciutta pasta
gli spaghetti al pomodoro ... with tomato sauce
i ravioli alla panna ...with cream sauce
le lasagne alla bolognese ...with tomato, meat, and white sauce
I cannelloni alla napoletana stuffed pasta with tomato sauce

LE BEVANDE *DRINKS*

la birra *beer*
il vino
l'ạcqua minerale
il ghiaccio *ice*

IL SECONDO PIATTO
SECOND COURSE

la bistecca steak
il pollo arrosto roast chicken
le scaloppine veal cutlets
l'arrosto di vitello roast veal
il pesce fritto fried fish
la sọgliola ai ferri grilled sole
la trota al burro trout

LE VERDURE *VEGETABLES*

l'insalata verde o mista (*mixed*)
le carote
i piselli peas
gli spinaci
le zucchine
le patate fritte fried potatoes
le melanzane eggplant
i brọccoli

Il dessert Il dolce: la torta (*cake, pie*), la torta al cioccolato, la torta di mele (*apple pie*), le paste (*pastries*), il gelato (al cioccolato, alla panna [*vanilla*], al limone [*lemon*]).
La frutta: la mela (*apple*), la pera (*pear*), l'arạncia, la banana, la frạgola (*strawberry*), la pesca (*peach*), l'uva (*grapes*); la macedonia di frutta (*fruit salad*).
Il formạggio (*cheese*).

In un bar-pasticceria.

A. Domande.

1. Ci sono molti o pochi clienti nel disegno?
2. Quanti camerieri ci sono?
3. Di sọlito, che cosa pọrtano i camerieri?
4. Con che cosa incomịncia un pranzo elegante in Itạlia?
5. Quanti e quali sono i pasti del giorno?
6. In Itạlia il pasto principale è il pranzo. Negli Stati Uniti è la stessa cosa?
7. Gli spaghetti in Itạlia sono un primo o un secondo piatto?
8. Se abbiamo ancora (*still*) fame dopo la carne o il pesce, che cosa ordiniamo?
9. Che cosa porta il cameriere alla fine (*at the end*) del pranzo?
10. Che cosa riceve dai clienti?

B. Che cosa ti piace? (*Choose six items from* "Stụdio di parole" *that you like and four that you dislike. Begin with* **Mi piace** *or* **Non mi piace** (+ *singular noun*)...; **Mi pịacciono** *or* **Non mi pịacciono** (+ *plural noun*)...

ESEMPIO **Mi piace il melone.**
Mi pịacciono le lasagne.
Non mi pịacciono le zucchine.

C. Al bar. *Play the roles of a waiter/waitress and two customers. Order different drinks or snacks.*

ESEMPIO
Cameriere —**I signori desịderano?**
1º Cliente —**Un cappuccino e una brioche, per favore.**
Cameriere —**Benịssimo, e Lei?**
2º Cliente —**Vorrei una birra e una pizzetta.**

D. Domande personali.

1. Lei vede gli amici a un ristorante elegante o alla mensa (*cafeteria*) dell'università?
2. Che cosa ọrdina Lei spesso?
3. Lei mạngia sempre le stesse cose?
4. Che cosa non mạngia una persona che ha paura d'ingrassare (*to get fat*): formạggio, pane, verdura, frutta, pesce fritto, paste?
5. Ha bisogno di vitamine o di calorie Lei?
6. Lei è vegetariano(a)?
7. In un ristorante Lei ọrdina del vino o dell'ạcqua minerale?

Che cosa sono?

Snack Bar Intermezzo

PRIMI PIATTI

LASAGNE AL FORNO	
PENNETTE ALLA BOSCAIOLA	
TORTELLI RAGU	
TORTELLI ERBETTE	
	L.6.000

PANINI

PROSCIUTTO	L. 4.000
SALAME	L. 3.500
MORTADELLA	L. 3.500
FORMAGGIO	L. 4.500

Ascoltiamo!

Una colazione. *Mr. Wilson is staying at an elegant* **pensione** *in Florence. After admiring the view of the city from his window he has come down to have breakfast. Listen to his conversation with the waitress who takes his order, then answer the following questions.*

Comprensione

1. Per che cosa è pronto il signor Wilson? **2.** È in una pensione o in un albergo? **3.** Com'è la città di Firenze la mattina? **4.** Sono freddi i panini e le brioche? Perchè? **5.** Che cosa desịdera mangiare il signor Wilson? **6.** Che succo di frutta ọrdina? Ọrdina anche caffè e latte? **7.** Quante marmellate ci sono sul tạvolo? Di che frutta sono? **8.** È contento il signor Wilson? Perchè?

Dialogo

Colazione alla pensione. *In groups of three play the roles of two customers and a waiter/waitress. It's 8:00 in the morning, and you order breakfast at the inn where you are staying.*

PUNTI GRAMMATICALI

I. Verbi regolari in *-ere* e *-ire:* il presente

Gabriella scrive a Filippo
Papà legge il giornale.

La mattina il signor Brambilla dorme troppo e perde l'autobus.

1. A chi scrive Gabriella?
2. Cosa legge il papà?
3. Perchè il signor Brambilla perde l'ạutobus?

scrịvere (*to write*)		**dormire** (*to sleep*)	
scriv **o**	scriv **iamo**	dorm **o**	dorm **iamo**
scriv **i**	scriv **ete**	dorm **i**	dorm **ite**
scriv **e**	scrịv **ono**	dorm **e**	dọrm **ono**

1. Verbs ending in **-ere** (second conjugation) and verbs ending in **-ire** (third conjugation) differ only in the ending of the **voi** form: **scriv*ete*, part*ite***. Both **-ere** and **-ire** verbs differ from **-are** verbs in the endings of the **lui**, **voi**, and **loro** forms: **parlare** → **parl*a*, parl*ate*, pạrl*ano***.

   Scrivo una lẹttera a Gino. { **I write *a letter to Gino.*** / **I am writing *a letter to Gino.*** / **I do write *a letter to Gino.*** }

   Dormi in classe? { **Do you sleep *in class?*** / **Are you sleeping *in class?*** }

2. Some common verbs ending in **-ere** are:

chiẹdere	*to ask*
chiụdere	*to close*
crẹdere	*to believe*
lẹggere	*to read*
pẹrdere	*to lose; to miss (the bus, etc.)*
prẹndere	*to take*
ricẹvere	*to receive*
ripẹtere	*to repeat*
rispọndere (a)	*to answer*
scrịvere	*to write*
vedere	*to see*
vịvere	*to live*

Che voti **ricevete** a scuola? — *What grades do you receive in school?*
Oggi **prendo** l'ạutobus. — *Today I'm taking the bus.*
Gli studenti non **rispọndono** alla domanda. — *The students don't answer the question.*

3. Some common verbs ending in **-ire** are:

aprire	*to open*
dormire	*to sleep*
offrire	*to offer*
partire (da)	*to leave (a place)*
seguire	*to follow, to take a course*
sentire	*to hear*
servire	*to serve*

Quanti corsi **sẹgui?** — *How many classes are you taking?*
Dorme soltanto cinque ore. — *He sleeps only five hours.*
Sentite il telẹfono? — *Do you hear the phone?*
Parto da Roma in treno. — *I leave Rome by train.*

Pratica

A. Le seguenti persone sẹntono il tẹlefono, ma non rispọndono. Seguite l'esẹmpio.

ESEMPIO Io
Io sento il telẹfono, ma non rispondo.

1. Gabriella
2. i signori Sordi
3. tu e Fạbio
4. Gianna e io
5. tu

B. Che cosa fanno le seguenti persone? Rispondete con una frase completa.

ESEMPIO la cameriera, ricẹvere la mạncia
La cameriera riceve la mạncia.

1. la signora Rossi, scrịvere una lẹttera **2.** noi, lẹggere il giornale **3.** il cameriere, servire i clienti **4.** voi, partire per Roma **5.** i ragazzi, seguire le spiegazioni del professore **6.** Alberto, dormire molte ore **7.** tu e Marisa, chiụdere le finestre **8.** i signori Gentile, offrire dolci al bambino

C. Completate le seguenti frasi. Seguite l'esẹmpio.

ESEMPIO il professore: —Ragazzi, che cosa _____ (vedere) dalla finestra?
—Ragazzi, che cosa vedete dalla finestra?

1. Al bar —Signori, cosa _____ (prẹndere) Loro?
—Io _____ una birra e la signora _____ un'ạcqua minerale.
2. A scuola —Quante pạgine _____ (lẹggere) tu in un'ora?
—Io _____ cinque pạgine, ma lui _____ dieci pạgine.
3. La mamma: —Pierino, i bravi bambini _____ (ricẹvere) bei voti.

—Ma io sono bravo! Non _____ (dormire) mai (*never*) in classe!

4. Nino: —Papà e mamma, perchè _____ (ripẹtere) sempre le stesse cose?
—Noi _____ perchè tu non ascolti.

D. Rispondete alle seguenti domande.

1. Quante ore dormi tu ogni notte? 2. Che cosa vedi dalla finestra della tua stanza? 3. Rispondi sempre alle lẹttere che ricevi? 4. Che giornale leggi quando hai tempo? 5. Che cosa chiedi al cameriere dopo il pranzo? 6. Cosa offri quando inviti degli amici? 7. Prendi il caffè con zụcchero o senza? 8. Ti piace vịvere in una grande città o in una pịccola città?

II. Il partitivo *(some, any)*

1. The partitive (**partitivo**) is used to indicate a part of a whole or an undetermined quantity or number. In English, it is expressed by *some* or *any*. In Italian, it is expressed by the contraction of **di** and the definite article in all its forms (**del, dello, dell'; della, dell'; dei, degli; delle**).

Vorrei **dell'**ạcqua minerale.	*I would like some mineral water.*
Luisa offre **delle** paste.	*Luisa is offering some pastry.*
Abbiamo **del** vino francese.	*We have some French wine.*
Ho **degli** amici simpạtici.	*I have some nice friends.*
Invitiamo **delle** ragazze americane.	*We are inviting some American girls.*

NOTE:
The partitive's plural forms may be considered the plural forms of the indefinite article **un, uno, una.**

Hai amici in Itạlia?	*Do you have friends in Italy?*
Sì, ho **un** amico a Roma e **degli** amici a Nạpoli.	*Yes, I have a friend in Rome and some friends in Naples.*

2. The partitive is omitted in negative sentences and is frequently omitted in interrogative sentences.

Non ho soldi; hai (**dei**) soldi tu?	*I don't have (any) money; do you have (any) money?*
Comprate (**delle**) mele?	*Are you buying (some) apples?*
No, non compriamo frutta, compriamo **del** gelato.	*No, we are not buying (any) fruit, we're buying (some) ice cream.*

Pratica

A. **Che cosa desịderi? Vorrei...** (*I would like...*) **Domanda e risposta.** Seguite l'esẹmpio.

ESEMPIO ạcqua minerale/latte **—Desịderi dell'ạcqua minerale?**
—No, vorrei del latte.

1. gelato/torta 2. spinaci/zucchine 3. pane e formạggio/frutta 4. tè/Coca-Cola 5. spaghetti/pizza 6. vino/birra 7. arrosto di vitello/scaloppine 8. insalata verde/pomodori 9. biscotti (*cookies*)/ paste

B. **Che cosa c'è in una città?** Rispondete alla domanda.

ESEMPIO treni **Ci sono dei treni.**

1. ạutobus 2. mạcchine 3. tram 4. biciclette 5. università 6. edifici 7. negozi 8. parchi 9. giardini 10. piazze 11. stazioni

C. **Che cosa porti? Domanda e risposta.** Tu e dei compagni di classe organizzate un picnic. Seguite l'esẹmpio.

ESEMPIO formạggio **—Porti del formạggio?**
—No, non porto formạggio. Porto della frutta.

1. pollo 2. pane 3. mele 4. caffè 5. prosciutto 6. bevande fredde 7. bicchieri 8. piatti di carta 9. insalata di pomodori 10. patatine fritte (*potato chips*) 11. dolci 12. gelato 13. panini

D. **La spesa.** Completate con una forma appropriata (*correct*) del partitivo o dell'artịcolo indeterminativo secondo il significato (*meaning*).

Oggi è giorno di spesa (*shopping*) per la signora Gianna. Ha bisogno di comprare ________ prosciutto, ________ frạgole, ________ ạcqua minerale, ________ pesce, ________ piselli, ________ bottịglia di vino bianco, ________ tè, ________ melone (*m.*), ________ rivista (*magazine*), ________ giornale (*m.*) e ________ fiori.

III. Alcuni, qualche, un po' di

—Cosa desịderi?
Ci sono alcune mele.
C'è anche un po'di torta.

1. **Alcuni, qualche**, and **un po' di** are other forms that translate into *some*. The adjective **alcuni** (**alcune**) is *always followed by a plural noun.* The adjective **qualche** is invariable and *is only followed by a singular noun.* Both may replace the partitive when *some* means *a few*.

Invitiamo	**alcuni** amici. **qualche** amico. **degli** amici.	*We invite some (a few) friends.*
Pio porta	**alcune** bottịglie. **qualche** bottịglia. **delle** bottịglie.	*Pio brings some (a few) bottles.*

2. **Un po' di (Un poco di)** may replace the partitive only when *some* means *a little, a bit of.*

Desịdero	**un po' di latte.** **del** latte.	*I would like some milk.*
Mạngio	**un po' di** pollo. **del** pollo.	*I eat some chicken.*

3. With nouns that indicate *an indivisible mass* or *quantity,* such as **pane, latte, carne, caffè, minestra**, etc., the partitive article **del, della, dello** cannot be replaced by **qualche** or **alcuni.**

A. **In una cartoleria. Domanda e risposta.** Rispondete con **qualche** e la forma appropriata del nome.

ESEMPIO libri **—Compri dei libri?**
—Sì, compro qualche libro.

1. matite 2. quaderni 3. penne blu 4. giornali 5. cartoline (*postcards*) 6. foto (*pl.*) di paesaggi 7. poster (*m. pl.*) di Venẹzia

B. **Al supermercato.** Che cosa prẹndono le seguenti persone? Rispondete con **alcuni, alcune** e la forma appropriata del nome.

ESEMPIO Anna, panino
Anna prende alcuni panini.

1. Marcello e Filippo, bottịglia di Asti spumante 2. io, rosa 3. Antọnio, mela 4. noi, pomodoro 5. i signori Rizzi, scạtola (*box*) di spaghetti 6. la signora Marini, etto (= 100 grammi) di prosciutto 7. voi, lattina (*can*) di Coca-Cola

C. **Hai fame? Desịderi...? Sì, vorrei un po' di... Domanda e risposta.** Seguite l'esẹmpio.

ESEMPIO pane **—Desịderi del pane?**
—Sì, vorrei un po' di pane.

1. formạggio Bel Paese 2. insalata di pomodori 3. pollo ai ferri 4. spinaci al burro 5. torta di mele 6. pesce fritto 7. macedọnia di frutta 8. minestra di verdure 9. gelato alla panna

D. Completate con **alcuni, alcune** o con una forma singolare, secondo il significato.

Oggi sono al supermercato e compro _____ bottịglie di ạcqua minerale, _____ latte, _____ scaloppine, _____ pane, _____ pasta, _____ melanzane, _____ formạggio parmigiano (*parmesan*) e _____ pịccolo regalo per la mamma: _____ paste.

E. **Quanto costa (cọstano)? Domanda e risposta.** Sei in un supermercato e domandi il costo in dollari e in centẹsimi (*cents*) dei seguenti gẹneri alimentari (*food*). Uno (Una) studente(ssa) risponde.

ESEMPIO 1 libbra (*pound*) di mele/$_____
—Quanto costa una libbra di mele?
—Costa un dọllaro e venti centẹsimi. (*o* ...)

1. 1 libbra di zụcchero/$_____ 2. 1 barattolo (*jar*) di marmellata/ $_____ 3. 1 libbra di gamberetti/$_____ 4. 1 libbra di pomodori/ $_____ 5. 1 bottịglia di ọlio d'oliva/$_____ 6. mezzo gallone di latte/ $_____ 7. 3 bottịglie di Coca-cola/$_____ 8. 1 fiasco di Chianti/ $_____ 9. 12 uova/$_____

IV. Molto, tanto, troppo, poco, tutto, ogni

—*Hai molta fame?*
—*Sì, ma ho pochi soldi.*

1. The following adjectives express quantity:

molto, molta; molti, molte	*much, a lot of; many*
tanto, tanta; tanti, tante	*much, so much; so many*
troppo, troppa; troppi, troppe	*too much; too many*
poco, poca; pochi, poche	*little; few*

Lavorate **molte** ore?	*Do you work many hours?*
Pensiamo a **tante** cose.	*We are thinking about (so) many things.*
I bambini mạngiano **troppo** gelato.	*Children eat too much ice cream.*
Lui invita **pochi** amici.	*He invites few friends.*

2. When **molto**, **tanto**, **troppo**, and **poco** modify an adjective or a verb, *they are adverbs* (**avverbi**). As adverbs, they are invariable.

L'Itạlia è **molto** bella.	*Italy is very beautiful.*
Gli studenti sono **tanto** bravi!	*The students are so good!*
Tu parli **troppo.**	*You talk too much.*
Lei è **poco** studiosa.	*She is not very studious.*

3. **Tutto, tutta; tutti, tutte** (*the whole; all, every*). When the adjective **tutto** is used in the singular, it means *the whole;* when it is used in the plural, it means *all, every*. The adjective **tutto** is followed by the definite article.

Tutti i ragazzi sono là.	*All the boys are there.*
Stụdio **tutti i** giorni.	*I study every day.*
Studi **tutto il** giorno?	*Are you studying the whole day?*

4. **Ogni** (*each, every*) is an *invariable* adjective. It is *always* followed by a singular noun.

Lavoriamo **ogni** giorno.	*We work every day.*
Ogni settimana gioco a tennis.	*Every week I play tennis.*

NOTE:
Tutto and **ogni** are often used interchangeably.

tutti i giorni } *every day*
ogni giorno }

Pratica

A. Completate con la forma corretta di **quanto, molto, poco, tutto, tanto** o **troppo.**

1. (troppo) Tu mangi _____ lasagne. **2.** (molto) Cuciniamo _____ spaghetti. **3.** (molto) Cọmprano _____ birra. **4.** (poco) Desịdero _____ minestra. **5.** (tutto) Guardiamo _____ i regali (*gifts*). **6.** (tutto) _____ le ragazze pạrlano francese. **7.** (poco) Ci sono _____ camerieri. **8.** (quanto) _____ pane mangi! **9.** (tutto) Nino suona la chitarra _____ il giorno. **10.** (poco) Desịdero _____ cose. **11.** (tanto) Nella biblioteca dell'università vediamo _____ libri.

B. Completate con **molto** (avverbio) o con la forma corretta di **molto** (aggettivo).

1. «Cucini _____?» «No, cucino poco.» **2.** Marcello ha _____ soldi e _____ amici. **3.** Mangiate sempre _____ frutta? **4.** Non siamo _____ stanchi. **5.** Gabriella è _____ preoccupata. **6.** Liliana non ama _____ cucinare. **7.** La mamma compra _____ latte. **8.** Una persona curiosa domanda _____ cose. **9.** Mia nonna (*grandmother*) cucina _____ verdure. 10. Mi piace _____ il gelato al cioccolato.

C. Tutti, tutte... Domanda e risposta. Seguite l'esẹmpio.

ESEMPIO i giọvani, amare lo sport
—È vero che i giọvani ạmano lo sport?
—Sì, tutti i giọvani ạmano lo sport. *o*
—No, non tutti i giọvani ạmano lo sport.

1. le donne (*women*), amare cucinare
2. i dolci, avere troppe calorie
3. i bambini, ricẹvere molti regali
4. i professori, lẹggere molti libri
5. i dottori, vedere molti pazienti
6. i ristoranti italiani, ẹssere popolari

Ricevuta Fiscale XA Nº 20930 /92

RICEVUTA FISCALE
Ristorante "NANNI"
di MAZZOLENI LUCIA & C. S.a.s.
Via Milite Ignoto, 2 - ☎ 33230
18039 VENTIMIGLIA - IM
Partita IVA 00887170082
№ 2795
li, 19/09/92

S

Natura, qualità e quantità dei servizi	IMPORTO
N. 2 PASTI A PREZZO FISSO L.	32000
N. COPERTI E PANE L.	
N. APERITIVO L.	
N. VINO L.	
N. 1+1 BIRRA - ACQUA M. L.	5000
N. ANTIPASTI L.	
N. PRIMI L.	
N. SECONDI DI PESCE L.	
N. SECONDI DI CARNE L.	
N. CONTORNI L.	
N. FORMAGGI L.	
N. DESSERT L.	
N. 2 CAFFE' L.	3000
N. LIQUORI L.	
Fr 182	
Totale corrispettivo IVA inclusa L.	40000

Aut. Min. Finanze n. 368141 del 23/11/79 - Tip. ALBA Via S. Secondo, 22 - Ventimiglia DD.MM. 13-10-79 - 18-1-80 - 2-7-80 - 18-9-81 - 28-1-83

Che cos'è?

D. Tutti(e)—Ogni. Domanda e risposta. Parlate di alcune attività di tutti i giorni.

ESEMPIO studiare, sere **—Studiate tutte le sere?**
—Sì, studiamo ogni sera. *o*
—No, non studiamo ogni sera.

1. lavorare, giorni **2.** ascoltare, spiegazioni (*explanations*) dei professori **3.** mangiare a casa, giorni **4.** preparare la colazione, mattine **5.** imparare, parole del vocabolạrio **6.** studiare, lezioni **7.** parlare, compagni di classe **8.** guardare la televisione, sere **9.** pagare, conti **10.** scrịvere, esercizi del libro d'italiano

E. Rispondete usando **molto** o **poco** nella forma corretta.

1. Ti piace mangiare al ristorante? **2.** Quanti amici hai? **3.** Quanto tempo libero hai? **4.** Quanti soldi hanno, in generale, gli studenti? **5.** Quanto pane mangi a cena? **6.** Ti piạcciono le verdure? **7.** Compri dei gelati? **8.** Quante lẹttere ricevi? **9.** Ti piace organizzare un picnic? **10.** Quante cose porti al picnic?

V. Le preposizioni avverbiali

A Firenze.
—Scusi, il Davide davanti al Palazzo Vecchio è l'originale?
—No, è una cọpia. L'originale è nel Museo dell'Accademia.
—Dov'è? È lontano da qui?
—No, è vicino al Museo di San Marco.

The following adverbs are often used as prepositions:

sopra	*above, on (top of)*	**davanti (a)**	*in front (of), before*
sotto	*under, below*	**dietro**	*behind, after*
dentro	*in, inside*	**vicino (a)**	*near, beside, next to*
fuori	*out, outside*	**lontano (da)**	*far (from)*

Sopra il letto c'è una foto. — *Above the bed there is a picture.*
Il giardino è **dietro** l'edificio. — *The garden is behind the building.*
Non è **lontano dal** centro. — *It is not far from downtown.*
Ạbito **fuori** città. — *I live outside the city.*

Pratica

A. **Dov'è...?** *With the help of the pictures below, answer the questions by using the prepositions* **sotto, sopra, dentro, davanti (a), dietro, vicino (a), lontano (da)**, *or other prepositions.*

1. Dov'è la lạmpada? E il cane?
2. Dov'è la fotografia? E il gatto?
3. Dov'è la sẹdia? E la ragazza?
4. Dov'è il tạvolo? E la tazza? (*cup*) E il caffè?

B. Guardate la carta geogrạfica d'Itạlia (*map section of this book*) e rispondete alle seguenti domande.

1. Milano è vicino all'ịsola di Capri, o lontano dall'ịsola di Capri? 2. Milano è vicino al lago di Como o lontano dal lago di Como? 3. Torino è vicino al fiume (*river*) Po, o lontano dal fiume Po? 4. Nạpoli è vicino al vulcano Vesụvio o lontano dal vulcano Vesụvio? 5. La Sardegna è sotto la Cọrsica o sopra la Cọrsica? 6. Pisa è vicino al mare Lịgure o al mare Adriạtico? 7. Quale regione è vicino all'ịsola d'Elba? 8. Quale regione è vicino alla Sicịlia?

LETTURA

Festa tra amici.

UNA FESTA DI COMPLEANNO

Domani Gabriella ha ventụn anni. Lucia organizza una festa e invita Filippo, il ragazzo di Gabriella, e tutti gli altri amici.

Lucia Marcello, tu *che* hai sempre *un sacco di soldi,* che cosa porti? — who/a lot of money

Marcello *Macchè* un sacco di soldi! Se aspetto i soldi di papà... Io compro alcune bottịglie di Asti spumante. Liliana e Antọnio *vẹngono* con me nella Ferrari. — No way; are coming

Lucia E loro, cosa pọrtano?

Marcello Liliana ha intenzione di portare dei panini al prosciutto perchè non ama cucinare. Antọnio, sempre *al verde,* porta Fido e la chitarra. — broke

Lucia Filippo, che cosa porti tu?

Filippo Del vino rosso e una torta Motta.* Va bene?

Marcello Molto bene. Con ventụn *candeline,* vero? E tu Lucia, che sei una *cuoca* molto brava, che cosa prepari? — candles; cook

Lucia Vorrei preparare un arrosto con delle patate fritte.

Marcello Perchè non offriamo *insieme* un regalo? Qualche disco, per esẹmpio, *dato che* Gabriella ama la mụsica. — together; since

Lucia D'accordo. E tu Filippo, *che cosa regali?* Che cos'è? Siamo curiosi. — what present are you bringing?

Filippo Ho due *biglietti* per l'ọpera, ma silẹnzio, per piacere. È una sorpresa! Ho anche il *biglietto di auguri*. Perchè non scrivete qualche parola anche voi? — tickets; birthday card

La sera della festa tutti gli amici sono a casa di Lucia e aspẹttano Gabriella e Filippo. Quando i due ạprono la porta gli amici *ạugurano*: «Buon compleanno, Gabriella!» — wish

---

*One of the most popular Italian brands of pastries and cakes.

Comprensione

1. Per chi organizza una festa Lucia? Perchè? 2. Chi invita Lucia? 3. Chi è Filippo? 4. È ricco o pọvero il padre di Marcello? 5. Che cosa porta Marcello? 6. Come arriva alla festa Marcello? Con chi? 7. Che cosa pọrtano Liliana e Antọnio? 8. Perchè Liliana porta dei panini? 9. Che cosa porta Filippo? 10. Quante candeline ci sono sulla torta? 11. Cucina bene Lucia? Che cosa prepara? 12. Che regalo desịderano comprare gli amici di Gabriella? 13. Che cosa regala Filippo? Perchè? 14. Che cosa ạugurano tutti gli amici quando Gabriella e Filippo ạprono la porta?

Domande personali

1. Che regalo desịdera Lei per il Suo (*your*) compleanno? Di sọlito, riceve molti o pochi regali? 2. Le pịacciono (*Do you like*) le sorprese?
3. Organizza molte o poche feste per gli amici? 4. Invita molte persone alla festa, o invita solo pochi amici? 5. Che cosa pọrtano gli amici?
6. Dimẹntica il compleanno di un amico (un'amica) o offre sempre un regalo? 7. Cosa ạugura al compleanno degli amici?

ATTIVITÀ SUPPLEMENTARI

A. **Al ristorante.** Siete in un ristorante italiano. Uno studente è il cameriere e porta il menù. Due o tre studenti ọrdinano un pranzo all'italiana (*Italian style*): antipasto, primo piatto, secondo piatto, ecc.

Antipasti:

- Assortiti al carrello 6500/7500
- Prosciutto con melone........................9500
- Insalatina tropicale............................8500
- Mezzo avocado con olio e limone............4000
- Cocktail di gamberetti........................9500

Minestre Del Giorno:

- Conchigliette con melanzane alla siciliana ..7500
- Risotto al pomodoro..........................7000
- Riso alla catalana.............................6500
- Risotto alla parmigiana......................6500
- Spaghetti alla carbonara......................7500
- Maccheroni alla fiorentina....................6500
- Spaghetti al pomodoro e basilico............6500
- Tagliatelle alla bolognese.....................6500
- Ravioli alla panna e prosciutto...............7000
- Ravioli della casa.............................7000
- Pasta e fagioli.................................6500
- Zuppa di verdure.............................6000

Piatti Del Giorno:

- Abbacchio alla romana.......................14000
- Fagottino di vitello alle punte d'asparagi ...16000
- Vitello tonnato ai capperi 14000
- Fegato di vitello con polenta.................14000
- Petto di pollo con punte d'asparagi 14000
- Melanzane alla siciliana 13000
- Scaloppine di vitello 16000
- Saltimbocca alla romana.....................13000

Ai Ferri:

- Bistecca alla fiorentina (min 2 pers) 24000
- Robespierre con trevisana (min 2 pers) ...32000

Pesce:

- Branzino bollito con maionese 20000
- Scampi giganti ai ferri........................20000
- Sogliola al burro.............................18500
- Sogliola ai ferri..............................18500
- Trota al burro................................14000
- Fritto di scampi e calamari 20000

Guarnizioni Piatti:

- Cavolfiori...spinaci...zucchine...piselli 4500
- Insalata mista...pomodori...fagiolini 5500
- Insalata verde di stagione...patate fritte 4000
- Insalata di carciofi............................5000

Dolce, Semifreddi, Gelati Misti:

- Carrello dolci...semifreddi...gelati misti ...5500
- Macedonia...4500 Frutta di stagione 5000
- Fragole a piacere...kiwi con gelato 7000
- Formaggio....................................5000

Pane, Coperto e Servizio...2000

B. **Domani è il compleanno di...** *One student announces to the class that tomorrow is ...'s birthday. He/she asks the students what they are going to bring. Each student will respond, telling what he/she will bring.*

C. **Un picnic.** Inventate una pịccola stọria sui giọvani seduti sull'erba. *(Imagine a story about the people seated on the grass. Indicate who these people are and what their names are, why they are celebrating today, and what the circumstances are. Be sure to indicate what elements this celebration includes, and where things are located.)*

D. **Come si dice in italiano?**

1. Today Mr. and Mrs. Buongusto are eating in a restaurant.
2. The waiter brings the menu and says (*dice*), "Today we don't have roast veal, but we have very good *scaloppine al marsala.*"
3. They order spaghetti with tomato sauce, two steaks, green salad, and a bottle of red wine.
4. While (*mentre*) they are waiting, Mr. and Mrs. Buongusto talk about (*di*) some friends.
5. We don't have many friends, but we do have good friends.
6. Why don't we invite Ornella and Pạolo to (*a*) play tennis with us (*noi*) tomorrow? They are very good because they play every day.
7. Mr. Buongusto is very hungry and he eats a lot.
8. At the end Mr. Buongusto pays the bill.
9. "Are you forgetting the tip for the (*al*) waiter?," asks Mrs. Buongusto.

Vocabolario

Nomi

il bicchiere	*glass*
il biscotto	*cookie*
la bottiglia	*bottle*
la caloria	*calorie*
la candelina	*little candle*
la canzone	*song*
la carne	*meat*
il centẹsimo	*cent*
il compleanno	*birthday*
la cucina	*kitchen; cooking, cuisine*
il cuoco, la cuoca	*cook*
il disco (*pl.* i dischi)	*record*
la fine	*end*
il frigorifero	*refrigerator*
i gẹneri alimentari	*food*
il giornale	*newspaper*
l'invito	*invitation*
la libreria	*bookstore*
il piatto	*dish, course*
il regalo	*gift, present*
il significato	*meaning*
il silẹnzio	*silence*
la sorpresa	*surprise*
la spiegazione	*explanation*
il supermercato	*supermarket*
la tazza	*cup*
la vitamina	*vitamin*
lo zụcchero	*sugar*

Aggettivi

alcuni(e)	*some, a few*
ogni (*inv.*)	*each, every*
pọco (*pl.* pochi)	*little; few*
qualche (*sing.*)	*some*
squisito	*delicious*
tanto	*much, so much*
troppo	*too much*
tutto	*the whole; all, every*
vegetariano	*vegetarian*

Verbi

amare	*to love*
aprire	*to open*
augurare	*to wish (somebody)*
chiẹdere	*to ask*
chiụdere	*to close*
costare	*to cost*
crẹdere	*to believe*
cucinare	*to cook*
dimenticare	*to forget*
dormire	*to sleep*
invitare	*to invite*
lẹggere	*to read*
offrire	*to offer*
ordinare	*to order*
organizzare	*to organize*
pagare	*to pay*
partire (da)	*to leave (a place)*
pẹrdere	*to lose*
portare	*to bring, to carry; to wear*
prẹndere	*to take, to catch*
preparare	*to prepare*
regalare	*to give a present*
ricẹvere	*to receive*
ripẹtere	*to repeat*
rispọndere	*to answer*
scrịvere	*to write*
seguire	*to follow*
sentire	*to hear*
servire	*to serve*
vedere	*to see*
vịvere	*to live*

Altre espressioni

avere intenzione (di)	*to intend*
Buon compleanno!	*Happy birthday!*
d'accordo	*OK, agreed*
davanti (a)	*in front (of)*
dentro	*in, inside*
dietro	*behind*
di sọlito	*usually, generally*
fuori	*out, outside*
là	*there, over there*
lontano (da)	*far (from)*
sopra	*on, on top of*
sotto	*under*
Ti piace (piạcciono)...?	*Do you like ...? (informal)*
Le piace (piạcciono) ...?	*Do you like ...? (formal)*
Mi piace (piạcciono) ...	*I like ...*
un po' di (un poco di)	*some, a bit of*
un sacco di	*a lot of*
vorrei	*I would like*

DOVE E COSA MANGIARE

La mattina gli Italiani *fanno una leggera* colazione: un espresso o un cappuccino o un caffelatte con una *brioche* o un panino. Se uno non ha tempo di preparare la colazione a casa, *si ferma brevemente* a uno dei molti bar della città.

have a light
croissant
stops shortly

A mezzogiorno molti Italiani ritọrnano a casa per il pasto principale, che consiste *quasi sempre* in *pastasciutta,* carne, verdura e frutta. Chi lavora lontano da casa va a un ristorante, a una *trattoria* o a una *tạvola calda.* Molti giọvani, per *mancanza* di soldi o di tempo, cọmprano un *tramezzino* o un panino in una *paninoteca* o in una *salumeria.* Oggi è molto popolare fra i giọvani il «fast food» all'americana, specialmente gli hamburger e le patatine fritte.

almost always
pasta with tomato sauce
informal restaurant
cafeteria/lack
sandwich with crustless bread/sandwich shop/ delicatessen

La sera *si cena verso* le otto, a casa, con un pasto più o meno leggero; o *si va* ad una pizzeria. Per finire la *giornata* di lavoro con *qualcosa di dolce,* c'è la gelateria-pasticceria che offre una grande varietà di gelati e di paste.

people have supper/at about/people go
day/ something sweet

Vicino al bar c'è una vendita di giornali e tabacchi.

Musicisti romani al bar.

Comprensione

1. La colazione degli Italiani è abbondante? In che cosa consiste?
2. A mezzogiorno che cosa mạngiano gli Italiani che hanno la fortuna di ritornare a casa?
3. Oltre ai (*Besides*) ristoranti, in quali altri luoghi (*places*) è possịbile mangiare?
4. Che cos'è una paninoteca?
5. A quale ristorante americano corrisponde la tạvola calda?

5 ATTIVITÀ E PASSATEMPI

Avete anche voi il telefonino (telefono cellulare)?

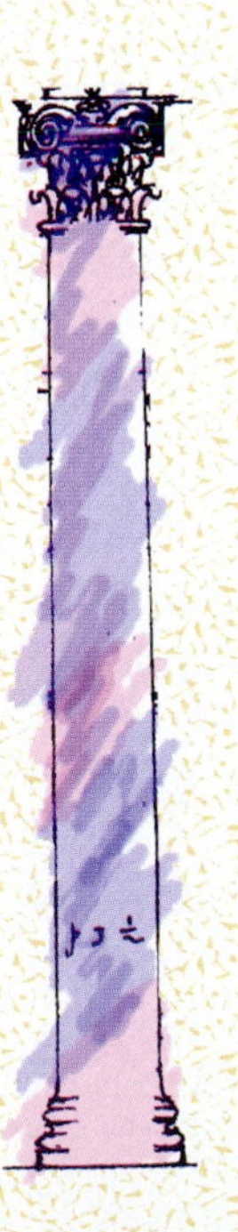

Punti di vista

Pronto? Chi parla?
Una telefonata d'affari

Punti grammaticali

I Verbi in *-ire* con il suffisso *-isc-*
II Verbi irregolari in *-are*
III I pronomi diretti *lo, la, li, le*
IV I giorni della settimana

Lettura

Una settimana molto occupata

Pagina culturale

Il sistema universitario

PUNTI DI VISTA

Dove giocano a tennis Gianna e Marisa?

PRONTO? CHI PARLA?

Gianna telẹfona all'amica Marisa. La mamma di Marisa, la signora Pini, risponde al telẹfono.

Signora Pini	Pronto?	
Gianna	Buon giorno, signora. Sono Gianna. C'è Marisa, per favore?	
Signora Pini	Sì, un momento, è qui.	
Marisa	Pronto? Ciao Gianna!	
Gianna	*Finalmente! Il tuo* telẹfono è sempre occupato!	finally!/your
Marisa	Da dove telẹfoni?	
Gianna	Sono a un telẹfono pụbblico vicino alla farmacia. E *devo* fare una telefonata breve perchè ho solo un *gettone,* e non ho *monete.**	I have to token coins
Marisa	*Allora, andiamo* al cịnema oggi *pomeriggio*?	so/are we going/ afternoon
Gianna	*Veramente io preferisco* giocare a tennis.	actually I prefer
Marisa	Va bene. Perchè non andiamo in bicicletta al *campo da tennis*? E quando ritorniamo andiamo a prẹndere un gelato.	tennis court
Gianna	Perfetto. Sono a casa tua *per le due.*	by two (o'clock)

---

*In Italy, phone calls from public telephones require tokens (*gettoni*), coins (*monete da 100 o 200 lire*), or a card (*carta telefọnica*). Tokens and telephone cards may be bought at a *Sale e Tabacchi* store or at a bar.

1. A chi telẹfona Gianna? 2. Chi risponde al telẹfono? 3. Perchè Gianna dice (*says*) «Finalmente»? 4. Da dove telẹfona Gianna? 5. Dov'è il telẹfono pụbblico? 6. È lunga la telefonata? Perchè? 7. Cosa desịdera fare Marisa? E Gianna?

Studio di parole

—Pronto. Chi parla?
—Sono Filippo. C'è Gabriella, per favore?

il telẹfono pụbblico
l'elenco telefọnico phone book
il nụmero di telẹfono
il prefisso area code
formare il nụmero to dial
fare una telefonata / **telefonare** / **chiamare** } to make a phone call, to phone
parlare al telẹfono to talk on the phone
rispọndere al telẹfono to answer the phone
lịbero free
occupato busy
il (la) centralinista operator
la telefonata interurbana long-distance phone call
il gettone token
la moneta coin
la carta telefọnica phone card
la segreteria telefọnica answering machine
la bolletta del telẹfono phone bill
il telẹfono cellulare cellular phone

una telefonata personale a personal phone call
una telefonata d'affari a business phone call
—Pronto? Sono... Hello. This is ...
—Vorrei parlare con... I would like to speak with ...
—C'è...? Is ... in?
—Mi dispiace, non c'è. I'm sorry, he/she is not in.
—Vorrei lasciare un messạggio. I would like to leave a message.
—Qual è il nụmero di telẹfono di...? What is the phone number of ...?

A. **Domande.**

1. Dove cerchiamo (*do we look for*) un numero di telefono?
2. Se un numero non è nell'elenco, chi chiama Lei?
3. Qual è il Suo (*your*) numero di telefono? (Il mio...)
4. Quando ha bisogno del prefisso Lei?
5. Negli Stati Uniti, abbiamo bisogno di un gettone per telefonare da un telefono pubblico? Che cosa usiamo?

B. **La telefonata di Filippo.** *Consider Filippo and his phone conversation, as shown in the* "Studio di parole," *then answer the following questions.*

1. Da dove telefona Filippo?
2. A chi desidera telefonare?
3. Il telefono di Gabriella è occupato?
4. Chi risponde al telefono, Gabriella o un'altra persona?
5. Cosa dice Filippo?
6. Filippo è a un telefono pubblico. Di cosa ha bisogno per fare la telefonata?
7. La telefonata di Filippo è una telefonata personale o una telefonata d'affari?

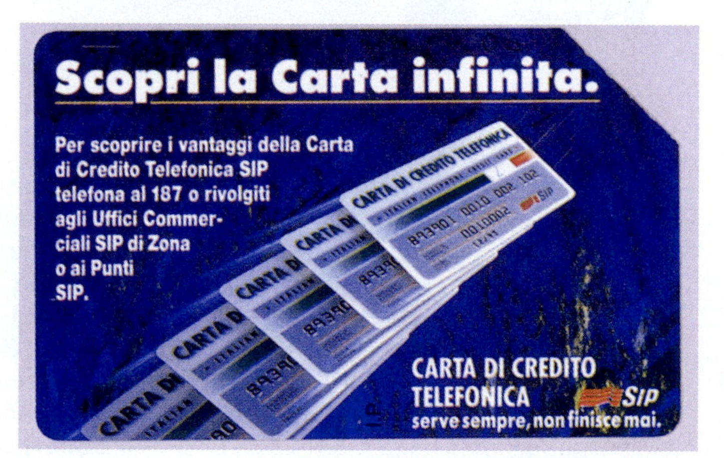

Hai una carta telefonica tu? Perchè?

C. Domande personali.

1. Fa molte telefonate Lei? (Fạccio...)
2. Come sono le Sue (*your*) telefonate? Brevi o lunghe? (Le mie telẹfonate...) Perchè?
3. Lei telẹfona o scrive una cartolina (*write a card*) a un amico (un'amica) per il suo compleanno?
4. Fa molte telefonate interurbane?
5. Chi paga la bolletta del telẹfono?
6. Ha una segreteria telefọnica? Una carta telefọnica? Un telẹfono cellulare?

D. Qual è il nụmero di telẹfono di...? *Ask a classmate for the phone numbers of the following people. Your classmate can respond, giving the numbers in groups of two digits, as Italians do.*

ESEMPIO Ạngela: 25-56-32
—Qual è il nụmero di telẹfono di Angela?
—È venticinque, cinquantasei, trentadue.

1. dottor Tommasi: 76-99-82
2. Luigi: 48-61-93
3. signorina Belli: 55-23-38
4. ? (*Make up a person and an imaginary phone number.)*

Ascoltiamo!

Una telefonata d'affari. *An architect, Gino Paoli, is making a business phone call to an engineer, Rusconi* (**l'ingegner Rusconi**), *about an appointment. Listen to his conversation with Rusconi's secretary, then answer the related questions.*

Comprensione

1. L'architetto Paoli telẹfona a casa o all'uffịcio dell'ingegner Rusconi? **2.** C'è l'ingegnere? **3.** Che cosa lạscia Paoli? **4.** Per quand'è l'appuntamento? **5.** L'uffịcio di Rusconi è nella stessa città da dove telẹfona Paoli? Perchè no? **6.** La telefonata di Paoli è una telefonata personale o d'affari?

Dialogo

Working in pairs, one student can make, the other receive, a business phone call. Expand on the dialogue "Una telefonata d'affari," *drawing from the vocabulary in* "Studio di parole" *and using your imagination.*

PUNTI GRAMMATICALI

—No, caro, preferisco la macchina!

I. Verbi in *-ire* con il suffisso *-isc-*

Many **-ire** verbs take the suffix **-isc-** between the stem and the endings of the **io, tu, lui,** and **loro** forms. In the vocabulary lists of this book and in the dictionary, these verbs are indicated in this way: **finire (-isc-).**

finire* (*to finish*)	
fin **isc** o	fin **iamo**
fin **isc** i	fin **ite**
fin **isc** e	fin **isc** ono

Some common verbs that follow this pattern are:

capire	*to understand*	**pulire**	*to clean*
costruire	*to build*	**restituire**	*to give back*
finire	*to finish*	**ubbidire**	*to obey*
preferire	*to prefer*		

Quando **finisci di** studiare? — *When do you finish studying?*
Preferiamo un esame facile. — *We prefer an easy exam.*
Pulisco la casa il sabato. — *I clean the house on Saturdays.*

***Finire** takes **di** before an infinitive.

A. Che cosa preferiscono come dessert le seguenti persone? Seguite l'esempio.

ESEMPIO Ornella, un gelato alla panna
Ornella preferisce un gelato alla panna.

1. i signori Golosi, della torta al cioccolato **2.** tu e la tua amica, delle fragole al marsala (*in sweet wine*) **3.** noi, una macedonia di frutta **4.** il signor Agrumi, un'arancia **5.** io, del gorgonzola (*sharp cheese*) e una pera **6.** e tu?

B. Completate con la forma corretta di uno dei seguenti verbi: **restituire, pulire, preferire, finire, capire, costruire, ubbidire.**

1. Tu _____ sempre quando il professore spiega? **2.** I bravi ragazzi _____ alla mamma e al papà. **3.** Voi _____ vedere un film o giocare a tennis? **4.** Quando _____ di studiare loro? **5.** Oggi io _____ la mia stanza. **6.** La studentessa _____ il dizionario alla professoressa. **7.** _____ studiare a casa o in biblioteca Lei? **8.** Quando _____ i compiti voi? **9.** Loro _____ una bella casa in montagna.

C. Qual è la domanda? Formulate le domande che corrispondono alle seguenti risposte.

ESEMPIO Paolo restituisce il computer *a Sergio*.
A chi restituisce il computer Paolo?

1. Io non capisco *la tua domanda.* **2.** I ragazzi partono *domani sera.* **3.** Liliana apre le finestre *perchè ha caldo.* **4.** Luisa e Anna finiscono gli studi *quest'anno.* **5.** Noi preferiamo partire *con la macchina.* **6.** Il signor Ricci costruisce una villa *a Rapallo.* **7.** Dino dorme ogni notte *dieci ore.* **8.** Mariella pulisce l'appartamento *molto bene.* **9.** Filippo offre una rosa rossa *a Gabriella.*

II. Verbi irregolari in *-are*

Che cosa fa Gino? Va al parco in bicicletta.

1. Sta a casa Gino? **2.** Come va al parco?

1. The following **-are** verbs are irregular in the present tense:

andare* (*to go*)		**fare** (*to do; to make*)		**dare** (*to give*)		**stare** (*to stay; to feel*)	
vado	andiamo	faccio	facciamo	do	diamo	sto	stiamo
vai	andate	fai	fate	dai	date	stai	state
va	vanno	fa	fanno	dà	danno	sta	stanno

Cosa **fai** stasera?	*What are you doing tonight?*
Faccio una telefonata interurbana.	*I am making a long-distance phone call.*
Vado a vedere un film.	*I am going to see a movie.*
Quando **danno** una festa?	*When are they giving a party?*
Come **sta** Maria?	*How is Maria?*
Maria **sta** a casa perchè **sta** male.	*Maria stays (is staying) home because she feels ill.*

2. **Fare** is used in many idiomatic expressions, some of which are listed below:

fare un regalo	*to give a present*
fare una passeggiata	*to take a walk*
fare le spese	*to go shopping*
fare la spesa	*to buy groceries*
fare il bagno, la doccia	*to take a bath, a shower*
fare colazione	*to have breakfast*
fare un viaggio	*to take a trip*
fare una domanda	*to ask a question*
fare una foto	*to take a picture*
fare attenzione	*to pay attention*
fare una gita	*to take a short trip*

Facciamo un viaggio in Italia.	*We are taking a trip to Italy.*
Faccio una passeggiata prima di mangiare.	*I take a walk before eating.*
Lui non **fa domande.**	*He does not ask questions.*
Perchè non **fate attenzione?**	*Why don't you pay attention?*

3. **Dare** is used in the following idiomatic expressions:

dare un esame	*to take an examination*
dare del «tu»	*to address someone informally*
dare del «Lei»	*to address someone formally*
dare la mano	*to shake hands*

Giovedì **do l'esame** di fisica.	*On Thursday I'll take the physics exam.*
Diamo del «tu» agli amici, ma **diamo del «Lei»** ai professori.	*We use "tu" with friends, but we use "Lei" with professors.*

*__Andare__ is followed by the preposition **a** before an infinitive.

4. **Stare** is used in the following idiomatic expressions:

stare bene (male)	*to feel well (badly, ill)*
stare attento(a)	*to be careful; to pay attention*

Stare per + *infinitive* translates as *to be about to (do something).*

I corsi **stanno per** finire. — *Classes are about to end.*

5. Contrary to English, **andare** is not used to express the immediate future. To convey this idea, Italian uses the present (or future) tense: **Parto.** = *I am going to leave.* **Andare a** + *infinitive* expresses motion:

Di solito **vado a mangiare** alla mensa. — *Usually I go to the cafeteria to eat.*

Pratica

A. **Cosa fanno queste persone?** Completate le frasi con le forme appropriate dei seguenti verbi. (*Complete the sentences with the correct forms of the following verbs.*)

1. *andare* Papà _____ in ufficio; la mamma e Tina _____ a una conferenza; Piero e io _____ in banca; e tu _____ a scuola.
2. *fare* I signori Profumo _____ la doccia; Antonella _____ una passeggiata; tu e Marco _____ alcune fotografie del giardino; io _____colazione e, dopo, tu e io _____ la spesa.
3. *dare* Io _____ la mancia alla cameriera; i signori Allegri _____ la mano al dottor Piccoli; Flavio _____ una festa per gli amici; e voi _____ l'esame d'italiano.

B. **Come stanno le seguenti persone?** Completate usando il verbo **stare.**

1. Stamattina il signor Neri _____ a letto perchè _____ male, ma i bambini _____ benissimo e cantano. **2.** Tu non _____ molto bene, ma hai un esame e non _____ a casa. **3.** Gli studenti _____ attenti alle domande del professore.

C. **Domanda e risposta.** Seguite gli esempi.

Dove vanno le seguenti persone?

ESEMPIO tu/dormire
—Dove vai tu?
—Vado a dormire.

1. la mamma/fare le spese **2.** il signor Rossi/comprare il giornale **3.** tu ed io stasera/vedere un film **4.** Gabriella e Filippo/ballare (*to dance*) alla discoteca

Che cosa stanno per fare le seguenti persone?

ESEMPIO tu/finire gli esercizi
—Cosa stai per fare tu?
—Sto per finire gli esercizi.

1. voi/fare il bagno **2.** la mamma e il papà/andare a teatro **3.** lo zio d'America/costruire una villa al mare (*sea*) **4.** tu/perdere la pazienza

D. **Domanda e risposta.** Completate e rispondete usando le forme appropriate dei verbi **andare, fare, dare** e **stare.**

ESEMPIO Dove _____ voi stasera? **—Dove andate voi stasera?**
—Andiamo al cịnema. (o...)

1. Come _____ tua mamma? **2.** Quando _____ una festa, tu? **3.** Dove _____ gli studenti quando non stanno bene? **4.** Tu _____ i cọmpiti solo(a) o con dei compagni? **5.** Preferite _____ una passeggiata o giocare a tennis? **6.** Tu _____ a casa oggi o _____ fuori? **7.** Che cosa _____ gli studenti alla fine del trimestre? **8.** Dopo le lezioni tu ed io _____ a comprare un gelato? **9.** A chi _____ del «tu»? **10.** Voi _____ a letto presto o tardi (*early or late*) la sera?

E. Rispondete usando le espressioni idiomạtiche con **fare**.

1. Cosa fai quando hai bisogno di frutta, verdura o carne? **2.** La mattina fai il bagno o la dọccia? **3.** Cosa fate se non capite la spiegazione del(la) professore(ssa)? **4.** Cosa fanno i turisti con la mạcchina fotogrạfica (*camera*)? **5.** Io vorrei fare un viạggio in Oriente, e tu? **6.** La sera ceniamo (*we have dinner*), e la mattina? **7.** Tu preferisci fare una passeggiata o fare il footing (*jogging*)? **8.** Cosa fanno i bravi studenti quando il professore spiega?

III. I pronomi diretti *lo, la, li, le**

L'amo, non l'amo; l'amo, non l'amo.

*In this chapter we are limiting the study of object pronouns to the most common. All the direct and indirect object pronouns are discussed in Chapter 10.

The direct object pronouns **lo, la, li,** and **le** are used to replace direct object nouns answering the questions *whom?* or *what?*

(*I call: whom? him, her, them*)		(*I visit: what? it, them*)	
Chiamo **il cameriere.**	**Lo** chiamo.	Visito **il museo.**	**Lo** visito.
Chiamo **la signora.**	**La** chiamo.	Visito **la chiesa.**	**La** visito.
Chiamo **gli amici.**	**Li** chiamo.	Visito **i giardini.**	**Li** visito.
Chiamo **le ragazze.**	**Le** chiamo.	Visito **le città.**	**Le** visito.

NOTE:

1. These pronouns immediately precede the conjugated verb even in the negative form.

   Conosci **la signora Galli?**
   No, non **la** conosco.

   Comprate **i giornali?**
   No, non **li** compriamo.

2. Usually the singular pronouns **lo** and **la** drop the final vowel before a verb beginning with a vowel sound.

   Inviti **Lucia?**
   Sì, **l'**invito.

   Ascolti **la radio?**
   No, non **l'**ascolto.

Pratica

Rispondete alle seguenti domande usando il pronome al posto del nome oggetto diretto.

ESEMPIO Aspetti il treno? **Sì, l'aspetto.** (*o...*)
No, non l'aspetto.

Cosa fai la domenica?
1. Incontri gli amici? **2.** Guardi la TV? **3.** Vedi la tua famiglia?
4. Fai i compiti? **5.** Pulisci l'appartamento?

Cosa mangi a pranzo?
1. Mangi la pastasciutta? **2.** Preferisci la carne con la verdura?
3. Mangi spesso le lasagne? **4.** Prendi il caffè alla fine del pranzo?
5. Ordini i ravioli al ristorante?

Marcello va a passare la domenica sul Lago di Como.

IV. I giorni della settimana

GENNAIO		
16	L	s Marcello
17	M	s Antonio
18	M	s Prisca
√19	G	s Mario
20	V	s Sebastiano
21	S	s Agnese
22	D	Sacra Famiglia

—Che giorno è oggi?
—Oggi è giovedì.

The days of the week are:

lunedì*	*Monday*
martedì	*Tuesday*
mercoledì	*Wednesday*
giovedì	*Thursday*
venerdì	*Friday*
sạbato	*Saturday*
domẹnica	*Sunday*

NOTE:
Days of the week are masculine except **domẹnica**, which is feminine. In Italian, they are not capitalized.

1. The preposition *on* is not expressed in Italian when used in expressions such as *on Monday, on Tuesday,* and so on.

   Lunedì il Prof. Bini dà una conferenza. — *On Monday Prof. Bini is giving a lecture.*

2. The definite article is used in the singular before the days of the week to express a habitual event.

   Il sạbato gioco al golf. — *On Saturdays (Every Saturday) I play golf.*

   BUT:
   Sạbato invito degli amici. — *(This) Saturday I am inviting some friends.*

3. The expressions **una volta a**, **due volte a**, etc., + *definite article* translate into English as *once a, twice a,* etc.

   Vado al cịnema **una volta alla settimana.** — *I go to the movies once a week.*
   Mangiamo **due volte al giorno.** — *We eat twice a day.*
   Andiamo a teatro **quattro volte all'anno.** — *We go to the theater four times a year.*

---

*In Italy **lunedì** is considered the first day of the week.

Per ricordare (*To remember*) quanti giorni ci sono in ogni mese, gli Italiani reçitano (*recite*) questo ritornello (*refrain*):

> Trenta giorni ha novembre,
> con aprile, giugno e settembre;
> di ventotto ce n'è uno,
> tutti gli altri ne hanno trentuno.

Pratica

A. **La settimana.** Rispondete alle seguenti domande.

1. Che giorno della settimana è oggi? 2. Con quale giorno incomịncia la settimana in Itạlia? 3. Qual è l'ụltimo (*last*) giorno della settimana? 4. Che cosa facciamo la domẹnica? 5. Quale giorno sẹgue il giovedì? 6. In che giorno gli Americani festeggiano il Thanksgiving? 7. Quanti giorni alla settimana vai a scuola tu? Quali? 8. Quale giorno della settimana preferisci e perchè? 9. Io vorrei avere un fine settimana di tre giorni, e tu? 10. Gli studenti italiani vanno a scuola anche il sạbato, e gli studenti americani?

B. Quante volte al giorno (alla settimana, al mese o all'anno) fate le seguenti cose?

1. mangiare della carne 2. fare le spese 3. scrịvere a un amico lontano 4. fare dello sport 5. andare al cịnema 6. andare in biblioteca 7. comprare un regalo per una persona cara 8. pulire la stanza (l'appartamento o la casa)

C. Ripetete le seguenti frasi e sostituite l'artịcolo determinativo con **ogni** e con **tutti**, **tutte**.

ESEMPIO Il venerdì sera fạccio molte telefonate.
Ogni venerdì sera fạccio molte telefonate.
Tutti i venerdì sera fạccio molte telefonate.

1. Il sạbato puliamo l'appartamento. 2. La domẹnica i signori Santi vanno in chiesa. 3. Il lunedì sera mio padre dorme davanti alla televisione. 4. Il giovedì Lella lavora in un negọzio. 5. La domẹnica pomeriggio facciamo una gita fuori città.

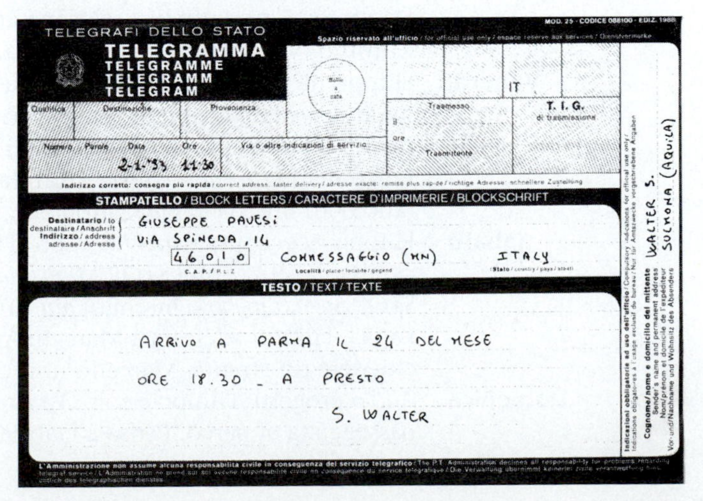

MOD. 25 - CODICE 088100 - EDIZ. 1988

TELEGRAFI DELLO STATO

TELEGRAMMA
TELEGRAMME
TELEGRAMM
TELEGRAM

Spazio riservato all'ufficio / for official use only / espace reservé aux services / Dienstvermerke

IT

Qualifica | Destinazione | Provenienza

Trasmesso il ... ore ... Trasmittente

T. I. G. di trasmissione

Numero | Parole | Data 2-1-'93 | Ore 11·30

Via o altre indicazioni di servizio

Indirizzo corretto: consegna più rapida / correct address, faster delivery / adresse exacte: remise plus rapide / richtige Adresse: schnellere Zustellung

STAMPATELLO / BLOCK LETTERS / CARACTERE D'IMPRIMERIE / BLOCKSCHRIFT

Destinatario / to / destinataire / Anschrift
Indirizzo / address / adresse / Adresse

GIUSEPPE PAVESI
VIA SPINEDA, 14
46010 COMMESSAGGIO (MN) ITALY

C.A.P. / P.L.Z. — Località / place / localité / gegend — Stato / country / pays / staat

TESTO / TEXT / TEXTE

ARRIVO A PARMA IL 24 DEL MESE
ORE 18.30 _ A PRESTO
S. WALTER

Indicazioni obbligatorie ad uso dell'ufficio / Compulsory indications for official use only / Indications obligatoires à l'usage exclusif du bureau / Nur für Amtszwecke vorgeschriebene Angaben

Cognome/nome e domicilio del mittente / Sender's name and permanent address / Nom/prénom et domicile de l'expéditeur / Vor- und Nachname und Wohnsitz des Absenders

WALTER S.
SULMONA (AQUILA)

L'Amministrazione non assume alcuna responsabilità civile in conseguenza del servizio telegrafico

LETTURA

Cosa facciamo sabato sera? Andiamo al cinema o alla discoteca?

UNA SETTIMANA MOLTO OCCUPATA

Lunedì	Filippo va all'università. Dopo le lezioni vede Gabriella e *lịtigano.* Gioca a tennis per un'ora. Va a casa e fa la dọccia. *Prima di* cena va in Galleria e prende un aperitivo con Marcello e Liliana.	quarrel before
Martedì	Filippo finisce il lavoro in uffịcio. Nel pomerịggio fa il footing e nuota in *piscina.* La sera vede gli amici al Caffè Sport: pạrlano di polịtica. Compra una carta telefọnica e fa una telefonata a Gabriella: Gabriella non risponde.	swimming pool
Mercoledì	Filippo sta alcune ore in uffịcio. Poi va in biblioteca. Legge e stụdia molto perchè domani ha un esame diffịcile. La sera telẹfona a Gabriella. Il telẹfono è sempre occupato.	
Giovedì	Filippo dà l'esame. L'esame è *un osso duro.* Non capisce alcune domande e non finisce. Da un telẹfono pụbblico telẹfona ad Antọnio. Vanno insieme al cịnema.	tough
Venerdì	Filippo ha grandi progetti per il week-end, ma è al verde. *Manda* un telegramma al padre: «Caro papà sono senza soldi STOP Prego mandare *sụbito* duecentomila (200.000) lire STOP *Baci* Filippo».	he sends immediately kisses
Sạbato	Filippo riceve una risposta: «Caro Filippo capisco la situazione STOP *Mi dispiace* STOP *Spendi meno* o *lavora di più* STOP Baci Papà». Filippo telẹfona a Marcello per chiẹdere un *prẹstito.* Marcello non c'è.	I am sorry spend less/work more loan
Domẹnica	*Addịo* progetti. Filippo è solo. Fa una passeggiata al parco. Pensa a Gabriella.	good-bye

Comprensione

1. Chi vede dopo le lezioni, Filippo? **2.** Cosa fanno Filippo e Gabriella? **3.** Cosa fa Filippo quando va a casa? **4.** Dove va Filippo prima di cena? **5.** Con chi prende un aperitivo? **6.** Dove lavora Filippo? **7.** Cosa fa nel pomeriggio di martedì? **8.** A chi telefona la sera di martedì e di mercoledì? **9.** Perchè Filippo va in biblioteca mercoledì? **10.** È facile l'esame? Filippo lo finisce? **11.** Dove va giovedì sera Filippo? Con chi? **12.** Perchè Filippo manda un telegramma al padre venerdì? **13.** È generoso il padre di Filippo? Perchè? **14.** Che cosa fa Filippo domenica sera?

Domande personali

1. Dov'è Lei il lunedì? il mercoledì? il venerdì? Perchè? **2.** Va all'università Lei tutti i giorni della settimana? Quali? **3.** Quando finisce i corsi Lei? La mattina o il pomeriggio? Dove va dopo i corsi? Perchè? **4.** Che cosa fa prima di cena? E dopo la cena? **5.** Di solito dov'è Lei il martedì pomeriggio? Perchè? **6.** Cosa fa Lei il sabato sera? Vede amici? **7.** Sta a casa Lei la domenica? Che cosa fa? **8.** Che cosa desidera fare Lei questo weekend? **9.** È al verde Lei qualche volta? Quando non ha soldi a chi li chiede?

ATTIVITÀ SUPPLEMENTARI

A. **Pronto? Che cosa fai?** Immaginate una conversazione telefonica fra due compagni(e) di classe. Soggetto: Un invito per la festa di compleanno di un amico (un'amica). Che giorno è la festa? Dove la fanno? Desiderate fare un regalo? Quale? Telefonate da un telefono pubblico e avete fretta perchè avete solo due gettoni.

B. **La vostra settimana.** Quali sono le vostre (*your*) attività per ogni giorno della settimana? Scrivete delle frasi complete. Incominciate con: **Il lunedì...** (*Follow the guidelines of* "Una settimana molto occupata.")

C. **Una giornata nella vita di Marisa.** Osservate i disegni e dite quali sono le attività di Marisa in una giornata. Usate la vostra immaginazione.

D. Come si dice in italiano?

1. On Fridays Giulia walks to the university with Maria.
2. Today, however, Maria is staying home because she is not well; so Giulia prefers to take the bus.
3. At the library she sees a friend: "Hi, Paola. What are you doing here?"
4. I am reading a book on (*sull'*) Italian art.
5. How many classes are you taking this (*questo*) quarter?
6. Three: a psychology class, an English class, and an art history class.
7. When Giulia finishes studying (*di studiare*), she takes a walk and then makes a phone call to Maria.
8. Maria answers: "Hello? Who is speaking?"
9. This is (I am) Giulia. How are you?
10. I am fine now, thank you.
11. Are we going to Gianni's party on Sunday?
12. Sorry, but on Sunday I am going to the movies with Cristina.

Vocabolario

Nomi

l'appuntamento	*appointment, date*
la discoteca	*discotheque*
la domẹnica	*Sunday*
la farmacia	*pharmacy*
il fine settimana	*weekend*
il giovedì	*Thursday*
l'invitato(a)	*guest*
la lẹttera	*letter*
la lira	*lira*
il lunedì	*Monday*
la mạcchina fotogrạfica	*camera*
il martedì	*Tuesday*
la mensa	*cafeteria*
il mercoledì	*Wednesday*
il momento	*moment*
la montagna	*mountain*
il padre	*father*
la pazienza	*patience*
la piscina	*swimming pool*
il pomeriggio	*afternoon*
il progetto	*project*
il sabato	*Saturday*
il venerdì	*Friday*

Aggettivi

breve	*brief, short*
pụbblico	*public*
sẹrio	*serious*
solo	*alone*

Verbi

andare	*to go*
ballare	*to dance*
capire (-isc)	*to understand*
chiamare	*to call, to phone*
costruire (-isc)	*to build*
dare	*to give*
fare	*to do; to make*
finire (-isc)	*to finish*
festeggiare	*to celebrate*
mandare	*to send*
nuotare	*to swim*
preferire (-isc)	*to prefer*
pulire (-isc)	*to clean*
restituire (-isc)	*to give back, to return (something)*
ritornare	*to return*
stare	*to stay; to feel*
ubbidire (-isc)	*to obey*
usare	*to use*

Altre espressioni

allora	*so, then*
dare un esame	*to take an exam*
dare del «tu»	*to address somebody in the «tu» form*
dare del «Lei»	*to address somebody in the «Lei» form*
dare la mano	*to shake hands*
ẹssere al verde	*to be broke*
fare attenzione	*to pay attention*
fare il bagno	*to take a bath*
fare colazione	*to have breakfast*
fare la dọccia	*to take a shower*
fare una domanda	*to ask a question*
fare una foto	*to take a picture*
fare una gita	*to take a short trip*
fare una passeggiata	*to take a walk*
fare un regalo	*to give a present*
fare la spesa	*to go shopping (for groceries)*
fare le spese	*to go shopping*
fare un viạggio	*to take a trip*
finalmente	*finally*
insieme	*together*
ora	*now*
però	*however, but*
poi	*then*
quante volte...?	*how many times...?*
una volta, due volte	*once, twice*
qui	*here*
senza	*without*
si trova, si trọvano	*it is, they are (location)*
stare attento(a)	*to be careful, to pay attention*
stare bene (male)	*to feel well (badly, ill)*
stare per...	*to be about to...*
va bene	*OK*

IL SISTEMA UNIVERSITẠRIO

In Itạlia ci sono *più di* quaranta università, quasi tutte *statali*. Le più grandi sono a Milano, Nạpoli e Roma, dove ci sono più di *sessantamila* studenti. La più antica università d'Italia e d'Europa è l'università di Bologna, *fondata* alla fine *del 1100*, e famosa nel *Medio Evo* per gli studi di *legge*. Oggi è nota per i corsi di medicina e di lẹttere.

more than
state schools
sixty thousand
founded/of the twelfth century/Middle Ages/law

Dopo il diploma della scuola mẹdia superiore, più del sessanta per cento degli studenti italiani contịnua gli studi all'università. La ragione: la difficoltà di trovare lavoro. Quando lo studente o la studentessa incomịncia gli studi universitari, *deve* decịdere immediatamente la sua *specializzazione, cioè,* a quale *facoltà* iscrịversi. Le facoltà più *affollate* sono Lẹttere, Lịngue e Letterature Straniere, Medicina, *Legge*, Scienze e *Economia e Commercio*.

must
major/that is
school/crowded
law
School of Business

I corsi sono in gẹnere *basati* su conferenze e *durano* un anno accadẹmico. I contatti con i professori non sono frequenti *a causa del* nụmero eccessivo di studenti. Alla fine dei corsi gli studenti danno degli esami scritti e orali: i voti vanno da diciotto (il minimo *per essere promossi*) a trenta *e lode*.

based/last
due to
to be promoted/with honors

Oggi esịstono tre tịtoli universitari: la lạurea breve (dopo due—tre anni di stụdio), la lạurea tradizionale (dopo quattro—sei anni di stụdio) e il dottorato di *ricerca*.

research

In Itạlia non esiste un vero «campus» universitạrio. L'università è spesso un insieme di vecchi edifici in città. Ci sono alcune «case dello studente» e dei *pensionati* che sẹrvono da «dormitọrio». *La maggior parte* degli studenti, però, vive in famịglia o in *camere d'affitto*.

boarding houses/most
rented rooms

Le tasse universitarie sono modeste. Lo stato *aiuta* i giọvani *meritevoli* e pọveri.

Tuition/helps
deserving

L'ora del pranzo alla Casa dello Studente.

Comprensione

Completate le seguenti frasi con le parole corrette.

1. Quasi tutte le università italiane sono...
   a. private **b.** a Milano **c.** statali
2. La più antica università italiana è...
   a. a Nạpoli **b.** a Bologna **c.** a Roma
3. I corsi universitari hanno la durata di...
   a. un semestre **b.** un trimestre **c.** un anno
4. Spesso l'università italiana si trova...
   a. fuori della città **b.** dentro la città **c.** lontano dalla città
5. La maggior parte degli studenti universitari vive...
   a. con la famịglia **b.** con compagni **c.** in pensionati per studenti
6. In gẹnere, gli studenti universitari pạrlano con i loro professori...
   a. ogni settimana **b.** spesso **c.** raramente
7. Il voto migliore (*best*) all'università è...
   a. trenta **b.** diciotto **c.** trenta e lode

6 LA FAMIGLIA E I PARENTI

Milano, Piazza Duomo. Madre, padre e bambini danno da mangiare ai piccioni..

Punti di vista

Una famiglia numerosa
A casa degli zii

Punti grammaticali

I Gli aggettivi possessivi
II I pronomi possessivi
III Verbi irregolari in *-ere*: il presente
IV Verbi irregolari in *-ire*: il presente
V *Sapere* e *conoscere*

Lettura

Chi viene a cena stasera?

Pagina culturale

La famiglia in Italia

PUNTI DI VISTA

Tre generazioni a tavola. Chi sono?

UNA FAMIGLIA NUMEROSA

È sạbato, e Ornella *va a trovare* gli zii che ạbitano *in cạmpagna*. Va in mạcchina, e la sua amica va con lei. — goes to visit/in the country

Bianca	Quante persone ci sono nella tua famịglia?	
Ornella	Mio padre, mia madre, mio fratello, le mie due sorelle ed io.	
Bianca	Hai una famịglia numerosa.	
Ornella	*Abbastanza.*	quite
Bianca	Come si chiama tuo fratello e quanti anni ha?	
Ornella	Marco ha venticinque anni, e *fa l'ụltimo anno di medicina* all'università di Bologna. È un bel ragazzo, intelligente. I suoi professori hanno un'opinione eccellente di lui. *Vuoi conọscerlo*?	he is in his last year of medical school; do you want to meet him?
Bianca	Sì, *volentieri*! Quando?	with pleasure
Ornella	Domani sera. *Possiamo uscire* insieme; tu con mio fratello e io con il mio ragazzo.	we can go out
Bianca	Splẹndido!	

Comprensione

1. Che giorno è? 2. Con chi va a trovare gli zii Ornella? 3. Quanti figli (*children*) ci sono nella famịglia di Ornella? 4. Come si chiama suo fratello? 5. Che opinione hanno i suoi professori? 6. Bianca vuole conọscere Marco o non vuole conọscerlo? 7. Secondo Lei, Bianca ha un ragazzo o non ha un ragazzo? 8. Con chi esce (*goes out*) Bianca domani sera?

Studio di parole

ALBERO GENEALOGICO

i genitori parents
il marito husband
la moglie wife
il fratello brother
la sorella sister
lo zio, la zia uncle, aunt
il cugino, la cugina cousin
il nipote grandson; nephew
la nipote granddaughter; niece
il (la) parente relative
i parenti relatives
i figli children
il suocero father-in-law
la suocera mother-in-law
il genero son-in-law
la nuora daughter-in-law
il cognato, la cognata brother-in-law, sister-in-law
nubile unmarried (single) female
celibe unmarried (single) male
sposato(a) married
divorziato(a) divorced

Applicazione

A. **Chi è?** Completate le seguenti frasi con l'espressione appropriata.

1. Il fratello di mio padre è mio __________.
2. La madre di mia madre è mia __________.
3. I nonni hanno un debole (*a weak spot*) per i loro __________.
4. La moglie di mio fratello è mia __________.
5. Rina non ha marito; è __________.
6. La figlia dello zio Piero è mia __________.

B. L'ạlbero genealọgico. Guardate l'ạlbero genealọgico e rispondete con una frase completa.

1. Luigi e Maria sono marito e mọglie. Chi sono i loro due figli? Chi è il loro gẹnero? Chi sono i loro nipoti?
2. Anna è la mọglie di Paolo. Chi è suo padre? Chi è suo fratello? Chi è sua cognata?
3. Luisa è la mọglie di Franco. Come si chiạmano i suoi figli? Chi è sua suọcera? Chi sono i suoi due nipoti?
4. Enzo è il fratello di Marina. Chi è suo nonno? Chi è sua zia? Chi sono i suoi cugini?

C. Domande personali.

1. Ha un fratello Lei?
2. Ha una sorella?
3. Quante persone ci sono nella Sua famịglia? (Nella mia...) Ha una famịglia numerosa?
4. Come si chiama Suo padre?
5. Va spesso a trovare i parenti?
6. Dove ạbitano i genitori, in città o in campagna?
7. Ha molti cugini?

Ascoltiamo!

A casa degli zii. *Ornella and her friend Bianca have just arrived at the house of her aunt and uncle in the country. Listen as everyone exchanges greetings and a few words, then answer the related questions.*

Comprensione

1. Dove arrịvano Ornella e la sua amica Bianca? **2.** Dove ạbitano gli zii? **3.** Cosa dice lo zio quando Ornella presenta la sua amica? **4.** Come stanno i genitori di Ornella? **5.** Dove lavora suo padre? **6.** Qual è la professione di sua madre? **7.** Cosa prepara la zia?

Dialogo

In groups of three, play the roles of Ornella, Bianca, and the uncle (or a grandfather or grandmother). Expand on the dialogue, drawing on the "Stụdio di parole." *For example, her uncle may ask Bianca if she is married and has children and what her husband's profession is. Or he could inquire if and where she works. He might also ask if she would like some coffee or tea, or some pastries.)*

PUNTI GRAMMATICALI

I. Gli aggettivi possessivi

Ecco Antonio, con la sua famiglia suo padre, sua madre, le sue sorelle, i suoi fratelli, e il suo cane. Alla parete c'è il ritratto dei suoi nonni.

1. È con i suoi amici o con la sua famiglia Antonio?
2. Quante persone ci sono nella sua famiglia?
3. Cosa c'è alla parete?

	Singular		*Plural*	
	Masculine	***Feminine***	***Masculine***	***Feminine***
my	il mio	la mia	i miei	le mie
your (familiar sing.)	il tuo	la tua	i tuoi	le tue
his, her, its	il suo	la sua	i suoi	le sue
your (formal sing.)	il Suo	la Sua	i Suoi	le Sue
our	il nostro	la nostra	i nostri	le nostre
your (familiar pl.)	il vostro	la vostra	i vostri	le vostre
their	il loro	la loro	i loro	le loro
your (formal pl.)	il Loro	la Loro	i Loro	le Loro

1. Possessive adjectives express ownership or relationship (*my, your, his,* etc.). They are preceded by the article and agree in gender and number with the noun that follows, *not* with the possessor. Remember that whenever certain prepositions precede a definite article, the two words contract (see Chapter 3): ***Nella mia* famiglia ci sono sei persone.**

   il mio amico — *my friend*
   i nostri nonni — *our grandparents*

la sua macchina	*his (her) car*
Telefona **dal Suo** ufficio?	*Are you calling from your office?*
Ritornano **dal loro** viaggio.	*They are returning from their trip.*
Rispondo **alla vostra** lettera.	*I am answering your letter.*

2. The article is *not* used when the possessive precedes a singular noun that refers to a relative.

mio zio Baldo	*my uncle Baldo*
nostra cugina Nella	*our cousin Nella*
suo fratello	*his (her) brother*

NOTE:
The article is used with the possessive if the noun referring to relatives is plural or if it is modified by an adjective or a suffix.

i miei zii e **le mie** cugine	*my uncles and my cousins*
la mia bella cugina Lia	*my beautiful cousin Lia*
il tuo fratellino	*your little brother*

3. **Loro** is invariable and is *always* preceded by the article.

la loro sorella	*their sister*
i loro vicini	*their neighbors*

4. Phrases such as *a friend of mine* and *some books of yours* translate as **un mio amico** and **alcuni tuoi libri.**

5. The idiomatic constructions **a casa mia, a casa tua,** etc., mean in English *at (to) my house, at (to) your house,* etc.

Pratica

A. Completate con la forma appropriata dell'aggettivo possessivo.

1. (*my*) Luisa, sai (*do you know*) dove sono _____ orologio, _____ penna e _____ appunti? Perdo sempre _____ cose.
2. (*our*) _____ compagni e _____ compagne sono simpatici. E _____ professore? È molto simpatico, ma un po' severo.
3. (*your, fam. sing.*) Conosco (*I know*) _____ sorella e _____ fratello, ma non conosco _____ genitori.
4. (*his*) Marco è alla stazione perchè aspetta _____ nonni. Dov'è _____ famiglia? _____ padre e _____ madre lavorano al museo e _____ sorelle vivono in un'altra città.
5. (*their*) Bice e Linda amano molto _____ zii e _____ cugina Paola.
6. (*your, fam. pl.*) Dove si trova _____ liceo? Sapete dove abitano _____ vecchi compagni di scuola?

B. **Chi portate a cena?** L'insegnante (*teacher*) invita i suoi studenti a cena. Ogni studente porta amici o parenti.

ESEMPIO amico **Io porto il mio amico.**

1. genitori 2. nonno 3. sorella 4. amiche 5. cugino 6. fratellino 7. compagne di classe 8. professore di tedesco 9. parenti italiani 10. cane 11. fratelli

C. Dov'è...? Domanda e risposta.

ESEMPIO libro d'italiano/tạvolo
—Dov'è il tuo libro d'italiano?
—Il mio libro d'italiano è sul tạvolo.

1. nonni/Assisi 2. compagno di stanza/lezione di filosofia 3. fratelli/ università 4. mạcchina/garage 5. famịglia/Grẹcia 6. fogli di appunti/ stụdio 7. fotografie/scrivania 8. calcolatrice/cassetto (*drawer*) 9. sorella/ristorante

D. Completate con la preposizione + l'aggettivo possessivo (con o senza artịcolo).

1. Io dimẹntico sempre molti oggetti (*on my*) _____ letto, _____ tạvolo e _____ sẹdie. 2. Lui mette i soldi (*in his*) _____ portafọglio (*wallet*) o _____ stanza. 3. Offriamo regali (*to our*) _____ amici e _____ parenti. 4. Stasera vẹngono tutti (*to our*) _____ festa. 5. Lei parla (di) (*about her*) _____ famịglia, _____ figli, _____ marito. 6. Le ragazze ascọltano l'opinione (*of their*) _____ genitori e _____ amiche. 7. Marcello ritorna (*from his*) _____ viạggio in campagna. 8. Se tu hai bisogno di soldi, scrivi (*to your*) _____ padre, _____ madre o _____ nonni? 9. Signor Mạuri, posso sapere l'indirizzo (*of your*) _____ fịglia?

E. Un(a) compagno(a) ti mostra (*is showing you*) delle foto, e tu fai delle domande.

ESEMPIO casa, nonno **—È la casa di tuo nonno?**
—Sì, è la sua casa.

1. mạcchina, genitori 2. fịglio, sorella 3. appartamento, cugini 4. mọglie, zio 5. fidanzata, fratello 6. madre, ragazzo 7. villa, zii 8. cane, cugina

F. **Domanda e risposta.** Uno studente (una studentessa) fa alcune domande alla signora Pini. Fate le due parti (*play the two roles*) e date del Lei alla signora.

ESEMPIO **—Signora Pini, chi è il Suo dentista?**
—Il mio dentista è il dottor Denti.

1. Signora Pini, qual è _____ nuovo nụmero di telẹfono? 2. Dove ạbitano _____ suọceri? 3. Dov'è _____ marito oggi? 4. Come sta _____ madre? 5. Che scuole frequẹntano _____ fịglie?

II. I pronomi possessivi

—*Mio figlio si chiama Luigi. E i Loro?*
—*I nostri si chiạmano:*
Mina, Lisa, Tino, Gino, Nino.

1. The possessive pronouns have the same forms as the possessive adjectives. They are preceded by the article, even when they refer to relatives.

mia madre e **la sua**	*my mother and his (hers)*
la tua casa e **la nostra**	*your house and ours*
i suoi amici e **i miei**	*his friends and mine*
Ecco mio fratello; dov'è **il Suo**?	*There is my brother; where is yours?*

2. When emphasizing possession after the verb **ẹssere**, the article is often omitted, except with **loro.**

Di chi è il disco sul tạvolo?	*Whose record is on the table?*
È mio.	*It is mine.*
Di chi sono i libri sulla sẹdia?	*Whose books are on the chair?*
Sono **suoi.**	*They are hers (his).*

Pratica

A. Sostituite le parole in corsivo (*italics*) con i pronomi possessivi appropriati.

ESEMPIO Ricordo mia madre e *tua madre.* **Ricordo mia madre e la tua.**

1. Conosco i tuoi genitori e anche *i genitori di Pietro.* 2. Io lavoro nel mio uffịcio e lui lavora *nel suo uffịcio.* 3. Voi raccontate le vostre stọrie e io racconto *le mie stọrie.* 4. Lui ha bisogno dei suoi soldi e anche *dei soldi dei genitori.* 5. Penso a mio padre e *a tuo padre.* 6. Ecco mia madre. Dov'è *la madre di Nino?* 7. Ecco la tua bicicletta. Dov'è *la mia bicicletta?*

B. Di chi...? Domanda e risposta. Seguite l'esẹmpio.

ESEMPIO libro di stọria/(*mine*) **—Di chi è il libro di stọria?**
—È mio.

1. i giornali sul tạvolo/(*hers*) **2.** la penna blu/(*his*) **3.** il bicchiere di latte sul tạvolo/(*yours, fam. sing.*) **4.** le sẹdie/(*ours*) **5.** i fogli sotto il tạvolo/ (*mine*) **6.** le due mạcchine davanti alla casa/(*ours*) **7.** i soldi/(*yours, fam. pl.*) **8.** l'appartamento sopra il negọzio/(*theirs*)

C. Come si chiama...? Domanda e risposta. Seguite l'esẹmpio.

ESEMPIO il nome della madre **—Come si chiama tua madre?**
—Mia madre si chiama..., e la tua?
—La mia si chiama...

1. il nome del cantante preferito **2.** il nome del padre **3.** il nome del liceo **4.** il nome delle attrici preferite **5.** il nome di un amico o di un'amica

III. Verbi irregolari in *-ere*: il presente

—Bevo alla tua salute!
—Cin cin!

The following verbs ending in **-ere** are irregular in the present tense.

bere (*to drink*)		**dovere** (*to have to, must; to owe*)		**potere** (*can, may, to be able to*)		**volere** (*to want*)	
bevo	beviamo	devo	dobbiamo	posso	possiamo	voglio	vogliamo
bevi	bevete	devi	dovete	puoi	potete	vuoi	volete
beve	bẹvono	deve	dẹvono	può	pọssono	vuole	vọgliono

Dovere and **potere** are followed by an infinitive. **Volere** may be followed by an infinitive or a noun.

Oggi **beviamo** del Chianti. — *Today we are drinking Chianti.*
Stasera **devo** uscire. — *Tonight I have to go out.*
Possiamo fare molte cose. — *We can do many things.*
Cosa **vuoi** mangiare? — *What do you want to eat?*
Vuole un succo d'arancia? — *Do you want (a glass of) orange juice?*

NOTE:
Dovere, followed by a noun, corresponds to the English *to owe.*

Devo 100 dollari a mia zia. — *I owe my aunt 100 dollars.*

Pratica

A. **Domanda e risposta.** Seguite l'esempio.

ESEMPIO i bambini **—Cosa preferiscono bere i bambini?**
—Bevono del latte. (o...)

1. una ragazza di 15 anni **2.** la nonna e il nonno **3.** io e tu **4.** una persona che (*who*) ha molta sete **5.** tu **6.** uno zio italiano

B. **Cosa possiamo fare con 1.000 dollari?** Un(a) compagno(a) dice che cosa vogliono fare le seguenti persone con mille (*one thousand*) dollari. Tu rispondi se possono o non possono.

ESEMPIO i miei genitori, andare in Italia **—I miei genitori vogliono andare in Italia.**
—I tuoi genitori non possono andare in Italia.

1. io, comprare una macchina fotografica **2.** mio fratello, fare un viaggio a New York **3.** mia sorella ed io, portare i nostri genitori all'opera **4.** i miei cugini, comprare una barca (*boat*) **5.** tu e io, dare una festa per tutti gli studenti **6.** io, affittare (*to rent*) una villa in Toscana per un mese **7.** mio marito ed io, fare una crociera (*cruise*) alle isole Hawaii **8.** tu, comprare un computer Macintosh

C. **Se...** Completate le frasi con la forma corretta di **dovere** e con un po' d'immaginazione.

ESEMPIO Se ho sete,... **Se ho sete, devo bere dell'acqua. (o...)**

1. Se gli studenti ricevono brutti voti,... **2.** Se io ho fame la mattina,... **3.** Se non stiamo bene,... **4.** Se hai sonno,... **5.** Se volete organizzare un picnic,... **6.** Se uno studente non capisce la spiegazione,... **7.** Se abbiamo bisogno di soldi,... **8.** Se un nostro amico non arriva all'appuntamento,...

D. **Che cosa devo a...?** Le seguenti persone hanno dei debiti (*debts*). Dite che cosa devono e a chi.

ESEMPIO (io) 20 dollari, nonno **Io devo venti dollari a mio nonno.**

1. (Filippo) molti soldi, padre **2.** (Gabriella) 1.000 (mille) lire, cugina **3.** (i signori Smith) 1.000 dollari, un parente **4.** (tu) 17 dollari, fratello **5.** (noi) mille ringraziamenti, genitori

IV. Verbi irregolari in *-ire*: il presente

Un proverbio dice: «Dopo la pioggia viene il sole.»

The following verbs ending in **-ire** are irregular in the present tense.

dire (*to say, to tell*)		**uscire*** (*to go out*)		**venire** (*to come*)	
dico	diciamo	esco	usciamo	vengo	veniamo
dici	dite	esci	uscite	vieni	venite
dice	dịcono	esce	ẹscono	viene	vẹngono

I genitori **dịcono** «Buon compleanno!» — *The parents are saying, "Happy birthday!"*
Veniamo domani. — *We'll come tomorrow.*
Esce tutte le sere. — *He (She) goes out every night.*
Lia **riesce** bene a scuola. — *Lia is very successful in school.*

NOTE:
The expression **voler(e) dire** translates as *to mean* in English.

Non capisco. Che cosa **vuoi dire**? — *I don't understand. What do you mean?*

---

*The verb **riuscire** (*to succeed*) is conjugated like **uscire**.

Pratica

A. **Cosa diciamo? Domanda e risposta.** Usate il verbo **dire.**

ESEMPIO tu, quando arrivi in classe —**Cosa dici tu quando arrivi in classe?**
—**Dico «Buon giorno». (o...)**

1. voi, al compleanno di un amico **2.** noi, quando rispondiamo al telẹfono **3.** i bambini, quando vanno a dormire **4.** i tuoi genitori, quando vẹdono i tuoi voti **5.** io, quando il cameriere porta un caffè **6.** tu, quando un tuo parente o un tuo amico parte **7.** tu, a un compagno prima di un esame diffịcile **8.** noi, quando il professore entra in classe **9.** voi, agli amici, la sera tardi (*late*) dopo una festa **10.** gli Italiani, quando fanno un brịndisi (*make a toast*)

B. Completate con le forme corrette di **uscire** e **venire**, secondo il caso (*according to the context*).

1. Questa sera io non _____ perchè i miei nonni _____ a cena. **2.** Tu e il tuo compagno _____ tutte le sere! Dove andate? **3.** Oggi mia madre non _____ di casa perchè aspetta sua sorella che _____ dall'Itạlia. **4.** Se noi _____ presto (*early*) dall'uffịcio, possiamo fare una passeggiata. **5.** Quando _____ a casa mia voi? **6.** Se volete, possiamo _____ insieme stasera.

C. Rispondete con una frase negativa o affermativa.

1. Esci domani sera? **2.** Venite a casa nostra questo pomerịggio? **3.** Dici sempre la verità o dici qualche bugia di convenienza (*white lie*)? **4.** Uscite spesso, tu e il tuo ragazzo (la tua ragazza)? **5.** Sei contento(a) se veniamo a casa tua? **6.** Vieni a cena domani sera? **7.** Uscite a fare la spesa? **8.** Ẹscono i ragazzi studiosi la sera prima di un esame importante?

V. Sapere e conọscere

—Pietro! Cosa fai!? Mia madre non sa nuotare!

In Italian there are two verbs that mean *to know* in English: **sapere** and **conọscere.** They are conjugated as follows:

sapere		**conoscere**	
so	sappiamo	conosco	conosciamo
sai	sapete	conosci	conoscete
sa	sanno	conosce	conọscono

1. **Sapere** is an irregular verb. It means *to know how to do something, to know a fact.*

   Sai la lezione? — *Do you know the lesson?*
   Nino **sa** suonare il piano. — *Nino knows how to play the piano.*

   Sai che Pietro è a Roma? — *Do you know Pietro is in Rome?*
   Sì, lo **so.** — *Yes, I know it.*

   Sapete quando ritorna? — *Do you know when he will come back?*
   No, non lo **sappiamo.** — *No, we do not know (it).*

2. **Conọscere** is a regular verb. It means *to be acquainted with a person or a place, to meet someone for the first time.*

   Non **conosco** il sig. Paoli. — *I don't know Mr. Paoli.*
   Conosciamo bene Venẹzia. — *We know Venice well.*
   Desịdero **conọscere** i tuoi genitori. — *I would like to meet your parents.*

Pratica

A. **Sapete...?** Rispondete alle seguenti domande.

   1. Sai che regalo desịdera tuo padre? **2.** I tuoi amici sanno giocare a tennis? **3.** Tu sai suonare il piano? **4.** Tuo padre sa che voti ricevi a scuola? **5.** Sapete sempre quando c'è un esame di italiano, o qualche volta è una sorpresa? **6.** Chi sa cucinare mẹglio (*better*), tu o tua madre? **7.** Sai che giorno è oggi, per favore?

B. **Un padre curioso.** Il padre di Gabriella domanda informazioni a un amico su (*about*) Filippo. Cominciate la domanda con **Sai...?** o **Conosci...?**

   ESEMPIO suo padre **Conosci suo padre?**

   1. dove ạbita **2.** con chi lavora **3.** la sua famịglia **4.** se è un ragazzo sẹrio **5.** i suoi amici **6.** quanti corsi sẹgue all'università **7.** i suoi genitori **8.** perchè vuole telefonare a Gabriella **9.** quanti anni ha **10.** quando viene a casa nostra **11.** sua madre **12.** quanti fratelli o quante sorelle ha **13.** quando finisce gli studi

LETTURA

Biglietto d'invito che accompagna una partecipazione di nozze.

CHI VIENE A CENA STASERA?

Gabriella parla di una serata speciale.

Stasera c'è una grande riunione a casa mia. Vẹngono i miei nonni Bettini e mio zio Baldo con sua mọglie. Viene anche Filippo: vuole conọscere i miei genitori e i miei parenti e annunciare il nostro *fidanzamento.*

Nella mia famịglia siamo solo in tre: mio padre, mia madre ed io. Mio padre è un uomo tranquillo e paziente, che ama fumare la pipa e lẹggere il giornale. Lavora in una *ditta di assicurazioni.* Mia madre è professoressa di mụsica; ama il teatro, ha molte amiche e sa cucinare meravigliosamente.

Mio zio Baldo è il fratello di mio padre. È un vẹcchio *marinạio* e conosce *diversi* paesi del *mondo.* Quando beve un po' troppo deve raccontare le sue avventure: parla allora di paesi *esọtici* e di donne meravigliose. Mia zia Teresina sorride: sa *queste* stọrie a memọria e sa che suo marito è un *sognatore.* I miei zii hanno due figli, Nino e Luisa. Mio cugino Nino è un «punk» *appassionato* di mụsica rock e viene a casa solo quando è al verde. Sua sorella scrive *poesie* e ha sempre *la testa fra le nuvole.* I miei nonni dịcono che sono *«un po' matti»* come il loro padre.

Oggi è una giornata molto importante per me. Sono felice, ma anche preoccupata. I miei genitori dịcono che Filippo ed io dobbiamo *prima* finire gli studi. Dịcono anche che siamo troppo giọvani e che non siamo *maturi* per il matrimọnio. Hanno torto!

engagement
insurance company
sailor/several/world
exotic
these
dreamer
crazy for
poetry
her head in the clouds
a little crazy
first
mature

Dopo la cerimonia del matrimonio, la coppia di giovani sposi posa per la tradizionale foto-ricordo.

Comprensione

Rispondete usando gli aggettivi possessivi.

1. Chi viene a casa di Gabriella stasera? **2.** Che cosa vọgliono annunciare stasera i due giọvani? **3.** Ha fratelli o sorelle Gabriella? **4.** Il padre di Gabriella esce la sera? **5.** La madre di Gabriella è una donna tranquilla come suo marito? **6.** Zio Baldo è il fratello della madre di Gabriella? **7.** Quando racconta stọrie interessanti lo zio di Gabriella? **8.** Quanti cugini ha Gabriella? **9.** Che mụsica preferisce Nino? **10.** Chi scrive poesie? **11.** Perchè Gabriella dice che è preoccupata stasera?

Domande personali

1. Ha molti parenti Lei? **2.** I Suoi nonni materni o paterni sono ancora (*still*) in vita? Li va a trovare qualche volta? **3.** Come sono i Suoi zii? **4.** I Suoi cugini sono molto giọvani o della Sua età (*age*)? Stụdiano o hanno già un diploma? **5.** Quando incontra i Suoi parenti? Spesso o in occasioni speciali (festa del Thanksgiving, Natale, compleanni, anniversari,...)? **6.** Quale dei Suoi parenti è particolarmente simpạtico? Perchè?

ATTIVITÀ SUPPLEMENTARI

A. **Una famiglia numerosa.** Descrivi la famiglia di Antonio: quanti sono, chi sono, quanti anni hanno, qual è la loro professione o attività scolastica. Descrivi anche il loro carattere (*temperament*) con alcuni aggettivi e con molta immaginazione

B. **Attività collettiva.** Form groups of 4 or 5. The students in each group pose as members of a family and take turns telling the rest of the class how they are related, how old they are, and what they do (work or school activities).

C. **Attività collettiva.** Uno studente (una studentessa) invita i compagni a casa sua per festeggiare il suo fidanzamento. Ogni compagno(a) può portare una persona. Fate delle domande allo studente (alla studentessa) sulla festa e dite chi portate.

D. **Come si dice in italiano?**

1. How many people are there in your (*fam. sing.*) family?
2. Only four: my father, my mother, my little brother, and myself (**io**).
3. Where do they live?
4. They live in New York.
5. If you are alone, why don't you come to my party tonight? It is at my house.
6. I'm sorry, but I can't because I have to meet a friend of mine.
7. Do I know your friend?
8. No. He is a quiet young man, but always happy. He also knows how to play the guitar wonderfully.
9. Is he your boyfriend?
10. Yes, and he wants to meet my family.
11. What do your parents say?
12. They say that we are too young and that we must wait.

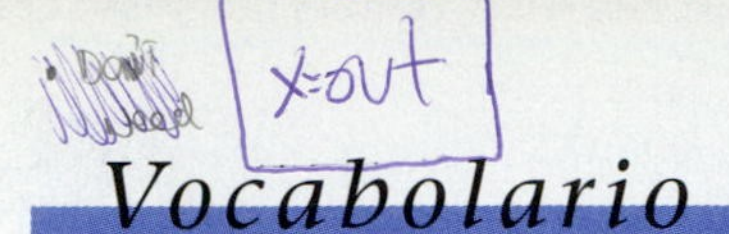

Vocabolario

Nomi

l'appartamento	*apartment*
l'avventura	*adventure*
la campagna	*countryside*
il carattere	*temperament*
il cassetto	*drawer*
la donna	*woman*
la famiglia	*family*
il fidanzamento	*engagement*
il fidanzato, la fidanzata	*fiancé, fiancée*
il fratellino, la sorellina	*little brother, little sister*
la generazione	*generation*
la giornata	*(the whole) day*
i giovani	*young people*
il gruppo	*group*
l'indirizzo	*address*
l'insegnante (*m.* & *f.*)	*teacher*
il lavoro	*work, job*
il matrimonio	*marriage, wedding*
il mondo	*world*
l'occasione (*f.*)	*occasion*
l'opinione (*f.*)	*opinion*
l'origine (*f.*)	*origin*
il paese	*country*
la persona	*person*
due o tre persone	*two or three people*
la pipa	*pipe*
il portafoglio	*wallet*
la riunione	*reunion*
la serata	*(the whole) evening*
l'uomo (*pl.* gli uomini)	*man*
la verità	*truth*

Aggettivi

eccellente	*excellent*
felice	*happy*
importante	*important*
matto	*crazy*
meraviglioso	*wonderful*
numeroso	*numerous*
speciale	*special*
strano	*strange*
tranquillo	*quiet*

Verbi

annunciare	*to announce*
bere	*to drink*
conoscere	*to know, to be acquainted with, to meet for the first time*
descrivere	*to describe*
dire	*to say, to tell*
dovere	*to have to, must; to owe*
entrare (in)	*to enter*
fumare	*to smoke*
incontrare	*to meet*
mettere	*to put*
passare	*to spend (time)*
potere	*to be able to, can, may*
raccontare	*to tell (a story)*
riuscire	*to succeed*
sapere	*to know, to know how*
sorridere	*to smile*
uscire	*to go out*
venire	*to come*
volere	*to want*

Altre espressioni

a memoria	*by heart*
andare a trovare	*to visit (people)*
a piedi	*on foot*
avere la testa fra le nuvole	*to have your head in the clouds*
come	*as, like*
fare una visita	*to pay a visit*
fare un brindisi	*to make a toast*
meravigliosamente	*wonderfully*
volentieri	*with pleasure*
voler dire	*to mean*
Cosa vuole dire...?	*What does ... mean?*

LA FAMỊGLIA IN ITẠLIA

La famịglia ọccupa un *posto* speciale nella società italiana. I *rapporti di parentela* sono sacri e ọffrono *l'aiuto* morale, fịsico ed econọmico che lo stato molte volte non può offrire.

place
family ties
help

Le vạrie generazioni—genitori, figli, nipoti, *pronipoti*—non vịvono, come nel passato, nella stessa casa. Il boom degli anni sessanta *ha trasformato* profondamente la vita e la struttura patriarcale della famịglia italiana. Molti giọvani *hanno abbandonato* la *campagna* e le pịccole città per vịvere nei grandi centri urbani.

great-grandchildren
has transformed
have abandoned
country

Nel 1970 un referendum *ha introdotto* in Itạlia il divọrzio. È vero *tuttavia* che il divọrzio non è così fạcile *da ottenere* come in altri paesi: gli sposi che vọgliono divorziare dẹvono vịvere separati per *almeno* tre anni.

has introduced
however
to obtain
at least

Oggi molte famịglie sono pịccole, con uno o due figli. Spesso anche la mọglie lavora. La solidarietà è tuttavia *ancora* grande fra i parenti che *si riuniscono* ancora *intorno a* una stessa tạvola, per la festa del santo patrono della città, per esẹmpio e per altre festività. *Quanto ai* figli, è normale la loro vita in famịglia *fino al* momento del loro matrimọnio. Quando *si sposano* non è raro vedere i giọvani sposi occupare un appartamento vicino all'appartamento dei genitori. Come risultato la solitudine dei «nonni» è meno grave in Itạlia che in altri paesi.

still/gather
around
As for
until
they get married

Giovani sposi e bambino davanti alla Basilica di San Pietro.

Comprensione

1. La società italiana consịdera la famịglia...
   a. poco importante b. molto importante c. senza importanza
2. Oggi i giọvani preferịscono vịvere e lavorare...
   a. in grandi città b. in campagna c. in piccoli centri urbani
3. In Italia...
   a. non è possịbile divorziare b. è molto fạcile divorziare c. è possịble divorziare
4. I figli di sọlito stanno in famịglia fino...
   a. al matrimọnio b. alla fine della scuola secondạria c. dopo (*after*) il matrimọnio
5. In generale la famịglia italiana di oggi è...
   a. patriarcale b. pịccola c. numerosa

Napoli. Padre e bambino fanno un giro in motorino.

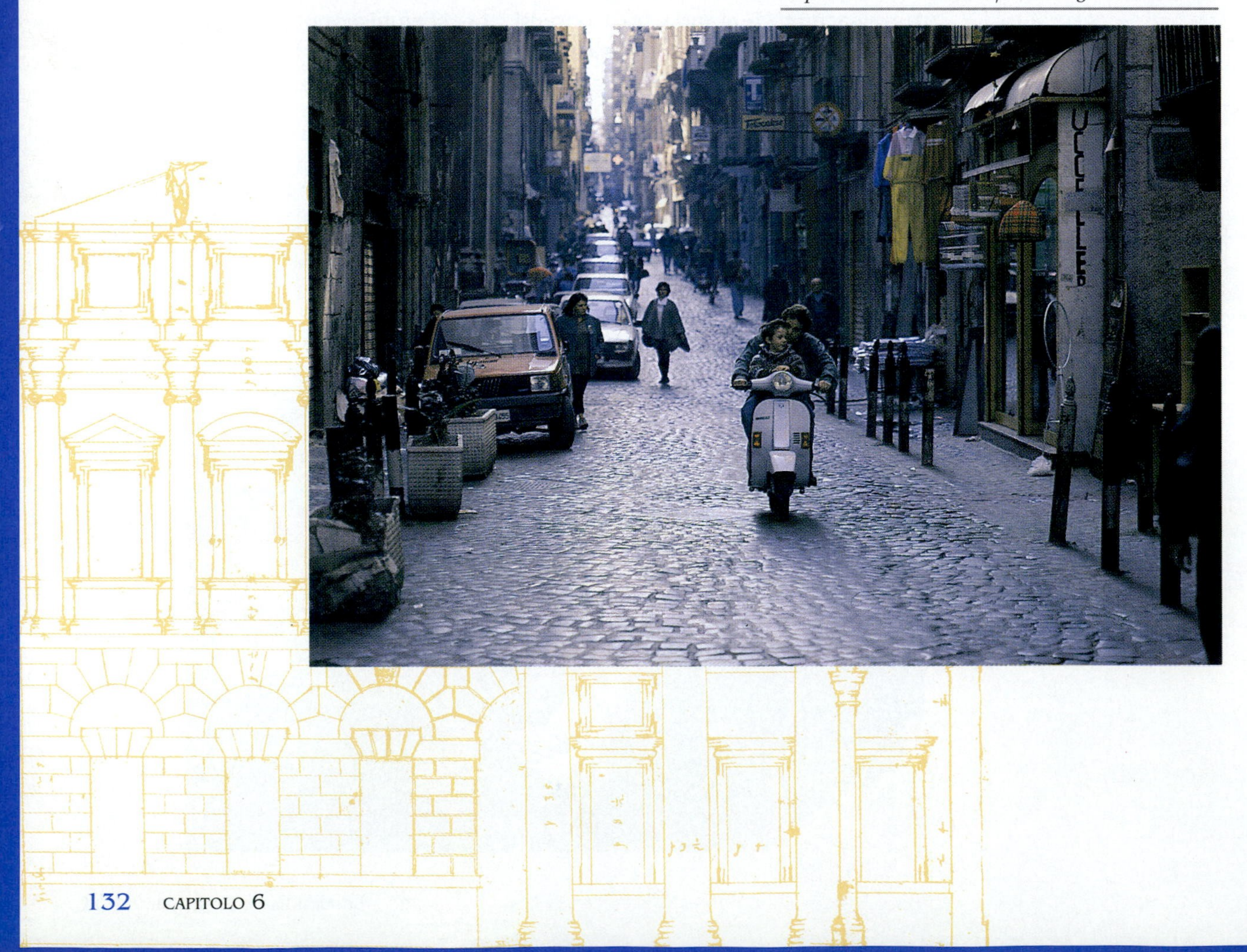

7 BUON VIAGGIO

Milano. Un'agenzia di viaggi in Galleria.

Punti di vista

Partiamo per il fine settimana
In treno

Punti grammaticali

I Il passato prossimo con *avere*
II Il passato prossimo con *essere*
III Espressioni di tempo nel passato
IV Usi di *a, in, da* e *per*

Lettura

Un viaggio di nozze

Pagina culturale

La Toscana

PUNTI DI VISTA

Viaggiatori in partenza e in arrivo, alla Stazione Centrale.

PARTIAMO PER IL FINE SETTIMANA

La famiglia Betti, padre, madre e figlio, sono alla stazione di Torino. I Betti vanno a *Rapallo* per il week-end. La stazione è *affollata*. — (resort town on the Italian Riviera)/crowded

Sig.ra Betti Rodolfo, hai i biglietti, vero?

Sig. Betti Sì, li ho, ma *non ho fatto* le prenotazioni. — I didn't make

Sig.ra Betti Oggi è venerdì. Ci sono molti viaggiatori. Perchè *non hai comprato* i biglietti di prima classe? — didn't you buy

Sig. Betti Perchè c'è una *bella* differenza di *prezzo* tra la prima e la seconda classe. E poi, non è un viaggio lungo. — big/price

Sig.ra Betti Ma l'impiegato dell'agenzia di viaggi *ha detto* che il venerdì i treni sono molto affollati. — said

Sig. Betti Sì, è vero, ma uno o due posti ci sono sempre.

Sig.ra Betti Sì, ma io non voglio viaggiare in uno *scompartimento* per *fumatori*... — compartment/smokers

Pippo Mamma, *hai messo* la mia racchetta da tennis nella valigia? — did you put

Sig.ra Betti Sì, e anche il tuo libro di storia.

Pippo Papà, il treno per Rapallo *è arrivato* sul *binario* 6. — has arrived / track

Sig. Betti Presto, *andiamo!* — let's go!

Comprensione

1. Dove vanno i Betti?
2. Da dove partono?
3. Perchè il padre non ha comprato i biglietti di prima classe?
4. Come sono i treni il venerdì?
5. Perchè la madre è preoccupata?
6. Che cosa desidera sapere Pippo? Perchè?
7. Su quale binario è arrivato il treno?

Studio di parole

ARRIVI E PARTENZE (*ARRIVALS AND DEPARTURES*)

il viaggio trip
viaggiare to travel
il viaggiatore, la viaggiatrice traveler
l'agenzia di viaggi travel agency
prenotare to reserve
la prenotazione reservation
il biglietto (di andata e ritorno) (round-trip ticket)
il volo flight
il posto seat
i bagagli luggage
l'orologio clock, watch
il binario track
il cartello sign
Vietato fumare No smoking
salire to get on
scendere to get off
la prima (seconda) classe first (second) class
la classe turistica economy class
lo scompartimento compartment
l'orario schedule
in orario on time
in ritardo late
il passaporto passport
la valigia suitcase
la dogana customs
l'arrivo arrival
la partenza departure
la gita short trip
la crociera cruise
all'estero abroad
depositare / **ritirare** } **i bagagli** — to check in / to pick up } luggage
perdere il treno (l'aereo, ecc.) to miss the train (the plane, etc.)

—**Scusi, sono liberi questi posti?** Excuse me, are these seats free?
—**No, sono occupati.** No, they are taken.
—**Dove scende Lei?** Where do you get off?

Alla dogana:
—Lei ha qualcosa da dichiarare?

Applicazione

A. **Guardate il disegno.**

1. Cosa fanno le persone in fila (*in line*) davanti alla biglietteria?
2. Un viaggiatore guarda l'orologio e corre (*runs*): di cosa ha paura?
3. Un uomo è all'ufficio bagagli: che cosa deposita?
4. Ha molte o poche valigie?
5. Che cosa nasconde (*is hiding*) il viaggiatore alla dogana? Perchè?
6. Se i viaggiatori vogliono essere sicuri (*sure*) di trovare un posto in treno (o in aereo o in albergo) che cosa devono fare?
7. Per viaggiare comodamente (*comfortably*), in quale classe devono viaggiare?
8. Di quale documento hanno bisogno se vanno all'estero?

B. Domande personali.

1. Lei preferisce viaggiare in treno o in macchina?
2. Lei preferisce passare il fine settimana a casa o fare un viaggio?
3. Dove desidera andare il prossimo (*next*) weekend? Con chi?
4. Quando Lei viaggia in treno, Lei preferisce viaggiare in prima classe, o non è molto importante per Lei?
5. Le piace viaggiare?
6. Di solito, Lei viaggia con molte o con poche valigie?
7. Preferisce viaggiare solo(a) o con altre persone?
8. Quando è in aereo, Lei dorme, legge o parla con altri viaggiatori?
9. Ha paura di viaggiare in aereo?
10. Che cosa dicono i Suoi amici quando Lei parte per un viaggio?

10 Segue **MILANO-PIACENZA-BOLOGNA-(Roma) (Lecce)**

10	69 TEE [1]	1171 EXP [1][2]	959 R [1]	705 EXP [1][2]	659 EXP. [1][2]	2507 D [1][2]	891 R [1]	1196 EXP [1][2]	1929 D [2]	10443 L [2]	295 EXP [1][2]	1511 D [1][2]	95 TEE [1]	2509 D [1][2]	4777 L [2]	2701 D [1][2]	4779 L [2]	2511 D [1][2]	93 TEE [1]	2971 D [1][2]	10445 L [2]	905 R [1][2]	573 EXP [1][2]	707 EXP [1][2]	2083 D [2]
MILANO C. ...p.	750	CC	815	825		830	...	CC	....	...	915	940	955	1025	...	1050	...	1110	1200	1205	...	1250	1255	1305	...
— P. Garibaldi				[X]			832	....	....	915					...		...				1206				1305
— Greco								...	...		CC				...	[X]	...						CC		
— Lambrate ..		757					840	848	855	924					...		...	1117	[X]		1215				1314
— P. Vittoria ..															...		...					[X]	[X]		
— P. Romana .															...		...								
— Rogoredo ...	✂	[X]								931			✂		...		...				1222	✂			
S. Giuliano	[X]														...		...								
Melegnano										941					...		...	1131			1231				
S. Zenone															...		...								
Tavazzano										949					...		...	1140			1239				
LODI						854				956				1052	...		...	1149			1247				1339
Secugnago										1006					...		...				1258				
Casalpusterl. ..										1013								1204			1307				1354
CODOGNO ...					....				940	1018								1212		1259	1313				1400
S. Stefano Lod.					...				661	1024										4781	1319				L
PIACENZA ... a.				906	910	922	928		EXP	1030		1030		1122		1142		1226		[2]	1326			1351	1411
PIACENZA ... p.				908	913	925	930		1004			1039		1126		1145		1229		1315	...			1354	1413
Pontenure										1109										1322	...				1420
Cadeo										EXP										1327	...				1426
Fiorenzuola					928				1018	[1][2]						1201		1245		1333	...				1432
Alseno																				1339	...				1439
FIDENZA ..... a.					938	947	951		1027			1104		1150	1201	1210	1235	1255		1344	....	1352		1414	1445
FIDENZA ..... p.					939	948	954		1028			1105		1152	1204	1212	1237	1304		1346	....	1353		1416	1450
Castelguelfo ...															1211		1244			1353	....				
PARMA ...... a.					953	1002	...		1040			1120		1207	1220	1227	1253	1320		1402	...			1431	
PARMA ...... p.					955	1005	...		1042	1103		1123		1211	...	1230	1256	1323		1420	...			1434	
S. Ilario d'E. ..															...		1305			1428	...				
Villa Cadè															...		1311			1433	....				
REGGIO E. ... a.					1012	1025			1056	1123		1141		1229		1248	1319	1341		1441	...			1453	
REGGIO E. ... p.					1014	1027			1057	1124		1143		1232	4023	1250	1328	1344		1443	...			1456	
Rubiera															D		1337			1452	...				
MODENA .... a.					1030	1043			1112	1141		1159		1248	[1][2]	1306	1346	1400		1501	...			1512	
MODENA .... p.					1032	1045			1113	1143		1202		1251	1257	1308	1348	1403		1503	...			1515	...
Castelfranco ...															1306		1357			1512	....				...
Samoggia															1313		1404			1519	....				...
Anzola d'E. ...															1317		1408			1523	....				...
Lavino																	1412			1527	....				...
BOLOGNA C. a.	935	1008	1015	1026	1058	1118		1130	1136	1207	1124	1229	1145	1324	1330	1336	1423	1430	1354	1536	....	1450	1459	1543	...
Firenze ... 11 a	1044	1131	...	1150	...	...		1315	♦ ...	...	...	...	1300	...		1518	♦ ...	...	...	...	....	1604	1637	1704	...
Roma Term. 11 a	1325	1438	...	1510	...	...		1638	...	...	...	...	1548	...		1907	...	...	...	...	....	1917	2005	◆ ...	...
Ancona ..13a.	....	....	1234	....	1332	1446		....	....	....	1256	1524	....	1700		....	....	1806	1610						
Pescara ..13a.	....	....	1409	....	Δ	1645		....	....	....	Δ	....	....	1900		....	....	2010	1747						
Bari .....13a.	....	....	1748	....	....	2112	....	....	....	....	...	....	....	016		....	...◊	2312	2120						
Lecce ....13a.	....	....	2000	....	....	....	...	....	....	....	...	....	....	252		....	....	....	....						
Note	SETTEBELLO (Prenotazione obbligatoria)	ITALIA EXPRESS (da Chiasso)	Prenotazione obbligatoria — per Lecce		da Torino (prosegue per Rimini via Ravenna dal 14-VII al 9-IX)	Si effettua dal 23-VI — per Bari	per Grosseto (Qdr. 22 e 34) — Si eff. dal 15-VII al 2-IX e il 23, 24 e 30-VI; 1, 7 e 8-VII; 8, 9, 15, 16, 22 e 23-IX	da Chiasso — Si eff. ven. dal 3 al 31-VIII, sab. dal 30-VI al 28-VII e dom. dall'1-VII al 2-IX — per Palermo la domen.	Sabato e festivi (per Mantova) — da Torino	da Genova (Qdr. 22 e 33)	da Chiasso — per Rimini	per Ancona	VESUVIO (Prenotazione obbligatoria) — per Napoli Merg.	per Lecce	da Salsomaggiore — da Verona	per Salerno	da Salsomaggiore	per Foggia	ADRIATICO (Prenotazione obbligatoria) — per Bari	per Mantova		per Napoli	per Palermo	per Foligno	per Salsomaggiore

♦ Firenze Campo di Marte. ◆ Roma Tiburtina. ◊ Foggia. Δ Rimini.

12

Orario ferroviario. Come si chiama il Trans-European Express (TEE) che parte per Napoli alle nove e cinquantacinque (9:55 A.M.)?

Ascoltiamo!

In treno. *The Betti family has gotten on the train for Rapallo. They are now in a compartment where there is already one other person, to whom they speak briefly. Listen to their conversation, then answer the related questions.*

Comprensione

1. Dove sono i Betti?
2. Di quanti posti hanno bisogno?
3. Dove scendono?
4. Con chi iniziano una conversazione?
5. Il loro compagno di viaggio va a Genova per un viaggio di piacere (*pleasure*) o per un viaggio d'affari (*business*)?
6. Che cosa domanda la signora Betti al viaggiatore?
7. Che cosa mostra (*shows*) il viaggiatore alla signora?
8. Perchè è contenta Maria Betti?

Dialogo

With another student, play the roles of two travelers, one who gets on a train and the other who is already in the compartment. Strike up a conversation; expand on the dialogue "In treno" *and use expressions from the* "Studio di parole."

PUNTI GRAMMATICALI

I. Il passato prossimo con *avere*

Jane ha comprato un biglietto per Roma.

A Roma ha ricevuto dei fiori da un amico romano.

Ha dormito in un albergo in piazza Navona.

1. Che cosa ha comprato Jane?
2. Che cosa ha ricevuto a Roma?
3. Dove ha dormito?

1. The **passato pròssimo** (*present perfect*) indicates an action completed in the recent past. Today, however, many Italians use it informally to indicate an action or an event that occurred in the recent or not-so-recent past. Like the present perfect tense, it is a compound tense. For most Italian verbs and all transitive verbs (verbs that take a direct object),* the **passato pròssimo** is conjugated with the present of the auxiliary verb **avere** + the *past participle* (**partićipio passato**) of the main verb.

   The **partićipio passato** of regular verbs is formed by replacing the infinitive endings **-are**, **-ere**, and **-ire** with **-ato**, **-uto**, and **-ito**, respectively.

   compr**are** — *comprato*
   ricẹv**ere** — *ricevuto*
   dorm**ire** — *dormito*

comprare		ricẹvere		dormire	
ho hai ha abbiamo avete hanno	comprato	ho hai ha abbiamo avete hanno	ricevuto	ho hai ha abbiamo avete hanno	dormito

2. The **passato pròssimo** is rendered in English in the following ways, depending on the context.

   Ho portato due valịgie. — *I have carried two suitcases.* / *I carried two suitcases.* / *I did carry two suitcases.*

3. The *negative form* is expressed by placing **non** in front of the auxiliary verb.

Hai telefonato all'agenzia di viaggi?	*Did you call the travel agency?*
Non ho avuto tempo.	*I did not have time.*
Non hai viaggiato con l'Alitạlia?	*Haven't you traveled with Alitalia?*
Non ha finito i suoi studi.	*He did not finish his studies.*
Non hanno ripetuto la domanda.	*They have not repeated the question.*

4. The past participle of a **passato pròssimo** conjugated with the auxiliary **avere** must agree in gender and number with the direct object pronouns **lo, la, li,** and **le**, that precede the verb.

Hai comprato **il giornale?**	Sì, **l'**ho **comprato.**	No, non **l'**ho **comprato.**
Hai comprato **la rivista?**	Sì, **l'**ho **comprata.**	No, non **l'**ho **comprata.**
Hai comprato **i biglietti?**	Sì, **li** ho **comprati.**	No, non **li** ho **comprati.**
Hai comprato **le vitamine?**	Sì, **le** ho **comprate.**	No, non **le** ho **comprate.**

*In the sentences **Mangio una mela** and **Saluto gli amici**, **mela** and **amici** are direct objects. (They answer directly the questions: *What?, Whom?*) The verbs **mangiare** and **salutare** are, therefore, transitive verbs.

La prenotazione? L'họ già **fatta**!	*The reservation? I already made it!*
Quando hai visto **i tuoi cugini?**	*When did you see your cousins?*
Li ho **visti** ieri.	*I saw them yesterday.*

AIR PULLMAN S. p. A.
Aeroporto della Malpensa - Telefono (02) 86.80.08
Servizio pubblico di linea senza fermate intermedie
MILANO
AEROPORTO MALPENSA
Esente da IVA a norma dell'art. 10 comma 14 del D.P.R. 26-10-1972 n. 633
Serie 86 Nº 95474 Lit. 6000
Il presente biglietto NON è rimborsabile.

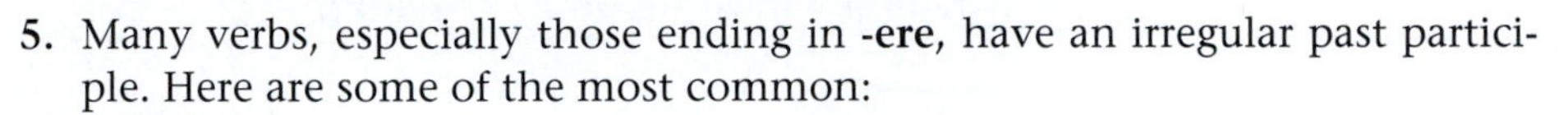

5. Many verbs, especially those ending in **-ere**, have an irregular past participle. Here are some of the most common:

fare (*to make*)	***fatto***
bere (*to drink*)	***bevuto***
chiẹdere (*to ask*)	***chiesto***
chiụdere (*to close*)	***chiuso***
conọscere (*to know*)	***conosciuto***
lẹggere (*to read*)	***letto***
mẹttere (*to put, to wear*)	***messo***
pẹrdere* (*to lose*)	***perduto (perso)***
prẹndere (*to take*)	***preso***
rispọndere (*to answer*)	***risposto***
scrịvere (*to write*)	***scritto***
spẹndere (*to spend*)	***speso***
vedere* (*to see*)	***veduto (visto)***
aprire (*to open*)	***aperto***
dire (*to say, to tell*)	***detto***
offrire (*to offer*)	***offerto***

Non **ha chiuso** la porta.	*He did not close the door.*
Hai letto il giornale?	*Did you read the newspaper?*
Abbiamo scritto ai nonni.	*We wrote to our grandparents.*
Hanno preso un tassì.	*They took a cab.*

NOTE:
Some verbs that are irregular in the present have a regular past participle: **dare:** *dato;* **avere:** *avuto;* **volere:** *voluto;* **potere:** *potuto;* **dovere:** *dovuto;* **sapere:** *saputo.*

***Perdere** and **vedere** have a regular and an irregular past participle. The two forms are interchangeable; however the irregular ones, **perso** and **visto**, are more frequently used.

A. Completate le risposte alle seguenti domande.

1. Che cosa *hanno regalato* a Peppino per Natale (*Christmas*)?
   Mia madre _____ un dizionạrio e mio padre _____ un libro per bambini. Roberto ed io _____ un orolọgio Swatch e voi _____ dei poster di Michael Jackson.
2. Che regalo *hanno ricevuto* le seguenti persone?
   Tu _____ dei dischi di Celentano e io _____ una mạcchina fotogrạfica. Mia cugina Lina _____ una valịgia blu e i miei zii _____ due biglietti per l'ọpera.
3. Quanto tempo *hanno dormito* le seguenti persone?
   Io _____ otto ore, ma Marco _____ solamente cinque ore. Voi _____ tutta la mattina e i vostri amici _____ tutta la giornata.

B. **Oggi/ieri.** Il fratello fa domande a Paolo sulle sue attività di oggi. Paolo risponde che le ha già (*already*) fatte ieri.

ESEMPIO parlare a papà **—Parli a papà oggi?**
—Ho parlato a papà ieri.

1. telefonare all'agenzia **2.** giocare a tennis **3.** nuotare in piscina **4.** lavorare in biblioteca **5.** vẹndere (*to sell*) lo stẹreo **6.** ricẹvere i soldi **7.** finire tutti i cọmpiti **8.** restituire i libri **9.** pulire lo stụdio

C. **Ho organizzato un viạggio!** (*Put the following sentences in logical sequence to say what you did to organize your trip. Express the verbs in the* **passato prọssimo**.)

1. salutare la mia famịglia **2.** preparare la valịgia **3.** telefonare all'agenzia di viaggi **4.** invitare un amico **5.** chiẹdere dei soldi a papà **6.** prẹndere l'aẹreo **7.** fare le prenotazioni **8.** comprare i biglietti

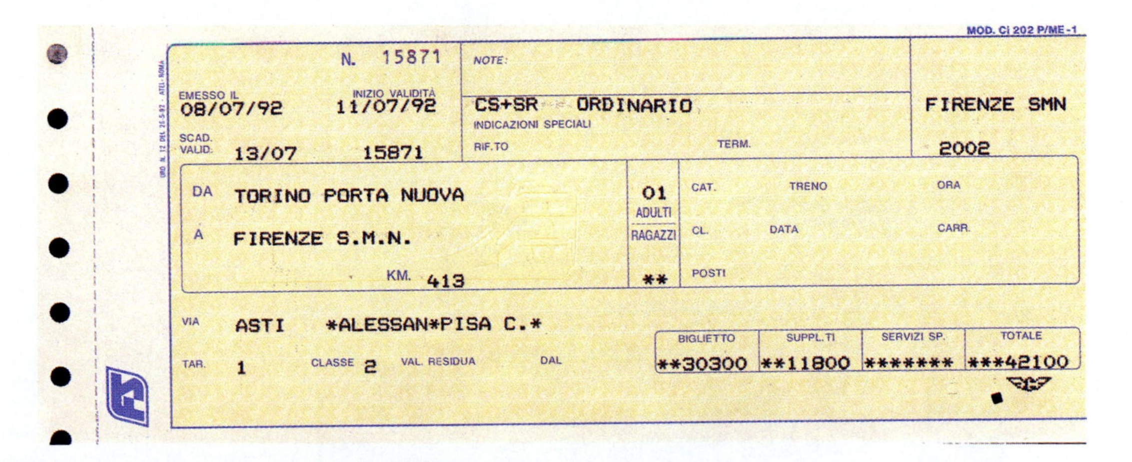

D. **Domanda e risposta.** Seguite l'esẹmpio.

ESEMPIO fare colazione stamattina
—Ha fatto colazione Lei stamattina?
—Sì, ho fatto colazione stamattina. *o*
—No, non ho fatto colazione stamattina.

1. vedere il film *JFK* 2. spẹndere troppi soldi questo mese 3. prẹndere l'aẹreo recentemente (*recently*) 4. avere tempo di studiare 5. potere fare i cọmpiti per oggi 6. lẹggere la *Divina Commẹdia* 7. scrịvere ai parenti 8. rispọndere a tutte le lẹttere

E. **Lei ha mai...?** (*Did you ever...?*) **Domanda e risposta.** Usate i pronomi **lo, la, li, le** invece del nome oggetto diretto. (Attenzione all'accordo del partecịpio passato.)

ESEMPIO mangiare i tortellini alla bolognese
—Lei ha mai mangiato i tortellini alla bolognese?
—Sì, li ho mangiati. (*o...*)
—No, non li ho mai mangiati.

1. prẹndere il cappuccino 2. cucinare gli spaghetti 3. mangiare la bistecca alla fiorentina 4. visitare la Toscana 5. sentire il nome di Niccolò Machiavelli 6. invitare gli amici a casa Sua 7. vedere il film *Via col vento* (Gone with the Wind) 8. bere l'ạcqua delle terme di Montecatini (*famous spa in Toscana*)

F. **Cosa avete fatto voi...?**

ESEMPIO in cucina **Abbiamo preparato un'insalata mista.** (*o...*)

1. al supermercato 2. all'agenzia di viaggi 3. al ristorante 4. in biblioteca 5. alla stazione dei treni 6. al telẹfono pụbblico 7. al caffè 8. alla piscina 9. alla conferenza del professore 10. al cịnema 11. al campo da tennis

II. Il passato prossimo con *essere*

Jane è andata a Roma. È partita dall'aeroporto Kennedy ed è arrivata all'aeroporto Leonardo da Vinci (Roma).

1. Dov'è andata Jane?
2. Da quale città ẹ partita?
3. A quale aeroporto è arrivata?

1. Most intransitive verbs (verbs that do not take a direct object) are conjugated with the auxiliary **ẹssere.** In this case, the past participle *must agree with the subject* in gender and number.

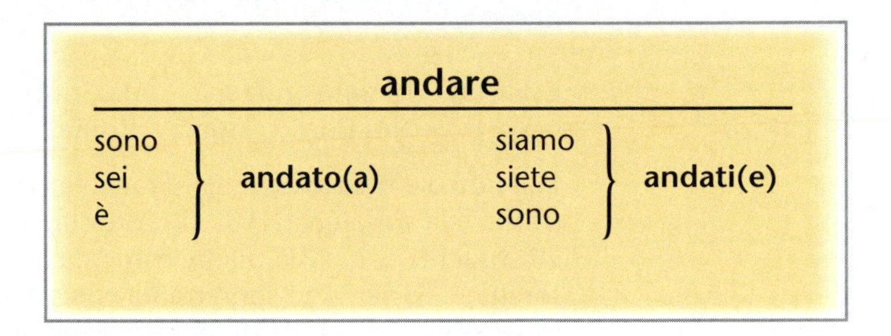

andare			
sono sei è	**andato(a)**	siamo siete sono	**andati(e)**

2. Most verbs that take the auxiliary **ẹssere** are verbs of coming and going. Here is a list of the most common ones:

andare (*to go*)	***andato***
venire (*to come*)	***venuto***
arrivare (*to arrive*)	***arrivato***
partire (*to leave*)	***partito***
(ri)tornare (*to return*)	***ritornato***
entrare (*to enter*)	***entrato***
uscire (*to go out*)	***uscito***
salire* (*to go up, to climb*)	***salito***
(di)scẹndere* (*to go down*)	***(di)sceso***
cadere (*to fall*)	***caduto***
nạscere (*to be born*)	***nato***
morire (*to die*)	***morto***
ẹssere (*to be*)	***stato***
stare (*to be, to stay*)	***stato***
restare (*to remain*)	***restato***
diventare (*to become*)	***diventato***

3. Note that **venire, discẹndere, nạscere, morire, ẹssere** have an irregular past participle.

Ieri **noi siamo andati** al cịnema.	*Yesterday **we went** to the movies.*
Maria **è uscita** con il suo ragazzo.	*Maria **went out** with her boyfriend.*
Giovanni **è stato** in Itạlia tre volte.	*Giovanni **has been** in Italy three times.*
Siete partiti in treno o in aẹreo?	***Did you leave** by train or by plane?*
Dove **sei nata?**	*Where **were you born?***
Ieri **non sono andata** all'università.	*Yesterday **I did not go** to the university.*

***Salire** and **(di)scendere** are conjugated with **avere** when they have a direct object: **Ho salito le scale.** *I climbed the stairs.*

A. Sostituite i soggetti con i soggetti in parentesi e fate i cambiamenti necessari.

ESEMPIO Io sono andata a Roma. (noi)
Noi siamo andati a Roma.

1. Franco è nato a Venẹzia. (Franco e Giovanni) 2. Anna è arrivata tardi. (Anna e la sua amica) 3. Il professore è entrato in classe. (il professore e gli studenti) 4. Mia madre è andata a Gẹnova. (mia madre e le mie sorelle) 5. Ieri sera sono uscita con gli amici. (Marco ed io) 6. Perchè tu sei stata a casa ieri? (tu e il tuo compagno) 7. Dov'è nato tuo nonno? (i tuoi nonni) 8. Sei venuto in aẹreo? (tu e Maria) 9. Marco è partito in mạcchina. (Marco ed io)

B. Completate con la forma corretta del **passato prọssimo.**

1. (andare) Maria _____ al mercato con sua madre. 2. (arrivare) Il treno _____ con venti minuti di ritardo. 3. (partire) Mio fratello ed io _____ la mattina presto. 4. (uscire) Con chi _____ tu, ieri sera? 5. (nạscere) I miei genitori _____ a Como, in Lombardia. 6. (stare) Ieri Anna _____ a casa dal lavoro. 7. (venire) Tu e Marco _____ in treno o in aẹreo? 8. (morire) I miei nonni _____ dieci anni fa. 9. (andare, stare) Quando Giovanni e Maria _____ in Itạlia, _____a Firenze per un anno. 10. (ẹssere) Dove _____ voi, l'altra sera?

C. **Un compagno curioso. Domanda e risposta.** Seguite l'esẹmpio.

ESEMPIO dove, ẹssere ieri sera
—Dove sei stato(a) ieri sera?
—Sono stato(a) al cịnema. (*o*...)

1. dove, nạscere 2. con chi, uscire sạbato scorso 3. come, ritornare a casa 4. dove, ẹssere domẹnica 5. come, venire all'università 6. in che giorno, andare in biblioteca 7. quando, partire per una vacanza 8. quando, andare al ristorante con i tuoi amici

D. Completate con la forma corretta del **passato prọssimo.**

1. Ieri sera noi _____ (mangiare) alla trattoria (*family run restaurant*). 2. La notte scorsa io non _____ (dormire) bene. 3. Gabriella _____ (scrịvere) una lẹttera. 4. Noi _____ (rispọndere) al telẹfono. 5. Gli sposi _____ (arrivare) a Nạpoli due giorni fa. 6. In che giorno _____ (partire) tua zia? 7. _____ (Capire) la domanda, tu? 8. La mia amica ed io _____ (vedere) un film di Bertolucci. 9. L'agente di viaggi _____ (dire) che non ci sono posti sull'aẹreo. 10. Io _____ (finire) di lavorare due giorni fa. 11. Ieri il bambino _____ (salire) sull'ạlbero. 12. La mọglie del mio amico _____ (ẹssere) in Sicịlia. 13. Per il compleanno di nostra sorella noi _____ (offrire) un biglietto per Roma.

E. **A Firenze.** Voi avete passato un giorno a Firenze. Che cosa avete fatto?

ESEMPIO viaggiare in aẹreo **—Ho viaggiato in aẹreo.**

1. arrivare all'aeroporto 2. scẹndere dall'aẹreo 3. prẹndere un tassì 4. dare l'indirizzo (*address*) dell'albergo al tassista 5. andare all'albergo 6. fare la dọccia 7. visitare Santa Maria del Fiore 8. mangiare in un buon ristorante 9. entrare nella Galleria degli Uffizi 10. camminare sul Ponte Vẹcchio 11. comprare dei regali per i parenti 12. scrịvere delle cartoline (*postcards*) 13. spẹndere molti soldi 14. bere un'aranciata 15. ritornare all'albergo 16. ordinare la cena 17. chiẹdere informazioni sulla città 18. uscire dall'albergo 19. passare alcune ore in Piazza della Signoria 20. andare a dormire, stanco(a) morto(a) (*dead tired*)

F. **Una storia triste.** Ripetete la stọria sostituendo (*substituting*) **Maria** con **le sorelle gemelle** (*twin sisters*). Fate i cambiamenti necessari.

Maria Caputo *è nata* in un villạggio vicino a Nạpoli. *È restata* in questo villạggio fino a quando (*until*) *è diventata* maestra.

È partita dal villạggio a 19 anni. *È andata* con la famịglia ad abitare a Bologna.

Dopo molti anni *è ritornata* al suo paese. *È arrivata* una sera bụia (*dark*). *È andata* alla vẹcchia casa, ora abbandonata. *È entrata, è salita* al primo piano. Poi *è discesa,* ma... *è caduta* dalle scale. Pọvera Maria! Non *è morta,* ma *è uscita* dalla vẹcchia casa con una gamba rotta (*broken leg*).

III. Espressioni di tempo nel passato

—L'anno scorso ho dovuto pagare un anno di studi per i miei due figli.

Here are some expressions that may be used when referring to actions or events that occurred recently or some time ago.

Quando?	*When?*
stamattina	*this morning*
ieri	*yesterday*
ieri mattina	*yesterday morning*
ieri pomeriggio	*yesterday afternoon*
ieri sera	*yesterday evening*
l'altro ieri	*the day before yesterday*
la notte scorsa	*last night*
domẹnica scorsa	*last Sunday*
la settimana scorsa	*last week*
il mese scorso	*last month*
l'anno scorso	*last year*

Quanto tempo fa?	*How long ago?*
poco tempo fa	*a little while ago, not long ago*
alcuni minuti fa	*a few minutes ago*
due ore fa	*two hours ago*
tre giorni fa	*three days ago*
quattro settimane fa	*four weeks ago*
molti mesi fa	*many months ago*
dieci anni fa	*ten years ago*

Pratica

A. **Quando...?** Rispondete alle seguenti domande, usando un'espressione di tempo al passato.

ESEMPIO **—Quando ha fatto colazione Lei? —Stamattina.** (*o...*)

1. Quando ha visto un film? **2.** Quando ha detto una buona parola a un amico triste? **3.** Quando ha mangiato pesce? **4.** Quando ha invitato parenti o amici al ristorante? **5.** Quando ha visitato una nuova città? **6.** Quando è andato(a) in aẹreo? **7.** Quando ha preso un tassì? **8.** Quando è entrato(a) in un'agenzia di viaggi? **9.** Quando ha dato un esame? **10.** Quando ha avuto un giorno lịbero?

B. **Quanto tempo fa...? Domanda e risposta.** Domandate a un(a) vostro(a) compagno(a) **quanto tempo fa** ha fatto le seguenti cose.

ESEMPIO andare in biblioteca —**Quanto tempo fa sei andato in biblioteca?**
—**Sono andato(a) in biblioteca due ore fa.** (*o...*)

1. finire la scuola elementare 2. incominciare gli studi universitari 3. arrivare all'università 4. entrare nell'ạula d'italiano 5. andare all'ẹstero 7. mangiare in un ristorante cinese 7. viaggiare con la tua famịglia 8. lẹggere il giornale

IV. Usi di *a, in, da, e per*

Marcello va a Firenze in macchina. Va da zia Rita.

1. The prepositions **a**, **in**, and **da** are used to indicate location or means of transportation. Each is used as follows:

The preposition **a**:
- before the names of cities and small islands;
- before nouns such as **casa, scuola, teatro, piedi** (*on foot*), **letto**, and **tạvola**:

Ạbitano **a** Venẹzia.	*They live in Venice.*
Siamo andati **a** Capri.	*We went to Capri.*
Sei venuta **a** scuola ieri?	*Did you come to school yesterday?*
No, sono restata **a** casa.	*No, I stayed (at) home.*
Andiamo **a** casa **a** piedi?	*Are we going home on foot?*
Vado **a** letto.	*I'm going to bed.*

The preposition **in**:
- before the names of continents, countries, states, regions, and large islands;*
- before nouns such as **classe, biblioteca, uffịcio, chiesa, città, montagna, campagna, viạggio, crociera,** and **vacanza;**
- before nouns indicating means of transportation such as **treno, aẹreo, mạcchina, bicicletta, ạutobus, tassì,** and **pullman** (*tour bus*):

*For more details on geographical names, see Chapter 15.

Siete stati **in** Europa?	*Have you been to Europe?*
Vorrei abitare **in** Toscana.	*I would like to live in Tuscany*
Vai **in** montagna?	*Are you going to the mountains?*
Vịvono **in** città o **in** campagna?	*Do they live in the city or in the country?*
Avete viaggiato **in** treno o **in** aẹreo?	*Did you travel by train or by plane?*
Siamo venuti **in** mạcchina.	*We came by car.*
Sono andati **in** vacanza **in** Sicịlia.	*They went on vacation to Sicily.*

The preposition **da:**

- before a person's name, title, or profession to indicate location when **da** means going to or being at that person's home or workplace;
- before a disjunctive pronoun to represent a person's home or workplace:

Stasera andiamo **da** Pietro.	*Tonight we are going to Pietro's.*
Vado **dalla** dottoressa Pini.	*I'm going to Doctor Pini's office.*
Mangiate **da** Maria stasera?	*Are you eating at Maria's house tonight?*
Venite **da** me domani?	*Are you coming to my house tomorrow?*

NOTE:
If the *definite article* is expressed, it contracts with **da.**

Vai **dal** tuo amico?	*Are you going to your friend's house?*

2. To indicate purpose, Italian uses **per** + *infinitive.* This construction corresponds to the English construction *(in order) to + infinitive.*

Stụdio **per** imparare.	*I study (in order) to learn.*
Lavoro **per** vịvere.	*I work (in order) to live.*

Pratica

A. Dove e come vanno le seguenti persone?

ESEMPIO Pietro, scuola, bicicletta **Pietro va a scuola in bicicletta.**

1. Gabriella e Filippo, teatro, tassì **2.** la signora Giạcomi, chiesa, piedi **3.** suo marito, città, ạutobus **4.** i signori Betti e il figlio, Rapallo, treno **5.** il signor Agnelli, montagna, aẹreo **6.** E Lei, dov'è andato(a), e come, stamattina?

B. Dove sono andate? L'anno scorso le seguenti persone hanno fatto un viaggio.

ESEMPIO Liliana, Inghilterra **Liliana è andata in Inghilterra.**

1. io, Ạustria **2.** voi, Alaska **3.** Gabriella e Filippo, Toscana, Roma, Nạpoli e Capri **4.** i signori Betti, Ligụria **5.** la famịglia Catalano, Sicịlia **6.** mio padre, Washington **7.** Marcello e suo zio, Ạfrica **8.** E Lei...?

C. Da chi è andato Marcello la settimana scorsa?

ESEMPIO lunedì mattina, signor Vari **Lunedì mattina è andato dal signor Vari.**

1. martedì pomeriggio, Filippo 2. martedì sera, nonni 3. mercoledì, sua zia 4. giovedì pomeriggio, dottore 5. venerdì mattina, Lucia 6. sabato, agente di viaggi 7. E Lei, da chi è andato(a) la settimana scorsa?

D. **In vacanza.** Completate con le preposizioni corrette.

L'anno scorso sono andata _____ vacanza _____ Italia. Ho viaggiato _____ aereo. Sono arrivata _____ Milano. Sono andata _____ macchina _____ mia madre. Sono restata _____ mia madre per tre settimane. Ho visitato la città _____ piedi e _____ autobus. Sono andata _____ miei nonni che abitano _____ campagna, e sono andata _____ sciare _____ montagna. Dopo tre settimane sono ritornata _____ California _____ aereo.

E. **Domanda e risposta.**

ESEMPIO venire, piedi —**Sei venuto(a) a piedi?**
—**No, sono venuto(a) in bicicletta.** (*o...*)

1. andare, montagna 2. partire, aereo 3. viaggiare, treno 4. essere, Roma 5. andare, Italia 6. abitare, California 7. restare, casa 8. andare, dottore 9. essere, Inghilterra

F. Unite le due frasi usando **per + l'infinito.**

ESEMPIO Studio. Imparo. **Studio per imparare.**

1. Telefono all'agenzia di viaggi. Domando informazioni. 2. La mamma ritorna. Prepara il pranzo. 3. Gli studenti stanno attenti. Capiscono la conferenza. 4. La signora prende il giornale. Legge le notizie (*news*). 5. Andiamo a una pizzeria. Mangiamo una pizza. 6. Io sto a casa. Faccio il compito d'italiano.

LETTURA

UN VIAGGIO DI NOZZE

Ieri Lucia ha ricevuto una lettera da Gabriella. L'amica *si è sposata* (got married) alcuni giorni fa e ora è in *viaggio di nozze* (honeymoon trip).

Ischia, 16 aprile

Cara Lucia,

Scrivo da *Ischia* (island in the gulf of Naples) *mentre* (while) aspetto l'*aliscafo* (hydrofoil boat) per Napoli. *Da quando* (Since) siamo partiti abbiamo visitato molti posti interessanti. Siamo stati solamente una notte a Firenze, perchè Filippo ha voluto visitare le *colline* (hills) toscane. Prima di Montefiascone* il nostro *pullman* (bus) ha

*Town near the lake of Bolsena, Lazio, famous for its wine called **Est, Est, Est.**

avuto *un guasto al motore* e noi tutti siamo scesi e abbiamo camminato per tre chilọmetri. Quando siamo arrivati a Montefiascone abbiamo bevuto un *fiasco* di vino locale.

Mercoledì siamo partiti per Roma. Hai ragione, Lucia: è una città magnịfica, ma il trạffico è impossịbile! Per andare all'albergo abbiamo preso un tassì, ma siamo arrivati dopo due ore perchè abbiamo avuto un pịccolo *incidente:* vicino al Colosseo un gatto nero *ha attraversato* la strada e *ha causato* una sẹrie di *tamponamenti.*

Ieri abbiamo preso il treno per Nạpoli. In treno abbiamo conosciuto due viaggiatori americani molto simpạtici e abbiamo parlato in inglese. È stata una conversazione un po' diffịcile, perchè abbiamo dimenticato molte delle espressioni che abbiamo studiato al liceo. *Ricordi?*

Stamattina siamo nella meravigliosa *ịsola* d'Ịschia davanti al golfo di Nạpoli.

Dopo una settimana di matrimọnio conosco *mẹglio* Filippo. Adesso so, per esẹmpio, che mio marito *russa* e che perde facilmente la pazienza. Stamattina *abbiamo litigato* per la prima volta. *Scherzo,* ma è vero che qualche volta gli uọmini sono *insopportabili.*

Un caro *abbraccio,*
Gabriella

breakdown
flask
accident
crossed/caused
collisions
Do you remember?
island
better
snores
we had a fight/I am joking/unbearable
hug

Isola d'Ischia (Golfo di Napoli). Veduta dall'aliscafo.

Comprensione

1. A chi ha scritto la lẹttera Gabriella?
2. Quanti giorni fa si è sposata Gabriella?
3. Chi è suo marito?
4. Da dove scrive Gabriella?
5. Che cosa hanno visitato i due sposi in Toscana?
6. Come sono arrivati a Montefiascone?
7. Che cosa hanno fatto quando sono arrivati a Montefiascone?
8. A Roma che cosa hanno preso per andare all'albergo?
9. Perchè hanno avuto un incidente vicino al Colosseo?
10. Chi hanno conosciuto in treno?
11. Perchè la loro conversazione in inglese è stata un po' diffịcile?
12. Con quale espressione ha finito la sua lẹttera Gabriella?

Domande personali

1. Ha fatto un viạggio Lei recentemente? Quanto tempo fa?
2. Dove è andato(a)? Come ha viaggiato?
3. Quale paese o quali paesi stranieri ha visitato Lei?
4. Ha viaggiato in treno Lei? Quando?
5. Ha incontrato persone interessanti durante un Suo viạggio? Dove?
6. Ha mai visitato Firenze? E Roma?
7. Quali sono, secondo Lei, le città più belle che ha visitato, all'ẹstero o negli Stati Uniti?
8. Preferisce fare un viạggio in Europa o una crociera nel mare dei Carạibi (*Caribbean*)?

ATTIVITÀ SUPPLEMENTARI

A. **Il viạggio di Marisa.** Guardate i seguenti disegni e dite dove è andata e cosa ha fatto Marisa. (Mettete i tempi al **passato prọssimo**).

B. **Le conversazioni di Marisa.** In gruppi (*groups*) di due, guardate i disegni dell'attività A, e immaginate:

1. la conversazione di Marisa con l'agente di viaggi (disegno 1);
2. la conversazione di Marisa e di Gino al telẹfono (disegni 7 e 8);
3. la conversazione di Marisa e di Gino quando s'incọntrano (*they meet*) davanti al bar (disegno 9);
4. la conversazione di Marisa e di Gino al ristorante: cosa ọrdinano, di cosa pạrlano, chi paga il conto? (disegno 10);
5. cosa dịcono Marisa e Gino alla stazione: cosa promette (*promises*) Gino e cosa promette Marisa? (disegno 11)

C. **Come si dice in italiano?**

1. I'm very tired because I didn't sleep much last night.
2. Why? Did you work late (**fino a tardi**)?
3. No, I came home five hours ago from a one-week trip to New York with my Aunt Jane.
4. Did you travel by plane or train?
5. By plane. But I didn't have to buy a (**il**) ticket. My Aunt Jane bought two first-class tickets, and our trip was very comfortable.
6. Did she reserve a room in a hotel?
7. No, we stayed at my grandparents' house, as we often do.
8. I don't know New York. How is it?
9. It's a great city with theaters and elegant shops. However, there are too many people and life isn't very simple.

Vocabolario

Nomi

l'aeroporto	*airport*
l'agente (*m.*)	*agent*
l'aranciata	*orange drink*
la cartolina	*postcard*
il chilometro	*kilometer*
la differenza	*difference*
il documento	*document*
l'espressione (*f.*)	*expression*
il fumatore, la fumatrice	*smoker*
il maestro, la maestra	*elementary school teacher*
la notizia	*news*
il posto	*place; seat*
il prezzo	*price*
il pullman	*tour bus*
la racchetta da tennis	*tennis racket*
lo sposo; la sposa	*groom; bride*
il tassì	*taxi*
il tassista	*taxi driver*
la tentazione	*temptation*
la trattoria	*restaurant*
il villaggio	*village*

Aggettivi

affollato	*crowded*
comodo	*comfortable*
impossibile	*impossible*
magnifico	*magnificient*
passato	*past*
possibile	*possible*
rapido	*fast*
scorso	*last*
semplice	*simple*
sicuro	*sure*

Verbi

cadere	*to fall*
camminare	*to walk*
causare	*to cause*
correre (*p.p.* corso)	*to run*
depositare	*to deposit*
(di)scendere (*p.p.* disceso)	*to descend, to go down*
diventare	*to become*
lasciare	*to leave (someone, something)*
mettere (*p.p.* messo)	*to put, to wear*
morire (*p.p.* morto)	*to die*
mostrare	*to show*
nascere (*p.p.* nato)	*to be born*
restare	*to remain*
ricordare	*to remember*
salire	*to climb, to go up*
sciare	*to ski*
spendere (*p.p.* speso)	*to spend (money)*
trovare	*to find*
vendere	*to sell*
visitare	*to visit*

Altre espressioni

Buon viaggio!	*Have a nice trip!*
comodamente	*comfortably*
fa	*ago*
facilmente	*easily*
ieri	*yesterday*
presto/Presto!	*early, fast, soon/Hurry up!*
Quanto tempo fa?	*How long ago?*
recentemente	*recently*
stamattina	*this morning*
stanco morto	*dead tired*
tardi	*late*
viaggio d'affari	*business trip*
di nozze	*honeymoon trip*
di piacere	*pleasure trip*

Firenze. Cupola e campanile della cattedrale di Santa Maria del Fiore. Dietro, le colline toscane.

LA TOSCANA

La Toscana è una delle regioni più affascinanti d'Italia. Il suo antico nome, «Tuscia», deriva dalla misteriosa *civiltà* etrusca, esistente prima di Roma. Firenze, fondata dai Romani sul *fiume* Arno, è il *capoluogo* della regione.

Nel 1300 (milletrecento) Firenze è uno dei centri principali d'Europa. Alcune delle città toscane rivali sono Siena, Lucca e Pisa, *ognuna* con una popolazione superiore alla popolazione di Londra di *quel* periodo. Molti Toscani sono *banchieri* e *prestano* la loro moneta, il «fiorino», a papi, imperatori e *re*. Dante, Petrarca e Boccaccio sono nati in Toscana e le loro *opere* sono diventate presto un modello per gli scrittori italiani e dell'Europa occidentale.

Anche il Rinascimento* è nato in Toscana. Le grandi famiglie toscane di questo periodo *conducono* una vita molto raffinata. La più famosa è la famiglia Medici, *signori* di Firenze e protettori

civilization
river
chief town
each
that/bankers
lend
kings
works
lead
rulers

*Rinascimento** means "Renaissance," that is, the "rebirth," or revival, of human values, art, literature, and learning after the prevailing religiosity of the Middle Ages.

delle arti; Donatello, Brunelleschi, il Beato Angẹlico, Botticelli, Michelạngelo e Leonardo da Vinci sono solo alcuni dei grandi artisti del Rinascimento toscano. Il contributo filosọfico, polịtico e scientịfico rinascimentale non è stato inferiore, se pensiamo, per esẹmpio, a Niccolò Machiavelli e a Galileo Galilei.

La stọria e la civiltà di quell'ẹpoca splẹndida hanno lasciato un'*impronta* speciale nel *paesạggio* toscano, straordinariamente ricco di castelli, *torri,* monasteri, chiese, piazze e palazzi. Oggi la tradizione artịstica dei grandi maestri contịnua a vịvere nell'*artigianato* delle *botteghe* e delle pịccole indụstrie toscane.

mark/landscape
towers
handicrafts
shops

Comprensione

1. Il nome di «Toscana» deriva dalla civiltà...
   a. romana b. rinascimentale c. etrusca
2. Il capoluogo della Toscana è...
   a. Siena b. Firenze c. Pisa
3. Dante è...
   a. uno scrittore b. un pittore c. uno scienziato
4. Il Rinascimento ha avuto orịgine...
   a. in Lombardia b. in Sicịlia c. in Toscana
5. Galileo Galilei, uno dei grandi nomi del Rinascimento toscano, ha contribuito...
   a. all'arte b. alle scienze c. alla polịtica
6. Nel Rinascimento i Mẹdici sono i signori della città di...
   a. Lucca b. Firenze c. Pisa

San Gimignano (Toscana). Alcune delle molte torri che dominano questa cittadina medioevale.

8 TEMPO E DENARO

Bergamo (Lombardia). Facciata della Banca Popolare.

Punti di vista

Un viaggio d'affari
In banca, allo sportello del cambio

Punti grammaticali

I I verbi riflessivi
II I verbi reciproci
III Il passato prossimo con i verbi riflessivi e reciproci
IV L'ora (time)
V Avverbi

Lettura

La giornata di un impiegato

Pagina culturale

Roma, «Città Eterna»

PUNTI DI VISTA

Roma. Cụpola del lussuoso albergo Excẹlsior lungo l'elegante Via Vẹneto.

UN VIAGGIO D'AFFARI

John White è un uomo d'affari americano. È arrivato a Roma e *soggiorna* (stays) all'albergo Excẹlsior, in via Vẹneto* dove ha prenotato una *cạmera sịngola* (single room) con dọccia. Dall'albergo telẹfona a Dạvide, un collega che lavora alla *filiale* (branch) di Roma.

John	Pronto, Dạvide? Sono John White. Come stai?	
Davide	*Salve* John! Come va? Hai fatto un buon viạggio?	hello
John	Sì, *abbastanza,* però è stato un viạggio lungo e *mi sono annoiato parẹcchio.*	quite / I got bored a lot
Davide	In che albergo stai? Hai una mạcchina?	
John	Sono all'Excẹlsior. No, *non ho noleggiato* la mạcchina. A Roma preferisco prẹndere il tassì.	I haven't rented
Davide	*Allora ci vediamo* per il pranzo? Al «Gladiatore»?	then/see each other
John	Sì, certo, però prima devo *lavarmi, vestirmi* e andare in banca per cambiare dei dọllari.	to wash/to get dressed
Davide	Allora *ci incontriamo* al ristorante *all'una.* Va bene?	we meet/at 1:00
John	D'accordo. A presto.	

---

*Street with luxury hotels and chic shops.

Comprensione

1. Chi è John White?
2. È venuto a Roma per un viạggio di piacere?
3. Dove soggiorna? Cosa ha prenotato all'albergo?
4. Dove lavora il suo collega Dạvide?
5. Perchè John si lamenta (*complains*) del viạggio?
6. Ha noleggiato una mạcchina? Perchè?
7. Prima di vedere Dạvide, John deve lavarsi, vestirsi e...
8. A che ora s'incọntrano John e Dạvide?

Studio di parole

un albergo hotel
una pensione boarding house
prenotare to reserve
una cạmera sịngola (dọppia) con dọccia a single (double) room with a shower
soggiornare to stay (in a hotel)
noleggiare una mạcchina to rent a car

il denaro, i soldi money
l'assegno check
il libretto degli assegni checkbook
depositare un assegno to deposit a check
riscuọtere un assegno to cash a check
il cạmbio exchange rate
cambiare un traveler's cheque to cash a traveler's check

mostrare un documento d'identità to show I.D.
la valuta currency
la firma signature
firmare to sign
la ricevuta receipt
lo sportello nụmero uno (due...) window number one (two...)
alla cassa to (at) the cashier
la carta di crẹdito credit card
in contanti cash

—Si accọmodi alla cassa. Please go to the cashier.

Mr. White: Vorrei cambiare un traveler's cheque di mille dollari.
Impiegato: Ha il passaporto, per favore?

Applicazione

A. Domande.

1. Se riceviamo un assegno di mille dọllari e non abbiamo bisogno di soldi, che cosa facciamo?
2. A quale sportello andiamo per cambiare i soldi?
3. Qual è il cambio del dọllaro in Itạlia adesso? Più o meno di 1.300 (milletrecento) lire?
4. Se in un negọzio paghiamo con un assegno, che cosa dobbiamo mostrare?
5. Cosa dobbiamo scrịvere sull'assegno?
6. In un paese straniero, qual è il nostro documento d'identità?

B. Dialogo.

Una telefonata intercontinentale tra un Americano (un'Americana) che desịdera stare a Roma tre giorni e l'impiegato di un albergo di Roma.

C. Domande personali.

1. Quando Lei vuole prenotare una cạmera in un albergo all'ẹstero, telẹfona all'albergo o scrive una lẹttera?
2. Come passa il tempo in aẹreo quando il viạggio è molto lungo?
3. Quando Lei è in un paese straniero, nolẹggia una mạcchina o usa i mezzi di trasporto (*means of transportation*) pụbblici?
4. Quando Lei compra qualcosa (*something*) in un negọzio, paga in contanti, con un assegno o con la carta di crẹdito?

I CAMBI DELLE VALUTE

VALUTE ESTERE	OGGI
Dollaro Usa	1526,49
ECU	1802,02
Marco tedesco	924,31
Franco francese	273,17
Sterlina	2198,45
Fiorino olandese	821,44
Franco belga	44,78
Peseta spagnola	13,026
Dollaro canadese	1207,57
Yen giapponese	12,271
Franco svizzero	999,67

Ascoltiamo!

In banca, allo sportello del cạmbio. *John White has arrived at the bank to change some American traveler's checks into* **lire.** *He is talking with the clerk at the exchange window. Listen to their conversation, then answer the related questions.*

Comprensione

1. Dov'è entrato il signor White?
2. Perchè è andato in banca?
3. Quanti dọllari vuole cambiare?
4. Secondo l'impiegato, è una settimana fortunata per il dọllaro? Perchè?
5. Quale documento ha voluto vedere l'impiegato?
6. Che cosa vuole sapere?
7. Come si chiama l'impiegato?
8. Il signor White ha ricevuto le lire in assegno o in contanti?

Dialogo

Una conversazione tra un viaggiatore americano (una viaggiatrice americana) che vuole cambiare dei dollari e l'impiegato di banca.

PUNTI GRAMMATICALI

I. I verbi riflessivi

Mi chiamo Gino; sono impiegato di banca. *Mi alzo alle sette.* *Mi lavo e mi vesto.* *Mi riposo la sera.*

1. Come si chiama l'impiegato di banca?
2. A che ora si alza?
3. Poi (*then*) che cosa fa?
4. Quando si riposa?

1. A verb is reflexive when the action expressed by the verb refers back to the subject. A transitive verb (a verb that takes a direct object) may be used in the reflexive construction.

Lavo la mącchina.	*I wash the car.* (transitive)
Mi lavo.	*I wash myself.* (reflexive)
Vedo la ragazza.	*I see the girl.* (transitive)
Mi vedo nello spęcchio.	*I see myself in the mirror.* (reflexive)

2. The infinitive of a reflexive verb is formed with the infinitive of the verb without the final **-e** (**lavar-**) + the reflexive pronoun **si** (*oneself*): **lavarsi** (*to wash oneself*). Reflexive verbs are recognizable in the dictionary by their endings: **-arsi**, **-ersi**, and **-irsi.**

prepar**arsi**	*to prepare oneself (to get ready)*
męțt**ersi**	*to put (on) oneself*
vest**irsi**	*to dress oneself (to get dressed)*

3. The reflexive pronouns are **mi, ti, ci, vi,** and **si.** They must always be expressed and agree with the subject, since the object and subject are the same. They precede the reflexive verb.

lavarsi (to wash oneself)	
mi lavo	I wash myself
ti lavi	you wash yourself
si lava	he/she/it washes himself/herself/itself
Si lava	you wash yourself (formal sing.)
ci laviamo	we wash ourselves
vi lavate	you wash yourselves
si lạvano	they wash themselves
Si lạvano	you wash yourselves (formal pl.)

4. Many Italian reflexive verbs are idiomatic and do not correspond literally to reflexives in English. Some verbs change their meaning when they are reflexive.

Teresa **chiama** Rosa. — *Teresa calls Rosa.*
Mi chiamo Rosa. — *My name is Rosa.*

Sento la mụsica. — *I hear the music.*
Mi sento bene. — *I feel fine.*

5. Some common reflexive verbs are:

chiamarsi	*to be called*	**annoiarsi**	*to get bored*
svegliarsi	*to wake up*	**sentirsi**	*to feel*
alzarsi	*to get up*	**fermarsi**	*to stop (oneself)*
lavarsi	*to wash oneself*	**riposarsi**	*to rest*
vestirsi	*to get dressed*	**addormentarsi**	*to fall alseep*
mẹttersi	*to put on*	**arrabbiarsi**	*to get angry*
prepararsi	*to get ready*	**scusarsi**	*to apologize*
divertirsi	*to have fun, to enjoy oneself*	**innamorarsi**	*to fall in love*
		sposarsi	*to get married*

(Noi) **ci alziamo** presto. — *We get up early.*
(Lei) **si veste** bene. — *She dresses well.*
Come **ti chiami?** — *What's your name?*
Mi svẹglio tutti i giorni alle otto. — *I wake up every day at eight.*

6. If the reflexive verb is used in an infinitive form, the appropriate reflexive pronoun is attached to the infinitive after dropping the final **-e.**

Desịdero divertir**mi**. — *I wish to enjoy myself (have a good time).*
Non dobbiamo alzar**ci** presto. — *We do not have to get (ourselves) up early.*
Oggi preferisce riposar**si.** — *Today she prefers to rest (herself).*

NOTE:
With **dovere**, **potere**, and **volere**, the reflexive pronoun may be placed *before* the conjugated verb:

Vọglio alzar**mi**.
Mi vọglio alzare. } *I want to get (myself) up.*

7. When the action involves parts of the body or clothing, Italian uses the reflexive construction instead of the possessive adjective. In this case, the possessive adjective is replaced by the definite article.

Mi lavo **le** mani.	*I wash my hands.* (Literally, *I wash the hands to myself.*)
Mi metto **il** vestito rosso.	*I put on my red dress.*

8. **Sedersi** (*to sit down*) has an irregular conjugation.

mi siedo	**ci sediamo**
ti siedi	**vi sedete**
si siede	**si siẹdono**

Passato prọssimo: *mi sono seduto(a)*

Pratica

A. Dove si divẹrtono le seguenti persone?

ESEMPIO mio zio, in montagna
Mio zio si diverte in montagna.

1. io, al caffè con gli amici 2. Mirella e Luisa, al campo da tennis 3. noi, alla discoteca 4. mia madre, a teatro 5. voi, al cịnema 6. mio padre e i suoi amici, davanti alla televisione 7. un topo di biblioteca, in una biblioteca 8. E tu, dove ti diverti?

B. Completate, seguendo l'esẹmpio.

ESEMPIO (alzarsi) Io _____ la mattina presto.
Io mi alzo la mattina presto.

1. (vestirsi) Mia sorella _____ molto rapidamente. 2. (chiamarsi) Noi _____ Rossi. 3. (divertirsi) Io _____ quando esco con gli amici. 4. (prepararsi) Voi _____ per partire. 5. (scusarsi) Tu _____ quando hai torto. 6. (svegliarsi) Io e il mio compagno _____ quando la svẹglia (*alarm clock*) suona (*rings*). 7. (arrabbiarsi) Io _____ quando i miei amici sono in ritardo. 8. (sentirsi) Come _____ tu oggi? 9. (innamorarsi) Tu _____ sempre a prima vista (*at first sight*). 10. (fermarsi) Io _____ al bar a prẹndere un caffè.

C. Rispondete alle seguenti domande con una frase completa.

a. *Come si vede Lei quando si guarda nello specchio?*

1. sorridente (*smiling*) o triste? 2. contento(a) o scontento(a)? 3. stanco(a) o riposato(a)? 4. giọvane o vẹcchio(a)? 5. preoccupato(a) o tranquillo(a)?

b. *Come si consịdera Lei quando pensa a se stesso(a)* (yourself)?

1. fortunato(a) o sfortunato(a)? 2. felice o infelice? 3. paziente o impaziente? 4. sẹmplice o complicato(a)? 5. un po' matto(a) o sạggio(a) (*wise*)? 6. cordiale o indifferente? 7. lento(a) o rạpido(a) nel lavoro? 8. ordinato(a) o disordinato(a)?

D. Domanda e risposta. Seguite l'esẹmpio.

ESEMPIO svegliarsi/presto o tardi
—Ti svegli presto o tardi?
—Mi svẹglio presto (tardi).

1. sentirsi/bene o male **2.** divertirsi/a una conferenza o a una festa **3.** annoiarsi/al cịnema o a teatro **4.** fermarsi/in biblioteca o al caffè **5.** arrabbiarsi/spesso o raramente **6.** alzarsi/presto o tardi **7.** innamorarsi/facilmente o difficilmente

E. Una questione di abitụdini (*habits*). Completate il parạgrafo.

Io _____ (chiamarsi) Alberto e il mio compagno _____ (chiamarsi) Stẹfano. Io _____ (svegliarsi) molto presto la mattina, ma Stẹfano _____ (svegliarsi) tardi. Io _____ (lavarsi) e _____ (vestirsi) rapidamente e lui _____ (lavarsi) e _____ (vestirsi) lentamente (*slowly*). Io non _____ (prepararsi) la colazione perchè non ho tempo, ma Stẹfano _____ (prepararsi) una colazione abbondante. Io _____ (divertirsi) quando gioco a tennis, ma Stẹfano non _____ (divertirsi). Io _____ (annoiarsi) quando guardo la TV e lui _____ (annoiarsi) quando è solo. Io _____ (innamorarsi) delle ragazze bionde e lui _____ (innamorarsi) delle ragazze brune. Io _____ (arrabbiarsi) perchè Stẹfano è sempre in ritardo, e lui _____ (arrabbiarsi) perchè io dimẹntico sempre i miei appuntamenti. A mezzogiorno Stẹfano ed io _____ (fermarsi) al caffè e mangiamo insieme. Poi noi _____ (riposarsi) al parco prima di ritornare al lavoro. La sera noi _____ (addormentarsi) presto perchè siamo stanchi morti.

F. Che cosa fate quando...? Rispondete alle domande scegliendo (*choosing*) il verbo riflessivo appropriato.

1. un amico è in ritardo?	**a.** mẹttersi un golf (*sweater*)
2. avete freddo?	**b.** addormentarsi
3. andate a una festa?	**c.** svegliarsi
4. ascoltate un discorso (*speech*) noioso?	**d.** divertirsi
5. siete stanchi(e) di camminare?	**e.** arrabbiarsi
6. la svẹglia suona?	**f.** annoiarsi
7. avete sonno?	**g.** fermarsi
8. vedete un amico (un'amica)?	**h.** sedersi

G. Che cosa preferiamo fare? Domanda e risposta. Seguite l'esẹmpio.

ESEMPIO tu, alzarsi/presto o tardi
—Ti alzi presto o tardi?
—Preferisco alzarmi presto (*o* **tardi**).

1. tu, vestirsi/rapidamente o lentamente **2.** voi, mẹttersi/dei vestiti (*clothes*) eleganti o dei jeans **3.** tu, svegliarsi/alle sette o alle otto **4.** i tuoi amici, divertirsi/la domẹnica o il sạbato **5.** voi, fermarsi/al caffè o al ristorante **6.** tu, riposarsi/il sạbato o la domẹnica

II. I verbi reciproci

Carlo e Maria si telẹfonano.

When a verb expresses reciprocal action (we know *one another,* you love *each other*), it follows the pattern of a reflexive verb. In this case, only the plural pronouns, **ci**, **vi**, and **si** are used.

Lia e Gino **si** salụtano. (Lia saluta Gino e Gino saluta Lia.)	*Lia and Gino greet each other.*
Noi **ci** scriviamo spesso.	*We write to each other often.*

Pratica

A. Due amici permalosi (*peevish*). Completate con la forma appropriata dei verbi in parentesi.

Gino e Franco, quando s'incọntrano, _____ (salutarsi) e _____ (parlarsi). Quando sono lontani, _____ (scrịversi) o _____ (telefonarsi) spesso. Quando hanno bisogno di aiuto, _____ (aiutarsi) volentieri. Ma quando s'arrạbbiano l'uno con l'altro, non _____ (guardarsi), non _____ (parlarsi), non _____ (salutarsi): insomma (*in short*), _____ (detestarsi), almeno (*at least*) per qualche tempo.

B. Domanda e risposta.

ESEMPIO tu e i tuoi amici, vedersi, in biblioteca
—Tu e i tuoi amici, vi vedete in biblioteca?
—No, non ci vediamo in biblioteca. Ci vediamo in classe.
(*o* **in una pizzeria;** *o*...)

1. tu e i tuoi genitori, scrịversi, ogni settimana **2.** tu e tua madre, telefonarsi, la domẹnica **3.** i veri amici, aiutarsi, raramente (*seldom*) **4.** tuo fratello e i suoi amici, incontrarsi, in centro **5.** io e tu, vedersi, stasera

C. Rispondete usando la costruzione reciproca.

1. Dove vi incontrate, tu e i tuoi compagni? 2. Dove vi vedete, tu e il tuo ragazzo (la tua ragazza)? 3. Quante volte all'anno vi scrivete, tu e i tuoi parenti? 4. Quando vi telefonate, tu e tua madre? 5. Quando sei arrabbiato(a) (*mad*) con il tuo compagno (la tua compagna) di stanza, vi parlate o non vi parlate? 6. Quando tu e i tuoi amici vi vedete, vi abbracciate o vi date la mano?

III. Il passato prossimo con i verbi riflessivi e reciproci

Pippo l'astuto si è seduto.

All reflexive and reciprocal verbs in the **passato prossimo** are conjugated with the auxiliary **essere.** The past participle must agree with the subject in gender and number.

lavarsi (*to wash oneself*)	
mi sono lavato(a)	*I washed myself*
ti sei lavato(a)	*you washed yourself*
si è lavato(a)	*he (she) washed himself (herself)*
ci siamo lavati(e)	*we washed ourselves*
vi siete lavati(e)	*you washed yourselves*
si sono lavati(e)	*they washed themselves*

Lia, **ti sei divertita** ieri?	*Lia, did you have fun yesterday?*
Ci siamo alzati alle sei.	*We got up at six.*
Il treno **si è fermato** a Parma.	*The train stopped in Parma.*
Le due ragazze **si sono salutate** e **si sono baciate.**	*The two girls greeted each other, and they kissed each other.*

Pratica

A. Domanda e risposta. Completate con il verbo riflessivo al **passato prossimo.**

ESEMPIO Ti alzi presto?

Sì, ma questa mattina (alzarsi) mi sono alzato(a) tardi.

1. Ti vesti rapidamente? Sì, ma oggi (vestirsi) _____ lentamente. **2.** Vi divertite alle feste? Sì, ma ieri sera noi (annoiarsi) _____ molto. **3.** Il tuo fratellino si addormenta presto? Sì, ma ieri lui (addormentarsi) _____ tardi. **4.** Vi fermate a salutare la nonna? No, perchè noi (fermarsi) _____ domenica pomeriggio. **5.** Quando si sposa tua sorella? Mia sorella (sposarsi) _____ due mesi fa. **6.** Ti annoi alle conferenze? Di solito no, ma alla conferenza di ieri io (annoiarsi) _____ terribilmente. **7.** Ti svegli presto la mattina? Sì, ma questa mattina io (svegliarsi) _____ tardi perchè la sveglia non ha funzionato.

B. Una storia d'amore. Raccontate la storia di Laura e Francesco al **passato prossimo.**

Un bel giorno Laura e Francesco s'incontrano. Si guardano e si parlano: s'innamorano a prima vista. Si scrivono e si rivedono spesso. Finalmente si fidanzano e, dopo pochi mesi, si sposano.

C. Vacanze romane. Completate le seguenti frasi usando il **passato prossimo.**

Raffaella _____ (arrivare) a Roma ieri sera per incontrare l'amica Marina. Stamattina Raffaella _____ (svegliarsi) presto, _____ (alzarsi) e _____ (telefonare) all'amica. Poi _____ (lavarsi) e _____ (vestirsi). Quando le due ragazze _____ (incontrarsi), _____ (salutarsi) con molto affetto e _____ (uscire) dall'albergo. Marina e Raffaella _____ (visitare) la città e _____ (divertirsi) molto. A mezzogiorno le due ragazze _____ (sentirsi) stanche e _____ (fermarsi) a una tavola calda (*snack bar*), dove _____ (riposarsi) per un'ora. Dopo il pranzo, Marina e Raffaella _____ (fare) le spese nei negozi e _____ (comprare) delle cartoline e dei francobolli (*postage stamps*). Poi le due amiche _____ (sedersi) a un caffè e _____ (scrivere) le cartoline ai loro parenti e amici.

D. **Ecco una cartolina di Raffaella.** Completate con il verbo al **passato prossimo.**

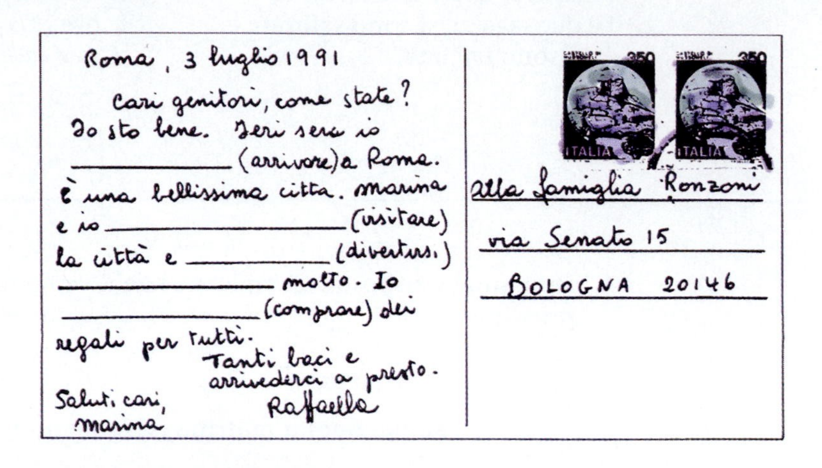
Roma, 3 luglio 1991

Cari genitori, come state?
Io sto bene. Ieri sera io
__________ (arrivare) a Roma.
È una bellissima città. Marina
e io __________ (visitare)
la città e __________ (divertirsi)
__________ molto. Io
__________ (comprare) dei
regali per tutti.
Tanti baci e
arrivederci a presto.
Raffaella

Saluti cari,
Marina

Alla famiglia Ronzoni
via Senato 15
BOLOGNA 20146

E. Rispondete alle seguenti domande.

1. Come ti chiami? **2.** A che ora ti sei alzato(a) stamattina? **3.** Hai avuto il tempo di prepararti la colazione? **4.** Ti arrabbi spesso? Quando ti sei arrabbiato(a) l'ultima volta? Perchè? **5.** Che cosa fai quando ti senti poco bene? **6.** Ti sei divertito(a) il week-end scorso? Come? **7.** Quando ti annoi? **8.** Quante volte al mese vi scrivete tu e i tuoi genitori? **9.** A che ora ti sei addormentato(a) ieri sera? **10.** Quando ti scusi? **11.** Quando vi telefonate tu e i tuoi amici (le tue amiche)? **12.** Quando ti vesti elegantemente? **13.** La mattina hai bisogno di una sveglia per svegliarti?

IV. L'ora (time)

1. The hour and its fractions are expressed in Italian as follows:

È l'una

È l'una e dieci.

È l'una e un quarto (*or* e quindici).

È l'una e mezzo (*or* e trenta).

Sono le due meno venti.

Sono le due meno un quarto (*or* meno quindici).

2. To ask what time it is, either of two expressions can be used:

Che ora è? *or* **Che ore sono?**

To answer, **è** is used in combination with **l'una**, **mezzogiorno**, and **mezzanotte. Sono le** is used to express all other hours.

È l'una.	*It is one o'clock.*
È mezzogiorno.	*It is noon.*
È mezzanotte.	*It is midnight.*
Sono le due, **le tre**, ecc.	*It is two o'clock, three o'clock,* etc.

To indicate A.M. and P.M., the expressions **di mattina**, **del pomeriggio**, **di sera**, and **di notte** are added after the hour.

Sono le cinque **di mattina.**	*It is 5:00 A.M.*
Sono le tre **del pomeriggio.**	*It is 3:00 P.M.*
Sono le dieci **di sera.**	*It is 10:00 P.M.*
È l'una **di notte.**	*It is 1:00 A.M.*

3. The question **A che ora?** (*At what time?*) is answered as follows:

A mezzogiorno (o mezzanotte).	*At noon (or midnight).*
All' una e mezzo.	*At 1:30.*
Alle sette di sera.	*At 7:00 P.M.*

4. Italians use the twenty-four-hour system for official time (travel schedules, museum hours, theater times).

La Galleria degli Uffizi apre **alle nove** e chiude **alle diciotto.**	*The Uffizi Gallery opens at 9:00 A.M. and closes at 6:00 P.M.*
L'aereo da Parigi arriva **alle diciassette.**	*The plane from Paris arrives at 5:00 P.M.*

5. The following expressions are associated with time:

la mattina	*in the morning*	**la sera**	*in the evening*
il pomeriggio	*in the afternoon*	**la notte**	*at night*
in anticipo	*ahead of time*	**in punto**	*sharp*
in orario	*on time*	**presto**	*early*
in ritardo	*late*	**tardi**	*late*

La mattina vado in biblioteca.	*In the morning I go to the library.*
La sera guardiamo la TV.	*In the evening we watch TV.*
Il treno è **in orario.**	*The train is on time.*
Sono le due **in punto.**	*It is two o'clock sharp.*
Franco è uscito **presto** ed è arrivato a scuola **in anticipo.**	*Franco left early and arrived at school ahead of time.*
Gina si è alzata **tardi** e ora è **in ritardo** all'appuntamento.	*Gina got up late and now she is late for her appointment.*

The adverbs **presto** and **tardi** are used with **essere** only when this verb is used in impersonal expressions.

È presto (tardi).	*It is early (late).*

6. The English word *time* is translated as **tempo, ora,** or **volta,** depending on context.

Non ho **tempo.**	*I don't have time.*
Che **ora** è?	*What time is it?*
Tre **volte** al giorno.	*Three times a day.*

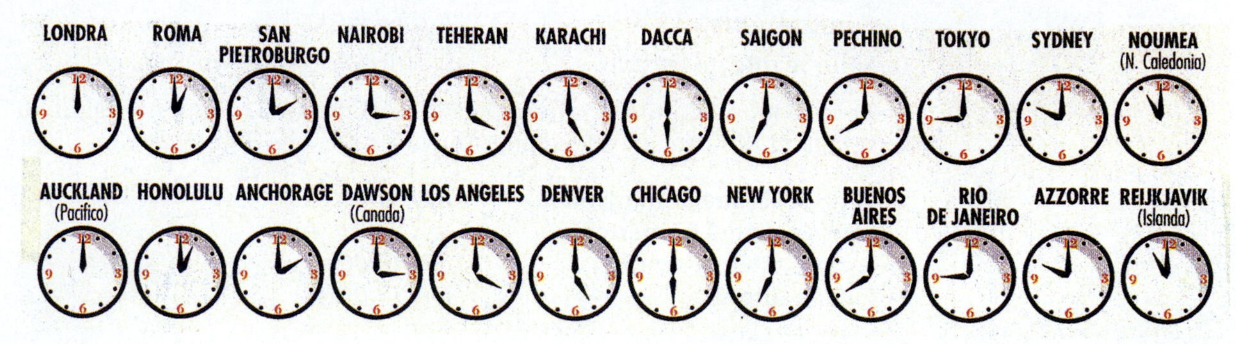

Quando a New York sono le 7 di sera, che ore sono a Roma?

Pratica

A. **Che ore sono?** Rispondete con una frase completa.

ESEMPIO 10:00 **—Sono le dieci.**

1. 12:15 3:10 12:00 6:30 9:45 6:20 7:35 1:05
2. 10:00 P.M. 5:30 P.M. 11:00 A.M. 2:00 A.M.

B. **Orari.** Voi leggete l'orạrio ferroviạrio (dei treni) e delle linee aẹree. Formate frasi complete, trasformando l'ora ufficiale in ora normale.

ESEMPIO aẹreo Parigi–New York, 17.20
L'aẹreo Parigi–New York parte alle cinque e venti del pomerịggio.

1. aẹreo Milano–Roma, 13.30 2. treno Bologna–Firenze, 21.50
3. treno Firenze–Nạpoli, 1.05 4. aẹreo Roma–New York, 11.45
5. aẹreo Torino–Londra, 14.35

C. **A che ora?** Domandate a un(a) compagno(a) a che ora fa di sọlito le seguenti attività.

1. svegliarsi la mattina 2. fare colazione 3. uscire di casa 4. arrivare al lavoro o a scuola 5. ritornare a casa 6. cenare 7. andare a letto

D. Rispondete usando l'espressione appropriata.

1. La lezione di matemạtica comịncia alle nove. Oggi Gianna è arrivata alle nove e un quarto. È arrivata in antịcipo? 2. Domẹnica scorsa Pippo si è alzato a mezzogiorno. Si è alzato presto? 3. Tu devi ẹssere dal dentista alle tre del pomerịggio e arrivi alle tre in punto. Sei in ritardo? 4. È sạbato. Noi ci svegliamo e guardiamo l'orolọgio: sono le sei di mattina. Ci addormentiamo di nuovo (*again*). Perchè?

V. Avverbi

La tartaruga e la lepre (hare) fanno una gara (race): la tartaruga cammina lentamente, l'altra corre velocemente.

1. In the preceding chapters, you have studied several adverbs (**molto, troppo, ora, presto**, etc). In Italian, many adverbs are formed by adding **-mente** to the feminine form of the adjective. The suffix **-mente** corresponds to the English adverbial suffix *-ly*.

attento	attenta	**attentamente** (*carefully*)
fortunato	fortunata	**fortunatamente** (*fortunately*)
lento	lenta	**lentamente** (*slowly*)
rạpido	rạpida	**rapidamente** (*rapidly*)

Adjectives ending in **-e** add **-mente** without changing the final vowel.

paziente	**pazientemente** (*patiently*)
sẹmplice	**semplicemente** (*simply*)
veloce	**velocemente** (*fast, quickly*)

Adjectives ending in **-le** and **-re** drop the final **-e** before taking **-mente.**

fạcile	**facilmente** (*easily*)
particolare	**particolarmente** (*particularly*)
probạbile	**probabilmente** (*probably*)

2. The following are some useful adverbs of time:

adesso, ora	*now*	≠	**dopo**	*later*
prima	*first, before*	≠	**poi**	*then*
presto	*early, soon*	≠	**tardi**	*late*
spesso	*often*	≠	{ **raramente** / **qualche volta**	*seldom* / *sometimes*
già	*already*	≠	**non...ancora**	*not...yet*
ancora	*still, more, again*	≠	**non...più**	*not...any longer, not...anymore*
sempre	*always*	≠	**non...mai***	*never*

*__Mai__ in an affirmative question means *ever:* **Hai *mai* visto Roma?**

3. Adverbs generally follow the verb.

Viaggio **spesso** per affari.	*I often travel for business.*
Vado **sempre** in aereo.	*I always go by plane.*
Scrivono **raramente.**	*They seldom write.*

With *compound tenses,* however, the following adverbs of time are placed *between* the auxiliary verb and the past participle: **già, non...ancora, non...più, non...mai,** and **sempre.**

Non sono **mai** andata in treno.	*I've never gone by train.*
Non ho **ancora** fatto colazione.	*I have not had breakfast yet.*
Hai **già** ricevuto i biglietti?	*Have you already received the tickets?*

Pratica

A. **Come...?** Rispondete con un avverbio, seguendo l'esempio.

ESEMPIO —Sei una persona cordiale: come saluti?
—**Saluto cordialmente.**

1. Sei molto rapido a leggere: come leggi? 2. Tua sorella è intelligente: come parla? 3. Stai attento quando il professore spiega: come ascolti? 4. Il tuo fratellino è rumoroso (*noisy*): come gioca? 5. Fai una vita tranquilla: come vivi? 6. Per te (*you*) è facile scrivere: come scrivi? 7. I tuoi saluti sono sempre cordiali: come saluti? 8. I tuoi vestiti (*clothes*) sono sempre eleganti: come ti vesti? 9. Il tuo amico mangia sempre dei pasti abbondanti: come mangia?

B. Riscrivete (*Rewrite*) la frase con l'avverbio al posto corretto.

1. (facilmente) Quando è con gli amici, ride (ridere: *laugh*). 2. (sempre) Ho viaggiato in prima classe. 3. (già) Hai prenotato il biglietto per Firenze? 4. (mai) Non so che cosa dire. 5. (spesso) Usciamo la domenica. 6. (più) Non ha visto i suoi parenti. 7. (ancora) È ritornata alla città dei suoi genitori. 8. (solamente) Mi sono riposato mezz'ora.

C. Rispondete alle domande usando uno dei seguenti avverbi: **non...mai, spesso, raramente, qualche volta, già, non...ancora, non...più.**

1. Hai visitato Roma? 2. Sei mai andato(a) in metropolitana (*subway*)? 3. Sei già salito(a) sulla torre (*tower*) di Pisa? 4. Hai viaggiato spesso quest'anno? 5. Hai già festeggiato il tuo compleanno quest'anno? 6. Hai mangiato qualche volta in una trattoria romana? 7. Sei già stato(a) a Capri? 8. Leggi ancora le favole (*fables*) per bambini?

LETTURA

Impiegati bancari al lavoro.

LA GIORNATA DI UN IMPIEGATO

L'ingegner Scotti ha dato un ultimatum al figlio: Marcello deve pensare seriamente a una *carriera.* Così, Marcello incomincia oggi la sua prima giornata di lavoro.

career

Stamattina si sveglia molto presto. Guarda la sveglia: sono *appena* le sette e un quarto. Non *è abituato* a svegliarsi così presto, ma oggi non può dormire. Non si sente molto bene. Marcello si alza, si lava e si veste: si mette un *completo* elegante. Di solito Marcello ha *una fame da lupo* e fa una colazione abbondante, ma oggi non ha fame e beve solo un espresso. Guarda l'orologio: sono le otto ed è ora di andare al lavoro.

only/accustomed
suit
he is as hungry as a wolf

In banca Marcello *fa la conoscenza* del *capoufficio* e dei *colleghi,* poi si siede e incomincia a lavorare. Alle dieci e mezzo *fa una pausa* e prende un caffè con un collega, poi *ricomincia* a lavorare. Ma è nervoso e fa degli errori. Il suo capoufficio prima è gentile, poi si arrabbia. Marcello guarda l'orologio con impazienza. Il tempo non passa mai! Finalmente arriva l'una del pomeriggio e Marcello esce dalla banca.

he makes the acquaintance/boss/colleagues
he takes a break
he starts again

(A casa, durante le cena.)

Papà *Allora,* com'è andata oggi? — So

Marcello Non molto bene. Mi sono annoiato terribilmente e mi sono quasi addormentato sulla calcolatrice.

Papà Caro ragazzo, incominci a capire che cosa vuol dire *guadagnarsi il pane. Finora* ti sei divertito; adesso è ora *di mettere la testa a posto* e di lavorare. — to earn one's living/ Until now/to settle down

Marcello *Ho fatto bene* a divertirmi perchè il lavoro è una bella *seccatura.* — I did the right thing / bore

Mantova 23 Marzo 1994 Lit. 350.000,00
BANCA NAZIONALE DEL LAVORO
ISTITUTO DI CREDITO DI DIRITTO PUBBLICO
MANTOVA
2 270 662 04
Pagate per questo assegno bancario a:
Payez contre ce chèque à:
Please pay against this cheque to:
Zahlen Sie gegen diesen Scheck an:
Enrico Bini
Lire it. Trecentocinquantamila
Claudia Storti

Comprensione

1. Perchè oggi è una giornata importante per Marcello?
2. A che ora si è svegliato?
3. Si svẹglia sempre così presto?
4. Perchè oggi non può dormire?
5. Quando si è alzato, che cosa ha fatto?
6. Come si è vestito?
7. A che ora è uscito di casa?
8. Chi ha conosciuto in uffịcio?
9. Perchè il suo capouffịcio si è arrabbiato?
10. Che cosa guarda Marcello impazientemente mentre (*while*) lavora?
11. Si è divertito oggi in uffịcio?
12. Che cosa pensa suo padre?

Domande personali

1. Lei ha incominciato a pensare seriamente alla Sua carriera?
2. Ha già lavorato? Dove? Lavora adesso?
3. Per il momento, Lei preferisce un lavoro a tempo pieno (*full time*) o un lavoro part-time?
4. Preferisce un lavoro in un uffịcio, o un lavoro all'ạria aperta (*outdoors*)?
5. Lei vuole cercare un lavoro immediatamente, quando finisce i Suoi studi, o preferisce divertirsi e viaggiare per qualche tempo?

ATTIVITÀ SUPPLEMENTARI

A. **Dịalogo a due.** Un(Un') amico(a) o collega è arrivato(a) nella tua città e ti telẹfona. Tu domandi com'è andato il vịaggio; in quale albergo si trova; se ha noleggiato una mạcchina. Fissate un appuntamento per il pranzo o la cena, a che ora e in quale ristorante vi incontrate. Esempio: il dịalogo *«Un vịaggio d'affari»*.

B. **Descrizione.** Osservate i disegni che sẹguono e descrivete una giornata nella vita del signor Felice. Usate il **passato prọssimo** e, tra altri verbi, alcuni verbi riflessivi e recịproci (**alzarsi**, **lavarsi**, **vestirsi**, **annoiarsi**, **arrabbiarsi**, **abbracciarsi**, **baciarsi**, **riposarsi**, **addormentarsi**, **divertirsi**).

C. **Attività collettiva.** Create e descrivete una persona immaginạria (come si chiama, dove ạbita, con chi, cosa fa, dove stụdia o lavora). Descrivete un giorno nella sua vita, dalla mattina alla sera. Ogni studente partecipa a turno (*taking turns*) all'attività.

D. **Proverbi.** Conoscete dei proverbi in inglese con un significato sịmile (*similar*) a questi? Con quali proverbi siete d'accordo (*do you agree*)?

1. Il tempo è denaro.
2. Il tempo è buon maestro.
3. I soldi non fanno la felicità.

E. **Come si dice in italiano?**

1. Marco and Vanna got married three years ago.
2. Marco found a good job at the Fiat plant (**fạbbrica**), and his wife continued to (**a**) work at the bank.
3. One day, two months ago, Marco lost (his) job, and their life became very difficult.
4. For a few weeks, Marco looked for a new job, but without success.
5. Finally, last Thursday, he phoned his father's friend, Anselmo Anselmi, one of the directors (**dirigente**) of Olivetti.
6. They met, and Anselmo offered Marco a job with (**nella**) his company (**ditta**).
7. Now, every morning Marco and his wife get up at 6:00; they wash and get dressed in a hurry.
8. They only have time (**di**) to drink a cup of coffee. Then they say goodbye to each other (**salutarsi**) and go to work.

Vocabolario

Nomi

l'affare (*m.*)	*business*
l'affetto	*affection*
il bạcio	*kiss*
il capoufficio	*boss*
la carriera	*career*
il (la) collega (*pl.* i colleghi; le colleghe)	*colleague*
il denaro	*money*
l'errore (*m.*)	*error, mistake*
il francobollo	*stamp*
il (la) giọvane	*young man, young woman*
il quarto	*quarter (of an hour)*
la spesa	*expense*
il successo	*success*
la svẹglia	*alarm clock*
la tạvola calda	*snack bar*

Aggettivi

abbondante	*abundant*
arrabbiato	*mad*
complicato	*complicated*
gentile	*kind*
indifferente	*indifferent*
lento	*slow*
nervoso	*nervous*
puntuale	*punctual*
ụltimo	*last*
veloce	*fast*

Verbi

abbracciarsi	*to embrace each other*
addormentarsi	*to fall asleep*
alzarsi	*to get up*
annoiarsi	*to get bored*
arrabbiarsi	*to get mad*
baciarsi	*to kiss each other*
cambiare	*to change, to exchange*
cercare	*to look for*
chiamarsi	*to be called*
considerarsi	*to consider oneself*
divertirsi	*to have fun, to enjoy oneself*
fermarsi	*to stop*
fidanzarsi	*to get engaged*
innamorarsi (di)	*to fall in love (with)*
lavarsi	*to wash (oneself)*
mẹttersi	*to put on, to wear*
prepararsi	*to prepare oneself, to get ready*
riposarsi	*to rest*
salutarsi	*to greet each other; to say good bye*
scusarsi	*to apologize*
sedersi	*to sit down*
sentirsi	*to feel*
soggiornare	*to stay (at a hotel, etc.)*
sposarsi	*to get married*
suonare	*to ring*
svegliarsi	*to wake up*
vestirsi	*to get dressed*

Altre espressioni

almeno	*at least*
ancora	*still, more, again*
di nuovo	*again*
è ora di (+ *inf.*)	*it is time to*
fare la conoscenza	*to make the acquaintance*
fare una pausa	*to take a break*
già	*already*
guadagnarsi il pane	*to earn one's living*
impazientemente	*impatiently*
in antịcipo	*early, ahead of time*
in punto	*sharp*
mentre	*while*
mezzo	*half*
non...ancora	*not...yet*
non...mai	*never*
non...più	*not...any longer, not... anymore*
per affari	*for business (on business)*
prima	*first, before*
a prima vista	*at first sight*
quasi	*almost*
raramente	*seldom*
Salve!	*Hello!*
seriamente	*seriously*
terribilmente	*terribly*
un uomo (una donna) d'affari	*a businessman(woman)*

▲ *Città del Vaticano. La grandiosa Piazza di San Pietro e il suo colonnato.*

◀ *Roma. L'antico e il moderno sono qui rappresentati dalle rovine del Foro e dal monumento a Vittorio Emanuele II (secondo).*

ROMA, «CITTÀ ETERNA»

Per il turista Roma è un'esperienza ụnica e un viạggio di *più di* 2.000 (duemila) anni nella stọria. *Lungo* la Via dei Fori Romani uno ha la possibilità di ammirare le *rovine* del Foro, centro commerciale, civile e religioso dell'antica Roma. Il gigantesco Colosseo* simbolizza la grandiosità dell'Impero Romano, *che comprendeva* buona parte del *mondo di allora.*

- more than/along
- ruins
- comprising
- world of that time

L'anno 313 (trecentotrẹdici) *dopo Cristo* rappresenta il trionfo del Cristianẹsimo e il declino dell'Impero Romano. Il Papa diventa l'alta autorità spirituale, l'*erede* della civiltà e della lingua di Roma (il latino**). La Roma dei Papi è ricca di basịliche e *campanili,* di palazzi e di innumerẹvoli *opere* d'arte. La più grande, e certamente la più maestosa, è la Basịlica di San Pietro, ọpera di molti artisti *fra cui* il Bramante, Michelạngelo, il Perugino, Raffaello e il Bernini.

- 313 A.D.
- heir
- bell towers
- works
- among them

Nel 1870 (milleottocentosettanta) tutta l'Itạlia è unificata e Roma diventa la capitale del nuovo Stato. Il

---

*So called because of the colossal statue of the emperor Nero erected nearby.
**The name "latino" comes from *Latium* (*Lazio:* the region where Rome was founded).

Papa deve ritirarsi nel Vaticano costruito *intorno* alla grande basịlica. Solamente nel 1929 (millenovecentoventinove) il Vaticano *diventerà* indipendente, il più pịccolo Stato del mondo, pịccola città nella grande città di Roma.

around

will become

La Roma moderna è rappresentata dall'*imponente* monumento a Vittọrio Emanuele II (secondo)* che domina Piazza Venẹzia, centro della città. Da qui incomịncia la famosa Via del Corso con superbi edifici e lussuosi negozi.

imposing

Questa grande varietà d'aspetti e di stili costituisce il *fascino* principale di Roma e giustifica il suo appellativo di «Città Eterna.»

charm

Comprensione

Completate le seguenti frasi con l'espressione corretta.

1. Il centro religioso e politico dell'antica Roma è
   a. il Colosseo **b.** il Foro **c.** Piazza Venezia
2. Il Colosseo simbolizza la grandiosità della Roma
   a. moderna **b.** papale **c.** antica
3. La lingua di Roma antica è
   a. l'italiano **b.** il romano **c.** il latino
4. Michelangelo ha partecipato alla costruzione
   a. del Foro romano **b.** della Basilica di San Pietro **c.** del monumento a Vittorio Emanuele II
5. Roma è diventata la capitale d'Italia nel
   a. 1770 **b.** 1870 **c.** 1929
6. Oggi la sede (*seat*) del Papa è
   a. Roma **b.** la Basilica di San Pietro **c.** il Vaticano

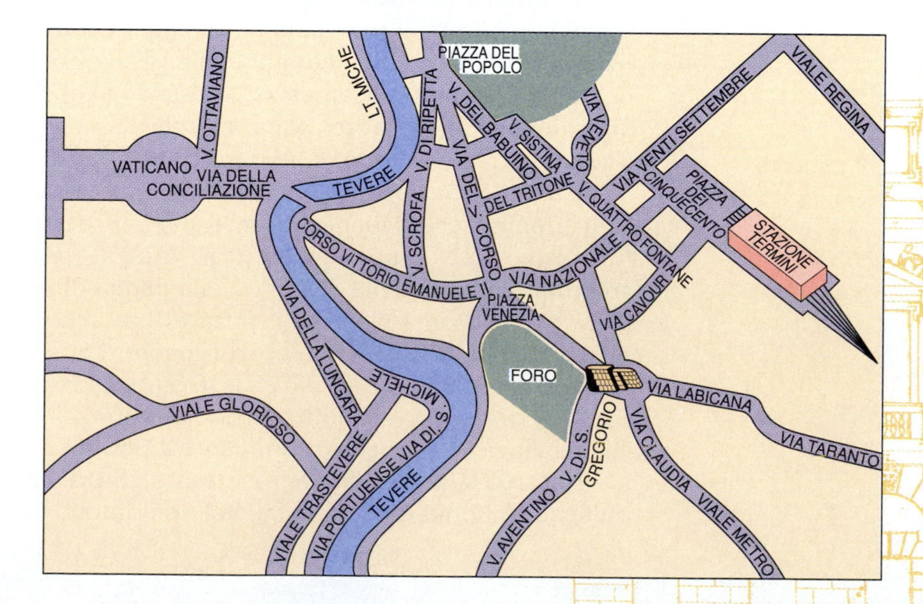

Il centro di Roma.

*First King of Italy from 1861 to 1878.

9 ABITI E STAGIONI

Una sfilata di moda di stilisti milanesi.

Punti di vista

Oggi facciamo le valigie
Che vestiti compriamo?

Punti grammaticali

I L'imperativo (*tu, noi, voi*)
II Aggettivi e pronomi dimostrativi
III Numeri cardinali e ordinali
IV I mesi e la data
V Le stagioni e il tempo

Lettura

Alla Rinascente

Pagina culturale

Alcune feste dell'anno

PUNTI DI VISTA

Perụgia. La pittoresca Piazza 4 Novembre, centro della città. Qui molti studenti dell'Università per Stranieri si ritrovano dopo i corsi.

OGGI *FACCIAMO LE VALIGIE* — we pack our suitcase

Terry e Jane si prepạrano per andare a studiare all'Università per Stranieri di Perụgia.* Oggi fanno le valịgie.

Terry	*Hai deciso* che cosa mẹttere nella valịgia?	have you decided
Jane	Poca *roba.* Non mi piace viaggiare con valịgie *pesanti.*	stuff; heavy
Terry	Io porto un impermeạbile perchè ho sentito dire che a Perụgia *piove* spesso in primavera.	it rains
Jane	E io porto un due pezzi di lana per quando *fa fresco;* questo vestito bianco e *quelle* due camicette, una di seta e l'altra di cotone.	it is cool; those
Terry	*Non dimenticare* di portare scarpe cọmode, perchè nelle città italiane *si gira* a piedi e non in mạcchina.	Don't forget; one goes around
Jane	Allora porto queste scarpe da tennis.	
Terry	Ma cos'è quel *barạttolo* che hai messo nella valịgia? Peanut butter?	jar
Jane	Sì, perchè ho sentito dire che non è fạcile trovarlo in Itạlia, e io non posso *farne a meno.*	live without it
Terry	Lo so, ma in Itạlia c'è la Nutella, una crema di cioccolato e *noccioline,* molto buona! E non dimenticare che a Perụgia ci sono i *Baci Perugina!*	peanuts; chocolate kisses from Perugia

*The oldest university for foreigners in Italy. It is situated in Perugia (Umbria), a charming medieval and Renaissance city, not too far from Assisi, town of St. Francis.

1. Perchè Terry e Jane hanno fatto le valigie?
2. Jane ha messo molta o poca roba nella sua valigia? Perchè?
3. Perchè Terry porta un impermeabile?
4. Perchè hanno bisogno di scarpe comode?
5. Perchè Terry è sorpresa?
6. Perchè Jane ha messo del *peanut butter* nella valigia?
7. Che cos'è la Nutella?

Studio di parole

ARTICOLI DI ABBIGLIAMENTO (*CLOTHING*)

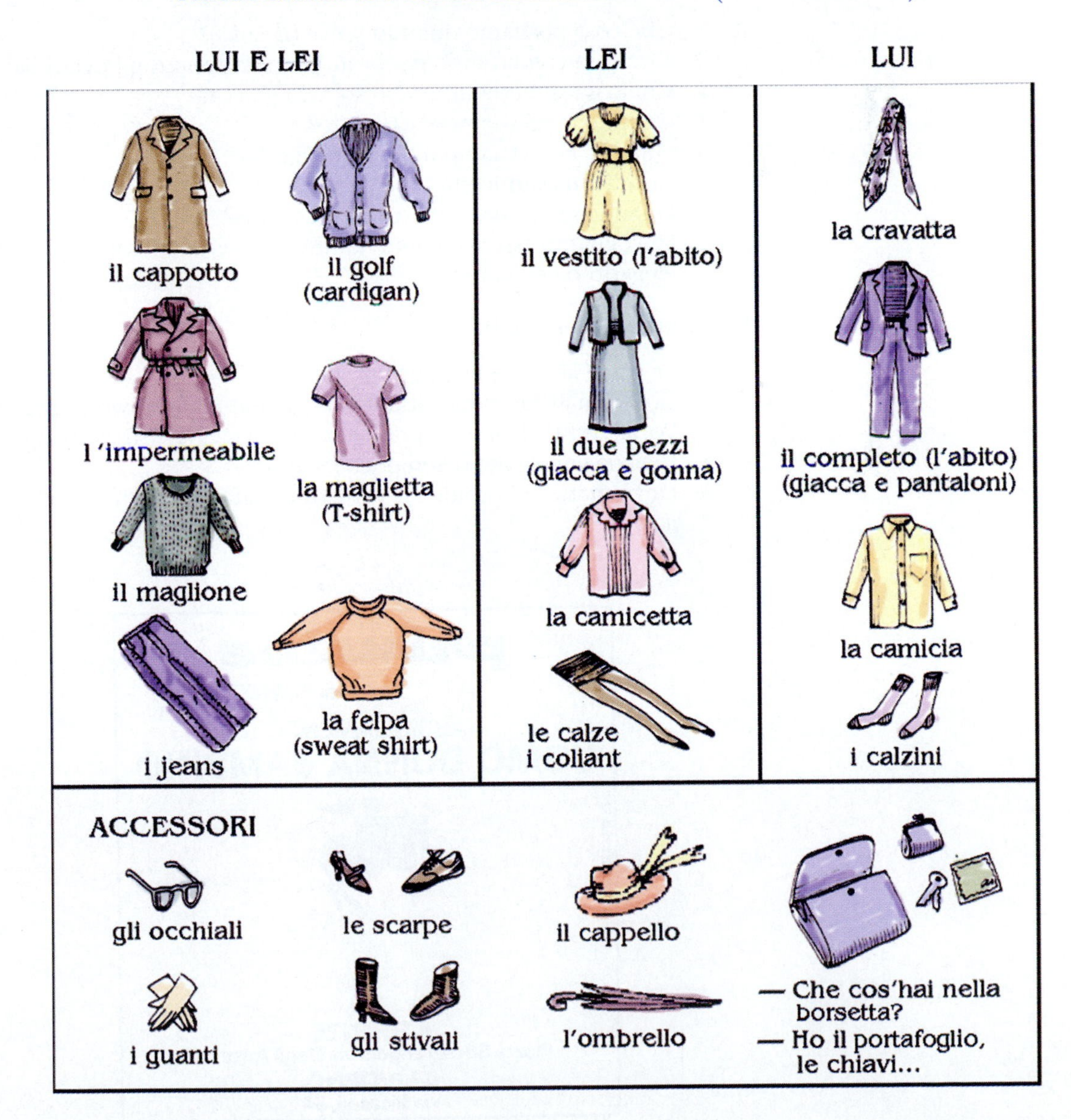

la moda fashion
mẹttersi to put on
portare to wear
provare to try on
i vestiti clothes
la tạglia size
un pạio di calze (scarpe, pantaloni) a pair of stockings (shoes, pants)
in svẹndita on sale
lo sconto discount

la seta silk
la lana wool
il cotone cotton
leggero light
pesante heavy
prạtico practical
a fiori floral (print)
a quadri checked
a righe striped
in tinta unita solid color

Applicazione

A. 1. Che cosa portiamo quando piove (*it rains*)?
2. Che cosa ci mettiamo per protẹggere (*to protect*) gli occhi dal sole?
3. Che cosa si mette un uomo sotto la giacca?
4. Quando ci mettiamo il cappotto?
5. Quando ci mettiamo un vestito leggero?
6. Com'è una camicetta di seta?
7. Quando ci mettiamo le scarpe da tennis?
8. Se vogliamo ẹssere cọmodi (*comfortable*) ci mettiamo dei pantaloni eleganti o dei jeans?

B. **Domande personali.**

1. Le piace la moda italiana?
2. Sa Lei quali sono due città italiane rinomate (*renowned*) per la moda?
3. Porta vestiti eleganti o prạtici quando viạggia? Che vestiti porta?
4. Viạggia con molte o con poche valịgie?
5. Dove mette Lei i soldi e le carte di crẹdito? Li mette in tasca (*in the pocket*)?

Ascoltiamo!

Che vestiti compriamo? *Terry and Jane have been in Perugia for several weeks. Today they are shopping for clothes in a store on the* **Corso Vannucci.** *Listen to their comments as Terry makes a decision about buying a blouse and talks with a clerk. Then answer the following questions.*

Comprensione

1. Dove sono Terry e Jane oggi? Perchè?
2. Che cosa ammirano le due ragazze?
3. Perchè Terry non compra la camicetta di seta?
4. C'è uno sconto sulla camicetta di poliestere? Di quanto?
5. Che taglia ha Terry?
6. Paga in contanti Terry?

Dialogo

Domandate a uno studente (una studentessa) come si veste quando va a una festa.

PUNTI GRAMMATICALI

I. L'imperativo (tu, noi, voi)

—Guarda, Luigi!
—Ma che cos'è?

1. The **imperativo** (*imperative mood*) is used to express a command, an invitation, an exhortation, or advice. The **tu**, **noi**, and **voi** forms are identical to those of the present indicative, except for the **tu** form of **-are** verbs, which changes the ending **-i** to **-a**.

	ascoltare		prẹndere		finire	
(tu)	ascolt**a**!	*listen!*	prend**i**!	*take!*	finisc**i**!	*finish!*
(noi)	ascolt**iamo**!	*let's listen!*	prend**iamo**!	*let's take!*	fin**iamo**!	*let's finish!*
(voi)	ascolt**ate**!	*listen!*	prend**ete**!	*take!*	fin**ite**!	*finish!*

NOTE:

a. Subject pronouns (**tu, noi, voi**) are not expressed.
b. The **noi** form corresponds to the English *let's + verb.*

2. The *negative imperative* for the **tu** form is expressed by **non** + *infinitive*. The **noi** and **voi** forms follow the general rule: **non** + *the conjugated verb.*

Mạngia la minestra! — *Eat the soup!*
Non mangiare dolci! — *Don't eat sweets!*

Leggi la lẹttera! — *Read the letter!*
Non lẹggere quella rivista! — *Don't read that magazine!*

Dormi un po'! — *Sleep a little!*
Non dormire troppo! — *Don't sleep too much!*

BUT:

Partiamo domani! — *Let's leave tomorrow!*
Non partiamo oggi! — *Let's not leave today!*

Guardate queste foto! — *Look at these pictures!*
Non guardate quelle! — *Don't look at those!*

3. Here are the **tu, noi**, and **voi** forms of some irregular verbs.

andare	va' (vai)	andiamo	andate
dare	da' (dai)	diamo	date
fare	fa' (fai)	facciamo	fate
stare	sta' (stai)	stiamo	state
dire	di'	diciamo	dite
avere	abbi	abbiamo	abbiate
ẹssere	sii	siamo	siate

NOTE:

a. The forms **va'**, **da'**, **fa'**, and **sta'** are abbreviations of the regular forms. Either form may be used.

b. **Ẹssere** and **avere** are irregular in the **tu** and **voi** forms. **Dire** is irregular in the **tu** form.

Va' avanti!	*Go ahead!*
Sta' zitto!	*Be quiet!*
Diciamo la verità!	*Let's tell the truth!*
Abbiate pazienza!	*Have patience!*
Non ẹssere maleducato!	*Don't be rude!*
Non avere paura!	*Don't be afraid!*

Pratica

A. Consigli di una madre al figlio (alla figlia).

ESEMPIO studiare **Studia!**

1. riordinare la stanza **2.** mẹttere a posto i tuoi vestiti **3.** prẹndere le vitamine **4.** finire i cọmpiti **5.** lẹggere buoni libri **6.** spẹndere poco **7.** venire a casa presto **8.** frequentare (*to go with*) buoni compagni

B. Esortazioni a degli amici. Usate la forma **tu** o **voi**, secondo il caso.

ESEMPIO Tino, stare zitto **—Tino, sta' zitto!**

1. Enrico, avere pazienza **2.** Gianna, ẹssere prudente al volante (*at the wheel*) **3.** bambini, fare attenzione al trạffico **4.** Paola, dare l'ombrello a Luisa **5.** Pippo, dire la verità **6.** Luisa e Roberta, ẹssere in orạrio **7.** Lucia, stare calma

C. Un moderno Amleto. Il fratello di Sergio è sempre indeciso (*indecisive*). Dice a Sergio di fare una cosa, poi gli dice di non farla.

ESEMPIO Prendi la mia mạcchina! **No, non prẹndere la mia mạcchina!**

1. Metti le scarpe da tennis! **2.** Va' al supermercato! **3.** Compra quel maglione rosso! **4.** Spedisci questa cartolina! **5.** Ascolta queste cassette! **6.** Ritorna in ạutobus! **7.** Vieni con me! **8.** Apri la finestra!

D. Un padre malcontento (*unhappy*) dei figli, li rimprovera.

ESEMPIO Stanno a letto fino a mezzogiorno.
Non state a letto fino a mezzogiorno!

1. Sono impazienti. **2.** Fanno troppe domande. **3.** Promẹttono cose che non vọgliono mantenere (*to keep*). **4.** Ẹscono tutte le sere. **5.** Fụmano. **6.** Vẹngono a casa a mezzanotte.

E. Progetti di fine settimana. Secondo il tempo che fa, tu e i tuoi amici proponete (*propose*) di fare o di non fare le seguenti cose.

ESEMPIO Fa molto caldo: uscire o giocare a carte?
—Non usciamo! Giochiamo a carte!

1. Piove: andare al mare o stare in città? **2.** Fa bel tempo: studiare in biblioteca o fare un giro (*to take a ride*) in bicicletta? **3.** Fa un freddo glaciale: nuotare in piscina o andare al cịnema? **4.** Nẹvica: giocare a tennis o incontrare gli amici al caffè?

II. Aggettivi e pronomi dimostrativi

Lucia: *Non è bello questo vestito rosso?*
Liliana: *Sì, ma preferisco quella giacca.*
Lucia: *Quanto costano quegli stivali?*

1. Che cosa preferisce Liliana?
2. Quale artịcolo (*item*) costa centoventimila lire?
3. Che cosa desịdera sapere Lucia?

1. The demonstrative adjectives (**aggettivi dimostrativi**) are **questo, questa** (*this*) and **quello, quella** (*that*). A demonstrative adjective always precedes the noun. As with all other adjectives, it must agree in gender and number with the noun.

   Questo has the following singular forms: **questo, questa, quest'** (before a singular noun beginning with a vowel); the plural forms are **questi, queste** and mean *these.*

Quanto hai pagato **questa** maglietta?	*How much did you pay for this T-shirt?*
Quest'anno vado in montagna.	*This year I'll go to the mountains.*
Queste scarpe sono larghe.	*These shoes are large.*

   Quello, quella have different endings like the adjective **bello** and the partitive (see Chapter 4.II). The singular forms are **quel, quello, quella, quell'**; the plural forms are **quei, quegli, quelle** and mean *those.*

Ti piace **quel** completo?	*Do you like that outfit?*
Preferisco **quell'**impermeạbile.	*I prefer that raincoat.*
Quella gonna è troppo lunga.	*That skirt is too long.*
Quegli stivali non sono più di moda.	*Those boots are no longer fashionable.*
Guarda **quei** vestiti!	*Look at those dresses!*
Quelle borsette sono italiane.	*Those handbags are from Italy.*

2. **Questo(a)** and **quello(a)** are also pronouns when used alone. **Questo(a)** means *this one* and **quello(a)** means *that one, that of,* or *the one of.* They have regular endings (**o, a, i, e**). For emphasis, **questo(a)** may be followed by **qui** (*here*) and **quello(a)** may be followed by **là** (*there*).

Compra questo vestito; **quello** rosso è caro.	*Buy this dress; the red one is expensive.*
Questa mạcchina è **quella** di Renzo.	*This car is Renzo's (that of Renzo).*
Ho provato queste scarpe e anche **quelle là.**	*I tried on these shoes and also those over there.*

Il tenore canta: —«Questa o quella per me pari sono (are the same)».

Pratica

A. **Questo...** Esprimete (*Express*) la vostra opinione sulle seguenti cose, usando l'aggettivo **questo** nella forma corretta.

ESEMPIO libri, interessante **Questi libri sono interessanti.**

1. vestiti, stretto **2.** magliette, bello **3.** cravatta, brutto **4.** scarpe, cọmodo **5.** maglione, pesante **6.** borsetta, elegante **7.** impermeạbile, troppo largo **8.** gonne, prạtico **9.** giacca, leggero **10.** pantaloni, corto

B. **Quello..** Completate con la forma corretta dell'aggettivo **quello.**

1. Vorrei _____ stivali e _____ scarpe marroni. **2.** Preferisci _____ gonna o _____ vestito? **3.** Ho bisogno di _____ impermeạbile e di _____ calzini. **4.** Dove hai comprato _____ occhiali da sole? **5.** _____ negọzio d'abbigliamento è troppo caro. **6.** Le piace _____ automọbile Fiat rossa? **7.** _____ commesse sono state poco gentili. **8.** _____ libri sono caduti dallo scaffale poco fa (*a little while ago*). **9.** _____ studenti sono veramente bravi!

C. **No!** Rispondete, secondo l'esẹmpio.

ESEMPIO (*Giovanni*) È il cappotto di Maria?
—No, è quello di Giovanni.

1. (*Maria*) Sono i bambini di Lucia? No, sono _____. **2.** (*Sig. Smith*) È l'assegno di Pietro? No, è _____. **3.** (*suo padre*) Sono le chiavi di Luigi? No, sono _____. **4.** (*Oggi*) Hai letto il giornale di ieri? No, ho letto _____. **5.** (*Puccini*) Preferisci le ọpere di Verdi? No, preferisco _____. **6.** (*Paolo*) Sono le scarpe di Pio? No, sono _____. **7.** (*Antonioni*) Desịderi vedere i film di Fellini? No, preferisco vedere _____.

D. **È Natale! Domanda e risposta.** Voi comprate dei regali di Natale (*Christmas*). Il commesso fa delle domande e voi rispondete secondo l'esẹmpio.

ESEMPIO disco **Desịdera questo disco o quello?**
—Preferisco questo. Lo compro.

1. guanti 2. portafoglio 3. camicetta 4. cravatte 5. profumo 6. libro di cucina 7. cartoline 8. calendario 9. ombrello 10. calcolatrice

E. **Preferenze. Domanda e risposta.** Due amici sono nel reparto abbigliamento ed esprimono le loro preferenze.

ESEMPIO camicia **—Mi piace molto questa camicia.**
—Io invece (*instead*) preferisco quella là.

1. scarpe 2. giacca 3. maglione 4. completo 5. pantaloni 6. cravatta

III. Numeri cardinali e ordinali

—O dividiamo i cento milioni o chiamo mio marito!

1. The *cardinal* numbers above 100 are:

101	centouno	2.000	duemila
200	duecento	3.000	tremila
300	trecento	100.000	centomila
1.000*	mille	1.000.000	un milione
1.001	milleuno	2.000.000	due milioni
1.100	millecento	1.000.000.000	un miliardo

NOTE:
The plural of **mille** is **mila.**

duemila chilometri — *two thousand kilometers*

In Italian, **cento** and **mille** are not preceded by the indefinite article **un.**

cento dollari — *a hundred dollars*
mille lire — *a thousand lire*

2. When **milione** (*pl.* **milioni**) and **miliardo** (*pl.* **miliardi**) are immediately followed by a noun, they take the preposition **di.**

Ci sono **due milioni di** abitanti a Milano? — *Are there two million inhabitants in Milan?*

*Note that in writing numbers of four or more digits, Italian uses a period instead of a comma.

3. *Ordinal numbers* (*first, second, third,* etc.) are adjectives and must agree in gender and number with the noun they modify. They are:

primo(a,i,e)*	**sesto**
secondo	**settimo**
terzo	**ottavo**
quarto	**nono**
quinto	**decimo**

From **undicẹsimo** (*eleventh*) on, the ordinal numbers are formed by dropping the final vowel of the cardinal number and adding the suffix **-esimo (a,i,e).** Exceptions: Numbers ending in **-trè (ventitrè, trentatrè,** etc.) and in **-sei (ventisei, trentasei,** etc.) preserve the final vowel.

quịndici	quindic**ẹsimo**	trentatrè	trentatre**ẹsimo**
venti	vent**ẹsimo**	ventisei	ventisei**ẹsimo**
trentuno	trentun**ẹsimo**	mille	mill**ẹsimo**

Ottobre è il **dẹcimo** mese dell'anno.	*October is the tenth month of the year.*
Hai letto le **prime** pạgine?	*Did you read the first pages?*
Ho detto di no, per la **millẹsima** volta.	*I said no, for the thousandth time.*

4. Ordinal numbers precede the noun they modify except when referring to popes and royalty. When referring to centuries, they may follow or precede the noun.

Papa Giovanni XXIII (ventitreẹsimo)	*Pope John XXIII*
Luigi XIV (quattordicẹsimo)	*Louis XIV*
il sẹcolo XX (ventẹsimo) *or* il ventẹsimo sẹcolo	*the twentieth century*

Pratica

A. Leggete le seguenti espressioni.

1. 560 giorni **2.** 3.000 chilọmetri **3.** 27.000 abitanti **4.** 580.000 dọllari **5.** 7.200.000 lire

B. **Per favore, vorrei il numero di... Domanda e risposta.** Voi chiedete alla centralinista il nụmero di telẹfono delle seguenti persone.

ESEMPIO Lino Ricci/35–500 **—Per favore, vorrei il nụmero di Lino Ricci.**
—Trentacinque-cinquecento.

1. Elsa Bettini/240–764 **2.** Luisa Bini/618–207 **3.** Gianni Cardinale/ 352–601 **4.** Emịlio Storti/41–909 **5.** Gigi Schicchi/33–46–104 **6.** Ornella Rei/17–92–888

*The abbreviated forms of ordinal numbers are: 1° **(primo)** or 1ª **(prima)**, 2° **(secondo)** or 2ª **(seconda)**, etc.

C. **Posso...? Domanda e risposta.** Due compagni di classe si scạmbiano il loro nụmero di telẹfono, incluso (*including*) il prefisso.

ESEMPIO **—Posso avere il tuo nụmero di telẹfono?**
—Ma certo (*certainly*). **Il mio nụmero di telẹfono è (415)245–0652. E il tuo?**
—Il mio è...

D. **Quanto costa (cọstano)...? Domanda e risposta.**

ESEMPIO camịcia/30.000 lire
—Quanto costa quella camịcia?
—Costa trentamila lire.

1. maglione/85.500 lire
2. scarpe/115 dọllari
3. mạcchina fotogrạfica/275.000 lire **4.** appartamento/150.000.000 di lire
5. biglietto aẹreo per Milano/980 dọllari **6.** torta/4.500 lire
7. jeans dello stilista Armani/148 dọllari
8. occhiali/65.750 lire
9. gelato/1 dọllaro

E. Leggete le seguenti espressioni, usando i nụmeri ordinali.

ESEMPIO 1, pạgina **la prima pạgina**

1. 5, strada **2.** 13, giorno **3.** 100, nụmero **4.** 24, ora **5.** 50, volta **6.** 1.000, parte (*f.*) **7.** 9, capịtolo **8.** 7, mese **9.** 10, giorno **10.** 3, maglietta

F. Completate le seguenti frasi con il numero ordinale appropriato.

1. Dopo il trentun marzo viene il _____ (1°) aprile. **2.** Machiavelli è vissuto (*lived*) nel sẹcolo _____ (XVI). **3.** Ora studiamo il _____ (9°) capitolo. 4. Papa Giovanni Paolo _____ (2°) è di orịgine polacca (*Polish*). **5.** Enrico _____ (VIII) ha avuto sette mogli. **6.** La regina (*queen*) d'Inghilterra è Elisabetta _____ (2ª). **7.** È la _____ (3ª) volta che ripeto la stessa cosa. **8.** Vittọrio Emanuele _____ (II) è stato il _____ (1°) re d'Itạlia.

G. Rispondete usando i nụmeri ordinali.

1. Quale pạgina del libro è questa? **2.** Quale capịtolo del libro è questo? **3.** Quale giorno della settimana è mercoledì? E venerdì? **4.** Aprile è il sesto mese dell'anno? E dicembre? **5.** In quale settimana di novembre festeggiamo il Thanksgiving? **6.** In quale settimana di settembre festeggiamo la Festa del Lavoro? **7.** Un minuto è la cinquantẹsima parte di un'ora? **8.** A che ora è la vostra prima lezione il lunedì? E la seconda lezione?

IV. I mesi e la data

—Il 32 marzo?!
Ma che calendario è questo!

1. In Italian, the months of the year are masculine and are *not* capitalized. They are:

gennạio	*January*	**lụglio**	*July*
febbrạio	*February*	**agosto**	*August*
marzo	*March*	**settembre**	*September*
aprile	*April*	**ottobre**	*October*
mạggio	*May*	**novembre**	*November*
giugno	*June*	**dicembre**	*December*

2. Dates are expressed according to the following pattern:

definite article	+	*number*	+	*month*	+	*year*
il		**20**		**marzo**		**1993**

The abbreviation of the above date would be written: **20/3/1993.** Note that in Italian, the day comes *before* the month (compare March 20, 1993, and 3/20/1993).

3. To express days of the month, *cardinal* numbers (1, 2, 3, etc.) are used except for the first of the month, which is indicated by the ordinal number **primo.**

Oggi è il **primo** (di) aprile.	*Today is April first.*
È il **quattọrdici** (di) lụglio.	*It is July fourteenth.*
Lia è nata il **sẹdici** ottobre.	*Lia was born on October sixteenth.*
Ạbito qui dal **tre** marzo 1980.	*I have been living here since March 3, 1980.*

4. To ask the day of the week, the day of the month, and the date, the following questions are used:

Che giorno è oggi?	*What day is today?*
Oggi è venerdì.	*Today is Friday.*

Quanti ne abbiamo oggi?	*How many (days of the month) do we have today?*
Oggi ne abbiamo trẹdici.	*Today we have thirteen (of them).*
Qual è la data di oggi?	*What is the date today?*
Oggi è il trẹdici (di) dicembre.	*Today is the thirteenth of December.*

5. The article **il** is used before the year.

Il 1992 è stato un anno bisestile.	*1992 was a leap year.*
Siamo nati **nel** 1962.	*We were born in 1962.*

Pratica

GIOVEDI 31 DICEMBRE
e VENERDI 1 GENNAIO

VEGLIONISSIMO DI S. SILVESTRO

spettacoli e cottillons orch. ILTER PELOSI

Andate anche voi al veglione di San Silvestro?

A. **Date.** Leggete queste date. Incominciate con **Oggi è il...**

1. 13/7 **2.** 1/4 **3.** 23/10 **4.** 29/5 **5.** 15/8 **6.** 17/2 **7.** 30/6 **8.** 1/1 **9.** 11/3 **10.** 18/11

B. Rispondete alle seguenti domande.

1. Quanti ne abbiamo oggi? **2.** Che giorno è oggi? **3.** Qual è la data di oggi? **4.** Quand'è il tuo compleanno? **5.** Quando incomịncia l'autunno? **6.** In che anno sei nato(a)? **7.** Quand'è Natale? **8.** Quand'è il compleanno di tua madre? **9.** Qual è l'ụltimo giorno dell'anno?

C. **Feste. Domanda e risposta.** Ecco le date di alcune feste civili e religiose in Itạlia. Incominciate le domande con **Quand'è...?**

1. Capodanno, 1/1 **2.** l'Epifania, 6/1 **3.** Pạsqua (*Easter*), in marzo o in aprile **4.** l'Anniversạrio della Liberazione, 25/4 **5.** la Festa del Lavoro, 1/5 **6.** Ferragosto*, 15/8 **7.** Tutti i Santi, 1/11 **8.** l'Immacolata Concezione, 8/12 **9.** Natale, 25/12

D. Abbinate (*Match*) le date e gli eventi e formate delle frasi complete.

25/12	Halloween
21/3	l'anno dell'unificazione d'Itạlia
1861	il primo giorno di primavera
1/1	l'anno della scoperta dell'Amẹrica
31/10	il giorno di Natale
1492	la data di dichiarazione dell'indipendenza americana
4/7	Capodanno

*Midsummer holiday

E. **Quanti anni ha?** Date l'età delle seguenti persone. Il loro anno di nascita (*birth*) è tra parentesi.

ESEMPIO mio padre (1930)
Mio padre è nato nel millenovecentotrenta; dunque (*therefore*) ha… anni.

1. la nonna di Marcello (1915) **2.** mio fratello (1973) **3.** la signora Cortese (1950) **4.** il marito della signora (1941) **5.** il cugino di Marco (1988) **6.** E tu?…

V. Le stagioni e il tempo

In primavera fa bel tempo. Ci sono molti fiori. *In estate fa caldo. C'è molto sole.* *In autunno fa brutto tempo. Piove e tira vento.* *In inverno fa freddo e nevica.*

1. The seasons are **la primavera** (*spring*); **l'estate** (*f.*) (*summer*); **l'autunno** (*autumn*); and **l'inverno** (*winter*). The article is used before these nouns except in the following expressions: **in primavera, in estate, in autunno, in inverno.***

L'autunno è molto bello.	*Fall is very beautiful.*
Vado in montagna **in estate.**	*I go to the mountains in the summer.*

2. **Fare** is used in the third person singular to express many weather conditions.

Che tempo fa?	*How is the weather?*
Fa bel tempo.	*The weather is nice.*
Fa brutto tempo.	*The weather is bad.*
Fa caldo.	*It is hot.*
Fa freddo.	*It is cold.*
Fa fresco.	*It is cool.*

3. Other common weather expressions are:

Piove. (piọvere)	*It is raining.*	**C'è nẹbbia.**	*It is foggy.*
Nẹvica. (nevicare)	*It is snowing.*	**È nuvoloso.**	*It is cloudy.*
Tira vento.	*It is windy.*	**È sereno.**	*It is clear.*
C'è il sole.	*It is sunny.*		

***Di** can be used in place of **in: d'estate; d'autunno.**

Che tempo fa a Firenze?
E in Sicilia?

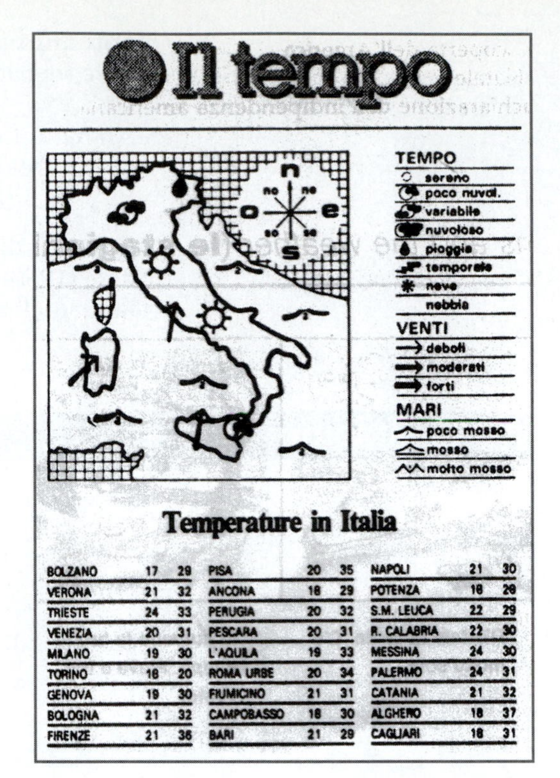

Temperature in Italia

BOLZANO	17	29	PISA	20	35	NAPOLI	21	30
VERONA	21	32	ANCONA	18	29	POTENZA	18	28
TRIESTE	24	33	PERUGIA	20	32	S.M. LEUCA	22	29
VENEZIA	20	31	PESCARA	20	31	R. CALABRIA	22	30
MILANO	19	30	L'AQUILA	19	33	MESSINA	24	30
TORINO	18	20	ROMA URBE	20	34	PALERMO	24	31
GENOVA	19	30	FIUMICINO	21	31	CATANIA	21	32
BOLOGNA	21	32	CAMPOBASSO	18	30	ALGHERO	18	37
FIRENZE	21	36	BARI	21	29	CAGLIARI	18	31

NOTE:
Piọvere and **nevicare** may be conjugated in the **passato prọssimo** with either **ẹssere** or **avere.**

Ieri ha piovuto *or* è piovuto.
Ieri ha nevicato *or* è nevicato.

Pratica

A. **Che tempo fa…? Domanda e risposta.** Nella domanda usate la preposizione appropriata.

ESEMPIO estate, New York —**Che tempo fa d'estate a New York?**
—**Fa molto caldo.**

1. agosto, Sicịlia **2.** primavera, Perụgia **3.** inverno, montagna **4.** novembre, Chicago **5.** dicembre, Florida **6.** autunno, Londra

B. **Variabilità del tempo.** Completate le frasi con l'espressione di tempo appropriata (con il verbo al **presente** o al **passato prọssimo**, secondo il caso).

1. Mi metto il cappotto perchè _____. **2.** Liliana porta l'ombrello perchè _____. **3.** L'inverno scorso _____ in montagna. **4.** In autunno a Milano, non vediamo bene perchè _____. **5.** Anche se è estate, a San Francisco abbiamo bisogno di un golf perchè _____. **6.** Fạccio lunghe passeggiate quando _____. **7.** D'estate mi metto un vestito leggero perchè _____. **8.** Non abbiamo bisogno dell'impermeạbile quando non _____. **9.** Chicago si chiama «*the windy city*» perchè _____. **10.** L'estate scorsa _____.

C. Rispondete alle seguenti domande.

1. Oggi è sereno o è nuvoloso? **2.** Ha piovuto la settimana scorsa? **3.** Che tempo ha fatto l'inverno scorso? **4.** Quando nẹvica nella Sua città? **5.** Ha nevicato in gennạio? **6.** In che mese fa molto caldo in questa città? **7.** Piove spesso o solo qualche volta qui? **8.** Qual è la stagione della piọggia in questa città? **9.** C'è mai nẹbbia qui? **10.** Tira vento? Quando?

D. Che cosa Le piace fare quando...? Combinate gli elementi delle due colonne e formate una frase completa. Incominciate sempre con **quando** e usate sempre l'espressione **mi piace...**

Quando	piove nẹvica tira vento fa bel tempo è nuvoloso è sereno fa caldo	**mi piace**	divertirmi con un aquilone (*kite*). guardare dalla finestra gli ombrelli delle persone. guardare il cielo. pensare all'ạlbero di Natale. camminare al sole. bere una bevanda fresca. stare a letto.

LETTURA

Firenze. Vetrina di un negozio d'abbigliamento per uomo.

ALLA *RINASCENTE* (department store)

Questa mattina Antọnio è andato alla Rinascente per comprarsi un completo nuovo. Di sọlito Antọnio porta jeans, camịcia e maglione, ma la settimana *prọssima* ha un *collọquio* importante, e gli amici gli hanno detto: «Antọnio, non dimenticare che la prima impressione è quella che conta!» *Ẹccolo* ora nel reparto abbigliamento maschile. Un commesso si avvicina.

next/interview

here he is

Commesso	Buon giorno. Desịdera un completo? Di che colore?	
Antonio	Non so, *forse* grigio.	perhaps
Commesso	In tinta unita o a righe?	
Antonio	Forse *è mẹglio* in tinta unita.	it is better
Commesso	Che tạglia porta?	
Antonio	Non lo so esattamente. Forse *52* o *54*.	(large sizes)
Commesso	Lo vuole pesante o *di mezza stagione?*	in-between-seasons
Antonio	Di mezza stagione; così può andare in tutte le stagioni.	
Commesso	Ecco un ạbito che *fa per Lei*, grigio *fumo*, di lana, non troppo pesante. È in svẹndita. Vuole provarlo?	suits you/smoke
Antonio	Okey. (*Dopo la prova*) La giacca mi va bene, ma i pantaloni sono lunghi.	
Commesso	*Nessun* problema. Li *accorciamo* e per sạbato sono pronti.	no/we will shorten
Antonio	Quanto costa?	
Commesso	Solo seicentocinquantamila lire. È un *affare!*	bargain
Antonio	Così caro?! Costa *un ọcchio della testa!*	a fortune
Commesso	Eh, caro signore, *oggigiorno* tutto costa caro. D'altra parte, viviamo *una volta sola!*	nowadays only once
Antonio	Ma sì, lo compro, e *addio risparmi!*	goodbye savings

Comprensione

1. Perchè Antọnio è andato in un negọzio di abbigliamento?
2. Perchè Antọnio ha bisogno di un completo nuovo?
3. Che cosa hanno detto gli amici ad Antọnio?
4. Quando Antọnio è nel negọzio, sa esattamente cosa vuole o è indeciso?
5. Di che colore è il completo che Antọnio prova? È pesante? È in svẹndita?
6. Vanno bene i pantaloni?
7. Antọnio trova il completo caro o a buon mercato (*cheap*)? Lo compra?

Domande personali

1. Lei va spesso a fare le spese in un negọzio di abbigliamento?
2. Ha un negọzio preferito? Come si chiama?
3. Come si veste Lei quando si presenta ad un collọquio?
4. Qual è il colore che Lei preferisce?
5. Porta dei vestiti leggeri d'inverno?
6. Fa molto freddo d'inverno nella Sua città? Piove molto? E d'estate, che tempo fa?
7. Spende molto Lei per vestirsi?
8. Ci sono molte svẹndite nel Suo negọzio d'abbigliamento preferito?

ATTIVITÀ SUPPLEMENTARI

A. **Nella vetrina.** Domanda al commesso (uno studente/una studentessa) quanto cọstano gli artịcoli d'abbigliamento nella vetrina (*shop window*) del negọzio. Usa l'aggettivo **quello** nelle sue forme appropriate. Il commesso risponde. (Il prezzo, approssimativo, è in dọllari).

ESEMPIO **—Scusi, per favore, quanto cọstano quelle scarpe?**
—Cọstano 65 dọllari.

B.Come ti vesti?

1. Il presidente degli Stati Uniti ti ha invitato(a) ad un pranzo ufficiale alla Casa Bianca.
2. Il tuo amico e la sua famịglia ti hanno invitato(a) a passare un fine settimana con loro nel loro cottage in montagna. È novembre e fa freddo.
3. Vai a un concerto rock con degli amici. È lụglio e fa molto caldo.
4. Sạbato c'è una riunione di famịglia al ristorante per festeggiare le nozze d'oro (*50-year wedding anniversary*) dei tuoi nonni.

C. **Diạlogo a due.** Il tuo fratello minore (*younger*) ti dice che vuole fare alcune cose. Tu lo consigli di farle o non farle perchè...

ESEMPIO *He would like to sleep for another hour./Tell him to get up because it is already eight o'clock.*
—Vorrei dormire un'altra ora.
—Ạlzati perchè sono già le otto.

1. *He would like to buy a brown suit./Advise him to buy the grey one because it is a bargain.*
2. *He wants to buy a pair of shoes./Advise him not to buy in that shop because it is too expensive.*
3. *He is taking the car to go downtown./Tell him to go, but to be careful because it is about to rain.*
4. *He is going out for a long walk./Advise him not to go out now because it is too hot.*
5. *Today he is coming home late./Tell him it is O.K., but not to be late for supper.*

D. Ecco le supermodelle! Immaginate di ẹssere alla sfilata di moda (*fashion show*) rappresentata nella foto a pạgina 179. Fate i vostri commenti:

Ti piace questa...?
Cosa pensi di quel...?
Mi piace quella...
Preferisco questi...
Non mi piacciono quei... perchè...

E. Che tạglia porti?

	Abiti da donna					Abiti da uomo				
Italia	36	38	40	42	44	44	46	48	50	52
USA	6	8	10	12	14	34	36	38	40	42

F. Come si dice in italiano?

1. Patrịzia, why don't we go shopping today?
2. Oh, not today. It is raining, and it is cold. Besides (**Inoltre**), I went shopping yesterday.
3. Really? What did you buy?
4. I bought these black boots.
5. They are very beautiful. Next week I plan to (**penso di**) go shopping, too (**anch'io**). Do you want to come with me?
6. Yes. What do you want to buy?
7. I would like to buy a two-piece suit for my birthday.
8. When exactly is your birthday? I know it is in May, but I forgot the exact (**esatta**) date.
9. I was born on June 17, 1964.
10. Oh, that's right! The other day I saw a beautiful silk blouse in Armani's window (**vetrina**), and I am planning to buy that blouse for your birthday.
11. Oh, Patrịzia, thank you.

Che cosa ammirano?

Vocabolario

Nomi

l'abitante (*m.* & *f.*)	*inhabitant*
agosto	*August*
aprile	*April*
l'artịcolo	*item*
l'autunno	*autumn, fall*
il calendạrio	*calendar*
il Capodanno	*New Year's Day*
il cielo	*sky*
il cioccolato	*chocolate*
il commesso, la commessa	*salesperson*
la data	*date*
dicembre	*December*
l'estate (*f.*)	*summer*
febbrạio	*February*
gennạio	*January*
giugno	*June*
l'inverno	*winter*
lụglio	*July*
mạggio	*May*
marzo	*March*
la moda	*fashion*
il Natale	*Christmas*
la nẹbbia	*fog*
la neve	*snow*
novembre	*November*
ottobre	*October*
la Pasqua	*Easter*
la piọggia	*rain*
la primavera	*spring*
il profumo	*perfume*
il reparto	*department (of a store)*
il resto	*change (money)*
la roba	*stuff, things*
settembre	*September*
il sole	*sun*
la stagione	*season*
lo, (la) stilista	*designer*
la tasca	*pocket*
il vento	*wind*
la vetrina	*display window*

Aggettivi

calmo	*calm*
elegante	*elegant*
indeciso	*indecisive*
largo (*pl.* larghi)	*large, wide*
lungo (*pl.* lunghi)	*long*
moderno	*modern*
prạtico	*practical*
prudente	*cautious*
quello	*that*
stretto	*narrow, tight*

Verbi

avvicinarsi	*to go near, to get closer*
consigliare	*to advise*
decịdere (*p.p.* deciso)	*to decide*
nevicare	*to snow*
piọvere	*to rain*
promẹttere (*p.p.* promesso)	*to promise*
spedire(-isc)	*to mail, to send*
sperare	*to hope*

Altre espressioni

a buon mercato	*cheap*
andare bene	*to fit*
C'è il sole.	*It is sunny.*
C'è nẹbbia.	*It is foggy.*
Così tanto!	*That much!*
costare un ọcchio della testa	*to cost a fortune*
di mezza stagione	*in-between-seasons*
di moda	*fashionable*
dunque	*so, therefore*
È nuvoloso.	*It is cloudy.*
È sereno.	*It is clear.*
È un affare.	*It is a bargain.*
È vero!	*That's right!*
Fa bel tempo.	*It is nice weather.*
Fa brutto tempo.	*It is bad weather.*
Fa caldo.	*It is hot.*
Fa freddo.	*It is cold.*
Fa fresco.	*It is cool.*
fare le valịgie	*to pack (suitcases)*
farne a meno	*to do without it*
Ho sentito dire che…	*I heard that…*
là	*over there*
mẹttere a posto	*to put in its place*
nessun problema	*no problem*
la settimana prossima	*next week*
scarpe da tennis	*tennis shoes*
stare zitto	*to be quiet*
Tira vento.	*It is windy.*
veramente	*truly, really*

Venezia. Maschere di Carnevale vicino al Ponte dei Sospiri.

ALCUNE FESTE DELL'ANNO

Il calendạrio italiano abbonda di giorni festivi. Le celebrazioni sono *legate* alle tradizioni religiose, popolari e... gastronọmiche.

tied to

L'anno incomịncia con la festa di Capodanno (1 gennạio). In questo giorno la gente *si scạmbia* gli auguri, dopo i divertimenti della notte di San Silvestro (31 dicembre). Il 6 gennạio è l'Epifania, festa che commẹmora la vịsita dei tre Re Magi al bambino Gesù. La notte dell'Epifania molti bambini aspẹttano l'arrivo della Befana che, secondo la leggenda, è una donna vẹcchia e brutta, ma generosa perchè porta *giocạttoli.*

exchange / toys

Sẹgue il Carnevale che contịnua *fino alla Quarẹsima.* La gente si diverte con banchetti, balli mascherati e *sfilate* di *carri* grotteschi; famosi sono il Carnevale di Viarẹggio, in Toscana, e quello di Venẹzia, città di orịgine delle *mạschere.* La *Pạsqua* (in primavera) è, con il Natale, la più solenne festa religiosa dell'anno.

until Lent / parades/floats / masks/Easter

Il Ferragosto (15 agosto) è la festa più importante dell'estate. *Essa* ha orịgine nell'*usanza* pagana di cele-

it/custom

Assisi (Umbria). Festa di Calendimaggio: la città festeggia l'arrivo del mese di maggio.

brare le feste (latino: «feriae») in onore dell'imperatore romano Augusto. In questo periodo gli Italiani abbandonano la città e partono per le vacanze.

Il Natale e il giorno seguente, Santo Stefano, hanno perso parte del loro carattere religioso. L'albero di Natale ha sostituito in molte case il *presepio,* usanza iniziata da San Francesco d'Assisi (1182–1226). Il dolce tipico di questi giorni è il *panettone.*

Nativity scene

sweet bread with raisins

Quasi ogni città, grande o piccola, celebra anche il suo santo protettore e la data di qualche *avvenimento* storico. Le antiche usanze restano *vive* nella vita italiana e ritornano ogni anno con i *costumi* di quell'epoca.

event
alive
customs

Comprensione

Rispondete alle seguenti domande.

1. In quale giorno auguriamo «Buon Anno»?
2. In quale periodo dell'anno molti Italiani portano costumi e maschere, e si divertono?
3. In quale festa la Befana porta giocattoli ai bambini?
4. Come si chiama la festa che la Chiesa celebra in primavera?
5. Gli Italiani aspettano con impazienza il 15 agosto. Perchè?
6. L'albero di Natale ha sostituito un'altra usanza: quale?

10 IN CUCINA

Un'ottima cuoca nella sua cucina.

Punti di vista

Il giorno di Pasqua
Dopo il pranzo

Punti grammaticali

I I pronomi diretti
II I pronomi indiretti
III I pronomi con l'infinito e *ecco!*
IV L'imperativo con un pronome (diretto, indiretto o riflessivo)
Esclamazioni comuni

Lettura

Una ricetta semplice: fusilli alla vesuviana

Pagina culturale

La cucina italiana

PUNTI DI VISTA

La colomba e le uova pasquali.

IL GIORNO DI *PASQUA*

Pasqua: Easter

Oggi è la domenica di Pasqua e, per festeggiar*la*, Marco e Paolo sono ritornati da Bologna, dove studiano medicina. Sono venuti per passare alcuni giorni con la loro famiglia. È l'ora del pranzo: i due fratelli *apparecchiano* la tavola.

la: it
apparecchiano: set

Paolo	Hai messo i piatti, le posate e i bicchieri?	
Marco	Sì, li ho già messi. E anche *i tovaglioli.*	napkins
Paolo	Hai preso l'ạcqua minerale dal frigo?	
Marco	Ma sì! L'ho presa! E tu, hai portato a casa *la colomba pasquale?*	Easter cake (in the shape of a dove)
Paolo	Certo, ho comprato una colomba Motta. E i fiori?	
Marco	Ho dimenticato di comprarli, ma ho preso un bell'uovo di cioccolato con la sorpresa*. Lo diamo adesso alla mamma?	
Paolo	*È mẹglio* aspettare la fine del pranzo.	It is better

E così, alla fine del pranzo, la mamma riceve un grosso uovo di cioccolato, con gli auguri di Pạsqua. Lei è sorpresa e dice *scherzando:*—Ma com'è pesante! Cosa c'è dentro? Un milione di lire?

scherzando: jokingly

---

*The chocolate Easter egg is hollow and contains a surprise.

1. Che giorno è oggi?
2. Sono cugini Marco e Paolo?
3. Da dove sono ritornati?
4. Cosa fanno a Bologna?
5. Con chi festeggiano il giorno di Pasqua?
6. Che cosa hanno messo sulla tavola?
7. Da dove ha preso l'acqua minerale Paolo?
8. Cosa ha comprato Paolo per la festa di Pasqua?
9. Marco ha comprato i fiori?
10. Cos'ha comprato?

Studio di parole

LA CUCINA E GLI INGREDIENTI

1 **i fornelli** 2 **il forno** 3 **la lavastoviglie** 4 **il lavandino** 5 **i cassetti** 6 **il frigo(rifero)** 7 **l'armadietto** 8 **la pentola** 9 **il piatto** 10 **il bicchiere** 11 **la tazza** 12 **le posate: il cucchiaio, il cucchiaino** (teaspoon), **il coltello, la forchetta** 13 **la tovaglia** 14 **il tovagliolo** 15 **il tavolo (la tavola)***

la farina flour
il burro butter
lo zucchero sugar
l'uovo (*pl.* **le uova**) egg(s)
il sale salt
il pepe pepper
l'olio oil
l'aceto vinegar
l'aglio garlic
la cipolla onion
condire to dress (a salad); to season
cucinare al forno to bake
asciugare to dry
rompere (*p.p.* **rotto**) to break

*__Tavola__ is used when referring to meals: **apparecchiare la tavola** (*to set the table*): **andiamo a tavola!**

Applicazione

A. Rispondete.

1. Guardate il disegno. Che cosa vedete su un fornello?
2. Che cosa vedete sotto i fornelli?
3. Quali ingredienti sono necessari per preparare una torta?
4. Dove mettiamo il latte per conservarlo (*to keep it*) fresco?
5. Quai ingredienti ụsano gli Italiani per condire l'insalata?
6. Che cosa mettiamo sulla tạvola per un pranzo elegante?
7. Dove mettiamo le posate quando sono lavate?

B. Descrivete.

1. È la festa del Thanksgiving e i vostri genitori sono venuti a trovarvi. Come apparecchiate la tạvola e cosa servite?

C. Domande personali.

1. Lei passa molto tempo o poco tempo in cucina?
2. Lei ha un forno a micro-onde (*microwave*)? Una lavastovịglie?
3. Cosa prepara per colazione? Delle uova?
4. Cosa beve? Un caffè? Un succo di frutta?...
5. A mezzogiorno va a casa (al dormitọrio) per il pranzo, o mạngia fuori?
6. Quando Lei ha degli invitati per un'occasione speciale, usa i tovaglioli di carta o quelli di cotone? Cucina una torta al forno o la compra dal pasticciere (*baker*)?

Ascoltiamo!

Dopo il pranzo. *Listen to Paolo's and Marco's conversation as they wash the dishes after Easter dinner, then answer the following questions.*

Comprensione

1. Paolo e Marco si ripọsano dopo il pranzo?
2. Cosa fanno i due ragazzi in cucina?
3. Perchè Marco vuole lavare i piatti domani?
4. Perchè non pọssono lavarli domani?
5. Che cosa pẹnsano di dire al papà? Perchè?
6. Quando pẹnsano di dirlo al papà?
7. Marco sta attento quando asciuga i piatti o è maldestro (*clumsy*)?

Dialogo

Domandate a un compagno (una compagna) com'è la cucina (*kitchen*) della sua famiglia.

PUNTI GRAMMATICALI

I I pronomi diretti

—Liliana, ti invito a cena.
—Inviti anche Maria e Teresa?
—Sì, le invito.
—Fai gli spaghetti?
—Sì, li fạccio.

1. Lucia invita le sue amiche a cena?
2. Prepara gli spaghetti?

1. You have already learned the direct object pronouns **lo, la, li, le** (Chapter 5). Remember that a direct object is a noun or a pronoun expressing the person(s) or thing(s) directly affected by the verb. It answers the question *whom?* or *what?*

   Here is a chart of all the direct object pronouns:

Singular			Plural		
mi (m')	*me*	**mi** chiamano	**ci**	*us*	**ci** chiamano
ti (t')	*you (familiar)*	**ti** chiamano	**vi**	*you (familiar)*	**vi** chiamano
lo (l')	*him, it*	**lo** chiamano	**li**	*them (m.)*	**li** chiamano
la (l')	*her, it*	**la** chiamano	**le**	*them (f.)*	**le** chiamano
La (L')*	*you (formal, m. & f.)*	**La** chiamano	**Li, Le**	*you (formal, m. & f.)*	**Li/Le** chiamano

*The formal pronoun **La (L')** is both masculine and feminine, as in **arrivederLa.**

Note that all the pronouns immediately precede the verb. This happens also in a negative sentence. The final vowel of a singular direct object pronoun may be dropped before a vowel or an *h*.

Apro il frigo. **L'**apro. — *I open the refrigerator. I open it.*
Leggo le lẹttere. **Le** leggo. — *I read the letters. I read them.*
Mi vẹdono? No, non **ti** vẹdono. — *Do they see me? No, they don't see you.*
Non **ci** invitano mai. — *They never invite us.*
Buona sera, dottore. **La** vedo domani. — *Good evening, Doctor. I'll see you tomorrow.*
Signori Bianchi, **Li** chịamano al telẹfono. — *Mr. and Mrs. Bianchi, they are calling you on the phone.*

2. In the case of a **passato prọssimo**, remember that:

   a) the pronoun comes before the auxiliary verb **avere;**

   b) the past participle must agree in gender and number with the direct object pronouns **lo, la, La, li, le, Li, Le.** Agreement with the other direct object pronouns is optional.

Hai cucinato le patate? — *Did you cook the potatoes?*
Sì, **le** ho cucinat**e**. — *Yes, I cooked them.*

Avete incontrato Luigi? — *Did you meet Luigi?*
No, non **l'**abbiamo incontrat**o**. — *No, we did not meet him.*

Hai accompagnato i ragazzi? — *Did you accompany the boys?*
Sì, **li** ho accompagnat**i**. — *Yes, I accompanied them.*

Signora Rossi, non **L'**ho vist**a**. — *Mrs. Rossi, I did not see you.*
Gina, **ti** ho aspettat**o** (aspettat**a**). — *Gina, I waited for you.*

3. Contrary to their English equivalents, verbs such as **ascoltare** (*to listen to*), **guardare** (*to look at*), **cercare** (*to look for*), and **aspettare** (*to wait for*) are not followed by a preposition; they therefore take a direct object.

Cerchi la ricetta? — *Are you looking for the recipe?*
Sì, **la** cerco. — *Yes, I'm looking for it.*
Guardi il ricettạrio? — *Are you looking at the cookbook?*
Sì, **lo** guardo. — *Yes, I'm looking at it.*
Vi aspetto stasera alle otto. — *I will be waiting for (expecting) you at eight o'clock tonight.*
Avete ascoltato le notịzie? — *Did you listen to the news?*
No, non **le** abbiamo ascoltate. — *No, we did not listen to it.*

4. **Sapere** takes the direct object pronoun **lo** to replace a dependent clause.

Sai **chi è Sophia Loren?** — *Do you know who Sophia Loren is?*
Sì, **lo** so. È un'attrice. — *Yes, I know (it). She is an actress.*
Sapete **quando è morto J.F.K.?** — *Do you know when J.F.K. died?*
No, non **lo** sappiamo. — *No, we do not know (it).*

Pratica

A. Voi siete in cucina e pensate ad alcune cose che dovete fare. Sostituite il nome in corsivo (*italics*) con il pronome appropriato.

ESEMPIO Aspetto *il mio amico* a cena. **Lo aspetto.**

1. Apparecchio *la tavola.* **2.** Metto *la tovaglia.* **3.** Metto *i piatti e i bicchieri.* **4.** Prendo *l'acqua minerale* dal frigo. **5.** Metto *le lasagne* nel forno. **6.** Lavo *l'insalata.* **7.** Apro *la porta* al mio amico. **8.** Servo *la cena.* **9.** Non servo *il dolce* perchè siamo a dieta (*we are on a diet*).

B. Domanda e risposta. Voi domandate a un(a) compagno(a) la sua opinione sulle seguenti cose. Il (La) compagno(a) risponde, usando il pronome appropriato.

ESEMPIO la pizza/buona, cattiva **—Come trovi la pizza?**
—La trovo buona (o cattiva).

1. il vino Valpolicella/eccellente, mediocre **2.** le ricette francesi/semplici, complicate **3.** la moda di quest'anno/elegante, inelegante **4.** lo studio dell'italiano/facile, difficile **5.** i professori dell'università/severi, indulgenti **6.** l'ultimo film di Bette Midler/divertente, noioso **7.** le sere d'inverno/lunghe, corte **8.** il caffè espresso/forte, debole **9.** i giorni di pioggia/tristi, allegri **10.** i mezzi di trasporto in Italia/efficienti, inefficienti

C. Lucio si lamenta (*complains*) perchè l'amico non è più cortese con lui. Gianni si difende (*defends himself*). Completate il dialogo con i pronomi appropriati.

Lucio —Tu non _____ guardi più, non _____ saluti quando _____ incontri, non _____ aspetti più dopo la lezione d'italiano e non _____ inviti più a bere un caffè insieme; insomma (*in short*), _____ ignori. Perchè? Che cosa ho fatto?

Gianni —Venerdì scorso _____ ho aspettato per mezz'ora. Più tardi (*later*), quando _____ ho cercato, non _____ ho trovato. Poi _____ ho visto al caffè con altri amici. _____ ho chiamato, ma tu hai fatto finta (*pretended*) di non vedermi. E adesso tu domandi che cosa hai fatto?

D. I genitori parlano con il figlio Aldo, giornalista, che è ritornato da un lungo viaggio. Completate il dialogo con i pronomi appropriati.

Aldo —Cari mamma e papà, finalmente _____ rivedo (*I see you again*)! Come state?

Il papà —Noi stiamo benone. Ma tu, come _____ trovi (*do you find us*)? Tristi e vecchi forse (*perhaps*)?

Aldo —Anzi (*on the contrary*), _____ trovo sempre giovani e in ottima forma, e _____ rivedo con tanto piacere!

E. Rispondete alle seguenti domande con i pronomi appropriati.

ESEMPIO —Dove lavi *i piatti?*
—Li lavo nella lavastoviglie.

1. Quando inviti *i tuoi amici?* 2. Dove cucini *l'arrosto?* 3. A chi mandi *gli inviti?* 4. Dove fai *la spesa?* 5. Dove trovi *le tue ricette?* 6. Come prepari *le uova?* Strapazzate (*scrambled*) o sode (*hard-boiled*)? 7. Usi *il burro* quando cucini? 8. Per una cena elegante, metti *la tovaglia?* 9. Metti *il formaggio* sui maccheroni?

F. **Domanda e risposta.** Tu hai perso alcune delle tue cose. Un amico (un'amica) ti domanda se le hai trovate. Tu rispondi negativamente.

ESEMPIO gli appunti **—Hai trovato i tuoi appunti?**
—No, non li ho trovati.

1. il portafoglio 2. le chiavi 3. gli occhiali da sole 4. la sveglia 5. l'orologio 6. la maglietta 7. il nuovo indirizzo 8. il biglietto dell'aereo 9. i soldi 10. le cravatte di seta

G. **Domanda e risposta.** Voi dovete apparecchiare (*to set*) la tavola. Vostra madre vi domanda se avete messo le seguenti cose.

ESEMPIO il vino **—Avete messo il vino?**
—Sì, l'abbiamo messo. *o*
—No, non l'abbiamo messo.

1. la tovaglia 2. i piatti nuovi 3. i bicchieri 4. le posate 5. i tovaglioli 6. il pane 7. il sale e il pepe 8. l'acqua minerale 9. i grissini (*bread sticks*) 10. le tazze

H. **Domanda e risposta.** Domandate a un(a) compagno(a) se oggi ha fatto le seguenti cose. Usate per ogni frase espressioni di tempo differenti.

ESEMPIO leggere il giornale **—Hai letto il giornale oggi?**
—No, l'ho letto ieri (domenica scorsa, venerdì mattina, ecc.).

1. mangiare le lasagne 2. ascoltare la radio 3. chiamare il tuo amico 4. salutare i compagni di classe 5. dare gli esami una settimana fa 6. prendere la macchina 7. vedere i tuoi genitori 8. fare i compiti.

II. I pronomi indiretti

—Marcello dà i cioccolatini a Lucia?
—No, le dà i fiori.

1. An indirect object pronoun replaces the person *to whom* the action is directed.

   It is used with verbs of *giving:* **dare, prestare, offrire, mandare, restituire, consigliare, regalare, portare**, etc., and with verbs of *oral* and *written communication:* **parlare, dire, domandare, chiẹdere, rispọndere, telefonare, scrịvere, insegnare, spiegare**, etc. The preposition **a** follows these verbs and precedes the name of the person to whom the action is directed.

   Scrivo **una lẹttera.** (*direct object*)
   Scrivo una lẹttera **a Lucia.** (*indirect object*)

   Here are the forms of the indirect object pronouns:

Singular			*Plural*		
mi (m')	*(to) me*	**mi** scrịvono	**ci**	*(to) us*	**ci** scrịvono
ti (t')	*(to) you (familiar)*	**ti** scrịvono	**vi**	*(to) you (familiar)*	**vi** scrịvono
gli	*(to) him*	**gli** scrịvono	**loro** *or* **gli**	*(to) them (m. & f.)*	(scrịvono **loro** (**gli** scrịvono)
le	*(to) her*	**le** scrịvono			
Le*	*(to) you (formal, m. & f.)*	**Le** scrịvono	**Loro** *or* **Gli***	*(to) you (formal, m. & f.)*	scrịvono **Loro** *(very formal)*

*The capital letter in **Le, Loro,** and **Gli** is optional and is used to avoid ambiguity.

2. Note that the pronouns **mi**, **ti**, **ci**, and **vi** can be used as direct and indirect object pronouns. Like the direct object pronouns, indirect object pronouns all precede the conjugated form of the verb, except **loro**, which always follows the verb. In negative sentences, **non** precedes the pronouns.

Mi dai un gettone?	*Will you give **me** a token?*
Chi **ti** telẹfona?	*Who is calling **you**?*
Non **gli** parlo.	*I am not speaking to **him**.*
Perchè non **ci** scrivete?	*Why don't you write **to us**?*
Le offro un caffè.	*I am offering **you** a cup of coffee.*
Domando **Loro** se è giusto.	*I am asking **you** if it is right.*

NOTE:
In contemporary Italian, the tendency is to replace **loro** with the plural **gli**.

Gli parlo. *or* Parlo **loro**.	*I am speaking **to them**.*

3. When a verb is conjugated in the **passato prọssimo**, the past participle *never* agrees with the indirect object pronoun.

Le ho parlat**o** ieri.	*I spoke **to her** yesterday.*
Non **gli** abbiamo telefonat**o**.	*We did not call **them**.*

4. Contrary to English, **telefonare** and **rispọndere** take an indirect object pronoun.

Quando telẹfoni a Lucia?	*When are you going to call Lucia?*
Le telẹfono stasera.	*I'll call her tonight.*
Hai risposto a Piero?	*Did you answer Piero?*
No, non **gli** ho risposto.	*No, I didn't answer him.*

Pratica

A. Sostituite le parole in corsivo con i pronomi appropriati.

1. Scrivo *a mia cugina.* **2.** Perchè non telẹfoni *a tuo fratello?* **3.** Lucia spiega una ricetta *a Liliana.* **4.** Presto il libro di cucina *al mio ragazzo.* **5.** Do cento dollari *a mia sorella.* **6.** I due ragazzi chiẹdono un favore *al padre.* **7.** Liliana scrive una cartolina *a sua madre.* **8.** Date spesso dei consigli *ai vostri amici?* **9.** Paolo manda dei fiori *alla sua ragazza.*

B. Ti piace telefonare e dici a chi telẹfoni e perchè.

ESEMPIO Pạolo, un piacere **Telẹfono a Pạolo e gli chiedo un piacere.**

1. mia madre, dei soldi **2.** mio padre, un consịglio **3.** i miei nonni, la mạcchina **4.** Maria, il nụmero di telẹfono di Lia **5.** Pạolo, l'indirizzo di Anna **6.** i miei zii, notịzie dei miei cugini **7.** la mia compagna di classe, gli appunti di chịmica **8.** l'agente di viaggi, informazioni **9.** i miei fratelli, un prẹstito (*loan*) **10.** la dottoressa, un appuntamento

C. **Domanda e risposta.** Seguite l'esẹmpio.

ESEMPIO portare (to take) a casa/se ho tempo **—Mi porti a casa?**
—Ti porto a casa se ho tempo.

1. ascoltare/se è una cosa breve 2. aspettare/se fai presto 3. invitare a cena/se paghi tu 4. dare l'indirizzo di Lucia/se lo trovo 5. prestare il libro di cucina/se non mi serve 6. offrire un caffè dopo la lezione/se non è troppo tardi 7. chiamare domani mattina/se è necessario 8. fare un favore/se posso

D. **Domanda e risposta.** Fate la parte (*play the role*) delle seguenti persone e completate con i pronomi appropriati.

ESEMPIO Signor Vita —Dottore, come **mi** trova?
Dottore —**La** trovo in ottima forma. (*excellent shape*).

1. Signora Verdi —Dottore, cosa _____ suggerisce di prendere?
   Dottore — ____ consiglio molte spremute d'arancia e aspirine.
2. Pierino —Antonio, _____ regali un libro per bambini?
   Antonio —Se fai il bravo (*are good*), _____ compro il libro di Pinocchio.
3. Cameriere —Cosa _____ porto, signorina?
   Signorina —Un cappuccino e una brioche, per favore.
4. Signora Neri —Cara signora Reggio, _____ ho chiamata ieri sera, ma nessuno (*nobody*) ha risposto.
   Signora Reggio —Signora, _____ prego (*I beg you*) di scusarmi, ma non ero (*was*) a casa.

E. Immaginate una conversazione tra un padre e i figli. Rispondete alle domande del padre affermativamente o negativamente.

ESEMPIO —Non vi porto spesso a teatro?
—Sì, ci porti spesso a teatro. *o*
—No, non ci porti spesso.

1. Non vi consiglio sempre bene? 2. Non vi do abbastanza soldi? 3. Non vi invito sempre al ristorante? 4. Non vi compro sempre cose nuove? 5. Non vi presto la macchina? 6. Non vi spiego l'algebra? 7. Non vi aiuto quando siete in difficoltà? 8. Non vi ascolto quando avete dei problemi?

F. **Domanda e risposta.**

ESEMPIO parlare, professore **—Quando parli al tuo professore?**
—Gli ho parlato l'altro ieri (*o* **venerdì**, *o...*).

1. rispondere, madre 2. chiedere un consiglio, padre 3. scrivere, sorelle 4. suggerire un ristorante, amico 5. telefonare, zio 6. chiedere un appuntamento, professoressa 7. dare l'indirizzo, parenti 8. offrire un pranzo, genitori 9. mandare un regalo, fratello 10. spiegare la situazione, compagne di classe

G. Rispondete alle domande sostituendo le parole in corsivo con i pronomi.

ESEMPIO —Quando dai dei consigli *al tuo amico?*/quando ha dei problemi
—Gli do dei consigli quando ha dei problemi.

1. Quando telẹfoni *a tua madre?*/la domẹnica 2. Quando *ci* mandi una cartolina?/quando arrivo a Roma 3. Quando presti il libro di cucina *alla tua amica?*/quando dà una festa 4. Quando scrivi *ai tuoi genitori?*/quando ho bisogno di soldi 5. Quando *mi* fai gli auguri?/il giorno del tuo compleanno 6. Quando *ci* offri un gelato?/dopo cena 7. Quando rispondi *ai tuoi parenti?*/quando ho tempo 8. Quando porti un regalo *a tua madre?*/per Natale

H. **La prova dell'amicịzia** (*Test of friendship*). Rispondete con una frase completa, sostituendo il **pronome diretto** o **indiretto** alle parole fra parentesi, secondo l'esẹmpio.

ESEMPIO Per il compleanno del tuo ragazzo (della tua ragazza):
a. hai portato (il tuo ragazzo, la tua ragazza) allo zoo?
b. hai portato (il tuo ragazzo, la tua ragazza) a cena e a teatro?
L'ho portato(a) a cena e a teatro. (*o...*)

1. Per il giorno di San Valentino:
   a. hai portato (*alla tua ragazza, al tuo ragazzo*) dei Baci Perugina (*chocolates from Perugia*)?
   b. hai portato (*alla tua ragazza, al tuo ragazzo*) dei Baci Perugina e un regalo?

2. Per Pạsqua:
   a. hai scritto una cartolina (*agli amici lontani*)?
   b. hai telefonato (*agli amici lontani*)?

3. I tuoi amici sono arrivati in ritardo a un appuntamento e tu:
   a. non hai aspettato (*i tuoi amici*)?
   b. hai aspettato (*i tuoi amici*)?

4. Quando tu e la tua amica (il tuo amico) avete litigato (*had an argument*):
   a. non hai telefonato (*alla tua amica, al tuo amico*) per fare la pace (*peace*)?
   b. hai telefonato (*alla tua amica, al tuo amico*) per fare la pace?

5. L'ụltima volta che sei andato al ristorante con gli amici:
   a. non hai pagato (*il conto*)?
   b. hai pagato (*il conto*) per tutti?

6. Quando un amico (un'amica) ti ha chiesto un favore:
   a. hai detto (*all'amico, all'amica*) di no?
   b. hai fatto il favore (*all'amico, all'amica*)?

7. Quando la tua amica (il tuo amico) ti ha chiesto un consịglio:
   a. hai detto (*alla tua amica, al tuo amico*) che non sei «Dear Abby».
   b. hai dato un consịglio (*alla tua amica, al tuo amico*).

Se hai totalizzato sette **b**, sei un vero amico (una vera amica); se hai totalizzato meno di (*fewer than*) quattro **b**, c'è sempre tempo per migliorare (*to improve*).

III. I pronomi con l'infinito e *ecco!*

—Che cos'è?
—Non lo so! Dobbiamo studiarlo bene.

1. When a direct or indirect pronoun is the object of an infinitive, it is attached to the infinitive, which drops the final **-e.**

Non desịdero veder**la.**	*I don't wish to see her.*
Preferisco scrịver**le.**	*I prefer to write to her.*

NOTE:
With the verbs **potere**, **volere**, **dovere**, and **sapere**, the object pronoun may be placed before the conjugated verb or attached to the infinitive.

Ti posso parlare?
Posso parlar**ti?** } *May I speak to you?*

2. A direct object pronoun is attached to the expression **ecco**!

Ẹcco**lo!**	*Here (There) he is!*
Ẹcco**mi!**	*Here I am!*

Pratica

A. Sostituite le espressioni in corsivo con il pronome appropriato.

1. Incomịncio a capire *questa lịngua.* **2.** Abbiamo bisogno di parlare *a Tonino.* **3.** Preferisco scrịvere *a Luisa* domani. **4.** Ho deciso di invitare *gli amici.* **5.** Ho dimenticato di comprare *le uova.* **6.** Quest'anno non posso fare molti regali *ai miei amici.* **7.** Desịdero invitare *le mie amiche* a una festa. **8.** Sapete parlare bene *lo spagnolo?* **9.** Vọglio trovare *le mie chiavi!* **10.** Non posso aspettare *mio fratello.* **11.** Devi prẹndere *la mạcchina?*

B. Domanda e risposta. Sei indeciso(a) e domandi a tuo fratello (a tua sorella) se (*whether*) devi fare le seguenti cose. Lui (Lei) risponde affermativamente, usando il pronome oggetto appropriato.

ESEMPIO studiare l'italiano —**Devo studiare l'italiano?**
—**Sì, devi studiarlo.** *o*
Sì, lo devi studiare.

1. lavare i bicchieri 2. preparare la cena 3. prẹndere l'ombrello 4. comprare i biglietti per il teatro 5. sentire le notịzie 6. chiamare la baby-sitter 7. aspettare la sua telefonata 8. offrire l'aperitivo agli ospiti

C. **Domanda e risposta.** Domandate dove sono le seguenti cose o persone. Lo (La) studente(ssa) che risponde usa **ecco** e il pronome appropriato.

ESEMPIO penna —**Dov'è la penna?**
—**Ẹccola!**

1. elenco telefọnico 2. orolọgio 3. chiavi 4. uscita (*exit*) 5. carta (*map*) d'Itạlia 6. tu 7. indirizzo di Marco 8. giornale di ieri 9. farina 10. soldi per la spesa 11. cucchiaini

IV. L'imperativo con un pronome (diretto, indiretto o riflessivo)

—Papà, prestami la tua auto stasera; se no, avrò un complesso di inferiorità.

1. Object and reflexive pronouns—except **loro**—are attached to the end of the **tu**, **noi**, and **voi** imperative forms.

Pạrla**le**!	*Talk to her!*
Cọmpra**li**!	*Buy them!*
Scriviạmo**gli** una lẹttera!	*Let's write him a letter!*
Fạte**ci** un favore!	*Do us a favor!*

BUT:

Parla **loro**!	*Speak to them!*

Note the imperative construction with reflexive and reciprocal verbs:

	fermarsi		scrivẹrsi	
(tu)	**fẹrmati!**	*stop!*		
(noi)	**fermiạmoci!**	*let's stop!*	**scriviạmoci!**	*let's write to each other!*
(voi)	**fermạtevi!**	*stop!*	**scrivẹtevi!**	*write to each other!*

2. When the pronouns are attached to the monosyllabic imperatives **va'**, **da'**, **fa'**, **sta'**, and **di'**, the initial consonant of the pronouns—except **gli**—is doubled.

Dammi la bicicletta! — *Give me the bike!*
Dicci qualcosa! — *Tell us something!*
Falle un regalo! — *Give her a gift!*

BUT:
Digli cosa fare! — *Tell him what to do!*

3. In the *negative imperative,* object and reflexive pronouns may precede or follow the imperative verb. When the pronouns follow an imperative verb in the **tu** form, the infinitive drops the final **-e.**

Non **ti** alzare! / Non alzar**ti!** — *Don't get up!*

Non **gli** diciamo niente! / Non diciạmo**gli** niente! — *Let's not tell him anything!*

Non **lo** perdete! / Non perdẹte**lo!** — *Don't lose it!*

Non **lo** fare! / Non far**lo!** — *Don't do it!*

Pratica

A. Fạbio si trasferisce nella tua città e ti chiede molte cose.

ESEMPIO aiutare **Per favore, aiụtami!**

1. dire dov'è l'uffịcio postale **2.** dare il nome di un bravo mẹdico **3.** suggerire un buon ristorante **4.** trovare una stanza **5.** mostrare dov'è l'università **6.** telefonare stasera

B. **La spesa.** Anna deve uscire e chiede alla mamma di che cosa ha bisogno in cucina.

ESEMPIO mele/sì **—Compro le mele?**
—Sì, cọmprale!

1. zụcchero/sì 2. sale/no 3. burro/sì 4. farina/no 5. cipolle/sì 6. uova/no 7. spinaci/no

C. **Dove?** Paolo e Marco dẹvono riordinare la cucina e domạndano alla mamma dove mẹttere certe cose.

ESEMPIO piatti/nell'armadietto sopra la lavastovịglie
—Dove mettiamo i piatti?
—Mettẹteli nell'armadietto sopra la lavastovịglie!

1. posate/nel cassetto di destra (*on the right*) 2. pẹntola rossa/sotto il lavandino 3. bicchieri/nell'armadietto vicino alla finestra 4. colomba pasquale/nel frigo 5. tovạglia/nel cassetto della tạvola 6. vaso di fiori/sulla tạvola

D. **Consigli.** Dite quali consigli dà una madre ai figli nelle seguenti situazioni.

ESEMPIO Hanno un corso alle otto e loro si ạlzano tardi.
—Alzạtevi presto!

1. Fa freddo e loro si mẹttono degli ạbiti leggeri. 2. È inverno e loro si lạvano con ạcqua fredda. 3. È l'ora di cena e loro si fẹrmano a chiacchierare (*to chat*) con amici. 4. È mezzanotte e loro si mẹttono (*start*) a studiare. 5. Vẹdono una ragazza e loro s'innamọrano. 6. È la fine del semestre e loro non si prepạrano per gli esami.

E. **Che fare?** Aldo ha litigato con la sua fidanzata, che gli ha restituito l'anello di fidanzamento (*engagement ring*). Aldo domanda al fratello se fare o non fare certe cose. Il fratello risponde di sì o di no.

ESEMPIO telefonare *alla mamma*/no **—Telẹfono alla mamma?**
—No, non telefonarle!

1. scrịvere *a papà*/no 2. parlare *ai nonni*/no 3. spiegare la situazione *alla zia*/no 4. dare la notịzia *agli amici*/no 5. chiẹdere scusa *a Anna*/sì 6. mandar*le* un mazzo di fiori/sì 7. telefonar*le*/no 8. scrịver*le* una lunga lẹttera/sì

Esclamazioni comuni

—Dimmi un po': cos'è?
—Mah! Chissà!

Here are some exclamations expressing a wish or a feeling. You have already encountered some of them.

Auguri! Best wishes!
Congratulazioni! Felicitazioni! Congratulations!
Buon Anno! Happy New Year!
Buon compleanno! Happy Birthday!
Buon appetito! Enjoy your meal!
Buon divertimento! Have fun!
Buona fortuna! Good luck!
In bocca al lupo! Break a leg! (*lit.:* In the wolf's mouth!)
Buona giornata! Have a good day (at work)!
Buon Natale! Merry Christmas!
Buona Pasqua! Happy Easter!
Buone vacanze! Have a nice vacation!
Buon viaggio! Have a nice trip!
Salute! Cin cin! Cheers!
Salute! God bless you! (when someone sneezes)
Aiuto! Help!
Attenzione! Watch out!
Bravo(a)! Well done!
Cạspita! Wow! Holy cow!
Chissà! Who knows!
Mah! Bah!
Ma va! Macchè! No way!
Magari! I wish it were true!
Meno male! Thank goodness!
Peccato! What a pity!
Su, dai! Come on!
Va bene! D'accordo! O.K.
Be' (Beh)... Well...

Pratica

Come si dice? Reagisci con una espressione esclamativa appropriata alle seguenti situazioni.

1. Tua cugina si sposa sạbato prọssimo. **2.** Bevi con amici un bicchiere di spumante. **3.** È l'ora di pranzo e tutti sono a tạvola. **4.** Vedi un pedone (*pedestrian*) che attraversa la strada in un momento di trạffico. **5.** Un parente ha vinto cinque milioni alla lotteria. **6.** Ti domạndano se andrai (*you will go*) in vacanza, ma tu sei incerto. **7.** Tuo fratello ha perduto il treno. **8.** Vuoi convịncere Alberto ad uscire con te. **9.** Domani tua sorella ha un esame importante.

LETTURA

Ingredienti necessari per un buon piatto di pastasciutta.

UNA RICETTA SEMPLICE: *FUSILLI ALLA VESUVIANA*

Noodles (in the form of coils), Vesuvio style

Domẹnica scorsa Liliana ha incontrato Marcello con una ragazza francese a casa di amici. Li ha invitati a cena per stasera. *Per fare bella figura* telẹfona a Lucia, cuoca esperta. Ẹccola ora che le parla.

To make a good impression

—Lucia, devi aiutarmi. Ho bisogno di te. Ho deciso di servire, come secondo, bistecca alla fiorentina e insalata mista. Sono ricette sẹmplici e so farle. E come dolce ho comprato un *semifreddo Motta.* Puoi consigliarmi cosa fare come primo piatto?

ice cream cake

—Perchè non prepari una pastasciutta sẹmplice, dei fusilli alla vesuviana, per esẹmpio.

—È fạcile?

—Molto fạcile. Ti do la ricetta di mia madre, che è napoletana e che la fa spesso. Ẹccola!

Dosi per quattro:

fusilli (o altra pasta)	450 grammi	about 1 lb
pomodori *maturi*	300 grammi (*tritati* e senza *semi*)	ripe/chopped/seeds
ọlio vẹrgine d'oliva	4 cucchiai	
basịlico fresco	1 o 2 cucchiai (tritato)	
orẹgano	1 cucchiaino	
sale	se lo vuoi	
mozzarella	100 grammi (*tagliata a dadi*)	diced
formạggio parmigiano	50 grammi (*gratuggiato*)	grated

Metti l'ọlio in una *padella, aggiungi* i pomodori, il basịlico, l'orẹgano e *fa' cuocere* per 15 minuti a fuoco mẹdio. Fa' cuọcere i fusilli in una grande pẹntola di ạcqua *bollente* e *mescola ogni tanto. Assaggia* la pasta: deve ẹssere *al dente. Fa' scolare* i fusilli e mẹttili in una casseruola. Aggiungi la salsa di pomodoro, la mozzarella e il parmigiano. Mescola bene e *fa' cuocere a fuoco basso* per qualche minuto. Una *spruzzatina* di pepe e... buon appetito! Va bene?

frying pan/add
cook
boiling/stir/once in a while/taste/just tender/drain
simmer
sprinkle

—Sì, mille grạzie. È una ricetta sẹmplice. La metto nel mio *ricettario.*

recipe collection

—*Da quando* hai un ricettạrio?

since when

—Da oggi.

Comprensione

1. Dove ha incontrato Marcello e la sua amica, Liliana?
2. Perchè telẹfona a Lucia?
3. Che cosa ha deciso di servire come secondo piatto Liliana?
4. Perchè ha deciso di servirlo?
5. Che cosa le consịglia Lucia come primo piatto?
6. Di dov'è la mamma di Lucia? Dov'è il Vesụvio?
7. Quali ingredienti ci vọgliono (*are necessary*) per preparare questa pastasciutta?
8. Deve ẹssere molto cotta la pasta?
9. Ha sempre avuto un ricettạrio Liliana?

Domande personali

1. Le piace cucinare?
2. Conosce alcune buone ricette? Quali?
3. Mạngia spesso la carne, o preferisce verdura e frutta?
4. Compra la verdura fresca o quella surgelata (*frozen*)?
5. Se Lei vuole fare bella figura quando ha degli ospiti, che cosa prepara per cena?
6. Quali ingredienti usa Lei per preparare una buona pastasciutta?
7. Le piạcciono i piatti piccanti (*spicy*)?
8. Ha un libro di cucina? Un ricettạrio?

ATTIVITÀ SUPPLEMENTARI

A. **Una ricetta.** Portate in classe una ricetta molto sẹmplice e scambiạtela (*exchange it*) con un(a) compagno(a). Dite se è un antipasto, un primo o un secondo piatto, oppure un dolce. Spiegate quali ingredienti ci vọgliono (*are necessary*). Dite se c'è bisogno del forno o del fornello e quanti minuti ci vọgliono per la cottura (*baking, cooking*). Se è un piatto freddo, dite quanti minuti ci vọgliono per la preparazione.

B. **Che cosa prepariamo?** Voi aspettate degli amici italiani e decidete di preparare un tịpico piatto americano, sẹmplice e alla buona (*informal*). Quale piatto? Forse un'insalata e... Quali ingredienti? *(One student is the organizer and directs the others to go..., to buy..., to wash..., to prepare... Use some imperatives.)* Attività per quattro studenti.

C. **Una tạvola elegante.** Descrivete com'è apparecchiata la tạvola della foto a pagina 221. Immaginate l'occasione e le portate (*entrées*). Che cosa vi piace o non vi piace su questa tạvola? Attività per due o tre studenti.

D. **Come si dice in italiano?**

1. Marc's parents intend to spend a few days in town, and Marc has invited them to dinner at his house.
2. Since (**poichè**) he does not know how to cook, he is worried.
3. He has phoned his girlfriend and asked her to give him a good recipe.
4. She has suggested preparing (**di preparare**) *spaghetti alla carbonara* and has explained to him how to make it (*pl.*).

5. It is a very easy recipe.
6. At seven o'clock, his parents arrive. Here they are!
7. Marc is very happy to (**di**) see them, but he does not want his mother in the kitchen.
8. Unfortunately, his girlfriend hasn't told him how much salt to use, and he has used it generously.
9. She also has forgotten (**di**) to tell him how long (**per quanto tempo**) to cook the spaghetti.
10. Tonight Marc and his parents are eating scrambled eggs and bacon (**pancetta**) with bread.

Tavola con il coperto per una persona.

E. LE PAROLE INCROCIATE.

Orizzontali

1. Molto tempo… (*ago*)
2. Preposizione sẹmplice
3. Strada
5. Il contrario di **sì**
6. Pronome personale
8. Preposizione semplice
9. Lo mangiamo freddo
10. Lo usiamo per tagliare la carne
11. In mezzo a… **dove**
12. Tra
13. Preposizione articolata (*to the*)
14. Seconda persona singolare del verbo **sapere**
15. Pronome (*to you*)
16. Pronome (*them*)
19. Terza pers. sing. del verbo **fare**
20. Pronome (*to us*)
21. Secon. pers. sing. del verbo **amare**
22. Adesso
24. Pronome personale
26. Lo mettiamo nel congelatore (*freezer*)
28. Vado a dormire perchè ho…
29. Pronome (*to me*)
30. Quando siamo ammalati la mamma prepara il… di pollo.

Verticali

1. La usiamo per mangiare gli spaghetti
2. La usiamo per cucinare
3. Il…Milano–New York è in ritardo
4. Kevin Costner e Paul Newman
5. Preposizione artic. (*in the*)
7. Le facciamo strapazzate
8. Artịcolo
9. Pronome oggetto (*to him*)
12. La usiamo per fare una torta
16. Il contrạrio di **stretto**
17. Lo usiamo per condire (*dress*) l'insalata
18. Lo cuciniamo con lo zafferano (*saffron*)
19. Lo usiamo per cucinare una torta
23. Le vocali in **mare**
25. Metà di **otto**
27. Artịcolo
28. Pronome riflessivo (terza pers.)

Vocabolario

Nomi

gli auguri	*wishes*
il brodo	*broth*
il cibo	*food*
i cioccolatini	*chocolate candies*
la dieta	*diet*
la dose	*amount*
il favore	*favor*
la forma	*form, shape*
i grissini	*bread sticks*
l'ingrediente (*m.*)	*ingredient*
il libro di cucina	*cookbook*
il mẹdico	*doctor*
l'ọspite (*m. & f.*)	*guest*
la padella	*frying pan*
il parmigiano	*Parmesan cheese*
il prẹstito	*loan*
la ricetta	*recipe*
il ricettạrio	*recipe collection, recipe book*
la salsa	*sauce*
la situazione	*situation*
l'uffịcio postale	*post office*
l'uscita	*exit*

Aggettivi

allegro	*cheerful, gay*
cotto	*cooked*
dẹbole	*weak*
efficiente	*efficient*
grosso	*big*
indulgente	*indulgent*
inefficiente	*inefficient*
ịntimo	*close*
misto	*mixed*
necessạrio	*necessary*
ọttimo	*excellent*
sorpreso	*surprised*
surgelato	*frozen*

Verbi

accompagnare	*to accompany*
aggiụngere (*p.p.* aggiunto)	*to add*
aiutare	*to help*
apparecchiare	*to set (the table)*
ignorare	*to ignore*
lamentarsi (di)	*to complain (about)*
litigare	*to have an argument, to argue*
mescolare	*to mix*
mettersi a(+*inf.*)	*to start*
pensare di (+*inf.*)	*to intend*
portare	*to take, to accompany*
prestare	*to lend*
punire (-isc)	*to punish*
rivedere	*to see again*
scambiare	*to exchange*
suggerire (-isc)	*to suggest*
tagliare	*to cut*

Altre espressioni

abbastanza	*enough*
al dente	*firm, not overcooked (pasta, rice)*
benone	*very well*
certo	*certainly*
ci vuole (+*sing. noun*) ci vọgliono (+*pl. noun*)	*it takes, it is necessary, they are necessary*
dire di no/sì	*to say* no/yes
è l'ora di pranzo (di cena)	*it is lunch (dinner) time*
ẹssere a dieta	*to be on a diet*
fare bella figura	*to make a good impression*
fare la pace	*to make up*
forse	*maybe, perhaps*
purtroppo	*unfortunately*

LA PIRAMIDE DELLA SALUTE

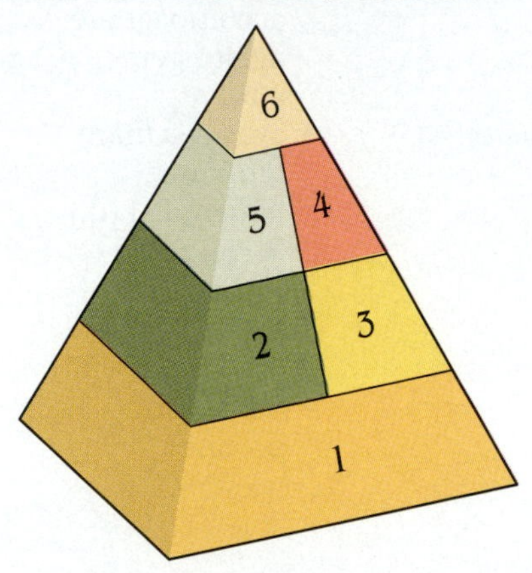

1. pane, pasta, riso...
2. verdura
3. frutta
4. carni
5. latti, formaggi
6. zucchero, dolci

LA CUCINA ITALIANA

La gastronomia italiana *vanta* una delle tradizioni più illustri d'Europa. Sono stati dei cuochi italiani che, nel Rinascimento, hanno insegnato ai Francesi l'arte culinaria. La cucina italiana è nota soprattutto per la varietà dei suoi primi piatti, a base di pasta.

È certo che non è stato Marco Polo ad importare gli spaghetti in Italia, come molti credono: esistono sull'*argomento* documenti anteriori al viaggio in Oriente di questo famoso Italiano.

Oggi troviamo la pasta in una varietà infinita di forme e di preparazioni, a seconda delle tradizioni locali. Può essere preparata in brodo con o *senza* verdure, con salse elaborate o condimenti semplici come l'olio d'oliva o il burro. Una delle regioni da visitare è l'Emilia-Romagna: la sua capitale, Bologna, è stata definita *«la dotta»* per la sua tradizione universitaria, ma anche «la grassa» per la ricchezza della sua cucina. In Emilia la lunga lista di paste fresche va dalle *tagliatelle* ai raffinati tortelli e cappelletti *ripieni di* carni o di verdure diverse.

Nelle città e nei paesi vicini al mare la pasta è condita spesso con *frutti di mare,* come i *vermicelli con le vongole* di Napoli—la città d'origine della pizza—o come la *pasta con le sarde* della Sicilia.

In diverse regioni del Nord sono popolari anche il riso, che è l'ingrediente base di diverse ricette di risotto, e la *polenta* che *si fa* con la farina di granoturco.

vanta: boasts
argomento: subject
senza: without
la dotta: learned
tagliatelle: thin ribbon noodles/
ripieni di: filled with
frutti di mare: seafood/
vermicelli con le vongole: noodles with baby clams
pasta con le sarde: macaroni and sardines
polenta: kind of corn mush/
si fa: is made

Comprensione

1. Gli Italiani hanno introdotto (*introduced*) la cucina italiana in Fr̦ancia nel șecolo...
   a. tredicęsimo b. sedicęsimo c. ventęsimo
2. La pasta è arrivata in Itạlia...
   a. quando Marco Polo è ritornato dall'Oriente b. dopo Marco Polo c. prima di (*before*) Marco Polo
3. Il condimento più sęmplice della pasta è...
   a. la carne b. la verdura c. l'ọlio
4. Bologna è chiamata «la dọtta» per
   a. la sua cucina b. la sua università c. la pizza
5. Nelle regioni lungo il mare la pasta è spesso condita con salse a base di...
   a. farina di granoturco b. carne c. frutti di mare

Bologna. Veduta aerea della città. Al centro, la Basilica di San Petronio.

11 LE VACANZE

Ragazzi sotto la tenda.

PUNTI DI VISTA

Bagnanti e ombrelloni sulla spiaggia di Rimini (Emilia-Romagna).

AL MARE

Due *bagnini* su una spiaggia dell'Adriatico parlano fra di loro. — lifeguards

Giovanni Hai visto quanti turisti ci sono quest'anno?
Lorenzo Sì, e molti altri arriveranno nelle prossime settimane.
Giovanni Arrivano con le loro tende e i loro camper da tutta l'Europa.
Lorenzo Il campeggio è un modo economico di fare le vacanze.
Giovanni Molti non hanno la tenda, ma solo uno *zaino* e un *sacco a pelo*. Quando sono stanchi di stare sulla spiaggia, fanno l'autostop e vanno in montagna. — back pack/sleeping bag
Lorenzo E hai visto come sono *attrezzati?* Hanno *tutto l'occorrente* per passare l'estate in Italia. — equipped/all that they need
Giovanni Sì, e viaggiano con le loro carte geografiche. Molti conoscono l'Italia *meglio di* noi. — better than
Lorenzo Quest'estate saremo più occupati *del solito*. Non ho mai visto tanta gente! — than usual
Giovanni È vero. Ma mi piace questo lavoro perchè posso ammirare lo spettacolo magnifico del mare.
Una voce Bagnino, *aiuto!* Aiuto! — help!
Lorenzo *Addio* spettacolo! — good-bye

1. Chi sono Giovanni e Lorenzo?
2. Dove sono?
3. Da dove arrivano i turisti sulle spiagge italiane?
4. Perchè preferiscono fare il campeggio?
5. Dove dormono?
6. Cosa fanno quando sono stanchi di stare sulla spiaggia?
7. Si perdono facilmente? Perchè no?
8. Mentre i due bagnini parlano, che cosa grida (*screams*) una bagnante?

Studio di parole

GITA TURISTICA O...VILLEGGIATURA

il mare sea
la spiaggia beach
la sabbia sand
la barca a vela sailboat
il (la) bagnante bather
il (la) bagnino(a) lifeguard
il costume da bagno bathing suit
il telo-bagno beach towel
asciugarsi to dry oneself
abbronzarsi to tan
nuotare to swim
il pericolo danger
pericoloso dangerous
annegare to drown
salvare to rescue
il salvataggio the rescue
il pullman tour bus
la carta geografica map
la guida* tour guide, guidebook
il bosco woods
la giacca a vento windbreaker
gil scarponi da montagna hiking boots
lo zaino backpack
il sacco a pelo sleeping bag
la tenda tent
montare le tende to pitch the tents
fare
- **l'autostop** to hitchhike
- **il campeggio** to go camping, to camp
- **un'escursione** *(f.)* to take an excursion
- **l'alpinismo** to climb a mountain

respirare to breathe

*__La guida__ is always feminine.

Applicazione

A. 1. Con quale mezzo di trasporto viaggiano i turisti nel disegno?
2. Chi seguono?
3. Perchè hanno fretta?
4. Alla spiaggia, chi salva le persone in pericolo di annegare?
5. Che cosa ci mettiamo quando andiamo a nuotare?
6. Cosa usiamo per asciugarci?
7. Perchè stiamo molte ore al sole?
8. Dove dormiamo quando facciamo il campeggio?
9. Respiriamo male in un bosco di montagna?
10. Siamo in montagna. Le previsioni del tempo (*weather forecast*) annunciano vento e pioggia: cosa ci mettiamo?
11. Quando ci perdiamo, di cosa abbiamo bisogno per ritrovare la strada?

B. Domande personali.

1. Le piace fare il campeggio?
2. Preferisce farlo al mare o in montagna?
3. Lei preferisce dormire sotto la tenda o in un bell'albergo?
4. Ha mai viaggiato in un camper Lei? Dov'è andato(a)?
5. Lei preferisce una vacanza a contatto con la natura, o un viaggio turistico in alcune città europee? Perchè?
6. Quando Lei è in vacanza al mare, fa una vita attiva? Nuota? Cammina sulla spiaggia? Gioca a pallavolo? Oppure preferisce riposarsi e prendere il sole?

Ascoltiamo!

Un salvataggio. *The lifeguards, Giovanni and Lorenzo, rush into the water to rescue the swimmer who seems to be drowning. They return to the beach, carrying an apparently lifeless woman. Listen to the ensuing conversation, then answer the related questions.*

Comprensione

1. Chi hanno salvato i due bagnini? Descrivetela.
2. Perchè Giovanni deve praticarle la respirazione artificiale?
3. Dopo qualche minuto che cosa fa la ragazza?
4. Dove si trova quando apre gli occhi?
5. È riconoscente (*grateful*) la ragazza? Che cosa dice a Giovanni?
6. Ha avuto paura di annegare perchè non sa nuotare?
7. Di che cosa ha bisogno ora la ragazza?
8. Dove l'accompagna Lorenzo?

Dialogo

In gruppi di due, progettate (*plan*) di passare una giornata al mare. Decidete come andare, cosa portare, come vestirvi e cosa fare alla spiaggia.

PUNTI GRAMMATICALI

I. Il futuro

Lia passerà le ferie al mare. *Tina si divertirà in montagna.*

1. Dove passerà le vacanze Lia? **2.** Chi andrà in montagna?
3. Si annoierà o si divertirà Tina?

1. The future (**futuro**) is a simple tense expressing an event that will take place in the future. It is formed by adding the endings of the future to the infinitive after dropping the final **-e**.

rispondere → risponder**ò** = *I will answer*
The future is conjugated as follows:

parlare	rispondere	partire
parler**ò**	risponder**ò**	partir**ò**
parler**ai**	risponder**ai**	partir**ai**
parler**à**	risponder**à**	partir**à**
parler**emo**	risponder**emo**	partir**emo**
parler**ete**	risponder**ete**	partir**ete**
parler**anno**	risponder**anno**	partir**anno**

The endings are the same for all conjugations. Note that for the first conjugation, the **-a** of the infinitive ending changes to **-e** before adding the future endings.

I turisti **prenderanno** il pullman. *The tourists will take the tour bus.*
Noi **visiteremo** un castello. *We will visit a castle.*
Che cosa mi **dirà?** *What will he/she say to me?*
Domani non **lavorerò.** *Tomorrow I will not work.*

2. The following groups of verbs are irregular in the future tense:

   a. Verbs that end in **-are** but that do not undergo a stem change:

      dare: **darò**, **darai**, ecc.
      fare: **farò**, **farai**, ecc.
      stare: **starò**, **starai**, ecc.

   b. Verbs that end in **-care**, **-gare**, **-ciare**, and **-giare** and that undergo a spelling change for phonetic reasons:

      dimenticare: **dimenticherò**, **dimenticherai**, ecc.
      pagare: **pagherò**, **pagherai**, ecc.
      cominciare: **comincerò**, **comincerai**, ecc.
      mangiare: **mangerò**, **mangerai**, ecc.

   c. Verbs that drop a stem vowel:

      andare: **andrò**, **andrai**, ecc.
      avere: **avrò**, **avrai**, ecc.
      cadere: **cadrò**, **cadrai**, ecc.
      dovere: **dovrò**, **dovrai**, ecc.
      potere: **potrò**, **potrai**, ecc.
      sapere: **saprò**, **saprai**, ecc.
      vedere: **vedrò**, **vedrai**, ecc.
      vivere: **vivrò**, **vivrai**, ecc.

—Dove cadrà?
—Chi vivrà, vedrà!

   d. Verbs that have an irregular stem:

      essere: **sarò**, **sarai**, ecc.
      bere: **berrò**, **berrai**, ecc.
      venire: **verrò**, **verrai**, ecc.
      volere: **vorrò**, **vorrai**, ecc.

Saremo pronti alle otto.	*We will be ready by eight.*
Dovrà studiare se **vorrà** riuscire.	*He will have to study if he wants to succeed.*
Pagherai tu il conto?	*Will you pay the bill?*
A che ora **mangerete?**	*At what time will you eat?*
Prometto che non **berrò** più.	*I promise that I will not drink any more.*

3. When the main verb of a sentence is in the future, the verb of a subordinate clause introduced by **se**, **quando**, or **appena** (*as soon as*) is also in the future.

Andremo alla spiaggia se **farà** bello.	*We will go to the beach if the weather is nice.*
Ti **racconterò** tutto quando ti **vedrò**.	*I will tell you everything when I see you.*
Mi **scriverà** appena **arriverà** a Roma.	*He will write to me as soon as he arrives in Rome.*

NOTE:
Colloquial Italian often uses the present tense to express the near future.

Quando **parti?**	*When are you leaving?*
Parto la settimana prossima.	*I am leaving next week.*

4. Here are a few expressions of time used with the future tense.

domani	tomorrow
dopodomani	the day after tomorrow
la settimana prossima	next week
l'anno (il mese) prossimo	next year (month)
fra 3 giorni (una settimana, ecc.)	in 3 days (a week, etc.)
fra poco	in a little while

Pratica

A. **Progetti di vacanze.** Rispondete alla domanda secondo l'esempio.

a. Cosa farai quando andrai in vacanza?

ESEMPIO andare a Portofino **Andrò a Portofino.**

1. stare in un bell'albergo **2.** mangiare nelle trattorie locali **3.** visitare i villaggi vicini **4.** nuotare nel mare **5.** abbronzarsi **6.** divertirsi con gli amici **7.** fare passeggiate sulla spiaggia **8.** dormire fino a tardi **9.** riposarsi **10.** andare in barca **11.** comprare dei ricordi (*souvenirs*) **12.** scrivere delle cartoline **13.** potere leggere

b. Cosa farete quando andrete in montagna?

ESEMPIO fare il campeggio **Faremo il campeggio.**

1. partire presto la mattina **2.** trovare un bel posto **3.** montare la tenda **4.** andare a pescare delle trote nel fiume (*river*) **5.** accendere (*to light*) il fuoco **6.** cucinare le trote sul fuoco **7.** mangiarle **8.** bere del tè **9.** cantare le canzoni della montagna **10.** ascoltare i rumori del bosco **11.** dormire nel sacco a pelo **12.** fermarsi alcuni giorni **13.** vivere all'aperto **14.** dimenticare i rumori della città

B. **In pullman.** Conversazione tra due passeggeri americani in gita turistica in Italia. Seguite l'esempio.

ESEMPIO mangiare le lasagne/Bologna **—Ha già mangiato le lasagne?**
—No, ma le mangerò a Bologna.

1. cambiare i dollari/fra poco 2. leggere la guida di Venezia/prima di sera 3. vedere la città di Firenze/dopodomani 4. visitare la Sicilia/l'anno prossimo 5. imparare alcune frasi in italiano/prima del ritorno 6. bere il vino di Frascati/a Roma

C. **I tuoi genitori faranno le seguenti cose quando avranno...** Seguite l'esempio.

ESEMPIO le ferie, riposarsi
Quando avranno le ferie, si riposeranno.

1. il camper, andare in campagna 2. una nuova macchina, volere fare lunghe gite 3. i soldi, comprarsi una barca a vela 4. la barca a vela, andare sul lago 5. il biglietto dell'aereo, partire per il Messico 6. una carta geografica, non perdersi più 7. una guida, capire facilmente le bellezze artistiche del paese

D. **Domanda e risposta.** Seguite l'esempio.

ESEMPIO prendere il sole
—Prenderai il sole?
—Lo prenderò se farà bel tempo. o

1. visitare l'Italia 2. vedere la Galleria degli Uffizi* 3. prendere il treno 4. fare l'autostop 5. assaggiare le tagliatelle alla bolognese 6. bere il caffè con ghiaccio 7. fare l'escursione Taormina–Monte Etna** 8. mandarmi una cartolina da Capri

Albergo ai piedi delle Dolomiti.

*A famous art museum in Florence.
**Taormina is a charming town on the east coast of Sicily, with an impressive view of Mount Etna.

II. Il futuro di probabilità

—*Perchè corre tutti i giorni in bicicletta?*
—*Si preparerà per il Giro d'Italia.*

The future tense may also be used to convey an idea of probability or conjecture. The future tense expresses probability in the present.

Dov'è la guida? **Sarà** al bar.	*Where is the tour guide? He is probably (He must be) in the bar.*
Che ore sono? **Saranno** le tre.	*What time is it? It is probably (It must be) three.*
Quanto costa una Ferrari? **Costerà** 100.000 dollari.	*How much does a Ferrari cost? It probably costs 100,000 dollars.*

Pratica

A. Indovinello (*Guessing game*). Dove saranno le seguenti persone e il gatto in questo momento? Completate le frasi con le espressioni appropriate delle due colonne.

1. La signora Soldi	in giardino, con un topo (*mouse*)
2. Alcuni studenti assenti	a Roma o in viaggio
3. Il gatto	in crociera
4. Il professore d'inglese	a casa a dormire
5. Il Presidente degli Stati Uniti	a casa a preparare un esame
6. Il Papa	alla Casa Bianca

B. Siete in pullman a Pompei, in partenza per la Sicilia. Mentre aspettate l'autista (*bus driver*) un turista fa un sacco di domande e di commenti. Voi reagite senza sapere con esattezza la risposta. Usate il futuro di probabilità.

ESEMPIO Che ore sono? **—Saranno le undici.** *o*

1. Ma dov'è l'autista? **2.** Ha visto? Quella ragazza porta uno zaino e un sacco a pelo. **3.** Cos'è quella carta che la ragazza legge attentamente? **4.** Com'è pallida la signora col (con il) bambino! **5.** Il bambino continua a mangiare. **6.** Quel signore dorme continuamente. **7.** Che tempo fa in Sicilia?

III. I pronomi tonici

—Ascolti me o guardi lei?

1. Disjunctive pronouns (**I pronomi tonici**) are personal pronouns that are used after a verb or a preposition. They are:

	Singular		Plural
me	*me; myself*	**noi**	*us; ourselves*
te	*you (familiar); yourself*	**voi**	*you (familiar); yourselves*
lui	*him*		
lei	*her*	**loro**	*them*
Lei	*you (formal)*	**Loro**	*you (formal)*
sè	*himself, herself, yourself*	**sè**	*themselves, yourselves*

2. As a direct or an indirect object, a disjunctive pronoun is used after the verb for emphasis, to avoid ambiguity, and when the verb has two or more objects.

Vedo **te!**	*I see you!*
Parlo **a lui**, non **a lei.**	*I'm speaking to him, not her.*
Ha scritto a Franco e **a me.**	*He wrote to Franco and me.*

3. It is frequently used as the object of a preposition.

Parto **con loro.**	*I'm leaving with them.*
L'invito è **per Lei.**	*The invitation is for you.*
Abita vicino **a noi.**	*He lives near us.*
Sono arrivati **prima di me.**	*They arrived before me.*
Siamo andati **da lei.**	*We went to her house.*
Luisa impara il francese **da sè.**	*Luisa is learning French by herself.*
Non mi preoccupo **di me**, ma **di voi.**	*I don't worry about myself, but about you.*

Pratica

A. Vostro fratello non capisce quello che (*what*) dite. Voi ripetete la frase, usando il pronome tonico. Seguite l'esempio.

ESEMPIO Ti ho visto alla spiaggia. **Ho visto te alla spiaggia.**

1. I nonni ci hanno scritto. **2.** Abbiamo invitato lo zio a pranzo, e non la cugina. **3.** Ho pensato a nostra sorella, non ai suoi bambini. **4.** Perchè non mi ascolti quando ho ragione? **5.** Devi parlare a nostro padre, non alla tua amica. **6.** Se ti ho chiamato, è perchè ti voglio parlare. **7.** Questo regalo non è per te, è per la mamma.

B. **Sì o no?** Rispondete, usando il pronome tonico.

ESEMPIO —Partirai con i tuoi genitori? **—Sì, partirò con loro.** *o* **—No, non partirò con loro.**

1. Sei arrivato(a) in classe prima degli altri compagni? **2.** Avrai bisogno del(la) professore(ssa) per alcune spiegazioni? **3.** A chi pensi? A una tua amica? **4.** Abiti vicino a Pietro (o...)? **5.** Noi andremo in vacanza fra due settimane. Verrai con noi? **6.** Vieni al ristorante con me domani sera? **7.** Hai bisogno di parlare a me? **8.** Hai fiducia (*confidence*) in me? E in te? **9.** Fai il compito d'italiano da te o con un compagno (una compagna)?

C. **Da...** Rispondete, usando **da** e il pronome tonico.

ESEMPIO —Vai a casa di Paolo oggi? **—Sì, vado da lui.** *o* **—No, non vado da lui.**

1. Ceni a casa dei tuoi zii stasera? **2.** Vieni a casa mia? **3.** Andrai a casa di... per le vacanze d'estate? **4.** Quando andrai dai tuoi genitori? **5.** Se hai bisogno di consigli, vai da tua madre? **6.** Quando vai dal dottore? **7.** Vieni da noi stasera? **8.** Quando hai bisogno di soldi, vai da tuo padre?

IV. Piacere

—Ti piace quella casa?

<table>
<tr><td>mi piace
ti piace
gli piace
le, Le piace</td><td>leggere</td><td>ci piace
vi piace
piace loro, Loro
(gli piace)</td><td>cantare</td></tr>
</table>

1. The irregular verb **piacere** means *to please.* It is used mainly in the third persons singular and plural (present: **piace, piacciono**), and it has an indirect construction that corresponds to the English construction *to be pleasing to.*

Mi piace la pasta.	*I like pasta. (Pasta is pleasing to me.)*
Ci piace l'appartamento.	*We like the apartment. (The apartment is pleasing to us.)*
Le piacciono queste scarpe?	*Do you like these shoes? (Are these shoes pleasing to you?)*

NOTE:

a. In Italian, the word order is *indirect object + verb + subject;* in English it is *subject + verb + direct object.*

b. The singular form **piace** is followed by a singular noun; the plural form **piacciono** is followed by a plural noun.

2. **Piacere** is in a singular form when followed by an infinitive.

Ti piace fare il campeggio?	*Do you like to go camping?*
Vi piacerà andare alla spiaggia.	*You will like to go to the beach.*

3. When the indirect object is a noun or a disjunctive pronoun, the preposition **a** is used.

Ai bambini piace il gelato.	*Children like ice cream.*
Ad Antonio piacerà la Sardegna.	*Antonio will like Sardinia.*
A me piacciono le feste.	*I like parties.*

4. The opposite of **piacere** is **non piacere. Dispiacere** has the same construction as **piacere**, but it translates as *to be sorry, to mind.*

Non mi piace la birra.	*I don't like beer.*
Non mi piacciono gli spinaci.	*I don't like spinach.*
Non sta bene? **Mi dispiace.**	*You are not well? I am sorry.*
Le dispiace se fumo?	*Do you mind if I smoke?*

5. The **passato prossimo** of **piacere** is conjugated with **essere.** Therefore, the past participle (**piaciuto**) agrees in gender and number with the subject.

Ti è piaciut**a** la sala?	*Did you like the living room?*
Non mi sono piaciut**i** i mobili.	*I did not like the furniture.*

Pratica

A. Rispondete a ogni domanda con due o tre attività.

1. Che cosa ti piace fare quando vai al mare? 2. Che cosa vi piace fare quando andate in montagna? 3. Che cosa piace fare ai turisti quando arrivano in Italia?

B. **Sì o no? Domanda e risposta.** Nella domanda usate la forma di cortesia: **Le piace...? Le piacciono...?**

ESEMPIO le lasagne **—Le piacciono le lasagne?**
—Sì, mi piacciono molto. *o*
—No, non mi piacciono tanto.

1. la cucina italiana **2.** le mele **3.** le fragole **4.** lavorare la domenica **5.** nuotare in piscina **6.** viaggiare **7.** i film italiani **8.** le vacanze al mare **9.** fare il campeggio **10.** i giorni di pioggia **11.** i mobili (*furniture*) antichi **12.** l'estate

C. **Domanda e risposta.** Rispondete usando i pronomi indiretti.

ESEMPIO ai bambini, giocare **—Ai bambini piace giocare?**
—Sì, gli piace giocare.

1. a te e a Mario, gli spaghetti **2.** a te, fare il campeggio **3.** ai tuoi genitori, i tuoi voti **4.** alla tua amica, il mare **5.** agli studenti di questa classe, studiare l'italiano **6.** a voi, il cappuccino **7.** a te, fare le spese

D. Rispondete alle seguenti domande.

ESEMPIO Cosa piace fare a tua sorella quando è a casa?
Le piace telefonare alle amiche. *o*

1. Cosa piace fare a tuo padre quando ha tempo libero? **2.** Che cosa piace fare a te quando arrivano le vacanze? **3.** A tua madre cosa piace ricevere per il «giorno della mamma»? **4.** Che cosa piace fare a te in una bella giornata di primavera? **5.** Cosa piace fare a te quando piove? **6.** Cosa piace fare ai bambini quando non studiano? **7.** E a te, che cosa piace fare?

E. **Domanda e risposta.** Domandate a uno(a) studente(ssa) se gli (le) sono piaciute le seguenti cose. Usate la forma di cortesia nella domanda.

ESEMPIO **—Le è piaciuto il film di ieri sera?**
—No, non mi è piaciuto. *o*
—Sì, mi è piaciuto molto.

1. il week-end scorso **2.** le vacanze dell'estate scorsa **3.** i regali che Lei ha ricevuto per Natale **4.** l'ultima gita che ha fatto **5.** il giorno del Suo compleanno **6.** il ristorante dove ha mangiato l'ultima volta **7.** gli anni che ha passato al liceo

F. **Tutti i gusti sono gusti.** Quali sono i gusti (*tastes*) delle seguenti persone? Usate **piacere** e il pronome tonico.

ESEMPIO Luisa preferisce cantare. **A lei piace cantare.**

1. Antonio preferisce insegnare. **2.** Noi preferiamo divertirci. **3.** La signora Tortora ha preferito le spiagge del mare Adriatico. **4.** Io ho preferito una casa al mare. **5.** Gabriella e Filippo hanno preferito un appartamento in città. **6.** So che voi preferite viaggiare in pullman. **7.** I miei genitori preferiscono stare in un albergo di prima categoria. **8.** Io, invece, preferisco dormire sotto la tenda.

V. Alcuni plurali irregolari*

Ecco una sfilata (parade) di cuochi: un cuoco, due cuochi...diversi cuochi.

1. Most nouns and adjectives that end in **-co** and **-go** form their plural with **-chi** and **-ghi**:

il cuoco	**i cuochi**	bianco	**bianchi**
il fuoco	**i fuochi**	fresco	**freschi**
il parco	**i parchi**	stanco	**stanchi**
l'albergo	**gli alberghi**	largo	**larghi**
il lago (*lake*)	**i laghi**	lungo	**lunghi**

NOTE:
The plural of most nouns and adjectives ending in **-ico** ends in **-ici:** l'amico, **gli amici**; il medico, **i medici**; simpatico, **simpatici;** pratico, **pratici.**

BUT: antico, **antichi.**

2. Most nouns and adjectives ending in **-ga** form their plural with **-ghe:**

la riga (*line*)	**le righe**	lunga	**lunghe**
la targa (*license plate*)	**le targhe**	larga	**larghe**

3. Nouns ending in **-io** with the stress on the last syllable form their plural with **-ii:**

lo zịo	**gli zii**
l'addịo	**gli addii**

*See also "Studio di parole" in chapter 17 for some irregular nouns that refer to parts of the body.

4. Nouns ending in **-cia** and **-gia** keep the **i** in the plural when the **i** is stressed; otherwise the plural is formed with **-ce** and **-ge:**

la farmacịa	**le farmacie**
la bugịa (*lie*)	**le bugie**

BUT:

l'arạncia	**le arance**
la ciliẹgia (*cherry*)	**le ciliege**
la piọggia	**le piogge**

5. Some masculine nouns ending in **-a** form their plural with **-i.** (They derive mainly from Greek. Most end in **-ma** or **-amma.**) The most common are:

il diploma	**i diplomi**
il problema	**i problemi**
il sistema	**i sistemi**
il programma	**i programmi**
il telegramma	**i telegrammi**
il poeta	**i poeti**

6. Nouns and adjectives ending in **-ista** can be either masculine or feminine. They form their plural in **-isti** (masculine) and **-iste** (feminine).

il/la dentista	**i dentisti/le dentiste**
il/la musicista	**i musicisti/le musiciste**
il/la turista	**i turisti/le turiste**
egoista (*selfish*)	**egoisti/egoiste**
idealista	**idealisti/idealiste**
ottimista	**ottimisti/ottimiste**

Pratica

A. Mettete le seguenti frasi al plurale.

1. L'ufficio turistico è chiuso oggi. **2.** Il turista e la turista hanno visitato il parco di Roma. **3.** L'acqua del lago è sporca (*dirty*). **4.** La camera dell'albergo è abbastanza larga. **5.** Non possiamo accendere un fuoco in questo bosco. **6.** Non ho mangiato quest'arancia perchè è mạrcia (*rotten*). **7.** Il tuo problema non è molto sẹrio.

B. Rispondete alle seguenti domande.

1. Come ti senti quando pensi al futuro? Ottimista o pessimista? E i tuoi amici, come si sentono? **2.** Quale programma televisivo ti piace guardare di più? **3.** Quale frutta ti piace di più? E le ciliege? **4.** Quando sei in ritardo, dici qualche bugịa di convenienza (*white lie*) per scusarti? Qual è il plurale di **bugịa?** **5.** Puoi nominare il nome di alcuni artisti e artiste famosi? **6.** Qual è la stagione delle piogge in questa città? **7.** Quando ci sentiamo stanchi, che cosa facciamo? Sei stanco(a) tu, ora? Perchè?

LETTURA

Sardegna. Parte della Costa Smeralda.

VACANZE IN SICILIA

L'estate è vicina e Antonio scrive una lettera ai nonni in Sicilia.

4 giugno

Carissimi nonni,

Come state? Noi in famiglia stiamo tutti bene, e così speriamo di voi. Le mie vacanze arriveranno presto, e io verrò *a trovarvi* per qualche settimana. Arriverò prima di ferragosto, *verso* il 2 o il 3 del mese. Purtroppo non potrò fermarmi *a lungo* perchè incomincerò a lavorare la prima settimana di settembre.

to visit you
around
for a long time

Vorrei chiedervi un favore: vorrei portare con me il mio amico Marcello. Prima, però, io e Marcello andremo in Sardegna, sulla Costa Smeralda* e staremo con i suoi genitori che hanno una villa poco lontano da Olbia. Resteremo là una settimana, poi partiremo per il sud. Viaggeremo con la macchina di Marcello. Pensate! Vostro nipote arriverà in una Ferrari nuova!

Siccome ha paura di *disturbarvi,* Marcello cercherà una camera con doccia in un albergo o in una *pensione.* Ma gli ho detto che per mangiare potrà venire da voi. Sono certo che Marcello vi piacerà. Non vedo l'ora di venire in Sicilia per rivedere voi, cari nonni, e tanti posti che amo. Visiterò certamente la Valle dei

since/to bother you
boarding house

*On the northeastern tip of the island. It has splendid beaches.

Templi e Siracusa. Sono sicuro che Marcello preferirà visitare la spiaggia di Taormina; perchè è innamorato del sole e del mare. Ma saliremo *tutti e due* sull'Etna e ci divertiremo *da matti.*

both

a lot

Aspetto una vostra telefonata per sapere se posso portare Marcello con me. Saluti *affettuosi** anche *da parte* dei miei genitori.

affectionate

from

Antonio

Comprensione

1. A chi scrive Antonio? Perchè?
2. Potrà fermarsi per molto tempo dai nonni? Perchè no?
3. Che favore vuole chiedere loro?
4. Antonio e Marcello andranno subito in Sicilia? Dove andranno prima?
5. Arriveranno in Sicilia in treno?
6. Perchè Marcello starà in una pensione o in un albergo?
7. Dove andranno a mangiare?
8. Antonio non vede l'ora di arrivare in Sicilia. Per quale ragione?
9. Perchè Marcello non visiterà con lui la Valle dei Templi?
10. Si annoieranno i due in Sicilia?
11. Dove saliranno?
12. Con quale saluto ha finito la sua lettera Antonio?

Domande personali

1. Dove ha passato le vacanze Lei l'anno scorso? Le sono piaciute?
2. Andrà in qualche posto l'estate prossima? Dove?
3. Visiterà qualche città americana? Quale (Quali)?
4. Andrà all'estero? È mai stato(a) Lei all'estero? Quando?
5. Con che mezzo di trasporto viaggerà?
6. Quale mezzo Le piace di più? Perchè?
7. Pensa di andare a trovare parenti o amici? Dove abitano?
8. Starà da loro o soggiornerà in un albergo (o una pensione)?
9. Se resterà a casa, come passerà il tempo libero?

ATTIVITÀ SUPPLEMENTARI

A. **Una gita.** Gli studenti della classe d'italiano organizzano una gita. Ogni studente contribuisce con qualche frase. Dove andrete? Quando partirete? Come viaggerete? Che cosa farete? Che cosa porterete con voi? Perchè? Chi telefonerà all'agenzia di viaggi?

B. **Dialogo a due.** Il mese prossimo un tuo cugino americano verrà in Italia e starà da te qualche settimana. Dà la notizia a un tuo amico. Lui ti fa molte domande. Vuole sapere, per esempio:

---

*See pages 150 and 168 for other informal letter salutations. Some expressions for formal endings are **Cordiali saluti** and **Distinti saluti.**

1. da quale città americana partirà;
2. quando arriverà;
3. quanto tempo resterà in Italia;
4. se sa parlare italiano;
5. se tu hai progetti precisi per divertirlo;
6. se sai come gli piace passare le vacanze;
7. quali luoghi visiterete;
8. con che mezzo viaggerete;
9. se lo porterai in montagna o al mare;
10. dove starete.

Alla fine il tuo amico ti esprimerà il desiderio di conoscere tuo cugino e di invitarlo a casa sua.

C. **Alpinismo.** Descrivete la scena: dite dove sono i due alpinisti, che tempo fa, cosa fanno, come sono vestiti, se è una scalata (*climb*) facile o difficile, se sono lontani dalla cima (*summit*). Immaginate cosa si diranno all'arrivo in cima.

D. **Campeggio.** Immaginate l'avventura di Pippo e di Franco. Dove sono in questo momento? Perchè sono scontenti? Che cosa aspettano per uscire? Che cosa si dicono? Dove vorrebbero (*would like*) essere? (Per questa attività guardate il disegno a pagina 255.)

E. **Una lettera.** Scrivete una breve lettera a dei parenti o amici per dire loro che andrete a trovarli durante le vacanze. Come incomincerete la lettera? Dite in quale giorno arriverete, se soli o con amici; quanto tempo (*how long*) resterete, ecc. Come finirete la vostra lettera? Seguite l'esempio della lettera di Antonio ai suoi nonni (pagine 241–242).

F. **Quale albergo?** Voi desiderate passare le vacanze in una località balneare (*seaside resort*) sul Mare Adriatico o Mare Jonio. Consultate la seguente lista di alberghi; quasi tutti fanno anche pensione. Discutete in gruppi di due quale promette di più per le vostre vacanze, e fate la vostra scelta (*choice*).

9 VACANZE E TURISMO

ALBERGHI-STAZ. CLIMATICHE 9.1

A Bovalino mare Jonio Hotel La Castelluccia 0964-66.837 - 61.435 camere servizi ristorante rinomato, prezzi particolari luglio-settembre, gratis viaggio.

A Cesenatico-Valverde, hotel Residence, tre stelle. Tel. 0547-87.170. Piscina con acquascivolo e palestra. Giardino, parcheggio. Feste. Menu scelta. Scuola nuoto. Ginnastica. Pensione completa ultima settimana agosto 60.000, settembre 49.000.

A Milano Marittima, Hotel Savini, 4 stelle sul mare. Spiaggia privata, piscina, idromassaggio, bocce, pallavolo, parcheggio, feste, spettacoli, piano-bar, buffet verdure e pasticceria. Servizio ristorante diretto da prestigioso maitre. Stanze dotate di servizi privati con vasca, doccia, balcone vista mare, telefono, cassaforte, televisore (frigo bar su richiesta). Vicino golf, centro ippico, 40 tennis. Via XVIII Traversa. Tel. 0544-99.47.19 - Fax 99.16.34.

A Milano Marittima, Lido di Savio, Hotel Palace Lido 3 stelle superiore sul mare, spiaggia privata, piscina, parcheggio custodito, piano bar, animazione, scelta menù uno sempre pesce, buffet verdure, pasticceria, colazione buffet. Sala panoramica. Tutte stanze vista mare con Tv color satellite, telefono, cassaforte. Fine agosto 70.000, settembre 54.000, speciale famiglie. Tel. 0544-94.92.23 - Fax 94.92.98.

ARISTON hotel, Igea Marina, 0541-33.01.17. Vicinissimo spiaggia. Dal 21 agosto 37.000.

CATTOLICA Ferie gratis Hotel Imperiale, tre stelle prospiciente mare, tel. 0541-961.334, piscina, due menù scelta, prima colazione buffet, parcheggio. Tre persone stessa camera pagheranno solo per due, la terza è gratis. Dal 24/8 64.000 settembre 50.000.

CATTOLICA ferie gratis Hotel Vendome, tre stelle tel. 0541-963.410, 50 metri mare, idromassaggio, aria condizionata, parcheggio, due menù scelta, colazione buffet. Tre per-

G. **Come si dice in italiano?**

1. It is August and Franca and Raffaella are beginning their vacation (**vacanze**, *f. pl.*) today.
2. Since they don't like to travel by train, they are traveling by car and will arrive tomorrow in the beautiful Dolomites (**Dolomiti**, *f. pl.*).
3. They will camp there for a week.
4. We will stop near a lake, so we will have water to (**per**) wash and cook.
5. I like your idea! And we will be able to swim every day!
6. Since it is my first camping experience (**esperienza**), you will pitch the tent and I will help you.
7. Then we will take the backpack and go for a short hike (**escursione**).
8. How is the weather in the mountains?
9. It is probably beautiful. The weather forecast (**le previsioni del tempo**) stated (**dire che**) it will be nice weather until next Friday.
10. Franca and Raffaella arrived and camped, but unfortunately it rained all week.

Vocabolario

Nomi

l'alpinista (*m.* & *f.*)	*mountain climber*
l'autista	*(bus) driver*
la bellezza	*beauty*
la canzone	*song*
la crociera	*cruise*
il desiderio	*wish, desire*
le ferie	*annual vacation*
il Ferragosto	*August holidays*
il fiume	*river*
il fuoco	*fire*
la gente	*people*
la gita (turistica)	*tour, trip*
il gusto	*taste*
l'indovinello	*puzzle, guessing game*
il lago	*lake*
il mezzo di trasporto	*means of transportation*
il modo	*way, manner*
la natura	*nature*
la pallavolo	*volleyball*
la pensione	*inn, boarding house*
il rumore	*noise*
il saluto	*greeting*
lo spettacolo	*spectacle, view, sight*
la vacanza	*vacation*
la villeggiatura	*summer vacation*

Aggettivi

affettuoso	*affectionate*
artistico	*artistic*
attivo	*active*
attrezzato	*equipped*
economico	*economical*
innamorato	*in love*
locale	*local*
occupato	*busy*
pallido	*pale*
preciso	*precise*
prossimo	*next*
riconoscente	*grateful*
siciliano	*Sicilian*
sporco	*dirty*

Verbi

accendere (*p.p.* acceso)	*to light*
ammirare	*to admire*
andare (venire) a trovare	*to visit (a person)*
contribuire (-isc)	*to contribute*
discutere (*p.p.* discusso)	*to discuss*
dispiacere	*to be sorry; to mind*
disturbare	*to disturb, to bother*
esprimere (*p.p.* espresso)	*to express*
gridare	*to scream*
perdersi	*to get lost*
pescare	*to fish*
piacere	*to like*
progettare	*to plan*
reagire	*to react*
ritrovare	*to find again*

Altre espressioni

Addio!	*Good-bye (forever)*
Aiuto!	*Help!*
all'aperto	*outdoors*
andare in vacanza	*to go on vacation*
avere fidụcia (in)	*to have confidence, to trust*
con esattezza	*exactly*
da matti	*a lot*
da parte di	*from*
del solito	*than usual*
dopodomani	*the day after tomorrow*
fra (tra) poco	*in a little while*
fra (tra) un mese (un anno)	*in a month (a year)*
non vedo l'ora di (+ *inf.*)	*I can't wait to...*
le previsioni del tempo	*weather forecast*
prima di	*before*
siccome	*since*
tutti(e) due	*both*
verso	*around; towards*

LA SICILIA: TERRA DI CONTRASTI

I turisti che sono innamorati del sole, del mare e del passato possono trovare tutto questo in Sicilia. La Sicilia è separata dal resto dell'Italia dallo stretto di Messina ed è la più grande isola del Mediterraneo. La sua posizione strategica è la ragione principale della sua storia complicata. Molti, infatti, sono i popoli che l'*hanno invasa* e *sfruttata:* i Greci, i Cartaginesi, i Romani, i Bizantini, gli Arabi, i Normanni, i Tedeschi, i Francesi e gli Spagnoli. Tutte queste dominazioni hanno lasciato l'isola *piena* di contrasti nell'arte, nella lingua e nel folclore.

invaded/exploited

full

La Sicilia è il museo archeologico d'Europa. Un viaggio in quest'isola significa anche un viaggio nel tempo, alla *scoperta* delle varie civiltà. La presenza di templi e di teatri greci ci ricorda che quasi tremila anni fa, *esistevano* nell'isola delle colonie greche molto importanti, come per esempio Agrigento e Siracusa. L'antico nome dell'isola, Trinacria, viene dal greco e significa triangolo, dalla sua forma. Le leggende siciliane sono piene di mostri e di divinità della mitologia greca. Il *dio* greco del fuoco, Vulcano, per esempio, *viveva* nell'interno del monte Etna, la *montagna ardente* (dal greco «aitho»). Secondo un'altra leggenda, *era* impossibile passare lo stretto di Messina *a causa* dei mostri Scilla e Cariddi—eccetto per l'eroe greco Ulisse.

discovery

existed

god

lived/mountain

burning

it was/because of

Gli Arabi hanno lasciato dei templi che *si riconoscono* dalle loro *cupole* sferiche. Il prefisso di diversi nomi di città deriva dall'arabo *Kalat* che significa «castello» (Calatafimi, Caltanissetta, Caltagirone). Marsala, la città del vino marsala, significa «porto di Dio» (dall'arabo «Marsah el Allah»). I Normanni hanno saputo adattare al loro stile l'arte bizantina e araba. Sotto di loro Palermo era una capitale splendida, con cattedrali e palazzi ricchi di mosaici e di giardini esotici. Nella prima *metà* del XIII secolo la corte di Palermo era *la più* brillante d'Europa. La prima scuola di *poesia* italiana è nata precisamente in questa città. Nei secoli successivi gli Spagnoli hanno introdotto in Sicilia lo stile barocco del loro paese. Purtroppo la dominazione spagnola ha anche determinato la decadenza dell'isola.

are recognizable/domes

half

the most

poetry

L'elemento umano rivela un *analogo* contrasto. L'aspetto fisico di molti Siciliani ricorda il tipo arabo. Ma è possibile ritrovare anche il tipo normanno in diversi abitanti dagli occhi azzurri e dai capelli biondi.

similar

Comprensione

Completate le seguenti frasi.

1. La Sicilia è considerata un museo archeologico a causa...
   a. delle sue leggende **b.** dei suoi templi **c.** dei resti di molte civiltà differenti
2. I templi di Agrigento rivelano tracce della civiltà...
   a. bizantina **b.** greca **c.** spagnola
3. L'antico nome della Sicilia, Trinacria, suggerisce (*suggests*) una forma...
   a. triangolare **b.** quadrata **c.** sferica
4. Secondo la leggenda, nel monte Etna abitava...
   a. il dio del fuoco **b.** un mostro **c.** un eroe greco
5. Nel secolo tredicesimo, Palermo era una capitale brillante, piena di palazzi, di arte, e di cultura, sotto la dominazione...
   a. francese **b.** spagnola **c.** normanna
6. La dominazione degli Spagnoli nell'isola ha contribuito...
   a. alla sua ricchezza **b.** alla sua civiltà **c.** alla sua decadenza
7. La Sicilia è divisa dal resto dell'Italia...
   a. dal monte Etna **b.** dallo stretto di Messina **c.** dai mostri Scilla e Cariddi

◀ *Palermo. La civiltà araba ha lasciato le sue tracce nel chiostro e nella chiesa di San Giovanni degli Eremiti.*

▼ *Agrigento. Uno dei templi greci dell'isola.*

12 LA POLITICA

Torino. Una dimostrazione contro la politica del governo italiano.

PUNTI DI VISTA

GLI EMBLEMI DEI MAGGIORI PARTITI POLITICI ITALIANI*

TEMPO DI ELEZIONI

Siamo ad Ancona, capoluogo delle Marche. Sui *muri* (walls) della città *sono affissi* (are posted) molti manifesti elettorali dei diversi partiti. Luciano rientra per il pranzo. Diletta, sua moglie, è già rientrata e l'abbraccia.

Diletta	Ciao, *tesoro*. Come mai sei in ritardo?	honey
Luciano	Sono venuto a casa a piedi. Hai visto quanti manifesti *c'erano* sui muri?	there were
Diletta	Sì, li ho visti, ma la gente non *si fermava* a leggerli. Gli Italiani sono pessimisti, in questi giorni. Ci sono troppi problemi: l'inflazione, la *disoccupazione*, i problemi ecologici…	did not stop; unemployment
Luciano	Hai già deciso per chi votare?	
Diletta	Sì, voterò per il partito dei Verdi.	
Luciano	E il nostro partito? Lo abbandoni?	
Diletta	Sì, perchè hanno parlato molto, ma hanno fatto troppo poco.	
Luciano	Allora, sei *davvero* per i Verdi!	really
Diletta	Sì, quello è un partito giovane, che si occupa attivamente dei problemi dell'*ambiente in cui* viviamo. E tu? Per chi voterai?	environment/in which
Luciano	Io voterò come ho sempre votato.	

*Summer 1993. The current restructuring of a few major parties may cause some modifications in the above names and symbols. The party known for more than forty years as *Democrazia Cristiana* will be renamed *Partito Popolare Italiano*.

Comprensione

1. In quale città abitano Diletta e Luciano?
2. Che ore saranno quando i due sposi rientrano a casa? Perchè rientrano?
3. Cosa c'era sui muri? La gente si fermava a leggerli?
4. Quali sono i problemi che preoccupano di più (*most*) gli Italiani?
5. Per quale partito vuole votare Diletta? Perchè?
6. Per quale partito voterà Luciano?

Studio di parole

il paese country
lo stato state
il governo government
la repubblica, repubblicano
la democrazia, democratico
la monarchia, monarchico
il re; la regina king; queen
il presidente; la presidentessa
il ministro (*m. & f.*)
il senatore; la senatrice
il deputato; la deputata congressman; congresswoman
vincere (*p.p.* **vinto**) to win
perdere to lose
la politica politics
politico political
il partito party
il partito di destra (*right*), **di sinistra** (*left*), **di centro**
il candidato; la candidata
le elezioni
eleggere (*p.p.* **eletto**) to elect
il voto
votare
il risultato
il manifesto

Applicazione

A. 1. Che cosa vediamo sui muri della città durante il periodo delle elezioni?
2. Quanti partiti sono rappresentati nel disegno?
3. Che cosa vuol dire «P.S.I.»? È un partito di destra o di sinistra?
4. Quanti e quali partiti ci sono negli Stati Uniti?

5. C'è una repubblica o una monarchia in Italia?
6. Come si chiama le regina d'Inghilterra?
7. Chi è il presidente degli Stati Uniti oggi?
8. Chi era il presidente degli Stati Uniti durante la seconda guerra mondiale?
9. Che cosa facciamo il giorno delle elezioni?
10. Per chi votiamo?
11. A che età possono votare gli Americani?

B. Domande personali.

1. Nella Sua città ci sono molti manifesti sui muri durante la campagna elettorale?
2. Quando ci sono state le ultime elezioni presidenziali?
3. Quale partito ha vinto? Chi è diventato presidente? Chi è diventato vice-presidente?
4. Quando ci saranno le prossime elezioni presidenziali?
5. Lei sa esattamente per quale partito votare o è indeciso(a)?
6. Lei discute con i Suoi amici dei problemi del Suo paese?
7. Quali sono i problemi che La preoccupano di più? (disoccupazione, inflazione, deficit dello Stato, troppe tasse, ecologia, violenza nelle città, droga, scuola...)

Ascoltiamo!

Dove vi siete conosciuti? *This evening Diletta and Luciano have invited a new colleague of Luciano's to dinner. While Diletta is in the kitchen, he asks Luciano a bit about himself and Diletta. Listen to the conversation, then answer the following questions.*

Comprensione

1. Come trova la moglie di Luciano il collega?
2. Dove si sono conosciuti Luciano e la moglie?
3. In quale facoltà erano (*were*) Luciano e Diletta?
4. Sono ancora idealisti, o non lo sono più? Perchè?
5. Si sono sposati prima della laurea?
6. Hanno fatto una bella carriera (*career*)? Perchè no?
7. Perchè si considerano fortunati?
8. Che cosa pensa il collega della situazione economica?

Dialogo

In gruppi di due, immaginate di essere i due candidati del vostro partito [presidente(ssa) e vice-presidente(ssa)]. Preparate una piccola piattaforma (*platform*), che presenterete agli studenti per convincerli a votare per voi. Verbi utili: **aumentare, diminuire, eliminare, incoraggiare, riformare, aiutare, migliorare** (*to improve*). Espressioni: **disoccupazione, inflazione, deficit dello Stato, tasse, ecologia, tecnologia, violenza nelle città, droga, scuola.**

PUNTI GRAMMATICALI

I. L'imperfetto

C'era una volta un burattino di legno (wooden puppet) che si chiamava Pinocchio. Aveva il naso molto lungo perchè diceva molte bugie...

1. Chi era Pinocchio?
2. Che naso aveva?
3. Perchè era così lungo?

1. The **imperfetto** (from the Latin *imperfectum*) means "imperfect," that is, incomplete. It is used to express an action that took place in the past and that cannot be framed within a precise time limit. It derives from the infinitive and has identical endings for all three conjugations.

   parlare → parla-**vo** = *I was speaking, I used to speak, I spoke*

parlare	ricevere	dormire
parla**vo**	riceve**vo**	dormi**vo**
parla**vi**	riceve**vi**	dormi**vi**
parla**va**	riceve**va**	dormi**va**
parla**vamo**	riceve**vamo**	dormi**vamo**
parla**vate**	riceve**vate**	dormi**vate**
parl**ạvano**	ricev**ẹvano**	dorm**ịvano**

2. The following verbs are irregular in the imperfect tense:

essere:	**ero, eri, era, eravamo, eravate, ẹrano**
fare:	**facevo, facevi, faceva, facevamo, facevate, facẹvano**
bere:	**bevevo, bevevi, beveva, bevevamo, bevevate, bevẹvano**
dire:	**dicevo, dicevi, diceva, dicevamo, dicevate, dicẹvano**

3. The imperfect tense is used to describe:

   a. Environment, time, weather; physical and mental states; and age in the past.

Il salone **era** pieno di gente.	*The hall was full of people.*
Erano le sette di sera.	*It was 7:00 P.M.*
Fuori **faceva** freddo e **pioveva.**	*Outside it was cold, and it was raining.*
La gente **aveva** fame.	*People were hungry.*
Antonio **era** preoccupato. Non **voleva** fare il discorso.	*Antonio was worried. He did not want to give a speech.*
Nel 1976 **avevo** dieci anni.	*In 1976 I was ten years old.*

   b. Habitual actions in the past.

Da bambino **andava** spesso al teatro dei burattini.	*As a child he often used to go to the marionette theater.*
Leggeva favole tutte le sere.	*He read (used to read) fables every night.*

   c. An action in progress while another action was taking place or was completed.

Mentre lui **parlava** il pubblico **si annoiava.**	*While he was speaking, the audience was getting bored.*
Lui **finiva** il discorso quando Marcello è entrato.	*He was finishing his speech when Marcello walked in.*

Pratica

A. Che cosa faceva tutti i giorni Franca quand'era a Venezia?

ESEMPIO visitare la città **Visitava la città.**

1. prendere il vaporetto (*motorboat*) **2.** ammirare i palazzi veneziani **3.** camminare lungo le calli (*narrow streets*) e i ponti (*bridges*) **4.** entrare nelle chiese e nei negozi **5.** fare delle spese **6.** scrivere cartoline ai parenti e agli amici **7.** la sera, sedersi a un caffè di Piazza San Marco **8.** bere un espresso o una bibita (*soft drink*) **9.** divertirsi a guardare la gente **10.** la notte, dormire molte ore

B. Ripetete l'esercizio A, usando come soggetto **I turisti.**

C. Domanda e risposta. Due vecchi amici ricordano gli anni della loro gioventù (*youth*).

ESEMPIO studiare molto/divertirsi
—Studiavi molto o ti divertivi?
—Studiavo molto. *o*
—Mi divertivo.

1. andare all'università tutti i giorni/andare quando avere voglia 2. prepararsi per gli esami/preferire andare al cinema 3. discutere con i compagni/uscire con gli amici per divertirsi 4. preoccuparsi del risultato degli esami/essere indifferente 5. alzarsi presto la mattina/dormire fino a tardi 6. telefonare a casa quando avere bisogno di soldi/cercare un lavoro 7. ascoltare attentamente le conferenze/annoiarsi

D. **Domanda e risposta.** Che cosa facevate tu e i tuoi amici quando eravate in vacanza?

ESEMPIO dove nuotare?
—Dove nuotavate?
—Nuotavamo nel fiume. (nel lago, in piscina,...)

1. a che ora svegliarsi? 2. leggere molto? 3. cosa fare con il bel tempo? 4. come divertirsi? 5. quando mettersi in costume da bagno? 6. cosa bere? 7. dove fare escursioni? 8. a che ora andare a letto?

E. Conversazione tra due persone: la prima persona parla della situazione al presente; la seconda persona risponde che le cose erano così anche nel passato.

ESEMPIO La vita è difficile. **—Oggi la vita è difficile.**
—Anche allora la vita era difficile.

1. I giovani vogliono cambiare le cose. 2. Molte madri lavorano fuori casa. 3. Le donne s'interessano di politica. 4. I padri ripetono le stesse cose. 5. I treni arrivano in ritardo. 6. Molti candidati politici dicono delle bugie. 7. Gli studi sono molto costosi.

F. Riscrivete al passato la lettura del Capitolo 2, *«Due amici differenti»* (pagine 47).

G. Sostituite l'infinito con la forma appropriata dell'**imperfetto.**

1. Mentre il deputato _____ (parlare), molte persone _____ (ascoltare) attentamente, ma altre _____ (annoiarsi). 2. Tutte le mattine, quando _____ (essere) le sette, marito e moglie _____ (salutarsi) e _____ (partire). 3. Quando Mussolini _____ (essere) primo ministro, l'Italia _____ (avere) un re, Vittorio Emanuele III. 4. Tutte le sere il giovane _____ (lavorare) come barista perchè _____ (dovere) pagarsi gli studi. 5. Quando noi _____ (essere) bambini, noi _____ (andare) al cinema tutte le settimane. 6. Io _____ (conoscere) una ragazza che _____ (volere) diventare deputata del Partito Democristiano (DC). 7. I miei nonni _____ (dire) sempre che ai loro tempi i figli _____ (seguire) i consigli dei genitori. 8. Mentre la mamma _____ (raccontare) la favola di *Cappuccetto Rosso* (*Little Red Riding Hood*), i bambini _____ (chiudere) gli occhi perchè _____ (avere) sonno.

H. Completate il seguente paragrafo con la forma appropriata dell'**imperfetto.**

Quando io e mia sorella ______ (essere) giovani, noi ______ (passare) ogni estate con i nonni. I nonni ______ (abitare) in una piccola casa in collina (*hill*). La casa ______ (essere) bianca, con un tetto (*roof*) rosso. Davanti alla casa ________ (esserci) un giardino molto grande. Ogni giorno, quando ______ (fare) caldo, noi ______ (stare) in giardino, e se noi ______ (avere) sete, la nonna _______ (portarci) del tè freddo. Il pomeriggio noi (divertirsi) a giocare a carte (*cards*) o _______ (fare) delle lunghe passeggiate nei campi (*fields*) con il vecchio cane. Alle sette la nonna ______ (chiamarci) per la cena, e noi _______ (aiutarla) ad apparecchiare la tavola. La sera noi ______ (andare) a letto, stanchi ma contenti.

I. Castelli in aria.* Mettete i verbi fra parentesi nella forma corretta dell'imperfetto o del futuro, secondo il caso.

C'era una volta una giovane contadina (*peasant*) che ________ (portare) al mercato del villaggio un secchio (*bucket*) pieno di latte. Mentre ________ (camminare) col secchio sulla testa ________(pensare): «Lo (vendere) e ________ (comprare) dei pulcini (*chicks*). Appena i pulcini ______ (diventare) dei bei polli, li ______ (vendere) e ______ (prendere) un vitellino (*calf*). Quando il vitellino ______ (essere) grasso, lo ______ (portare) al mercato, lo ______ (vendere) e con il guadagno (*earnings*) ______ (comprarsi) un bel vestito. Allora il figlio del re mi ________ (vedere) e ______ (innamorarsi) di me. Dopo il matrimonio, io ______ (andare) dal re. Il mio principe (*prince*) mi _________ (presentare) a suo padre, ed io ______(fare) un bell'inchino (*bow*), così...» Mentre______ (pensare), la ragazza ha fatto un bell'inchino, e il secchio di latte è caduto. La ragazza aveva fatto dei castelli in aria!

II. Contrasto tra imperfetto e passato prossimo

—Hai sentito le previsioni del tempo (weather forecast)?
—Sì, dicevano «sereno su tutta l'Italia».

***Fare dei castelli in aria** means *to daydream.*

Both the **passato prossimo** and the **imperfetto** present events and facts that took place in the past. However, they are not interchangeable.

a. If a past action took place only *once,* was repeated a *specific* number of times, or was performed within a *definite* time period, the **passato prossimo** is used.

b. If a past action was *habitual,* was repeated an *unspecified* number of times, or was performed in an *indefinite* time period (with no beginning or end indicated), the **imperfetto** is used. It is also used to *describe* all *circumstances* surrounding a past action or event (time, weather, physical appearance, age, feelings, attitudes, etc.).

The sentence below illustrates graphically the time relationship between these two tenses:

Quando **sono entrato,**

Antonio **parlava.**

The **passato prossimo** is represented by the dot (•), which symbolizes the *specific point in time* the action (**sono entrato**) occurred. The **imperfetto** is represented by an uninterrupted line (⟶), which symbolizes the *indefinite duration in time* of the action (**parlava**), that is, of *what was going on.*

The following sets of sentences illustrate further the contrast between these two tenses. (Dots and lines are used as a helping device.)

Ieri sera **ho ascoltato** la radio. (•, *one occurrence*)	*Last night I listened to the radio.*
Tutte le sere **ascoltavo** la radio. (⟶, *habitual*)	*Every evening I would (= used to) listen to the radio.*
La settimana scorsa Gianni mi **ha telefonato** tre volte. (•••, *specific number of repetitions*)	*Last week Gianni phoned me three times.*
Prima mi **telefonava** molto spesso. (⟶, *unspecified number of repetitions*)	*Before he used to phone me very often.*
L'estate scorsa **ho fatto** del tennis tutti i giorni. (•, *definite time period:* **l'estate scorsa**)	*Last summer I played tennis every day.*
Quando **ero** giovane, **facevo** del tennis tutti i giorni. (⇉, *indefinite time period* **quando ero giovane**)	*When I was young I would (= used to) play tennis every day.*
Gina **ha preso** l'impermeabile ed **è uscita.** (••, *two successive single occurrences*)	*Gina took her raincoat and went out.*
Gina **ha preso** l'impermeabile perchè **pioveva.** (•⟶, *one occurrence; one factual description with length of time unspecified*)	*Gina took her raincoat because it was raining.*

A. Sei stato(a) testimone (*witness*) a una discussione di politica, e adesso la racconti a un(a) amico(a). Usa il **passato prossimo** o **l'imperfetto**, a seconda del caso *(according to the context).*

1. È il primo giugno. **2.** Sono le otto di sera. **3.** Piove. **4.** Entro al Caffè Repubblica. **5.** Ordino un espresso. **6.** Un giovane arriva al bar. **7.** Ha circa vent'anni. **8.** Porta un vecchio impermeabile. **9.** Incomincia a parlare male del governo. **10.** Un cliente s'arrabbia. **11.** I due litigano. **12.** La confusione è grande. **13.** Un cameriere telefona alla polizia.

B. Descrivete quello che le seguenti persone facevano abitualmente e quello che hanno fatto in un'occasione particolare.

ESEMPIO Antonio, di solito prendere l'autobus/ieri andare a piedi
Antonio di solito prendeva l'autobus, ma ieri è andato a piedi.

1. Io, ogni estate lavorare/quest'estate fare un lungo viaggio **2.** Ornella, la domenica andare alla spiaggia/domenica scorsa non uscire di casa **3.** I commessi, di solito stare nel negozio fino alle (*until*) sei/quel giorno chiuderlo all'una per il brutto tempo **4.** Roberto, ogni agosto partire per le Dolomiti*/quest'anno passare il Ferragosto in Svizzera **5.** I miei genitori, il sabato sera andare al cinema/sabato scorso preferire andare all'opera

C. **Perchè?** Dite che cosa hanno fatto le seguenti persone e perchè.

ESEMPIO Lucia va a letto presto.
Lucia è andata a letto presto perchè aveva sonno.

1. Filippo e Gabriella entrano nella pasticceria. **2.** Mio padre si addormenta nella poltrona. **3.** Il dottore non viene alla clinica. **4.** Marcello non esce con la macchina. **5.** Liliana manda una cartolina a un caro amico.

D. **Che cosa hanno visto o fatto** le seguenti persone mentre camminavano per la strada? Mettete i verbi al passato.

ESEMPIO Antonio vede un giovane che attacca (*is hanging*) manifesti.
Antonio ha visto un giovane che attaccava manifesti.

1. Noi incontriamo un gruppo di lavoratori che gridano «Abbasso (*down with*) il governo!» **2.** Patrizia si ferma ad ascoltare un vecchio che suona il violino. **3.** Io parlo con della gente che discute di politica. **4.** Umberto ammira una bella ragazza che esce da un bar. **5.** Un giovane saluta un signore che porta un abito nero.

E. Sostituite all'infinito la forma corretta dell'**imperfetto** o del **passato prossimo**, a seconda del significato (*according to the meaning*).

---

*Part of the eastern Alps, south of the Austrian border.

1. Questo pomeriggio io _____ (vedere) molte persone: _____ (essere) sul marciapiede e _____ (leggere) dei manifesti. **2.** Quando Graziella _____ (uscire) stamattina, il marito _____ (dormire) ancora. **3.** Ieri Luisa _____ (andare) in campagna: _____ (fare) bel tempo. **4.** Quando noi _____ (svegliarsi), _____ (essere) le sei. **5.** Oggi Paolo _____ (incontrare) la sua ragazza: lei_____ (portare) un vestito rosso. **6.** L'Italia _____ (diventare) una repubblica perchè gli Italiani _____ (essere) scontenti della monarchia. **7.** Lo scrittore italiano Carlo Collodi _____ (scrivere) Pinocchio perchè _____ (avere) bisogno di soldi. **8.** Ieri noi _____ (camminare) lungo la strada quando _____ (vedere) un incidente automobilistico. **9.** La ragazza americana _____ (restare) all'Università per Stranieri di Perugia tre mesi perchè _____ (desiderare) imparare l'italiano.

III. Contrasto tra imperfetto e passato prossimo con alcuni verbi

—Ho dovuto lavorare, anche se non stavo bene.

Certain verbs such as **dovere**, **potere**, **sapere**, **volere**, and **conoscere** have different meanings depending on whether they are used in the **imperfetto** or in the **passato prossimo;** the former stresses the state, the latter the action.

Doveva lavorare, ma non stava bene.	*He (She) was supposed to work, but he (she) was not well.*
Ha dovuto lavorare anche se non stava bene.	*He had to work even if he was not well.*
Potevo uscire, ma non ne avevo voglia.	*I could have gone out, but I did not feel like it.*
Ho potuto finire il lavoro in un'ora.	*I was able to finish the job in one hour.*
Sapevamo che le elezioni erano in giugno.	*We knew the elections were in June.*

Abbiamo saputo che i socialisti non hanno vinto.	*We found out that the Socialists didn't win.*
Lui **voleva** divertirsi, ma non aveva soldi.	*He wanted to have fun, but he did not have any money.*
Maria **ha voluto** comprare una casa in Riviera.	*Maria wanted to buy a house on the Riviera (and she did).*
Conoscevo il senator Fabbri.	*I knew Senator Fabbri.*
Ieri **ho conosciuto** suo padre.	*Yesterday I met his father (for the first time)*

Pratica

A. **Domanda e risposta.** Ecco una conversazione tra due compagni di classe. Seguite l'esempio.

ESEMPIO dovere studiare ieri sera/sì, ma preferire uscire
—Dovevi studiare ieri sera?
—Sì, ma ho preferito uscire.

1. non potere restare a casa/sì, ma decidere di uscire **2.** non volere leggere queste pagine/sì, ma un amico telefonarmi **3.** sapere che l'Italia è una repubblica/sì, leggerlo nel mio libro di storia **4.** sapere il nome del primo re d'Italia/no, ma impararlo qualche mese fa **5.** non dovere scrivere alcuni esercizi di questo capitolo/sì, ma leggere solo il dialogo

B. Sostituite l'infinito tra parentesi con la forma corretta del **passato prossimo** o dell'**imperfetto.**

1. La bambina _____ (volere) giocare, ma la mamma le ha detto di studiare. **2.** Il deputato è ritornato contento: _____ (potere) visitare il Giappone. **3.** Due giorni fa noi_____ (conoscere) il candidato del Partito Socialista. **4.** _____ (Sapere) Lei che l'Italia è diventata una repubblica nel 1946? **5.** Domenica scorsa noi _____ (dovere) partire, ma pioveva e siamo restati a casa. **6.** Ieri io _____ (sapere) che Marcello non lavora più in banca. **7.** Sono ritornato(a) a casa tardi perchè _____ (dovere) prendere un libro in biblioteca.

C. **Rispondete.**

1. Conoscevi già i tuoi compagni di classe o li hai conosciuti all'inizio del trimestre? **2.** Hai dovuto fare recentemente qualche cosa anche se non avevi voglia di farla? Che cosa? Perchè? **3.** Sapevi che l'ultimo re d'Italia si chiamava Umberto II? Quando l'hai saputo? **4.** Tu volevi forse comprare un regalo per Natale, ma non hai potuto. Che regalo? Perchè non hai potuto comprarlo?

IV. Da quanto tempo? Da quando?

—Da quanto tempo aspetta l'autobus?
—Da secoli.

1. To ask *how long* (**da quanto tempo?**) something has been going on, the following construction is used:

Da	+	**(quanto tempo)**	+	*present tense*
Da		**quanti anni**		**abiti** qui?
(For) How		*many years*		*have you been living here?*

To answer, the following construction is used:

present tense	+	**da**	+	**(tempo)**
Abito qui		**da**		**dieci anni.**
I have been living here		*(for)*		*ten years.*

Da quanti giorni sei a Roma?	*How many days have you been in Rome?*
Sono a Roma **da tre giorni.**	*I have been in Rome (for) three days.*
Da quanto tempo siete sposati?	*How long have you been married?*
Siamo sposati **da due anni.**	*We have been married (for) two years.*

2. If the question is **da quando?** (*since when?*), **da** means *since.*

Da quando studi l'italiano?	*Since when have you been studying Italian?*
Studio l'italiano **dall'anno scorso.**	*I have been studying Italian since last year.*

3. The **imperfetto + da** is used to express an action that started at some point in the past and was still in progress when another action was completed.

Parlava da trenta minuti quando l'amico è arrivato.	*He had been speaking for thirty minutes when his friend arrived.*

NOTE:
The **passato prossimo + per** is used when the action began and was completed in the past.

Ha parlato per trenta minuti.	*He spoke for thirty minutes.*

A. Da quanto tempo? Domanda e risposta.

ESEMPIO abitare in questa città —**Da quanto tempo abiti in questa città?**
—**Abito in questa città da sei mesi (un anno, due anni, ecc.).**

1. frequentare l'università **2.** studiare l'italiano **3.** essere alla lezione d'italiano **4.** abitare all'indirizzo attuale (*present*) **5.** non vedere la tua famiglia **6.** non andare a un buon ristorante **7.** avere la patente (*driver's license*) **8.** parlare una lingua straniera

B. Da quando? Completate le frasi.

ESEMPIO Abito in questa città, 1985 **Abito in questa città dal 1985.**

1. L'Alaska è uno stato americano, 1958 **2.** L'Italia non è più una monarchia, 1946 **3.** La Costituzione americana esiste, 1789 **4.** L'Italia è una nazione unita, 1871 **5.** La California fa parte degli Stati Uniti, 1850

C. Leggete le seguenti frasi e dite **da quanto tempo** non facevate le seguenti cose. Seguite l'esempio.

ESEMPIO Oggi sono andato(a) al ristorante.
Non andavo al ristorante da tre mesi. *o*

1. La settimana scorsa ho parlato di politica. **2.** Venerdì sera sono andato(a) al cinema. **3.** Sabato ho pulito la mia stanza. **4.** Domenica ho fatto il footing. **5.** Ieri ho visto i miei zii. **6.** La notte scorsa ho dormito bene. **7.** Oggi ho bevuto latte.

V. Il trapassato prossimo

—Perchè sei ritornato in prigione?
—Perchè mia moglie aveva venduto la casa!

The **trapassato prossimo** (*pluperfect*) expresses an action that took place prior to an action in the past. It is a compound tense formed with the *imperfect tense* of the auxiliary (**avere** or **essere**) + *the past participle* of the main verb.

avevo ascoltato = *I had listened*

It is conjugated as follows:

parlare		partire		alzarsi	
avevo	parlato	ero	partito(a)	mi ero	alzato(a)
avevi		eri		ti eri	
aveva		era		si era	
avevamo		eravamo	partiti(e)	ci eravamo	alzati(e)
avevate		eravate		vi eravate	
avevano		erano		si erano	

Non aveva fame perchè **aveva** già **mangiato.**	*She wasn't hungry because she had already eaten.*
Non siamo andati a San Remo perchè c'**eravamo** già **stati** l'anno scorso.	*We didn't go to San Remo because we had already been there last year.*

Pratica

A. **Domanda e risposta.** Perchè non hai fatto le seguenti cose? Rispondete secondo l'esempio e usate pronomi, se possibile.

ESEMPIO mangiare con noi **—Perchè non hai mangiato con noi?**
—Perchè avevo già mangiato.

1. telefonare al tuo amico **2.** leggere i manifesti **3.** guardare la TV **4.** scrivere al senatore **5.** salutare le compagne di classe **6.** prendere un giorno di vacanza **7.** scusarti con il tuo collega

B. Completate con il **trapassato prossimo.**

1. Gino parlava bene l'italiano perchè _____ (studiare) lingue all'università. **2.** Le ho fatto un bel regalo perchè lei _____ (farmi) un favore. **3.** Ieri non siamo usciti perchè il giorno prima noi _____ (stancarsi) molto. **4.** Mi ha detto che quella sera lui _____ (aspettarmi) per tre ore e poi _____ (andare) a casa. **5.** Le ho portato dei cioccolatini perchè lei _____ (invitarmi) a cena la settimana prima. **6.** Quando tu sei arrivato, lei _____ (arrivare, già)? **7.** Io non l'ho visto, ma ho saputo che lui _____ (venire) a cercarmi.

C. **Troppo tardi!** Spiegate cos' è avvenuto (*happened*) alle seguenti persone.

ESEMPIO Filippo si sveglia. Gabriella è uscita.
Quando Filippo si è svegliato, Gabriella era già uscita.

1. La signora ritorna a casa. Il ladro ha rubato (*stole*) tutti i gioielli (*jewels*).
2. Entriamo in cucina. Il gatto ha mangiato le salsicce (*sausages*).
3. Andiamo dal fornaio. Il fornaio ha venduto tutto il pane.
4. Trovo la sala della riunione. Il candidato ha finito il suo discorso.

UNA POESIA DIALETTALE

Er compagno scompagno	*Il cattivo* compagno	comrade
Un Gatto, che faceva er socialista	Un Gatto, che *faceva* il socialista	pretended to be
Solo a lo scopo d'arivà' in un posto,	*solo allo scopo* d'arrivare a un *posto,*	just in order to position
Se stava lavoranno un pollo arosto	*si lavorava* un pollo arrosto	was eating
Ne la cucina d'un capitalista.	nella cucina d'un capitalista.	
Quanno da un finestrino su per aria	Quando *da un finestrino su per aria*	at a small narrow window from above
S'affacciò un antro Gatto:— Amico mio.	*s'affaccia* un altro Gatto:— Amico mio,	appears
Pensa—je disse—che ce so' pur'io	—gli dice—pensa che sono qui anch'io	
Ch'appartengo a la classe proletaria!	e che *appartengo* alla classe proletaria.	I belong
Io che conosco bene l'idee tue	Io che conosco bene le idee tue	
So' certo che quer pollo che te magni,	sono certo che quel pollo che tu mangi,	
Se vengo giù, sarà diviso in due:	se vengo *giù, sarà diviso* in due:	down/it will be divided
Mezzo a te mezzo a me... Semo compagni!	mezzo a te, mezzo a me... Siamo compagni!...	
—No, no:—rispose er Gatto senza core—	—No, no:—risponde il Gatto *senza cuore*—	heartless
Io nun divido gnente co' nessuno:	Io non divido *niente* con *nessuno:*	nothing nobody
Fo er socialista quanno sto a diggiuno,	faccio il socialista quando *sto a digiuno,*	I am starving
Ma quanno magno so' conservatore!	ma quando mangio sono conservatore!	

Satira in dialetto romano del poeta Trilussa (1871–1950)

LETTURA

LA COMUNITÀ EUROPEA

Filippo, Gabriella, Marcello e la sua amica Jane Clark sono seduti ad un caffè vicino a Piazza del Duomo. Hanno un'aria seria: parlano di politica.

Marcello In Italia abbiamo bisogno di riforme e di un governo *stabile,* se vogliamo essere pronti per l'unione monetaria europea del 1997. — stable

Jane Per favore, spiegatemi la differenza tra il Mercato Comune Europeo e la Comunità Europea.

Marcello *Nessuna* differenza, veramente. La seconda guerra mondiale aveva lasciato l'Europa *occidentale* mezzo *distrutta* e i paesi avevano bisogno di ricostruire la loro economia. Così, sei nazioni, *fra cui* l'Italia, hanno formato un mercato comune che permetteva la libera circolazione delle persone, delle *merci* e dei capitali. Nel 1957, con il *Trattato* di Roma, nasceva la CEE o Comunità Economica Europea. Più tardi, altri paesi si sono uniti alla CEE, e nel 1979 hanno eletto un Parlamento Europeo che ha deciso di creare una moneta unica europea, l'*Ecu.* — no; western/destroyed; among which; goods; treaty; EuropeanCurrency Unit

Filippo L'idea era di realizzare un'unione economica e monetaria, e di integrare un giorno anche le politiche sociali ed *estere* dei paesi *partecipanti.* — foreign; participating

Gabriella	Penso che non sarà facile. Siamo troppo *attaccati* al nostro paese: abbiamo una lingua, delle tradizioni e una cultura diverse. Io mi sentirò sempre e soltanto italiana.	attached
Jane	Anche il mio paese è formato di gente di origini e di culture diverse, *eppure* ci sentiamo americani.	and yet
Filippo	In Europa forse sarà possibile una confederazione economica, ma *niente di più*.	nothing more

Strasburgo (Francia). Il Parlamento della CEE.

Comprensione

1. Di cosa parlano i quattro amici?
2. Di cosa hanno bisogno gli Italiani per essere pronti per l'unione monetaria europea?
3. Quando è nato il Mercato Comune Europeo?
4. Qual era il suo scopo (*aim*)?
5. Che cosa significa CEE?
6. In che anno e dove è nata questa organizzazione?
7. I paesi che partecipano alla CEE desiderano solamente un'unione economica e monetaria? A cosa sperano di arrivare?
8. Perchè Gabriella e Filippo esprimono un certo pessimismo?
9. Chi sembra (*seems*) ottimista? Perchè?

Domande personali

1. Lei aveva già sentito parlare della CEE? Sapeva il significato di questa sigla (*abbreviation*)?
2. Secondo Lei, un'unione economica e politica delle nazioni europee, sarà una realtà o resterà un'utopia? Perchè?
3. Un'integrazione dei sistemi economici dei paesi della CEE avrà conseguenze positive o negative per l'economia degli Stati Uniti?
4. Gli studenti universitari americani s'interessano di politica internazionale?
5. Lei legge giornali o riviste (*magazines*) che riportano notizie di politica estera? Quali?

ATTIVITÀ SUPPLEMENTARI

A. **Elezioni.** Parlate delle ultime elezioni presidenziali. (Ogni studente contribuisce con qualche frase.) Chi erano i candidati? Di quale partito erano? Com'erano? Qual era il candidato favorito? Perchè? Chi ha vinto le elezioni? Secondo voi, perchè ha vinto? Chi è diventato vice-presidente?

B. **La famiglia Brambilla.** (disegno numero 1) Che cosa facevano di solito i Brambilla, padre e figlia, la sera? E il cane? Dov'era la signora? Descrivete usando l'imperfetto. (**poltrona**, *armchair*)

C. **Passatempi.** (disegno numero 2) Che cosa facevano le persone quando andavano al parco? Descrivete usando l'imperfetto (**i piccioni**, *pigeons;* **dare da mangiare**, *to feed;* **panchina**, *bench;* **innamorati**, *lovers*).

D. **Pagina di un diario** (*diary*). Lei è andato(a) a una riunione politica (o a una conferenza, o...). Descriva quello che ha visto e sentito. Che giorno era? Che tempo faceva? Dov'era Lei? Perchè era là? Che cosa è successo? (*What happened?*) Che cosa ha detto l'oratore (*speaker*)?

E. **Attività in gruppi di due.** Intervistate un compagno (una compagna) sulla sua conoscenza di politica nazionale ed estera.

Incominciate le vostre domande con "**Sai...?**"

1. ... in che anno è finita la seconda guerra mondiale?
2. ... chi era dittatore in Italia allora?
3. ... chi erano i due scienziati, uno americano, l'altro italiano, che hanno contribuito alla costruzione della bomba atomica?
4. ... come si chiamava il presidente eletto dopo Eisenhower?
5. ... in quale paese e in quale città si trovava il muro infame (*infamous wall*) che è caduto alcuni anni fa?

6. ... quale uomo politico russo ha contribuito con le sue idee alla caduta del comunismo?
7. ... in quale città alcuni capi (*leaders*) europei hanno firmato il trattato che ha dato origine alla CEE?
8. ... il nome di alcuni paesi della CEE?
9. ... dove si trova il Parlamento della Comunità Europea?
10. ... cos'è l'Ecu?

BOSNIA-ERZEGOVINA

Pioggia di granate sulla città, nove morti

Sarajevo, in fiamme l'hotel dei profughi

Incertezza sulla data

Bossi: «Presto ci saranno le elezioni»

VARESE. «In questo momento non c'è possibilità di fare accordi politici col pds ma può essere che i forti siano interessati a non far crollare il Paese. Se ci

ITERVISTA AL PRESIDENTE

«Il socialismo non è morto»

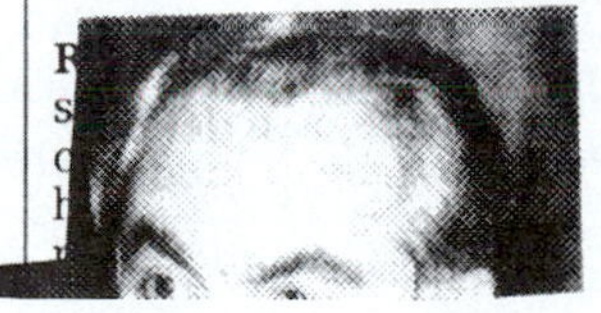

ROMA. Il presidente del Consiglio Giuliano Amato non crede che il psi sia al capolinea dopo la crisi scaturita da Tangentopoli. «Non penso che l'idea stessa di socialismo sia

F. **Come si dice in italiano?**

1. I am reading from the diary of a young cynic (**cinico**).
2. The other day my friends and I were listening to a political speech.
3. The candidate who (**che**) was giving (**fare**) the speech was a Christian Democrat; he was about fifty and was wearing a gray suit and glasses.
4. He was saying that Italy needed to change and that we had to vote for his party.
5. I had heard these same lies last week from a socialist candidate.
6. At one time (**una volta**), I used to listen to these speeches.
7. Suddenly, we heard the voice of a young man.
8. He was asking the candidate if his speeches were always so interesting.
9. When we went out, it was raining.
10. We all went to the Caffè Sport.

Vocabolario

Nomi

il barista	*barman*
la bibita	*soft drink*
la bugia	*lie*
il/la cliente	*client*
il/la comunista	*communist*
la confusione	*confusion*
la conoscenza	*knowledge*
la cultura	*culture*
il democristiano, la democristiana	*Christian democrat*
la destra	*right*
il diario	*diary*
il discorso	*speech*
la discussione	*discussion*
la disoccupazione	*unemployment*
la droga	*drug*
l'ecologia	*ecology*
l'economia	*economy*
la favola	*fable*
la guerra	*war*
l'idealista (*m., f.*)	*idealist*
l'incidente (*m.*)	*accident*
l'inflazione (*f.*)	*inflation*
il muro	*wall*
la nazione	*nation*
l'ottimista (*m., f.*)	*optimist*
il passato	*past*
il/la pessimista	*pessimist*
la polizia	*police*
il ponte	*bridge*
il problema	*problem*
il/la realista	*realist*
la realtà	*reality*
la sinistra	*left*
il/la socialista	*socialist*
la tassa	*tax*
la tradizione	*tradition*
l'unione (*f.*)	*union*
la violenza	*violence*
la voce	*voice*

Aggettivi

comune	*common*
costoso	*expensive*
diverso	*various; different*
ecologico	*ecological*
estero	*foreign*
internazionale	*international*
pieno	*full*
presidenziale	*presidential*
scontento	*unhappy*
unito	*united*
utile	*useful*

Verbi

abbandonare	*to abandon*
attaccare	*to hang; to attach*
aumentare	*to increase*
diminuire (-isc)	*to diminish, to reduce*
esistere (*p.p.* esistito)	*to exist*
migliorare	*to improve*
interessarsi (di)	*to be interested in*
occuparsi (di)	*to devote oneself to*
preoccupare	*to worry*
preoccuparsi (di)	*to be worried about*

Altre espressioni

Abbasso!	*Down with*
abitualmente	*usually*
avere un'aria	*to look like*
c'era una volta	*once upon a time*
da bambino(a)	*as a child*
davvero	*really*
durante	*during*
esattamente	*exactly*
fino a	*until*
giocare a carte	*to play cards*
improvvisamente	*suddenly*
parlare male (di)	*to say bad things about*
la seconda guerra mondiale	*World War II*
tesoro	*honey; sweetheart*

LA REPUBBLICA ITALIANA

L'Italia è un paese che *vanta* una storia e una civiltà antiche. Come stato *tuttavia*, è nata solamente nel 1861, con il nome di *Regno* d'Italia.

boasts / however / kingdom

La dittatura fascista iniziata nel 1922 ha accettato la presenza del re, ma ha centralizzato il *potere* nelle *mani* di Mussolini. La fine della seconda guerra mondiale ha visto anche la fine del fascismo e della monarchia. Infatti, il 2 giugno 1946 gli Italiani si sono presentati alle *urne* per la prima volta *per scegliere* la forma del nuovo governo: la repubblica.

power / hands / polls/to choose

Oggi l'Italia è una repubblica parlamentare. Il Parlamento è formato dalla *Camera dei Deputati* e da *quella dei Senatori*. Questi hanno *il potere* di fare *le leggi*, di eleggere il Presidente e di approvare un nuovo governo. Il Presidente è il capo dello Stato e *resta in carica* sette anni. Il capo del governo è il Primo Ministro, *che* è nominato dal Presidente e che ha l'autorità *di scegliere* i suoi collaboratori, *cioè* i membri del Consiglio dei Ministri.

the House of Representatives/that of the Senate/power / laws / is appointed for / who / to choose/that is

Diversi partiti siedono nelle due camere. Tra i principali sono la Democrazia Cristiana (DC), che ha dominato la scena politica fino al 1983; il Partito Repubblicano (PRI), il Partito Liberale (PLI), il Partito Socialista (PSI), il Partito Social-Democratico (PSDI) e il Partito Comunista, ora diviso in due: Partito Democratico della Sinistra (PDS) e Partito della Rifondazione Comunista. Negli ultimi anni si sono formati altri partiti: i più notevoli sono il Partito dei Verdi, che si occupa di ecologia e quello della Lega Nord, che favorisce l'autonomia regionale. Questa pluralità di partiti è una delle cause principali dell'instabilità del governo italiano. *In seguito a* una grave crisi dei partiti al governo, gli Italiani hanno votato per una riforma del sistema elettorale (referendum dell'aprile 1993).

following

Comprensione

Vero o falso? Se le seguenti frasi sono false, correggetele.

1. L'Italia è diventata uno stato molti secoli fa.
2. Il fascismo ha trasformato l'Italia in repubblica.
3. Nel 1946 gli Italiani hanno votato e hanno scelto come forma di governo la repubblica.
4. Il popolo italiano vota per eleggere i vari ministri e il presidente della Repubblica.
5. Il presidente è anche il capo del governo.
6. Il PDS è un partito di centro.
7. Il Partito dei Verdi favorisce l'autonomia delle regioni.

Roma. Piazza del Campidoglio e in fondo, il Palazzo del Senato. ▲

Oscar Luigi Scalfaro, Presidente della Repubblica Italiana (1993). ▶

13 LA CASA

Elegante salotto di una casa in Sicilia.

Punti di vista

Il nuovo appartamento
Il giorno del trasloco

Punti grammaticali

I *Ne*
II *Ci*
III I pronomi doppi
IV I pronomi doppi con i verbi riflessivi

Lettura

Si affitta appartamento ammobiliato

Pagina culturale

Le abitazioni in Italia

PUNTI DI VISTA

Moderni appartamenti a Marina di Carrara (Toscana).

IL NUOVO APPARTAMENTO

Emanuela e Franco abitano a Napoli,* dove Franco lavora come guida turistica. Da alcune settimane Emanuela cercava un appartamento. Ora ne ha trovato uno e lo dice al marito.

—Franco, ho trovato un appartamento *bellissimo!* È in	very beautiful
via Nazionale, al terzo *piano.*	floor
—Quante stanze ci sono?	
—Ce ne sono tre, con un bel bagno, e la cucina è abbastanza grande.	
—Quante finestre ci sono nella sala?	
—Ce ne sono due. Tutto l'appartamento ha molta *luce.*	light
—È *ammobiliato* o vuoto?	furnished
—È ammobiliato.	
—*Magnifico!* Ed è già libero?	wonderful
—Sì, e *il padrone di casa* dice che dobbiamo firmare il contratto per almeno sei mesi.	landlord
—Va bene, glielo firmeremo. Quant'è l'*affitto?*	rent
—900.000 lire al mese, *comprese le spese.*	with expenses
—Possiamo portare il nostro gatto?	
—Non gliel'ho domandato, ma *penso di sì.***	I think so
—Allora potremo *traslocare* il primo del mese!	to move

*Napoli is the chief city of Campania and the second port of Italy. It is situated near the volcano Vesuvio and the archeological ruins of Pompei and Ercolano.

Verbs such as **pensare, **credere** and **dire**, take **di** when affirming or denying something: **Penso di no** = *I don't think so;* ***Ha detto di sì*** = *He said yes.*

Comprensione

1. Da quanto tempo Emanuela e Franco cercavano un appartamento?
2. A che piano si trova quello in via Nazionale?
3. Quante stanze ci sono in quell'appartamento?
4. Perchè c'è molta luce nella sala?
5. Dovranno comprare i mobili Emanuela e Franco? Perchè no?
6. Quanto vuole d'affitto il padrone di casa?
7. Emanuela vuole lasciare il gatto a un parente o desidera portarlo nel nuovo appartamento?
8. Quando potranno traslocare?

Studio di parole

I MOBILI (*FURNITURE*)

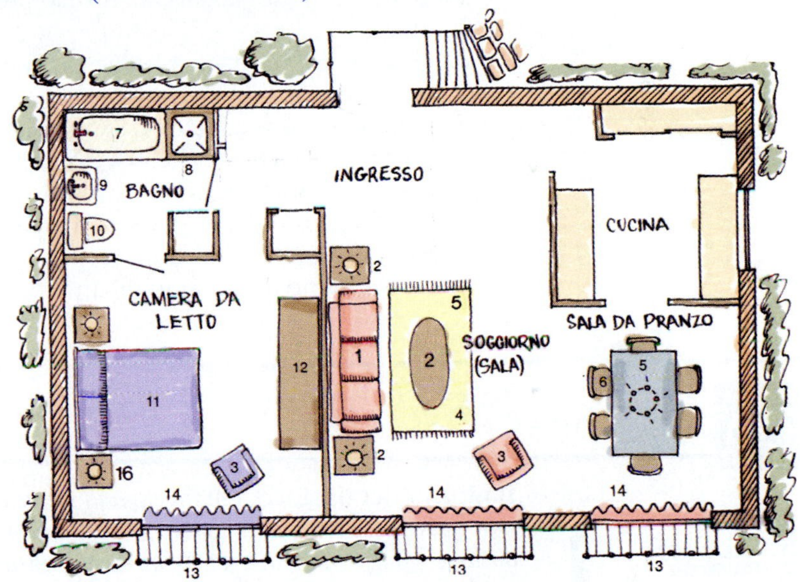

1 **il divano** sofa
2 **il tavolino** end table, coffee table
3 **la poltrona** armchair
4 **il tappeto** rug
5 **la tavola** table (dining table)
6 **la sedia** chair
7 **la vasca da bagno** bath tub
8 **la doccia** shower
9 **il lavabo** sink
10 **il W.C.** toilet (water closet)
11 **il letto** bed
il letto singolo single bed
il letto matrimoniale double bed
12 **l'armadio** wardrobe
13 **il balcone** balcony
14 **le tende** draperies

LA BIANCHERIA

la coperta blanket
il lenzuolo (*pl.* **le lenzuola**) sheet
il cuscino pillow

la roba household articles

l'affitto rent
affittare to rent

il trasloco move
traslocare to move
la cauzione deposit
il padrone di casa landlord
l'inquilino tenant

A. Guardate il disegno.

1. Quante camere da letto ci sono in quest'appartamento?
2. Dove sono la tavola e le sei sedie?
3. Che mobili ci sono nel soggiorno?
4. Cosa c'è sotto il tavolino davanti al divano?
5. La camera da letto è per una o per due persone? Come lo sa?
6. Da dove riceve la luce la camera da letto?
7. Mangiamo in cucina quando abbiamo degli invitati?
8. Che biancheria è necessaria per fare il letto?

B. Domande personali.

1. Lei preferisce abitare in una casa o in un appartamento?
2. Se Lei affitta un appartamento, lo preferisce ai primi piani o ai piani alti?
3. Quando Lei immagina la Sua casa ideale, la preferisce in città, al mare, in montagna o in campagna?
4. Quante camere da letto ci sono nella Sua casa ideale?
5. Quali mobili ci sono nel soggiorno?
6. In quale stanza mette Lei la televisione?
7. Nel soggiorno, Lei preferisce i tappeti orientali o la moquette (*wall-to-wall carpet*)?
8. Le piacciono di più i mobili antichi o i mobili moderni?

Ascoltiamo!

Il giorno del trasloco. *Emanuela and Franco, exhausted from moving into their new apartment today, are taking a break and talking about what they have yet to do and what it has all cost them. Listen to their conversation, then answer the following questions.*

Comprensione

1. Emanuela e Franco hanno dimenticato qualche cosa nel vecchio appartamento? Hanno portato tutta la loro roba?
2. Che cos'hanno portato nel nuovo appartamento?
3. Chi è Mimì? Dove sarà?
4. Perchè Franco sembra preoccupato? Che cosa ha dovuto dare al padrone di casa?
5. Emanuela ha fretta di fare altre spese? Come si sente?
6. Mentre loro parlano, chi arriva? Sembra contento o scontento lui? Perchè, secondo Lei?

Dialogo

In gruppi di due, immaginate che avete affittato insieme un appartamento vuoto di due locali *(rooms)*, e ora dovete arredarlo *(to furnish it)*. Discutete insieme quali mobili comprare e dove metterli.

PUNTI GRAMMATICALI

I. Ne

Antonio fa la spesa.
—Quante pere desidera?
—Ne desidero un chilo.
—Desidera uva, mele, fragole?
—No, non ne ho bisogno.

1. Desidera molti chili di pere Antonio?
2. Desidera altra frutta?

1. **Ne** is an invariable pronoun that has several meanings: *some (of it, of them); any (of it, of them); about it, about them; of it, of them.* **Ne** can be used to replace a noun used in a partitive sense or a noun introduced by a number or expression of quantity, such as **poco**, **molto**, **tanto**, **chilo**, **cestino** *(basket)*, **bottiglia**, etc.

Hai **del vino bianco?** No, non **ne** ho.	*Do you have some white wine?* *No, I don't have any (of it).*
Volevo **delle pesche.** **Ne** volevo alcune.	*I wanted some peaches.* *I wanted some (of them).*
Quante **stanze** hai? **Ne** ho tre.	*How many rooms do you have?* *I have three (of them).*
Quanti **anni** hai? **Ne** ho ventitrè.	*How old are you?* *I am twenty-three.*
Hai molti **vestiti?** Sì, **ne** ho molti.	*Do you have many dresses?* *Yes, I have many.*
Vorrei **due cestini di fragole.** **Ne** vorrei due cestini.	*I would like two baskets of strawberries.* *I would like two baskets (of them).*

2. **Ne** replaces the noun or infinitive used after verbs such as **avere bisogno di, avere paura di, essere contento di, parlare di,** and **pensare di** (when asking for an opinion).

Hai bisogno **di lavorare?**	*Do you need to work?*
No, non **ne** ho bisogno.	*No, I do not need to.*
Parlavate **dell'affitto?**	*Were you talking about the rent?*
Sì, **ne** parlavamo.	*Yes, we were talking about it.*
Che pensi **di quel film?**	*What do you think of that movie?*
Che **ne** pensi?	*What do you think of it?*

3. **Ne** has the same position as that of object pronouns.

Quante **camere** avevi?	*How many rooms did you have?*
Ne avevo cinque.	*I had five (of them).*
Vuoi comprare **delle arance?**	*Do you want to buy some oranges?*
Voglio comprar**ne** 4 o 5. / **Ne** voglio comprare 4 o 5.	*I want to buy 4 or 5 (of them).*
Cọmpra**ne** due chili!	*Buy two kilos (of them)!*

4. When **ne** is used with the **passato prossimo**, the past participle agrees with the noun replaced by **ne** only when this noun is a direct object.

Quanti **annunci** hai letto?	*How many ads have you read?* (direct object)
Ne ho lett**i** molti.	*I have read many (of them).*

But if the noun replaced by **ne** is *not* a direct object, there is no agreement.

Abbiamo parlato **delle elezioni.**	*We talked about the elections.*
Ne abbiamo parlato.	*We talked about them.*

Pratica

A. **Domanda e risposta.** In un negozio di frutta e verdura. Seguite l'esempio.

ESEMPIO pesche **—Vorrei delle pesche.**
—Quante ne desidera?
—Ne vorrei quattro. *o*

1. fragole **2.** uva bianca **3.** mele **4.** pomodori **5.** piselli **6.** patate **7.** pere **8.** funghi (*mushrooms*)

B. Rispondete, usando il pronome **ne.**

1. Quanti corsi hai questo trimestre (semestre)? **2.** Quante camere da letto hai? **3.** Quanti amici hai? **4.** Hai dei fratelli? Quanti? **5.** Leggi molti o pochi libri? **6.** Quanti anni avevi quando hai incominciato le scuole elementari? **7.** Quanti giocattoli (*toys*) avevi quando eri bambino? **8.** Dicevi molte bugie da bambino(a)?

C. Rispondete affermativamente o negativamente, usando il pronome **ne.**

ESEMPIO Abbiamo bisogno di carta per scrivere? **—Sì, ne abbiamo bisogno.**

1. Abbiamo bisogno del passaporto per andare in Messico? **2.** Abbiamo bisogno di mangiare per vivere? **3.** Abbiamo bisogno di soldi per essere felici? **4.** E tu, desideri avere molti soldi? **5.** Parli qualche volta della tua famiglia? **6.** Parli di politica durante le elezioni? **7.** Con chi parli dei tuoi problemi personali? **8.** Vuoi parlare dei tuoi problemi ora? **9.** Ha paura Lei di una guerra? **10.** Ha paura del terremoto (*earthquake*)? **11.** Ha paura degli esami?

D. **Domanda e risposta.** Conversazione con un amico (un'amica) che è ritornato(a) da un viaggio in Italia. Seguite l'esempio.

ESEMPIO conoscere persone interessanti —**Hai conosciuto delle persone interessanti?**
—**Ne ho conosciute molte (poche, una...).** *o*
—**Non ne ho conosciute.**

1. vedere molte città **2.** visitare dei musei **3.** incontrare molti turisti americani **4.** fare delle telefonate negli Stati Uniti **5.** bere dell'acqua minerale San Pellegrino **6.** mangiare molta pasta **7.** essere contento del viaggio

E. Rispondete affermativamente usando **lo**, **la**, **li**, **le** o **ne**, secondo il caso.

ESEMPIO —Hai comprato i libri? —**Sì, li ho comprati.**
—Hai comprato dei libri?—**Sì, ne ho comprati.**

1. Hai veduto le fontane di Roma? **2.** Hai veduto delle fontane a Roma? **3.** Hai visitato dei musei? **4.** Hai visitato i musei Vaticani? **5.** Hai bevuto il Frascati? **6.** Hai bevuto del Frascati? **7.** Hai preso dell'acqua minerale? **8.** Hai preso l'acqua minerale? **9.** Hai incontrato i turisti americani? **10.** Hai incontrato dei turisti americani?

II. Ci

—Quanti piani ci sono?
—Ce ne sono troppi!

1. The adverb **ci** means *there* when it is used in the expressions **c'è** and **ci sono.**

Scusi, **c'è** una galleria d'arte?	*Excuse me, is there an art gallery?*
Ci sono due lampade in sala.	*There are two lamps in the living room.*

2. **Ci** is also used to replace an expression indicating location and introduced by **a, in, su,** or **da.** It has the same position as that of object pronouns.

Quando vieni **da me?**	*When are you coming to my house?*
Ci vengo stasera.	*I am coming (there) tonight.*
Sei stato(a) **in Italia?**	*Have you been to Italy?*
No, non **ci** sono mai stato.	*No, I have never been there.*
Voglio andar**ci**. / **Ci** voglio andare.	*I want to go there.*

3. **Ci** may also replace a prepositional phrase governed by **a** after verbs such as **credere** (*to believe in*) and **pensare** (*to think about*).

Credi **all'astrologia?**	*Do you believe in astrology?*
No, non **ci** credo.	*No, I don't believe in it.*
Devi pensare **al futuro!**	*You have to think about the future!*
Pens**aci** bene!	*Think well about it!*
Non voglio pensar**ci**! / Non **ci** voglio pensare!	*I don't want to think about it!*

4. **Ci** + **vuole** or **vogliono** acquires the idiomatic meaning of *it takes* or *one needs.*

ci vuole + *singular noun:*

Ci vuole un'ora per andare da Bologna a Firenze.	*It takes one hour to go from Bologna to Florence.*

ci vogliono + *plural noun:*

Ci vogliono 20 minuti per andare da Firenze a Fiesole.	*It takes 20 minutes to go from Florence to Fiesole.*

5. When **ci** is followed by a direct object pronoun or **ne**, it becomes **ce.**

Ci sono quadri in sala?	*Are there paintings in the living room?*
Sì, **ce ne** sono quattro.	*Yes, there are four.*
Hai la chiave in tasca?	*Do you have the key in your pocket?*
Sì, **ce** l'ho.	*Yes, I have it.*

Pratica

A. **Domanda e risposta.** Quando sei stato(a) in questi posti?

ESEMPIO a Los Angeles **—Quando sei stato(a) a Los Angeles?**
—Ci sono stato(a) l'estate scorsa. *o*
—Non ci sono mai stato(a).

1. in Europa **2.** a un museo **3.** a teatro **4.** dal dentista **5.** dal medico (dottore) **6.** dai tuoi nonni **7.** al cinema **8.** all'ospedale **9.** in Sardegna **10.** in montagna a sciare (*to ski*)

B. **Domanda e risposta.** Pensi mai alle seguenti cose o situazioni? Seguite l'esempio.

ESEMPIO la politica **—Pensi mai alla politica?**
—Sì, ci penso spesso (qualche volta). *o*
—No, non ci penso mai.

1. il costo della vita **2.** il nostro governo **3.** le elezioni **4.** la probabilità di una guerra **5.** la morte (*death*) **6.** l'inflazione **7.** i senzatetto (*homeless*) **8.** il tuo futuro **9.** i problemi ecologici

C. Rispondete alle domande e sostituite i nomi con i pronomi appropriati.

ESEMPIO Quante sedie ci sono nella tua cucina? **—Ce ne sono quattro.**
o
—Non ce ne sono.

1. Quanti studenti ci sono oggi in classe? E ieri? **2.** Quanti giorni ci sono in un anno? **3.** Quante finestre ci sono nella tua camera da letto? **4.** Quante poltrone (o sedie) ci sono nel tuo soggiorno? **5.** Ci sono quadri nella tua camera da letto? Quanti? **6.** Quanti tappeti orientali ci sono nella tua casa ideale? **7.** Quante persone ci sono nella tua famiglia?

D. Rispondete e usate i pronomi **ci** or **ne**, secondo il caso.

1. Preferisci parlare dei tuoi progetti con gli amici o con la tua famiglia? **2.** Quando hai deciso di andare in Europa? **3.** Quante settimane pensi di restare in Italia? **4.** Quanti regali pensi di ricevere a Natale? Quanti regali hai ricevuto l'anno scorso? **5.** Sei andato al cinema la settimana scorsa? Pensi di andare al cinema sabato o domenica? **6.** Quante settimane di vacanza speravi di avere quest'anno? Quante settimane avrai?

E. Rispondete alle seguenti domande.

1. Quanto tempo ci vuole per andare dall'università al centro della vostra città? **2.** Quanti dollari ci vogliono per comprare un bel maglione di lana? **3.** Quanti soldi ci vogliono per affittare un appartamento bilocale (di due stanze)? **4.** Quante ore ci vogliono per andare in aereo dalla vostra città in Europa? **5.** Quanti minuti ci vogliono per rispondere a queste domande?

III. I pronomi doppi

—Mi leggi gli annunci pubblicitari?
—Sì, te li leggo subito.

—Ci mostra l'appartamento?
—Sì, ve lo mostro volentieri.

1. When two object pronouns occur with the same verb, the word order is the following:

indirect object +	*direct object* +	*verb*
Me	**lo**	**leggi?**

(Mi leggi il giornale?)

Me lo leggi?	*Will you read it to me?*
Sì, **te lo** leggo.	*Yes, I'll read it to you.*

Here are all the possible combinations.

mi	+ lo, la, li, le, ne =	**me lo, me la, me li, me le, me ne**
ti	+ lo, la, li, le, ne =	**te lo, te la, te li, te le, te ne**
ci	+ lo, la, li, le, ne =	**ce lo, ce la, ce li, ce le, ce ne**
vi	+ lo, la, li, le, ne =	**ve lo, ve la, ve li, ve le, ve ne**
gli le (Le)	+ lo, la, li, le, ne =	**glielo, gliela, glieli, gliele, gliene**

NOTE:

a. **Mi**, **ti**, **ci**, and **vi** change the ending **-i** to **-e** before **lo**, **la**, **li**, **le**, **ne** (for phonetic reasons).
b. **Gli**, **le**, and **Le** become **glie-** when they combine with direct object pronouns.
c. **Loro** does *not* combine with direct object pronouns and always follows the verb.

Do loro il quadro.	*I give the painting to them.*
Lo do **loro.**	*I give it to them.*

Quando mi dà il libro?	*When will you give me the book?*
Quando **me lo** dà?	*When will you give it to me?*
Gli ho affittato la casa.	*I rented him the house.*
Gliela ho affittata.	*I rented it to him.*
Le offro centomila lire.	*I offer you one hundred thousand lire.*
Gliene offro centomila.	*I offer you one hundred thousand (of them).*
Non ci ha letto la lettera.	*He did not read us the letter.*
Non **ce l'**ha letta.	*He did not read it to us.*
Non le abbiamo dato le chiavi?	*Didn't we give her the keys?*
Non **gliele** abbiamo date?	*Didn't we give them to her?*

2. The position of the double object pronouns is the same as that of the single object pronouns. They precede a conjugated verb; they are attached to the **tu, noi,** and **voi** imperative forms and to the infinitive. Note that if the infinitive is governed by **dovere, volere,** or **potere** the double pronouns may be expressed either before these verbs or may be attached to the infinitive.

Spero di affittarLe l'appartamento.	*I hope to rent you the apartment.*
Spero di affittar**glielo.**	*I hope to rent it to you.*
Voglio mostrarti gli annunci.	*I want to show you the ads.*
Voglio mostrar**teli.** / **Te li** voglio mostrare.	*I want to show them to you.*

Ripeti la domanda! Ripetimi la domanda! Ripeti**mela!**
Date il giornale a Lucia! Datele il giornale! Date**glielo!**
Dammi il tuo indirizzo! Da**mmelo!**

Pratica

A. **Domanda e risposta.** Pierino è a letto con il raffreddore (*cold*) e chiama la mamma continuamente. Seguite l'esempio.

ESEMPIO portare il succo d'arancia
—Mamma, mi porti il succo d'arancia? Me lo porti, per favore?
—Sì, te lo porto.

1. raccontare la favola di Pinocchio 2. portare le matite colorate 3. dare il quaderno verde 4. portare l'altro cuscino 5. preparare la cioccolata calda 6. dare dei fazzoletti (*handerkchiefs*)

B. Ad una trattoria, durante l'ora del pranzo. Seguite l'esempio.

ESEMPIO gelato al caffè
—Cameriere, mi porta il gelato al caffè, per favore?
—Glielo porto subito, signore (signora, signorina)!

1. ravioli alla panna 2. tagliatelle alla bolognese 3. spinaci al burro 4. scaloppine al marsala 5. insalata di pomodori 6. formaggio Bel Paese 7. frutta di stagione

C. Rispondete affermativamente o negativamente. Usate i pronomi doppi.

1. Diamo la mancia a un commesso? 2. Offriamo la nostra poltrona a una vecchia signora? 3. Facciamo dei regali a persone antipatiche? 4. Diciamo delle cattive parole a un bravo bambino? 5. Parliamo del nostro lavoro a un amico? 6. Apriamo la porta ai nostri invitati? 7. Prestiamo le nostre cose a un compagno di classe? 8. Diamo i nostri consigli a un amico (un'amica) in difficoltà?

D. **Prima del trasloco. Domanda e risposta.** Emanuela e Franco vogliono sbarazzarsi (*get rid*) di vecchie cose e ne parlano. Seguite l'esempio.

ESEMPIO questa sedia/a Maria?
—Guarda questa sedia! Possiamo darla a Maria?
—Sì, diạmogliela!

1. questi tuoi stivali/a mio fratello? 2. questo tavolino/al nostro vicino? 3. queste vecchie riviste/ai ragazzi del secondo piano? 4. questa brutta poltrona/al signor Lisi? 5. queste pentole rosse/alla portinaia (*concierge*)?

E. Come risponde una persona egoista alle seguenti domande? Seguite l'esempio.

ESEMPIO —Puoi prestarci la macchina?
—Mi dispiace, ma non posso prestạrvela.

1. Vuoi darci il tuo numero di telefono? 2. Vuoi mostrarci i tuoi appunti? 3. Puoi presentarci i tuoi amici? 4. Vuoi prestare alcuni dollari a Silvia? 5. Puoi farci questo favore?

F. **Che cosa aspetti? Domanda e risposta.** Vostra sorella vi domanda se avete già fatto le seguenti cose. Voi rispondete di no. Lei vi dice di farle. Seguite l'esempio.

ESEMPIO dare il libro a Pietro? **—Hai già dato il libro a Pietro?**
—No, non glielo ho ancora dato.
—Allora, dạglielo.

1. pagare l'affitto al padrone di casa? 2. vendere la bicicletta al cugino Lucio? 3. parlare del problema al capoufficio? 4. mandare le notizie della famiglia agli zii? 5. offrire il tuo aiuto agli amici che traslocano? 6. restituire il computer all'amico Luca? 7. farmi la lista della spesa?

IV. I pronomi doppi con i verbi riflessivi

—Mi metto il cappello o non me lo metto?

1. With reflexive verbs, the reflexive pronouns combine with the direct object pronouns **lo**, **la**, **li**, **le**, and **ne**, and follow the same word order as double object pronouns.

Mi metto		**Me lo** metto.
Ti metti		**Te lo** metti.
Si mette	il vestito. =	**Se lo** mette.
Ci mettiamo		**Ce lo** mettiamo.
Vi mettete		**Ve lo** mettete.
Si mettono		**Se lo** mettono.

   Note that when a reflexive pronoun precedes a direct object pronoun, the ending **-i** changes to **-e**.

2. In Italian, reflexive pronouns take the place of the English possessive adjectives when referring to parts of the body or articles of clothing.

   Mi lavo la faccia. — *I wash my face.*
   Si mette l'impermeabile. — *She is putting on her raincoat.*

3. If the reflexive verb is in a compound tense, the past participle must agree with the *direct object pronoun* that precedes the verb.

   Gino si è lavato **le mani.** — *Gino washed his hands.*
   Gino se **le** è lavat**e**. — *Gino washed them.*

   Maria si è tagliata **i capelli.** — *Maria cut her hair.*
   Maria se **li** è tagliat**i**. — *Maria cut it.*

   Note that **li** and **le** function as direct object pronouns and therefore require agreement with the past participle.

Pratica

A. **Quando ti metti...?** Rispondete e sostituite i seguenti nomi con il pronome appropriato.

   ESEMPIO i guanti di lana **—Quando ti metti i guanti di lana?**
   —Me li metto quando fa freddo.

1. il golf o il maglione di lana 2. gli occhiali da sole 3. le scarpe da tennis 4. l'impermeabile 5. il cappotto e gli stivali 6. il vestito da sera 7. la maglietta leggera 8. il costume da bagno 9. gli scarponi da montagna 10. i pantaloni corti (pantaloncini) 11. le scarpe comode

B. Che cosa hanno fatto questi studenti **prima di...** (*before...*)? Ripetete le frasi e sostituite le espressioni in corsivo con il pronome appropriato.

ESEMPIO Prima di uscire, Maria si è messa *il cappello.*
Prima di uscire, Maria se lo è messo.

1. Prima di colazione io mi sono lavato(a) *le mani.* 2. Tu, invece, non ti sei lavato(a) *le mani.* 3. Prima di partire mi sono tagliato(a) *i capelli.* 4. Prima di cena io e la mia compagna ci siamo messe *il vestito da sera.* 5. Prima di andare a letto Lucia si è lavata *i capelli.* 6. Prima dell'appuntamento lui si è pulito *le scarpe nere.* 7. Prima di andare in bicicletta, noi ci siamo messi *i pantaloncini.* 8. Prima di uscire mi sono messo(a) *il cappotto.*

AFFITTI OFFERTI

TORINO CITTA'

A.A. CASAFFITTI offre contratti transitori foresteria e patti in deroga in Torino. Tel. 503.097 - 507.029.
A. CASAFFITTI offre in corso Giulio Cesare panoramico mq 70/80 vuoto contratto patto in deroga. Tel. 501.813.
ABBIAMO alloggi vuoti arredati uffici stessa casa possibilità di medie e lunghe locazioni. Interpellateci. Interacta 568.3629.
ABBIAMO vuoto zona Nuovo Tribunale 3 camere tinello cucinino bagno. Sarcase 385.4581.
ABITARE & FINANZIARE 581.7643 via Airasca (S. Paolo) alloggio di camera cucina bagno con rate pari affitto.
ADIACENTE corso Tassoni via Tenivelli vuoto salone 3 camere cucina biservizi piano 4° L. 1.100.000. Tel. 745.010.
ADIACENZE Mirafiori privato affitta 580.000 mensili camera tinello cucinino bagno ingresso 2 terrazzi. Tel. 318.0440.
AFFITTASI ammobiliato monolocale corso Sempione. Telefonare 434.2720.
AFFITTASI ammobiliato via Ozegna camera cucina servizi. Telefonare 434.2720.
AFFITTASI appartamento vuoto volendo arredato a persona referenziata. Tel. 436.0006.
AFFITTASI a referenziati corso D'Azeglio arredato salone 2 camere cucina doppi servizi. Tel. 0337 204.666.
AFFITTASI arredato 3 camere cucina e servizio adatto a studenti. Tel. 537.109.
AFFITTASI corso Cosenza salone 2 camere cucina biservizi posto auto stabile signorile. Tel. 547.470 Eurocase.
AFFITTASI corso Peschiera uso foresteria alloggio ristrutturato ed arredato di mq 66. Serim 562.9801.
AFFITTASI corso Tassoni piano rialzato uso studio 4 vani L. 1.350.000. Telefonare al 365.852.
AFFITTASI piazza Bengasi 3 vani e servizi arredato uso transitorio adatto a studenti. Tel. 537.109.
AFFITTASI recente alloggio arredato nuovo 2 camere e servizi a studentesse o studenti zona Politecnico. Tel. 992.1845.
ALLOGGIO Gran Madre (liceo Segrè) panoramico mq 120 in palazzina affittasi L. 1.500.000. Furbatto 544.566 - 540.909.
ALLOGGIO libero affittasi zona Mirafiori composto di 2 camere tinello e servizi a coppia entrambi occupati. Tel. 226.0350.
ALPINA affitta appartamento vuoto/arreda-

APPARTAMENTI IN TORINO

ADIACENZE VIA BORGARO DA RISTRUTTURARE INGRESSO 2 CAMERE CUCINA SERVIZI CANTINA.
(RIF. 04882025) **TEL. 011 - 226 78 56**
C.SO BELGIO PANORAMICO 3 CAMERE CUCINA SERVIZI AMPIA METRATURA OCCUPATO CON SFRATTO IN CORSO L. 129.000.000.
(RIF. 03262134) **TEL. 011 - 248 77 11**
C.SO CASALE ADIACENZE LIBERO RESIDENZIALE SOGGIORNO CAMERA CUCINA SERVIZI RIPOSTIGLIO TERRAZZINO BOX PIU' POSTO AUTO GIARDINO CONDOMINIALE MQ 6.000 CA.
(RIF. 00012144) **TEL. 011 - 50 59 17**
C.SO MONTE CUCCO RECENTE INGRESSO CAMERA TINELLO CUCININO BAGNO OTTIMO STATO 2 ARIE.
(RIF. 03361006) **TEL. 011 - 385 05 10**
C.SO NOVARA ADIACENZE LIBERO 2 CAMERE CUCINA SERVIZI COMPLETAMENTE RISTRUTTURATO RISCALDAMENTO AUTONOMO.
(RIF. 03262139) **TEL. 011 - 248 77 11**
C.SO POTENZA ADIACENZE IN STABILE DI NUOVA COSTRUZIONE APPARTAMENTO DI INGRESSO CAMERA SALONE TINELLO CUCININO. DISIMPEGNO SERVIZI CANTINA TERRAZZO BOX PER 2 POSTI AUTO AMPIA METRATURA OTTIME RIFINITURE.
(RIF. 0488931002) **TEL. 011 - 226 78 56**
C.SO RACCONIGI (VIA VERZUOLO) 4° PIANO NO ASCENSORE RISTRUTTURATO INGRESSO LIVING SU SALONE ANGOLO COTTURA 2 CAMERE BAGNO L. 175.000.000.
(RIF. 03360152) **TEL. 011 - 385 05 10**
C.SO SEBASTOPOLI ADIACENZE APPARTAMENTI DI CAMERA CUCINA SERVIZI INGRESSO A PARTIRE DA L. 116.000.000.
(RIF. 04739310060124) **TEL. 011 - 324 18 41**
C.SO TRAIANO LUMINOSO PIANO ALTO RISTRUTTURATO INGRESSO LI-

LUNGO PO ANTONELLI ADIACENZE LIBERO SUBITO 6° PIANO PANORAMICO CAMERA TINELLO CUCININO SERVIZI.
(RIF. 03262144) **TEL. 011 - 248 77 11**
SANTA RITA LIBERI PIANI ALTI 2 CAMERE TINELLO CUCININO SERVIZI RIPOSTIGLIO INGRESSO BOX AUTO.
(RIF. 04730117931002) **TEL. 011 - 324 18 41**
STRADA S.MAURO ADIACENZE LIBERO RECENTE SALONE 2 CAMERE CUCINA BISERVIZI BOX AUTO GIARDINO CONDOMINIALE.
(RIF. 0326931006) **TEL. 011 - 248 77 11**
VIA BORGARO OTTIMO STABILE SIGNORILE INGRESSO 2 CAMERE CUCINA SERVIZI RIPOSTIGLIO CANTINA 5° PIANO ASCENSORE.
(RIF. 04882023) **TEL. 011 - 226 78 56**
VIA BREGLIO ULTIMO PIANO ATTICO DI 1 CAMERA TINELLO CUCININO SERVIZI RIPOSTIGLIO INGRESSO CANTINA TERRAZZO STABILE OTTIME CONDIZIONI.
(RIF. 04882013) **TEL. 011 - 226 78 56**
VIA GENOVA SIGNORILE PIANO ALTO 2 CAMERE TINELLO CUCINOTTA SERVIZI 2 RIPOSTIGLI INGRESSO POSSIBILITA' BOX AUTO.
(RIF. 04730104) **TEL. 011 - 324 18 41**
VIA GORIZIA ADIACENZE CAMERA TINELLO CON ANGOLO COTTURA SERVIZI INGRESSO RISTRUTTURATO L. 129.000.000.
(RIF. 04730113) **TEL. 011 - 324 18 41**
VIA GUIDO RENI ADIACENZE IN STABILE CON GIARDINO CONDOMINIALE 3 CAMERE SOGGIORNO CUCINA ABITABILE BISERVIZI RIPOSTIGLIO INGRESSO AMPI BALCONI POSSIBILITA' BOX AUTO DOPPIO.
(RIF. 0473931001) **TEL. 011 - 324 18 41**
VIA ISONZO ADIACENZE C.SO PESCHIERA INGRESSO 2 CAMERE CUCINA SERVIZIO INTERAMENTE RISTRUTTURATO TERMOAUTONOMO MQ 75.
(RIF. 0336149) **TEL. 011 - 385 05 10**
VIA PEYRON LIBERI ABBINABILI 2 APPARTAMENTI MANSARDATI COMPLETAMENTE RISTRUTTURATI DI MQ 150 CA. E DI MQ 80 CA. CON BOX.
(RIF. 0001210221021) **TEL. 011 - 50 59 17**
VIA PINELLI PIANO RIALZATO TOTALMENTE RISTRUTTURATO 2 CAMERE CUCINA BAGNO IN-

LETTURA

SI AFFITTA APPARTAMENTO AMMOBILIATO

Un mese fa Antonio ha incominciato a insegnare in una scuola media come *supplente*. Il giovane è ora pieno di entusiasmo e di progetti. Eccolo che ne parla a Marcello. — substitute

—Sai, ho intenzione di cercarmi un appartamentino ammobiliato e di *rendermi* indipendente. — to become
—Ehi! Super! Così possiamo dare *un sacco* di feste! Hai guardato gli annunci pubblicitari sul *Corriere della Sera?** — a lot
—No, non ancora... eccoli!
—Non ce ne sono molti. Te ne leggo uno: Appartamento *signorile* 4 locali *doppi servizi* libero... — deluxe/two baths
—Sei matto?! *Mi basta* una cucina-soggiorno con bagno. — is enough for me
—Eccone uno che va bene:... monolocale Lambrate.**
—Sì, mi piace. Quant'è l'affitto?
—Non lo dice. Perchè non *fissiamo* un appuntamento e ci andiamo? (Il monolocale si trova al terzo piano di un modesto edificio senza ascensore. Il *portinaio*, svegliato dalla siesta, glielo mostra *malvolentieri*.) — set up / concierge / reluctantly
—Scusi, ha una lettera di referenze?
—Certamente, *interviene* Marcello. Mio padre, l'ingegner Scotti della *ditta* Scotti e Figli, è pronto a scrivergliene una. — interrupts / company
—Grazie, Marcello. Che ne pensi?
—Mah! Mi sembra un *buco*...con dei mobili *preistorici*. — a hole/prehistoric
—Caro mio, io non ho la *grana* di tuo padre; per uno come me che ha *condiviso* fino a oggi la stanza con due fratelli, quest'appartamento sembra un palazzo! — dough (slang) / shared

Comprensione

Usate i pronomi quando è possibile.

1. In che scuola ha incominciato ad insegnare Antonio?
2. Da quanto tempo ci insegna?
3. Che cosa pensa di fare ora?
4. Perchè vuole cercarsi un appartamento?
5. Lo vuole vuoto o ammobiliato?
6. Perchè Marcello è entusiasta dell'idea dell'amico?
7. Dove suggerisce di cercare gli annunci Marcello?
8. Perchè il primo annuncio che Marcello legge non piace ad Antonio? Di quante stanze ha bisogno?
9. Nell'annuncio c'è il costo dell'affitto?

---

*Well-known Italian newspaper.
**Small town near Milano.

10. Com'è l'appartamento che Antonio decide di andare a vedere? Dove si trova?
11. Chi mostra l'appartamento ai due amici?
12. Perchè il portinaio è di malumore? Cosa chiede ad Antonio?
13. Chi è disposto (*willing*) a scrivergli una lettera di referenze?
14. Piace a Marcello quell'appartamento?
15. Che ne pensa Antonio? Perchè?

Domande personali

1. Se Lei ha bisogno di cercarsi un appartamento, mette un annuncio sul giornale? Risponde a un annuncio? O cosa fa?
2. Preferisce affittare un appartamento soltanto per sè (*for yourself*), o condividerlo con un'altra persona e dividere le spese?
3. Se Lei affitta un appartamento per sè, ha il vantaggio di avere della privacy. Qual è lo svantaggio?
4. In generale gli studenti preferiscono affittare un appartamento vuoto o ammobiliato?
5. Dove abita Lei adesso? Le piace starci o ha intenzione di traslocare?
6. Cosa Le piace e cosa non Le piace del Suo alloggio (*housing*)?
7. Può avere degli animali domestici (*pets*)? Ne ha?

ATTIVITÀ SUPPLEMENTARI

A. **La casa ideale.** Descrivete la casa ideale. Ogni studente partecipa alla descrizione. Dov'è la casa (in campagna, in città, vicino al mare)? Quanti piani ci sono? Quali sono le stanze? Come sono i mobili? ecc.

B. **Descrivete** i due disegni che seguono e immaginate un breve dialogo fra le due persone. (Usate un po' di fantasia e qualche pronome.)

1. Chi sono Emanuela e Franco? In che stanza sono? Cosa fanno? Dove sono seduti? Che ore sono? Non hanno ancora cenato? Che cosa si diranno dopo la fatica (*toil*) del trasloco?
2. Antonio è andato dalla fruttivendola (*greengrocer*). Ha una borsa al braccio. Perchè? Di che cosa ha bisogno? Che cosa vedete sul banco della fruttivendola? Immaginate il dialogo dei due e usate il pronome **ne.**

C. **Attività in gruppi di due:** un padrone di casa e un eventuale (*probable*) inquilino (inquilina). Voi cercate un appartamento in affitto e leggete nel giornale il seguente annuncio:

> Affittiamo bellissimi appartamenti nuovi e ristrutturati, vuoti o arredati, monolocali, 2-3-4 locali, primo-settimo piano, cucina-soggiorno, doppi servizi, balcone. Alcuni appartamenti con garage privato. Zona tranquilla, vicinanza metropolitana. Telefonate al 02/47–817–25 durante ore ufficio.

Telefonate al numero indicato, specificate l'appartamento che cercate e discutete le condizioni dell'affitto con il padrone (la padrona) di casa.

D. **Come si dice in italiano?**

1. Giulia has been living in San Francisco with her friend Kathy for a month, and now she wants to rent an apartment.
2. Today Kathy is helping her find one, and she is reading her the newspaper ads.
3. I found one that I like: Studio, Golden Gate park. Available immediately. $550.
4. How big is a studio? How many rooms are there?
5. There is only one, with a bathroom.
6. Now, here they are near Golden Gate park to see the studio.
7. The manager (**l'amministratore**, *m.*) shows it willingly to them.
8. Giulia is enthusiastic about (**di**) the studio and asks Kathy what (**cosa**) she thinks about it.
9. I like it a lot, because there are big windows with the view (**veduta**) of the park.
10. Next Saturday Giulia can move to (**nel**) her new apartment.

AIRASCA VILLA ANGOLARE IN FINIZIONE SALONE 2 CAMERE CUCINA MANSARDA TAVERNA GIARDINO 500 MQ L. 325.000.000.
(RIF. 00315210) **TEL. 011 - 640 83 26**

AVIGLIANA PRENOTASI VILLE SALONE 4 CAMERE CUCINA QUADRISERVIZITAVERNETTA GARAGE GIARDINO DA L. 520.000.000.
(RIF. 0315931048) **TEL. 011 - 640 83 26**

CASELLE VILLA DISPOSTA SU 3 PIANI COMPOSTA PIANO TERRA: SOGGIORNO 2 CAMERE RIPOSTIGLIO SERVIZIO. PIANO 1°: SALONE 2 CAMERE CUCINA SERVIZI TERRAZZO. PIANO 2°: SOGGIORNO 2 CAMERE CUCINA SERVIZI. BOX DOPPIO 1.000 MQ DI TERRENO.
(RIF. 0450326931007) **TEL. 011 - 403 44 04**

CASTIGLIONE ALTO VILLA PANORAMICA DISPOSTA SU 3 PIANI UNI/BIFAMILIARE PIANO 1°: SALONE 4 CAMERE CUCINA BISERVIZI INGRESSO TERRAZZO. PIANO 2°: INGRESSO INDIPENDENTE SALONE ANGOLO CUCINA 2 CAMERE SERVIZI TERRAZZO. AUTORIMESSA LAVANDERIA. 2.800 MQ DI PARCO.
(RIF. 04500012133) **TEL. 011 - 403 44 04**

GIAVENO IN ZONA RESIDENZIALE PRESTIGIOSA VILLA DISPOSTA SU 4 LIVELLI UNI/BIFAMILIARE DI 650 MQ DOTATA DI PALESTRA SAUNA AMPIA MANSARDA BOX TRIPLO PARCO 1.000 MQ CIRCA.
(RIF. 04502097) **TEL. 011 - 403 44 04**

LEINI' (ZONA RONCHI) VILLA COMPLETAMENTE RISTRUTTURATA INDIPENDENTE SU 4 LATI CON MQ 1.000 DI TERRENO RECINTATO COMPOSTA DA SEMINTERRATO DI 150 MQ. PIANO TERRENO DI 150 MQ. MANSARDA ABITABILE DI 90 MQ CON SERVIZIO E 60 MQ DI TERRAZZO.
(RIF. 0001336144) **TEL. 011 - 50 59 17**

REAGLIE PANORAMICISSIMA VILLA DISPOSTA SU 2 PIANI SALONE 5 CAMERE CUCINA BISERVIZI INGRESSO AMPIO TERRAZZO PIU' PIANO CANTINATO BOX 3/4 AUTO TERRENO MQ 1.700 CA. POSSIBILITA' SUDDIVISIONE BIFAMILIARE.
(RIF. 00012143) **TEL. 011 - 50 59 17**

RIVOLI COLLINA PANORAMICA VILLA BIFAMILIARE 460 MQ PISCINA BARBECUE TAVERNETTA GIARDINO 1.500 MQ L. 1.400.000.000.
(RIF. 0039212800) **TEL. 011 - 640 83 26**

ROSTA COLLINA VILLA UNI-BIFAMILIARE 470 MQ MANSARDA PATIO CAPPELLETTA PRIVATA PARCO 1.500 MQ L. 1.000.000.000.
(RIF. 0039008900) **TEL. 011 - 640 83 26**

L. 1 milione mensili più spese.

GRIMALDI 505.917 affittasi uso transitorio appartamento semicentrale di salone 3 camere cucina doppi servizi box.

MANSARDA signorile zona corso Trapani salone camera tinello bagno L. 700 mila referenziati. Agenzia 562.3811.

MARE' affitta Gran Madre signorile appartamento in palazzotto d'epoca mq 130 piano alto posto auto. Tel. 542.933.

MARE' affitta via Garibaldi in palazzo del '700 salone cucina camera con camino studio 2 bagni posto auto. Tel. 542.933.

MEC CASE 533.025 affitta appartamento arredato 2 camere cucina servizi in stabile recente semicentrale.

PRECOLLINA villa unifamiliare perfettamente rifinita ampi spazi interni giardino libera subito. Studio Mapi 898.1724.

SPAI A corso Belgio, appartamento, piano alto vista prestigiosa, composto di: ingresso, salone, 2 camere, cucina e 2 bagni arredati, ripostiglio, 2 terrazzi, cantina, box, posto auto. Tel. 812.7177.

SPAI B via Garibaldi/piazza Castello in stabile signorile appartamenti uso abitazione di mq 70 e mq 80 di ingresso, 3 camere, cucina, bagno. Tel. 812.7177.

S. PAOLO alloggio di camera cucina cucinotta bagno con rate pari affitto. Abitare & Finanziare 581.7745.

S. RITA via Barletta affittasi uso abitazione 2 camere tinello cucinino termo bagno ascensore. Affare 562.9262.

TORINO sud via Amari/Vigliani ben arredato 3 camere soggiorno doppi servizi box, transitorio. Tel. 318.0696.

VALSALICE affittasi signorile uso abitazione salone 2 camere cucina biservizi mansarda box auto. Affaire 562.9262.

VIA Po piano alto nuovissimo ben arredato bilocale uso foresteria. Pastore Immobili 434.4645.

VIA Vigliani stesso stabile alloggi vuoti ingresso 2/3 camere cucina bagno volendo box. Silpa affitta 616.648.

VUOTI Mirafiori sud salone living 2 camere 2 bagni box altri stessa casa cucina 2 camere 1 bagno. Sarcase 385.4581.

ZONA Crimea affitto da 3 a 11 vani stessa casa foresteria ufficio. Tel. 669.8918/21.

Vocabolario

Nomi

l'alloggio	*housing*
l'annuncio pubblicitario	*ad*
l'ascensore	*elevator*
il banco	*stand; counter*
la borsa	*shopping bag*
il cestino	*basket*
la chiave	*key*
il contratto	*contract*
il costo	*cost*
la difficoltà	*difficulty*
la ditta	*firm, company*
l'entusiasmo	*enthusiasm*
la faccia	*face*
il fazzoletto	*handkerchief*
la fruttivendola	*greengrocer*
il fungo	*mushroom*
il giocattolo	*toy*
il locale	*room*
la luce	*light*
la mano (*pl.* le mani)	*hand*
il marsala	*sweet Sicilian wine*
il mobile	*piece of furniture*
il monolocale	*studio apartment*
la moquette	*wall-to-wall carpet*
la morte	*death*
il palazzo	*palace; building*
i pantaloncini	*shorts*
il piano	*floor; story*
il portinaio, la portinaia	*concierge*
il quadro	*painting, picture*
il raffreddore	*cold*
i senzatetto	*homeless people*
lo svantaggio	*disadvantage*
il terremoto	*earthquake*
il vantaggio	*advantage*
la vicinanza	*vicinity*

Aggettivi

ammobiliato	*furnished*
arredato	*furnished*
antico	*antique; ancient*
doppio	*double*
entusiasta (di)	*enthusiastic (about)*
indipendente	*independent*
libero	*free; vacant*
modesto	*modest*
vuoto	*vacant, empty*

Verbi

arredare	*to furnish*
condividere (*p.p.* condiviso)	*to share*
sembrare	*to seem; to look like*
trovarsi	*to find oneself; to be located*

Altre espressioni

certamente	*certainly*
ci vuole, ci vogliono	*it takes*
così	*so, this way*
doppi servizi	*two baths*
essere disposto (a)	*to be willing (to)*
fissare un appuntamento	*to set (make) an appointment*
di malumore	*in a bad mood*
in affitto	*for rent*
in vendita	*for sale*
malvolentieri	*reluctantly*
penso di sì/penso di no	*I think so/I don't think so*
prima di (+ *inf.*)	*before...*
rendersi indipendente	*to become independent*
va bene	*it is right*

PAGINA CULTURALE

LE ABITAZIONI IN ITALIA

I vecchi palazzi delle città italiane hanno avuto come prototipo l'antica casa romana. *Essi* sono uniti l'uno all'altro. Al centro di ogni facciata un *portone ad arco dà* su un *cortile* interno. All'esterno, il *pianterreno* è occupato da negozi o da uffici, mentre gli altri piani sono occupati, in genere, da appartamenti. Gli *artigiani* e i commercianti abitano spesso nell'appartamento sopra il loro negozio. Nel vecchio centro urbano convivono diverse classi sociali e questo contribuisce alla vitalità del centro cittadino.

They
arched front gate opens
courtyard/ground floor
artisans

Fra gli anni 1950 e 1970 i *cambiamenti* economici e sociali hanno determinato un'espansione notevole dei centri urbani. *Intorno* alla vecchia città ne è nata una interamente moderna, fatta di edifici a molti piani e di *villette.* Per correggere la grave crisi di abitazioni del dopoguerra, il governo ha preso molti *provvedimenti.* Ha finanziato la costruzione di condomini e di abitazioni economiche, e ha stabilito dei *mutui* per incoraggiare gli Italiani a diventare proprietari del loro appartamento.

changes
around
small villas
measures
mortgage loans

Durante la prosperità degli anni sessanta-ottanta molti Italiani hanno potuto «*farsi*» una seconda casa o un appartamentino in *zone di villeggiatura.* Interi villaggi di condomini *sono sorti* senza un *piano regolatore,* causando *eccessivo affollamento* nei periodi di vacanze. Gli *amanti* della campagna hanno ristrutturato vecchie case e *fienili, trasformandoli* in confortevoli rifugi lontano dalla vita cittadina.

buy
resort areas
arose/town plan
overcrowding
lovers
barns/changing them

In Puglia molti trulli sono stati rimodernati per uso turistico. I trulli sono *strane abitazioni* circolari di *pietra,* attribuite alla civiltà preistorica araba. Il centro della zona dei trulli è la *cittadina* di Alberobello in provincia di Bari, dove sono preservati nella loro antica forma.

strange dwellings
stone
small town

Comprensione

Completate le seguenti frasi.

1. Come le antiche case romane, i vecchi palazzi italiani hanno un cortile...
   a. davanti **b.** dietro **c.** all'interno
2. La coabitazione di diverse classi sociali dà vita...
   a. agli uffici **b.** ai cortili dei palazzi **c.** al vecchio centro urbano
3. Dopo la seconda guerra mondiale il governo italiano ha...
   a. aumentato gli affitti **b.** finanziato la costruzione di case **c.** limitato la costruzione di case
4. Molti Italiani si sono fatti una seconda casa, stimolati (*spurred*)...
   a. dal costo economico delle costruzioni **b.** da un periodo di economia favorevole **c.** dall'amore per la villeggiatura
5. I trulli sono abitazioni...
   a. moderne **b.** vecchie **c.** antiche
6. Alberobello si trova nell'Italia...
   a. del Sud **b.** del Nord **c.** del Centro

Alcuni trulli di Alberobello (Bari).

14 MESTIERI E PROFESSIONI

Nell'ufficio di un commercialista (CPA).

Punti di vista

Una scelta difficile
Una decisione pratica

Punti grammaticali

I Il condizionale presente
II Il condizionale passato
III Uso di ***dovere, potere, volere*** nel condizionale
IV Verbi e espressioni verbali + infinito

Lettura

In cerca di un impiego

Pagina culturale

Il lavoro e la donna

PUNTI DI VISTA

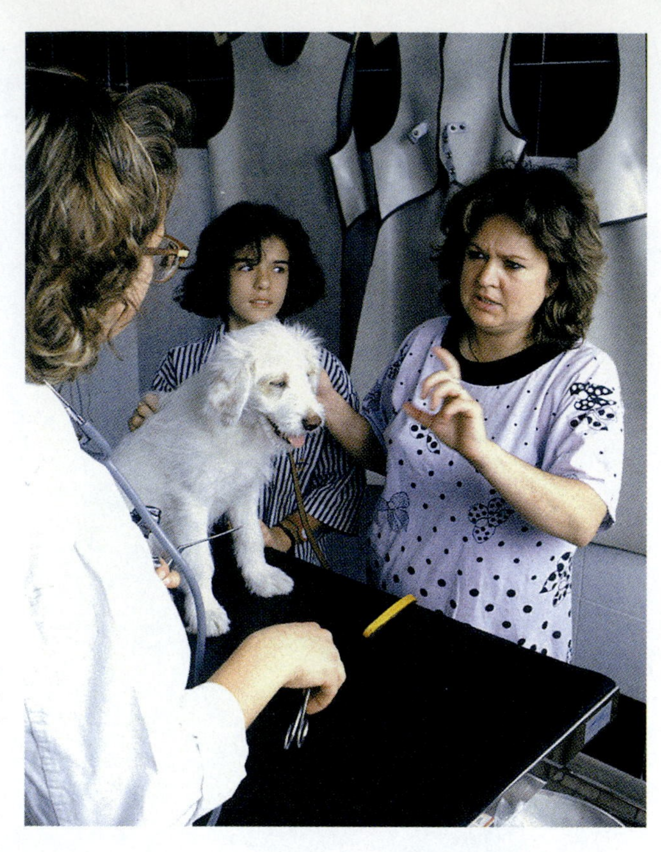

Che cosa fa la signora con il camice bianco e gli occhiali?

UNA *SCELTA* DIFFICILE

choice

Laura e Franco frequentano l'ultimo anno di liceo e parlano del loro futuro.

Franco Non so a quale facoltà *iscrivermi*. Tu cosa mi consigli Laura? — to register
Laura Cosa *ti piacerebbe* fare nella vita? — would you like
Franco Mi piacerebbe insegnare matematica.
Laura Devi considerare che ci sono vantaggi e svantaggi nell'insegnamento, come nelle altre professioni. I vantaggi? *Faresti* un lavoro che ti piace e d'estate avresti tre mesi di vacanza. *Potresti* viaggiare, riposarti o dedicarti ad altre attività. — *Faresti*: you would do; *Potresti*: you could
Franco E gli svantaggi, quali sono?
Laura Lo sai anche tu che non è facile trovare lavoro nell'insegnamento. E sai anche che lo stipendio degli insegnanti è basso.
Franco Hai ragione. E tu hai deciso a quale facoltà iscriverti?
Laura Sì, farò il veterinario.
Franco *Davvero?* Ti piacciono così tanto gli animali? — really
Laura Oh, sì, moltissimo! A casa mia ho un piccolo zoo: due cani, quattro gatti, un *coniglio* e due *porcellini d'India*. — *coniglio*: rabbit; *porcellini d'India*: guinea pigs

Comprensione

1. Che anno di liceo frequentano Laura e Franco?
2. Che cosa deve decidere Franco?
3. Che cosa gli piacerebbe fare?
4. Quali sono i vantaggi nell'insegnamento? Quali sono gli svantaggi?
5. Anche Laura è indecisa sulla sua professione?
6. Che cosa vuole fare? Perchè?
7. Cos'ha a casa sua?

Studio di parole

I MESTIERI *TRADES*

l'elettricista (*m.*) electrician
l'idraulico plumber
il meccanico
l'operaio, l'operaia factory worker, laborer
il parrucchiere, la parrucchiera hairdresser
il barbiere barber
il salumiere delicatessen man
il postino, la postina mail carrier
il lavoratore, la lavoratrice worker

LE PROFESSIONI

il dottore, la dottoressa; il medico (*m. & f.*)
il chirurgo surgeon
l'oculista (*m. & f.*) eye doctor
il (la) farmacista
il (la) consulente consultant
il (la) dentista
l'avvocato, l'avvocatessa lawyer
il direttore, la direttrice director, manager
l'ingegnere engineer
il ragioniere, la ragioniera accountant
il programmatore (la programmatrice) di computer computer programmer
l'uomo (la donna) d'affari business man/woman
l'impiegato, l'impiegata clerk
il segretario, la segretaria secretary
fare il (la)... to be a... (profession or trade)

il colloquio interview
l'impiego employment, job
il lavoro job
un lavoro a tempo pieno full-time job
un lavoro part-time part-time job
un posto a position
fare domanda to apply
guadagnare to earn
il salario, **lo stipendio** salary, wages

l'aumento raise
disoccupato unemployed
la disoccupazione unemployment
fare sciopero to strike
la casalinga homemaker
il pensionato, la pensionata retiree
andare in pensione to retire

l'uniforme the uniform
la tuta overall

Applicazione

A. 1. Guardate il disegno: che cosa vogliono le persone che fanno la fila (*stand in line*) davanti all'agenzia di collocamento? Perchè? ______________

2. Chi chiama Lei se non ha l'elettricità in casa? ______________
3. Se ha bisogno di occhiali, da quale specialista va?
4. Se Lei vuole mangiare un bel panino al prosciutto, dove va a comprarlo? ______________ ______________
5. Se i Suoi capelli sono troppo lunghi, chi glieli taglia? ______________ ______________
6. Quando un lavoratore (una lavoratrice) arriva a sessantacinque anni ed è stanco(a) di lavorare, cosa fa? ______________ ______________
7. Che cosa riceve alla fine del mese una persona che lavora?
8. Di tutte le professioni o i mestieri sopra elencati (*listed above*), qual è, secondo Lei, la (il) più difficile (*the most difficult*)? Perchè?
9. Se i lavoratori non sono soddisfatti delle loro condizioni di lavoro, cosa fanno?

B. **Cosa fanno?** Dite quale mestiere o professione fanno le seguenti persone.

1. Scrive lettere e tiene (*keeps*) in ordine i documenti in ufficio.
2. È una donna che non conosce orario nè (*nor*) stipendio.
3. Fa la nostra conoscenza in momenti gravi della nostra vita.
4. Lavora in una fabbrica (*factory*).
5. Porta la posta ai vari indirizzi.
6. Dirige una grande ditta.
7. Ha finito di lavorare e ora dovrebbe (*should*) riposare e... divertirsi.
8. Prepara programmi per una macchina elettronica.

C. **Domande personali.**

1. Che professione o mestiere fa, o pensa di fare Lei?
2. La Sua scelta è stata facile o difficile?
3. Che cosa l'ha influenzato(a) di più? L'interesse economico o la Sua inclinazione?
4. Se Lei ha la scelta, in quale stato degli Stati Uniti preferisce lavorare? Perchè?
5. Se Lei ha la possibilità di lavorare all'estero, quale paese dell'Europa o dell'Asia preferisce? Perchè?
6. Se Lei fa domanda per un impiego, quali sono i fattori che influenzano la Sua scelta? Il clima? La famiglia? Lo stipendio? Le condizioni di lavoro? Il costo degli alloggi?
7. Attualmente (*At present*) dov'è più facile trovare un impiego: nell'industria, nel commercio, nel governo, nell'insegnamento?

Ascoltiamo!

Una decisione pratica. *Paola has just run into Luigi, an old friend from the* **liceo.** *Listen to their conversation, as they each catch up on what the other is doing. Then answer the following questions.*

Comprensione

1. Com'è vestito Luigi? Perchè?
2. Che cosa voleva fare Luigi quand'era al liceo? Perchè ha cambiato idea (*did he change his mind*)?
3. Che cosa cerca Paola? Perchè?
4. Adesso che cosa vorrebbe fare anche Paola?
5. Secondo Lei, Paola parla seriamente o scherza (*is joking*)?

Dialogo

Avete incontrato un amico (un'amica) che è disoccupato(a) e che cerca lavoro. In gruppi di due, domandate cosa sa fare. Consultate insieme le offerte di lavoro sul giornale, e decidete a quali rispondere (pagine 295-307).

LAVORO OFFERTE

OPERAI AUTISTI FATTORINI

AGGIUSTATORE stampi plastica e pressofusione cercasi. Telefonare ore ufficio al 707.2333/4.

IMPIEGATI

A. A AZIENDA leader seleziona ambosessi automuniti anche part-time. Richiedesi massima serietà bella presenza e buona dialettica, offresi ottimi guadagni L. 3 milioni e possibilità di carriera. Telefonare 434.3038.

ASSUME studio notarile veloce dattilografa 1° impiego. Tel. 546.254.

AZIENDA meccanica zona Torino Nord cerca persona esperta gestione commesse programmazione officina e fornitori, approvvigionamento materiali, pratica PC. Scrivere: Publikompass 8646 - 10100 Torino.

CERCHIAMO ambosessi da addestrare e specializzare nel campo investigativo inserimento per i prescelti. Tel. 581.8122.

CORSI

per un impiego sicuro: Contabilità Iva, Paghe e Contributi, Operatori office Automation, Cad (Computer Aided Design). Presa d'Atto regionale. Istituto Vagnone via Vagnone 7 Torino. Tel. 488.994.

E.A.U. per apertura nuove sedi in Italia cerca personale fortemente motivato ad esprimere al meglio le proprie capacità personali proiettato ad un miglioramento a livelli manageriali automunito minimo 24enne. tel. 562.4826.

PERSONALE PUBBLICI ESERCIZI

NEGOZIO Peppermint cerca commessa abbigliamento buona volontà e spirito di collaborazione. Presentarsi lunedì 25/01/93 ore 9/12 Centro Commerciale Auchan corso Romania, 460 Torino.

IMPIEGATI

AFFERMATA azienda seleziona per assunzione full-time signora/ina diplomata e/o laureata per gestione ufficio settore servizi. Sede di lavoro Novara. Scrivere: Publikompass 7031 - 10100 Torino.

AGENZIA generale primaria compagnia di assicurazioni cerca ambosessi con esperienza di vendita a cui affidare settore di sviluppo. Tel. 355.055.

ASSUMESI geometra referenziato pratico amministrazione stabili e contabilità. Scrivere: Publikompass 8606 - 10100 Torino.

AZIENDA italiana ricerca 4 giovani per attività esterna commerciale non di vendita. Guadagno minimo garantito mensile 1.700.000 con anticipazioni. Tel. 677.752.

AZIENDA settore metalmeccanico cintura Sud cerca per inserimento proprio organico contabile provata esperienza, addetto profilatura nastri d'acciaio, addetto magazzino ricevimento merci. Scrivere: Publikompass 5021 - 10100 Torino.

PUNTI GRAMMATICALI

I. Il condizionale presente

Il muratore preferirebbe riposarsi. *Al postino piacerebbe andare in macchina.*

1. Il muratore preferirebbe lavorare o riposarsi?
2. Che cosa piacerebbe fare al postino?

1. The present conditional (**condizionale presente**) expresses an intention, a preference, a wish, or a polite request; it is the equivalent of the English *would* + verb. Like the future, it derives from the infinitive, and its stem is always the same as the future stem. Also like the future, **-are** verbs change the **-a** to **-e.**

   partire ⟶ **partirei** = *I would* leave*

   It is conjugated as follows:

parlare	rispondere	partire
parler**ei**	risponder**ei**	partir**ei**
parler**esti**	risponder**esti**	partir**esti**
parler**ebbe**	risponder**ebbe**	partir**ebbe**
parler**emmo**	risponder**emmo**	partir**emmo**
parler**este**	risponder**este**	partir**este**
parler**ẹbbero**	risponder**ẹbbero**	partir**ẹbbero**

NOTE:
The endings of the present conditional are the same for all conjugations.

Mi **piacerebbe** essere ricco.	*I would like to be rich.*
Preferirebbe lavorare.	*She would prefer to work.*
Ci **aiuteresti?**	*Would you help us?*

---

*When "would" indicates a habitual action in the past, Italian uses the imperfect tense. *When I was a child, I would (I used to) go to the beach every summer.* = **Da bambino, andavo alla spiaggia tutte le estati.**

2. Verbs that are irregular in the future are also irregular in the conditional. Here is a comprehensive list.

dare:	**darei, daresti**, ecc.
fare:	**farei, faresti**, ecc.
stare:	**starei, staresti**, ecc.
andare:	**andrei, andresti**, ecc.
avere:	**avrei, avresti**, ecc.
cadere:	**cadrei, cadresti**, ecc.
dovere:	**dovrei, dovresti**, ecc.
potere:	**potrei, potresti**, ecc.
sapere:	**saprei, sapresti**, ecc.
vedere:	**vedrei, vedresti**, ecc.
vivere:	**vivrei, vivresti**, ecc.
essere:	**sarei, saresti**, ecc.
bere:	**berrei, berresti**, ecc.
venire:	**verrei, verresti**, ecc.
volere:	**vorrei, vorresti**, ecc.

Verresti al cinema con me?
Would you come with me to the movies?
Mi **darebbe** alcuni consigli?
Would you give me some advice?
Che cosa **vorrebbe** fare Paolo?
What would Paolo like to be?
Io **vorrei** fare l'oculista.
I would like to be an eye doctor.

—Vorrebbe l'anestesia?

3. Verbs ending in **-care**, **-gare**, **-ciare**, and **-giare** undergo a spelling change for phonetic reasons, as in the future tense (see Chapter 11, I).

cercare: **Cercherei** un lavoro.	*I would look for a job.*
pagare: **Pagherei** molto.	*I would pay a lot.*
cominciare: **Comincerei** a lavorare.	*I would start working.*
mangiare: **Mangerei** della frutta.	*I would eat fruit.*

Pratica

A. Cosa faresti durante le vacanze? Rispondete secondo l'esempio.

ESEMPIO vedere gli amici **Vedrei gli amici.**

1. dormire fino a tardi **2.** fare delle passeggiate **3.** leggere molti libri **4.** mangiare al ristorante **5.** guardare la TV **6.** divertirsi **7.** scrivere delle lettere **8.** andare al cinema **9.** stare alla spiaggia tutto il giorno **10.** uscire con gli amici **11.** riposarsi **12.** giocare a tennis

B. **Domanda e risposta.** Un vostro amico spera di vincere alla lotteria. Aiutatelo con le vostre domande a esprimere i suoi sogni (*dreams*).

ESEMPIO fare un viaggio in Florida
—Faresti un viaggio in Florida?
—No, farei un viaggio in Oriente. *o*

1. passare i week-end in città **2.** viaggiare in treno **3.** mangiare al McDonald's? **4.** vivere in un appartamentino di due o tre locali **5.** comprare una Fiat **6.** spendere tutti i soldi in un anno **7.** prestarmi mille dollari

C. **Domanda e risposta.** Uno studente domanda a te e ad altri compagni se vorreste fare alcune cose. Tu rispondi anche per loro. Seguite l'esempio.

ESEMPIO venire al cinema
—Verreste al cinema?
—No, ma verremmo volentieri alla discoteca.

1. bere un succo d'arancia **2.** mangiare una pizza **3.** giocare a carte **4.** andare a vedere il film *Profumo di donna* con Al Pacino **5.** fare un giro (*to take a ride*) in bicicletta **6.** darmi il vostro indirizzo

D. Leggete e completate con il **condizionale presente.**

1. A un caffè di Viareggio, in Toscana.
   —Ragazzi, io _____ (prendere) un espresso lungo (*weak*). E voi?
   —Con questo caldo? Noi _____ (bere) volentieri qualcosa di fresco.
   —Sì, mi _____ (piacere) bere un succo di pompelmo. E a te?
   —Per me la stessa cosa.
2. Un turista in una banca di Bari, in Puglia.
   —Scusi, Lei _____ (potere) cambiarmi un assegno di cento dollari?
   —Non a questo sportello; Lei _____ (dovere) andare allo sportello del Cambio.
3. All'ingresso di un albergo di Verona, nel Veneto.
   —Che camera _____ (volere) i signori? Una sul davanti?
   —Sì, _____ (andare) bene, se non c'è troppo rumore però.
   —Possono stare tranquilli. _____ (Potere) darmi un Loro documento?
   —Ecco il passaporto.

E. **Cosa faresti tu in questa situazione?** Scegliete (*Choose*) l'espressione corretta della seconda colonna e rispondete usando il verbo al **condizionale.**

1. Sei in ritardo a un appuntamento.
2. La macchina non funziona.
3. Un amico ti chiede un favore.
4. Il padrone di casa aumenta l'affitto dell'appartamento.
5. Un collega d'ufficio riceve una promozione.
6. Devi spedire un pacco (*package*), e all'ufficio postale ci sono molte persone.
7. Devi presentarti ad un colloquio.
8. Il tuo direttore ti dà un aumento di stipendio.

protestare (o cambiare casa)
fargli le mie congratulazioni
fargliela
scusarsi
portarla dal meccanico
fare la fila e aspettare
ringraziarlo
preparare il mio curriculum vitae

NEO-LAUREATI
IN CHIMICA INDUSTRIALE
O INGEGNERIA CHIMICA

Rif. 352

Si richiede per entrambe le posizioni:
— età non superiore a 35 anni;
— disponibilità a frequenti spostamenti.
La conoscenza della lingua inglese costituirà titolo preferenziale.
Sede di lavoro: **Lamezia Terme (CZ).**
Si offre l'inserimento in un ambiente dinamico ed in fase di espansione, con notevoli possibilità di crescita professionale sostenute da adeguati interventi formativi.

Gli interessati sono pregati di inviare dettagliato curriculum, corredato di recapito telefonico e di fotografia, alla **PA Consulting Group** - Via Turati 40 - 20121 Milano citando il riferimento di interesse anche sulla busta e indicando «Riservato» se nella lettera sono elencate società con le quali non si desidera entrare in contatto.
La selezione verrà effettuata direttamente dall'Azienda.

PA Consulting Group
Creating Business Advantage

II. Il condizionale passato

Michele avrebbe voluto diventare un grande pittore... invece fa l'imbianchino.

1. The conditional perfect (**condizionale passato**) is the equivalent of the English *would have* + past participle. It is formed with the present conditional of **avere** or **essere** + the past participle of the main verb.

   avrei finito = *I would have finished*

It is conjugated as follows:

parlare		rispondere		partire	
avrei	parlato	avrei	risposto	sarei	partito(a)
avresti		avresti		saresti	
avrebbe		avrebbe		sarebbe	
avremmo		avremmo		saremmo	partiti(e)
avreste		avreste		sareste	
avrẹbbero		avrẹbbero		sarẹbbero	

Avrei scritto, ma non avevo l'indirizzo — *I would have written, but I did not have the address.*
Avresti accettato l'invito? — *Would you have accepted the invitation?*

2. In indirect discourse with verbs such as **dire**, **rispondere**, **scrivere**, **telefonare**, **spiegare**, Italian uses the conditional perfect to express a future action that is seen from a point in the past. Compare the constructions in Italian with those in English:

Ha detto che **sarebbe andato.** — *He said he would go.*
Hanno scritto che **sarebbero venuti.** — *They wrote they would come.*
Ha risposto che non **avrebbe aspettato.** — *He answered he would not wait.*

Pratica

A. Le seguenti persone hanno agito in un certo modo (*way*). Altre, invece, avrebbero agito diversamente (*differently*). Dite come.

ESEMPIO Lisa ha comprato un cappotto./Marco...
Marco, invece, avrebbe comprato un impermeabile. *o*

1. Silvio ha ordinato lasagne al forno./Noi... **2.** L'ingegner Scotti è partito in aereo./La signora Scotti... **3.** Il direttore della ditta è andato in vacanza a Miami./La sua segretaria... **4.** Gabriella e Filippo hanno bevuto una bottiglia di Frascati./Tu... **5.** Io mi sono alzato tardi./I miei fratelli... **6.** I miei genitori hanno preferito un appartamento in centro./Io...

B. **Hanno detto che...**Usate il discorso indiretto (*indirect discourse*) e il **condizionale passato.**

ESEMPIO La mia fidanzata mi ha detto: —Ti telefonerò alle tre.
La mia fidanzata mi ha detto che m'avrebbe telefonato alle tre.

1. Lorenzo mi ha detto: —Comprerò un computer. **2.** I miei zii mi hanno detto: —Verremo presto a trovarti. **3.** Liliana ha detto a Lucia: —Mi presenterò per un colloquio. **4.** Luigi ha detto a Paola: —Farò l'architetto o l'ingegnere. **5.** La segretaria ha detto alla sua amica: —Chiederò un aumento di stipendio.

C. Domanda e risposta. Cosa avresti fatto nelle seguenti situazioni?

ESEMPIO al lago
—Cosa avresti fatto al lago?
—Avrei preso il sole. *o*

1. a Roma **2.** dopo un esame difficile **3.** prima di un colloquio per un impiego **4.** in caso di cattivo tempo **5.** per il compleanno del tuo ragazzo (della tua ragazza) **6.** il giorno delle elezioni **7.** dopo un trasloco

D. Formate delle frasi complete con il primo verbo al **condizionale passato** e il secondo verbo all'**imperfetto.**

ESEMPIO Lia (fare) un viaggio, non (avere) soldi
Lia avrebbe fatto un viaggio, ma non aveva soldi.

1. io (prestarti) la macchina, non (funzionare) **2.** lui (cambiare) lavoro, (essere) difficile trovarne un altro **3.** noi (prendere) il treno, (esserci) lo sciopero dei treni **4.** lei (fare) medicina, ma gli studi (essere) troppo lunghi **5.** il nostro amico (partire), non (stare) bene **6.** io (preferire) un lavoro a tempo pieno, (esserci) solo lavori part-time

E. Completate con il **condizionale presente** o **passato.**

1. Io (*would go*) _____ in vacanza, ma sono al verde. **2.** Noi (would go out) _____, ma piove. **3.** (*Would you live*) _____ in campagna Lei? **4.** Loro (*would be*) _____ contenti di stare a casa oggi. **5.** Gino (*would have left*) _____ con il treno delle sei, ma la sua valigia non era pronta. **6.** Che cosa (*would you answer*) _____ a un amico che ti domanda un favore? **7.** (*Would you like*) _____ fare il chirurgo? **8.** Hai scritto a Pietro? (*I would have written to him*) _____, ma lui non ha risposto alla mia ultima lettera.

III. Uso di *dovere, potere, volere* nel condizionale

—Potrebbe darmi un aumento?

1. The present conditional of **dovere**, **potere**, and **volere** is used instead of the present indicative to make a request sound more polite or a statement less forceful. It has the following meanings:

   dovrei = *I should, I ought to*
   potrei = *I could, I might*
   vorrei = *I would want, I would like*

   Compare:

Devi aiutare la gente.	*You must help people.*
Dovresti aiutare la gente.	*You should (you ought to) help people.*
Non **voglio** vivere qui.	*I don't want to live here.*
Non **vorrei** vivere qui.	*I would not want (I would not like) to live here.*
Può aiutarmi?	*Can you help me?*
Potrebbe aiutarmi?	*Could you help me?*

2. The Italian constructions of **potere**, **volere**, and **dovere** in the conditional perfect correspond to the following English constructions:

   avrei dovuto + *infinitive* = *I should have* + past participle
   avrei potuto + *infinitive* = *I could have* + past participle
   avrei voluto + *infinitive* = *I would have liked* + infinitive

Avrei dovuto parlare all'avvocato.	*I should have spoken to the lawyer.*
Avrebbe potuto laurearsi l'anno scorso.	*She could have graduated last year.*
Avrebbe voluto fare un viaggio.	*He would have liked to take a trip.*

Pratica

A. Attenuate (*Make less forceful*) il significato delle seguenti frasi, usando il **condizionale presente.**

   1. I due turisti: —Vogliamo due camere singole con doccia. Può prepararci il conto per stasera? **2.** Il direttore di una ditta: —Dobbiamo assumere una persona competente. Può inviarci (*send us*) il Suo curriculum vitae? **3.** Il capoufficio: —Deve pensare al Suo futuro. Vuole una lettera di raccomandazione? **4.** Un lavoratore part-time: —Oggi voglio finire prima. Devo andare all'agenzia di collocamento. **5.** Gli studenti d'italiano: —Possiamo uscire mezz'ora prima? Può ripetere le spiegazioni sul condizionale domani?

B. Cosa direste nelle seguenti situazioni? Usate il **condizionale** di **dovere**, **volere** o **potere.**

   1. Lei ha portato il cane dal veterinario, ma non può pagare perchè ha dimenticato a casa il portafoglio. **2.** Lei ha perduto l'autobus e sa che un compagno ha la macchina. **3.** Un turista straniero Le chiede dov'è possibile fare una telefonata. **4.** Oggi Lei non può aspettare la fine dell'ora d'italiano perchè non si sente bene.

C. Dite che cosa avrebbero dovuto (voluto o potuto) fare queste persone nelle seguenti situazioni.

ESEMPIO Lei ha ricevuto un brutto voto all'esame. Che cosa avrebbe dovuto fare?
—**Avrei dovuto studiare di più.**

1. Il signor Brambilla era stanco di lavorare. Che cosa avrebbe voluto fare?
2. Non avevate notizie di una vostra amica. Che cosa avreste potuto fare?
3. Avevi un appuntamento, ma non ci potevi andare. Che cosa avresti potuto fare? **4.** Sei arrivato(a) in ritardo a scuola. Che cosa avresti dovuto fare? **5.** Un amico Le ha telefonato perchè era in gravi difficoltà finanziarie. Che cosa avrebbe potuto fare? **6.** L'altro giorno Lei è andato(a) in ufficio; il computer non funzionava, faceva troppo caldo e il direttore era di cattivo umore. Cosa avrebbe voluto fare? **7.** Ieri era una bellissima giornata. A scuola c'era un esame difficile; tu e il tuo compagno (la tua compagna) non eravate preparati(e), e non avevate voglia di andare in classe. Cosa avreste voluto fare?

D. Completate le frasi al **condizionale passato.**

1. Voi (*should have waited for us*) _____ anche se eravamo un po' in ritardo. **2.** Tu (*should have spoken about it*) _____ al tuo avvocato. **3.** Io (*should have gone*) _____ dal dentista, anche se avevo paura. **4.** Mio padre (*would have wanted*) _____ andare in pensione, ma non aveva ancora 60 anni. **5.** Mia sorella (*could have found*) _____ un buon impiego, ma ha preferito continuare gli studi. **6.** (*Would you have preferred*) _____ essere una casalinga o fare carriera in una professione? **7.** (*I would have liked*) _____ fare architettura, ma ho dovuto cercarmi un lavoro appena mi sono diplomato(a).

IV. Verbi e espressioni verbali + infinito

Mentre Beethoven continuava a soffrire (to suffer) il padre incominciava a perdere la pazienza (patience).

1. Perchè Beethoven continuava a soffrire?
2. Che cosa incominciava a perdere il padre?

1. Some verbs and verbal expressions are followed by an infinitive without any preposition. Among the most common are:

   a. Semiauxiliary verbs: **dovere, potere, volere, sapere**
   b. Verbs of *liking* or *disliking:* **amare, detestare** (*to hate*), **piacere, desiderare, preferire**
   c. Impersonal verbal expressions with the verb **essere**, such as: **è facile (difficile), è possibile (impossibile), è necessario, è bello**

Potresti aiutarmi?	*Could you help me?*
Mi **piace** ascoltare i dischi di Pavarotti.	*I like to listen to Pavarotti's records.*
È facile sbagliarsi.	*It is easy to make a mistake.*
È possibile laurearsi in quattro anni.	*It is possible to graduate in four years.*
È bello camminare sotto la pioggia.	*It is nice to walk in the rain.*

2. Some verbs and verbal expressions require the preposition **di** + *infinitive*. Among the most common are:

   a. **essere** + *adjective*: **contento, felice, soddisfatto, stanco**
   b. **avere** + *noun*: **paura, bisogno, intenzione, tempo, voglia**
   c. Verbs of *saying*: **dire, domandare, chiedere, consigliare, promettere**
   d. Verbs of *thinking*: **credere, pensare, ricordarsi, sperare, decidere**
   e. Other verbs: **dimenticare, dispiacere, cercare** (*to try*), **finire**

Sono contento di vederLa.	*I am glad to see you.*
Mi dispiace di sentire questa brutta notizia.	*I am sorry to hear this bad news.*
Non ha intenzione di assumermi.	*He doesn't intend to hire me.*
Sperava di diventare un grande pittore.	*He was hoping to become a great painter.*
Ti **prometto di** studiare.	*I promise you to (that I will) study.*
Non ci siamo ricordati di pagare l'affitto.	*We didn't remember to pay the rent.*

3. Some verbs require the preposition **a** + *infinitive*. Among the most common are:

aiutare	**imparare**	**mettersi**
andare	**(in)cominciare**	**riuscire**
continuare	**insegnare**	**venire**
fermarsi	**invitare**	

Non riesco a capire.	*I cannot understand.*
Abbiamo continuato a camminare.	*We continued walking.*
Mi **sono messo(a) a** leggere.	*I started reading.*
Ha imparato a scrivere a macchina.	*He learned to type.*
Mi **ha insegnato a** leggere.	*She taught me to read.*
Mi sono fermato a salutarlo.	*I stopped to say hello to him.*
Vorrei **venire a** trovarti.	*I would like to come visit you.*

NOTE:
A more complete list of verbs and verbal expressions + infinitive may be found in Appendix 2.

Pratica

A. Completate con le preposizioni **a**, **di** o **per**, se necessario.

Pierino impara ______ suonare il piano. Detesta ______ studiare. Preferisce ______ giocare con gli amici. Dopo la scuola incomincia ______ studiare e spera _______ finire presto perchè vuole _______ andare _______ giocare al pallone. Quando è fuori, continua _______ giocare e dimentica _______ ritornare presto per la cena. Dopo cena Pierino chiede _______ guardare la televisione, ma non può ________ guardarla per molto tempo perchè ha sonno e desidera ________ dormire. La mattina del giorno dopo deve ________ alzarsi presto ______ finire i compiti.

B. Cambiate le frasi seguenti secondo l'esempio e usate le preposizioni appropriate quando sono necessarie.

ESEMPIO Ci iscriviamo all'università. (speriamo) **Speriamo di iscriverci all'università.**

1. Beviamo un cappuccino. (vorremmo) **2.** Vai in Italia? (sei contento) **3.** I lavoratori aspettavano un aumento. (erano stanchi) **4.** Ho riparato la macchina da scrivere. (ho cercato) **5.** Il giovane cerca un lavoro. (si mette) **6.** Lucia guarda le vetrine. (si è fermata) **7.** Ti accompagno a casa? (posso) **8.** Lei leggeva fino a tardi. (le piaceva) **9.** Non faccio molto sport. (mi dispiace) **10.** Lavoriamo per vivere. (è necessario)

C. Un amico (Un'amica) non fa quello che (*what*) dovrebbe fare. Date alcuni buoni consigli, secondo l'esempio.

ESEMPIO (mangia poco) cercare **Devi cercare di mangiare!**

1. (non parla italiano) imparare **2.** (non è paziente) cercare **3.** (studia poco) promettere **4.** (non si preoccupa degli esami) incominciare **5.** (non chiude mai la porta) ricordarsi **6.** (non è mai in orario) incominciare **7.** (non risparmia) riuscire **8.** (non va più dal medico) continuare

D. Completate le seguenti frasi secondo il significato. Usate le preposizioni appropriate quando è necessario.

ESEMPIO Il professore ha sonno. Desidera... **Desidera dormire.** *o*

1. Il padre di Marcello ha 65 anni. Pensa... **2.** Il segretario ha perso l'impiego. Ha paura... **3.** Noi partiremo alle cinque di mattina. Dovremo... **4.** Liliana fa il secondo anno di legge. Ha intenzione... **5.** Gli operai sono scontenti del loro salario. Vorrebbero... **6.** A Marcello non piaceva il lavoro in banca. Non voleva continuare... **7.** È marzo e piove quasi ogni giorno. Io non dimentico mai... **8.** Non mi laureerò quest'anno. Mi dispiace... **9.** Filippo riceve uno stipendio modesto. Lui e Gabriella non riescono...

E. Rispondete.

1. Cos'hai intenzione di fare l'estate prossima? **2.** Speri di fare un viaggio? Dove desideri andare? **3.** Chiederai a tuo padre di aiutarti a pagare le tue vacanze? **4.** Hai mai cercato di risparmiare? È facile risparmiare? Perchè? **5.** Quanti anni avevi quando hai cominciato a guadagnare? **6.** Hai un lavoro adesso? È a tempo pieno? Se l'hai, sei soddisfatto(a) di averlo? Perchè?

LETTURA

IN CERCA DI UN IMPIEGO

In search of

Oggi Liliana si è presentata nello studio dell'avvocato Rizzi per un colloquio.

Rizzi *Dunque,* signorina, quali sarebbero le Sue qualifiche? — *so*

Liliana Lei vuol dire se ho esperienza?

Rizzi *Appunto.* Ha mai lavorato in un ufficio come questo? — *Exactly.*

Liliana No, mai. Ma ho lavorato per alcuni mesi in una ditta di import-export.

Rizzi Allora Lei sa usare il computer.

Liliana No, ma so scrivere a macchina.

Rizzi Velocemente?

Liliana Non troppo.

Rizzi *Viva la sincerità,* signorina. Ma, francamente, perchè vorrebbe lavorare da noi? — *hurrah for your frankness*

Liliana Sono studentessa in legge e mi piacerebbe vedere come funziona uno studio legale.

Rizzi Ah! Lei fa legge! Brava! E quando finirà gli studi?

Liliana Se tutto va bene, li finirò *fra* due anni. — *within*

Rizzi Ancora due anni, eh? Fra due anni una bella ragazza come Lei potrebbe incontrare un bel giovanotto, sposarsi e avere...

Liliana Avvocato, Lei mi offende! Se Lei *insinua* che non ho intenzioni serie perchè sono una donna, Lei si sbaglia. Ho sempre avuto l'intenzione di diventare avvocato, e un giorno lo diventerò, anche se esistono *certi pregiudizi.* — *suggest*; *certain biases*

Rizzi Mi scusi, signorina, *scherzavo!* Ma avrebbe dovuto presentarsi qualche giorno fa. Adesso è troppo tardi. Abbiamo già assunto un'altra signorina, molto esperta in lavori d'ufficio. Vuole un consiglio? Dovrebbe prima finire i Suoi studi e poi ritornare, e allora, chissà... potremmo avere bisogno del Suo aiuto. — *I was joking*

1.

FISIM SPA

immobiliare ricerca acquisitori/trici per filiale di Torino. Gradita esperienza commerciale anche non di settore. Corso di formazione retribuito (4 milioni) fisso mensile, adeguate provvigioni, istruzione tecnica. Tel. 568.1312.

OFFFRIAMO addestramento su computer settore segretariato contabilità e disegno computerizzato finalizzato ad assunzione inserimento regolato da contratto. Tel. 771.4156.

SEGRETARIA pratica uso PC, ottime referenze, massima disponibilità per lavoro impegnativo cercasi. Inviare curriculum a: Publikompass 7101 - 10100 Torino.

PERSONALE DOMESTICO BABY SITTER

CERCASI domestica fissa referenziata di qualsiasi età presso famiglia di 2 persone alto guadagno. Tel. 011 650.5822.

LAVORI VARI E PART TIME

PRIMARIA agenzia moda pubblicità seleziona indossatrici/tori, modelle/i per rapido inserimento lavorativo. Possibilità di qualificazione professionale. Telefonare ore ufficio allo 011 562.9138.

AGENTI E RAPPRESENTANTI

AZIENDA industriale e commerciale cerca agenti, anche 1° esperienza, automuniti, militesenti, max 35enni. Vendita articoli largo consumo nella ristorazione, industria comunità per provincia di To At Al e Valle d'Aosta. Offresi fisso mensile, più provvigioni, incentivi, esclusiva di zona, addestramento iniziale. Per appuntamento tel. 0322 844.623 Effepi group Borgomanero (No).

CERCASI abili venditori per nuovo prodotto ecologico, fisso mensile. Vendita su appuntamento. Tel. 854.210.

2.

IMPIEGATI

A. ESPERTA amministrazione contabilità bilanci fiscali, cerca occupazione responsabilità media azienda Torino Sud. Tel. 605.1333.

DIPLOMATA lingue inglese, francese, spagnolo, simpatica, presenza, cultura, esperta pubbliche relazioni, occuperebbesi seria ditta. Tel. 647.3006.

IMPIEGATA 26enne esperienza pluriennale gestione autonoma ufficio commerciale inglese buon livello offresi a seria azienda. Tel. 229.6555.

PENSIONATO 57enne già responsabile gestione acquisti e magazzino offresi anche part-time. Tel. 953.0309 ore pasti.

PERITO informatico 21enne pratico lavori di ufficio cerca lavoro. Tel. 011 886.976 ore pasti.

PRATICA uso Pc cerca lavoro buona cultura lingua madre spagnolo discreta conoscenza inglese. Tel. 988.7265 serali.

SEGRETARIA di direzione 25enne con esperienza, pratica lavori ufficio e uso Pc offresi. Passaggio diretto. Tel. 011 447.1988.

29ENNE libera subito, esperienza pluriennale import/export, ufficio commerciale, ottimo inglese/francese, buon tedesco/spagnolo, referenziata, offresi. Tel. 904.6084.

TECNICI

ELETTROMECCANICO cablatore provata esperienza bordo macchina automazione offresi a seria azienda per Italia ed estero. Tel. 770.9047.

PERSONALE DOMESTICO BABY SITTER

RAGAZZA 30enne cerca lavoro come collaboratrice familiare oppure pulizie ufficio. Tel. 650.5367.

Annunci pubblicitari:
1. offerte d'impiego
2. domande d'impiego.

Comprensione

1. Perchè Liliana si è presentata ad uno studio legale?
2. Ha mai lavorato in un ufficio Liliana?
3. Sarebbe una segretaria esperta? Perchè?
4. Per quali ragioni vorrebbe fare la segretaria in uno studio legale?
5. Ha già finito gli studi di legge? Fra quanto tempo li finirà?
6. Secondo l'avvocato, che cosa potrebbe succedere (*happen*) a Liliana prima della laurea?
7. Ha dei pregiudizi verso le donne l'avvocato? Parlava seriamente?
8. Ha ottenuto (*obtained*) l'impiego Liliana? Perchè no?
9. Quale consiglio le dà l'avvocato?

Domande personali

1. Si è mai presentato(a) a un colloquio Lei? Com'è andato?
2. Che cosa Le hanno chiesto? Le hanno chiesto anche il curriculum vitae?
3. Ha ottenuto l'impiego?
4. Le piacerebbe fare l'impiegato(a)? Perchè?
5. Sa usare il computer e scrivere a macchina rapidamente?
6. Se non ha ancora un lavoro, quale mestiere o professione vorrebbe fare? Perchè?
7. Se Lei ha già un impiego, è soddisfatto(a) del Suo stipendio? Lo spende tutto o riesce a risparmiare un po' di soldi?
8. Se Lei non ha un impiego, è perchè Lei è disoccupato(a), molto ricco(a), in pensione, o perchè prima avrebbe intenzione di finire gli studi?

ATTIVITÀ SUPPLEMENTARI

A. **Cerchiamo lavoro.** Immaginate di essere in un'agenzia di collocamento. Gli studenti si dividono in due gruppi: quelli che offrono il lavoro e quelli che lo cercano. I colloqui incominciano: Che lavoro è? Quali sono le condizioni: per esempio, l'orario, lo stipendio, gli studi, l'esperienza, le referenze?

B. **Curriculum vitae.** Immaginate di scrivere un breve riassunto *(resumé)* della vostra vita.

1. nome e cognome
2. data di nascita
3. indirizzo e numero di telefono
4. titolo di studio (diploma o laurea, nome della scuola o dell'università)
5. esperienza di lavoro (dove, quando, quanto tempo)
6. altre qualifiche
7. lettere di raccomandazione (da chi: nome, qualifica, scuola o ditta)

C. **Il futuro.** Due amici (amiche) parlano dei loro progetti per il futuro: quale mestiere o professione, per quale ragione, vantaggi e svantaggi, ecc. Prendete come esempio il dialogo *«Una scelta difficile»*.

D. **Cercate un compagno (una compagna) ideale?** Leggete queste inserzioni (*ads*) matrimoniali e usatele come modello per scrivere il vostro annuncio al giornale.

E. **La giornata di una superdonna.** Presentate la signora Bravi (professione e famiglia, tre gemelli) e descrivete la sua giornata, seguendo i disegni secondo l'ordine suggerito dall'orologio.

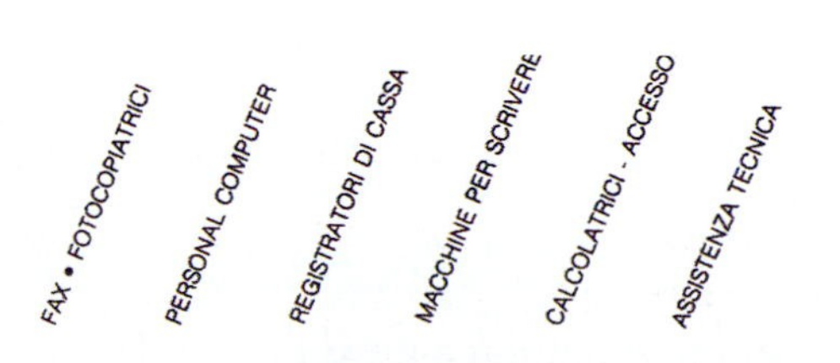

MATRIMONIALI

ATTRAENTE, sportivo, 55enne, ottimo livello socio/culturale, sposerebbe bella signora/ina, snella, fine, pulita, 30/50enne, anche straniera. Scrivere: Publikompass 8549 - 10100 Torino.

CELIBE 36enne operaio, presenza, cerca signora/ina scopo matrimonio. Scrivere: Publikompass 7024 - 10100 Torino.

INCONTRI Agenzia Matrimoniale. requisiti richiesti: classe, cultura, serietà d'intenti. Via Vespucci 34 bis (To). Tel. 568.3242.

LIBERA 45enne laureata posizionata giovane attraente conoscerebbe scopo matrimonio, laureato, colto, solida posizione economica, bella presenza, moralità irreprensibile, senza figli, inanonimi, telefono. Scrivere: Publikompass 1526 - 43100 Parma.

PENSIONATO 84enne cerca scopo matrimonio pensionata sensibile seria. Scrivere: Publikompass 5019 - 10100 Torino.

RAGAZZA nubile trentenne relazionerebbe scopo matrimonio con coetaneo. Scrivere: Publikompass 8548 - 10100 Torino.

30ENNE bella presenza alto 1,85, diplomato, cerca scopo matrimonio bella e diplomata. Scrivere: Publikompass 8601 - 10100 Torino.

30ENNE ex modella contatterebbe solo scopo matrimonio settentrionale laureato industriale professionista. Scrivere: Publikompass 5016 - 10100 Torino.

33ENNE bella presenza, romantico, buon lavoro, sposerebbe ragazza carina, affettuosa, lavoratrice, anche nullatenente massimo trentenne, possibilmente residente in Torino. Gradito tel. Scrivere: Publikompass 8602 - 10100 Torino.

42ENNE celibe, serio, conoscerebbe seria, carina, scopo matrimonio. Scrivere: Publikompass 8551 - 10100 Torino.

51ENNE vedovo cerca signora/ina o vedova 40/48enne seria scopo matrimonio max serietà, no perditempo. Scrivere: Publikompass 7022 - 10100 Torino.

58ENNE vedova indipendente cerca massimo 60enne alto, bella presenza, fumatore, indipendente, scopo matrimonio. Scrivere: Publikompass 8603 - 10100 Torino.

63ENNE pensionato solo casa propria conoscerebbe signora scopo matrimonio. Scrivere: Publikompass 7028 - 10100 Torino.

F. Come si dice in italiano?

1. Roberto S. is a young lawyer who (**che**) lost (his) job.
2. Since he would like to find a new one, today he is in an employment agency for an interview.
3. Would you have a job for a person with my qualifications (**qualifiche**, *f. pl.*)?
4. Well (**beh!**), the C. & C. brothers are building a wall (**muro**) around their property (**proprietà**) and will be hiring several people.
5. I would prefer to work in an office: I can type…
6. Well, maybe you should come back next month; we might have another job.
7. I can't wait. I will take this job, though (**però**) I would have preferred a more (**più**) intellectual job.
8. Who knows? Today you start as (a) laborer, and tomorrow you might become the president of C. & C.

Vocabolario

Nomi

l'agenzia di collocamento	*employment agency*
il commercio	*commerce*
la condizione	*condition*
il coniglio	*rabbit*
il davanti	*front*
l'elettricità	*electricity*
l'esperienza	*experience*
la fabbrica	*factory*
il fattore	*factor, element*
il giovanotto	*young man*
l'inclinazione (*f.*)	*inclination*
l'industria	*industry*
l'insegnamento	*teaching*
l'interesse (*m.*)	*interest*
la lettera di raccomandazione	*letter of recommendation*
il mestiere	*trade*
il muratore	*brick layer*
l'offerta	*offer*
la posta	*mail*
il pregiudizio	*prejudice, bias*
il (la) professionista	*professional (person)*
la promozione	*promotion*
la qualifica	*qualification*
la referenza	*reference*
la scelta	*choice*
il sogno	*dream*
lo (la) specialista	*specialist*
il titolo di studio	*degree*
il veterinario	*veterinary*

Aggettivi

competente	*competent*
elettronico	*electronic*
esperto	*experienced, expert*
grave	*grave, serious*
inesperto	*inexperienced*
legale	*legal*
soddisfatto	*satisfied*

Verbi

agire (-isc)	*to act*
assumere (*p.p.* assunto)	*to hire*
cercare di (+inf.)	*to try*
consultare	*to consult*
detestare	*to hate*
diplomarsi	*to graduate (from high school)*
funzionare	*to function, to work*
influenzare	*to influence*
iscriversi	*to enroll, to register*
laurearsi	*to graduate (from university or college)*
licenziare	*to fire*
offendere (p.p. offeso)	*to offend*
ottenere	*to obtain*
presentarsi	*to introduce (present) one-self*
protestare	*to protest*
ringraziare	*to thank*
riparare	*to repair*
risparmiare	*to save (money)*
sbagliarsi	*to make a mistake*
scegliere (*p.p.* scelto)	*to choose*
scherzare	*to joke*
scrivere a macchina	*to type*
succedere (*p.p.* successo)	*to happen*

Altre espressioni

appena	*as soon as*
attualmente	*at present*
cambiare idea	*to change one's mind*
di cattivo umore	*in a bad mood*
fare la fila	*to stand in line*
Guarda chi si vede!	*Look who is here!*
invece	*instead*
intorno a	*around*
qualcosa	*something*
Viva la sincerità!	*Hurrah for frankness!*

La giornalista e scrittrice Oriana Fallaci.

IL LAVORO E LA DONNA

Da alcuni anni l'Italia *attraversa* una grave crisi economica. L'inflazione, la disoccupazione e il deficit dello Stato sono saliti in maniera allarmante. I giovani che si iscrivono all'università trovano difficilmente lavoro alla fine degli studi. *Eppure* i turisti stranieri che leggono le statistiche dei giornali, sono sorpresi di *constatare* l'abbondanza e la qualità dei prodotti *disponibili* nei negozi, *come anche* l'eleganza della gente che *affolla* ristoranti, teatri, centri di villeggiatura.

attraversa: has been experiencing
Eppure: yet
constatare: to see
disponibili: available
come anche/affolla: as well as/crowd

In realtà, il governo italiano ha continuato per anni una politica sociale molto generosa. Fino al 1992, per esempio, le pensioni erano garantite a tutti i cittadini a un'età relativamente giovane (55 anni per la donna, 60 anni per l'uomo) e potevano *raggiungere* il 90 per cento dell'ultimo stipendio per gli *statali.* Il governo, tuttavia, ha introdotto varie riforme.*

raggiungere: reach
statali: government employees

Nel 1946 la donna ha votato per la prima volta; da allora *ha fatto molta strada* nella conquista dei suoi *diritti.* Le casalinghe hanno ottenuto il diritto alla pensione sociale e le lavoratrici il diritto a cinque mesi di *congedo* pagato in caso di maternità. *Inoltre, si* può dire che oggi le donne competono con gli uomini in tutte le professioni una volta esclusivamente maschili. La donna può *essere magistrato* o fare la giornalista, può dedicarsi all'insegnamento universitario o fare il chirurgo. Diverse donne siedono nella Camera dei Deputati e nel Senato; alcune hanno fatto o fanno parte del Consiglio dei Ministri.

ha fatto molta strada: has gone a long way
diritti: rights
congedo/Inoltre/si: leave/Moreover/one
essere magistrato: sit on the Bench

*Starting in 1996 the retirement age will be 60 for women and 65 for men.

La senatrice Nilde Jotti, ex-presidente della Camera dei Deputati.

La donna italiana è entrata come *dirigente* anche nelle ditte commerciali e industriali, *malgrado* una certa resistenza. Le scuole per le future manager sono *sempre più* numerose in Italia. Il periodo fascista, che confinava la donna al ruolo di casalinga e di madre, è *ormai* molto lontano.

manager
in spite of
more and more
by now

Comprensione

Rispondete alle seguenti domande.

1. Quali sono le prove della crisi economica italiana?
2. È facile per i giovani trovare lavoro?
3. A che età potevano andare in pensione gli Italiani prima del 1993?
4. In che anno le donne italiane hanno votato per la prima volta?
5. A che cosa hanno diritto le lavoratrici?
6. Che cosa possono diventare le donne italiane nel campo della politica?
7. Qual è la dimostrazione che la donna italiana può fare carriera anche nel campo commerciale e industriale?

15 PAESI E PAESAGGI

Vista notturna del golfo di Napoli e, in parte, del Vesuvio.

Punti di vista

Una gita scolastica
Un incontro

Punti grammaticali

I I comparativi
II I superlativi
III Comparativi e superlativi irregolari
IV Uso dell'articolo determinativo

Lettura

Una lezione di geografia

Pagina culturale

L'Italia: un mosaico di paesaggi

PUNTI DI VISTA

Cortina d'Ampezzo (Veneto). Campi di neve e, sullo sfondo, le Dolomiti.

UNA *GITA SCOLASTICA* — field trip

Alcuni professori del liceo «M» dell'Aquila* hanno organizzato una gita scolastica a Roccaraso. Così Tina e i compagni vanno in montagna a passare la settimana bianca.** Ora i ragazzi sono in pullman, *eccitati* (excited) e felici.

Tina Mi piace viaggiare in pullman, e a te?

Stefano Mi piace *di più* (more) viaggiare in treno.

Riccardo Sapete cosa mi piacerebbe fare? Un viaggio in aereo. Siete mai andati in aereo voi?

Lisa Sì, io ci sono andata l'anno scorso, ma è *meno* interessante *di quel che* (less... than) tu pensi.

Stefano *Sono d'accordo* con te. Un viaggio in treno è *molto più* (I agree/much more) piacevole: dal treno puoi vedere *pianure,* (plains) colline, laghi, fiumi, mentre dall'aereo non vedi niente.

Tina E poi io non prenderei mai l'aereo, perchè soffro di claustrofobia e *avrei una paura da morire!* (I would be scared to death)

Riccardo *Ma va!* Tu hai paura di *tutto! Come mai* (come on!/everything/how come) non hai paura di sciare?

---

*L'Aquila, chief town of the region Abruzzi, is surrounded by the highest mountains of the Appennini. South of L'Aquila is Roccaraso, a summer and winter resort town.

**A winter vacation on the snow.

Tina	Perchè sciare mi piace moltissimo. E poi mio padre mi ha comprato un paio di *sci* per Natale.	skis
Lisa	*A proposito,* ho bisogno di comprare alcune cose appena arriviamo al paese.	by the way
Tina	Di cosa hai bisogno?	
Lisa	Ho dimenticato a casa *il sacchetto del trucco.*	make-up case
Tina	Ma per tre giorni non puoi *farne a meno?*	do without it
Lisa	Sì, posso fare a meno *di truccarmi,* ma il fatto è che nel sacchetto c'erano *lo spazzolino da denti* e *il dentifricio.*	to put on my make-up; toothbrush; toothpaste
Tina	Allora appena arriveremo al paese, cercheremo una farmacia.	

Comprensione

1. Dove vanno Tina e i suoi compagni?
2. A Stefano piace di più viaggiare in treno o in pullman?
3. Quando è andata in aereo Lisa? Le è piaciuto viaggiare in aereo?
4. Stefano dice che un viaggio in aereo è meno interessante di un viaggio in treno. Perchè?
5. Secondo Riccardo, è una ragazza coraggiosa Tina? Perchè no?
6. Di cosa non ha paura Tina? Perchè?
7. Che cosa ha lasciato a casa Lisa?
8. Lisa si preoccupa solo perchè non potrà truccarsi, o si preoccupa per un'altra ragione? Quale?
9. Perchè dovrà cercare una farmacia Lisa?

Studio di parole

TERMINI GEOGRAFICI

Tutto il mondo... in cinquanta parole.

la terra earth
la montagna mountain
il monte
la catena chain
la collina hill
il vulcano volcano
la valle valley
la pianura plain
la costa coast
il continente continent
il paese country; town
l'isola island
la penisola peninsula
il fiume river

il porto port
il golfo gulf
il lago lake
il mare sea
l'oceano ocean
il territorio territory
la superficie area
attraversare to cross
confinare (con) to border
settentrionale = del nord northern
meridionale = del sud southern
orientale = dell'est eastern
occidentale = dell'ovest western

lo spazio space
l'atmosfera atmosphere
il cielo sky
il sole sun
la luna moon

la stella star
il pianeta planet
lo strato dell'ozono ozone layer
l'effetto serra greenhouse effect

illuminare to light
Il sole sorge (*rises*) **alle...e tramonta** (*sets*) **alle...**
l'alba dawn
il tramonto sunset

Applicazione

A. **Geografia.**

1. La Sardegna è un'isola o una penisola?
2. Da che cosa è circondata l'Italia?
3. Che cosa attraversiamo per andare dall'Austria all'Italia?
4. È più lunga la catena degli Appennini o quella delle Alpi?
5. Che cosa sono il Po, l'Arno e il Tevere?
6. È più grande la superficie dell'Italia o quella dell'Alaska?
7. Sa quali sono i paesi che confinano con l'Italia? Se non lo sa, Lei può guardare le carte geografiche che si trovano all'inizio (*beginning*) di questo libro.

B. **Il cielo.**

1. Che cosa illumina il cielo la notte?
2. A che ora sorge il sole in questi giorni?
3. Di che colore è il cielo sull'oceano quando il sole tramonta?
4. L'effetto serra riscalda o raffredda la terra?
5. Che cosa protegge (*protects*) l'atmosfera dai raggi (*rays*) ultravioletti?

C. **Domande personali.**

1. Ha mai partecipato Lei a una gita scolastica? Dov'è stato(a) e con che mezzo ha viaggiato?
2. Le piace di più viaggiare in aereo o in treno? Perchè?
3. Ha mai attraversato gli Stati Uniti in treno? Sa quanti giorni ci vogliono?
4. Secondo Lei, è più attraente la costa orientale degli Stati Uniti o quella occidentale?
5. Conosce il nome di un vulcano attivo in Italia? Sa dov'è?
6. Conosce il nome di due belle isole nel golfo di Napoli?
7. Sa qual è il monte più alto d'Europa?

Ascoltiamo!

Un incontro. *Lisa has stopped at a pharmacy in Roccaraso to buy a toothbrush and toothpaste. There, she runs into Giovanni, an old school friend whom she has not seen for several years. Listen to their conversation, then answer the following questions.*

Comprensione

1. Che sorpresa ha avuto Lisa quando è entrata nella farmacia?
2. Con chi è venuto in montagna Giovanni? Perchè?
3. In quale periodo dell'anno Lisa e Giovanni venivano in montagna con le loro famiglie?
4. Lisa era una brava sciatrice quand'era bambina? Perchè Giovanni rideva?
5. Perchè Giovanni non potrà vedere Lisa sugli sci domani?
6. Che cosa vuole sapere Giovanni da Lisa? Perchè?

Dialogo

In gruppi di due: Immaginate di incontrare un vecchio amico (una vecchia amica), che non vedevate da molto tempo, in un posto di villeggiatura. Abbracciatevi e scambiatevi (*exchange*) notizie e indirizzi.

PUNTI GRAMMATICALI

I. I comparativi

La Sardegna è quasi grande quanto la Sicilia. Il Po è più lungo del Tevere. Gli Appennini sono meno alti delle Alpi.

L'Italia ha una superficie di 116.305 miglia quadrate (sq. mi.) e una lunghezza di circa 800 miglia.

1. Il Tevere è più lungo o più corto del Po?
2. Le Alpi sono meno alte o più alte degli Appennini?
3. La Sardegna è più grande della Sicilia?

There are two types of comparisons: the comparisons of equality, and the comparisons of inequality.

1. The expressions for the comparison of equality are as follows:

(così)...come	*as...as*
(tanto)...quanto	*as...as, as much...as*

Both may be used either before an adjective or before an adverb. In these cases, **così** and **tanto** may be omitted. Before a noun, **tanto...quanto** must be used. In that case, **tanto** must agree with the noun it modifies and cannot be omitted.

Roma è **(tanto)** bella **quanto** Firenze.	*Rome is as beautiful as Florence.*
Studio **(così)** diligentemente **come** Giulia.	*I study as diligently as Giulia.*
Io ho **tanta** pazienza **quanto** Lei.	*I have as much patience as you.*
Ho **tanti** amici **quanto** Luigi.	*I have as many friends as Luigi.*

2. The expressions for the comparisons of inequality are:

più...di, più...che	*more...than*
meno...di, meno...che	*less...than*

a. **Più...di** and **meno...di** are used when two persons or things are compared in terms of the same quality or performance.

La California è **più** grande **dell'**Italia.	*California is bigger than Italy.*
Una Fiat è **meno** cara **di** una Ferrari.	*A Fiat is less expensive than a Ferrari.*
Gli aerei viaggiano **più** rapidamente **dei** treni.	*Planes travel faster than trains.*
Tu hai **più** soldi **di** me.	*You have more money than I.*

NOTE:
Di (*than*) combines with the article. Also, if the second term of comparison is a personal pronoun, a disjunctive pronoun must be used (**me**, **te**, ecc.).

b. **Più di** and **meno di** are used also in front of numerals.

Avrò letto **più di trenta** annunci.	*I probably read more than thirty ads.*
Il bambino pesa **meno di quattro** chili.	*The baby weighs less than four kilos.*

c. **Più...che** and **meno...che** are used when two adjectives, adverbs, infinitives, or nouns are directly compared and are related to the same subject.

L'Italia è **più** lunga **che** larga.	*Italy is longer than it is wide.*
Studia **più** diligentemente **che** intelligentemente.	*He studies more diligently than intelligently.*
Mi piace **meno** studiare **che** divertirmi.	*I like studying less than having fun.*
Luigi ha **più** nemici **che** amici.	*Luigi has more enemies than friends.*

Pratica

A. Paragonate (*Compare*) le seguenti persone (o posti o cose) usando **(tanto)... quanto** o **(così)...come.**

ESEMPIO (alto) Teresa, Gina **Teresa è (tanto) alta quanto Gina.** *o* **Teresa è (così) alta come Gina.**

1. (bello) l'isola di Capri, l'isola d'Ischia **2.** (grande) la tua camera, la mia camera **3.** (elegante) le donne italiane, le donne americane **4.** (preoccupato) la mamma, il papà **5.** (presto) questo pullman arriva, il treno **6.** (serio) il problema della disoccupazione, quello dell'inflazione

B. **Domanda e risposta.** Rispondete usando **più di** o **meno di** e scegliendo (*choosing*) una delle due alternative.

ESEMPIO (popolato) l'Italia, la California
—L'Italia è più popolata o meno popolata della California?
—L'Italia è più popolata della California.

1. (riservato) gli Italiani, gli Inglesi **2.** (lungo) le notti d'inverno, le notti d'estate **3.** (leggero) un vestito di lana, un vestito di seta **4.** (rapido) l'aereo, il treno **5.** (necessario) la salute, i soldi **6.** (pericoloso) la bicicletta, la motocicletta **7.** (vecchio) il nonno, il nipotino **8.** (comodo) una poltrona, una sedia

C. Rispondete usando **più...di** o **meno...di.**

ESEMPIO Chi ha più soldi? I Rockefeller o Lei?
—I Rockefeller hanno più soldi di me. *o*
—I Rockefeller hanno meno soldi di me.

1. Chi ha più preoccupazioni? I Suoi genitori o Lei? **2.** Chi ha più clienti? Gli avvocati o i dottori? **3.** Chi cucina più spaghetti? Gli Italiani o i Francesi? **4.** Chi cambia la macchina più spesso? Gli Europei o gli Americani? **5.** Chi ha ricevuto più voti nelle ultime elezioni? I repubblicani o i democratici? **6.** Chi guadagna più soldi? Un professore o un idraulico? **7.** Chi va più volentieri al ristorante? La moglie o il marito? **8.** Chi ha un lavoro più faticoso (*tiring*)? Un meccanico o un postino?

D. **Indovinello.** Rispondete approssimativamente alle seguenti domande, usando **più...di** o **meno...di.**

ESEMPIO Quanti anni avrà Lisa? **—Ne avrà meno di venti.**

1. Quanto tempo ci vorrà per andare da casa tua all'università? **2.** Quanto costerà un buon computer? **3.** Quanti libri ci saranno nella stanza di un topo di biblioteca? **4.** Quanti soldi ci saranno nel portafoglio di...? **5.** Quanti anni avrà...?

E. Rispondete secondo l'esempio.

ESEMPIO Milano è industriale o artistica? **Milano è più industriale che artistica.**

1. La Maserati è sportiva o pratica? **2.** L'Amaretto di Saronno è dolce o amaro? **3.** Venezia ha strade o canali? **4.** A un bambino piace studiare o giocare? **5.** Lei mangia carne o verdura? **6.** Le piace sciare o andare a un concerto? **7.** Lavora volentieri dentro o all'aperto, Lei? **8.** Per Lei è interessante viaggiare negli Stati Uniti o all'estero?

F. Completate le frasi usando **come, quanto, di** (con o senza articolo), **che.**

1. La tua stanza è tanto grande ______ la mia. **2.** Ho scritto più ______ dieci pagine. **3.** La sua sorellina è più bella ______ lei. **4.** È meno faticoso camminare in pianura ______ camminare in collina. **5.** La moda di quest'anno è meno attraente (*attractive*) ______ moda degli anni scorsi. **6.** Non siamo mai stati così poveri ______ adesso. **7.** Pescare è più riposante ______ nuotare. **8.** I bambini sono più semplici ______ adulti. **9.** L'italiano è più facile ______ cinese.

II. I superlativi

Con i suoi canali, i suoi ponti, e le sue gondole, Venezia è la città più romantica d'Italia.

There are two types of superlatives: the relative superlative (**superlativo relativo**) and the absolute superlative (**superlativo assoluto**).

1. The relative superlative in English means *the most..., the least... the (...)est.* It is formed by placing the definite article before the comparatives of inequality.

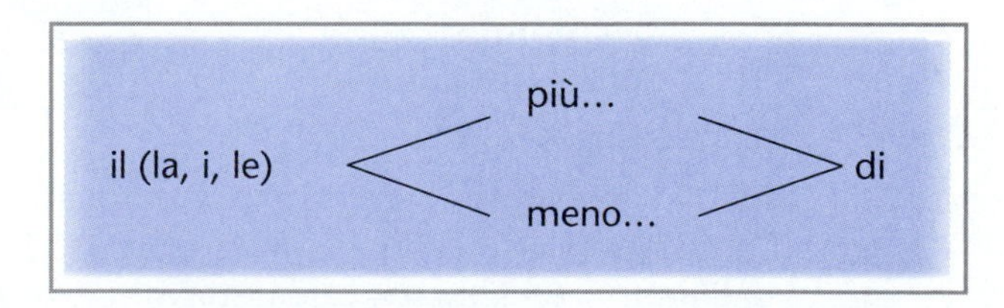

Firenze è **la più** bella città d'Italia.	*Florence is the most beautiful city in Italy.*
Pierino è **il meno** studioso della classe.	*Pierino is the least studious in the class.*
Il Monte Bianco è **il più** alto d'Europa.	*Mont Blanc is the highest mountain in Europe.*

Note that the English preposition *in* is rendered in Italian by **di** or **di** + definite article.

The position of the superlative in relation to the noun depends on the adjective. If the adjective follows the noun, the superlative also follows the noun. In this case, the article is placed *before* the noun.

Roma è **la più grande** città d'Italia. *or* Roma è **la** città **più grande** d'Italia.	*Rome is the largest city in Italy.*
Genova e Napoli sono **i** porti **più importanti** del Mare Tirreno.	*Genoa and Naples are the most important ports in the Tyrrhenian Sea.*

2. The absolute superlative in English means *very* or *extremely* + adjective or adverb. It is formed in the following ways:

   a. By placing **molto** before the adjective or the adverb:

Capri è un'isola **molto bella.**	*Capri is a very beautiful island.*
Lui impara le lingue **molto facilmente.**	*He learns languages very easily.*

   b. By adding the suffix **-ssimo** (**-ssima, -ssimi, - ssime**) to the masculine plural form of the adjectives. This absolute superlative is more emphatic.

È stata una **bellissima** serata.	*It was a very beautiful evening.*
Ho passato delle vacanze **interessantissime.**	*I spent a very interesting vacation.*
Roma è una città **antichissima.**	*Rome is a very ancient city.*

NOTE:
The superlative of **presto** and **tardi** are **prestissimo** and **tardissimo.**

Pratica

A. Più o meno? Domanda e risposta. Rispondete usando il **superlativo relativo**, secondo l'esempio.

ESEMPIO I vini francesi, famosi, mondo
—I vini francesi sono i più famosi o i meno famosi del mondo?
—Sono i più famosi.

1. Lo stato di Rhode Island, grande, Stati Uniti **2.** Il baseball, popolare, sport americani **3.** Un chirurgo, caro, professionisti **4.** Febbraio, lungo, mesi **5.** Il 21 dicembre, breve, giorni dell'anno **6.** L'estate, calda, stagioni **7.** Il jogging, pericoloso, sport **8.** Il «Concorde», veloce, aerei di linea **9.** Il Po, lungo, fiumi italiani **10.** Il cane, fedele, animali

B. Secondo te...? Domanda e risposta. Seguite l'esempio.

ESEMPIO il giorno, bello, settimana
—Secondo te, qual è il giorno più bello della settimana?
—Secondo me, il giorno più bello della settimana è il sabato.

1. il programma, popolare, televisione 2. la città, attraente, Stati Uniti 3. le attrici, brave, Hollywood 4. il ristorante, caro, questa città 5. la moda, elegante, Europa 6. la stagione, bella, anno

C. **Domanda e risposta.** Rispondete formando il **superlativo assoluto** dell'aggettivo.

ESEMPIO bravo, Maria —**È brava Maria?**
—**È bravissima.**

1. bello, l'isola di Capri 2. veloce, la Lamborghini 3. stanco, gli studenti 4. ordinato, la tua stanza 5. lungo, quest'ora 6. alto, i grattacieli 7. antico, Roma 8. simpatico, gli Italiani 9. nervoso, gli studenti prima degli esami 10. affollato, i negozi durante il periodo di Natale

III. Comparativi e superlativi irregolari

È il peggior pianista della città. Suona peggio degli altri.

1. Some adjectives have irregular comparative and superlative forms in addition to regular forms (**più** + adjective; **il/la più** + adjective). The most common are:

Adjective	Comparative		Relative superlative	
buono	migliore	*better*	il migliore	*the best*
cattivo	peggiore	*worse*	il peggiore	*the worst*
grande	maggiore	*bigger, greater*	il maggiore	*the biggest, the greatest*
piccolo	minore	*smaller*	il minore	*the smallest*

Although the regular and irregular forms are sometimes interchangeable, the choice is often determined by the context. The regular forms are used more often in a literal sense, to express size and physical or moral qualities, for example. The irregular forms are generally used to express figurative qualities or values, such as skills, greatness, or importance.

Come studentessa Franca è **migliore** di Claudia, ma Claudia è **più buona** di Franca.	*Franca is a better student than Claudia, but Claudia is better (nicer) than Franca.*
Il Lago di Como è **più piccolo** del Lago di Garda.	*Lake Como is smaller than Lake Garda.*
Le autostrade italiane sono tra **le migliori** d'Europa.	*Italian highways are among the best in Europe.*
Dante è **il maggior*** poeta italiano.	*Dante is the greatest Italian poet.*
La tua è **la peggiore** delle scuse.	*Yours is the worst of the excuses.*

NOTE:

a. When referring to people's age (in a family), *older (the oldest)* and *younger (the youngest)* are frequently expressed by **maggiore (il maggiore)** and **minore (il minore).**

Tuo fratello è **maggiore** o **minore** di te?	*Is your brother older or younger than you?*
Franca è **la minore** delle sorelle.	*Franca is the youngest of the sisters.*

b. When referring to food or beverages, *better (the best),* and *worse (the worst)* may be expressed by the regular or irregular form.

Il vino bianco è **migliore (più buono)** quando è refrigerato.	*White wine is better when it is chilled.*
Secondo me, la margarina è **peggiore (più cattiva)** del burro.	*In my opinion margarine is worse than butter.*
A Napoli si mangia **la migliore (la più buona)** pizza d'Italia.	*The best pizza in Italy is eaten in Naples.*

2. The *absolute superlatives* of these adjectives are formed regularly:

buono	→	**buonissimo, ottimo**	*very good*
cattivo	→	**cattivissimo, pessimo**	*very bad*
grande	→	**grandissimo, massimo**	*very big, very great*
piccolo	→	**piccolissimo, minimo**	*very small*

La tagliatelle alla bolognese sono **buonissime (ottime).**	*Tagliatelle alla bolognese are very good.*
La Russia è un paese **grandissimo.**	*Russia is a very large country.*
Capri è un'isola **piccolissima.**	*Capri is a very small island.*
Non ho la **minima** idea di cosa farò.	*I haven't the slightest idea what I will do.*
La tua è un'**ottima** soluzione.	*Yours is a very good solution.*
D'inverno il clima di Milano è **pessimo.**	*In winter the climate in Milan is very bad.*

---

*__Migliore__, __peggiore__, __maggiore__, and __minore__ may drop the final __-e__ before a noun not beginning with __z__ or with __s__ + *consonant.*

3. The adverbs **bene, male, molto,** and **poco** have the following comparative and superlative forms:

Adverb	Comparative		Relative superlative	
bene	meglio	*better*	il meglio	*the best*
male	peggio	*worse*	il peggio	*the worst*
molto	più, di più*	*more*	il più	*the most*
poco	meno, di meno*	*less*	il meno	*the least*

Lei conosce gli Stati Uniti **meglio** di me. — *You know the United States better than I do.*

Viaggio **più** d'estate che d'inverno. — *I travel more in summer than in winter.*

Parlerò **il meno** possibile. — *I will speak the least possible.*

Guadagni come me? No, guadagno **di più.** — *Do you earn as much as I (do)? No, I earn more.*

È **meglio** partire ora. — *It is better to leave now.*

NOTE:
The *absolute superlatives* of these adverbs are formed regularly:

bene → **benissimo** — *very well*
male → **malissimo** — *very badly*
molto → **moltissimo** — *very much*
poco → **pochissimo** — *very little*

Qui si mangia **benissimo.** — *Here one eats very well.*
Ho dormito **pochissimo.** — *I slept very little.*

Pratica

A. Domanda e risposta. Secondo te...

a. Quale dei due è **migliore?**

ESEMPIO il clima della California, il clima dell'Oregon
—**Secondo te, è migliore il clima della California o il clima dell'Oregon?**
—**Il clima della California è migliore del clima dell'Oregon.**

1. una vacanza al mare, una vacanza in montagna **2.** un gelato al cioccolato, un gelato alla vaniglia **3.** la musica classica, la musica rock **4.** la cucina italiana, la cucina francese

b. Quale dei due è **peggiore?**

1. la noia (*boredom*), il troppo lavoro **2.** un padre avaro, un padre severo **3.** la pioggia, il vento **4.** un chirurgo nervoso, un chirurgo lento

---

***Di più** and **di meno** are used when the second term of comparison is not expressed.

c. Quale dei due è **maggiore?**

1. un figlio di vent'anni, un figlio di tredici anni 2. la popolazione dello stato di New York, quella della California 3. il costo di un biglietto per le Hawaii, uno per l'Inghilterra 4. la responsabilità di un padre, quella di un figlio

d. Quale dei due è **minore?**

1. la distanza Milano–Roma, quella Milano–Napoli 2. i problemi di uno studente, quelli di un padre di famiglia 3. il peso di una libbra, quello di un chilo 4. l'autorità di un deputato, quella del primo ministro

B. Formate una frase completa con il **comparativo** dell'avverbio in corsivo, seguendo l'esempio.

ESEMPIO Maria canta *bene,* Elvira. **Maria canta meglio di Elvira.**

1. Un povero mangia *male,* un ricco. 2. Un avvocato guadagna *molto,* un impiegato. 3. Un barista (*barman*) va a letto *tardi,* un elettricista. 4. Un neonato (*newborn*) mangia *spesso,* un ragazzo. 5. Uno studente pigro studia *poco,* uno studente diligente. 6. Una segretaria scrive a macchina *velocemente,* una professoressa. 7. Mia madre cucina *bene,* me.

C. Rispondete usando il **superlativo assoluto** dell'aggettivo o dell'avverbio.

1. Canta bene Pavarotti? 2. Le piace molto viaggiare? 3. Mangia poco quando è a dieta? 4. Sta male quando riceve una brutta notizia? 5. È cattivo l'olio di ricino (*castor oil*)? 6. È grande l'Oceano Pacifico? 7. È piccolo un atomo? 8. Sono buoni i dolci italiani?

D. **Opinioni.** Al ritorno dalla breve vacanza sulla neve, a Cortina d'Ampezzo,* Tina e Riccardo parlano dell'albergo dove hanno alloggiato e fanno diversi paragoni (*comparisons*). Completate il loro dialogo.

R. Quest'anno il nostro albergo era (*better*) _____ di quello dell'anno scorso, non ti pare?

T. Sì, era (*more attractive*) _____, ma la mia camera era (*smaller*) _____ della tua. L'anno scorso io sono stata (*better*) _____ di questa volta.

R. Però non puoi negare (*deny*) che la cucina del ristorante era (*very good*) _____.

T. Hai ragione. I primi piatti erano tutti (*good*) _____, ma i tortellini erano (*the best*) _____. Purtroppo, il cameriere che ci serviva era (*the worst*) _____ di tutto il ristorante.

R. Tina, cerca di criticare (*less*) _____. Il poveretto era austriaco e parlava (*very badly*) _____ l'italiano.

E. Rispondete.

1. Chi è il più alto della tua famiglia? E il più giovane? 2. Qual è stata la temperatura massima di ieri? E la minima? 3. Qual esame del tuo programma di studi è stato il peggiore di tutti? 4. Secondo te, è meglio vivere una vita breve ma interessantissima, o vivere una vita lunga ma insignificante? 5. È meglio andare in Europa con un viaggio organizzato o da soli (*by yourselves*)? Perchè?

---

*A renowned and fashionable resort town in the heart of the Dolomiti.

F. **Proverbi.** Quali sono i proverbi in inglese che hanno un significato simile a questi?

1. Meglio tardi che mai. **2.** È meglio un asino (*donkey*) vivo che un dottore morto. **3.** È meglio un uovo oggi che una gallina (*hen*) domani. **4.** Non c'è peggior sordo (*deaf*) di chi non vuol sentire.

IV. Uso dell'articolo determinativo

La gente non è mai contenta. La signora Scontenti vorrebbe andare in macchina. Il signor Scontenti vorrebbe fare una passeggiata a piedi.

1. We have already seen that the definite article is used with titles, days of the week, possessive adjectives, reflexive constructions, and dates and seasons.

2. The definite article is also required with:

   a. Nouns used in a general or an abstract sense, whereas in English it is often omitted.

I bambini amano **gli animali.**	*Children love animals.*
La gente ammira **il coraggio.**	*People admire courage.*
Il tempo è prezioso.	*Time is precious.*

   b. Names of languages (except when immediately preceded by the verb **parlare**).

Ho incominciato a studiare **l'italiano.** Parlo inglese.	*I began to study Italian. I speak English.*

   c. Geographical names indicating continents, countries, states, regions, large islands, and mountains. Names ending in **-a** are generally feminine and take a feminine article; those ending in a different vowel or in a consonant are masculine and take a masculine article.

L'Everest è il monte più alto del mondo.	*Mount Everest is the highest mountain in the world.*
La capitale de**gli Stati Uniti** è Washington.	*The capital of the United States is Washington.*
L'Asia è più grande del**l'Europa**.	*Asia is larger than Europe.*
I miei genitori vengono dal**la Sicilia.**	*My parents come from Sicily.*
Il Texas è ricco di petrolio.	*Texas is rich in oil.*
Il Piemonte confina con **la Liguria.**	*Piedmont borders on Liguria.*
La Sicilia è una bellissima isola.	*Sicily is a very beautiful island.*

NOTE:
When a feminine noun indicating a continent, country, region, or large island is preceded by the preposition **in** (*in, to*), the article is omitted unless the noun is modified.

Andrete **in Italia** questa estate?	*Will you go to Italy this summer?*
Sì, andremo **nell'Italia meridionale.**	*Yes, we will go to southern Italy.*

Pratica

A. Mirella parla di sè e del marito. Completate il suo discorso con l'**articolo determinativo**, se necessario.

Io amo _______ musica classica, lui ama _______ calcio. A me piacciono _____ acqua minerale e _____ frutta; a lui piacciono _____ panini al salame e _______ vino rosso. Io preferisco _______ lettura e lui preferisce _______ TV. _____ mia stagione favorita è _____ autunno; _____ sua è _____ estate. Io ho imparato ______ francese ed anche ______ inglese; lui ha studiato solamente ______ spagnolo. ______ mio padre è fiorentino e ______ suo padre è romano. _____ Toscana è _____ mia regione; _____ Lazio è _____ sua. Io vedo sempre ______ mie amiche ______ venerdì e lui vede ______ suoi amici ______ sabato. Ma ______ domenica prossima non ci saranno differenze e partiremo insieme per _____ Grecia.

B. Dove si trova...? Domanda e risposta. Seguite l'esempio.

ESEMPIO Cina/Asia **—Dove si trova la Cina?**
—La Cina si trova in Asia.

1. Portogallo/Europa **2.** Brasile/America del Sud **3.** Monte Etna/Sicilia **4.** Russia/Europa Orientale **5.** Calabria/Italia meridionale **6.** Monte Bianco/Alpi occidentali **7.** Stati Uniti/America del Nord **8.** Maine/Stati Uniti dell'Est **9.** Chicago/Illinois **10.** Denver/Colorado

LETTURA

UNA LEZIONE DI GEOGRAFIA

Liliana ha potuto trovare diverse lezioni private. Fra i suoi *allievi* c'è Tim, un *ragazzino* californiano. Il padre di Tim è impiegato in una società multinazionale *con sede* a Milano e si trova in Italia da più di un anno, con la famiglia.

pupils/young boy
based

Oggi si parla di geografia.

—Timmy, che cosa sono queste?
—Due mappe, una dell'Italia, l'altra degli Stati Uniti.
—Attento: si dice «carte geografiche». Se paragoni l'Italia agli Stati Uniti, che cosa vedi?
—Vedo che l'Italia è piccolissima, molto più piccola degli Stati Uniti. Vedo anche che ha una forma strana e che è molto più lunga che larga.
—Bravissimo! Infatti ha la forma di uno stivale. Ora, se guardi il tuo stato, la California, che cosa mi puoi dire?
—L'Italia è quasi grande quanto la California.
—Benissimo. La superficie dell'Italia è più di due terzi quella della California. Ti posso dire di più: Milano dista da Roma quanto San Francisco dista da Los Angeles.
—Però quando *si va* in macchina da Milano a Roma, non sembra così lontano.

one goes

—Perchè dici così?
—Perchè *si vedono* tante città. Anche l'Autostrada del Sole sembra più piccola, paragonata alle autostrade americane.

one sees

—E Milano, come ti sembra, se la paragoni a San Francisco?
—Meno bella, *naturalmente*. Più vecchia di San Francisco, e con le case più grigie. E d'inverno fa più freddo a Milano che a San Francisco, mentre d'estate fa più caldo.

of course

—Insomma, cosa ti piace di questa città?
—Mi piace la cucina. Da quando siamo qui, mangiamo molto meglio: ogni giorno un piatto diverso di pastasciutta. E le torte sono migliori qui che negli Stati Uniti.
—*Meno male* che ti piace qualche cosa. Ma... parlavamo della superficie dell'Italia, che è quasi uguale a quella della California.* Lo sai quanti abitanti ci sono in California?

thank goodness

—Mio padre dice che ci sono più di trenta milioni di Californiani e che sono troppi.
—Sì, ho letto che la California è lo stato più popolato degli Stati Uniti. Ma lo sai, Tim, che in Italia ci sono quasi sessanta milioni di abitanti?

---

*L'Italia misura più di 116.000 miglia quadrate e ha una popolazione di più di 57.000.000 di abitanti.

L'Autostrada del Sole parte da Milano e attraversa tutta la penisola.

Comprensione

1. A chi ha incominciato a dare lezioni private Liliana? Da quanto tempo si trova in Italia?
2. Di quali paesi parlano? Che cosa guardano per paragonarli?
3. È meno grande la California dell'Italia?
4. La distanza fra Milano e Roma è maggiore o minore di quella fra San Francisco e Los Angeles?
5. Secondo Tim, Milano sarebbe più bella o meno bella di San Francisco? Perchè?
6. Com'è il clima di Milano paragonato a quello di San Francisco?
7. Secondo il ragazzino, come sarebbe la cucina italiana paragonata a quella americana?
8. Ci sono più o meno di 50 milioni di abitanti in Italia?
9. L'Italia è più popolata o meno popolata della California?

Domande personali

1. È mai stato(a) in Italia Lei, o ha mai viaggiato in un altro paese straniero? Quale?
2. Se Lei lo paragona al Suo stato, quali differenze vi ha notato? Per esempio, il Suo stato è più grande o più piccolo? Più popolato o meno popolato?
3. Ha notato altre differenze? Quali? (La moda, i prezzi, le autostrade...)
4. Come ha trovato gli abitanti di quel paese: molto cordiali o poco cordiali? Desiderosi di comunicare con gli stranieri o indifferenti?
5. Come Le è sembrato il tenore di vita (*standard of living*): alto o basso? O più o meno come quello del Suo paese?
6. Com'era la cucina: migliore o peggiore di quella del Suo paese?
7. Quali aspetti l'hanno particolarmente sorpreso(a)?

ItaliaNostra

Lezioni in libertà

Paesaggi e beni culturali da conoscere: questo lo scopo dei nostri campi-scuola, soggiorni escursionistici di particolare interesse ambientale, in cui i partecipanti vengono guidati e stimolati ad un rapporto diretto, attivo e consapevole con la natura. Le località prescelte sono tra le più affascinanti della nostra ancora bella Italia

Associazione nazionale per la tutela del patrimonio storico, artistico e naturale. Via Massena 71 - 10128 TORINO, tel. 011/50.00.56

ATTIVITÀ SUPPLEMENTARI

A. **Descrivete la geografia di questo stato.** Quali sono gli stati che lo circondano (*surround it*)? Quali ne sono le caratteristiche fisiche, il clima, ecc.? Dite che cosa vi piace di più di questo stato, che cosa non vi piace, e perchè. (Ogni studente dovrebbe contribuire con le sue osservazioni.)

B. **Dialogo a due.** Scegliete due città che vi piacciono di più e paragonatele l'una all'altra, dal punto di vista delle bellezze naturali o artistiche, del clima, dei vantaggi culturali, sportivi, economici, gastronomici, ecc.

C. **Identificate le foto a pagina 332, 333.**

Foto numero 1: Riconoscete la città? In quale regione si trova? Come si chiama il fiume che l'attraversa? Sapete il nome del suo ponte famoso (visibile nella foto)? Potete nominare una statua, una chiesa o un museo di questa città? Come si chiama il movimento umanistico nato nel '400 in questa città? Ricordate il nome di alcuni dei suoi più illustri cittadini nel campo dell'arte o della letteratura? (Vedi *«Pagina culturale»*, capitolo 7.)

Foto numero 2: Riconoscete questa piazza? Si trova nel più piccolo stato del mondo. Quale? In quale regione si trova la città che lo circonda? È una regione dell'Italia settentrionale? Come si chiama il fiume che attraversa la città? Conoscete il nome di alcuni artisti che hanno contribuito alla ricchezza artistica e architettonica di questa città? (Vedi *«Pagina culturale»*, capitolo 8.)

Foto numero 3: In che città si trova questa cattedrale? Come si chiama? Di che stile è? In che regione si trova questa città? La regione si trova in una valle molto fertile che prende il nome dal fiume che l'attraversa. Come si chiama? Perchè questa città si chiama «la capitale industriale d'Italia»? Potete nominare alcune industrie che esportano i loro prodotti all'estero? (Vedi *«Pagina culturale»*, capitolo 1.)

Se voi poteste (*If you could*) visitare soltanto una delle tre città, quale scegliereste, e perchè?

D. **Dialogo a quattro.** Consultate la carta d'Italia e organizzate un viaggio in bicicletta, alla scoperta (*discovery*) di una o più regioni italiane. Discutete l'itinerario, la stagione e la durata del viaggio; il punto di partenza e il punto d'arrivo; i luoghi in cui vi piacerebbe fermarvi, dove alloggereste la notte, dove andreste a mangiare, e che cosa vorreste vedere.

1.

2.

3.

E. **Come si dice in italiano?**

1. Gino Campana and Gennaro De Filippo are two mechanics who work at the Fiat plant (**fabbrica**) in Torino.
2. Gennaro often speaks about his region, Campania, and his city, Napoli, to his friend Gino.
3. Napoli is the most beautiful city in the world, with its fantastic gulf, Capri, Ischia...
4. Yes, Gennarino, but you must admit (**ammettere**) that Torino is more industrial and richer than Napoli.
5. But the climate is not as good as that of Napoli. In winter it is much colder, and in summer it is more humid.
6. You are right. Life is more pleasant in Napoli than in Torino for very rich people.
7. If one wants to earn more money, it is better to live in Torino. There are better jobs, and salaries are higher.
8. In fact, my younger brother, who is an engineer, has been working only three years, and he earns more than I.
9. I will work in Torino until (**fino a quando**) it is time to retire, and then I will return to my very beautiful city.
10. So, Gennarino, it is true what (**quello che**) they say: *Vedi Napoli, e poi muori.*

Vocabolario

Nomi

l'adulto, adulta	*adult*
l'allievo, allieva	*pupil*
l'autorità	*authority*
il canale	*canal, channel*
la caratteristica	*characteristic*
il clima	*climate*
il codice postale	*zip code*
il dentifricio	*toothpaste*
la distanza	*distance*
la gita scolastica	*field trip*
il grattacielo	*skyscraper*
il luogo	*place*
il miglio (*pl.* le miglia)	*mile*
il mondo	*world*
la noia	*boredom*
il paragone	*comparison*
il paesaggio	*landscape*
il peso	*weight*
la popolazione	*population*
la preoccupazione	*worry*
la presenza	*presence*
la responsabilità	*responsibility*
la ricchezza	*richness*
gli sci	*skis*
la società	*company, society*
lo spazzolino da denti	*toothbrush*

Aggettivi

amaro	*bitter*
attraente	*attractive*
austriaco	*Austrian*
centrale	*central*
coraggioso	*courageous*
cordiale	*friendly, warm*
culturale	*cultural*
desideroso	*eager*
dolce	*sweet*
eccitato	*excited*
faticoso	*tiring*
fedele	*faithful*
fisico	*physical*
industriale	*industrial*
maggiore	*larger, greater*
massimo	*greatest*
migliore	*better*
minimo	*smallest*
minore	*smaller; younger*
peggiore	*worse*
pessimo	*terrible, very bad*
popolare	*popular*
popolato	*populated*
prezioso	*precious*
privato	*private*
riposante	*relaxing*
romantico	*romantic*
riservato	*reserved*
uguale	*equal*

Verbi

circondare	*to surround*
criticare	*to criticize*
distare	*to be distant, to be far (from)*
negare	*to deny*
nominare	*to name*
paragonare	*to compare*
partecipare(a)	*to take part (in)*
proteggere (*p.p.* protetto)	*to protect*
raffreddare	*to cool*
riconoscere	*to recognize*
riscaldare	*to warm*
soffrire (*p.p.* sofferto)	*to suffer*
truccarsi	*to put on makeup*

Altre espressioni

approssimativamente	*approximately*
a proposito	*by the way*
Come mai?	*How come?*
così...come	*as...as*
essere d'accordo	*to agree*
fare a meno di	*to do without*
infatti	*in fact*
meno...di	*less than*
il meno possibile	*the least possible*
meglio (*adv.*)	*better*
naturalmente	*naturally, of course*
niente	*nothing*
peggio (*adv.*)	*worse*
più...di (che)	*more...than*
avere una paura da morire	*to be scared to death*
tanto...quanto	*as (much)...as*
non ti pare?	*don't you think?*
più o meno	*more or less*

Lago di Carezza (Trentino–Alto Adige). Minuscolo lago alpino, incorniciato da boschi di pini e dalle Dolomiti.

L'ITALIA: UN MOSAICO DI PAESAGGI

L'Italia è un piccolo paese con *confini* naturali ben definiti. Al nord la catena *maestosa* delle Alpi la separa dal resto dell'Europa. All'ovest, al sud e all'est, invece, la circondano il Mare Ligure, il Mare Tirreno, il Mare Ionio e il Mare Adriatico. Dentro questi confini sta un mosaico di *paesaggi* che permette al viaggiatore di ammirare panorami continuamente diversi.

boundaries
majestic
landscapes

Il paesaggio della regione alpina è ricco di *ghiacciai,* di grandi e piccoli laghi, e di valli coperte di *pinete.* Nelle Alpi occidentali si alza la montagna più alta d'Europa, il Monte Bianco (4.810 metri*). Poi viene la zona dei grandi laghi: i più importanti sono il Lago Maggiore, il Lago di Como e il Lago di Garda, che *attirano* i turisti in ogni stagione. Infatti, il clima qui è mite e permette l'esistenza di una vegetazione che si trova di solito lungo le coste del mare: ulivi, aranci, limoni e palme.

glaciers
pine forests
attract

*15,781 ft.

Dalle Alpi occidentali nasce il Po, il fiume più lungo d'Italia. Il Po attraversa la Pianura Padana (del Po) ed entra nell'Adriatico. La Valle Padana è la pianura più grande d'Italia. L'abbondanza dell'acqua fa di essa la zona più ricca d'Italia. La campagna *vi* è fertilissima e l'agricoltura *vi raggiunge* un alto livello di *sviluppo*. La catena dei Monti Appennini limita la Pianura Padana al sud e attraversa tutta la penisola.

here
reaches (here)
development

Da questa catena nascono i due fiumi Arno e Tevere che attraversano rispettivamente Firenze e Roma, prima di finire nel Tirreno. Gli Appennini sono di origine vulcanica. Una zona particolarmente instabile è quella compresa fra il Vesuvio, vicino a Napoli, e l'Etna, nella Sicilia orientale. Questi due vulcani hanno una lunga storia di distruzione. Il Vesuvio *ha sepolto* nel 79 dopo Cristo le città romane di Pompei e Ercolano; l'Etna *ha distrutto* diverse volte la città di Catania. Nelle regioni settentrionali, il paesaggio appenninico ha un aspetto dolce e civilizzato, mentre *acquista* una bellezza selvaggia *più si* procede verso il sud.

buried
destroyed
acquires/the more one

Anche le coste italiane differiscono nel loro aspetto fisico. Quelle occidentali sono in genere alte e *rocciose*. Particolarmente pittoresche sono la Riviera Ligure, che continua la Riviera Francese; la Costa Amalfitana, al sud di Napoli; e le coste settentrionale e orientale della Sicilia. Le coste dell'Adriatico sono in genere più basse, con ampie spiagge *sabbiose* che attirano d'estate *folle di bagnanti*.

rocky
sandy
crowds of sunbathers

Oltre alla Sicilia, fanno parte dell'Italia l'isola di Sardegna e molte altre isole minori. Vicino alla Toscana si trova l'isola d'Elba. Nel golfo di Napoli ci sono le isole di Capri e Ischia, due delle più belle isole del Mediterraneo.

Comprensione

Rispondete alle seguenti domande.

1. Che cosa divide l'Italia dall'Europa? Quale catena di monti corre lungo tutta la penisola italiana?
2. Dite il nome dei mari che bagnano (*wash*) le coste dell'Italia occidentale.
3. Quali grandi laghi si trovano ai piedi delle Alpi? Che vegetazione c'è in questa zona?
4. Come si chiama il fiume più lungo d'Italia? Che pianura bagna (*does it flow through*)?
5. Che cosa sono il Vesuvio e l'Etna? Dove sono situati?
6. Perchè ricordiamo i nomi di Pompei e Ercolano?
7. Dove si trovano le coste più pittoresche del paese? Come si chiamano?
8. Dite il nome di un'isola situata vicino alla costa toscana.
9. Perchè il titolo della lettura dice: *«L'Italia: un mosaico di paesaggi»?*

Riviera Ligure. Camogli.

16 GLI SPORT

Santa Margherita Ligure, sulla Riviera di Levante (a est di Genova). Luogo di sport nautici.

PUNTI DI VISTA

Una partita di pallacanestro.

GIOVANI SPORTIVI

Marisa ha incontrato Alberto, un ragazzo *con cui* suo fratello faceva dello sport alcuni anni fa. — with whom

Marisa	Come va, Alberto? Sempre appassionato di *pallacanestro?*	basketball
Alberto	Più che mai! Ho *appena* finito di giocare contro la *squadra* torinese.	just team
Marisa	E chi ha vinto la *partita?*	game
Alberto	La mia squadra, naturalmente! Il nostro gioco è stato migliore. E poi, siamo più alti; cosa che aiuta, *non ti pare?*	don't you think so?
Marisa	Eh, direi!	
Alberto	E voi, cosa c'è di nuovo?	
Marisa	*Nessuna novità,* almeno per me. Ma mio fratello ha ricevuto una lettera, *in cui* gli offrono un posto come istruttore sportivo per l'estate prossima.	nothing new in which
Alberto	E dove lavorerà?	
Marisa	In uno dei villaggi turistici della Calabria.	
Alberto	Magnifico! Là potrà praticare tutti gli sport che piacciono a lui, *compresi* il surf e il windsurf.	including
Marisa	Eh, sì. Sono due degli sport di maggior successo oggi.	
Alberto	Ma tu, con un fratello così attivo negli sport, non ne pratichi *qualcuno?*	any
Marisa	Certo, ma sono gli sport dei poveri. Faccio del footing e molto ciclismo. Chissà, un giorno forse parteciperò al Giro d'Italia delle donne.	

1. Chi è Alberto? Quale sport pratica?
2. La sua squadra ha vinto o perso contro la squadra di Torino?
3. Cosa c'è di nuovo per Marisa?
4. Che novità ci sono per il fratello di Marisa?
5. In quale regione andrà a lavorare? Dove si trova questa regione?
6. Quali sport potrà praticare al mare il fratello di Marisa?
7. Quali sport pratica Marisa?
8. Che cosa spera di fare un giorno?

Studio di parole

il giocatore di pallacanestro **il/la ciclista** **il pugile**

il calcio soccer
il canottaggio rowing
il ciclismo bicycling
l'equitazione (*f.*) horseback riding
la ginnastica aerobica aerobics
il nuoto swimming
la pallacanestro, il basket basketball
la pallavolo volleyball
il pattinaggio skating
la pesistica weightlifting
il culturismo bodybuilding
il pugilato boxing
lo sci **nautico** water skiing; **di discesa** downhill; **di fondo** cross-country
il tennis
fare della vela to go sailing
lo stadio stadium
la palestra gym(nasium)
il giocatore, la giocatrice player
l'atleta (*m. & f.*) athlete
la squadra team
la partita match, game
il gioco game
la gara race, competition
la tuta da ginnastica sweatsuit
l'allenatore, allenatrice coach; trainer
l'arbitro referee
lo spettatore, la spettatrice spectator
il (la) tifoso(a) fan
fare il tifo (per) to be a fan (of)
fare dello sport
praticare uno sport (lo sci...ecc.**)**
giocare a
allenare to coach; to train
allenarsi to practice; to train
andare in bicicletta to ride a bike
correre (*p.p.* **corso)** to run
il premio prize
vincere (*p.p.* **vinto)** to win
segnare to score
Forza! Come on!

A. 1. Nominate alcuni degli sport americani più popolari.
2. Quale genere di sci si fa al mare?
3. A che cosa giocano i *Globetrotter?*
4. Dove si pratica il canottaggio?
5. Quali sono gli sport che si fanno sulla neve o sul ghiaccio?
6. Come si chiamano gli appassionati di uno sport?
7. Chi allena i giocatori nella loro preparazione sportiva?
8. Dove si allenano i giocatori?
9. Chi ricorda dove hanno avuto luogo (*took place*) le Olimpiadi invernali del 1992? E quelle estive?
10. Cosa si mette Lei quando va in palestra o fa il jogging?

B. **Domande personali.**

1. È attivo(a) Lei negli sport? Qual è lo sport che Le piace di più? Quando lo pratica?
2. Qual è lo sport che Le piace di meno? Perchè?
3. Gioca a pallacanestro Lei? Fa del footing? Quante volte alla settimana?
4. Sa sciare Lei? Andava a sciare con la Sua famiglia da bambino(a)? È uno sciatore (una sciatrice) esperto(a)? Preferisce lo sci di discesa o lo sci di fondo?
5. Quante ore di macchina ci vogliono per raggiungere (*to reach*) le montagne, da dove abita Lei?
6. Quali sono due degli sport più popolari tra i Suoi amici? Quali sport vorrebbe vedere di più alla TV?
7. Lei sa quale sport in Italia ha il maggior numero di tifosi?
8. Fa il tifo per una squadra o per un giocatore Lei? Quale?
9. Ha mai vinto un premio Lei (primo, secondo, terzo... o il premio di consolazione)?

CONCORSO 29

TOTOCALCIO CONI

COMITATO OLIMPICO NAZIONALE ITALIANO

Totocalcio

"AL SERVIZIO DELLO SPORT"

PARTITE DEL 7/3/93

	squadra 1ª	squadra 2ª
1	Ancona	Genoa
2	Atalanta	Inter
3	Foggia	Brescia
4	Juventus	Napoli
5	Milan	Fiorentina
6	Parma	Lazio
7	Pescara	Udinese
8	Roma	Cagliari
9	Sampdoria	Torino
10	Cesena	Cosenza
11	Lucchese	Piacenza
12	Carpi	Empoli
13	Catania	Perugia

fonte Gaudianello

fonte Gaudianel

Una schedina del totocalcio.

Ascoltiamo!

Alla partita di pallacanestro. *Marisa and Alberto are watching a basketball game between the Brescia and Trieste teams. Marisa's boyfriend, Gino, plays on the Trieste team. She is cheering him and his team on and also exchanging opinions with Alberto. Listen to what they are saying, then answer the related questions.*

Comprensione

1. Che partita c'è questa sera?
2. Perchè Marisa è venuta a vedere la partita? Per chi fa il tifo Marisa?
3. Secondo Marisa, la squadra del suo ragazzo vincerà o perderà? Alberto è della stessa opinione?
4. Dove si sono allenati il ragazzo di Marisa e gli altri giocatori?
5. Che cosa pagherà Marisa ad Alberto se la squadra di Trieste perderà?
6. Come si conclude la partita?

Dialogo

In gruppi di due. Avete del tempo libero durante la settimana e vorreste dedicarvi a una nuova attività sportiva. Consultate lo «*Studio di parole*» e decidete insieme quale sport scegliere, perchè, quando e dove allenarvi.

PUNTI GRAMMATICALI

I. I pronomi relativi

Ecco la squadra che giocherà domani.

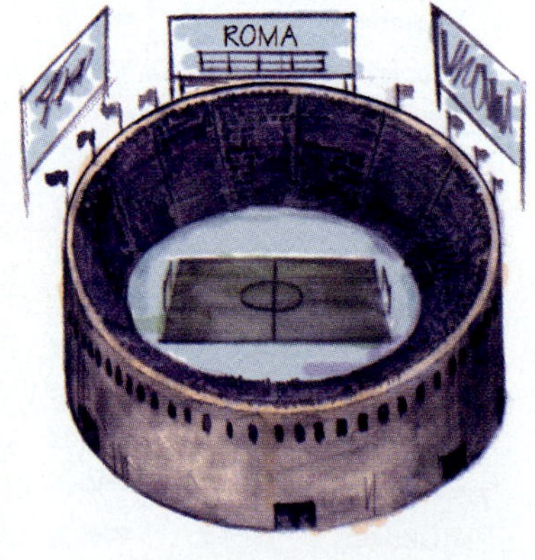

Ecco lo stadio in cui giocherà.

1. Chi sono gli Azzurri?
2. Dove si trova lo stadio in cui giocheranno?

1. The relative pronouns are **che, cui, quello che (ciò che),** and **chi.** They are used to link two clauses.

Questa è la squadra italiana. Ha giocato a Roma.
Questa è la squadra italiana **che** ha giocato a Roma.

2. **Che** is the equivalent of the English *who, whom, that, which* and is used either as a subject or as a direct object. It is invariable, cannot be omitted, and must *never* be used after a preposition.

Il ragazzo **che** gioca è brasiliano.	*The boy who is playing is Brazilian.*
La macchina **che** ho comprato è usata.	*The car (that) I bought is used.*
Le signore **che** ho visto sono le zie di Pino.	*The ladies (whom) I saw are Pino's aunts.*

3. **Cui** is the equivalent of the English *whom* and *which* as objects of prepositions. It is invariable and must be *preceded* by a preposition.

Ecco i signori **con cui** abbiamo viaggiato.	*Here are the gentlemen we traveled with (with whom we traveled).*
Il pugile **di cui** ti ho parlato è il migliore.	*The boxer I spoke to you about (about whom I spoke to you) is the best.*
L'amico **a cui** ho scritto si chiama Gianfranco.	*The friend I wrote to (to whom I wrote) is Gianfranco.*

NOTE:

a. **In cui** translates as *when* in expressions of time and as *where* in expressions of place. In the latter case, it may be replaced by **dove.**

Il giorno **in cui** sono nato...	*The day (when) I was born...*
La casa **in cui (dove)** sono nato...	*The house in which (where) I was born*

b. **Per cui** translates as *why* in the expression *the reason why (that).*

Ecco la ragione **per cui** ti ho scritto.	*Here is the reason (why) I wrote to you.*

4. **Quello che (quel che)** or **ciò che** mean *what* denoting *that which.* They are invariable.

Quello che (Ciò che) dici è vero.	*What you are saying is true.*
Non so **quello che (ciò che)** farò.	*I don't know what I will do.*

5. **Chi** translates as *the one(s) who, he who,* and *those who.* It is invariable.

Chi studierà avrà un bel voto.	*He who studies will receive a good grade.*
Chi arriverà ultimo avrà un premio di consolazione.	*He who arrives last will receive a consolation prize.*
Chi più spende, meno spende.	*Cheapest is dearest. (lit.: He who spends more, spends less.)*

Pratica

A. **Chi è...? Domanda e risposta.** Un tuo amico ti ha invitato a una festa a casa sua. Tu desideri sapere chi sono alcune delle persone presenti.

ESEMPIO ragazza, parlare con tua madre
—Chi è quella ragazza che parla con tua madre?
—È mia sorella Angelina.

1. signore, essere seduto vicino alla finestra **2.** signorina, ballare con il ragazzo biondo **3.** ragazzo, parlare spagnolo **4.** vecchio signore, dormire nella poltrona **5.** signora, mangiare un grissino (*bread stick*) **6.** uomo, parlare al telefono

B. **Domanda e risposta.** Esprimete (*Express*) la vostra preferenza per le seguenti cose, secondo l'esempio.

ESEMPIO il nuoto/lo sport... **—Ti piace il nuoto?**
—No, lo sport che mi piace è il canottaggio. (o...)

1. il giallo/il colore... **2.** le mele/la frutta... **3.** il Chianti/il vino... **4.** la Volvo/l'automobile... **5.** i gatti/gli animali... **6.** il pugilato/gli sport... **7.** il tè/la bevanda... **8.** il Capodanno/la festa...

C. Dite se parlate **spesso, raramente, qualche volta**, o **mai** dei seguenti argomenti (*topics*).

ESEMPIO la politica **La politica è un argomento (*subject*) di cui non parlo mai.** (o...)

1. il football **2.** la crisi economica **3.** le previsioni del tempo **4.** le vacanze **5.** il matrimonio **6.** i divertimenti **7.** la moda **8.** i miei problemi personali

D. Completate le seguenti frasi usando **cui** preceduto (*preceded*) dalla preposizione appropriata.

ESEMPIO Ricordi gli sposi _____ ti ho parlato?
Ricordi gli sposi di cui ti ho parlato?

1. Ecco la chiesa _____ si sono sposati. **2.** Questa è la città _____ si sono conosciuti. **3.** Quello è il monumento vicino _____ si incontravano. Ecco il negozio _____ lui lavorava. **5.** Quelli sono gli amici _____ hanno passato molte ore divertenti. **6.** Non so esattamente la ragione _____ hanno litigato. **7.** Ricordo molto bene il biglietto (*card*) _____ lei mi annunciava la loro separazione.

E. Completate le frasi usando uno dei seguenti pronomi relativi: **che, cui** (preceduto da una preposizione) o **quello che.**

1. Lo sport _____ preferisco è il tennis. **2.** L'anno _____ sono nato era bisestile (*leap year*). **3.** Non capisco _____ dici. **4.** La festa _____ hai dato è stata un successo. **5.** Il libro _____ ti ho parlato è in biblioteca. **6.** La signorina _____ abbiamo incontrato è americana. **7.** La signora _____ abbiamo parlato è canadese. **8.** Il pranzo _____ mi hanno invitato era al ristorante Pappagallo di Bologna. **9.** È proprio il vestito _____ ho bisogno. **10.** Non ho sentito _____ ha detto il professore.

F. **Proverbi.** Quali proverbi inglesi hanno un significato simile a questi proverbi?

1. Chi non lavora, non mangia. **2.** Chi troppo vuole, niente ha. **3.** Chi dorme, non prende pesci.

II. I pronomi indefiniti

—C'è qualcuno in casa?

In Chapter 4, you studied the indefinite adjectives **qualche**, **alcuni(e)** (*some*); **tutti(e)** (*all*); and **ogni** (*every*). Here are some common indefinite pronouns:

alcuni(e)	*some*		
qualcuno	*someone, anyone (in a question)*	**ognuno**	*everyone, each one*
		tutti(e)	*everybody, all*
qualcosa	*something, anything (in a question)*	**tutto**	*everything*

Alcuni sono rimasti, altri sono partiti. — *Some stayed, others left.*
Conosco **qualcuno** a Roma. — *I know someone in Rome.*
Hai bisogno di **qualcosa?** — *Do you need anything?*
Ognuno ha fatto una domanda. — *Each one asked a question.*
C'erano **tutti.** — *Everybody was there.*
Ho visto **tutto.** — *I saw everything.*

NOTE:
Qualcosa takes **di** before an adjective and **da** before an infinitive.

Ho qualcosa **di** interessante **da** dirti. — *I have something interesting to tell you.*

Pratica

A. Completate scegliendo una delle seguenti espressioni: **qualche, alcuni, alcune, qualcuno, qualcosa.**

1. Mi piacciono tutte le attività sportive, ma ho solamente _____ domeniche libere e pratico solamente _____ sport leggero. **2.** Ieri sono andato allo stadio e ho visto _____ di interessante. C'erano degli atleti che si allenavano per le Olimpiadi: _____ erano spettacolari. **3.** _____ mi ha detto che la nostra squadra di calcio ha una buona possibilità di vincere e che abbiamo anche _____atlete bravissime. **4.** Franco, c'è _____ al telefono che vuole domandarti _____. **5.** _____ volta è difficile ammettere (*to admit*) di avere torto.

B. **È qualcuno... Domanda e risposta.** Seguite l'esempio.

ESEMPIO un allenatore **—Che cos'è un allenatore?**
—È qualcuno che allena gli atleti.

1. un giornalista **2.** un ciclista **3.** un ottimista **4.** un architetto **5.** un disoccupato **6.** una persona elegante **7.** una persona pigra **8.** uno sportivo **9.** un tifoso **10.** un pessimista

C. **È qualcosa... Domanda e risposta.** Seguite l'esempio.

ESEMPIO una palla **—Che cos'è una palla?**
—È qualcosa con cui si gioca (*one plays*).

1. una pentola **2.** un paio di scarponi **3.** una penna **4.** i pattini **5.** una valigia **6.** l'ascensore **7.** un bicchiere **8.** gli occhiali **9.** un cucchiaio **10.** un coltello

D. Completate le frasi usando **ogni, ognuno, tutto** o **tutti.**

1. Ho mangiato _____. **2.** _____ può fare questo lavoro. **3.** _____ sono venuti. **4.** _____ volta che la vedevo, mi sorrideva (*she was smiling*). **5.** _____ erano presenti e _____ ha potuto esprimere la sua opinione. **6.** I tifosi applaudivano _____ gol della squadra. **7.** Ho fatto _____ quello che dovevo fare. **8.** _____ gli hanno augurato buon viaggio. **9.** _____ giorno vado in bicicletta.

E. **Qualcosa di... Domanda e risposta.** Seguite l'esempio.

ESEMPIO dire/brutto **—Che cos'hai da dirmi?**
—Ho qualcosa di brutto da dirti.

1. dare/carino **2.** mostrare/meraviglioso **3.** raccontare/divertente **4.** regalare/bello **5.** annunciare (*announce*)/interessante **6.** portare/buono **7.** prestare/comodo **8.** offrire/caldo **9.** domandare/importante

III. Espressioni negative

Il frigo è vuoto e il signor Goloso protesta: —Non c'è mai niente da mangiare in questa casa!

1. You have already studied (Chapter 8) some negative expressions: **non...più, non...mai, non...ancora.** The following are other common expressions that take a *double negative* construction:

nessuno	*nobody, no one, not...anyone*
niente (nulla)	*nothing, not...anything*
neanche (neppure, nemmeno)	*not even; neither*
nè...nè	*neither...nor*

Non è venuto **nessuno.**	*Nobody came.*
Non abbiamo visto **nessuno.**	*We did not see anyone.*
Non ho mangiato **niente.**	*I did not eat anything.*
Non c'era **neanche** Pietro.	*Not even Pietro was there.*
Io **non** posso andare, e **neanche** lui!	*I can't go, and neither can he.*
Non voglio **nè** carne **nè** pesce.	*I want neither meat nor fish.*

2. The expressions **nessuno, niente, nè...nè** may precede the verb. When they do, **non** is omitted.

Nessuno vuole parlare.	*Nobody wants to talk.*
Niente è pronto.	*Nothing is ready.*
Nè Giovanni **nè** Maria vogliono venire.	*Neither Giovanni nor Maria wants to come.*

Note that with **nè...nè**, Italian uses a plural form of the verb (**vogliono**), whereas English uses a singular form (*wants*).

3. When **nessuno** is used as an adjective, it has the same endings as the indefinite article **un.** The noun that follows is in the singular.

Non ho **nessun** amico.	*I have no friends.*
Non vedo **nessuna** sedia.	*I don't see any chairs.*

4. **Niente** takes **di** before an adjective and **da** before an infinitive.

Non ho **niente di** buono **da** darti.	*I have nothing good to offer you.*

A. Completate le frasi scegliendo fra **nessuno, niente, neanche** o **nè...nè.**

1. Non ho invitato ______ per il mio compleanno; non ho invitato ______ il mio ragazzo. **2.** Non c'è mai ______ d'interessante da vedere alla TV. **3.** Siamo andati all'appuntamento, ma non c'era ______. **4.** Non ho visto ______ tuo cugino ______tuo fratello. **5.** Ha detto qualcosa? No, non ho detto ______. **6.** Se tu non vai alla partita, non vado ______ io. **7.** Mi dispiace, ma non ho ______ da offrirti. **8.** Non ho visto ______ atleta. **9.** ______ è venuto a trovarmi. **10.** ______ i giocatori ______ l'allenatore erano allo stadio. **11.** ______ va bene oggi! **12.** Non hanno costruito ______ nuovo edificio. **13.** Questo mese non ho risparmiato ______ una lira! **14.** Gina non mi ha mandato ______ una lettera ______una cartolina.

B. Voi siete di cattivo umore. Rispondete usando **non** con un'altra espressione negativa.

1. C'è qualcosa di buono in casa? **2.** Hai comprato qualcosa da mangiare? **3.** Vuoi qualcosa da bere? **4.** Desideri leggere il giornale o riposare? **5.** Hai incontrato qualcuno in piscina? **6.** Ti ha parlato qualcuno? **7.** Farai della pallacanestro o del nuoto questo week-end? **8.** Hai mai fatto del ciclismo? **9.** Farai mai della pesistica? **10.** Uscirai con qualcuno domenica?

C. **Domanda e risposta.** Rispondete negativamente.

ESEMPIO partecipare a una gara di nuoto
—Hai partecipato a una gara di nuoto?
—Non ho partecipato a nessuna gara di nuoto.

1. allenarsi allo stadio o in palestra **2.** capire tutto **3.** conoscere qualcuno a Firenze **4.** vedere alcune città italiane **5.** vincere un trofeo (*trophy*) **6.** telefonare a qualcuno ieri sera **7.** andare al cinema o alla partita **8.** mangiare qualcosa di buono **9.** scrivere cartoline a qualcuno

IV. Il «si» impersonale

*Dante. Divina Commedia, Inferno, Canto III**

*At the beginning of his mystic journey, Dante comes to the gate of hell and reads the following solemn inscription: "Through me one goes to the grieving city. Through me one goes to the eternal sorrow, Through me one goes among the lost souls."

The impersonal **si** + *verb* in the third person singular is used:

1. In general statements corresponding to the English words *one, you, we, they,* and *people* + verb.

Come **si dice** «...»?	*How do you say "..."?*
Se **si studia, s'impara.**	*If one studies, one learns.*

2. In conversational style, meaning **noi.**

Che **si fa** stasera?	*What are we doing tonight?*
Si va in palestra?	*Shall we go to the gym?*

3. As the equivalent of the passive construction. In this case the verb is in the singular or plural form depending on whether the noun that follows is singular or plural.

In Francia **si parla** francese.	*In France, French is spoken.*
In Svizzera, **si parlano** diverse lingue.	*In Switzerland, several languages are spoken.*

Pratica

A. Riscrivete le seguenti frasi usando il **si** impersonale.

1. Mangiamo bene in quel ristorante. **2.** Se tu studi, impari. **3.** In montagna, la gente va a dormire presto. **4.** Se vuoi mangiare, devi lavorare. **5.** Andiamo al cinema stasera? **6.** Se vogliamo un aumento di stipendio, dobbiamo chiederlo. **7.** Oggi la gente non ha più pazienza. **8.** Mangiamo per vivere, non viviamo per mangiare.

B. **Dove...? Domanda e risposta.** Seguite l'esempio.

ESEMPIO comprare i libri **—Dove si comprano i libri?**
—Si comprano in una libreria.

1. fare ginnastica **2.** praticare il windsurf **3.** potere telefonare **4.** comprare i gettoni **5.** giocare a calcio **6.** pagare il conto

C. Rispondete alle domande usando il **si** impersonale + il verbo.

ESEMPIO al cinema **—Che cosa si fa al cinema?**
—Si guarda un film.

1. a un concerto? **2.** in cucina? **3.** in biblioteca? **4.** in banca? **5.** a una discoteca? **6.** a una scrivania? **7.** al ristorante? **8.** all'università? **9.** al supermercato? **10.** in un negozio di abbigliamento? **11.** durante le elezioni? **12.** in montagna? **13.** in piscina?

LETTURA

La Vespa, un tipo di motorino.

GIOVANI *RIBELLI*

ribelli: rebels

A casa di Gabriella e Filippo. Gli amici reagiscono ad Antonio che ha espresso l'intenzione di comprarsi un motorino.

Marcello	Sei matto? Un motorino a Milano? Con tutte le brutte notizie che si leggono sui giornali *a proposito* di motoscooter e motociclette?	about
Filippo	Non vorrai *farti membro* dei «biker»?	to become a member
Mary Clark	Chi sono questi «biker» di cui parli con ironia?	
Antonio	Per essere precisi, i «biker» sono delle *bande* di ribelli, mentre io desidero semplicemente avere un mezzo di rapida comunicazione tra casa mia e il lavoro.	gangs
Mary Clark	E cosa fanno i «biker»?	
Filippo	Escono dalle città su moto spesso *riciclate* e vanno a dei *raduni* motociclistici, in cui si divertono con musica rock e molta birra.	recycled rallies
Mary Clark	Insomma, sono degli Hell's Angels all'italiana.	
Antonio	Infatti portano dei nomi americani come «Red Skin», «Hurricane» *e così via*. Esistono	and so on

altre bande che si ispirano all'America, le bande «rapper», per esempio. Ce ne sono almeno *una cinquantina* in tutta Italia. — about fifty

Filippo Anche i rapper italiani sono contro il sistema e lo esprimono *cantando in cantilena* e quasi sempre nel dialetto della loro regione. — by sing-song

Gabriella Ma abbiamo anche altri ribelli...

Marcello Mary, non tutti i giovani sono così. La maggior parte sono più o meno come noi. Ma..., per ritornare ad Antonio, perchè non ti compri una macchina usata? Senza dubbio è *più sicura* del motorino. Ti do *lezioni di guida* io! — safer; driving lessons

Antonio Perchè no? Ma prima di risponderti dovrò controllare le mie finanze.

Comprensione

1. Che desiderio ha espresso Antonio?
2. Che ne pensa Marcello? Perchè?
3. Che cosa gli domanda Filippo? Parla seriamente o scherza?
4. Perchè Antonio vorrebbe comprarsi un motorino?
5. Chi sono i biker e cosa fanno quando si riuniscono?
6. A quali bande americane si potrebbero paragonare?
7. Ci sono altre bande di giovani ribelli che imitano l'America? Quali?
8. Che cosa dovrebbe fare Antonio per risolvere (*to solve*) il suo problema?
9. E Marcello, che cosa dovrebbe fare per aiutare l'amico?

Domande personali

1. Ha mai guidato un motoscooter o una motocicletta Lei? Se non li ha mai guidati, Le piacerebbe guidarli?
2. Antonio vorrebbe comprarsi un motorino per andare al lavoro. Secondo Lei, sarebbe una buona idea, o no? Perchè?
3. I giovani americani che incominciano a lavorare, quale mezzo di trasporto si comprano? Una motocicletta? Lei cosa si è comprato, o cosa si comprerà?
4. Se i soldi non costituiscono un problema per Lei, cosa vorrebbe comprarsi?
5. Lei è membro, o è stato membro di qualche banda di ribelli?
6. Conosce il nome di una banda? Sa contro (*against*) cosa si ribellano? Contro le istituzioni sociali (*establishment*)?

ATTIVITÀ SUPPLEMENTARI

A. **Quale sport?** Ogni studente sceglie uno sport, senza dire quale e lo descrive: dove si pratica, con che cosa, in quale stagione, come uno si veste per questo sport, se è uno sport individuale o di squadra. Gli altri studenti devono indovinare il nome dello sport.

B. **Identificate** gli sport delle seguenti foto e rispondete alle domande.

Foto numero 1: Gli Italiani lo chiamano anche «football», ma qual è il vero nome italiano di questo sport? Sai quanti giocatori giocano nella squadra? È uno sport per cui fanno il tifo i paesi europei e quelli dell'America Latina. È popolare anche negli Stati Uniti? Più popolare del football? Perchè?

Foto numero 2: Di che sport si tratta? Qual è l'equipaggiamento necessario per praticarlo? Quali varietà di questo sport conosci? Se lo pratichi, racconta la tua ultima esperienza (dove sei andato(a), quando, con chi, per quanto tempo, dove hai alloggiato, che tempo faceva, ecc.).

Foto numero 3: Come si chiama questo sport? Hai una bicicletta? Di che marca (*make*) è? Quando la usi? La usi come divertimento o come mezzo di trasporto? Quali sono i vantaggi e gli svantaggi della bicicletta rispetto alla macchina? Quale delle due è migliore per la salute (*health*) e per l'ambiente? Meno pericolosa, più economica, più divertente?

1.

2.

3.

C. **Conversazione** con un compagno (una compagna) di classe. Praticate qualche sport? Quale? (Quali?) Oppure vi interessate a qualcosa d'altro? Quando e come avete incominciato? Qualcuno o qualcosa vi ha influenzato nella scelta? (Spiegate.) Dedicate (*Do you devote*) molte ore del vostro tempo libero a...? È una passione seria oppure è soltanto un passatempo? È qualcosa di costoso? Se avete dovuto smettere (*stop*), dite perchè.

D. **Siete stanchi di sport?** Leggete la seguente poesia, molto semplice. Non descrive niente di preciso, ma suggerisce (*suggests*) una storia molto comune: la fine di un amore. Anche voi potete essere poeti «impressionisti»; scrivete alcune righe e seguite sempre lo stesso ordine di parole: **nome** + *pronome relativo* + *qualcuno* + **passato prossimo.** (Ogni soggetto va bene: biblioteca, aula, stanza dove studiate, ecc.)

La ragazza che qualcuno ha amato
La stanza in cui qualcuno è entrato
Il bacio che qualcuno ha dato
Il sole che qualcuno ha portato
La sedia su cui qualcuno si è riposato
Il giornale che qualcuno ha letto
Le parole che qualcuno ha detto
L'orologio che qualcuno ha guardato
La porta che qualcuno ha aperto
La *pena* che qualcuno ha sofferto

grief

E. **Come si dice in italiano?**

1. Paul is a student at the University of..., which is one of the best universities on the West Coast.
2. He is also a football player who plays on (**in**) the school team.
3. Today he is sitting (**è seduto**) in the (**alla**) cafeteria.
4. John, the friend with whom he is speaking, is a basketball player.
5. Someone said that he is so good that one day he will certainly take part in the Olympic games.
6. Today he needs to talk to Paul because he wants to ask him for yesterday's notes.
7. But Paul didn't go to class.
8. John, did you do anything interesting yesterday?
9. No, I didn't do anything interesting. I practiced for a few hours in (the) gym. And you?
10. I was supposed to meet my coach and some other players at the stadium, but no one was there.
11. Will you come tomorrow to see the game?
12. I don't know yet what I will do. I hope to be able to come. Anyhow (**comunque**), good luck!

Vocabolario

Nomi

la banda	*gang*
la crisi	*crisis*
il divertimento	*fun*
l'equipaggiamento	*equipment*
le finanze	*money*
il genere	*kind*
il ghiaccio	*ice*
l'ironia	*irony*
l'istruttore, l'istruttrice	*instructor*
la marca	*make, brand name*
il membro	*member*
il motorino	*motorscooter*
i pattini	*skates*
la possibilità	*possibility*
la preparazione	*preparation*
la ragione	*reason*
il ribelle	*rebel*
lo sciatore, la sciatrice	*skier*
la separazione	*separation*
il sistema	*system; establishment*

Aggettivi

appassionato (di)	*fond (of)*
estivo	*summer*
invernale	*winter*
olimpico	*Olympic*
personale	*personal*
sicuro	*safe*
spettacolare	*spectacular*
sportivo	*sports, sporty, athletic*
usato	*used*

Verbi

ammettere (*p.p.* ammesso)	*to admit*
applaudire	*to applaud*
concludersi	*to end, to conclude itself*
costituire (-isc)	*to represent*
dedicarsi	*to devote oneself*
guidare	*to ride (a motor vehicle)*
imitare	*to imitate*
indovinare	*to guess*
ispirarsi	*to be inspired by*
protestare	*to complain*
raggiungere (*p.p.* raggiunto)	*to reach*
ribellarsi	*to rebel*
riunirsi	*to gather*

Altre espressioni

a proposito di	*about*
avere luogo	*to take place*
contro	*against*
essere seduto(a)	*to be sitting*
insomma	*in short*
la maggior parte (di)	*most (of)*
nè...nè	*neither...nor*
neanche, nemmeno	*not even, neither*
nessuna novità	*nothing new*
nessuno	*nobody, no one*
niente	*nothing*
ognuno	*everyone; each one*
per esempio	*for instance*
proprio	*exactly, really, indeed*
qualcuno	*someone*
senza dubbio	*undoubtedly*
tutti	*everybody*
tutto	*everything*
veramente	*actually*

GLI SPORT IN ITALIA

Come nel passato, gli Italiani continuano ad essere *accaniti* tifosi del calcio. Incominciano a praticarlo da bambini nei *cortili* delle scuole o nel campo della loro *parrocchia.* In famiglia e fuori assistono alle discussioni dei *grandi* che il sabato *compilano* la *schedina* del Totocalcio* e predicono la vittoria della loro squadra nella partita della domenica. Le discussioni diventano polemiche durante e dopo la partita e possono trasformarsi in vere *battaglie.* Il lunedì le polemiche si calmano per *riaccendersi* la domenica dopo. Purtroppo, i calciatori di questi ultimi anni sembrano *alzarsi* raramente al livello dei campioni di una volta. D'altra parte, nuovi campioni *sono apparsi* negli sport individuali, specialmente nel tennis, nello sci e nel ciclismo.

keen
courtyards
parish
grown-ups/fill in
form
fights
to catch fire again
to rise
have appeared

La bicicletta è praticata da moltissimi, come risposta ai problemi dell'ambiente e al consiglio degli *igienisti.* Ma altri sport sono nati, *rendendo* gli Italiani *sempre più* attivi. Sono sport d'importazione USA, che i giovani *hanno accolto* con entusiasmo insieme al loro nome straniero. Così molti si dedicano al weightlifting («pesistica» per i puristi della lingua), al karate, al jogging, al footing («camminata aerobica»), mentre qualcuno coltiva il bodybuilding («culturismo»). La donna pratica specialmente l'aerobica, lo yoga, lo stretching e altre forme di ginnastica leggera.

health experts/making
more and more
have welcomed

Si sa che d'estate moltissimi Italiani si concentrano lungo le coste, attratti dal mare. Diversi giovani vi praticano la pallanuoto, il beach-volley (un tempo chiamato «pallavolo»), il surf, il windsurf e il sub («pesca subacquea»). Altri preferiscono lo skateboard. Una mania di questi ultimi tempi è la barca a vela o a motore, che nel mondo dei *vip* assume le proporzioni del yacht.

V.I.P.

Per finire, si deve parlare di un nuovo sport, nato dal *crescente* interesse per i problemi ecologici: l'agriturismo. D'estate, intere famiglie passano le loro vacanze in aziende agrituristiche** a contatto con la natura e in attività varie, fra cui l'equitazione, usata come mezzo di scoperta dell'ambiente (*trekking*).

growing

---

*A popular lottery related to the soccer game.
**These are usually restructured farm houses, with horses, swimming pools, and good country cooking.

Comprensione

Rispondete alle seguenti domande.

1. In quale giorno della settimana si giocano le partite di calcio? Come si chiama la lotteria legata (*tied*) al gioco del calcio?
2. Perchè è così popolare il ciclismo oggi?
3. A quale paese si ispira sopratutto la gioventù per i suoi sport?
4. Che cos'è la pesistica? E la camminata aerobica? E il culturismo?
5. Quali sono gli sport preferiti al mare?
6. In questi ultimi anni, che cosa preferiscono fare diverse famiglie durante le vacanze estive?
7. Come si chiama l'equitazione praticata per studiare l'ambiente?

Vacanze a cavallo, alla scoperta dell'ambiente.

17 MEDICI E PAZIENTI

Arte e medicine in una vecchia farmacia italiana.

Punti di vista

Dalla dottoressa
Una telefonata

Punti grammaticali

I Il passato remoto
II Suffissi con nomi e aggettivi
III La forma passiva
IV Il gerundio e la forma progressiva

Lettura

La nonna è ammalata

Pagina culturale

L'assistenza medica per tutti

PUNTI DI VISTA

In sala operatoria.

DALLA DOTTORESSA

Nello studio della dottoressa Rovelli, a Bari.*

Signor Pini	Buon giorno, dottoressa.	
La dottoressa	Buon giorno, signor Pini, come andiamo oggi?	
Signor Pini	Eh, non molto bene, purtroppo. Ho mal di testa, un terribile *raffreddore*, e la *tosse*.	cold/cough
La dottoressa	Ha anche la *febbre?*	temperature
Signor Pini	Sì, l'ho misurata ed è alta: *trentanove*.	39° centigradi-102.2° F
La dottoressa	Vedo che Lei ha una bella influenza. Le scrivo una *ricetta* che Lei presenterà in farmacia. Sono gli stessi antibiotici che Le *diedi* l'anno scorso.	prescription / I gave
Signor Pini	E per la tosse? La notte non posso dormire *a causa* della tosse.	because of
La dottoressa	Per la tosse prenderà questa medicina.	
Signor Pini	*Mi fanno male* anche le spalle, le braccia e le gambe.	my...ache
La dottoressa	*Prenda* delle aspirine e vedrà che fra due o tre giorni starà meglio.	take
Signor Pini	Se non morirò prima...	
La dottoressa	Che *fifone!* Lei è *sano come un pesce!*	chicken (lit. *funk*) / "as healthy as a horse" (lit. *as a fish*)

*Regional capital of Puglia and port on the Adriatic Sea.

Comprensione

1. In quale città si trova lo studio della dottoressa Rovelli?
2. Perchè il signor Pini va dalla dottoressa?
3. Quali sono i suoi sintomi?
4. Ha la febbre alta o bassa il signor Pini?
5. Qual è la diagnosi della dottoressa?
6. Che cosa scrive la dottoressa?
7. Dove deve portare la ricetta il signor Pini?
8. Perchè non può dormire la notte il signor Pini?
9. Che altri dolori ha?
10. Che cosa prescrive la dottoressa per tutti i dolori?
11. Perchè la dottoressa lo prende in giro (*does...tease him*)?

Studio di parole

avere mal di...testa to have a...headache
denti toothache
stomaco stomachache
schiena backache
gola sore throat
avere il raffreddore to have a cold
avere la febbre to have a fever
misurare la febbre to take one's temperature
avere la tosse to have a cough
mi fa male la testa (lo stomaco, ecc.) my head hurts (my stomach..., etc.)
mi fanno male i denti (le spalle, ecc.) my teeth hurt (my shoulders..., etc.)
farsi male to hurt oneself
rompersi (*p.p.* **rotto) un braccio (una gamba)** to break an arm (a leg)
dimagrire (-isc) to lose weight
Sono dimagrito(a) di due chili. I lost 2 kilos.
ingrassare to gain weight
Sono ingrassato(a) di una libbra. I gained 1 pound.
ingessare to put a cast
guarire (-isc) to recover

IL CORPO

The following nouns that refer to the body are masculine in the singular and feminine in the plural.

il braccio	**le braccia**	la mano, f.	**le mani**
il dito	**le dita**	l'orecchio	**le orecchie**
il ginocchio	**le ginocchia**	l'osso (*bone*)	**le ossa**
il labbro (*lip*)	**le labbra**		

A. 1. Quando si va dal dentista?
2. Se uno va a sciare e cade, cosa si può rompere?
3. Se mangiamo troppo, che cosa succede?
4. Se qualcuno lavora tutto il giorno in giardino, come si sente la sera?
5. Se qualcuno festeggia un'occasione speciale e beve molti bicchieri di vino, che cos'ha il giorno dopo?
6. Quando portiamo un paio di scarpe strette, che cosa ci fa male?
7. Che cosa incidono (*carve*) sugli alberi gli innamorati romantici?
8. Che cosa si deve fare quando non si sta bene?
9. Cosa si prende quando si ha il raffreddore?
10. Quando si usa il termometro?
11. Quando si ha l'influenza, si bevono molti o pochi liquidi?

B. Completate le frasi seguenti.

1. Il mese scorso sono andato(a) a sciare e (*I broke my leg*) _____.
2. Ieri sono stato(a) a casa perchè (*I had a fever*) _____.
3. Mia sorella è caduta dalla bicicletta e (*she hurt herself*) _____.
4. L'altro ieri ho camminato per 4 ore e oggi (*my feet hurt*) _____.
5. Se (*you have a toothache*) _____, perchè non vai dal dentista?
6. Dottore, non mi sento bene: (*I have a cold and a sore throat*) _____.
7. Mia madre è preoccupata perchè (*I lost weight*) _____ di tre chili.
8. Ho scritto a macchina tutto il giorno e ora (*my arms, my hands, and my fingers hurt*) _____.

C. **Domande personali.**

1. Ha spesso il raffreddore Lei? Quante volte all'anno?
2. In quale stagione è facile prenderlo (*to get it*)?
3. Quanto tempo fa ha avuto l'influenza Lei? Che cosa Le faceva male?
4. Ha mai fatto l'iniezione Lei per prevenire (*to prevent*) l'influenza?
5. Quanto tempo ci vuole per guarirne?
6. Il Suo medico Le ha mai ordinato di prendere degli antibiotici? Se li ha presi, Le hanno fatto bene?
7. Lei va dal dottore quando ha il raffreddore o l'influenza?
8. Che cosa fa di solito un fifone quando sta male? Si considera un fifone (una fifona) Lei?

AVVERTENZE

1 - La tessera costituisce il documento attestante l'iscrizione al Servizio Sanitario Nazionale
2 - Essa deve essere presentata all'atto della richiesta di qualsiasi prestazione sanitaria (medicina generica, specialistica, farmaceutica, ospedaliera)
3 - La struttura sanitaria erogante la prestazione potrà richiedere l'esibizione di un idoneo documento di identificazione
4 - In caso di smarrimento della tessera o di variazione dei dati in essa contenuti presentarsi alla struttura competente della U.S.S.L.

SERVIZIO SANITARIO NAZIONALE

Ascoltiamo!

Una telefonata. *Lisa receives a phone call from Giovanni, an old friend she ran into a few weeks earlier while on vacation in Roccaraso. Listen to their conversation, then answer the following questions.*

Comprensione

1. Dove si sono incontrati Lisa e Giovanni?
2. Lisa ha delle buone novità?
3. Che cosa è successo a Lisa mentre sciava?
4. Si è anche fatta male alla testa?
5. Dove le hanno ingessato il braccio? Il braccio ingessato è il destro o il sinistro?
6. Perchè Giovanni ha telefonato a Lisa?
7. Quando si vedranno Lisa e Giovanni?

Dialogo

Un incidente *(accident).* In gruppi di due, immaginate di telefonare a un amico (un'amica) e di raccontargli(le) un incidente che vi è successo mentre praticavate uno sport o in un'altra occasione.

PUNTI GRAMMATICALI

I. Passato remoto

Il nonno di Lucia nacque a Cosenza nel 1910.*

Visse in Calabria fino al 1933.

A ventitrè anni emigrò in America.

Morì a Brooklyn nel 1975.

1. Dove nacque il nonno di Lucia?
2. Quando partì dalla sua città?
3. In quale paese emigrò?
4. In che anno morì?

---

*Città della Calabria.

1. The **passato remoto** is a past tense that corresponds to the English past absolute. It is formed by adding the appropriate endings to the infinitive stem.

   parlare → parl**ai** = *I spoke, I did speak*
   It is conjugated as follows:

parlare	ricevere	partire
parl**ai**	ricev**ei** (ricevetti)	part**ii**
parl**asti**	ricev**esti**	part**isti**
parl**ò**	ricev**è** (ricevette)	part**ì**
parl**ammo**	ricev**emmo**	part**immo**
parl**aste**	ricev**este**	part**iste**
parl**arono**	ricev**erono** (ricevettero)	part**irono**

   Many regular **-ere** verbs have an alternate ending for the first person singular and for the third person singular and plural.

2. The **passato remoto**, like the **passato prossimo**, expresses an action that was completed in the past. However, the **passato prossimo** is generally used to express actions that took place in a not-too-distant past. The **passato remoto** relates past actions and events completely detached from the present. It is most commonly found in narrative and historical writings. The **passato remoto** is used less frequently in spoken Italian, although this varies from region to region. Use of the **passato remoto** in conversation indicates that the speaker perceives the action described as distant from or unrelated to the present.

Dante **morì** nel 1321.	*Dante died in 1321.*
Il dottore **entrò** e **visitò** il malato.	*The doctor came in and examined the patient.*
Roma **diventò** la capitale d'Italia nel 1870.	*Rome became the capital of Italy in 1870.*

3. **Essere** and the following verbs are irregular in all their forms in the **passato remoto**:

essere:	**fui, fosti, fu, fummo, foste, furono**
bere:	**bevvi, bevesti, bevve, bevemmo, beveste, bevvero**
dare:	**diedi, desti, diede, demmo, deste, diedero**
dire:	**dissi, dicesti, disse, dicemmo, diceste, dissero**
fare:	**feci, facesti, fece, facemmo, faceste, fecero**
stare:	**stetti, stesti, stette, stemmo, steste, stettero**

4. **Avere** and the following verbs are irregular only in the **io**, **lei**, and **loro** forms. To conjugate these forms, add the endings **-i**, **-e**, and **-ero** to the irregular stem.

avere: **ebb*i***, avesti, **ebb*e***, avemmo, aveste, **ebb*ero***
cadere: **cadd*i***, cadesti, **cadd*e***, cademmo, cadeste, **cadd*ero***

chiedere	chiesi	rispondere	risposi
chiudere	chiusi	rompere	ruppi
conoscere	conobbi	sapere	seppi
decidere	decisi	scrivere	scrissi
leggere	lessi	vedere	vidi
mettere	misi	venire	venni
nascere	nacqui	vivere	vissi
prendere	presi	volere	volli

5. The **passato remoto**, like the **passato prossimo**, may be used in combination with the imperfect tense to express an action that was completed while another action or situation was occurring.

Gli **diedi** un bacio mentre uscivo.	*I gave him a kiss while I was going out.*
Scrissero al padre perchè non avevano più soldi.	*They wrote to their father because they didn't have any more money.*

Pratica

A. Cosa fecero i membri di questa famiglia l'anno scorso? Rispondete secondo l'esempio.

ESEMPIO tu, andare in America **Tu andasti in America.**

1. io, laurearsi **2.** Marco, ricevere una borsa di studio (*grant*) **3.** Pino, partire per il Marocco **4.** le nostre due sorelle, passare due settimane a Cortina **5.** il nostro cane, morire **6.** nostra madre, andare a trovare zia Maria **7.** finalmente tu e la mamma, ritornare

B. **Domanda e risposta.** Immaginate l'intervista di una giornalista a un vecchio professore italo-americano. La giornalista usa solo il **passato prossimo**; il professore risponde col **passato remoto** e con i **pronomi** appropriati.

ESEMPIO quando, venire negli Stati Uniti/cinquant'anni fa
—Professore, quando è venuto negli Stati Uniti?
—Ci venni cinquant'anni fa.

1. fare i Suoi studi secondari in questo paese/no, in Italia **2.** quando, leggere la *Divina Commedia*/quand'ero studente di liceo **3.** dove, frequentare l'università/negli Stati Uniti **4.** conoscere italiani importanti in questo paese/uno all'Università di Chicago: Enrico Fermi **5.** parlare con Enrico Fermi/sì, a lungo **6.** ritornare mai in Italia/sì, spesso **7.** rivedere i Suoi parenti/solamente alcuni **8.** come, trovare l'Italia/molto cambiata e più prospera

C. **La gente non è mai contenta.** Leggete la storia con i verbi al **passato remoto.**

Un giorno la Madonna, San Giuseppe e il Bambino Gesù *partono* da Gerusalemme con il loro asino (*donkey*). San Giuseppe *mette* la Madonna e il Bambino Gesù sull'asino. Lui *va* a piedi. *Arrivano* ad un paese. La gente *guarda* i tre viaggiatori e *dice* «Che vergogna (*What a shame*)! La giovane donna e il bambino sono sull'asino, e il povero vecchio cammina!» Allora la Madonna e il Bambino *smontano* dall'asino e *incominciano* a camminare, mentre San Giuseppe *sale* sull'asino. *Arrivano* ad un altro paese e *sentono* altri commenti della gente: «Che vergogna! L'uomo forte è sull'asino e la povera donna con il bambino cammina!» Allora tutti e tre *montano* sull'asino. Ma *arrivano* ad un terzo paese e la gente *commenta* ancora: «Che vergogna! Tre persone sopra un povero asino!» E i tre *smontano* dall'asino e lo *portano* sulle spalle. Quando *arrivano* ad un altro paese gli abitanti *fanno* ancora commenti. «Che stupidi! Tre persone che portano un asino!»

D. **Cappuccetto Rosso.** Completate con il verbo fra parentesi al **passato remoto** o all'**imperfetto**, secondo il caso.

C'era una volta una bambina che (chiamarsi) Cappuccetto Rosso. Un giorno la mamma (preparare) un cestino di cose buone per la nonna che (essere) ammalata. Cappuccetto Rosso (partire), (entrare) nel bosco e (fermarsi) a raccogliere (*to pick*) dei fiori. Improvvisamente un grosso lupo (uscire) da dietro un albero e le (domandare) dove (andare). Quando seppe che (andare) dalla nonna, la (salutare) e (andare) via (*away*). Cappuccetto Rosso (arrivare) dalla nonna, (entrare) e (trovare) la nonna a letto.

—Nonna, nonna, che orecchie lunghe hai...(dire) la bambina.
—Per sentirti meglio! (rispondere) la nonna.
—Nonna, nonna, che bocca grande hai...
—Per mangiarti meglio!
E il lupo (saltare) (*to jump*) dal letto e la (divorare).

E. Mettete i verbi in corsivo al **passato remoto** o all'**imperfetto**, secondo il caso.

In una piccola città di provincia un contadino *festeggia* il suo centesimo compleanno. Un giornalista *va* a casa sua per intervistarlo. *Vuole* conoscere il segreto della sua longevità.
—Qual è il segreto di una lunga vita? —gli *domanda* il giornalista.
Il contadino, che *si sente* importante, *pensa* un po', e poi *risponde:*
—È molto semplice: non fumo, vado a letto presto la sera e, sopratutto, non bevo vino. Non ho mai bevuto una goccia (*drop*) di vino in tutta la mia vita: ecco il segreto.

Mentre i due uomini *parlano, sentono* un gran rumore che *viene* dalle scale.
—Che cosa succede? —*chiede* il giornalista.
—Oh, non è niente, —*dice* il contadino, —è mio padre che ritorna a casa ubriaco (*drunk*) tutte le sere.

F. **Alcuni Italiani famosi.** Quanti nomi di esploratori (*explorers*) e di scienziati (*scientists*) italiani potete abbinare (*to match*) con le frasi che seguono?

Marco Polo (1254–1324)	Luigi Galvani (1737–1798)
Leonardo da Vinci (1452–1519)	Alessandro Volta (1745–1827)
Amerigo Vespucci (1454–1512)	Guglielmo Marconi (1874–1937)
Galileo Galilei (1564–1642)	Enrico Fermi (1901–1954)

1. Cinque secoli fa disegnò molte macchine moderne, fra cui l'elicottero, l'aereo e il carro armato (*tank*).
2. Con l'aiuto del telescopio, confermò la teoria che la terra gira intorno al sole. La Chiesa lo condannò come eretico.
3. Nel 1938 ricevè il premio Nobel per le sue ricerche nel campo (*field*) dell'energia nucleare.
4. Fece esperimenti sugli animali e stabilì le basi dell'elettrofisiologia.
5. Esplorò le coste del «Nuovo Mondo» e diede il suo nome al nuovo continente.
6. Inventò il telegrafo senza fili (*wireless*), e nel 1909 ottenne il premio Nobel per la fisica.
7. Visitò l'Asia e descrisse il suo viaggio nel famoso libro *Il Milione.*
8. Fu l'inventore della pila (*battery*) elettrica.

II. Suffissi con nomi e aggettivi

—Che bel nasino!
—Che brutto nasone!

In Italian, the meaning of a noun or an adjective can be altered by attaching a particular suffix to it. The suffix is added after the final vowel of the word is dropped. The most common suffixes are:

a. **-ino(a); -etto(a); -ello(a).** They convey an idea of smallness or indicate endearment.

fratello	fratell**ino** (*dear little brother*)
Luigi	Luig**ino** (*dear little Luigi*)
piccolo	piccol**ino** (*very small and cute*)
casa	cas**etta** (*small, cute little house*)
vino	vin**ello** (*light, but good, wine*)

b. **-one (-ona, -oni, -one).** It conveys a meaning of largeness, weight, or importance. When a feminine noun takes this suffix, it sometimes becomes masculine.

naso	nas**one** (*huge nose*)
dottore	dottor**one** (*well-known doctor*)
pigro	pigr**one** (*very lazy*)
una donna	un donn**one** (*a big woman*)

c. **-accio (-accia, -acci, -acce).** It gives the noun or the adjective a pejorative connotation.

parola	parol**accia** (*dirty word*)
ragazzo	ragazz**accio** (*bad boy*)
tempo	temp**accio** (*very bad weather*)

NOTE:
The choice of these suffixes is idiomatic and cannot be made at random. It is best that you limit their use to the examples read in reliable sources or heard from native speakers.

Pratica

A. **Aggiungete** a ogni parola in corsivo il **suffisso** che è necessario per rendere (*to convey*) il significato della frase.

1. un *tempo* con molta pioggia **2.** un *libro* di mille pagine **3.** il *naso* di un bambino **4.** un *ragazzo* grande e grosso **5.** una *villa* piccola e carina **6.** un *vestito* di poco valore (*value*) **7.** due lunghe *giornate* faticose **8.** il *giornale* dei piccoli (bambini) **9.** un *ragazzo* cattivo **10.** le grosse *scarpe* da montagna **11.** un *professore* molto famoso **12.** una brutta *parola*

B. Date l'equivalente inglese delle espressioni in corsivo.

1. Hanno comprato *una macchinetta rossa.* **2.** Vai alla spiaggia? *Porta l'ombrellone!* **3.** Antonio ci ha raccontato *una storiella divertente.* **4.** Se voglio i libri dell'ultimo scaffale, *ho bisogno della scaletta.* **5.** *Era una serataccia* fredda, con vento e pioggia. **6.** Ho incontrato Marcello: *era con una biondina.* **7.** Un ragazzo come te non dovrebbe leggere quel *giornalaccio.* **8.** Nel giardino ci sono due *alberelli di mele.*

III. La forma passiva

La tragedia Amleto *è stata scritta da Shakespeare.*

The passive form is possible only with transitive verbs (verbs that take a direct object). When an active sentence is put into the passive form, the direct object becomes the subject of the new sentence. The subject becomes the agent, introduced by **da.**

The passive form of a verb consists of **essere** (in the required tense) + *the past participle* of the verb. As for all verbs conjugated with **essere,** the past participle must agree with the subject in number and gender.

Active form	Passive form
Nino **canta** la canzone.	La canzone **è cantata** da Nino.
Nino **cantava** la canzone	La canzone **era cantata** da Nino.
Nino **cantò** la canzone.	La canzone **fu cantata** da Nino.
Nino **canterà** la canzone.	La canzone **sarà cantata** da Nino.
Lisa **ha scritto** il diario.	Il diario **è stato scritto** da Lisa.
Lisa **aveva scritto** il diario.	Il diario **era stato scritto** da Lisa.

Il paziente **è curato** dal medico. — *The patient is treated by the physician.*

Quelle ville **sono state costruite** dall'architetto Nervi. — *Those villas were built by the architect Nervi.*

Questo libro **sarà pubblicato** da un editore di Fort Worth. — *This book will be published by a publisher in Fort Worth.*

Pratica

A. All'ospedale. Mettete le seguenti frasi alla forma passiva.

ESEMPIO Il bambino chiama la mamma.
La mamma è chiamata dal bambino.

1. Il chirurgo opera un paziente. **2.** Un medico visita un malato. **3.** Un altro medico ordina gli antibiotici. **4.** Un infermiere aiuta un vecchio signore. **5.** Un ragazzo ha portato i fiori. **6.** Un'infermiera ha preso la pressione del sangue (*blood*). **7.** Il radiologo esaminerà la radiografia. **8.** La capoinfermiera metterà in ordine le cartelle (*charts*) dei malati.

B. Un quiz. Rispondete usando la forma **passiva.**

ESEMPIO Chi ha dipinto *La Gioconda?* **—La Gioconda è stata dipinta da Leonardo.**

1. Chi ha scolpito *La Pietà?* **2.** Chi ha composto l'*Aida?* **3.** Chi ha scoperto l'America? **4.** Chi ha inventato la teoria della relatività? **5.** Chi ha formulato la teoria dell'evoluzione dell'uomo? **6.** Chi governava l'Egitto ai tempi di Cesare? **7.** Quale eroina del Medioevo salvò la Francia dagli Inglesi? **8.** Chi scrisse la tragedia *Giulietta e Romeo?* **9.** Chi ha scoperto la penicillina? **10.** Chi inventò il telefono? (Meucci)

IV. Il gerundio e la forma progressiva

—Che cosa fa Pulcinella?
—Sta dando una lezione a Arlecchino.

1. The gerund (**il gerundio**) corresponds to the **-ing** form of English verbs. The gerund is formed by adding **-ando** to the stem of first conjugation (**-are**) verbs and **-endo** to the stem of second and third conjugation (**-ere** and **-ire**) verbs. It is invariable. The compound tense, the *past gerund,* is composed of the gerund of **avere** or **essere** + *past participle* of the verb.

Gerund		Past gerund	
parl**ando**	*speaking*	**avendo** parlato	*having spoken*
ripet**endo**	*repeating*	**avendo** ripetuto	*having repeated*
usc**endo**	*going out*	**essendo** uscito (**a,i,e**)	*having gone out*

Note that verbs with an irregular stem in the imperfect also have an irregular stem in the gerund.

bere: **bevendo** dire: **dicendo** fare: **facendo**

2. The gerund may be used alone in a subordinate clause to express the conditions (time, cause, means, manner) that govern the main action. It corresponds to the English gerund, which is usually preceded by the prepositions *while, upon, on, in,* or *by*.

Camminando per la strada, ho visto un incidente d'auto.	*While walking on the street, I saw a car accident.*
Studiando, s'impara.	*By studying, one learns.*
Leggendo attentamente, capirete meglio.	*By reading carefully, you will understand better.*
Avendo lavorato per quarant'anni, ha guadagnato molti soldi.	*Having worked for forty years, he has earned a lot of money.*

Note that the subject of the gerund and the subject of the main verb are the same.

3. **Stare + the gerund** expresses an action in progress in the present, in the past, or in the future. It stresses the point in time in which the action occurs; therefore it is less commonly used in Italian than in English.

Che cosa **stai facendo?**	*What are you doing (at this very moment)?*
Sto leggendo.	*I'm reading.*
Che cosa **stavate facendo** ieri sera, a quest'ora?	*What were you doing last night at this time?*
Stavamo cenando.	*We were having dinner.*
Domani, a quest'ora, Stefania **starà viaggiando.**	*Tomorrow at this time, Stefania will be traveling.*

4. With the progressive form (**stare** + *gerund*) object and reflexive pronouns may precede **stare** or follow the gerund. When the gerund stands alone, the pronouns are attached to it.

Mi stai ascoltando? *or:* Stai ascoltando**mi**?	*Are you listening to me?*
Il medico stava visitando**lo.**	*The doctor was examining him.*
La ringraziò, alzando**si.**	*He thanked her while getting up.*

5. Contrary to English, Italian uses an infinitive instead of a gerund as a noun (subject or object of another verb).

Nuotare (il nuoto) fa bene alla salute.	*Swimming* (subj.) *is good for your health.*
Preferisco **nuotare** (il nuoto).	*I prefer swimming* (obj.).

Pratica

A. **Un malato immaginario. Domanda e risposta.** Il vostro amico rivela la sua ossessione delle malattie quando risponde alle vostre domande. Usate **stare + il gerundio**, secondo l'esempio.

ESEMPIO scrivere alla tua ragazza/fare la lista dei miei mali (*aches*)
—Stai scrivendo alla tua ragazza?
—No, sto facendo la lista dei miei mali.

1. leggere un libro divertente/consultare un libro di medicina 2. prendere un aperitivo/bere uno sciroppo per la tosse 3. mangiare un cioccolatino/masticare (*chew*) una pastiglia (*tablet*) contro il mal di stomaco 4. fare l'aerobica/esercitare le braccia per migliorare l'artrite 5. dormire/praticare lo yoga contro la depressione

B. Rispondete alle domande usando **stare + il gerundio.**

1. Quale lingua state parlando? 2. Quale capitolo del libro state studiando? 3. Chi stai ascoltando adesso? 4. Che cosa stanno facendo alcuni studenti in questo momento? 5. Che cosa facevano gli studenti quando sei entrato(a) nell'aula? 6. Cosa facevi tu alle otto stamattina? E a mezzanotte? 7. Che cosa farai domenica a quest'ora?

C. Parliamo di Filippo e di Gabriella. Leggete le seguenti frasi, sostituendo il gerundio alle espressioni in corsivo.

1. *Dato che sono* molto innamorati, Filippo e Gabriella non vorrebbero stare lontani l'uno dall'altra. 2. Al mattino, *quando si lasciano* per andare al lavoro, si danno sempre un bacio. 3. La sera, *mentre preparano* la cena, si raccontano i fatti della giornata. 4. Un giorno, *mentre saliva* le scale di casa, Filippo è caduto e si è fatto male alla schiena. 5. L'altro giorno, *siccome aveva* il raffreddore, Gabriella non è uscita di casa. 6. Ma adesso, *poichè sono guariti* tutti e due, hanno intenzione di divertirsi un po'.

D. Sostituite il nome in corsivo con l'**infinito** corrispondente.

ESEMPIO *Il lavoro* fa bene allo spirito e alla salute.
Lavorare fa bene allo spirito e alla salute.

1. *Lo sci* è divertente. 2. *Il riso* (*laughter*) fa buon sangue. 3. *Il fumo* fa male ai polmoni (*lungs*). 4. Vorrei *una bevanda.* 5. Ho bisogno di *riposo.* 6. Ti piacerebbe *una passeggiata* in campagna? 7. *Il divertimento* è necessario quanto *lo studio.* 8. I bambini preferiscono *il gioco.*

E. Completate le seguenti frasi, scegliendo tra il **gerundio** e l'**infinito.**

1. _____ (*Walking*) per la strada, ho incontrato Maria. 2. _____ (*Hearing*) quella canzone, ho avuto nostalgia del mio paese. 3. Mi piace _____ (*swimming*). 4. _____ (*Skiing*) è molto costoso. 5. _____ (*Walking*) tutti i giorni è un buon esercizio. 6. Pietro è andato a scuola _____ (*running*). 7. _____ (*Having*) molti soldi non significa essere felici. 8. _____ (*Having*) molti soldi, Dino è partito per le Hawaii.

LETTURA

LA NONNA È AMMALATA

Antonio è andato in Sicilia a trovare nonna Caterina che è ammalata da molti mesi.

Antonio Come ti senti, nonnina?
nonna Eh, figlio mio, non troppo bene. Mi fanno male tutte le ossa e *faccio fatica a* camminare. — I find it difficult to
Antonio Ma non hai chiamato il medico?
nonna Ma sì, Tonino, il dottor Gaetani venne molte volte l'inverno scorso.
Antonio E che cosa ti disse *allora* il medico? — at that time
nonna Mi disse che ho l'artrite e mi trovò la pressione alta.
Antonio Che cosa ti ordinò?
nonna Delle iniezioni. Mi diede anche delle pillole per calmare un po' il dolore e controllare la pressione. Mi raccomandò anche di stare a dieta.
Antonio E la cura non ha fatto niente?
nonna Ho fatto, e sto ancora facendo, delle iniezioni, ma, che vuoi, ragazzo mio, gli anni sono tanti...
nonno Tua nonna parla sempre di anni e ascolta troppo i medici. Dovrebbe ascoltare me e bere questo vinello rosso dell'Etna. *L'hai assaggiato?* — Did you taste it?
Antonio Sì, lo trovo ottimo. È della tua *vigna,* nonno? — vineyard
nonno No, questo mi è stato dato da un mio amico. Che ne dici, Tonino, non c'è dentro il fuoco dell'Etna?
Antonio Hai ragione, nonno. Incomincio già ad avere caldo.
nonno È quello che dico sempre a tua nonna: due bicchieri di vino al giorno e *ti levi il medico d'intorno.* Ma lei ha la testa dura e preferisce ascoltare i dottori. — you keep the doctor away

Comprensione

1. Perchè Antonio è andato a trovare nonna Caterina?
2. Come si sentiva la nonna?
3. Che cosa le faceva male?
4. Cosa le disse il medico che la visitò?
5. Che medicine le ordinò il medico?
6. Il medico disse che poteva mangiare tutto quello che voleva? Cosa doveva fare?
7. Come si sente la nonna?
8. Secondo la nonna, quale sarebbe la vera ragione dei suoi disturbi (*ailments*)?
9. Secondo il nonno, cosa dovrebbe fare la nonna per guarire?
10. Come trova quel vinello Antonio? Come si sente dopo che l'ha bevuto?
11. Quale proverbio ripete sempre il nonno?
12. Perchè, secondo lui, la nonna ha la testa dura?

1. Com'è la Sua salute? Che medicina prende quando ha mal di testa?
2. Lei può mangiare tutto o deve stare a dieta?
3. Com'è la salute dei Suoi genitori? Si preoccupa per loro quando sono malati?
4. Che cosa pensa Lei dei medici? Ha fiducia in loro (*Do you trust them*)?
5. Se il Suo medico Le ordina una medicina, che cosa fa Lei? E se Le dà un consiglio?
6. È d'accordo Lei con il proverbio del nonno di Antonio? Cosa pensa Lei della filosofia del nonno?

ATTIVITÀ SUPPLEMENTARI

A. **La signora e il medico.** La signora è a letto e il medico è venuto a visitarla. Immaginate il dialogo fra i due. Due studenti fanno la parte dei due personaggi (*characters*).

B. **Disegno senza titolo.** (Attività in gruppi di due). Immaginate di essere i due personaggi del disegno e di pensare ad alta voce. Dite, ognuno dei due, quello che avete fatto, che state facendo e quali ne sono le conseguenze. Dite anche cosa pensate dell'altra persona. Date un titolo al disegno.

C. **La depressione, malattia del nostro secolo.** In gruppi di due, leggete il seguente articoletto, che riporta i sintomi della depressione. Ne avete qualcuno? Immaginate di essere uno psicologo e un(a) paziente. Il (la) paziente sceglie alcuni sintomi e li comunica allo psicologo, che gli (le) dà dei consigli per guarire dalla depressione.

Non sottovalutarne i sintomi

La depressione è diagnosticabile con certezza solo dallo specialista. Comunque la presenza di questi sintomi (almeno cinque e perduranti da almeno due settimane) può segnalare uno stato depressivo. Ed è necessario rivolgersi al medico per una valutazione esatta.

SEGNALI PSICOLOGICI

- tristezza, irritabilità, malinconia continua e immotivata
- insonnia o eccessivo bisogno di sonno
- disinteresse per la cura della propria persona
- crisi di pianto
- sensi di colpa (eccessivi e immotivati) — feelings of guilt
- perdita di interesse per ogni attività (di lavoro e di svago) — loss
- perdita della memoria e della capacità di concentrazione
- ricorrenti pensieri di morte (e talvolta propositi suicidi)

SEGNALI FISICI

- mal di testa cronico
- sensazione di non riuscire a respirare (compressione sul torace e alla gola)
- affaticabilità — fatigue
- eccessiva sudorazione — perspiration
- disturbi sessuali
- dolori (addominali, articolari)
- notevole perdita di capelli
- tachicardia (aumento del battito cardiaco) — heart beat
- perdita o aumento sensibile di peso (in assenza di diete)

D. **Come si dice in italiano?**

1. Here is a question that the Sphinx (**la Sfinge**) asked a great hero (**eroe,** *m.*): "Which is the animal who in the morning walks on four legs, at noon on two, and in the evening on three?" The hero knew how to answer. Do you? (**E Lei?**)
2. One day an old peasant told the doctor who had treated him for a serious earache, "I feel completely cured (**guarito**). How much do I owe you?" The doctor answered, "One hundred thousand lire." The old man put (his) hand close to (**vicino a**) (his) ear and asked, "What did you say? Two hundred thousand lire?" So, the doctor shouted (**gridare**): "No, three hundred thousand lire!"

Vocabolario

Nomi

l'antibiotico	*antibiotic*
l'artrite (*f.*)	*arthritis*
l'aspirina	*aspirine*
la borsa di studio	*scholarship; grant*
il calmante	*sedative*
la cartella	*chart*
il contadino, la contadina	*peasant, farmer*
la cura	*treatment; care*
la depressione	*depression*
il dente	*tooth*
la diagnosi	*diagnosis*
il disturbo	*ailment; trouble*
il dolore	*pain, ache*
il (la) giornalista	*journalist*
l'infermiere(a)	*nurse*
l'influenza	*flu*
l'iniezione (*f.*)	*injection*
l'innamorato, l'innamorata	*lover*
l'intervista	*interview*
il malato, la malata	*sick person; patient*
la malattia	*disease, illness*
la medicina	*medicine, medication*
la novità	*news*
l'occasione (*f.*)	*occasion, circumstance*
la pastiglia	*tablet*
il (la) paziente	*patient*
il peso	*weight*
la pillola	*pill*
la pressione	*blood pressure*
lo psicologo, la psicologa	*psychologist*
la radiografia	*X-ray*
la ricerca	*research*
la ricetta	*prescription*
la salute	*health*
il segreto	*secret*
il sintomo	*symptom*
la teoria	*theory*
il termometro	*thermometer*

Aggettivi

(am)malato	*ill, sick*
duro	*hard*
gratuito	*free (of charge)*
medico	*medical*
sano	*healthy*
terribile	*terrible*
ubriaco	*drunk*

Verbi

ammalarsi	*to get sick*
calmare	*to calm*
commentare	*to make a comment, to remark*
controllare	*to check; to keep under control*
curare	*to treat*
emigrare	*to emigrate*
esplorare	*to explore*
guarire (-isc)	*to cure; to be cured; to recover*
intervistare	*to interview*
inventare	*to invent*
operare	*to operate*
ordinare	*to prescribe*
raccommandare	*to recommend*
saltare	*to jump*
scoprire (*p.p.* scoperto)	*to discover*
smontare	*to dismount*
visitare	*to examine*

Altre espressioni

a lungo	*for a long time*
andare via	*to go away*
avere la testa dura	*to be stubborn*
a causa di	*because of*
Che fifone!	*What a funk!*
Che vergogna!	*What a shame!*
Come andiamo?	*How are we doing?*
fare fatica a (+ *inf.*)	*to find it difficult to*
prendere il raffreddore	*to catch a cold*
prendere in giro	*to tease*
sano come un pesce	*healthy as a horse* (lit. fish)
sopratutto	*above all*
stare a dieta	*to be on a diet*

Atletica leggera anche per le donne della terza età.

L'ASSISTENZA MEDICA PER TUTTI

La Costituzione italiana assicura a tutti gli Italiani l'assistenza medica «come fondamentale *diritto* dell'individuo ed interesse della collettività». I contributi sono pagati dal *datore di lavoro* per le persone che hanno un lavoro. Tutti gli altri pagano un contributo *attraverso* le tasse; i poveri ricevono l'assistenza medica *gratuita*.

diritto: right
datore di lavoro: employer
attraverso: through
gratuita: free

Ogni cittadino possiede *una tessera sanitaria* che presenta per le visite mediche e tutti gli altri servizi sanitari. Ognuno è libero di scegliere il medico che preferisce; di solito questo è un medico generico che assiste tutta la famiglia. La continuità del *rapporto* di assistenza stabilisce *legami* di rispettosa amicizia, per cui il medico diventa veramente «il medico di famiglia». Quando una persona è ammalata, il medico viene a casa per la visita e, se necessario, ritorna nei giorni successivi. Purtroppo, la medicina socializzata rappresenta per lo stato un grave *peso* economico, e crea difficoltà nella costruzione di nuovi ospedali adeguati.*

una tessera sanitaria: health card
rapporto: relation
legami: ties
peso: burden

Grande importanza è data alla prevenzione delle malattie. Un'istituzione che fu creata durante l'epoca fascista e che è ancora molto popolare in Italia è quella delle *colonie* estive per i giovanissimi. *Enti* governativi, privati e religiosi organizzano per i bambini vacanze economiche o anche gratuite in località marine o montane.

colonie/Enti: camps/Agencies

Le migliorate condizioni di vita e un'assistenza sanitaria costante hanno allungato la vita media, che è oggi di circa settantacinque anni. Si parla così della «terza età», cioè, del periodo della vita che comincia verso i sessant'anni, in cui uomini e donne, liberi da rapporti di lavoro e da preoccupazioni economiche, possono *dedicarsi* a nuove attività. In questi ultimi anni, molte università hanno aperto le loro porte a questa nuova categoria di studenti.

dedicarsi: devote themselves

La dottoressa Rita Levi Montalcini, vincitrice di un premio internazionale per le scienze mediche.

Comprensione

Rispondete alle seguenti domande.

1. Chi paga i contributi per l'assistenza medica?
2. Che cos'è una tessera sanitaria?
3. Se una persona si ammala, che cosa fa il medico di famiglia?
4. Chi organizza le colonie estive per i ragazzi?
5. Quali fattori hanno allungato la vita media?
6. Chi sono i cittadini della terza età?
7. Sono liberi da preoccupazioni economiche?
8. A quale (o quali) attività si dedicano (*devote*) secondo voi?

18 LA MACCHINA E L'ECOLOGIA

Milano. Vigili urbani regolano il traffico.

Punti di vista

Ha controllato la macchina?
Aria inquinata

Punti grammaticali

I Il congiuntivo presente
II Il congiuntivo presente dei verbi irregolari
III L'imperativo *(Lei e Loro)*
IV Il congiuntivo passato

Lettura

Una lezione di guida

Pagina culturale

Problemi ecologici

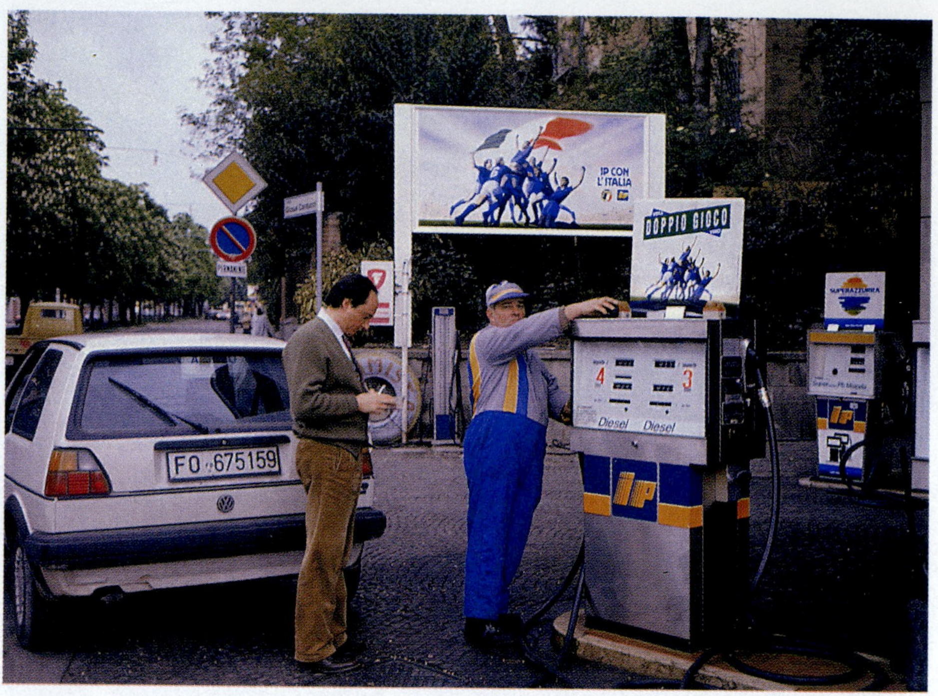

Un automobilista ha fatto il pieno a un distributore di benzina.

HA CONTROLLATO LA MACCHINA?

A Milano, dal meccanico.

Sig.na Meucci	Paolo, ha già controllato la mia macchina?	
Paolo	*Ma sicuro,* signorina. È pronta da un'ora.	of course
Sig.na Meucci	Spero che tutto *sia a posto.* Devo partire per Roma e non vorrei avere *noie* sull'autostrada.	is in order trouble
Paolo	*Stia tranquilla,* signorina. Ho verificato tutto, anche i *freni* e le gomme.	relax brakes
Sig.na Meucci	E il motore?	
Paolo	Aveva bisogno di una *revisione,* ma ora va come un orologio. *Lo metta in moto* e sentirà.	tune-up turn it on
Sig.na Meucci	Bravo Paolo!	
Paolo	*Non dimentichi di fare il pieno.* Non credo che *ci sia* più di un litro di benzina nel *serbatoio.*	don't forget to fill it up there is gas tank
Sig.na Meucci	Lo farò al primo distributore. Quanto Le devo?	
Paolo	Vediamo...duecentomila lire in tutto.	
Sig.na Meucci	Ecco a Lei. Scusi, Paolo, qual è la strada più breve per arrivare all'autostrada?	

Paolo	Vada *diritto* per sette o ottocento metri, fino a via Matteotti. *Giri a destra* in via Matteotti e continui fino a quando vedrà l'indicazione «Autostrada».	straight head turn right
Sig.na Meucci	Quante ore ci vogliono, più o meno?	
Paolo	Ci vorranno sei o sette ore.	
Sig.na Meucci	Grazie mille, e arrivederLa.	
Paolo	Grazie a Lei. Buon viaggio, signorina...e *mi saluti* San Pietro.	say "hello" for me to

Comprensione

1. Che mestiere fa Paolo?
2. Perchè la signorina Meucci spera che la sua automobile sia a posto?
3. Quale parte della macchina aveva bisogno di una revisione?
4. Perchè Paolo ricorda alla signorina di fare il pieno?
5. Dove farà benzina la signorina?
6. Quanti soldi deve al meccanico?
7. Che cosa vuole sapere la signorina prima di partire?
8. Quando la signorina arriverà in via Matteotti, dovrà girare a destra o a sinistra per prendere l'autostrada?
9. Quante ore ci vogliono per arrivare a Roma?
10. Perchè il meccanico dice: —Mi saluti San Pietro?

Studio di parole

LA MACCHINA

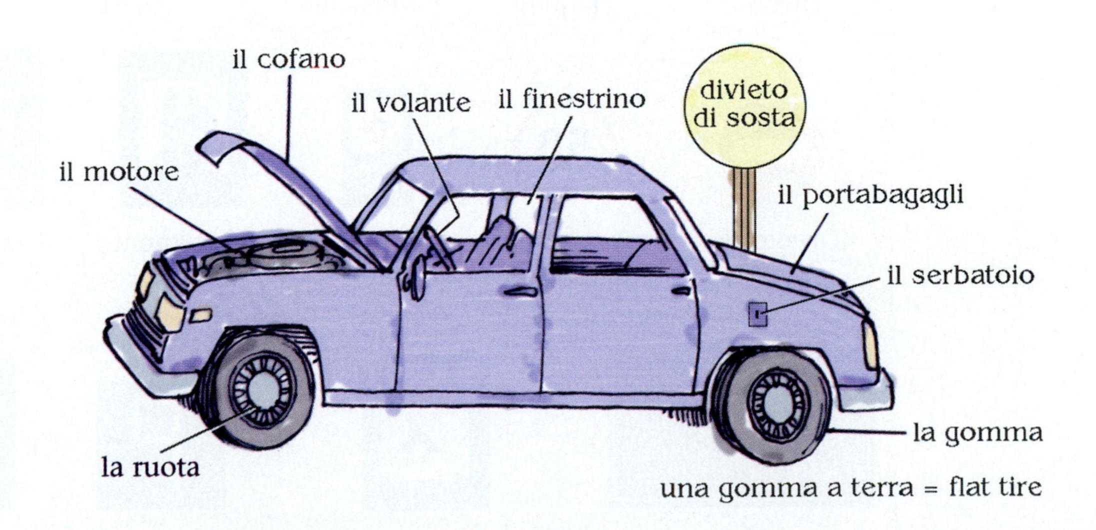

l'automobilista (*m. & f.*) driver
la patente driver's license
la targa license plate
la benzina gasoline
la benzina senza piombo unleaded gasoline
il distributore di benzina gasoline pump
fare il pieno to fill up
controllare (l'olio, l'acqua) to check (the oil, the water)
avere un guasto al motore to have a car breakdown
allacciare la cintura di sicurezza to fasten the safety belt
mettere in moto to start the car
guidare to drive
accelerare to accelerate
rallentare to slow down
superare to exceed
il limite di velocità speed limit
i freni brakes
frenare to brake
il vigile traffic policeman
il poliziotto policeman
la multa fine
il parcheggio parking, parking lot
parcheggiare to park
dare un passaggio to give a lift
un pedone pedestrian

la natura nature
l'aria air
l'ossigeno oxygen
respirare to breathe
l'ambiente environment
l'ambientalista (*m. & f.*) environmentalist
inquinare to pollute
l'inquinamento pollution

ALCUNI SEGNALI STRADALI

Lavori

Bambini

Pericolo

Pedoni

Stop!

Divieto di accesso

Limite massimo di velocita

Pronto soccorso

Rifornimento

Ospedale

Polizia stradale

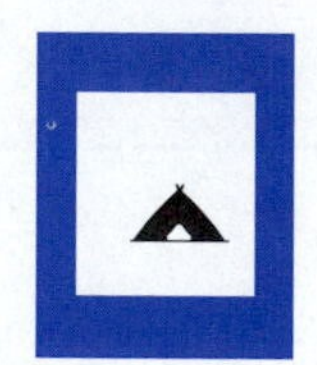
Campeggio

Parcheggio

Assistenza

A. 1. Qual è il documento indispensabile per guidare la macchina?
2. Quali parti della macchina domandiamo al meccanico di controllare?
3. Che cosa facciamo quando andiamo ad un distributore di benzina?
4. Che cosa ci dà un vigile se parcheggiamo dove c'è un divieto di sosta (*no parking*)?
5. Dove mettiamo le valigie quando facciamo un viaggio in auto?
6. Che cosa dobbiamo allacciare prima di mettere la macchina in moto?
7. Per fermare la macchina che cosa si deve fare?
8. Qual è il segnale stradale che si vede spesso nelle vicinanze (*in the vicinity*) di una scuola?
9. Se Lei è al volante e un pedone sta attraversando la strada, che cosa fa?
10. Se Lei o qualcuno con Lei si sente male, quale segnale spera di vedere?
11. Quando si fa il pieno, che benzina si deve mettere per migliorare la qualità dell'aria che respiriamo?

B. Domande personali.

1. Ha la macchina Lei? Che macchina Le piacerebbe avere?
2. Le piace guidare?
3. Ha mai superato il limite di velocità?
4. È mai stato(a) in un incidente di macchina? Era un incidente grave? È arrivata l'ambulanza?
5. Ha mai avuto una gomma a terra? Cos'ha fatto?
6. Da quando ha la patente?
7. È facile parcheggiare nella Sua città? Dove parcheggia: lungo la strada o in un parcheggio a pagamento?
8. C'è molto smog dove abita Lei? Secondo Lei, cosa dovrebbero fare gli automobilisti per diminuire l'inquinamento dell'aria?

Ascoltiamo!

Aria inquinata. *Two young men, who are also waiting for Paolo, the garage mechanic, have overheard Signorina Meucci's conversation with him. Fervent environmentalists, they react critically to her plans to drive to Rome. Listen to their comments, then answer the following questions.*

Comprensione

1. Chi sta facendo commenti sulla conversazione della signorina Meucci?
2. Secondo loro, come sono gli automobilisti? Responsabili o egoisti?
3. Per arrivare più presto a Roma, che mezzo di trasporto sarebbe consigliabile (*advisable*)?
4. Un biglietto ferroviario da Milano a Roma costerebbe di più o di meno di un pieno di benzina?
5. Che tipo di benzina potrebbe migliorare l'aria?
6. La benzina senza piombo è obbligatoria (*compulsory*) in Italia?
7. Oltre (*beside*) al treno, che altri mezzi di trasporto si potrebbero usare?

Dialogo

Immaginate, in gruppi di tre, di trovarvi per la strada con una gomma a terra, e di non avere una gomma di ricambio *(spare tire)*. Discutete cosa fare e come risolvere il vostro problema.

PUNTI GRAMMATICALI

I. Il Congiuntivo presente

Pierino, l'ottimista:
—Papà, spero che tu mi compri una Ferrari per il mio compleanno.

1. The subjunctive mood (**il congiuntivo**) expresses points of view and feelings, volition, uncertainty, possibility, and doubt. The indicative mood (**l'indicativo**) expresses facts, indicating what is objectively real. Compare the following sentences:

   (fact) L'acqua **è** inquinata.
   So che l'acqua **è** inquinata.

   (belief) **Credo** }
   (doubt) **Dubito** } che l'acqua **sia** inquinata.
   (fear) **Ho paura** }

   Unlike in English, the subjunctive is very common in Italian, in both speaking and writing.

2. The subjunctive is used mainly in subordinate clauses introduced by **che**, when the subjects of the main clause and the subordinate clause are different. If the subject is the same, the infinitive is used. Compare the following sentences:

Spero **che tu compri** una macchina.	*I hope you buy a car.*
Spero **di comprare** una macchina.	*I hope to buy a car.*

3. Here are the present subjunctive (**congiuntivo presente**) forms of regular verbs.

Main clause	Subordinate clause				
		ascoltare	**leggere**	**partire**	**finire**
	che io	ascolt**i**	legg**a**	part**a**	fin**isca**
Sperano	che tu	ascolt**i**	legg**a**	part**a**	fin**isca**
	che lui/lei	ascolt**i**	legg**a**	part**a**	fin**isca**
	che noi	ascolt**iamo**	legg**iamo**	part**iamo**	fin**iamo**
Vuole	che voi	ascolt**iate**	legg**iate**	part**iate**	fin**iate**
	che loro	ascolt**ino**	legg**ano**	part**ano**	fin**iscano**

   a. Note that the first, second, and third persons singular are identical. To avoid ambiguity, the subject pronouns are usually expressed.
   b. Verbs ending in **-care** and **-gare** insert an **h** between the stem and the endings: dimentic**hi**, dimentic**hiamo**, dimentic**hiate**, dimentic**hino**; pag**hi**, pag**hiamo**, pag**hiate**, pag**hino**.
   c. Verbs ending in **-iare** drop the **i** of the stem: **cominci**, **cominciamo**, **cominciate**, **comincino**.

4. The following verbs and expressions usually require the subjunctive in a dependent clause:

Verbs of volition	Verbs of opinion, doubt, uncertainty	Expressions of emotion
volere	credere	avere paura
desiderare	pensare	temere (*to fear*)
preferire	dubitare	essere contento/felice
sperare	non essere certo/sicuro	dispiacere

Impersonal expressions (implying a personal attitude)	
bisogna (*it is necessary*)	è importante
è necessario	è ora (*it is time*)
è (im)probabile	basta (*it is enough*)
è (im)possibile	pare/sembra (*it seems*)
è bene	può darsi (*it may be*)
è meglio	(è un) peccato (*too bad*)

Vogliamo che tu **impari** a guidare.	*We want you to learn how to drive.*
Credo che Antonio **cerchi** una macchina usata.	*I believe Antonio is looking for a used car.*
Sono felice che i miei genitori mi **capiscano.**	*I am happy that my parents understand me.*
Bisogna che tu **studi** di più.	*It is necessary that you study more.*
È probabile che domani **piova.**	*It is probable that tomorrow it will rain.*
Peccato che il televisore non **funzioni.**	*(It's) too bad that the TV set is not working.*

NOTE:

When no subject is expressed, the infinitive is used also after an impersonal expression.

È necessario **lavorare.**	*It is necessary to work.*
È ora di **partire.**	*It is time to leave.*

Pratica

A. Di' a un amico quello che tuo padre ti raccomanda di fare.

ESEMPIO verificare la macchina più spesso
Mio padre vuole che io verifichi la macchina più spesso.

1. comprare la benzina senza piombo 2. guidare più attentamente 3. non dimenticare di fare il pieno 4. controllare l'olio più spesso 5. fermarmi al segnale dello *Stop!!* 6. Parcheggiare con più attenzione 7. mettere in moto la macchina e frenare più dolcemente 8. non

superare i limiti di velocità **9.** lavare la macchina una volta alla settimana **10.** vendere il motorino

B. Di che cosa ha paura una madre per i suoi figli?

ESEMPIO studiare poco
Ha paura che studino poco.

1. non mangiare abbastanza **2.** spendere troppo **3.** divertirsi invece di studiare **4.** ricevere brutti voti **5.** ritornare tardi la sera **6.** frequentare cattive compagnie **7.** non finire nè il lavoro nè i compiti **8.** guidare troppo velocemente **9.** attraversare con il semaforo rosso **10.** prendere una multa

C. Il professore parla ad alcuni studenti che hanno poca voglia di studiare. Seguite l'esempio.

ESEMPIO È necessario leggere di più.
È necessario che leggiate di più.

1. È bene divertirsi. **2.** Basta studiare alcune ore al giorno. **3.** È importante riuscire. **4.** Non è possibile finire i compiti in un'ora. **5.** È necessario organizzare meglio il tempo. **6.** Bisogna alzarsi presto la mattina. **7.** È ora di prendere le cose seriamente.

D. Vostra sorella risponde alle vostre domande sui signori Zani, ma non è sempre sicura delle sue risposte. Completate le frasi scegliendo tra l'**indicativo** e il **congiuntivo.**

1. So che adesso i signori Zani _____ (abitare) a Torino. **2.** Mi pare che _____ (lavorare) tutti e due alla Fiat. **3.** Sembra che la moglie _____ (aspettare) un altro bambino. **4.** È certo che i due _____ (scrivere) spesso alla zia. **5.** Secondo la zia, è probabile che il mese prossimo i signori Zani _____ (ritornare) per alcuni giorni in questa città. **6.** Dice anche che _____ (essere) contenti del loro lavoro e che _____ (avere) una macchina nuova. **7.** Spero che i signori Zani non _____ (dimenticare) di venire a trovarci.

AGOSTO.
TUTTO CHIUSO
PER FERIE.

FIAT APERTA PER VOI.

E. **Oggi parliamo di politica.** Completate le seguenti frasi con i verbi in parentesi, scegliendo tra il **congiuntivo** e l'**infinito.**

1. I Verdi vogliono che il governo _____ (prendere) nuovi provvedimenti (*measures*) contro l'inquinamento dei fiumi. 2. Il governo preferisce _____ (occuparsi) di altri problemi. 3. È probabile che il valore della lira _____ (discendere). 4. Il primo ministro dice che bisogna _____ (aumentare) le tasse. 5. Alcuni politici credono che gli Italiani non _____ (capire) la gravità della situazione. 6. Gli Italiani non sono contenti di _____ (pagare) altre tasse. 7. Tutti sperano che la crisi del paese _____ (finire) presto.

II. Il Congiuntivo presente dei verbi irregolari

—Credo che il nostro professore abbia la testa fra le nuvole. È sempre così distratto!

Here is the present subjunctive of the most common irregular verbs:

andare:	**vada,** andiamo, **andiate, vadano**
avere:	**abbia,** abbiamo, **abbiate, ąbbiano**
bere:	**beva,** beviamo, **beviate, bẹvano**
dare:	**dia,** diamo, **diate, dịano**
dire:	**dica,** diciamo, **diciate, dịcano**
dovere:	**deva (debba),** dobbiamo, **dobbiate, dẹvano (dẹbbano)**
essere:	**sia,** siamo, **siate, sịano**
fare:	**faccia,** facciamo, **facciate, fạcciano**
potere:	**possa,** possiamo, **possiate, pọssano**
sapere:	**sappia,** sappiamo, **sappiate, sạppiano**
stare:	**stia,** stiamo, **stiate, stịano**
uscire:	**esca,** usciamo, **usciate, ẹscano**
venire:	**venga,** veniamo, **veniate, vẹngano**
volere:	**voglia,** vogliamo, **vogliate, vọgliano**

Spero che Lei **abbia** la patente.	*I hope you have a driver's license.*
Desidero che tu **stia** attento al semaforo.	*I would like you to pay attention to the traffic light.*
È ora che tutti **siano** responsabili.	*It is time that everybody be responsible.*
La mamma non vuole che **beviate** vino.	*Mother does not want you to drink wine.*
Dubita che **sappiamo** guidare bene.	*He (She) doubts that we know how to drive well.*
Non crede che **dicano** la verità.	*He (She) does not believe (that) they are telling the truth.*

Pratica

A. Esprimete la vostra opinione sulle seguenti affermazioni (*statements*) incominciando la frase con **Credo che** o **Non credo che.**

1. È difficile guidare in Italia. **2.** Gli Italiani bevono molto latte. **3.** Il governo vuole aumentare le tasse. **4.** L'inflazione può aumentare ancora. **5.** Le donne hanno gli stessi diritti (*rights*) degli uomini. **6.** Molti Europei vengono a passare le loro vacanze negli Stati Uniti. **7.** La benzina è più cara negli Stati Uniti che in Italia. **8.** Gli ambientalisti hanno ragione. **9.** Uno studente diligente esce tutte le sere.

B. Marta impone (*imposes*) i suoi desideri a tutti, fratelli e amici. Completate le frasi secondo l'esempio.

ESEMPIO Desidero che tu (stare)... —**Desidero che tu stia attento.** *o...*

1. Non voglio che voi (bere)... **2.** Desidero che tu non (uscire)... **3.** Voglio che tu (fare)... **4.** Spero che Lisa non (andare)... **5.** Non desidero che Roberto (venire)... **6.** Insisto che Marco e Pino (stare)... **7.** Non voglio che tu (dire)... **8.** Spero che tu non (volere)...

C. Marcello rifiuta (*refuses*) di fare quello che suo padre gli dice di fare. Due studenti fanno la parte di Marcello e del padre.

ESEMPIO fare l'ingegnere **Padre: Voglio che tu faccia l'ingegnere.**
Marcello: Mi dispiace, ma non voglio fare l'ingegnere!

1. vendere la Ferrari **2.** stare a casa la sera **3.** laurearti quest'anno **4.** lavorare nella ditta Scotti e Figli **5.** iscriverti a un corso per manager **6.** venire a lavorare con me

D. Commenti di un Americano di ritorno dall'Italia. Completate le frasi, scegliendo il presente dell'**indicativo** o del **congiuntivo.**

1. Ora sono sicuro che gli Italiani _____ (guidare) pericolosamente. **2.** Ho paura che gli stranieri _____ (avere) molti problemi quando _____ (guidare) in Italia. **3.** È certo che l'Italia _____ (essere) un bellissimo paese. **4.** Credo che la gente là _____ (sapere) vivere bene, malgrado l'inflazione. **5.** Peccato che gli alberghi italiani _____ (essere) così cari. **6.** Pare che l'economia italiana non _____ (andare) troppo bene. **7.** Spero almeno che il nuovo governo _____ (potere) controllare l'inflazione.

E. Il testamento del vecchio conte di Altavilla. Completate la storiella con le forme appropriate del **congiuntivo**.

Cara moglie,

Queste sono le mie ultime volontà. Spero che tu _______ (seguire) tutte le mie istruzioni. Desidero che tu _______ (dare) il tappeto del mio studio alla cameriera perchè mi ha sempre servito bene. Voglio che tu ______ (regalare) la mia collezione di francobolli al mio maggiordomo (*butler*) per la sua fedeltà e che tu ______ (pagare) al giardiniere la somma di un milione di lire.

Preferisco che il cugino Cosimo ______ (avere) il mio orologio d'oro (*gold*) e che le zie Rosa e Linda _______ (ricevere) tutte le bottiglie di vino della mia cantina. Spero che così loro ______ (consolarsi) della mia morte. Desidero che il mio castello, i miei mobili, le mie cinque macchine e tutte le mie proprietà ______ (andare) al mio autista che mi è stato amico fedele per quarant'anni. A te, cara moglie, che hai protestato per quarant'anni, lascio i miei occhiali e la mia dentiera (*denture*). Spero che tu ne ______ (essere) contenta.

Tuo Alfredo

III. L'imperativo (*Lei* e *Loro*)

—Guardi dove va! Freni! Stia attento!

1. The polite imperative forms of all verbs (regular and irregular) are identical to the *Lei* and *Loro* forms of the present subjunctive.

   a. Regular verbs:

parlare	scrivere	partire	finire
(Lei) parli!	scriva!	parta!	finisca!
(Loro) parlino!	scrivano!	partano!	finiscano!

b. Irregular verbs:

	Lei	**Loro**
andare:	vada!	vạdano!
avere:	abbia!	ạbbiano!
bere:	beva!	bẹvano!
dare:	dia!	dịano!
dire:	dica!	dịcano!
essere:	sia!	sịano!
fare:	faccia!	fạcciano!
sapere:	sappia!	sạppiano!
sedersi:	si sieda!	si siẹdano!
stare:	stia!	stịano!
uscire:	esca!	ẹscano!
venire:	venga!	vẹngano!
volere:	voglia!	vọgliano!

2. In the negative forms **non** precedes the verb.

Non vada! **Non** vadano!	*Don't go!*
Non lo ascolti! **Non** lo ascoltino!	*Don't listen to him!*

3. Direct object, indirect object, and reflexive pronouns—except **loro**—precede these imperative forms.

Mi dica!	*Tell me!*
Mi scusi!	*Excuse me!*
Si siedano!	*Sit down!*
Si accomodi!	*Make yourself comfortable!*
Mi facciano un favore!	*Do me a favor!*
Gli scriva una lettera!	*Write him a letter!*
Gliela scriva!	*Write it to him!*
Dica **loro** di entrare!	*Tell them to come in!*

Pratica

A. La signorina Renzi è andata dal medico, che le ha detto di fare le seguenti cose.

ESEMPIO accomodarsi **Si accomodi!**

1. stare a dieta **2.** mangiare molta verdura e frutta **3.** evitare (*avoid*) la carne **4.** non mangiare dolci **5.** fare lunghe camminate **6.** bere otto bicchieri d'acqua al giorno **7.** non bere caffè e non fumare **8.** andare in farmacia e comprare delle vitamine **9.** avere pazienza **10.** ritornare a vedermi tra due settimane

B. Ecco alcuni consigli che un istruttore (un'istruttrice) di guida (*driving instructor*) dà al signor e alla signora Fabbri. Usate la forma **Loro** dell'**imperativo** al posto della forma **voi**, e fate i cambiamenti necessari.

1. Non superate mai il limite di velocità! **2.** Fate sempre attenzione al semaforo! **3.** State sempre attenti al traffico e ai pedoni! **4.** Segnalate prima di girare a destra o a sinistra! **5.** Non parcheggiate dove c'è il divieto di parcheggio! **6.** Non sorpassate quando c'è il divieto di sorpasso! **7.** Non siate mai distratti quando siete al volante! **8.** Sopratutto, non bevete bevande alcooliche se dovete guidare!

C. Immaginate di essere il (la) professore(ssa) e dite a uno (una) studente(ssa) di fare o non fare le seguenti cose. Usate la forma **Lei** al posto della forma **tu**.

ESEMPIO Non arrivare in ritardo! **Non arrivi in ritardo!**

1. Sii paziente! **2.** Vieni alla lavagna! **3.** Fa' attenzione! **4.** Non parlare in inglese, parla in italiano! **5.** Non fare troppe domande! **6.** Ascolta attentamente! **7.** Non avere paura di sbagliare!

D. Rispondete con la forma **Lei** dell'**imperativo**, sostituendo le parole in corsivo con i pronomi appropriati.

ESEMPIO Posso darLe *un consiglio?* **—Sì, me lo dia pure!**

1. Posso seder*mi?* **2.** Posso aprire *le finestre?* **3.** Posso darle *il mio numero di telefono?* **4.** Posso portare *un amico alla festa?* **5.** Posso andare *a vedere la partita?* **6.** Posso dirLe *una cosa?* **7.** Posso guidare *la Sua macchina?* **8.** Posso fare *una passeggiata?* **9.** Posso parlarLe *del mio problema?* **10.** Posso presentarLe *i miei amici?*

E. Le seguenti persone dicono a... di fare alcune cose.

ESEMPIO La signorina Baetti chiede al cameriere di portarle un gelato alla vaniglia.
Cameriere, per favore mi porti un gelato alla vaniglia.

1. La signora Meucci domanda al meccanico di dirle la via più breve per arrivare all'autostrada. **2.** Il ministro dell'Ambiente dice al suo segretario, signor Cini, di telefonare al ministro dell'Interno e di chiedergli un appuntamento. **3.** Il dentista dice alla signorina Franchi di aprire la bocca e di non muoversi (*move*). **4.** Il dottor Aspirina dice alla sua infermiera di andare a prendere la cartella medica del signor Neri e di portargliela. **5.** Il poliziotto risponde alle turiste (che gli hanno domandato dove si trova San Pietro), di prendere il ponte di Sant'Angelo, di girare a sinistra e poi di andare diritto in Via della Conciliazione. **6.** Alcuni giornalisti chiedono all'onorevole X, deputato dei Verdi, di spiegare loro il programma del partito.

IV. Il congiuntivo passato

—Credo che la mamma ci abbia detto di non guardare la televisione.

1. The past subjunctive **(congiuntivo passato)** is a compound tense formed with the present subjunctive of the auxiliary verb **avere** or **essere** + the *past participle* of the main verb.

	studiare		partire	
Franco crede	che io **abbia**	studiato	che io **sia**	partito(a)
	che tu **abbia**		che tu **sia**	
	che lui/lei **abbia**		che lui/lei **sia**	
	che noi **abbiamo**		che noi **siamo**	partiti(e)
	che voi **abbiate**		che voi **siate**	
	che loro **abbiano**		che loro **siano**	

Spero che **abbiate ascoltato** il telegiornale. — *I hope you listened to the TV news.*

Non penso che i miei genitori **siano** già **arrivati.** — *I don't think my parents have arrived yet.*

2. The **congiuntivo passato** is used when the verb of the main clause requires the subjunctive, and the subordinate clause expresses an action that precedes the action of the main clause.

COMPARE:

Mi dispiace che zia Teresa non **venga** oggi. — *I'm sorry Aunt Teresa is not coming today.*

Mi dispiace che zia Teresa non **sia venuta** ieri. — *I'm sorry Aunt Teresa didn't come yesterday.*

Temo che non ti **piaccia** questo film.	*I'm afraid you will not like this movie.*
Temo che non ti **sia piaciuto** il film di domenica.	*I'm afraid you did not like last Sunday's movie.*

3. When the suject of the main verb and the subject of the subordinate verb are the same, the past infinitive is used.

   Past infinitive: **avere** or **essere** + *past participle* of the verb used

Spero di **aver(e) fatto** tutto.	*I hope I did everything.*
Siamo contenti di **essere ritornati.**	*We are happy we came back.*
Crede di **averla vista.**	*He thinks he saw her.*

Pratica

A. Alcuni amici commentano quello che è successo la settimana scorsa. Sostituite il **congiuntivo passato** al **congiuntivo presente.**

1. Spero che Giovanni trovi un buon posto. **2.** Siamo contenti che anche lui traslochi. **3.** Mi dispiace che Franca non venga con noi alla festa di domenica. **4.** È possibile che sia ammalata. **5.** Peccato che Marina e Lisa partano per la Svizzera. **6.** Non credo che i loro genitori siano contenti della loro partenza.

B. Il signor Fanti sta leggendo alcune notizie alla moglie e aggiunge ogni volta il suo commento.

ESEMPIO Il presidente ha fatto un discorso davanti al Senato. (Pare che...)
Pare che il presidente abbia fatto un discorso davanti al Senato.

1. I Verdi hanno presentato il loro programma per la protezione dell'ambiente. (Sono contento che...) **2.** Delle squadre di volontari (*volunteers*) hanno pulito le spiagge sporche (*dirty*). (Pare che...) **3.** Il ministro dell'Ambiente non è andato al Convegno (*conference*) mondiale di ecologia. (È un peccato che...) **4.** I rappresentanti dell'OPEC hanno deciso di aumentare il costo della benzina. (Mi dispiace che...) **5.** La fabbrica X ha inquinato l'acqua di una parte della città. (Pare che...) **6.** Alcuni leader dei Verdi sono partiti per studiare la situazione. (È bene che...)

C. Filippo e Gabriella stanno parlando di Antonio e Marcello. Riscrivete le frasi sostituendo il **congiuntivo passato** all'**indicativo**, quando necessario.

ESEMPIO Antonio è arrivato ieri. (Spero)
Spero che Antonio sia arrivato ieri.

Antonio è arrivato ieri. (Sono sicuro)
Sono sicuro che Antonio è arrivato ieri.

1. Antonio ha rinunciato (*gave up*) all'idea del motorino. (Marcello dice) **2.** Marcello ha dato lezioni di guida ad Antonio. (Pare) **3.** Ha già imparato a guidare? (Credi) **4.** Antonio non ha avuto abbastanza tempo libero per pensare alla macchina. (Penso) **5.** Ha lavorato troppo quest'anno. (È vero) **6.** Marcello ha cercato nel giornale occasioni di macchine usate. (Sembra) **7.** Non ha trovato niente d'interessante. (Dice)

D. Esprimete i sentimenti (*feelings*) di queste persone. Di due frasi formatene una usando **di + infinito** o **che + congiuntivo.**

ESEMPIO Paolo è contento. È guarito.
Paolo è contento di essere guarito.
Paolo è contento. Suo padre è guarito.
Paolo è contento che suo padre sia guarito.

1. Ho paura. Non ho capito la domanda. **2.** Gabriella è felice. Filippo ha vinto due milioni al Totocalcio. **3.** Mi dispiace. Ho dimenticato di telefonarti. **4.** Antonio è contento. È riuscito all'esame di guida. **5.** Sono felice. I miei genitori sono venuti a trovarmi. **6.** Mi dispiace. Tu non ti sei divertito.

E. **Che bugiardo(a)!** Vi piace esagerare quando parlate di voi, ma gli amici non vi credono. Completate le frasi usando il **congiuntivo presente** o **passato.**

ESEMPI

Domani partirò.../Non credo...
—Domani partirò per Roma.
—Non credo che tu parta per Roma.

Ieri ho visto.../Dubito...
—Ieri ho visto Michael Jackson.
—Dubito che tu l'abbia visto.

1. Il week-end scorso ho vinto.../È impossibile... **2.** Per Natale i miei zii mi regaleranno.../Ho paura... **3.** Il mese scorso sono andato(a).../Non credo... **4.** Due anni fa sono stato(a).../Non è possibile... **5.** L'estate prossima mio padre mi darà.../Non penso... **6.** L'estate scorsa ho guadagnato.../Non credo... **7.** Ho partecipato a una gara di... e ho ricevuto.../ Mi sembra impossibile... **8.** Fra qualche anno sarò.../ Dubito...

LETTURA

UNA LEZIONE DI *GUIDA*

driving

Marcello vuole che Antonio impari a guidare. Ora i due amici si trovano lungo una strada di molto traffico e il povero Antonio non sa come fare.

—*Insomma,* Tonino, è ora che tu guardi davanti a te! Frena, per piacere! Non hai visto che il semaforo è rosso e che i pedoni attraversano la strada?

for heaven's sake

—Hai ragione, mi dispiace.

—Dai, va' adesso! È possibile che tu non abbia visto che il semaforo è diventato verde? Va' diritto! Non girare a destra! Non vedi che quel cartello dice *«Senso vietato»?* Fammi un piacere: bisogna che tu stia attento!

wrong way

—Insomma, cosa vuoi che faccia!? Se desideri che io impari a guidare, devi *smettere* di criticarmi. Ho già il mal di testa. È meglio tornare a casa. È stata una pessima idea imparare a guidare durante le *ore di punta.* E poi...incomincio a dubitare che tu sia un buon istruttore. ...

stop

rush hours

—Sta' zitto, *somaro*. Ma che cosa hai fatto? Hai accelerato e non hai visto che c'era il segnale di limite di velocità! Spero almeno che nessun poliziotto ti abbia visto.

dumbbell

(Troppo tardi. I due sentono già la sirena: la macchina della polizia è dietro di loro.)

—Marcello, cosa faccio?

—Eh! Che cosa vuoi fare? Rallenta e fermati vicino al marciapiede.

L'agente si avvicina alla macchina e dice ad Antonio:

—Mi dia la patente, prego.

—Mi permetta di spiegarLe. ... (È Marcello che parla.)

—Preferisco che Lei stia zitto. *Quanto a* Lei, come si chiama?

as for

—Antonio Catalano.

Le cose *si complicano* e il povero Antonio deve *rinunciare* a guidare per il momento.

become complicated

give up

Che cosa fanno queste due agenti della polizia urbana?

Comprensione

1. Chi vuole che Antonio impari a guidare la macchina?
2. Com'è la strada dove Antonio sta guidando?
3. A che cosa deve fare attenzione Antonio?
4. Perchè non può girare a destra?
5. Perchè si lamenta?
6. Secondo Lei, è paziente o impaziente Marcello?
7. Perchè è difficile guidare durante le ore di punta?
8. Che cosa è necessario che faccia Antonio?
9. Che grave errore ha fatto?
10. Che cosa spera Marcello?
11. Perchè Antonio ha dovuto fermare la macchina vicino al marciapiede?
12. Che cosa vuole vedere il poliziotto?
13. Il poliziotto permette a Marcello di parlare? Cosa gli dice?
14. Che cosa succederà, secondo Lei? Perchè?

Domande personali

1. Ha già preso la patente Lei? L'ha ricevuta la prima volta che ha fatto l'esame?
2. Qual è l'età minima per prendere la patente nel Suo stato? Lei pensa che sia troppo presto prenderla a 15 anni?
3. Lei ha dovuto prendere molte lezioni di guida? Era paziente il Suo istruttore?
4. Con chi ha fatto pratica di guida? Dove?
5. Ha avuto paura le prime volte che ha guidato da solo(a) (*by yourself*)?
6. Quali accessori Le piacerebbe avere nella Sua macchina? Lo stereo? I C.D.? L'aria condizionata? Il telefonino? Il tetto apribile (*sun roof*)?

ATTIVITÀ SUPPLEMENTARI

A. **Il traffico.** In gruppi di quattro o cinque studenti, descrivete il problema del traffico in una città moderna e le sue conseguenze. Esprimete le vostre opinioni per migliorarne la situazione.

B. **Indicazioni** (*Directions*). In piccoli gruppi, spiegate come arrivare a casa vostra.

ESEMPIO Se volete venire a casa mia da San Francisco, prendete l'autostrada 280 che va verso San Jose. Uscite dall'autostrada all'uscita (*exit*) con l'indicazione «Los Altos». Prendete la seconda strada a sinistra. Andate diritto fino al primo semaforo, poi girate a destra in via Cascade. La prima strada a sinistra è la strada dove io abito.

C. **Dal meccanico.** Preparate una scenetta: uno fa la parte dell'automobilista che ha un guasto alla macchina e l'altro fa la parte del meccanico che cerca di trovare il problema. Dopo che la macchina è riparata, i due discutono il costo della riparazione.

D. Attività in gruppi di due. Immaginate di essere un agente di polizia e un automobilista. L'agente ha fermato l'automobilista per una o più infrazioni del Codice stradale (scegliete quale/quali nella tabella che segue) e si prepara a dargli una multa. L'automobilista si difende con delle scuse, per evitare di pagare la multa. Ci riesce?

Ecco le nuove maximulte

La tabella confronta le sanzioni previste dal nuovo Codice con quelle esistenti in precedenza per le infrazioni più frequenti, nel caso di pagamento entro i 60 giorni.

VIOLAZIONE	MULTE	
	Ieri	***Oggi***
Non rispettare la precedenza	*50.000*	*100.000*
Circolare contromano in curva o in caso di scarsa visibilità	*50.000*	*200.000**
Non segnalare il cambio di direzione	*12.500*	*50.000*
Sorpassare a destra	*penale*	*50.000*
Sorpassare in prossimità di curve o dossi	*penale*	*100.000*
Non rispettare la distanza di sicurezza	*25.000*	*50.000*
Non utilizzare le cinture di sicurezza (da parte di ogni passeggero)	*25.000 12.500***	*50.000*
Inversione di marcia pericolosa	*12.500*	*100.000*
Uso improprio del clacson	*12.500*	*50.000*
Attraversare o invertire il senso di marcia in autostrada	*25.000*	*penale*
Circolare sulla corsia d'emergenza	*25.000*	*500.000*
Non avere con sé patente o libretto	*12.500*	*50.000*
Guidare con la patente scaduta	*125.000*	*200.000*

** Oltre alla sospensione della patente. ** In città*

contromano *wrong way*
penale *penalty*
marcia *direction*
clacson *horn*
corsia *lane*
scaduta *expired*

E. **Segnali stradali.** Voi vi trovate in prossimità dei seguenti segnali stradali. Identificateli e dite cosa dovete fare.

F. **Come si dice in italiano?**

1. Mr. and Mrs. Smith arrived in Rome yesterday and rented a Fiat.
2. Mr. Smith's wife is afraid that he may have an accident and continually tells him: "Go slowly! Pay attention!"
3. "If you must complain so much (**così tanto**), next time I prefer that you stay home."
4. "Look, Jim, those beautiful fountains! That is Piazza Navona. Let's stop!"
5. "With this traffic? Let's first look for a parking lot."
6. So, Mr. and Mrs. Smith drove for one hour, and finally, they were able to park (their) car.
7. "Where are we now? I doubt that it is possible to walk to (**fino a**) Piazza Navona. It is too far!"
8. "Listen, Liz, since you have studied Italian, go into that coffee shop and ask how to go to Piazza Navona."
9. Mrs. Smith went in and asked the barman.
10. "Tell me how to find Piazza Navona, please."
11. "I am afraid you have to take the bus. Go straight for one hundred meters, and then turn to the left. You will see the bus stop (**la fermata dell'autobus**) at the street corner."

Vocabolario

Nomi

l'affermazione (*f.*)	*statement*
l'ambulanza	*ambulance*
l'angolo	*corner*
il bugiardo	*liar*
il commento	*comment*
la compagnia	*company*
il diritto	*right*
il divieto	*prohibition; no...*
l'eccesso	*excess*
la fedeltà	*loyalty*
il giardiniere	*gardener*
la gravità	*seriousness*
l'indicazione (*f.*)	*direction, sign*
l'infrazione (*f.*)	*violation*
il litro	*liter*
il marciapiede	*sidewalk*
la proprietà	*property*
la revisione	*tune-up*
la riparazione	*repair*
il semaforo	*traffic light*
il sentimento	*feeling*
la sirena	*siren*
l'uscita	*exit*
la vicinanza	*vicinity*
la volontà	*will*

Aggettivi

alcoolico	*alcoholic*
consigliabile	*advisable*
fedele	*faithful*
ferroviario	*railroad*
indispensabile	*indispensable*
irresponsabile	*irresponsible*
obbligatorio	*compulsory*
onorevole	*honorable (title for members of the Parliament)*
responsabile	*responsible*

Verbi

accomodarsi	*to make oneself comfortable*
consolarsi	*to console oneself*
difendersi	*to defend oneself*
esagerare	*to exaggerate*
evitare	*to avoid*
girare	*to turn*
muoversi	*to move*
permettere (*p.p.* permesso)	*to allow*
rinunciare(a)	*to renounce, give up*
risolvere (*p.p.* risolto)	*to solve*
rispettare	*to respect*
segnalare	*to signal*
smettere di (+ *inf.*)	*to stop (doing something)*
sorpassare	*to pass (a car)*
temere	*to fear*
verificare	*to verify*

Altre espressioni

adagio	*slowly*
a destra	*to the right*
a posto	*in order*
a sinistra	*to the left*
diritto	*straight ahead*
avere delle noie	*to have troubles*
basta (*impers.*)	*it is enough*
bisogna (*impers.*)	*it is necessary*
dolcemente	*gradually, gently*
(È un) peccato...	*too bad...*
fare la parte di	*to play the role of*
insomma	*for heaven's sake; in short*
invece di (+ *inf.*)	*instead of*
malgrado	*in spite of*
oltre a	*beside*
le ore di punta	*rush hours*
pare (*impers.*)	*it seems*
può darsi (*impers.*)	*it may be*
pure	*please do...* (entra pure! *please come in!)*
quanto a	*as for*
sembra (*impers.*)	*it seems*
seriamente	*seriously*
sopratutto	*above all*
Stia (Sta: *famil.*) tranquillo!	*Relax!*

Riciclaggio delle bottiglie di vetro.

PROBLEMI ECOLOGICI

Da alcuni anni gli Italiani si preoccupano della necessità di difendere l'ambiente. Il notevole *sviluppo* industriale e agricolo *minaccia* costantemente il paesaggio e le acque con i prodotti chimici. In tutta Italia l'alta densità della popolazione contribuisce all'inquinamento della natura, con i *rifiuti* e *detersivi* casalinghi e con l'uso delle macchine. L'*afflusso* dei turisti peggiora una situazione già seria. Per esempio, d'estate le coste del Lago di Garda (170.000 residenti) sono invase da circa due milioni di *villeggianti,* quasi tutti motorizzati; 25 milioni circa di innamorati del mare *affollano* i 7.000 chilometri di coste italiane.

development
threatens
waste/detergents
influx
vacationers
overcrowd

Un piccolo paese come l'Italia deve amministrare un patrimonio artistico che, per la sua ricchezza, non ha paragone al mondo. Purtroppo, l'inquinamento tipico del nostro secolo, e l'azione del tempo, *hanno annerito* e danneggiato buona parte dei suoi monumenti. Il Colosseo, per esempio, è in pericolo, situato com'è in mezzo alle vie di maggior traffico della capitale; il terreno su cui è costruito, *trema* ogni volta che passano i treni della metropolitana. Il *Comune* di Roma ha deciso di deviare il traffico ad altre strade, ma soltanto un progetto molto ambizioso potrebbe salvare il Colosseo: trasformare l'area dei Fori in parco archeologico. Per questo e altri progetti è necessario trovare «sponsor» privati, com'è *avvenuto* per la

blackened
shakes
Town Council
it happened

famosa Fontana di Trevi. In molte città il Centro Storico è inaccessibile alle macchine, che devono parcheggiare fuori delle *mura.* In altre città si parla di limitare i posti di parcheggio e di *vietare* la circolazione alle auto dei non-residenti.

city walls

prohibiting

Quanto ai fiumi, il governo *fa del suo meglio* per purificare le loro acque. Varie associazioni ambientaliste si sono formate per proteggere le acque del mare e organizzare la *pulizia* di diverse località costiere. Da qualche anno molti Italiani preferiscono scegliere le vacanze ecologiche e vanno alla *scoperta* della natura e dell'arte meno conosciuta con mezzi inoffensivi: a piedi, in bicicletta o *a cavallo.*

As for/does its best

cleaning

discovery

on horseback

Comprensione

Rispondete alle seguenti domande.

1. Che influenza hanno l'agricoltura e l'industria sull'ambiente?
2. Anche l'alta densità della popolazione minaccia la natura. Come?
3. I turisti contribuiscono a questa minaccia? Perchè?
4. L'aria inquinata che effetto produce sulle opere d'arte?
5. Perchè il Colosseo è in pericolo? Come si potrebbe salvarlo?
6. Che cosa hanno fatto molte città e cittadine per proteggere l'arte e l'ambiente?
7. Quali vacanze preferiscono molti Italiani preoccupati dell'ambiente?

Chi ha la precedenza (right of way): le mucche o la macchina?

19 MEZZI DI DIFFUSIONE

Antica biblioteca universitaria.

Punti di vista

Che novità ci sono?
I gemelli

Punti grammaticali

I Congiunzioni + congiuntivo
II L'imperfetto del congiuntivo
III Il trapassato del congiuntivo

Lettura

Soldi e amore

Pagina culturale

Mezzi di diffusione italiani

PUNTI DI VISTA

Alcuni quotidiani.

CHE NOVITÀ CI SONO?

La signora Ferri sorride, immersa nella lettura di una rivista, e non sente il marito che è entrato in salotto, di ritorno da un viaggio d'affari all'estero.

Signor Ferri	Ciao, cara, credevo che tu *fossi* in città.	were
Signora Ferri	Oh, Giulio! *Ben tornato!* Che hai di nuovo da raccontarmi?	welcome home!
Signor Ferri	Nessuna novità. Mentre ero in aereo ho letto *La Stampa* di Torino. Pare che il governo abbia proposto nuove tasse. E io credevo che *non avessero più niente* da tassare!	they had nothing else
Signora Ferri	Stavo leggendo la stessa cosa su *Panorama* di questa settimana. C'è anche un articolo interessante sui nostri uomini politici. *Figurati* che un disegnatore satirico ha fatto la caricatura dei più noti, disegnandoli come alcuni personaggi di Walt Disney. Ci sono anche *Topolino* e *Paperino*...	imagine; Micky Mouse/Donald Duck
Signor Ferri	Voglio leggere anch'io l'articolo... Speriamo che il telefono mi lasci in pace!	

Comprensione

1. Che cosa stava leggendo la signora Ferri quando è entrato il marito?
2. Era divertente o noioso quello che leggeva? Perchè lo sappiamo?
3. Dov'era stato suo marito?
4. Come lo ha salutato lei?
5. Che articolo aveva letto in aereo il signor Ferri? Su quale giornale?
6. Era deluso (*disappointed*)? Perchè?
7. Di chi parlava l'articolo in *Panorama?*

8. Perchè era satirico?
9. Il signor Ferri desiderava che la moglie gli raccontasse di più? Che cosa speravа di fare se non lo volevano al telefono?

Studio di parole

Oggi si gira... «Via col vento!»

IL GIORNALE

il (la) giornalista reporter
il quotidiano daily newspaper
il settimanale weekly
la rivista magazine
l'intervista interview
le notizie news
la pubblicità advertising
pubblicare to publish

IL LIBRO

l'autore, l'autrice author
lo scrittore, la scrittrice writer
il critico critic
la biografia biography
l'autobiografia autobiography
il saggio essay
la favola fable
il racconto short story
il romanzo novel
il romanzo { **rosa** love story / **giallo** mystery / **di fantascienza** science friction / **di avventure** }
la trama plot
il riassunto summary
l'editore, l'editrice publisher
il lettore, la lettrice reader
il personaggio character

LA TELEVISIONE

il televisore TV set
il canale channel
l'annunciatore, l'annunciatrice anchor person
il telegiornale TV news
il programma televisivo (*pl.* i programmi...) TV program
il teleromanzo soap opera
il telefilm
il documentario
in diretta live
accendere (*p.p.* acceso) to turn on
spegnere (*p.p.* spento) to turn off

IL CINEMA

filmare / **girare un film** } to make a movie
l'attore, l'attrice actor, actress
il (la) regista director
il produttore, la produttrice producer
lo spettatore, la spettatrice member of the audience/spectator
le didascalie subtitles
il cartone animato cartoon
a colori/in bianco e nero in color/in black and white
l'articolo (il libro, il film) tratta di... the article, (book, movie) deals with...
si tratta di... it is about...
fare la parte to play the role

Applicazione

A. 1. *Newsweek* e *Panorama* sono quotidiani o settimanali?
2. Che cosa fa un giornalista?
3. Chi era Steinbeck? Può nominare il titolo di qualche suo romanzo?
4. Chi esprime un giudizio (*critique*) su uno scrittore o attore?
5. Quale film si gira nel disegno di *«Studio di parole»?* Come si chiamavano gli attori e i personaggi principali del film?
6. Se andiamo a vedere un film straniero, che cosa ci aiuta a capirne il dialogo?
7. Che cosa presenta il telegiornale? Chi lo presenta?
8. Per quale ragione molte compagnie commerciali finanziano programmi televisivi?
9. Lei si è mai domandato(a) come passavano le serate d'inverno i nostri nonni, quando la televisione non esisteva ancora? Come?
10. Che cosa fa un editore?

B. Sapete dire il titolo originale in inglese dei seguenti film?

1. *La Bella e la Bestia* di Walt Disney
2. *Balla coi lupi* con Kevin Costner
3. *Il mio piede sinistro* con Daniel Day Lewis
4. *Harry, ti presento Sally* con Billy Cristal
5. *Qualcuno volò sul nido del cuculo* con Jack Nicholson
6. *Il Principe delle maree* con Barbra Streisand
7. *Il silenzio degli innocenti* con Jodie Foster
8. *Il Padre della sposa* con Steve Martin
9. *Il mio piccolo genio* con Jodie Foster
10. *Capitan Uncino* con Robin William e Dustin Hoffman

C. **Domande personali.**

1. Quale giornale o rivista legge Lei di solito? Perchè? Quali articoli preferisce leggere? Di politica, economia, cinema, musica, sport..., o letteratura (*literature*)?
2. Che articolo o che libro ha letto Lei recentemente? Di chi era? Come l'ha trovato?
3. Ha mai pensato Lei di avere talento come scrittore (scrittrice)? Ha scritto qualcosa? Cosa?
4. Che programmi Le piace guardare alla TV? Che cosa guardava quand'era ragazzino(a)?
5. Le piaceva seguire le avventure di Topolino e Paperino? Perchè?
6. Immagini di essere un regista e di voler girare un film. Quale soggetto e quali attori sceglierebbe?

I gemelli (*The twins*). *Mr. and Mrs. Ferri are looking at their TV guide and trying to decide what to watch this evening. Listen to their conversation as they consider the choices, then answer the related questions.*

Comprensione

1. Per quale ragione il signor Ferri ha letto la guida della TV?
2. Che cosa presentava il canale UNO?
3. Desideravano vederlo i Ferri? Perchè? Che cosa preferivano?
4. Che scelta avevano? Chi era l'attrice del film *Ieri, oggi, domani?* Perchè non voleva vederlo la signora?
5. Quale dei due film hanno scelto? Che cosa significa «fratelli gemelli»? Quali attori fanno la parte dei gemelli?
6. Perchè sono strani i due personaggi? Chi fa la parte dell'imbroglione (*swindler*)?
7. Ha visto Lei questo film? Se sì, come l'ha trovato?

Dialogo

In gruppi di due, date un'occhiata (*take a look*) ai programmi di questa sera (sotto). Quale di questi programmi vorreste vedere? Avete un solo televisore e gusti (*tastes*) diversi. Discutete tra di voi e decidete.

20,00 Telegiornale Uno.

20,25 Telegiornale Uno sport

20,40 FILM–Western
"Un dollaro d'onore" (USA '59)
Con John Wayne, Dean Martin.
Uno sceriffo fa rispettare la legge a una banda di cowboys in una cittadina del West.
CAPOLAVORO DEL GENERE.

22,35 Telegiornale Uno.

22,50 Musicale. "Omaggio a Rossini"
Dal Teatro "Rossini" di Pesaro.

0,10 Oggi al Parlamento.

19,00 Quiz. "La ruota della fortuna."
Con Mike

20,00 Tg 5 – Sera.

20,30 FILM–Commedia
"Baby Boom" (USA '87)
Con Diane Keaton.
J.C.W. è consulente finanziaria in una importante società e sta facendo una brillante carriera. Un giorno riceve un'eredità da un cugino morto in un incidente stradale: una bambina di un anno. Incomincia per la donna un periodo infernale che la obbliga a cambiare vita.

22,15 Musicale. "Anteprima Michael Jackson"

23,15 Tg 5 – Notte

23,30 Telefilm – Murphy Brown.

PUNTI GRAMMATICALI

I. Congiunzioni + congiuntivo

—Ti do i soldi del cinema, purchè tu lavi la macchina.

1. The following conjunctions *must* be followed by the subjunctive:

affinchè, perchè	*so that*
benchè, per quanto, sebbene	*although*
a meno che...(non)	*unless*
prima che	*before*
purchè	*provided that*
senza che	*without*

Scrivimi una nota **affinchè** me ne **ricordi.**	*Write me a note so that I will remember it.*
Benchè mio zio **sia** ricco, è molto avaro.	*Although my uncle is rich, he is very stingy.*
Compra i biglietti **a meno che** Paolo (non) li **abbia** già **comprati.**	*Buy the tickets unless Paolo has already bought them.*
Ritorniamo a casa **prima che piova.**	*Let's go home before it rains.*
Andranno alla spiaggia **purchè faccia** bel tempo.	*They'll go to the beach, provided that the weather is fine.*

2. The prepositions **per**, **prima di**, and **senza** + *infinitive* are used instead of **affinchè (perchè)**, **prima che**, and **senza che** when the subject of the two clauses is the same. Compare:

Lavoro **per pagarmi** gli studi.	*I work (in order) to pay my studies.*
Lavoro **perchè tu possa** continuare gli studi.	*I work so that you'll be able to continue your studies.*

Telefonami **prima di uscire.**	*Phone me before going out.*
Telefonami **prima che io esca.**	*Phone me before I go out.*
Partono **senza salutarci.**	*They leave without saying good-bye to us.*
Partono **senza che noi** li **salutiamo.**	*They leave without our saying good-bye to them.*

Pratica

A. **Domanda e risposta.** Conversazione fra due fratelli. Seguite l'esempio.

a. Tu farai le seguenti cose benchè...

ESEMPIO —Pulirai la stanza?/essere stanco(a)
—La pulirò benchè sia stanco(a).

1. Andrai dal dentista?/avere paura **2.** Farai la spesa?/non sentirmi bene **3.** Andrai anche dai nonni?/nevicare **4.** Mi aiuterai?/non essere sicuro(a) di poterlo fare **5.** Ritornerai presto?/dovere fare molte cose **6.** Comprerai la macchina fotografica?/costare molto

b. Tu farai le seguenti cose prima che...

ESEMPIO —Quando ti laureerai?/essere troppo tardi
—Mi laureerò prima che sia troppo tardi.

1. Quando partirai per il lavoro?/la mamma, alzarsi **2.** Quando andrai alla posta?/esserci troppa gente **3.** Quando ritornerai?/tu, uscire **4.** Quando cenerai?/gli altri, ritornare **5.** Quando studierai?/voi, fratelli, accendere la televisione **6.** Quando leggerai l'articolo sul regista Fellini?/tu, leggerlo

B. Unite le due frasi, usando la congiunzione tra parentesi.

ESEMPIO Paolo esce stasera.. È malato. (benchè) **Paolo esce stasera benchè sia malato.**

1. Ti presto diecimila lire. Me le restituisci. (purchè) **2.** Ti vedrò al caffè. Sei già partito. (a meno che) **3.** Luigino aiuta in casa. La mamma glielo chiede. (senza che) **4.** Il padre lavora. I figli possono andare all'università. (perchè) **5.** Leggo ancora. È già mezzanotte. (sebbene) **6.** Andrò a vedere il film *Il nuovo cinema Paradiso* di Giuseppe Tornatore. L'ho già visto due volte. (benchè) **7.** Il professore parla ad alta voce. Tutti lo capiscono. (affinchè)

C. Riscrivete il paragrafo sostituendo **se + l'indicativo** con **purchè + il congiuntivo.**

Il regista Pellini vuol girare un film se riesce a trovare un produttore. Desidera offrire la parte principale all'attrice Sonia Sorel se non deve pagarla troppo. Per la parte maschile vuole invitare l'attore americano Neal Puman se è libero. Tutto va bene e si gira il film, ma un bel giorno i due attori principali litigano. Il povero regista finirà il film se i due attori faranno la pace.

D. Povero Beppe! Riscrivete il paragrafo sostituendo **anche se + l'indicativo** con **benchè (per quanto, sebbene) + il congiuntivo.**

Questa mattina Beppe deve andare al lavoro anche se la macchina non funziona. Decide di andare a piedi anche se l'ufficio è lontano. Arriva in ritardo e il suo capoufficio lo rimprovera anche se lui ha dato una buona giustificazione. Deve scrivere molte lettere a macchina anche se non sa scrivere a macchina velocemente. Deve portare molti pacchi (*parcels*) alla posta anche se non si sente bene. Deve fare molte telefonate anche se ha mal di testa. La sera deve portare i bambini al cinema anche se ha lavorato tutto il giorno ed è stanco.

E. Intervista. Immaginate di essere un(a) giornalista e di fare le seguenti domande ad un'attrice straniera che ha appena finito di girare un film in Italia. Completate le domande e rispondete in modo personale.

G. Signora, quando pensa (*to leave*) __________ Roma?
A. ...
G. Le dispiace (*that the movie is already finished*) __________?
A. ...
G. Desidera (*to work again*) __________ con il regista Pellini?
A. ...
G. Partirà (*without visiting*) __________ altre città italiane?
A. ...
G. (*Before arriving*) __________ in Italia, come immaginava Lei questo paese?
A. ...
G. Suo marito verrà a raggiungerLa (*to join you*) (*before you leave*) __________?
A. ...
G. Grazie, signora, e i miei migliori auguri di buon viaggio!
A. ...

II. L'imperfetto del congiuntivo

Il signor Placido sperava che quelle vacanze non finissero più!

1. The imperfect subjunctive (**imperfetto del congiuntivo**) is formed by adding the endings **-ssi, -ssi, -sse, -ssimo, -ste, -ssero** to the infinitive form of the verb after dropping **-re.**

   che io **parlassi** = *that I spoke, might speak, would speak*

		parlare	leggere	dormire
	che io	parla**ssi**	legge**ssi**	dormi**ssi**
Volevano	che tu	parla**ssi**	legge**ssi**	dormi**ssi**
	che lui/lei	parla**sse**	legge**sse**	dormi**sse**
	che noi	parla**ssimo**	legge**ssimo**	dormi**ssimo**
Era bene	che voi	parla**ste**	legge**ste**	dormi**ste**
	che loro	parla**ssero**	legge**ssero**	dormi**ssero**

2. The imperfect subjunctive is governed by the same verbs and conjunctions that govern the present and present perfect subjunctive. It expresses an action that is *simultaneous* or *subsequent* to that of the main clause and is used when the verb of the main clause is in a *past tense* or in the *conditional.*

Pia desiderava che il suo ragazzo le **scrivesse.**	*Pia wanted her boyfriend to write to her.*
Le due autrici speravano che molti **comprassero** il loro libro.	*The two authors were hoping that many would buy their book.*
È uscito benchè **piovesse.**	*He went out although it was raining.*
Fece dei sacrifici perchè suo figlio **andasse** all'università.	*He made sacrifices so that his son might go to the university.*
Vorrei che tu mi **ascoltassi.**	*I would like you to listen to me.*
Speravo che tu **pagassi** meno tasse.	*I was hoping you would pay fewer taxes.*
Volevamo che i nostri figli **andassero** d'accordo.	*We wanted our children to get along.*

   The following verbs are irregular in the imperfect subjunctive:

essere:	**fossi, fossi, fosse, fossimo, foste, fossero**
dare:	**dessi, dessi, desse, dessimo, deste, dessero**
stare:	**stessi, stessi, stesse, stessimo, steste, stessero**
fare:	**facessi, facessi, facesse, facessimo, faceste, facessero**
dire:	**dicessi, dicessi, dicesse, dicessimo, diceste, dicessero**
bere:	**bevessi, bevessi, bevesse, bevessimo, beveste, bevessero**

Mi piacerebbe che tu **stessi** a casa più spesso.	*I would like (for) you to stay home more often.*
Sarebbe bene che lui **bevesse** meno.	*It would be good if he drank less.*
Lesse il racconto sebbene **fosse** mezzanotte.	*He read the short story although it was midnight.*

Pratica

A. Mettete le frasi **al passato**, secondo l'esempio.

ESEMPIO Ho paura che lui sia malato. **Avevo paura che lui fosse malato.**

1. Peccato che il computer non funzioni. **2.** Ho paura che la farmacia sia chiusa. **3.** È una bella giornata benchè faccia freddo. **4.** È necessario che tu vada in biblioteca. **5.** Devo comprare un televisore, sebbene costi molto. **6.** È bene che non beviamo troppo. **7.** Credo che lui non stia bene. **8.** Il padre si sacrifica affinchè i figli si istruiscano. **9.** Sono contenta che i miei genitori siano d'accordo (*agree*) con me. **10.** Penso che ci vogliano tre ore per finire questo lavoro.

B. Incominciate ogni frase con **Luisa sperava che...**, e fate i cambiamenti necessari.

ESEMPIO qualcuno invitarla ad un recital di poesie
—Luisa sperara che qualcuno l'invitasse ad un recital di poesie.

1. il suo professore prestarle il settimanale *Oggi*. **2.** esserci degli articoli interessanti **3.** sua madre non avere bisogno di lei in casa **4.** la sua amica dare una festa **5.** il vestito rosso andarle bene **6.** qualcuno dirle «sei bella!» **7.** il professor Bini correggerle il saggio sul cinema italiano **8.** le tasse universitarie (*tuition*) essere meno costose **9.** il professore essere di buon umore (*in a good mood*) e dare a tutti un bel voto **10.** lei e la sua nuova compagna andare d'accordo (*to get along*)

C. Se tu potessi (*If you could*) cambiare le cose, cosa vorresti cambiare?

ESEMPIO il week-end durare... **Vorrei che il week-end durasse tre giorni.** (o...)

1. la vita essere... **2.** i professori dare... **3.** mio padre capire... **4.** gli amici dire... **5.** mia sorella non leggere... **6.** i corsi finire... **7.** la televisione eliminare... **8.** i film essere...

D. Che cosa vorresti dalla vita? Incomincia con **Vorrei che...** Ogni studente esprime un desiderio.

III. Il trapassato del congiuntivo

—Hai visto? Un nuovo romanzo di Romani!
—E io credevo che non avesse più scritto niente dopo il divorzio!

1. The pluperfect subjunctive (**trapassato del congiuntivo**) is a compound tense. It is formed with the imperfect subjunctive of **avere** or **essere** + the *past participle* of the main verb.

		dormire		partire	
Non era vero	che io	avessi	dormito	fossi	partito(a)
	che tu	avessi		fossi	
	che lui/lei	avesse		fosse	
	che noi	avessimo		fossimo	partiti(e)
	che voi	aveste		foste	
	che loro	avessero		fossero	

2. The pluperfect subjunctive, as well as the imperfect subjunctive, is used when the verb of the main clause is in a *past tense* or in the *conditional*. However, the pluperfect subjunctive expresses an action that occurred *prior* to the action of the main clause.

Non sapevo che Marco Polo **avesse scritto** *Il Milione* in prigione. — *I did not know Marco Polo had written* Il Milione *in prison.*

Benchè i Fiorentini l'avessero **mandato** in esilio, Dante continuò ad amare Firenze. — *Although the Florentines had sent him into exile, Dante continued to love Florence.*

A. Luisa è con Gabriella e Filippo e sta facendo loro una serie di domande. Completate secondo l'esempio.

ESEMPIO Sapete se Antonio ha già preso la patente? Sì? Credevo che non l'__avesse__ ancora __presa__.

1. Gabriella, hai telefonato a Liliana? No? Speravo che tu le _____ già _____. 2. Come mai Liliana non è ancora ritornata a casa? Pensavo che a quest'ora _____ già _____. 3. Sapete se ha già ricevuto la lettera dagli Stati Uniti? No? Come mai? Speravo che l'_____ già _____. 4. Filippo, sai se Marcello ha già trovato una macchinetta per Antonio? Sì? Credevo che non l'_____ ancora _____. 5. Come? Non avete ancora visto *Mediterraneo,* il film che ha ricevuto un Oscar nel '92? Mi pareva che l'_____ già _____. 6. Vi siete già abbonati alla rivista *L'Europeo?* No? Credevo che _____ qualche mese fa.

B. **Pensieri di un compagno di studi.** Completate mettendo l'infinito al **congiuntivo passato** o **trapassato**, secondo il caso.

1. Dubito che Paolo (finire) _____ gli studi l'anno scorso. 2. Pensavo che Marco (andare) _____ alla biblioteca ieri. 3. È un peccato che Fulvio non (venire) _____ al cinema con me domenica scorsa. 4. Sarebbe stato meglio che (accompagnarmi) _____: mi sarei divertito di più. 5. Mi dispiace che suo fratello (rompersi) _____ una gamba quando è andato a sciare. 6. Avevo paura che (rompersi) _____ anche un braccio.

LETTURA

SOLDI E AMORE

Ieri Liliana ha ricevuto la visita di Gabriella, che non vedeva da molto tempo, e le ha domandato se era felice.

—Sì, Filippo e io *ci vogliamo molto bene.* Certo che la vita oggi è molto cara ed i soldi non *bastano* mai.

we love each other very much
are (never) enough

—*Come mai?* Credevo che anche tu lavorassi e che ci fossero due stipendi in famiglia.

How come?

—Sì, è vero. Sono riuscita a trovare un lavoro presso la ditta O, che mi permetterà di continuare i miei studi in psicologia.

—Sono molto contenta che tu l'abbia trovato, ma è difficile pensare che con due stipendi voi abbiate dei problemi economici.

—Il fatto è che Filippo ed io desideriamo risparmiare perchè vorremmo comprare un appartamentino. Purtroppo non siamo d'accordo *per quanto riguarda* il risparmio. Da quando ci siamo sposati, io sono diventata più economa, e lui mi sembra che sia diventato più *spendaccione.* Devo sempre raccomandargli di stare

about
spendthrift

Lo scrittore Alberto Moravia (1907–1990), autore di molti romanzi, fra cui "La Ciociara," che ha ispirato il film "Two Women."

attento a non spendere.

—Credo che molte coppie litighino *a causa dei* soldi. Il tuo problema mi fa pensare a un racconto di Moravia* *il cui* titolo è *appunto «Sciupone»*. In questa storia il marito era economo e la moglie pensava invece che fosse avaro. Siccome lui l'amava molto, *bastava* che lei gli dicesse che era avaro perchè lui pagasse senza protestare. Sperava che un giorno sua moglie capisse che lui era, invece, generoso.

because of

whose/precisely/"spendthrift"

it was enough

—E com'è finito il racconto?

—È successo che lui è andato *in rovina* e che la moglie l'ha lasciato dicendo a tutti che lui era uno spendaccione.

bankrupt

—*Poverino!* È una storia molto triste. Per fortuna, il nostro caso è differente.

Poor man

Compensione

1. Si vedono spesso Liliana e Gabriella?
2. Benchè Gabriella e Filippo si vogliano molto bene, c'è qualcosa che li preoccupa. Cos'è?
3. Perchè, secondo Liliana, è difficile pensare che Gabriella abbia problemi economici?
4. Per quale ragione i due sposi vogliono risparmiare?
5. Sono d'accordo in tutto o c'è un punto su cui hanno delle discussioni?
6. C'è stato un cambiamento (*change*) in Filippo e Gabriella dopo il loro matrimonio?
7. Che cosa vorrebbe Gabriella che suo marito facesse?
8. Quale scrittore tratta il problema dei soldi? In quale racconto?
9. Era avaro o spendaccione il protagonista del racconto?
10. Perchè pagava senza protestare?
11. È finito bene il racconto? Perchè?
12. Qual è il commento di Gabriella alla storia che Liliana le ha raccontato?

*Alberto Moravia is one of the foremost Italian writers of our century. In his novels and short stories, he depicts contemporary Rome and the struggles and faults of its people.

Domande personali

1. Si considera uno(a) spendaccione(a) o una persona economa Lei?
2. In che cosa spende molto?
3. Supponiamo (*Let's suppose*) che Lei abbia uno zio ricchissimo: alla sua morte le lascia un milione di dollari purchè Lei li spenda in un mese. Cosa ne farebbe?
4. Supponiamo che Lei non abbia bisogno di lavorare per vivere: come passerebbe il Suo tempo?
5. Ha mai letto Lei l'opera (*work*) di un autore italiano? Se sì, quale? In italiano o in inglese?
6. Lei pensa che le discussioni di soldi in famiglia siano rare?
7. Le succede qualche volta di discutere di soldi con uno dei Suoi genitori (o con il Suo ragazzo/la Sua ragazza)? Perchè?

ATTIVITÀ SUPPLEMENTARI

A. **Telegiornale.** Immaginate di essere telegiornalisti. In piccoli gruppi preparate le notizie più importanti del giorno (politica nazionale e internazionale, fatti di cronaca (*news items*) della vostra città, tempo, sport), e organizzatevi per presentarle come se foste alla televisione.

B. **Giornalino dell'università.** In collaborazione con altri studenti scrivete articoletti di poche righe che trattino di notizie, critica e pubblicità locali da mandare al vostro giornale.

C. **Film.** Lei ha visto un film che Le è piaciuto. Ne faccia un breve riassunto. (Era americano o straniero? Qual era il titolo? Chi ne erano il regista e gli attori principali?) Descriva brevemente la trama, la fine e la Sua reazione.

D. **Intervista.** Immaginate di intervistare un attore (un' attrice) italiano(a) che è andato(a) a Hollywood per girare un film. (Titolo del film; nome del regista e di altri attori; dove si gira; impressioni sui compagni di lavoro, sulla vita a Hollywood e sull'America in generale). Collaborate in gruppi di tre o quattro.

E. **Fumetti.** Ecco una storiella a fumetti (*a comic strip*). Riempite (*Fill in*) ogni fumetto (*bubble*) secondo il dialogo.

Dialogo: Il Signor Speranza fa una dichiarazione d'amore alla signorina Prudenza. La signorina gli fa diverse domande su:

Fumetto numero 1: la sua famiglia
Fumetto numero 2: i suoi passatempi
Fumetto numero 3: la sua posizione sociale
Fumetto numero 4: le sue idee politiche
Fumetto numero 5: Il signor Speranza, stanco di tutte le domande, manda al diavolo la signorina Prudenza.
Fumetto numero 6: Cosa dirà la signorina Prudenza?

F. Scrivete una breve autobiografia o un breve racconto.

G. Discussione collettiva. Esprimete la vostra opinione sui seguenti punti:

1. È bene o male che i bambini passino ore e ore davanti alla televisione? Perchè?
2. Quale crede Lei che sia migliore per l'immaginazione di un bambino: un buon libro o un programma televisivo? Perchè?
3. Suggerite alcuni libri o programmi televisivi che potrebbero essere utili alla formazione dei bambini.

H. Come si dice in italiano?

(Here is a letter from Veronica to her friend Lina.)

Dear Lina,

How are you? Since I saw you, a terrible thing happened. I am very worried because Pio has quit school. Although he is a good student and has always received good grades, he decided to (**di**) work because he needed money. Pio is a spendthrift and was afraid that his father would not lend him money because he is stingy. Pio's best friend, Jim, who is a representative (**rappresentante**) for (**di**) a publisher, wanted Pio to work for his company. According to Jim, it is a field (**campo**) in which Pio could earn a lot of money. It is possible that his friend is right, but I think it is better for Pio to go back to school. I would like him to understand that without an education (**istruzione**), it is difficult to get (**ottenere**) a good job. I hope that you give me some advice and answer me as soon as possible.

Love (**con affetto**),
Veronica

Vocabolario

Nomi

la caricatura	*caricature*
la coppia	*couple*
il disegnatore, la disegnatrice	*designer*
il divorzio	*divorce*
il fumetto	*bubble*
i fumetti	*comic strips*
i gemelli	*twins*
la giustificazione	*justification*
la letteratura	*literature*
i mezzi di diffusione	*mass-media*
la parte	*role*
la reazione	*reaction*
il sacrificio	*sacrifice*
il salotto	*living room*
la serie	*series, succession*
il talento	*talent*
il titolo	*title*

Aggettivi

comico	*funny*
costoso	*expensive*
deluso	*disappointed*
economo	*thrifty*
imbroglione	*cheater*
innocente	*innocent*
intitolato	*entitled*
noto	*renowned*
originale	*original*
principale	*main*
recente	*recent*
satirico	*satirical*
spendaccione	*spendthrift*

Verbi

abbonarsi	*to subscribe*
bastare	*to suffice; to be enough*
disegnare	*to draw*
domandarsi	*to wonder*
durare	*to last*
eliminare	*to eliminate*
finanziare	*to finance*
istruirsi	*to educate oneself*
proporre (*p.p.* proposto)	*to propose*
rimproverare	*to scold*
sacrificarsi	*to sacrifice*
tassare	*to tax*
trattarsi	*to be about*
volersi bene	*to love each other*

Altre espressioni

ad alta voce	*aloud*
affinchè (perchè) (+*subj.*)	*so that*
a meno che (+*subj.*)	*unless*
andare d'accordo	*to get along*
appunto	*precisely*
benchè (+ *subj.*)	*although*
Ben tornato!	*Welcome back!*
Come?	*What?*
dare un'occhiata	*to take a look*
di buon umore	*in a good mood*
essere d'accordo	*to agree*
fare la pace	*to make up*
Figurati!	*Imagine!*
lasciare in pace	*to leave alone*
mandare al diavolo	*to send to the devil*
per fortuna	*luckily*
per quanto (+*subj.*)	*although*
per quanto riguarda	*as for*
più niente	*nothing else*
prima che (+ *subj.*)	*before*
purchè (+ *subj.*)	*provided that*
sebbene (+*subj.*)	*although*
senza che (+*subj.*)	*without*
le tasse universitarie	*tuition*

Copertine di due settimanali.

MEZZI DI DIFFUSIONE ITALIANI

La *stampa*, la radio, la televisione e il cinema sono i fattori che, con la scuola, hanno maggiormente influenzato il processo di unificazione della lingua italiana. — press

I quotidiani e i settimanali entrano sempre più spesso nelle case e nelle scuole. Sebbene quasi ogni città abbia il suo giornale locale, i quotidiani più letti del paese sono *La Repubblica, Il Corriere della Sera, Il Messaggero* e *La Stampa.* Anche i partiti politici hanno il loro giornale: i socialisti, per esempio, sono fedeli lettori dell'*Avanti. Quanto ai* tifosi dello sport, leggono la *Gazzetta delio Sport.* Per la gente che preferisce una maggior varietà di articoli esiste un'ampia scelta di riviste (settimanali illustrati). Fra le più popolari sono *Panorama, Epoca, L'Espresso, L'Europeo e Oggi.* Tra le riviste femminili più lette sono *Grazia, La Donna moderna* e *Più bella.* — *Quanto ai*: as for the

La sera è il telegiornale che entra in tutte le famiglie italiane e che *riassume* per i più pigri le notizie del giorno. In questi ultimi vent'anni la radiotelevisione di stato (RAI–TV) ha visto la nascita di molte stazioni teleradio private. Dopo diversi anni di monopolio dello stato, è nata ufficialmente in Italia anche la televisione commerciale, alla maniera americana. La differenza fra i due paesi è che gli *utenti* italiani sono *tassati* annualmente dallo stato per un servizio pubblico che non è più esclusivamente dello stato. I telespettatori italiani hanno oggi a loro disposizione un'ampia scelta di film, *spettacoli* e programmi d'informazione che sono offerti, *oltre che* dalle *reti* dello stato, da canali privati, nazionali o locali, e da canali esteri (Montecarlo, Svizzera).

summarizes
consumers
taxed
shows
besides/networks

A causa della popolarità della TV, l'industria cinematografica è in crisi. I grandi maestri del neorealismo del *dopoguerra,* De Sica, Rossellini e Visconti, sono morti. Dopo di loro, due *giganti* hanno dominato la scena cinematografica italiana; Antonioni e Fellini, sempre pronti a sperimentare nuovi *temi* e nuove forme. Fellini è un regista che *ha ritratto* l'Italia e gli Italiani con l'occhio del visionario. Diversi titoli dei suoi film sono diventati parte del linguaggio comune: *vitellone, bidonista,* la dolce vita, *amarcord.* Una nuova generazione di registi sembra continuare le tendenze del neorealismo e *si serve* della macchina da presa per documentare la realtà sociale. Fra questi registi sono Bernardo Bertolucci, Francesco Rosi, Elio Petri, Ettore Scola, i fratelli Taviani e anche due donne, Lina Wertmuller e Liliana Cavani. Bertolucci ha ricevuto l'Oscar per il miglior film del 1987, *L'ultimo Imperatore.* Più recentemente, due film italiani hanno ricevuto l'Oscar per il miglior film straniero: *Il nuovo cinema Paradiso* di Giuseppe Tornatore (1990) e *Mediterraneo* di Gabriele Salvatores (1992).

postwar
giants
themes
has portrayed
lazy good-for-nothing/swindler/I remember (Northern dialect)
uses

Comprensione

A. 1. *Il Corriere della Sera* è un giornale che esce una volta...
   a. al giorno b. alla settimana c. al mese

2. La RAI–TV è una sigla che rappresenta...
   a. una stazione teleradio privata b. una rete dello stato c. la radio-televisone dello stato

3. Per avere il diritto di guardare la televisione, gli Italiani devono...
   a. ascoltare programmi d'informazione b. vedere canali esteri c. pagare una tassa annuale

4. Un grande regista ancora vivente è...
   a. Marcello Mastroianni b. Luchino Visconti c. Federico Fellini

5. La dolce vita significa...
   a. una vita di lotta (*struggle*) sociale b. una vita facile e superficiale c. la vita del dopoguerra

B. 1. Spiegate perchè i mezzi di diffusione hanno contribuito all'unificazione della lingua italiana. (Ricordate la prima lettura culturale?)

2. Che cos'è *Il Messaggero? Panorama? Grazia?*

3. Molti Italiani considerano ingiusta la tassa sulla televisione. Perchè?

4. Chi era Rossellini? Che cosa fece il neorealismo italiano del dopoguerra?

5. In che modo il successo di Federico Fellini ha influenzato la lingua italiana?

6. Quali film italiani furono premiati (*were awarded*) con l'Oscar in questi ultimi anni?

1993. Il regista Federico Fellini riceve un Oscar speciale. Al suo fianco sono gli attori Sophia Loren e Marcello Mastroianni.

20 ARTE E TEATRO

Milano. Opera al Teatro alla Scala.

Punti di vista

Musica operistica o musica elettronica?
Se tu fossi pittore...

Punti grammaticali

I «Se» con le frasi ipotetiche
II Congiuntivo: uso dei tempi
III *Fare* + infinito

Lettura

La commedia è finita

Pagina culturale

L'opera italiana e la commedia dell'arte

PUNTI DI VISTA

MUSICA OPERISTICA O MUSICA ELETTRONICA?

Giuseppe Piccoli e tre suoi amici hanno messo insieme un piccolo gruppo rock che ha un certo successo. Giuseppe suona la chitarra elettrica, e gli altri tre suonano la *batteria*, il piano, e la chitarra. Oggi i quattro ragazzi sono a casa di Giuseppe e suonano i loro strumenti un po' troppo entusiasticamente. Dopo un paio d'ore la mamma entra nel soggiorno.

drums

—Scusa, Giuseppe, ma *mi avete fatto venire* un grosso mal di testa!

you caused me

—Ti prego, mamma, *lasciaci* suonare ancora un po'. E poi... lo sai che adesso mi chiamo Paco Pank!

let us

—Paco Pank? Che bisogno avevi di cambiarti il nome? Giuseppe Piccoli non ti andava bene?

—Se non avessi cambiato il nome, non sarei diventato famoso.

—Beh, famoso... è troppo presto per dirlo. Ricordati che riesce solo chi ha talento.

—In questa casa nessuno mi capisce! A papà, per esempio, piace solo la musica operistica e non vuole ascoltare *nient'altro*. Però se un giorno diventerò famoso, *grazie alla* musica rock, tu e papà sarete *orgogliosi* di me.

nothing else
thanks to
proud

—Va bene, ma per il momento sarei contenta se tu suonassi meno *forte;* mi sembra che questo sia *fracasso,* non musica.

loud/loud noise

—È inutile discutere con voi! Siete rimasti all'epoca di Giuseppe Verdi.

Comprensione

1. Cos'hanno messo insieme i quattro amici?
2. Quali strumenti suonano?
3. Cosa fanno oggi? Dove?
4. Perchè la mamma di Giuseppe ha mal di testa?
5. Paco Pank è un nome vero o un nome d'arte? Qual è, in questo caso, il nome vero?
6. Perchè ha deciso di cambiarsi il nome Giuseppe?
7. Per diventare famoso, basta che Giuseppe si cambi il nome, o ci vuole qualcos'altro? Che cosa?
8. Piace a suo padre la musica rock? Perchè no?
9. Cosa vorrebbe la madre di Giuseppe, per il momento?
10. Qual è, secondo Giuseppe, il problema dei suoi genitori per quanto riguarda (*regarding*) la musica?
11. Lei sa chi era Giuseppe Verdi?

Studio di parole

LE ARTI

la musica...classica
operistica
sinfonica
leggera
l'opera
la sinfonia symphony
la canzone song
il compositore, la compositrice
il (la) cantante singer
il coro chorus
il (la) musicista musician
il direttore d'orchestra (*m. & f.*) orchestra conductor
Strumenti musicali:
il pianoforte
il violino violin
il violoncello cello
il flauto flute
la tromba trumpet
la chitarra guitar
la batteria drums

la pittura painting
il pittore, la pittrice
la scultura sculpture
lo scultore, la scultrice
l'architettura architecture
l'architetto (*m. & f.*) architect
il quadro painting, picture
il ritratto portrait
il paesaggio landscape...
la natura morta still life
l'affresco fresco
la statua statue
la mostra show, exhibition
dipingere (*p.p.* **dipinto)** to paint
scolpire (-isc) to sculpt
disegnare to draw

IL TEATRO

la commedia play, comedy
la tragedia tragedy
l'atto act
la scena scene
il comico comedian

il commediografo playwright
il palcoscenico stage
il pubblico audience
recitare to act/to play
applaudire to applaud
fischiare to boo (*lit.*, to whistle)

Che gelida manina…(What a tiny frozen hand…) (Puccini, La Bohème. Atto I.)

Applicazione

A. **1.** Che cosa compose Beethoven?
2. Paganini era un famoso musicista dell'Ottocento. Quale strumento suonava alla perfezione?
3. Louis Armstrong, suonava il flauto o la tromba?
4. Milioni di turisti visitano la Cappella Sistina in Vaticano. Perchè?
5. Chi era Botticelli?
6. Che tipo di quadro è *La Gioconda* (*Monna Lisa*)? Dove si trova?
7. Che cosa rappresenta una natura morta?
8. Che tipo di quadri preferivano dipingere gli Impressionisti?
9. In quali parti è divisa un'opera di teatro?
10. Su quale parte del teatro si rappresenta un'opera teatrale?
11. Cosa fa il pubblico alla fine di un atto?

B. Abbinate gli elementi delle due colonne in una frase completa, scegliendo la forma appropriata dei verbi che seguono.

scrisse, scolpì, compose, dipinse, fu, è

Shakespeare	*La Bohème*
Michelangelo	*La Gioconda*
Giuseppe Verdi	un cantante operistico
Arturo Toscanini	*La Pietà*
Puccini	*Amleto*
Leonardo da Vinci	un celebre direttore d'orchestra
Luciano Pavarotti	un compositore di sinfonie e concerti
Vivaldi	*L'Aida*

C. **Domande personali.**

1. Lei sa suonare qualche strumento? Se sì, quale?
2. Ha mai preso lezioni di pianoforte o di…?
3. Ha mai suonato in un'orchestra o in un gruppo?
4. Se Lei suonasse o cantasse in un gruppo rock, ne sarebbero contenti o scontenti i Suoi genitori? Perchè?

5. Le differenze di gusti e di opinioni sono frequenti fra la vecchia generazione e la nuova? Per esempio, su che cosa la Sua famiglia e Lei non vanno d'accordo?
6. Quale musica e quali cantanti preferiscono i Suoi genitori? E Lei?
7. Lei crede che la musica sia utile nella vita? Spieghi la Sua risposta.

Ascoltiamo!

Se tu fossi pittore... *Luisa has been taking an art course and must do a painting of her own as an assignment. She is trying to decide what to paint, and asks her older brother Alberto for advice. Listen as he makes various suggestions, then answer the related questions.*

Comprensione

1. Che cosa deve fare Luisa per lunedì? A chi ha domandato aiuto? **2.** È pittore Alberto? Se fosse pittore che cosa dipingerebbe? **3.** Quali elementi dovrebbe avere l'angolo (*corner*) di giardino che Alberto consiglia di disegnare? **4.** Luisa segue il consiglio del fratello? Perchè? **5.** Alberto le suggerisce una seconda idea. Quale? **6.** Alla fine, Alberto che cosa ha detto di dipingere? **7.** Crede Lei che Luisa abbia veramente talento artistico?

Dialogo

In gruppi di due, immaginate di essere pittori. Scegliereste un soggetto come quello del quadro in questa pagina, o un altro soggetto? Quale?

I. "Se" con le frasi ipotetiche

—Giotto, se studierai pittura, diventerai un gran pittore.

—Se non avesse i baffi, sembrerebbe il ritratto di zia Clotilde!

1. Che cosa dice un vecchio pittore al giovane Giotto?
2. Com'è il cerchio che il ragazzo disegna?
3. In quale caso il ritratto sembrerebbe quello della zia del turista?

1. In a real or probable situation, the *if* clause is *always* in the indicative. The *result* clause is also in the indicative.

If clause		Result clause
present indicative	→	*present indicative*
Se studiamo,		impariamo.
future	→	*future*
Se studieremo,		impareremo.

Se **mangi** troppo, **ingrassi**. — *If you eat too much, you become fat.*
Se **andremo** a Roma, **visiteremo** i Musei Vaticani. — *If we go to Rome, we will visit the Vatican Museums.*

2. In a hypothetical situation that is possible, but unlikely to occur (in the present or in the future), the *if* clause is in the imperfect subjunctive, and the *result* clause is in the present conditional.

   In a hypothetical situation that did not occur, the *if* clause is in the pluperfect subjunctive, and the *result* clause is in the past conditional.

If clause		Result clause
imperfect subjunctive	→	*present conditional*
Se studiassi,	→	imparerei. (*still possible*)
pluperfect subjunctive	→	*past conditional*
Se avessi studiato,	→	avrei imparato. (*no longer possible*)

Se **avessi** tempo, **seguirei** un corso di pittura.	*If I had the time, I would take a course in painting.*
Se **fossi** milionario, **farei** il giro del mondo.	*If I were a millionaire, I would take a trip around the world.*
Se **avesse avuto** più talento, **sarebbe diventata** una grande scultrice.	*If she had had more talent, she would have become a great sculptor.*

Pratica

A. Due amici parlano. Ogni volta che il primo annuncia qualcosa di probabile, il secondo esprime «ipoteticamente» il suo desiderio.

ESEMPIO Se Maria ha (avrà) un mese di vacanze, va (andrà) in Italia.
Se avessi un mese di vacanze ci andrei anch'io.

1. Se oggi ho tempo, visito la mostra del pittore Carrà. **2.** Se stasera c'è un film di Bertolucci, voglio vederlo. **3.** Se i miei genitori possono comprare due biglietti, vanno a vedere *La Traviata* di Verdi. **4.** Se mio fratello riceverà un aumento di stipendio, comprerà un'Alfa Romeo. **5.** Se mia sorella reciterà in *Giulietta e Romeo,* tutta la famiglia andrà a vederla.

B. Rispondete con frasi complete alle seguenti situazioni ipotetiche.

1. Se tu avessi un milione, che cosa faresti? **2.** Se tu avessi uno yacht, dove andresti? **3.** Se tu potessi scegliere, dove vorresti vivere? **4.** Se tu ricevessi in eredità (*inheritance*) un quadro di De Chirico,* che cosa ne faresti? **5.** Se tu ti trovassi su un'isola deserta, che cosa faresti? **6.** Se fossi pittore, che cosa dipingeresti? **7.** Se tu potessi rivivere un anno della tua vita, quale sceglieresti? **8.** Se tu fossi il presidente degli Stati Uniti, cosa faresti per prima cosa? **9.** Se tu avessi una bacchetta magica (*magic wand*), quali cose ti piacerebbe avere?

C. **Se...** Che cosa avrebbero fatto le seguenti persone?

ESEMPIO Se fossi stato a Firenze, (vedere) il Davide.
Se fossi stato a Firenze, avrei visto il Davide.

1. Se avessimo avuto tempo, (leggere) un romanzo di Moravia. **2.** Se tu mi avessi aspettato, (noi uscire) insieme. **3.** Se io fossi arrivato in orario alla stazione, non (perdere) il treno. **4.** Sei lui avesse studiato il Rinascimento, (imparare) molto sull'arte italiana. **5.** Se tu avessi cercato attentamente, (trovare) il libro perduto. **6.** Se io non avessi dimenticato il tuo indirizzo, ti (scrivere) una cartolina. **7.** Se Gabriella non fosse stata ammalata, (andare) a teatro. **8.** Se il padrone di casa mi avesse aumentato l'affitto, (cercarmi) un altro appartamento.

D. Completate le seguenti frasi con un po' di fantasia.

1. Se mi piacesse la musica... **2.** Se avessi una bella voce... **3.** Se sapessi scrivere con facilità... **4.** Se fossi in Italia d'inverno... **5.** Se mi invitassero al ristorante Pappagallo di Bologna... **6.** Se non ci fossero più esami...

---

*Giorgio de Chirico (1888–1978). One of the most outstanding Italian painters of our century; he gave impetus to the surrealist movement and influenced many contemporary artists, including the Spanish painter Salvador Dali.

II. Congiuntivo: uso dei tempi

L'uomo delle caverne era felice che ci fossero le pietre.

Nei secoli scorsi erano felici che esistessero la penna e l'inchiostro.

Oggi siamo felici che abbiano inventato il computer.

The following chart summarizes the relationship of tenses between the main clause and the dependent clause in the subjunctive.

Main clause	Subordinate clause
present, future, imperative	*present subjunctive* (*simultaneous or future action*) *past subjunctive* (*prior action*)
all past tenses, conditional	*imperfect subjunctive* (*simultaneous or future action*) *pluperfect subjunctive* (*prior action*)

Now look at the following examples:

Sono contento che Lei **venga** stasera.	*I am happy you are coming tonight.*
Sono contento che Lei **sia venuto** ieri sera.	*I am happy you came last night.*
Sarà bene che tu **ritorni** presto.	*It will be good if you return soon.*
Al mio arrivo, sarà bene che tu **sia** già **ritornato.**	*Upon my arrival, it will be good if you will have already returned.*
Era meglio che **studiasse** l'italiano.	*It was better for him to study Italian.*
Era meglio che **avesse studiato** l'italiano.	*It was better for him to have studied Italian.*

Aveva paura che lo **licenziassero.**	*He was afraid they might fire him.*
Aveva paura che lo **avessero licenziato.**	*He was afraid they had fired him.*
In quel momento pensai che il treno **fosse** in ritardo.	*At that moment I thought the train was late.*
In quel momento pensai che il treno **fosse** già **arrivato.**	*At that moment I thought the train had already arrived.*
Vorrei che tu **seguissi** i miei consigli.	*I would like you to follow my advice.*
Vorrei che tu **avessi seguito** i miei consigli.	*I wish you had followed my advice.*

Pratica

A. **Dialogo tra madre e figlio.** Completate mettendo l'infinito al **congiuntivo presente** o **imperfetto**, secondo il caso.

F. Mamma, partirò benchè (fare) _______ brutto tempo. Non mi piace, ma è necessario che io (andare) ______.

M. Sei veramente ostinato. Preferivo che tu (restare) ______ a casa, ma se proprio bisogna che tu (partire) ______, va' pure. Vorrei almeno che (metterti) ______ l'impermeabile.

F. Non preoccuparti! Ti telefonerò non appena arriverò perchè tu (potere) ______ stare con il cuore in pace.

B. Liliana va a trovare la mamma. Ecco i suoi pensieri mentre sta arrivando alla stazione ferroviaria. Completate le frasi con il **congiuntivo passato** o **trapassato.**

1. Spero che il treno non ______ (già, partire). **2.** È un peccato che Lucia non ______ (venire) al concerto di ieri sera. **3.** Mi ha detto che era stanca, sebbene ______ (fare) vacanza due giorni. **4.** Vorrei che anche lei ______ (sentire) l'orchestra dell'Angelicum: ha suonato magnificamente! **5.** Spero che mia madre ______ (curarsi) della brutta influenza che aveva e che ora stia meglio.

C. Il robot **I.C.P.** Riscrivete la storiella cambiando i tempi dal **presente** al **passato.** Incominciate con: *L'anno scorso...*

Lo scrittore Carlo Speranza manda all'editore il suo primo romanzo intitolato *Il robot I.C.P.* perchè glielo pubblichi. Si tratta di una storia di fantascienza. I due personaggi principali sono uno scienziato, il dottor Ivan Inventovich, e il suo assistente. Il professore vuole che il suo assistente lo aiuti a perfezionare il modello di un robot: il cameriere perfetto. È importante che l'esperimento riesca perchè il professore spera che tutto il mondo riconosca finalmente il suo genio (*genius*). I.C.P. è un cameriere perfetto. La mattina prepara il caffè prima che i due uomini si alzino. A mezzogiorno cucina senza che glielo domandino. La sera non va a letto a meno che non abbia lavato i piatti. Tutto va bene finchè un giorno un transistor di I.C.P. non funziona. I.C.P. deve fare la frittata (*omelette*), ma invece di rompere due uova, rompe la testa al professore e al suo assistente.

III. Fare + infinito

La volpe (fox) pensava —Devo farlo cantare per fargli cadere il formaggio.

1. The construction **fare** + *infinitive* is used to express the idea of having something done or having someone do something.

Faccio cantare una canzone.	*I have a song sung.*
Faccio cantare i bambini.	*I have (make) the children sing.*
Faccio cantare una canzone ai bambini.	*I have the children sing a song.*

When the construction has only one object, the object is direct.

Fa suonare **un disco.** — *He has a record played.*
Fa suonare **Pietro.** — *He has (makes) Pietro play.*

When this construction has two objects, the person who performs the action is always the indirect object.

Fa suonare **un disco a Pietro.** — *He has (makes) Pietro play a record.*

2. When the objects are nouns, as seen above, they *always* follow the infinitive. When the objects are pronouns, they precede the verb fare.

Farò riparare **il piano.** — *I will have the piano repaired.*
Lo farò riparare. — *I will have it repaired.*
Farò riparare **il piano a Pietro.** — *I will have Pietro repair the piano.*
Glielo farò riparare. — *I will have him repair it.*
Ho fatto venire **i miei amici.** — *I had my friends come.*
Li ho fatti venire. — *I had them come.*

If **fare** is in the *imperative* (**tu, noi, voi** forms) or in the *infinitive,* the pronouns follow **fare** and are attached to it.

Fa cantare **i bambini!**	*Have the children sing!*
Falli cantare!	*Have them sing!*
Mi piacerebbe fare dipingere **la casa.**	*I would like to have the house painted.*
Mi piacerebbe far**la** dipingere.	*I would like to have it painted.*

3. The verb **fare** is used in a reflexive form when the action is done on behalf of the subject. The name of the person performing the action is preceded by **da.** In compound tenses **essere** is used.

Lisa **si farà** aiutare da Luigi.	*Lisa will have Luigi help her (Lisa will have herself helped by Luigi).*
Lisa **si è fatta** aiutare da Luigi.	*Lisa had Luigi help her (Lisa had herself helped by Luigi).*
Il bambino **si fa** lavare la faccia dalla mamma.	*The child is having his face washed by his mother.*
Il bambino **se la fa** lavare dalla mamma.	*The child is having it washed by his mother.*

Pratica

A. Che cosa fanno fare le seguenti persone o cose?

ESEMPIO dieta, dimagrire, signora **La dieta fa dimagrire la signora.**

1. bambini, aspettare, madre **2.** direttore d'orchestra, ripetere, sinfonia **3.** smog, star male, gente **4.** tragedia, piangere, pubblico **5.** preoccupazioni, dormire male, genitori **6.** comico, ridere, spettatori

B. Dite sei cose che il professore (la professoressa) d'italiano vi fa fare.

ESEMPIO **Ci fa leggere ad alta voce. Ci fa...**

C. **Domanda e risposta.** Farai tu le seguenti azioni?

ESEMPIO comprare il giornale **—Comprerai tu il giornale?**
—No, lo farò comprare a mio padre.

1. pulire la casa **2.** tagliare l'erba **3.** preparare i panini al prosciutto **4.** riparare il rubinetto (*faucet*) della cucina **5.** cucinare le bistecche **6.** dipingere la tua stanza da letto

D. **Domanda e risposta.** Pierino si lamenta perchè la mamma è troppo esigente.

ESEMPIO mangiare gli spinaci/sì **—Ti fa mangiare gli spinaci?**
—Sì, me li fa mangiare.

1. fare tutti i compiti/sì **2.** vedere i cartoni animati/no **3.** ripetere le lezioni/sì **4.** leggere i giornali a fumetti/no **5.** riordinare la stanza/sì **6.** lavare le orecchie tutti i giorni/sì

E. Il marito fa delle osservazioni alla moglie perchè i figli non l'aiutano. Seguite l'esempio.

ESEMPIO Fa' lavorare Ornella! —**Falla lavorare!**
Fa' fare la spesa a Maria! —**Falle fare la spesa!**

1. Fa' studiare i ragazzi! **2.** Fa' leggere Pierino! **4.** Fa' pulire il giardino a Guido! **4.** Fa' apparecchiare la tavola a Ornella! **5.** Fa' lavare i piatti a Maria! **6.** Non fare uscire i ragazzi di sera!

F. **Domanda e risposta.** Da chi ti sei fatto fare le seguenti cose?

ESEMPIO tagliare i capelli —**Da chi ti sei fatto(a) tagliare i capelli?**
—**Me li sono fatti tagliare dal parrucchiere.**

1. regalare l'orologio d'oro (*gold*) **2.** scrivere a macchina il saggio **3.** esaminare gli occhi **4.** prescrivere gli antibiotici **5.** scrivere la lettera di raccomandazione **6.** prestare la bicicletta

G. **Rispondete.**

1. Ti fanno piangere o ridere i film comici? **2.** Che cosa ti fa piangere? **3.** Quante volte all'anno ti fai tagliare i capelli? **4.** Quando ascolti la televisione, che cosa ti fa arrabbiare? **5.** Che cosa ti faresti regalare da tuo padre se fosse miliardario (*billionaire*)?

H. Completate le frasi in maniera logica e con un po' d'immaginazione.

ESEMPIO Vorrei una casa al mare. Vado da un architetto e...
—Vado da un architetto e me la faccio costruire.

1. La mia Fiat è rotta. Vado dal meccanico e... **2.** Sono rimasto(a) senza soldi. Vado da un amico e... **3.** Ho solo dollari, ma avrei bisogno di lire. Vado in banca e... **4.** Non ho capito il passivo. Vado dal(la) professore(ssa) e... **5.** Vado all'università a Chicago. Ho dimenticato il mio cappotto a New York. Telefono a mia madre e... **6.** Vorrei un bicchiere di latte, ma non posso alzarmi dal divano perchè ho una gamba ingessata (*in a cast*). Chiamo il mio fratellino e... **7.** Sto cercando un appartamento. Ne ho trovato uno sul giornale. Vado dal portinaio e... **8.** Ho voglia di mangiare due uova strapazzate. Chiamo il cuoco e...

LETTURA

LA COMMEDIA È FINITA

Liliana ha ricevuto una borsa di studio che le permetterà di studiare per un anno negli Stati Uniti. Oggi gli amici si sono riuniti per festeggiare l'avvenimento, prima che lei parta. Infatti hanno organizzato una serata in suo onore: l'hanno invitata all'Odeon dove si rappresenta una commedia di Pirandello perchè sanno che le piace andare a teatro. Dopo la rappresentazione ci sarà una cenetta elegante al ristorante Biffi.

Uscendo dal teatro gli amici discutono la commedia che hanno visto, *Sei personaggi in cerca d'autore.*

Lucia	Mi è piaciuta molto l'idea di far uscire i sei personaggi dal pubblico e di farli salire ad uno ad uno sul palcoscenico.
Marcello	Già, ma perchè?
Antonio	Se tu avessi studiato meglio Pirandello, avresti capito perchè.
Liliana	Be', bisognerebbe parlare della filosofia di Pirandello, che non è molto semplice.*
Filippo	La storia che ognuno dei sei personaggi ha raccontato era molto deprimente. Chissà perchè è stata chiamata commedia. Questa è una vera tragedia familiare.
Gabriella	Ehi, anche noi siamo sei personaggi, ognuno con una sua storia!
Antonio	In cerca d'autore?
Gabriella	A proposito, Liliana, se visiterai la California, va' a salutare le due signore che sono state gentili con noi.
Antonio	Be', veramente, con me non sono state tanto gentili. Sono stato descritto brutto e con il naso storto.
	(*Coro di proteste.*)
	—E io che sono stata confinata diverse volte in cucina?
	—E io che sono stato presentato come un bel ragazzo, ma superficiale?
	—E io? Sembra che viva solo per lo studio e la carriera!
Gabriella	Ma insomma, perchè ci lamentiamo? L'hanno fatto scherzando, ma con affetto.

Dopo la cenetta al Biffi gli amici si abbracciano affettuosamente.

—Buon viaggio, Liliana!
—Arrivederci all'anno prossimo.
—Scrivici presto!
—Ciao!
—Ciao!

Luigi Pirandello, grande commediografo, romanziere e saggista.

*Pirandello (1867–1936) is internationally famous, particularly for his theater. His plays introduce the artistic philosophy of relativity in all aspects of life and are open to different interpretations. In 1934, Pirandello was awarded the Nobel Prize for literature.

Comprensione

1. Dove andrà Liliana? Perchè?
2. Che cosa hanno deciso di fare i suoi amici, prima che lei parta?
3. In che modo passeranno la serata?
4. Che cosa fanno mentre stanno uscendo dal teatro?
5. Da quale parte del teatro sono saliti sul palcoscenico i personaggi della commedia?
6. È comica questa commedia di Pirandello?
7. Che paragone fa Gabriella fra gli amici e i personaggi della commedia?
8. Chi dovrebbe andare a salutare in America Liliana?
9. Riconoscete il nome di chi protesta dalle descrizioni che sono state fatte?
10. Chi sono, secondo voi, le due signore?

Domande personali

1. Ha mai recitato Lei in una commedia? Quale? Che parte ha fatto?
2. Se Lei fosse un attore (un'attrice), preferirebbe recitare una parte drammatica, comica o sentimentale?
3. Lei ha mai visto o letto un'opera teatrale di Pirandello? Quale? In italiano o in inglese?
4. Se un amico (un'amica) dovesse partire per un lungo viaggio, come festeggerebbe Lei la sua partenza? L'inviterebbe a teatro? O che cosa farebbe?
5. Lei va qualche volta a teatro con gli amici? Perchè? Che cosa va a vedere?
6. Ha letto Lei qualche tragedia di Shakespeare? Quale o quali?

ATTIVITÀ SUPPLEMENTARI

A. **Che musica preferisci?** In gruppi di due a tre, ogni studente parla del tipo di musica che preferisce (classica, operistica, jazz, popolare) e spiega quando l'ascolta, dove, se va all'opera o ai concerti. Se uno studente suona uno strumento musicale, dice quale, spiega da quanto tempo lo suona, se fa parte di un gruppo, se ha una collezione di dischi, chi è il suo (la sua) cantante preferito(a).

B. **Oggi si recita!** Improvvisatevi commediografi e, in collaborazione con altri compagni (compagne), scrivete una breve scena che poi reciterete davanti alla classe.

C. **Un avvenimento** (*event*) **artistico.** Descrivete una vostra esperienza: un'opera alla quale avete assistito, un concerto che avete ascoltato, un museo che avete visitato.

D. **Intervista.** Immaginate che Liliana e una sua amica siano già ritornate dai loro studi in America. Scegliete due studentesse che facciano la loro parte. Gli altri studenti faranno la parte degli amici che chiedono informazioni sulla loro esperienza americana.

E. **Pensiamo al futuro di...** Cercate di immaginare quale sarà il futuro di Marcello e di Antonio. Incominciate qualche frase con **penso che..., credo che...**, ecc.

F. Osservate questi quadri. Il primo è di Botticelli (1447–1515). È un particolare della *Primavera*. Il secondo è il *Bacco* di Caravaggio (1571–1610). Il terzo è *Donna dagli occhi blu* di Modigliani (1884–1920). Il quarto è *Ettore e Andromaca* di De Chirico (1888–1978). Quale vi piace di più? Perchè?

1.

2.

3.

4.

G. Come si dice in italiano?

1. One day a friend told Michelangelo: "Too bad you did not marry. If you had married, you would have had children and you would have left them your masterpieces." The great sculptor answered: "I have the most beautiful wife. My children are the works of art I will leave; if they are great, I will live for a long time."
2. While Michelangelo was painting *The Last Judgment (Il Giudizio Universale),* a cardinal (**cardinale**) bothered him every day. Michelangelo got angry at (**con**) the cardinal and, since he was painting hell, decided to put him there. The cardinal went to the Pope to complain, but the Pope answered him: "If you were in purgatory (**purgatorio**), I could do something for you, but no one can free (**liberare**) you from hell." Who (**Chi**) looks at the *Last Judgment* can see the portrait of the cardinal in the left corner (**nell'angolo di sinistra**).

Vocabolario

Nomi

l'affetto	*affection*
l'assistente (*m.* & *f.*)	*assistant*
l'avvenimento	*happening; event*
i baffi	*moustache*
la banda	*band*
il capolavoro	*masterpiece*
il cerchio	*circle*
l'epoca	*epoch*
l'eredità	*inheritance*
l'esperimento	*experiment*
la facilità	*ease*
il fracasso	*loud noise*
la frittata	*omelette*
la generazione	*generation*
il genio	*genius*
il gruppo	*group*
il miliardario	*billionaire*
il modello	*model*
l'oro	*gold*
la perfezione	*perfection*
la pietra	*stone*
la rappresentazione	*performance*
la stampa	*print*
il tema	*theme*

Aggettivi

artistico	*artistic*
astratto	*abstract*
deprimente	*depressing*
deserto	*inhabited*
drammatico	*dramatic*
elettrico	*electric*
esigente	*demanding*
familiare	*of the family*
inutile	*useless*
operistico	*of the opera*
orgoglioso	*proud*
ostinato	*stubborn*
sentimentale	*sentimental*
teatrale	*theatrical, theater*

Verbi

assistere	*to attend*
comporre (*p.p.* composto)	*to compose*
inventare	*to invent*
lasciare	*to let*
perfezionare	*to perfect*
piangere (*p.p.* pianto)	*to cry*
rappresentare	*to stage*
ridere (*p.p.* riso)	*to laugh*
rimanere (*p.p.* rimasto)	*to remain*
rivivere	*to relive, to live again*
riunirsi	*to gather*
sembrare	*to look like*

Altre espressioni

ad uno ad uno	*one by one*
affettuosamente	*affectionately*
a proposito	*by the way*
entusiasticamente	*enthusiastically*
far(e) venire il mal di testa	*to cause a headache*
finchè	*until*
grazie a	*thanks to*
in cerca di	*in search of*
nome d'arte	*stage name*
non appena	*as soon as*
un paio d'ore	*a couple of hours*
proprio	*indeed*
l'uomo delle caverne	*caveman*

Il tenore Luciano Pavarotti, famoso interprete dell'opera italiana.

L'OPERA ITALIANA E LA COMMEDIA DELL'ARTE

L'opera nacque in Italia alla fine del Cinquecento. La prima fu *L'Orfeo* di Claudio Monteverdi, rappresentata nel 1606 alla corte dei duchi Gonzaga di Mantova. Ma è a Napoli che l'opera diventò quella che il mondo *definisce* oggi «opera italiana». Napoli si identificò con il «bel canto», la melodia cantata. Fra i grandi maestri napoletani del Seicento e del Settecento furono Stradella, Scarlatti e Pergolesi. Dall'Italia l'opera italiana partì alla conquista del mondo ed influenzò geni come Mozart, che scrisse opere italiane di stile e di libretto.

defines as

Il periodo del bel canto continuò *a fiorire* nell'Ottocento con Rossini, Bellini e Donizetti. Questo secolo fu dominato *tuttavia* dal genio drammatico di Giuseppe Verdi. Le prime opere di Verdi si ispirarono a temi nazionali, e Verdi fu considerato come l'interprete del *sogno* politico degli Italiani. I patrioti italiani diedero alle lettere del suo nome la seguente interpretazione: *V*(ittorio) *E*(manuele) *R*(e) *D*(i) *I*(talia), e il suo nome diventò il loro *grido di battaglia*. Il grande musicista fu insuperabile nella creazione di arie e di cori che accompagnano grandi scene drammatiche. Basti ricordare di lui alcune opere come *Rigoletto, Il Trovatore, La Traviata, Aida* e *Otello*.

to flourish
however
dream
battle cry

Alla fine del secolo l'opera *si fece* più realista, e Giacomo Puccini, autore della *Bohème,* ne fu l'interprete più popolare. Da allora altri compositori hanno scritto opere, ma nessuno si è avvicinato al successo di Verdi e di Puccini.

became

La Commedia dell'arte *si sviluppò* in Italia nella seconda metà del Cinquecento. Essa nacque dall'arte degli attori che improvvisavano le scene di una commedia, seguendo una trama prestabilita (lo scenario). I più *abili* si specializzarono in una parte e crearono un *tipo* che aveva *gesti* ed espressioni particolari. Nacquero così le maschere che si presentavano al pubblico vestendo il costume e la *maschera* che le distinguevano.

developed
clever
stock character/gestures
mask

Tutta l'Italia è rappresentata nel teatro delle maschere. Venezia ha dato Pantalone, il tipo del vecchio mercante geloso e anche del padre avaro e tiranno. Di origine veneta è probabilmente anche *la più nota* delle maschere femminili, Colombina, *servetta* piena di brio e di *astuzia.* Da Bologna, la città universitaria, viene il Dottore, cioè il pedante a cui piace mostrare la sua erudizione. La maschera napoletana più famosa è Pulcinella, brutto e *amante* delle donne e del vino.

the best known
young maid
cleverness
fond

Da un città lombarda, Bergamo, è venuto Arlecchino, servitore simpatico *nonostante* i suoi molti *difetti.* Arlecchino è la maschera più facile da riconoscersi per il suo costume *variopinto.*

in spite of
faults
multicolored

La commedia italiana ebbe successo in tutta l'Europa. I suoi comici, *oltre a* saper recitare, si distinguevano come acrobati, ballerini e musicisti. In Francia le loro fantasie e invenzioni ispirarono il grande Molière. Nel Settecento la letteratura italiana ebbe il suo primo grande commediografo nel veneziano Carlo Goldoni. Goldoni riformò la commedia dell'arte, che era diventata troppo libera, eliminando gli scenari. Le sue commedie si rappresentano ancora oggi e *hanno conservato* il movimento e la comicità della commedia dell'arte.

besides
retained

Le antiche maschere italiane continuano a vivere per il divertimento dei bambini nel teatro delle marionette. *Inoltre,* i loro costumi ritornano ogni anno durante le feste del carnevale.

furthermore

Comprensione

A. 1. L'opera nacque in Italia e il primo compositore ne fu...
   a. Monteverdi   b. Bellini   c. Scarlatti
2. Il libretto contiene...
   a. la musica dell'opera   b. le parole dell'opera   c. le istruzioni ai cantanti
3. La città che diventò famosa per «il bel canto» fu...
   a. Mantova   b. Milano   c. Napoli
4. Il maggiore compositore di opere del diciannovesimo secolo fu...
   a. Rossini   b. Verdi   c. Puccini
5. Verdi entusiasmò i patrioti italiani specialmente...
   a. per la creazione delle sue arie   b. per la sua ispirazione drammatica   c. per la scelta di temi nazionali

B. 1. Dove e in che secolo nacque la Commedia dell'arte?
2. Le commedie che gli attori recitavano erano scritte? Che cosa facevano gli attori?
3. Perchè la Commedia dell'arte si chiama anche Commedia delle maschere?
4. Che maschere ha dato il Veneto? Che personaggi rappresentavano?
5. Perchè il Dottore è bolognese?
6. Di dov'è Pulcinella e com'è?
7. Qual è la maschera più riconoscibile (*recognizable*)? Perchè?
8. Sapevano soltanto recitare questi attori?
9. Chi trasformò lo scenario in commedia scritta? Perchè?
10. Dove e quando si possono ancora vedere le maschere italiane?

Le maschere italiane: 1. *Pulcinella* 2. *Pantalone* 3. *Colombina* 4. *Arlecchino* 5. *Il Dottore*

APPENDIXES

APPENDIX 1 (For recognition purposes)

A. Futuro anteriore

1. The **futuro anteriore** (*future perfect tense*) expresses a future action taking place before another future action. It is a compound tense formed with the future of the auxiliary **avere** or **essere** + the past participle of the conjugated verb, and is usually introduced by conjunctions such as **se**, **quando**, **appena**, and **dopo che**.

   avrò finito = I will have finished

   It is conjugated as follows:

parlare		rispondere		partire	
avrò	parlato	avrò	risposto	sarò	partito (a)
avrai		avrai		sarai	
avrà		avrà		sarà	
avremo		avremo		saremo	partiti(e)
avrete		avrete		sarete	
avranno		avranno		saranno	

Avrò finito alle cinque.	***I will have finished** by five.*
Usciremo dopo che **avremo cenato**.	*We will go out after **we have dinner.***
Visiterò la città appena **sarò arrivata**.	*I will visit the city as soon as **I have arrived.***

2. The future perfect tense expresses also probability in the past.

Che bella macchina ha Luigi! **Avrà ereditato** dallo zio d'America.	*What a beautiful car Luigi has! **He must have inherited** from his rich uncle in America.*
Com'è abbronzata! **Sarà stata** alla spiaggia.	*How tan she is! **She must have been** at the beach.*
Non è ancora arrivato? No, **si sarà fermato** con gli amici.	*Hasn't he arrived yet? No **he must have stopped** with his friends.*

B. Trapassato remoto

1. The **trapassato remoto** (*past perfect*) is a compound tense. It is formed with the **passato remoto** of the auxiliary verb **essere** or **avere** + the past participle of the main verb.

   ebbi parlato = *I had spoken*

   fui partito = *I had left*

parlare		**partire**	
ebbi	parlato	fui	partito(a)
avesti		fosti	
ebbe		fu	
avemmo		fummo	partiti(e)
aveste		foste	
ẹbbero		fụrono	

2. The **trapassato remoto** is used in combination with the **passato remoto** and after conjunctions of time such as **quando**, **dopo che**, and **appena** (*as soon as*) to express an action prior to another past action. It is a tense found mainly in literary language.

Quando **ebbe finito**, salutò i colleghi e uscì.	*When **he (had) finished**, he said good-bye to his colleagues and left.*
Appena **fu uscito**, tutti cominciarono a ridere.	*As soon as **he (had) left**, they all began to laugh.*

3. When the subject of the two clauses is the same, the **trapassato remoto** is often replaced by **dopo** (**di**) + the past infinitive.

   Dopo che ebbe mangiato, uscì. *or* **Dopo** (**di**) **aver**(**e**) **mangiato**, uscì.

APPENDIX 2

COMMON VERBS AND EXPRESSIONS REQUIRING A PREPOSITION BEFORE AN INFINITIVE

A. Verbs and expressions + **a** + infinitive

abituarsi	*to get used*	Mi sono abituato ad alzarmi presto.
aiutare	*to help*	Aiutiamo la mamma a cucinare.
andare	*to go*	La signora va a fare la spesa ogni giorno.
continuare	*to continue*	Continuano a parlare di politica.
divertirsi	*to have a good time*	Ci siamo divertiti a cantare molte canzoni.
essere pronto	*to be ready*	Siete pronti a rispondere alla domanda?
imparare	*to learn*	Quando hai imparato a giocare a tennis?
(in)cominciare	*to begin*	Incomincio a lavorare domani.
insegnare	*to teach*	Mi insegni a usare il computer?
invitare	*to invite*	Vi invito a prendere un espresso.
mandare	*to send*	L'ho mandato a comprare una pizza.
prepararsi	*to get ready*	Ci prepariamo a fare un lungo viaggio.
riuscire	*to succeed*	Sei riuscito a trovare gli appunti d'inglese?
venire	*to come*	Luisa è venuta a salutare i suoi nonni.
mettersi	*to start*	Mi sono messo(a) a leggere il giornale.

B. Verbs and expressions + **di** + infinitive.

accettare	*to accept*	Accetti di aiutarlo?
ammettere	*to admit*	Lei ammette di volere troppo.
aspettare	*to wait*	Aspettano di ricevere una risposta.
cercare	*to try*	Cerco di arrivare in orario.
chiedere	*to ask*	Mi ha chiesto di prestargli dei soldi.
consigliare	*to advise*	Che cosa mi consigli di fare?
credere	*to believe*	Crede di avere ragione.
decidere	*to decide*	Ha deciso di fare medicina.
dimenticare	*to forget*	Non dimenticare di comprare della frutta!
(di)mostrare	*to show*	Lucia ha dimostrato di essere generosa.
dire	*to say, to tell*	Gli ho detto di stare zitto.
dubitare	*to doubt*	Dubita di riuscire.
finire	*to finish*	Ha finito di lavorare alle dieci di sera.
lamentarsi	*to complain*	Si lamentano di avere poco tempo.
ordinare	*to order*	Il medico mi ha ordinato di prendere delle vitamine.
pensare	*to think*	Quando pensi di partire?

permettere	*to allow*	Mi permetti di dire la verità?
pregare	*to pray, to beg*	La prego di scusarmi.
preoccuparsi	*to worry*	Si preoccupa solamente di finire.
proibire	*to forbid*	Mio padre mi proibisce di usare la macchina.
promettere	*to promise*	Ci hanno promesso di venire stasera.
raccomandare	*to recommend*	Ti raccomando di scrivermi subito.
riconoscere	*to recognize*	Riconosco di avere torto.
ricordare	*to remember; to remind*	Ricordami di telefonarle!
ripetere	*to repeat*	Vi ripeto sempre di fare attenzione.
scegliere	*to choose*	Perchè hai scelto di andare a Firenze?
scrivere	*to write*	Le ho scritto di venire in treno.
smettere	*to stop*	Ho smesso di bere caffè.
sperare	*to hope*	Loro sperano di vederti.
suggerire	*to suggest*	Filippo suggerisce di andare al ristorante.
temere	*to fear*	Lei teme di non sapere abbastanza.
avere bisogno	*to need*	Abbiamo bisogno di dormire.
avere paura	*to be afraid*	Hai paura di viaggiare in aereo?
avere ragione	*to be right*	Hanno avuto ragione di partire presto.
avere torto	*to be wrong*	Non ha torto di parlare così.
avere voglia	*to feel like*	Ho voglia di mangiare un gelato.
essere certo (sicuro)	*to be certain*	Sei sicuro di avere abbastanza soldi?
essere contento (felice)	*to be happy*	Nino, sei contento di andare in Europa?
essere curioso	*to be curious*	Siamo curiosi di sapere la verità.
essere fortunato	*to be lucky*	È fortunata di avere un padre ricco.
essere impaziente	*to be anxious*	Lui è impaziente di vederla.
essere libero	*to be free*	È libera di uscire.
essere orgoglioso	*to be proud*	Siamo orgogliosi di essere americani.
essere spiacente	*to be sorry*	Sono spiacenti di non essere qui.
essere stanco	*to be tired*	Sono stanca di aspettare.
è ora	*it is time*	È ora di partire.

APPENDIX 3

A. Auxiliary verbs: avere, essere

SIMPLE TENSES

Infinito (*infinitive*)	**avere**		**essere**	
Presente (*present indicative*)	ho hai ha	abbiamo avete hanno	sono sei è	siamo siete sono
Imperfetto (*imperfect indicative*)	avevo avevi aveva	avevamo avevate avẹvano	ero eri era	eravamo eravate ẹrano
Passato remoto (*past absolute*)	ebbi avesti ebbe	avemmo aveste ẹbbero	fui fosti fu	fummo foste fụrono
Futuro (*future*)	avrò avrai avrà	avremo avrete avranno	sarò sarai sarà	saremo sarete saranno
Condizionale presente (*present conditional*)	avrei avresti avrebbe	avremmo avreste avrẹbbero	sarei saresti sarebbe	saremmo sareste sarẹbbero
Imperativo (*imperative*)	— abbi ạbbia	abbiamo abbiate ạbbiano	— sii sia	siamo siate sịano
Congiuntivo presente (*present subjunctive*)	ạbbia ạbbia ạbbia	abbiamo abbiate ạbbiano	sia sia sia	siamo siate sịano
Imperfetto del congiuntivo (*imperfect subjunctive*)	avessi avessi avesse	avẹssimo aveste avẹssero	fossi fossi fosse	fọssimo foste fọssero
Gerụndio (*gerund*)	avendo		essendo	

COMPOUND TENSES

Partic̣ipio passato (*past participle*)	avuto		stato (a, i, e)	
Infinito passato (*past infinitive*)	avere avuto		esere stato (a, i,e)	
Passato prọssimo (*present perfect indicative*)	ho	avuto	sono	stato (a)
	hai		sei	
	ha		è	
	abbiamo		siamo	stati (e)
	avete		siete	
	hanno		sono	
Trapassato prọssimo (*pluperfect*)	avevo	avuto	ero	stato (a)
	avevi		eri	
	aveva		era	
	avevamo		eravamo	stati (e)
	avevate		eravate	
	avẹvano		ẹrano	
Trapassato remoto (*past perfect indicative*)	ebbi	avuto	fui	stato (a)
	avesti		fosti	
	ebbe		fu	
	avemmo		fummo	stati (e)
	aveste		foste	
	ẹbbero		fụrono	
Futuro anteriore (*future perfect*)	avrò	avuto	sarò	stato (a)
	avrai		sarai	
	avrà		sarà	
	avremo		saremo	stati (e)
	avrete		sarete	
	avranno		saranno	
Condizionale passato (*conditional perfect*)	avrei	avuto	sarei	stato (a)
	avresti		saresti	
	avrebbe		sarebbe	
	avremmo		saremmo	stati (e)
	avreste		sareste	
	avrẹbbero		sarẹbbero	

Congiuntivo passato (*present perfect subjunctive*)	ạbbia ạbbia ạbbia abbiamo abbiate ạbbiano	avuto	sia sia sia	stato (a)
			siamo siate sịano	stati (e)
Trapassato del congiuntivo (*pluperfect subjunctive*)	avessi avessi avesse avẹssimo aveste avẹssero	avuto	fossi fossi fosse	stato (a)
			fọssimo foste fọssero	stati (e)
Gerundio passato (*past gerund*)	avendo avuto		essendo stato (a, i, e)	

B. Regular Verbs

SIMPLE TENSES

Infinito (*infinitive*)	-**are** **cantare**	-**ere** **ripetere**	-**ire** **partire**	-**ire** (-**isc**-) **finire**
Presente (*present indicative*)	cant **o** cant **i** cant **a** cant **iamo** cant **ate** cạnt **ano**	ripet **o** ripet **i** ripet **e** ripet **iamo** ripet **ete** ripẹt **ono**	part **o** part **i** part **e** part **iamo** par **ite** pạrt **ono**	fin isc **o** fin isc **i** fin isc **e** fin **iamo** fin **ite** fin ịsc **ono**
Imperfetto (*imperfect indicative*)	canta **vo** canta **vi** canta **va** canta **vamo** canta **vate** cantạ **vano**	ripete **vo** ripete **vi** ripete **va** ripete **vamo** ripete **vate** ripetẹ **vano**	parti **vo** parti **vi** parti **va** parti **vamo** parti **vate** partị **vano**	fini **vo** fini **vi** fini **va** fini **vamo** fini **vate** finị **vano**
Passato remoto (*past absolute*)	cant **ai** cant **asti** cant **ò** cant **ammo** cant **aste** cant **ạrono**	ripet **ei** ripet **esti** ripet **è** ripet **emmo** ripet **este** ripet **ẹrono**	part **ii** part **isti** part **ì** part **immo** part **iste** part **ịrono**	fin **ii** fin **isti** fin **ì** fin **immo** fin **iste** fin **ịrono**

Futuro	canter ò	ripeter ò	partir ò	finir ò
(*future*)	canter **ai**	ripeter **ai**	partir **ai**	finir **ai**
	canter **à**	ripeter **à**	partir **à**	finir **à**
	canter **emo**	ripeter **emo**	partir **emo**	finir **emo**
	canter **ete**	ripeter **ete**	partir **ete**	finir **ete**
	canter **anno**	ripeter **anno**	partir **anno**	finir **anno**
Condizionale presente	canter **ei**	ripeter **ei**	partir **ei**	finir **ei**
(*present conditional*)	canter **esti**	ripeter **esti**	partir **esti**	finir **esti**
	canter **ebbe**	ripeter **ebbe**	partir **ebbe**	finir **ebbe**
	canter **emmo**	ripeter **emmo**	partir **emmo**	finir **emmo**
	canter **este**	ripeter **este**	partir **este**	finir **este**
	canter **ẹbbero**	ripeter **ẹbbero**	partir **ẹbbero**	finir **ẹbbero**
Imperativo	—	—	—	—
(*imperative*)	cant **a**	ripet **i**	part **i**	fin isc **i**
	cant **i**	ripet **a**	part **a**	fin isc **a**
	cant **iamo**	ripet **iamo**	part **iamo**	fin **iamo**
	cant **ate**	ripet **ete**	part **ite**	fin **ite**
	cạnt **ino**	ripẹt **ano**	pạrt **ano**	fin ịsc **ano**
Congiuntivo presente	cant **i**	ripet **a**	part **a**	fin isc **a**
(*present subjunctive*)	cant **i**	ripet **a**	part **a**	fin isc **a**
	cant **i**	ripet **a**	part **a**	fin isc **a**
	cant **iamo**	ripet **iamo**	part **iamo**	fin **iamo**
	cant **iate**	ripet **iate**	part **iate**	fin **iate**
	cạnt **ino**	ripẹt **ano**	pạrt **ano**	fin ịsc **ano**
Imperfetto del congiuntivo	cant **assi**	ripet **essi**	part **issi**	fin **issi**
(*imperfect subjunctive*)	cant **assi**	ripet **essi**	part **issi**	fin **issi**
	cant **asse**	ripet **esse**	part **isse**	fin **isse**
	cant **ạssimo**	ripet **ẹssimo**	part **issimo**	fin **ịssimo**
	cant **aste**	ripet **este**	part **iste**	fin **iste**
	cant **ạssero**	ripet **ẹssero**	part **ịssero**	fin **ịssero**
Gerundio	cant **ando**	ripet **endo**	part **endo**	fin **endo**
(*gerund*)				

COMPOUND TENSES

Particịpio passato (*past participle*)	cant **ato**	ripet **uto**	part **ito**	fin **ito**
Infinito passato (*past infinitive*)	avere cantato	avere ripetuto	essere partito (a, i, e)	avere finito
Passato prọssimo (*present perfect indicative*)	ho hai ha abbiamo avete hanno } cantato	ho hai ha abbiamo avete hanno } ripetuto	sono sei è } partito(a) siamo siete sono } partiti(e)	ho hai ha abbiamo avete hanno } finito
Trapassato prossimo (*pluperfect*)	avevo avevi aveva avevamo avevate avẹvano } cantato	avevo avevi aveva avevamo avevate avẹvano } ripetuto	ero eri era } partito(a) eravamo eravate ẹrano } partiti(e)	avevo avevi aveva avevamo avevate avẹvano } finito
Trapassato remoto (*past perfect indicative*)	ebbi avesti ebbe avemmo aveste ẹbbero } cantato	ebbi avesti ebbe avemmo aveste ẹbbero } ripetuto	fui fosti fu } partito(a) fummo foste fụrono } partiti(e)	ebbi avesti ebbe avemmo aveste ẹbbero } finito
Futuro anteriore (*future perfect*)	avrò avrai avrà avremo avrete avranno } cantato	avrò avrai avrà avremo avrete avranno } ripetuto	sarò sarai sarà } partito(a) saremo sarete saranno } partiti(e)	avrò avrai avrà avremo avrete avranno } finito
Condizionale passato (*conditional perfect*)	avrei avresti avrebbe avremmo avreste avrẹbbero } cantato	avrei avresti avrebbe avremmo avreste avrẹbbero } ripetuto	sarei saresti sarebbe } partito(a) saremmo sareste sarẹbbero } partiti(e)	avrei avresti avrebbe avremmo avreste avrẹbbero } finito

Congiuntivo passato (*present perfect subjunctive*)	ạbbia, ạbbia, ạbbia, abbiamo, abbiate, ạbbiano — cantato	ạbbia, ạbbia, ạbbia, abbiamo, abbiate, ạbbiano — ripetuto	sia, sia, sia — partito(a); siamo, siate, sịano — partiti(e)	ạbbia, ạbbia, ạbbia, abbiamo, abbiate, ạbbiano — finito
Trapassato del congiuntivo (*pluperfect subjunctive*)	avessi, avessi, avesse, avẹssimo, aveste, avẹssero — cantato	avessi, avessi, avesse, avẹssimo, aveste, avẹssero — ripetuto	fossi, fossi, fosse — partito(a); fọssimo, foste, fọssero — partiti(e)	avessi, avessi, avesse, avẹssimo, aveste, avẹssero — finito
Gerụndio passato (*past gerund*)	avendo cantato	avendo ripetuto	essendo partito (a, i, e)	avendo finito

APPENDIX 4

Irregular Verbs

Only the irregular forms are given.

andare *to go*

present indicative: vado, vai, va, andiamo, andate, vanno
future: andrò, andrai, andrà, andremo, andrete, andranno
conditional: andrei, andresti, andrebbe, andremmo, andreste, andrẹbbero
imperative: va' (vai), vada, andiamo, andate, vạdano
present subjunctive: vada, vada, vada, andiamo, andiate, vạdano

aprire *to open*

past participle: aperto

assụmere to hire

past absolute: assunsi, assumesti, assunse, assumemmo, assumeste, assụnsero
past participle: assunto

bere *to drink*

present indicative: bevo, bevi, beve, beviamo, bevete, bẹvono
imperfect indicative: bevevo, bevevi, beveva, bevevamo, bevevate, bevẹvano
past absolute: bevvi, bevesti, bevve, bevemmo, beveste, bẹvvero
future: berrò, berrai, berrà, berremo, berrete, berranno
conditional: berrei, berresti, berrebbe, berremmo, berreste, berrẹbbero
imperative: bevi, beva, beviamo, bevete, bẹvano
present subjunctive: beva, beva, beva, beviamo, beviate, bẹvano
imperfect subjunctive: bevessi, bevessi, bevesse, bevẹssimo, beveste, bevẹssero
past participle: bevuto
gerund: bevendo

cadere *to fall*

past absolute: caddi, cadesti, cadde, cademmo, cadeste, cạddero
future: cadrò, cadrai, cadrà, cadremo, cadrete, cadranno
conditional: cadrei, cadresti, cadrebbe, cadremmo, cadreste, cadrẹbbero

chiẹdere *to ask*

past absolute: chiesi, chiedesti, chiese, chiedemmo, chiedeste, chiẹsero
past participle: chiesto

chiụdere *to close*

past absolute: chiusi, chiudesti, chiuse, chiudemmo, chiudeste, chiụsero
part participle: chiuso

conọscere *to know*

past absolute: conobbi, conoscesti, conobbe, conoscemmo, conosceste, conọbbero
past participle: conosciuto

cọrrere *to run*

past absolute: corsi, corresti, corse, corremmo, correste, cọrsero
past participle: corso

dare *to give*

present indicative: do, dai, dà, diamo, date, danno
past absolute: diedi, desti, diede, demmo, deste, dịedero
future: darò, darai, darà, daremo, darete, daranno
conditional: darei, daresti, darebbe, daremmo, dareste, darẹbbero
imperative: da' (dai), dia, diamo, date, dịano
present subjunctive: dia, dia, dia, diamo, diate, dịano
imperfect subjunctive: dessi, dessi, desse, dẹssimo, deste, dẹssero

decịdere *to decide*

past absolute: decisi, decidesti, decise, decidemmo, decideste, decịsero
past participle: deciso

dipingere *to paint*

past absolute: dipinsi, dipingesti, dipinse, dipingemmo, dipingeste, dipịnsero
past participle : dipinto

dire *to say*

present indicative: dico, dici, dice, diciamo, dite, dịcono
imperfect indicative: dicevo, dicevi, diceva, dicevamo, dicevate, dicẹvano
past absolute: dissi, dicesti, disse, dicemmo, diceste, dịssero
imperative: di', dica, diciamo, dite, dịcano
present subjunctive: dica, dica, dica, diciamo, diciate, dịcano
imperfect subjunctive: dicessi, dicessi, dicesse, dicẹssimo', diceste, dicẹssero
past participle: detto
gerund: dicendo

discụtere *to discuss*

past absolute: discussi, discutesti, discusse, discutemmo, discuteste, discụssero
past participle: discusso

dovere *must, to have to*

present indicative: devo, devi, deve, dobbiamo, dovete, dẹvono
future: dovrò, dovrai, dovrà, dovremo, dovrete, dovranno
conditional: dovrei, dovresti, dovrebbe, dovremmo, dovreste, dovrẹbbero
present subjunctive: debba, debba, debba, dobbiamo, dobbiate, dẹbbano *or* deva, deva, deva, dobbiamo, dobbiate, dẹvano

fare *to do, to make*

present indicative: fạccio, fai, fa, facciamo, fate, fanno
imperfect indicative: facevo, facevi, faceva, facevamo, facevate, facẹvano
past absolute: feci, facesti, fece, facemmo, faceste, fẹcero
future: farò, farai, farà, faremo, farete, faranno
conditional: farei, faresti, farebbe, faremmo, fareste, farẹbbero
imperative: fa' (fai), fạccia, facciamo, fate, fạcciano
present subjunctive: fạccia, fạccia, fạccia, facciamo, facciate, fạcciano
imperfect subjunctive: facessi, facessi, facesse, facẹssimo, faceste, facẹssero
past participle: fatto
gerund: facendo

lẹggere *to read*

past absolute: lessi, leggesti, lesse, leggemmo, leggeste, lẹssero
past participle: letto

mẹttere *to put*

past absolute: misi, mettesti, mise, mettemmo, metteste, mịsero
past participle: messo

morire *to die*

present indicative: muọio, muori, muore, moriamo, morite, muọiono
imperative: muori, muọia, moriamo, morite, muọiano
present subjunctive: muọia, muọia, muọia, moriamo, moriate, muọiano
past participle morto

nạscere *to be born*

past absolute: nacqui, nascesti, nacque, nascemmo, nasceste, nạcquero
past participle: nato

offẹndere *to offend*

past absolute:	offesi, offendesti, offese, offendemmo, offendeste, offẹsero
past participle:	offeso

offrire *to offer*

past participle:	offerto

piacere *to be pleasing*

present indicative:	piạccio, piaci, piace, piacciamo, piacete, piạcciono
past absolute:	piạcqui, piacesti, piạcque, piacemmo, piaceste, piạcquero
imperative:	piaci, piạccia, piacciamo, piacete, piạcciano
present subjunctive:	piạccia, piạccia, piạccia, piacciamo, piacciate, piạcciano
past participle:	piaciuto

potere *to be able to*

present indicative:	posso, puoi, può, possiamo, potete, pọssono
future:	potrò, potrai, potrà, potremo, potrete, potranno
conditional:	potrei, potresti, potrebbe, potremmo, potreste, potrẹbbero
Present subjunctive:	possa, possa, possa, possiamo, possiate, pọssano

prẹndere *to take*

past absolute:	presi, prendesti, prese, prendemmo, prendeste, prẹsero
past participle:	preso

rịdere *to laugh*

past absolute:	risi, ridesti, rise, ridemmo, rideste, rịsero
past participle:	riso

rimanere *to remain*

present indicative:	rimango, rimani, rimane, rimaniamo, rimanete, rimạngono
past absolute:	rimasi, rimanesti, rimase, rimanemmo, rimaneste, rimạsero
future:	rimarrò, rimarrai, rimarrà, rimarremo, rimarrete, rimarranno
conditional:	rimarrei, rimarresti, rimarrebbe, rimarremmo, rimarreste, rimarrẹbbero
imperative:	rimani, rimanga, rimaniamo, rimanete, rimạngano
present subjunctive:	rimanga, rimanga, rimanga, rimaniamo, rimaniate, rimạngano
past participle:	rimasto

rispọndere *to answer*

past absolute:	risposi, rispondesti, rispose, rispondemmo, rispondeste, rispọsero
past participle:	risposto

rọmpere *to break*

past absolute:	ruppi, rompesti, ruppe, rompemmo, rompeste, rụppero
past participle:	rotto

salire *to go up*

present indicative:	salgo, sali, sale, saliamo, salite, sạlgono
imperative:	sali, salga, saliamo, salite, sạlgano
present subjunctive:	salga, salga, salga, saliamo, saliate, sạlgano

sapere *to know*

present indicative:	so, sai, sa, sappiamo, sapete, sanno
past absolute:	seppi, sapesti, seppe, sapemmo, sapeste, sẹppero
future:	saprò, saprai, saprà, sapremo, saprete, sapranno
conditional:	saprei, sapresti, saprebbe, sapremmo, sapreste, saprẹbbero
imperative:	sappi, sappia, sappiamo, sappiate, sạppiano
present subjunctive:	sạppia, sạppia, sạppia, sappiamo, sappiate, sạppiano

scẹgliere *to choose*

present indicative:	scelgo, scegli, scẹglie, scegliamo, scegliete, scẹlgono
past absolute:	scelsi, scegliesti, scelse, scegliemmo, sceglieste, scẹlsero
imperative:	scegli, scelga, scegliamo, scegliete, scẹlgano
present subjunctive:	scelga, scelga, scelga, scegliamo, scegliate, scẹlgano
past participle:	scelto

scẹndere *to descend*

past absolute:	scesi, scendesti, scese, scendemmo, scendeste, scẹsero
past participle:	sceso

scoprire *to discover*

past participle:	scoperto

scrịvere *to write*

past absolute:	scrissi, scrivesti, scrisse, scrivemmo, scriveste, scrịssero
past participle:	scritto

sedere *to sit down*

present indicative:	siedo, siedi, siede, sediamo, sedete, siędono
imperative:	siedi, sieda, sediamo, sedete, siędano
present subjunctive:	sieda, sieda, sieda, sediamo, sediate, siędano

spẹndere *to spend*

past absolute: spesi, spendesti, spese, spendemmo, spendeste, spẹsero
past participle: speso

stare *to stay*

present indicative: sto, stai, sta, stiamo, state, stanno
past absolute: stetti, stesti, stette, stemmo, steste, stẹttero
future: starò, starai, starà, staremo, starete, staranno
conditional: starei, staresti, starebbe, staremmo, stareste, starẹbbero
imperative: sta' (stai), stia, stiamo, state, stiano
present subjunctive: stia, stia, stia, stiamo, stiate, stịano
imperfect subjunctive: stessi, stessi, stesse, stẹssimo, steste, stẹssero

succẹdere *to happen*

past absolute: successe
past participle: successo

tenere *to happen*

present indicative: tengo, tieni, tiene, teniamo, tenete, tẹngono
past absolute: tenni, tenesti, tenne, tenemmo, teneste, tẹnnero
future: terrò, terrai, terrà, terremo, terrete, terranno
conditional terrei, terresti, terrebbe, terremmo, terreste, terrẹbbero
imperative: tieni, tenga, teniamo, tenete, tẹngano
present subjunctive: tenga, tenga, tenga, teniamo, teniate, tẹngano

uccịdere *to kill*

past absolute: uccisi, uccidesti, uccise, uccidemmo, uccideste, uccịsero
past participle: ucciso

uscire *to go out*

present indicative: esco, esci, esce, usciamo, uscite, ẹscono
imperative: esci, esca, usciamo, uscite, ẹscano
present subjunctive: esca, esca, esca, usciamo, usciate, ẹscano

vedere *to see*

past absolute: vidi, vedesti, vide, vedemmo, vedeste, vịdero
future: vedrò, vedrai, vedrà, vedremo, vedrete, vedranno
conditional: vedrei, vedresti, vedrebbe, vedremmo, vedreste, vedrẹbbero
past participle: visto (veduto)

venire *to come*

present indicative: vengo, vieni, viene, veniamo, venite, vẹngono
past absolute: venni, venisti, venne, venimmo, veniste, vẹnnero
future: verrò, verrai, verrà, verremo, verrete, verranno
conditional: verrei, verresti, verrebbe, verremmo, verreste, verrẹbbero
imperative: vieni, venga, veniamo, venite, vẹngano
present subjunctive: venga, venga, venga, veniamo, veniate, vẹngano
past participle: venuto

vịncere *to win*

past absolute: vinsi, vincesti, vinse, vincemmo, vinceste, vịnsero
past participle: vinto

vịvere *to live*

past absolute: vissi, vivesti, visse, vivemmo, viveste, vịssero
future: vivrò, vivrai, vivrà, vivremo, vivrete, vivranno
conditional: vivrei, vivresti, vivrebbe, vivremmo, vivreste, vivrẹbbero
past participle: vissuto

volere *to want*

present indicative: vọglio, vuoi, vuole, vogliamo, volete, vọgliono
past absolute: volli, volesti, volle, volemmo, voleste, vọllero
future: vorrò, vorrai, vorrà, vorremo, vorrete, vorranno
conditional: vorrei, vorresti, vorrebbe, vorremmo, vorreste, vorrẹbbero
present subjunctive: vọglia, vọglia, vọglia, vogliamo, vogliate, vọgliano

ITALIAN–ENGLISH VOCABULARY

The Italian-English vocabulary contains most of the basic words and expressions used in each chapter. Stress is indicated by a dot under the stressed vowel. An asterisk * following an infinitive indicates that the verb is conjugated with **essere** in compound tenses. The **-isc-** after an **-ire** verb means that the verb requires **-isc-** in the present indicative, present subjunctive, and imperative conjugations.

The following abbreviations are used:

adj.	adjective	*inv.*	invariable
adv.	adverb	*m.*	masculine
colloq.	colloquial	*p.p.*	past participle
def. art.	definite article	*pl.*	plural
f.	feminine	*prep.*	preposition
fam.	familiar	*pron.*	pronoun
form.	formal	*conj.*	conjunction
inf.	infinitive		

A

a in, at, to
abbandonare to abandon
abbasso down with
abbastanza enough, sufficiently
l'abbigliamento clothing, apparel
abbonarsi* to subscribe
abbondante abundant
abbracciare to embrace
l'abbraccio hug
abbronzarsi to tan
l'abitante *(m. & f.)* inhabitant
abitare to live
abitualmente usually
abituarsi* to get used to
abituato accustomed
l'abitudine *(f.)* habit
accelerare to accelerate
accendere (*p.p.* **acceso**) to light, to turn on
l'accento accent, stress
accomodarsi* to make oneself comfortable
accompagnare to accompany
l'accordo agreement;
d'accordo OK, agreed
l'aceto vinegar
l'acqua water;
l'acqua minerale mineral water
adagio slowly
adesso now
addio good-bye (forever)
addormentarsi to fall asleep;
addormentato asleep
l'adulto, l'adulta adult
l'aereo, l'aeroplano airplane
l'aeroporto airport
l'affare *(m.)* business;
per affari on business;
È un affare! It is a bargain!;
uomo (donna) d'affari business man (woman)
affascinante fascinating
affatto not at all
l'affermazione *(f.)* statement
l'affetto affection;
con affetto love
affinchè so that, in order that
affittare to rent, to lease
l'affitto rent, rental;
in affitto for rent
affollato crowded
l'affresco fresco
l'agente *(m. & f.)* **di viaggi** travel agent
l'agenzia di collocamento employment agency;
l'agenzia di viaggi travel agency
l'aggettivo adjective
agire (-isc) to act
aggiungere (*p.p.* **aggiunto**) to add
l'aglio garlic
agosto August
aiutare to help
l'aiuto help

l'alba dawn
l'albergo hotel
l'ạlbero tree
alcuni (alcune) some, a few
alcoọlico alcoholic
allacciare (le cinture di sicurezza) to fasten (the seat belts)
allegro cheerful
allenare to coach;
allenarsi* to practice, to train, to make oneself fit
l'allenatore, l'allenatrice coach
l'allievo, l'allieva pupil
l'allọggio housing
allora then, well then, so;
da allora since then
allungare to prolong
almeno at least
le Alpi Alps
l'alpinismo mountain climbing
l'alpinista *(m.& f.)* mountain climber
alto tall, high
altro other
alzarsi* to get up
amare to love
amaro bitter
l'ambientalista *(m.& f)* environmentalist
l'ambiente environment
l'ambulanza ambulance
americano American
l'amicịzia friendship
l'amico, l'amica friend
ammalarsi* to become ill
ammalato ill, sick
ammẹttere to admit
ammirare to admire
ammobiliato furnished
l'amore *(m.)* love
l'anạlisi *(f.)* analysis
anạlogo similar
anche also, too;
anche se even if
ancora still, more, again;
non ancora not yet
andare* to go;
andare d'accordo to get along;
andare bene to fit;
andare in bicicletta to ride a bicycle;
andare in cerca di to go in search of;
andare al cịnema to go to the movies;
andare in pensione to retire;
andare a piedi to walk;
andare a trovare to visit a person;
andare via to go away
l'ạngolo corner
l'animale *(m.)* animal
annegare to drawn
l'anno year;
avere... anni to be ... years old
annoiarsi* to get bored
annunciare to announce
l'annunciatore, l'annunciatrice TV announcer
l'annụncio pubblicitario ad
ansiosamente anxiously
l'antibiọtico antibiotic
l'antịcipo advance;
in antịcipo ahead of time, in advance
antico (*pl.* **antichi**) ancient, antique
l'antipasto hors d'oeuvre
antipạtico unpleasant
anziano elderly
l'aperitivo aperitif
aperto open;
all'aperto outdoors
apparecchiare to set the table
l'appartamento apartment
appassionato (*di*) fond of
appena as soon as; only
gli Appennini Apennine Mountains
appennịnico of the Apennines
l'appetito appetite
applaudire to applaud
apprezzare to appreciate
approssimativamente approximately
l'appuntamento appointment, date
gli appunti notes
aprile April
aprire to open
ạrabo Arabic;
gli Ạrabi Arabs
l'arạncia orange
l'aranciata orange drink
l'ạrbitro referee
l'architetto architect
l'architettura architecture
l'argomento subject
l'ạria air, appearance;
avere un'ạria to look
l'armadietto cabinet
l'armạdio wardrobe;
armạdio a muro closet
arrabbiarsi* to get angry
arrabbiato angry
arredare to furnish
arredato furnished
arrivare* to arrive
arrivederci! *(fam.)*;
ArrivederLa! *(form.)* Good-bye!
l'arrivo arrival
l'arrosto roast;
l'arrosto di vitello roast veal
l'arte *(f.)* art;
ọpera d'arte work of art;
Le Belle Arti Fine Arts
l'artịcolo article, item
l'artigianato handicraft
l'artigiano artisan
l'artista *(m. & f.)* artist
artịstico artistic
l'artrite *(f.)* arthritis
l'ascensore *(m.)* elevator
l'asciugamano towel
asciugarsi* to dry oneself
ascoltare to listen to
aspettare to wait for
l'aspirina aspirine
assaggiare to taste

l'assegno check
assente absent
assistere (*p.p.* **assistito**) to attend, to assist
assumere (*p.p.* **assunto**) to hire
astratto abstract
l'astrologia astrology
l'atleta *(m. & f.)* athlete
l'atmosfera atmosphere
attaccare to hang
attento careful;
  stare attento to pay attention
l'attenzione *(f.)* attention;
  fare attenzione to be careful
l'attività *(f.)* activity
attivo active
l'atto act
l'attore; l'attrice actor; actress
attraente attractive
attraversare to cross
attraverso across; through
attrezzato equipped
attualmente at present
augurare to wish
l'augurio wish;
  Tanti auguri! Best wishes!
l'aula classroom
aumentare to increase
l'aumento increase
l'autista *(m. & f.)* driver
l'autobiografia autobiography
l'autobus *(m.)* (*pl.* **gli autobus**) bus
l'automobile *(f.)* car
l'automobilista *(m. & f.)* motorist
l'autore; l'autrice author
l'autorità authority
l'autostop hitchhiking; **fare l'autostop** to hitchhike
l'autostrada freeway
l'autunno autumn, fall
Avanti! Come in;
  avanti straight ahead
avaro stingy
avere to have;
  avere... anni to be ... years old;
  avere un'aria to look;
  avere bisogno (di) to need;
  avere caldo to be hot;
  avere fame to be hungry;
  avere la febbre to have a temperature;
  avere freddo to be cold;
  avere fretta to be in a hurry;
  avere dei guasti al motore to have a car breakdown;
  avere intenzione (di) to intend;
  avere luogo to take place;
  avere mal di (denti, schiena, stomaco, testa, gola) to have a (toothache, backache, stomachache, headache, sore throat);
  avere paura di to be afraid of;
  avere il raffreddore to have a cold;
  avere ragione to be right;
  avere sete to be thirsty;
  avere sonno to be sleepy;
  avere torto to be wrong;
  avere la tosse to have a cough;
  avere voglia (di) to feel like
l'avvenimento event
l'avventura adventure
l'avverbio adverb
avvicinarsi* (a) to get near, to approach
avvincente fascinating
l'avvocato; l'avvocatessa lawyer
l'azione *(f.)* action
azzurro light blue

B

baciare to kiss
il bacio kiss
i baffi mustache
i bagagli baggage, luggage
il/la bagnante bather
il bagnino; la bagnina lifeguard
il bagno bath; bathroom;
  fare il bagno to take a bath
il balcone balcony
ballare to dance
il bambino; la bambina child, little boy, little girl;
  da bambino as a child
la banca bank
il banco stand, counter; student desk
la banda band
la bandiera flag
il bar bar;
  bar con tavola calda snack bar
la barba beard;
  farsi la barba to shave
la barca boat;
  la barca a vela sailboat
il barista barman
barocco baroque
basso short, low
bastare to suffice, to be enough
la batteria drums
be' (bene) well
la bellezza beauty
bello beautiful, handsome
benchè although
bene well, fine;
  va bene OK, very well;
  è bene che it's a good thing that;
  benissimo very well;
  benone! great!

la benzina gasoline; **il distributore di benzina** gasoline pump; **fare benzina** to fill up; **la benzina senza piombo** unleaded gasoline

bere (*p. p.* **bevuto)** to drink

la bevanda drink; **bevanda alcọolica** alcoholic beverage

la biancheria da letto linens

bianco (*pl.* **bianchi)** white

la bibita soft drink

la biblioteca library

il bicchiere glass

la bicicletta bicycle

il biglietto ticket, card; **biglietto di andata e ritorno** round-trip ticket

il binạrio (railway) track

la biologia biology

biondo blond

la birra beer

bisognare to be necessary

il bisogno need; **avere bisogno di** to need

la bistecca steak

blu (*inv.*) blue

la bocca mouth

la bolletta bill (telephone, utilities)

la borsa bag; **borsa di studio** grant, scholarship

la borsetta handbag

il bosco wood, forest

la bottịglia bottle

il brạccio (*pl.* **le brạccia)** arm

bravo good

breve short, brief

il brodo broth

bruno dark-haired

brutto ugly, bad

la bugia lie; **dire le bugie** to lie

bugiardo liar

bụio dark, darkness

buono good

il burattino puppet

il burro butter

la busta envelope

C

cadere* to fall

il caffè coffee, cafe, coffee shop

il cạlcio soccer

la calcolatrice calculator

caldo hot; **avere caldo** to be hot; **fa caldo** it is hot (weather)

il calendạrio calendar

il calmante sedative

calmare to calm

calmo calm

la caloria calorie

la calza stocking

il calzino sock

cambiare to change, to exchange; **cambiare idea** to change one's mind

il cạmbio change, exchange

la cạmera room; **cạmera da letto** bedroom; **cạmera singola (doppia)** single (double) room

il cameriere; la cameriera waiter; waitress; maid

la camịcetta blouse

la camịcia (*pl.* **le camịcie)** shirt

camminare to walk

la campagna country, countryside; **campagna elettorale** election campaign

il campanile bell tower

il campẹggio camping; **fare il campẹggio** to go camping

il campionato championship

il campione; la campionessa champion

il campo field; **campo da tennis** tennis court

canadese Canadian

il canale channel, canal (Venice)

la candela candle

il candidato, la candidata candidate

il cane dog

i cannelloni stuffed pasta

il canottạggio boating, rowing

il (la) cantante singer

cantare to sing

il canto singing

la canzone song

i capelli hair

capire (-isc-) to understand

la capitale capital

il capịtolo chapter

il capo head, leader

il Capodanno New Year's day

il capolavoro masterpiece

il capoluogo chief town

il cappello hat

il cappotto winter coat

il cappuccino coffee with steamed milk

il capouffịcio boss

il carạttere temperament

la caratterịstica characteristic, feature

la caricatura caricature

carino pretty, cute

la carne meat

caro dear, expensive

la carota carrot

la carriera career; **fare carriera** to have a successful career

la carta paper;
carta geografica map;
la carta di credito credit card;
la carta telefonica telephone card
la carta d'identità identification card
la cartella chart
il cartello sign
la cartoleria stationary store
la cartolina postcard
il cartone animato animated cartoon
la casa house, home;
a casa, in casa at home;
a casa di at the house of;
a casa sua at his/her house;
fatto in casa homemade
la casalinga housewife
il caso case;
per caso by any chance;
secondo il caso according to the case
la cassa case, cashier's desk
il cassetto drawer
castano brown (eyes, hair)
il castello castle
la catena chain
cattivo bad, mean
la causa cause;
a causa di because of
causare to cause
c'è (ci sono) there is (are)
la cauzione deposit
celebrare to celebrate
celibe *(m.)* unmarried, single
la cena dinner
cenare to have supper
il centesimo cent
cento one hundred
centrale central
il (la) centralinista telephone operator
il centro center;
in centro downtown
cercare to look for;
cercare di + *inf.* to try
i cereali cereals
certamente certainly
certo certain; *(adv.)* certainly
il cestino basket
che? who; whom;
che ...! what (a) ...!
che *(cong.)* that;
che; che cosa, cosa? what?;
più ... che more ... than
chi? who?, whom?
di chi è? whose is it?
chiamare to call;
chiamarsi* to be called
la chiave key
chiedere *(p.p.* **chiesto)** to ask (for)
la chiesa church
il chilogrammo kilogram
il chilometro kilometer
la chimica chemistry
il chirurgo surgeon
chissà! who knows
la chitarra guitar
chiudere *(p.p.* **chiuso)** to close
ciao hello, hi, good-bye
il cibo food
il ciclismo bicycling
il (la) ciclista cyclist
il cielo sky
il cinematografo movie theater
cinese Chinese
la cintura di sicurezza safety belt
il cioccolato chocolate
il cioccolatino chocolate candy
cioè that is
la cipolla onion
circa about, approximately
circondare to surround
la circostanza occasion
la città city, town
il cittadino citizen
la civilizzazione civilization
la civiltà civilization
la classe class, classroom
classico classic
il (la) cliente customer
il clima climate
il codice postale zip code
il cofano hood (car)
il cognato, la cognata brother-in-law; sister-in law
il cognome last name
la colazione breakfast
fare colazione to have breakfast
i collant pantyhose
collaborare to collaborate
il (la) collega colleague
la collina hill
il collo neck
il colloquio interview
il colore color
il coltello knife
come as, like;
Come? How?;
Come sta? *(form. s.)*, **Come stai?** *(fam. s.)*, **Come va?** How are you?
Com'è? How does he (she, it) look like?
Come mai? How come?
il comico comedian;
comico *(adj.)* comic
la commedia comedy, play
il commediografo playwright
commentare to make a comment
il commento comment
il commercio commerce
il commesso, la commessa salesperson
comodamente comfortably
la comodità comfort
comodo comfortable
la compagnia company
il compagno, la compagna companion;
compagno(a) di classe classmate;
compagno(a) di stanza roommate;
competente competent
il compito homework, task

il compleanno birthday;
Buon compleanno! Happy birthday!
completamente fully, completely
completare to complete
il completo suit
complicato complicated
comporre (*p.p.* **composto**) to compose
il compositore, la compositrice composer
comprare to buy
comune common
comunicare to communicate
il (la) comunista communist
con with
il concerto concert
conclụdersi* (*p.p.* **concluso**) to end; to conclude itself
la conclusione conclusion
condire to dress (salad, food)
condivịdere (*p.p.* **condiviso**) to share
la condizione condition
la conferenza lecture
confinare to border, to confine
la confusione confusion
Congratulazioni! Congratulations!
il conịglio rabbit
la conoscenza knowledge
conọscere (*p.p.* **conosciuto**) to know, to meet, to be acquainted with
considerarsi* to consider oneself
consigliare to advise
il consịglio advice
consolare to console
la consonante consonant
il (la) consulente consultant
consultare to consult
consumare to consume
il contadino, la contadina peasant; farmer
contare to count
contento happy, glad; pleased
il continente continent
continuare to continue
il conto check, bill
il contrạrio opposite
il contrasto contrast
il contratto contract
contribuire (-isc) to contribute
contro against
controllare to check
la conversazione conversation
la coperta blanket; cover
la cọpia copy
la cọppia couple, pair
il corạggio courage
corạggio! come on!
coraggioso courageous; brave
cordiale cordial
il coro chorus
il corpo body
corrẹggere (*p.p.* **corretto**) to correct
correre (*p.p.* **corso**) to run
la corsa run, race
il corso course (studies); main street
il cortile courtyard
corto short
la cosa thing
così so;
così-così so-so;
così tanto! that much!
così ... come as ... as
la costa coast;
la Costa Azzurra French Riviera
costare to cost;
quanto costa? how much is it?
il costo cost, price
costoso expensive
costruire (-isc-) to build
il costume costume;
il costume da bagno bathing suit
il cotone cotton
cotto cooked
la cravatta tie
creare to create
crẹdere to believe
la crisi crisis
la crịtica criticism, critique, review
criticare to criticize
il crịtico critic; (*adj.*) critical
la crociera cruise;
fare una crociera to go on a cruise
il cucchịaio spoon
il cucchiaino tea spoon
la cucina kitchen; cooking; cuisine
cucinare to cook;
cucinare al forno to bake
il cugino, la cugina cousin
cui (*pron.*) whom, which;
la ragazza con cui esco the girl with whom I go out
la cultura culture
culturale cultural
il culturismo body building
cuọcere (*p.p.* **cotto**) to cook
il cuoco, la cuoca cook
il cuore heart
la cura treatment; care
curare to treat
curioso curious
la curva curve
il cuscino pillow

D

da from, by;
lavoro da un mese I have been working for a month
d'accordo OK, agreed;
ẹssere d'accordo to agree
Dai! Come on! (*fam.*)

dare to give;
dare un esame to take an exam;
dare fastidio to bother;
dare un passaggio to give a lift;
dare del tu (Lei) use the tu (Lei) form; **dare la mano** to shake hands
la data date (calendar)
il dattilọgrafo, la dattilọgrafa typist
davanti (a) in front of, before
davvero really, indeed
dẹbole weak
decịdere (*p.p.* **deciso)** to decide
la decisione decision
dedicarsi* to devote oneself
la delusione disappointment
deluso disappointed
democrạtico democratic
la democrazia democracy
democristiano Christian Democrat
il denaro money
il dente tooth;
al dente firm, not overcooked
il dentifricio toothpaste
il (la) dentista dentist
dentro in, inside
depositare to deposit;
depositare un assegno to deposit a check
il depọsito deposit;
depọsito bagagli baggage room
la depressione depression
deprimente depressing
il deputato congressman;
la deputata congresswoman
descrịvere (*p.p.* **descritto)** to describe
la descrizione description
desiderare to wish, want;
desịdera? may I help you?
il desidẹrio wish, desire
desideroso eager
la destra right;
a destra to the right;
il braccio destro the right arm
detestare to hate
di of, from; **di** + *def. art.* some, any;
di chi è? whose is it?
di dov'è? where is he/she from?
la diạgnosi diagnosis
il dialetto dialect
il diạlogo (*pl.* **diạloghi**) dialogue
il diạrio diary
dicembre *(m.)* December
le didascalie (*f. pl.*) (*cinema*) subtitles
la dieta diet;
stare a dieta to be on a diet
dietro behind
difẹndersi* to defend oneself
la differenza difference;
a differenza di unlike
difficile difficult
la difficoltà difficulty
diligente diligent
dimagrire (-isc-) to lose weight
dimenticare to forget
diminuire (-isc-) to diminish; to reduce
dimostrare to show, to express
dipẹndere (*p.p.* **dipeso)** to depend;
dipẹnde (da) it depends (on)
dipịngere (*p.p.* **dipinto)** to paint, to portray
il diploma certificate, diploma
diplomarsi* to graduate from high school
dire *(p.p.* **detto)** to say, to tell;
dire di no to say no;
voler dire to mean
direttamente directly
il direttore, la direttrice director; administrator
direttore d'orchestra orchestra conductor
diritto, dritto (*adj.*) straight; (*adv.*) straight ahead
il diritto right
discendere* (*p.p.* **disceso**) to descend, to go (come) down
il disco (*pl.* **dischi**) record
il discorso speech
la discoteca discoteque
la discussione discussion
discụtere (*p.p.* **discusso**) to discuss
disegnare to draw
il disegnatore, la disegnatrice designer
il disegno drawing, pattern plan
disoccupato unemployed
la disoccupazione unemployment
disordinato messy
dispiacere* **(***p.p.* **dispiaciuto)** to mind, to be sorry;
mi dispiace I am sorry
disposto willing;
essere disposto to be willing
la distanza distance
distare to be distant, to be far from
distratto absent-minded
il distributore di benzina gasoline pump
disturbare to bother
il disturbo ailment, trouble
il dito (*pl.* **le dita)** finger;
dito del piede toe
la ditta firm
il divano sofa, couch
diventare* to become
diverso different;
diversi giorni several days
divertente amusing
divertimento amusement;
buon divertimento! have fun!

divertire to amuse;
divertirsi* to have fun, to enjoy oneself
divịdere (*p.p.* **diviso**) to share, to divide
il divieto prohibition;
divieto di fumare no smoking;
divieto di parchẹggio no parking
divorziato (a) divorced
il divọrzio divorce
il dizionạrio dictionary
la dọccia shower;
fare la dọccia to take a shower
il documentạrio documentary film
il documento document;
documento d'identità I.D.
la dogana customs
il dolce dessert, candy; (*adj.*) sweet
dolcemente gradually, gently
il dọllaro dollar
il dolore pain, ache
la domanda question;
fare una domanda to ask a question
domandare to ask;
domandarsi* to wonder
domani tomorrow
la domẹnica Sunday
la donna woman
dopo after, afterwards
dopodomani the day after tomorrow
doppio double
dormire to sleep
la dose amount
il dottore, la dottoressa doctor, university graduate
dove? where?;
di dove sei? where are you from?
il dovere duty
dovere to have to, must, to owe
il dramma drama, play
drammạtico dramatic
la droga drug
il dubbio doubt;
senza dubbio undoubedly
dubitare to doubt
dunque therefore; well now!
il duomo cathedral
durante during
durare* to last
duro hard;
avere la testa dura to be stubborn

E

e, ed and
eccellente excellent
l'eccesso excess
eccẹtera etcetera
eccetto except
l'eccezione (*f.*) exception
eccitato excited
ecco! here is! here are!;
ẹccomi here I am
l'ecologia ecology
ecolọgico ecological
l'economia economy
econọmico economic(al), cheap
ecọnomo thrifty
l'edifịcio building
l'editore, l'editrice publisher
educato polite
l'effetto effect;
effetto serra greenhouse effect
efficiente efficient
elegante elegant, fashionable
elẹggere (*p.p.* **eletto**) to elect
elementare elementary
l'elenco telefọnico phone book
l'elettricista electrician
l'elettricità electricity
elettrọnico electronic
l'elezione (*f.*) election
eliminare to eliminate
emigrare to emigrate
entrare* to enter
l'entrata entrance
l'entusiasmo enthusiasm
entusiasta enthusiastic
l'ẹpoca period
l'equipaggiamento equipment
l'equitazione (*f.*) horse riding
l'erba grass
l'eredità inheritance
ereditare to inherit
l'errore (*m.*) error, mistake
esagerare to exaggerate
l'esame (*m.*) exam;
dare un esame to take an exam
esattamente exactly
esatto exact
l'esclamazione (*f.*) exclamation
l'escursione (*f.*) excursion
l'esẹmpio example;
ad (per) esẹmpio for example
esercitare to exercise
l'esercịzio exercise
esigente demanding
l'esịlio exile
esịstere* (*p. p.* **esistito**) to exist
esọtico exotic
l'esperienza experience
l'esperimento experiment
esperto experienced
esplorare to explore
l'espressione expression;
espressione di cortesia greetings
l'espresso expresso coffee
esprịmere (*p.p.* **espresso**) to express

ẹssere* (*p.p.* **stato**) to be;
ẹssere d'accordo to agree;
ẹssere in antịcipo to be early;
ẹssere a dieta to be on a diet;
ẹssere in orạrio to be on time;
ẹssere promosso to be promoted;
ẹssere in ritardo to be late;
ẹssere al verde to be broke
l'est east
l'estate (*f.*) summer
esterno exterior
ẹstero foreign;
commẹrcio estero foreign trade;
all'estero abroad
estivo (*adj.*) summer
l'età age;
l'età della pietra stone age
l'Europa Europe
europeo European
evitare to avoid

F

fa ago;
un anno fa one year ago
fa caldo (freddo, fresco, bel tempo, brutto tempo) it is hot (cold, cool, nice weather, bad weather);
fa (*math.*) equals
la fạbbrica factory
la fạccia face
fạcile easy
facilmente easily
la facoltà di legge (medicina, ecc.) law (medical, etc.) school
i fagiolini green beans
falso false
la fame hunger;
avere fame to be hungry
la famịglia family
familiare familiar
famoso famous
la fantascienza science fiction
la fantasia fantasy; imagination
fare (*p.p.* **fatto**) to do, to make;
fare attenzione to pay attention;
fare gli auguri to send good wishes;
fare l'autostop to hitchhike;
fare il bagno to take a bath;
fare un brindisi to make a toast;
fare il campeggio to go camping;
fare colazione to have breakfast;
fare la conoscenza (di) to make the acquaintance (of);
fare la dọccia to take a shower;
fare una domanda to ask a question;
fare domanda to apply; **fare il dottore (l'ingegnere, ecc.)** to be a doctor (an engineer, etc);
fare un'escursione to make an excursion;
fare bella figura to make a good impression;
fare la fila to stand in line;
fare una foto to take a picture;
fare una gita to take a short trip;
fare legge (matematica, medicina, ecc.) to study law (mathematics, medicine, etc);
fare la pace to make up;
fare parte(di) to take part (in);
fare una passeggiata to take a walk;
fare una pausa to take a break;
fare il pieno to fill it up;
fare presto to hurry;
fare un regalo to give a present;
fare sciopero to be on strike;
fare la siesta to take a nap;
fare la spesa to buy groceries;
fare le spese to go shopping;
fare lo spiritoso to clown around;
fare dello sport to practice sports;
fare una telefonata to make a phone call;
fare il tifo to be a fan;
fare le valịgie to pack;
fare un viạggio to take a trip;
fare una vịsita to pay a visit;
farne a meno to do without it;
farsi* male to hurt oneself
la farina flour
la farmacia pharmacy
il (la) farmacista pharmacist
il fascismo fascism
faticoso tiring
il fatto fact; event
il fattore factor, element
la fạvola fable
il favore favor;
per favore please
il fazzoletto handkerchief
febbrạio February
la febbre fever
fedele faithful; loyal
la fedeltà loyalty
felice happy
la felicità happiness
la felpa sweat shirt
femminile ferninine
le fẹrie paid annual vacation

ai ferri broiled
fermare to stop someone (something);
  fermarsi* to stop
fermo still, stopped
il Ferragosto August holiday
la ferrovia railroad
ferroviạrio of the railroad
la festa holiday, party
festeggiare to celebrate
la fetta slice
il fidanzamento engagement
fidanzarsi* to become engaged
il fidanzato, la fidanzata fiance, fiancee
la fidụcia trust; **avere fiducia** to trust
il fịglio, la fịglia son, daughter;
  fịglio (a) ụnico (a) only child;
  i fịgli children
la figura figure;
  fare bella figura to make a good impression
la fila line;
  fare la fila to stand in line
il film movie;
  dare un film to show a movie
filmare to make a movie
finalmente finally, at last
finanziare to finance
finchè until
la fine end
il fine settimana weekend
la finestra window
il finestrino window (car, bus, train, etc.)
finire (-isc-) to finish, to end
fino a until; as far as
il fiore flower
fiorentino Florentine
Firenze Florence
la firma signature
firmare to sign; **firmare una ricevuta** to sign a receipt
fischiare to whistle; to boo
la fịsica physics
fịsico physical
fissare un appuntamento to set an appointment
il fiume river
il flạuto flute
il foglio sheet;
  il foglio di carta sheet of paper
la folla crowd
fondare to found
la fontana fountain
la forchetta fork
la forma form, shape
il formạggio cheese
formare to form;
  formare il nụmero to dial
il fornaio baker
i fornelli range (stove)
il forno oven
forse maybe, perhaps
forte strong
la fortuna fortune, luck;
  buona fortuna good luck;
  per fortuna luckily
fortunato lucky
la forza strength;
  forza! come on!
la foto(grafia) picture, photography;
  fare una foto to take a picture
fra between, among, in
la frạgola strawberry
francamente frankly, honestly
francese French
il francobollo stamp
la frase sentence
il fratello brother
il freddo cold;
  avere freddo to be cold;
  fa freddo it is cold;
  (adj.) **il caffè freddo** cold coffee
frenare to brake
i freni brakes
frequentare to attend (school)
fresco cool, fresh
la fretta hurry;
  avere fretta to be in a hurry;
  in fretta in a hurry
il frigo (rịfero) refrigerator
la frittata omelette
la frutta fruit
fumare to smoke
il fumatore, la fumatrice smoker
il fumetto bubble;
  i fumetti comic strips
il fungo (*pl.* funghi) mushroom
funzionare to function
il fuoco (*pl.* **fuochi**) fire
fuori (di) out (of), outside
il futuro future

G

la galleria arcade; gallery; balcony;
  la galleria d'arte art gallery
la gamba leg
il gamberetto shrimp
la gara race; competition
i1 gatto cat
il gelato ice cream
i gemelli twins
generale general;
  in generale in general
la generazione generation
il gẹnere gender;
  in gẹnere generally
i gẹneri alimentari grocery
il gẹnero son-in-law
generoso generous
il gẹnio genius
il genitore parent
gennạio January
Gẹnova Genoa
la gente people
gentile kind
la geografia geography

geografico geographic
la Germania Germany
il gesso chalk
il gettone token (telephone)
il ghiaccio ice
già already; yes; sure
la giacca coat, jacket;
la giacca a vento windbreaker
giallo yellow
il Giappone Japan
giapponese Japanese
il giardino garden;
i giardini pubblici park
la ginnastica gymnastics
il ginocchio knee
giocare (a) to play (*a game*);
giocare a carte to play cards
il giocatore, la giocatrice player
il giocattolo toy
il gioco (*pl.* **giochi**) game
il giornale newspaper
il (la) giornalista journalist
la giornata the whole day
il giorno day;
buon giorno good morning, good day
giovane young;
il giovane young man;
i giovani young people
il giovanotto young man
il giovedì Thursday
la gioventù youth
il giradischi record player
girare to turn; to tour;
girare un film to make a movie
il giro tour
la gita trip, excursion, tour
la gita scolastica field trip
il giudizio judgement, sentence
giugno June
la giustificazione justification
giusto just, right
la gola throat;
il mal di gola sore throat
il golf sweater (cardigan)
il golfo gulf
la gomma tire;
una gomma a terra flat tire
la gonna skirt
gotico gothic
governare to rule
il governo government
il grammo gram
grande big, wide, large, great;
da grande as an adult
grasso fat
grassottello chubby
il grattacielo skyscraper
gratuito free (of charge)
grave grave; serious
grazie thank you;
grazie a thanks to;
mille grazie thanks a lot
greco (*pl.* **greci**) Greek
gridare to shout
grigio grey
i grissini bread sticks
grosso huge, big
il gruppo group
guadagnare to earn;
guadagnarsi* il pane to earn one's living
i guanti (*pl.*) gloves
guardare to look at, to watch
guarire (-isc-) to cure, to recover
la guerra war
la guida guide, tourist guide; guidebook; driving
guidare to drive
il gusto taste; preference

I

l'idea idea
ideale ideal
l'idealista idealist
l'idraulico plumber
ieri yesterday;
l'altro ieri the day before yesterday;
ieri sera last night
l'igienista (*m.& f.*) hygienist
ignorante ignorant
ignorare to ignore
illuminare to illuminate, to light
l'imbroglione cheater, swindler
imitare to imitate
immaginare to imagine
immaginario imaginary
l'immaginazione (*f.*) imagination
immediatamente immediately
imparare to learn
impaziente impatient
l'impazienza impatience
l'impermeabile (*m.*) raincoat
l'impiegato, l'impiegata clerk
l'impiego employment, job
importante important
l'importanza importance
importare to be important, to matter;
non importa! never mind!
l'importazione (*f.*) import
impossibile impossible
improvvisamente suddenly
in in, at, to
incantevole charming
incassare to cash
l'inchiostro ink
l'incidente (*m.*) accident
l'inclinazione (*f.*) inclination
incominciare to begin
incontrare to meet
l'incontro encounter; meeting
l'incrocio intersection
indeciso undecided; indecisive
l'indicazione (*f.*) direction
indifferente indifferent
indipendente independent
l'indipendenza independence
l'indirizzo address
indispensabile indispensable

indovinare to guess
l'indovinello puzzle; guessing game
l'indụstria industry
industriale industrial
inefficiente inefficient
inesperto inexperienced
infatti in fact
infelice unhappy
l'infermiere, l'infermiera nurse
l'inferno hell
l'inflazione (*f.*) inflation
l'influenza flu
influenzare to influence; to affect
l'informạtica computer science
l'informazione (*f.*) information
l'infrazione (f.) violation
l'ingegnere *(m.)* engineer
l'ingegneria engineering
ingessare to put in a cast
l'Inghilterra England
inglese English
ingrassare to gain weight
l'ingrediente *(m.)* ingredient
l'ingresso entrance, entry
l'iniezione *(f.)* injection
l'inzio beginning
innamorarsi* (di) to fall in love (with)
l'innamorato, l'innamorata lover
innocente innocent
inoltre besides
l'inquilino, l'inquilina tenant
l'inquinamento pollution
inquinare to pollute
l'insalata salad
l'insegnamento teaching
l'insegnante *(m.& f.)* teacher, instructor
insegnare to teach
insieme together
insinuare to hint at, to suggest
insomma for heaven's sake; in short
intelligente intelligent
l'intenzione *(f.)* intention;
avere intenzione di + inf. to intend
interessante interesting
interessare to interest;
interessarsi* di (a) to be interested in
l'interesse *(m.)* interest
l'intermezzo intermission
internazionale international
interno internal, interior, domestic
l'interpretazione *(f.)* interpretation
l'intervista interview
intervistare to interview
ịntimo close, intimate
intitolato entitled
intorno a around
introdurre (*p.p.* **introdotto**) to introduce
l'introduzione introduction
inụtile useless
invece instead
inventare to invent
l'inventore, l'inventrice inventor
invernale (*adj.*) winter
l'inverno winter
invitare to invite
l'invitato guest
l'invito invitation
irlandese Irish
l'ironia irony
irregolare irregular
irresponsạbile irresponsible
iscriversi* (*p.p.* **iscritto**) to enroll, to register
l'ịsola island
ispirare to inspire;
ispirarsi* to get inspired
istruire to educate, to instruct, to teach;
istruirsi* to educate oneself
l'istruttore, l'istruttrice instructor
l'istruzione *(f.)* instruction, education
l'Italia Italy
italiano Italian;
l'italiano Italian language;
l'Italiano/l'Italiana Italian person
all'italiana in the Italian way

L

là there, over there
il labbro (*pl.* **le labbra**) lip
il ladro, la ladra thief
il lago (*pl.* **laghi**) lake
lamentarsi* (di) to complain (about)
la lạmpada lamp
il lampadạrio chandelier
la lana wool;
di lana woolen
largo (*pl.* **larghi**) large, wide
lasciare to leave (*someone or something*); to quit; to let, to allow
il latte milk
la lạurea university degree
laurearsi* to graduate
il laureato university graduate
il lavabo sink
la lavagna blackboard
il lavandino sink
lavare to wash;
lavarsi* to get washed
la lavastoviglie dish washer
la lavatrice washing machine
lavorare to work
il lavoratore, la lavoratrice worker
il lavoro work, job;
lavoro a tempo pieno full time job

legale legal;
studio legale law office
la legge law;
facoltà di legge law school
lẹggere (*p.p.* **letto**) to read
leggero light
il legno wood
di legno wooden
lento slow;
il lenzuolo (*pl.* **le lenzuola**) sheet
il leone lion
la lẹttera letter;
le Lẹttere humanities
la letteratura literature
il letto bed;
letto singolo (matrimoniale): single (double) bed
camera da letto bedroom
il lettore, la lettrice reader
la lettura reading
la lezione lesson; class
lì there
la libbra pound
lịbero free, available; vacant (apartment)
la libertà freedom
la libreria bookstore
il libro book;
libro di cucina cookbook
licenziare to fire
il liceo high school
il lịmite limit;
limite di velocità speed limit
il limone lemon
la lịngua language; tongue;
le lingue straniere foreign languages
la lira lira (Italian currency)
la lista list
litigare to fight
il locale room;
locale (*adj.*) local
la località place
la Lombardia Lombardy
Londra London
lontano (da) far (from)
la luce light; electricity
lụglio July
la luna moon
il lunedì Monday
lungo (*pl.* **lunghi**) long; (*adv.*) along;
a lungo for a long time
il luogo (*pl.* **luoghi**) place;
avere luogo to take place
lussuoso sumptuous

M

ma but
la mạcchina car, machine, engine;
mạcchina fotogrạfica camera;
mạcchina da presa movie camera;
mạcchina da scrịvere typewriter
la macedọnia di frutta fruit salad
la madre mother
maestoso majestic
il maestro, la maestra elementary school teacher
mạggio May
la maggioranza majority
maggiore bigger, greater, older;
la maggior parte most (of)
la maglietta T-shirt
il maglione heavy sweater
magnifico magnificent, splendid
magro thin; skinny
mai ever;
non mai never
il malato sick person; (*adj.*) sick, ill
la malattia illness, disease
il male ache;
male di denti toothache
male badly;
non c'è male not bad
maleducato impolite
malgrado in spite of
il malumore bad mood;
essere di malumore to be in a bad mood
malvolentieri reluctantly
la mamma mom
la mạncia tip;
dare la mạncia to tip
mandare to send
mangiare to eat
il manifesto poster;
manifesto elettorale campaign poster
la mano (*pl.* **le mani**) hand;
dare la mano to shake hands
il manoscritto manuscript
la marca make; brand name
il marciapiede sidewalk
mạrcio rotten
il mare sea;
al mare at the seashore;
il Mar Tirreno Tyrrhenian Sea
la margarina margarine
il marinạio sailor
il marito husband
la marmellata jam
il marmo marble
marrone brown
il martedì Tuesday
marzo March
la mạschera mask, masked character
maschile masculine
mạssimo greatest, maximum;
al mạssimo at the most
la matemạtica mathematics
la matẹria subject (scholastic)
la matita pencil
il matrimọnio marriage, wedding
la mattina, il mattino morning;
di mattina in the morning

matto crazy;
da matti a lot
il mattone brick
maturo mature; ripe
il meccạnico mechanic
la medicina medicine
il mẹdico doctor, physician
il Mẹdio Evo Middle Ages
mẹglio (*adv.*) better
la mela apple
la melanzana eggplant
il melone cantaloupe
il membro member
la memọria memory;
a memọria by heart
meno less; minus
a meno che unless
la mensa cafeteria
mensile monthly
mentre while
il menù menu
meravigliosamente wonderfully
meraviglioso wonderful
il mercato market
a buon mercato cheap
il mercoledì Wednesday
meridionale southern
mescolare to mix
il mese month
il messạggio message
messicano Mexican
il mestiere trade
la metà half
la metropolitana subway
mẹttere to put, to place, to wear;
mẹttersi* to put on, wear;
mẹttersi* a to start;
mẹttere a posto to put in order;
mẹttere in moto to start (car)
la mezzanotte midnight
i mezzi di diffusione mass media;
i mezzi di trasporto means of transportation
mezzo (*adj.*) half
il mezzo means; middle;
per mezzo di by means of;
il mezzogiorno noon;
il Mezzogiorno Southern Italy
il miglio (*f. pl.* **miglia**) mile
migliorare to improve
migliore (*adj.*) better
Milano Milan
il miliardario billionaire
il milionạrio millionaire
mille (*pl.* **mila**) thousand;
Mille grazie! Thanks a lot!
la minestra soup
il minestrone vegetable soup
mịnimo smallest
il ministro (*m. & f.*) minister
minore smaller, younger
il minuto minute
misto mixed
misurare to measure
mite mild
il mọbile piece of furniture
la moda fashion;
di moda fashionable
il modello, la modella model
moderno modern
modesto modest
il modo way, manner;
ad ogni modo anyway
la mọglie wife
molto much, a lot of; (*inv.*) very
il momento moment
la monarchia monarchy
mondiale worldwide
il mondo world
la moneta coin
il monolocale studio apartment
la montagna mountain
il monte mount
il monumento monument
la moquette wall-to-wall carpet
morire* (*p.p.* **morto**) to die
la morte death
la mostra exhibition
mostrare to show
il moto motion, movement;
mẹttere in moto to start (the car)
la moto(cicletta) motorcycle
il motore motor
il motorino motorscooter
la multa fine
il muratore mason
il muro (exterior) wall;
le mura city walls
il museo museum
la mụsica music;
mụsica folkloristica folklore music;
mụsica operịstica opera music;
mụsica classica classical music;
mụsica leggera light music
il (la) musicista musician

N

napoletano Neapolitan
Nạpoli Naples
nạscere* (*p.p.* **nato**) to be born
la nạscita birth
il naso nose
Natale Christmas;
Babbo Natale Santa Claus;
Buon Natale! Merry Christmas!
la natura nature;
la natura morta still life
naturalmente naturally
nazionale national
la nazionalità nationality
la nazione nation
nè … nè neither … nor
neanche not even
la nẹbbia fog;
c'è nẹbbia it is foggy

necessario necessary
negare to deny
negativo negative
il negozio store, shop
nemmeno not even
nero black
nervoso nervous
nessuno nobody, no one, not anyone
la neve snow
nevicare to snow
niente nothing, not anything
il nipote nephew, grandchild; **la nipote** niece, granddaughter; **i nipoti** grandchildren
no no
la noia boredom; (*pl.*) trouble
noioso boring
noleggiare to rent (a car, a bicycle, skis)
il nome noun, name
nominare to name
non not
il nonno, la nonna grandfather, grandmother; **i nonni** grandparents
nonostante in spite of
il nord north
notevole remarkable
la notizia news
noto well-known
la notte night
novembre (*m.*) November
la novità news; **nessuna novità** nothing new
le nozze wedding; **viaggio di nozze** honeymoon trip
nubile (*f.*) unmarried, single
il numero number; **numero di telefono** phone number
numeroso numerous
la nuora daughter-in-law
nuotare to swim
il nuoto swimming
nuovo new; **di nuovo** again
la nuvola cloud; **avere la testa fra le nuvole** to be absent-minded
nuvoloso cloudy

O

o or
obbligatorio compulsory
l'occasione (*f.*) opportunity; **approfittare dell'occasione** to take advantage of
gli occhiali (*pl.*) eyeglasses; **occhiali da sole** sunglasses
l'occhio eye; **costare un occhio della testa** to cost a fortune; **dare un'occhiata** to take a look
occidentale western
occupare to occupy; **occuparsi*** to occupy oneself with
occupato busy
l'oceano ocean
l'oculista (*m. & f.*) eye doctor
offendere (*p.p.* **offeso**) to offend
l'offerta offer
offrire (*p.p.* **offerto**) to offer
l'oggetto object
oggi today
ogni each, every
ognuno everyone, each one
olimpico Olympic
l'olio oil; **olio d'oliva** olive oil
oltre a besides
l'ombrello umbrella
l'onore (*m.*) honor
l'opera work, opera; **l'opera d'arte** work of art; **cantante d'opera** opera singer
l'operaio (a) factory worker, laborer
operare to operate
l'opinione (*f.*) opinion
oppure or
ora now
l'ora hour, time; (*adv.*) now
è ora che it is time that; **è ora di** it is time to; **le ore di punta** rush hours; **non vedo l'ora** I can't wait
l'orario schedule; **in orario** on time
l'orchestra orchestra
ordinare to order, to prescribe
ordinato neat
l'ordine order
l'orecchio (*pl.* **le orecchie**) ear
organizzare to organize
orgoglioso proud
orientale oriental, eastern
originale original
l'origine (*f.*) origin
l'oro gold; **d'oro** golden
l'orologio watch, clock
l'ospedale (*m.*) hospital
l'ospite (*m. & f.*) guest, host
l'ossigeno oxygen
l'osso (*pl. f.* **le ossa**) bone
ostinato stubborn
ottenere to obtain
l'ottimista optimist
ottimo excellent
ottobre October
l'ovest West
l'ozono ozone; **lo strato dell'ozono** ozone layer

P

il pacco package, parcel
la pace peace; **fare la pace** to make up

la padella frying pan
il padre father
il padrone owner, boss;
  padrone di casa landlord
il paesạggio landscape, scenery
il paese country, town, village
pagare to pay
la pạgina page
il pạio (*pl. f.* **le paia**) pair
il palazzo palace, building
il palcoscẹnico stage
la palestra gym
la palla ball
la pallacanestro basketball
la pallavolo volleyball
pạllido pale
il pallone ball (soccer)
la panchina bench
il pane bread
il panino roll;
  panino imbottito sandwich
la panna cream
i pantaloni pants, trousers
il Papa Pope
il papà dad
paragonare to compare
il paragone comparison
parcheggiare to park
il parchẹggio parking
il parco park
il (la) parente relative;
  i parenti relatives
parere (*p.p.* **parso**) to seem
  non ti pare? don't you think so?
la parete (interior) wall
Parigi Paris
parlare to speak, to talk;
  parlare male (bene) di to say bad (good) things about
il parmigiano Parmesan cheese
la parola word
il parrucchiere, la parrucchiera hairdresser
la parte part, role;
  fare la parte to play the role;
  da parte di from

partecipare a to take part in
la partenza departure
partire* to leave, to depart
la partita match, game
il partito political party
la Pạsqua Easter
il passạggio passage, lift;
  dare un passạggio to give a lift
il passaporto passport
passare to pass, to pass by; to spend (time)
il passatempo pastime, hobby
il passato past
  passato (*adj.*) last, past
il passeggero, la passeggera passenger
la passeggiata walk;
  fare una passeggiata to take a walk
la passione passion
la pasta dough, pasta, pastry;
  le paste (*pl.*) pastries
la pastasciutta pasta dish
la pasticceria pastry shop
la pastịglia tablet
il pasto meal
la patata potato;
  patate fritte fried potatoes
la patente driver's license
il pattinạggio skating
i pạttini skates
la paura fear;
  avere paura to be afraid;
  avere una paura da morire to be scared to death
il pavimento floor
paziente patient
il (la) paziente patient
la pazienza patience;
  avere pazienza to be patient
Peccato! Too bad!
il pedone pedestrian
peggio (*adv.*) worse
peggiore (*adj.*) worse
la pelle skin; leather
la penịsola peninsula
la penna pen

pensare to think;
  pensare a to think about;
  pensare di + *inf.* to plan, to intend (*to do something*);
  penso di sì I think so
il pensiero thought
il pensionato senior citizen
la pensione pension; boardinghouse;
  andare in pensione to retire
la pẹntola pot
il pepe pepper
per for;
  per (+*inf.*) in order to;
  per caso by any chance
la pera pear
perchè why; because
pẹrdere (*p.p.* **perduto, perso**) to lose, to waste (time);
  perdersi* to get lost
perfetto perfect
la perfezione perfection
il perịcolo danger
pericoloso dangerous
la periferia outskirts, periphery
il perịodo period (time)
la permanente *(f.)* permanent;
  farsi la permanente to get a perm
Permesso? May I come in?
permẹttere (*p.p.* **permesso**) to allow
però but, however
la persona person
il personạggio character
personale personal
pesante heavy
la pesca peach; fishing
pescare to fish
il pesce fish;
  pesce fritto fried fish
la pesịstica weight lifting
il peso weight
il (la) pessimista pessimist
pettinarsi* to comb one's hair
il pezzo piece;
  un due pezzi a two-piece suit

il piacere *(m.)* pleasure;
con piacere with pleasure, gladly;
per piacere please;
Piacere! Pleased to meet you!
piacere* (*p.p.* **piaciuto**) to like, to be pleasing
piacẹvole pleasant
il pianeta planet
piạngere (*p.p.* **pianto**) to cry, to weep
il piano floor, plan;
il pianterreno ground floor
il piano(forte) piano
la pianura plain
il piatto dish;
primo piatto first course;
secondo piatto second course
la piazza square
pịccolo little, small
il piede *(m.)* foot;
a piedi on foot
il Piemonte Piedmont
pieno (di) full (of); **fare il pieno** to fill up
la pietra stone
pigro lazy
la pịllola pill
la piọggia rain
piọvere to rain
la pipa pipe
la piscina swimming pool
i piselli peas
il pittore, la pittrice painter
la pittura painting
più more;
non più no longer;
più o meno more or less
più ... di more ... than
piuttosto rather
poco little, few;
un po' di some; a little bit of
il poema poem
la poesia poetry; poem
il poeta, la poetessa poet, poetess
poi then, afterwards
poichè since
polịtico political
la polịtica politics
la Polizia Police Station
il poliziotto policemen
il pollo chicken;
pollo arrosto roast chicken
la poltrona arm chair; orchestra seat
il pomerịggio afternoon
il pomodoro tomato
il pompelmo grapefruit
il ponte bridge
popolare popular
popolato populated
la popolazione population
il popolo people, inhabitants
la porta door
il portabagagli trunk (of a car)
il portafọglio wallet
portare to carry, to bring; to wear; to take
il portinạio concierge
il porto port, harbor
le posate silverware
possịbile possible;
il meno possịbile as little as possible
la possibilità possibility
il postino mailman
la posta post office; mail
postale (*adj.*) post, mail;
cassetta postale mailbox;
codice postale zip code
il posto place, seat, position
il potere power;
potere to be able to, can, may;
può darsi it may be that
povero poor
Poverino! Poor thing!
pranzare to have dinner
il pranzo dinner;
sala da pranzo dining room;
l'ora del pranzo lunch (dinner) time
praticare to practice a sport
pratico practical
preciso precise
preferịbile preferable
preferire (-isc-) to prefer
preferito favorite
il prefisso area code (phone)
pregare to pray, to beg
il pregiudizio prejudice
Prego! Please!, You are welcome!, Don't mention it!
il prẹmio prize, award
prẹndere (*p.p.* **preso**) to take, to pick up;
prendere in giro to tease
prenotare to reserve
la prenotazione reservation
preoccuparsi* (di) to worry (about)
preoccupato worried
la preoccupazione worry
preparare to prepare;
prepararsi* to prepare oneself, to get ready
la preparazione preparation
prescrịvere (*p. p.* **prescritto**) to prescribe
presentare to introduce;
presentarsi* to introduce onself
presente present
la presenza presence
il presidente, la presidentessa president
prestare to lend
la pressione pressure;
la pressione del sangue blood pressure
il prestito loan
presto early, fast, soon, quickly;
il più presto possibile as soon as possible;
(Fa') presto! Hurry up!
la previsione forecast
prezioso precious
il prezzo price
prima before, earlier, first;
prima di before
la primavera spring

primo first
principale main; leading
privato private
probạbile probable
la probabilità probability
il problema (*pl.* **problemi**) problem
il produttore, la produttrice producer
la professione profession
il (la) professionista professional man/woman
il professore, la professoressa professor, teacher
il profumo perfume, scent
progettare to plan
il progetto project, plan
il programma (*pl.* **programmi**) program; schedule
il programmatore, la programmatrice programmer
il progresso progress
proibire (-isc-) to prohibit
promẹttere (*p.p.* **promesso**) to promise
la promozione promotion
il pronome pronoun
pronto ready;
  Pronto! Hello! (telephone)
proporre (*p.p.* **proposto**) to propose
il propọsito purpose;
  a propọsito by the way
il proprietạrio, la proprietạria owner
prọprio (*adv.*) exactly, indeed
la prosa prose
il prosciutto cured Italian ham
prọssimo next
il (la) protagonista main character
protẹggere (*p.p.* **protetto**) to protect
protestare to protest, to complain
provare to try, to try on
il proverbio proverb
la provịncia province
prudente prudent, cautious
lo psicọlogo, la psicọloga psychologist
pubblicare to publish
la pubblicità advertising
il pụbblico public, audience; (*adj.*) public
il pụgile boxer
il pugilato boxing
pulire (-isc-) to clean
pulito clean
il pullman tour bus
punire (-isc-) to punish
il punto point;
  punto di vista point of view;
  in punto on the dot
puntuale punctual
purchè provided that (+ *sub.*)
pure by all means
purtroppo unfortunately

Q

il quaderno notebook
il quadro painting, picture;
  a quadri checked
qualche some
qualcosa something
qualcuno someone
quale? which?; which one?
la qualịfica qualification
la qualità quality
quando when;
  da quando? since when?
quanto how much;
  per quanto although;
  quanto a concerning, as for;
  quanto tempo fa? How long ago?
il quarto quarter (*of an hour*); (*adj.*) fourth
quasi almost
quello that
questo this
qui here
il quotidiano daily newspaper

la racchetta da tennis tennis racquet
raccomandare to warn
la raccomandazione recommendation
raccontare to tell, to relate
il racconto short story, tale
rạdersi* (*p.p.* **raso**) to shave
la rạdio radio
la radiografia X-ray
raffreddare to cool
il raffreddore cold;
  prẹndere il raffreddore to catch a cold
il ragazzo, la ragazza boy, young man; girl, young woman; boy- or girlfriend
raggiụngere (*p.p.* **raggiunto**) to reach
la ragione reason;
  avere ragione to be right
il ragioniere, la ragioniera accountant
rallentare to slow down
rạpido (*adj.*) fast, quick;
  il rạpido express train
rappresentare to represent; stage (theater)
la rappresentazione performance (theater)
raramente rarely, seldom
raro rare
il re, la regina king, queen
reagire to react
il (la) realista realist
la realtà reality
la reazione reaction
recente recent
recentemente recently
recitare to act out; to play
la recitazione recitation, performance
la referenza reference
regalare to give a present
il regalo gift, present

la regione region
il (la) regista movie director
il registratore tape recorder
la regola rule
il regolamento regulation
regolare regular
rẹndersi* conto (*p.p.* **reso**) to realize
il reparto department (store)
la repubblica republic
repụbblicano republican
respirare to breathe
responsạbile responsible
la responsabilità responsibility
restare* to stay, to remain
restituire (-isc-) to return (something)
il resto change (money); rest
la rete network
la revisione tune-up
riassụmere to summarize
il riassunto summary
ribellarsi* to rebel
ribelle rebel
la ricchezza wealth
ricco (*pl.* **ricchi**) rich
la ricerca research
la ricetta recipe, prescription
il ricettạrio recipe book
ricẹvere to receive
la ricevuta receipt
riciclare to recycle
riconoscente grateful
ricordare to remember;
  ricordarsi* to remember
rịdere (*p.p.* **riso**) to laugh
rifare il letto to make the bed
la riga (*pl.* **righe**) line;
  a righe striped
rimanẹre (*p.p.* **rimasto**) to remain
rimproverare to scold, to reproach
il Rinascimento Renaissance
ringraziare to thank
rinunciare (a) to renounce
riparare to repair, to fix
ripassare to review
ripẹtere to repeat
riposante relaxing
riposare to rest;
  riposarsi* to rest
riscaldare to warm
riscuọtere (*p.p.* **riscosso**) to cash
riservato reserved
il riso rice; laughter
risparmiare to save
il rispạrmio saving
rispettare to respect
rispọndere (*p.p.* **risposto**) to answer, to reply
la risposta answer, reply
il ristorante restaurant
il risultato result, outcome
il ritardo delay;
  in ritardo late
ritirare to withdraw
ritornare to return, to come back
il ritorno return
il ritratto picture, portrait
ritrovare to find again
la riunione reunion, meeting
  riunirsi* (isc-) to gather
riuscire* (a) to succeed (in)
rivedere (*p.p.* **rivisto**) to see again
la rivista magazine
la roba stuff
Roma Rome
romano Roman
romạntico romantic
il romanzo novel;
  romanzo rosa (giallo, di fantascienza, di avventure) love story (mystery, science-fiction, adventure)
rọmpere (*p.p.* **rotto**) to break;
  rompersi* un braccio to break an arm
rosa (*inv.*) pink
la rosa rose
rosso red
rovinare to ruin; to damage
la rovina ruin, fall,
  andare in rovina to go bankrupt
rubare to steal
il rumore noise
il ruolo role
la ruota wheel
russo Russian

S

il sạbato Saturday
la sạbbia sand
il sacco bag, sack;
  sacco a pelo sleeping bag;
  un sacco di a lot of
sacrificarsi* to sacrifice oneself
il sạggio essay
la sala living room;
la sala da pranzo dining room
il salạrio salary
il sale salt
salire* to climb, to go up, to get on
il salone hall
il salotto living rooms
la salsa sauce
saltare to jump; to skip
il salumiere delicatessen man
salutare to greet, to say good-bye;
  salutarsi* to greet each other
la salute health
il saluto greeting;
  saluti cordiali kind regards;
  distinti saluti sincerely
salvare to save; to rescue
il salvatạggio rescue
Salve! Hello!
sano healthy
  sano come un pesce as healthy as a horse
sapere to know, to know how (to do something)
la Sardegna Sardinia

satịrico satirical
sbadigliare to yawn
sbagliarsi* to make a mistake
sbagliato wrong, incorrect;
è sbagliato it is wrong
lo scaffale shelf
la scala ladder; staircase
scambiare to exchange
lo scạmbio exchange
lo scạpolo bachelor; (*adj.*) single
la scạrpa shoe
gli scarponi da montagna hiking boots
scẹgliere (*p.p.* scelto) to choose
la scelta choice
la scena scene
scẹndere* (*p.p.* sceso) to descend, to come down; to get off
scherzare to joke
lo scherzo joke
la schiena back
lo sci (*inv.*) ski;
lo sci acquạtico water ski;
lo sci di discesa down hill ski;
lo sci di fondo cross country ski
sciare to ski
lo sciatore, la sciatrice skier
scientịfico scientific
la scienza science;
le scienze polịtiche political science
lo scienziato scientist
scioperare to strike
lo sciọpero strike;
fare sciọpero to go on strike
scolpire to sculpt, to carve
lo scompartimento compartment
sconosciuto unknown
scontento unhappy
lo sconto discount;
sconto del venti per cento twenty-percent discount
la scoperta discovery
scoprire (*p.p.* scoperto)
scorso last;
il mese scorso last month
lo scrittore, la scrittrice writer
la scrivanịa desk
scrịvere (*p.p.* scritto) to write;
scrịvere a mạcchina to type
lo scultore, la scultrice sculptor, sculptress
la scultura sculpture
la scuola school;
scuola elementare elementary school;
scuola mẹdia junior high school
la scusa excuse;
scusarsi* to apologize;
Scusa! (*fam.s.*); **Scusi!** (*form.s.*) Excuse me!
se if;
anche se even if
sebbene although
secco dry
il sẹcolo century
secondo according to; (*adj.*) second
sedẹrsi* to sit down
la sẹdia chair
segnalare to signal
il segnale signal; sign
segnare (sports) to score
il segretạrio, la segretạria secretary
la segreteria telefọnica answering machine
il segreto secret
seguire to follow, to take (a course)
il semạforo traffic light
sembrare to seem
il semestre semester
sẹmplice simple
sempre always
il senatore, la senatrice senator
il senso sense, meaning; direction;
senso unico one way (direction)
sentimentale sentimental
il sentimento feeling
sentire to hear, to feel, to smell;
sentirsi* bene (male) to feel well (sick)
sentir dire to hear say
senza without
i senzatetto homeless people
separare to divide;
separarsi* to separate, to part
la separazione separation
la sera evening;
la (di) sera in the evening (duration)
la serata evening (duration)
il serbatọio oil tank
sereno clear (weather)
seriamente seriously
la sẹrie series
sẹrio serious
servire to serve;
servirsi* (di) to use
il servịzio service;
i doppi servizi two baths
il sesso sex
la seta silk
la sete thirst;
avere sete to be thirsty
settembre September
settentrionale Northern
la settimana week;
fra una settimana in a week
il settimanale weekly magazine
severo strict
sfavorẹvole unfavorable
la sfilata fashion show
la sfortuna bad luck
sfortunato unfortunate
sì yes
si va? shall we go?;
si mangia bene qui one eats well here
sia...che both....and
siccome since, because

Sicilia Sicily
siciliano Sicilian
sicuro sure; safe
la siesta siesta, nap;
 fare la siesta to take a nap
la sigaretta cigarette
significare to mean
il significato meaning
la signora lady, Mrs., ma'am
il signore gentleman, Mr., sir
la signorina young lady, miss
il silenzio silence
la sillaba syllable
il simbolo symbol
simile similar
simpatico nice
la sincerità sincerity
sincero sincere
la sinfonia symphony
la sinistra left;
 a sinistra to the left
il sintomo symptom
la sirena siren
il sistema (*pl.* **sistemi**) system
situato situated, located
la situazione situation
smettere (*p.p.* **smesso**) to stop
snello slim, slender
socialista socialist
la società society, company
la sociologia sociology
soddisfatto satisfied
soffrire (*p.p.* **sofferto**) to suffer
soggiornare to stay (in a hotel)
il soggiorno (la sala) living room; stay
la sogliola sole
sognare to dream
il sogno dream
solamente only
i soldi money;
 un sacco di soldi a lot of money
il sole sun;
 c'è il sole it is sunny;
 prendere il sole to sunbathe
solito usual;
 al solito as usual;
 del solito than usual;
 di solito usually, generally
la solitudine loneliness
solo alone; (*adv.*) only;
 da solo by oneself
soltanto only
la somma sum, addition, total
il sonno sleep;
 avere sonno to be sleepy
sopra above, on top of
il (la) soprano soprano
sopratutto above all
la sorella sister
sorgere (*p.p.* **sorto**) to rise
sorpassare to pass (a car)
la sorpresa surprise
sorpreso surprised
sorridere (*p.p.* **sorriso**) to smile
sotto under, below
sottolineare to underline
spagnolo Spanish
la spalla shoulder
lo spazio space
spazioso spacious
lo spazzolino da denti toothbrush
lo specchio mirror
speciale special
lo (la) specialista specialist
specializzarsi* (in) to specialize
la specializzazione major
specialmente especially
spedire (-isc-) to send; to mail
spegnere (*p.p.* **spento**) to turn off
lo spendaccione spendthrift
spendere (*p.p.* **speso**) to spend
sperare to hope
la spesa expense;
 fare la spesa to go (grocery) shopping
spesso often
spettacolare spectacular
lo spettacolo show, performance; sight
lo spettatore, la spettatrice spectator
la spiaggia beach
spiegare to explain
la spiegazione explanation
gli spinaci spinach
spiritoso witty, funny
sporco dirty
lo sportello (teller) window
sportivo athletic, sporty
sposare to marry;
 sposarsi* to get married
sposato (a) married
lo sposo, la sposa groom, bride; **gli sposi** newlyweds
lo spumante sparkling wine
lo spuntino snack
la squadra team
squisito exquisite, delicious
lo stadio stadium
la stagione season;
 di mezza stagione in between seasons
stamattina this morning
la stampa press, print
stancare to tire;
 stancarsi* to get tired
stanco tired;
 stanco morto dead tired
la stanza room
stare* to stay;
 stare attento to be careful;
 stare bene to be well, to feel well;
 stare a dieta to be on a diet;
 stare male to feel ill;
 stare per to be about to;
 stare zitto to be quiet
stasera this evening, tonight
statale of the state
lo stato state
la statua statue
la stazione station
la stella star
stesso same;
 lo stesso the same
lo stile style
lo (la) stilista designer
lo stipendio salary
lo stivale boot

lo stọmaco stomach

la stọria history; story

stọrico historical

storto crooked

la strada street, road

stradale of the road or street

straniero (*adj.*) foreign

lo straniero, la straniera foreigner

strano strange

stretto narrow, tight

lo strumento instrument;

strumento musicale musical instrument

lo studente, la studentessa student

studiare to study

lo studio study; study room

studioso studious

stupendo magnificent, splendid

stụpido stupid

su above, on top of;

Su! Come on!

sụbito immediately

succẹdere (*p.p.* **successo**) to happen;

Cos'è successo? What happened?

il successo success

il succo juice;

succo d'arạncia orange juice

il sud South

il suffisso suffix

il suggerimento suggestion

suggerire (-isc-) to suggest

il suọcero, la suọcera father-in-law, mother-in-law

suonare to play an instrument, to ring

il suono sound

superare to exceed (speed); to overcome

superficiale superficial

la superfịcie area

superiore superior

il supermercato supermarket

surgelato frozen

lo svantạggio disadvantage

la svẹglia alarm clock

svegliarsi* to wake up

la svẹndita sale

lo sviluppo development

la Svịzzera Switzerland

svịzzero Swiss

T

la tạglia size

tagliare to cut;

tagliarsi* to cut oneself;

tagliarsi i baffi to cut one's mustache

le tagliatelle pasta (cut into thin strips)

il talento talent

tanto much, so much;

Così tanto! That much!;

tanto ...quanto as much as

il tappeto rug

tardi late;

è tardi it is late

la targa license plate

la tasca pocket

la tassa tax;

tassa universitạria tuition

il tassì (*inv.*) taxi, cab

il tassista cab driver

la tạvola, il tạvolo table;

A tạvola! Dinner's ready!;

la tạvola calda snack bar;

tạvola da pranzo dinner table;

tạvolo da disegno drawing table;

il tavolino end table;

tavolino da tè coffee table

la tazza cup

il tè tea

teatrale theatrical, (of the) theater

il teatro theater

la tẹcnica technique

tedesco (*pl.* **tedeschi**) German

la telecạmera TV camera

il telefilm TV movie

telefonare to phone;

la telefonata phone call;

telefonata interurbana long-distance phone call

il telẹfono telephone

telẹfono cellulare (telefonino) cellular phone

il telegiornale TV news

il telegramma telegram

il teleromanzo soap opera

il telespettatore, la telespettatrice TV viewer

la televisione television;

alla televisione on TV

il televisore TV set

il telo-bagno beach towel

il tema (*pl.* **temi**) theme, composition

temere to fear

la temperatura temperature

il tempo time; weather;

tempo pieno full-time;

a tempo ridotto part-time;

Che tempạccio! What bad weather!

la tenda tent;

montare la tenda to pitch the tent

le tende curtains

il tenore tenor (singer);

il tenore di vita way of living

la tentazione temptation

la teoria theory

terminare to finish, to end

il tẹrmine term

il termọmetro thermometer

la terra earth, ground, land;

per terra on the floor

il terremoto earthquake

terrịbile terrible

terribilmente terribly

il territọrio territory

il tesoro treasure;

tesoro! (*affect.*) honey, sweetheart

la tẹssera card;
la tẹssera sanitaria medical card
la testa head
il tetto roof
il Tẹvere Tiber river
il tifo (sports) enthusiasm;
fare il tifo per to be a fan of
tifoso fan
tịmido timid, shy
la tinta color; dye;
in tinta unita solid color
il tipo guy; type, kind
tirare to pull;
tirare vento to be windy
il tịtolo title;
il tịtolo di studio college degree
la tivù (*colloq.*) television
il topo mouse;
Topolino Mickey Mouse
Torino Turin
tornare to return;
Ben tornato! Welcome back!
la torre tower
la torta cake; pie
torto wrong;
avere torto to be wrong
toscano Tuscan
la tosse cough
il totale total
il Totocạlcio soccer pool;
schedina del Totocạlcio soccer lottery ticket
la tovạglia tablecloth
il tovagliolo napkin
tra (*or* **fra**) between, among;
tra un'ora in one hour
tradizionale traditional
la tradizione tradition
tradurre (*p.p.* **tradotto**) to translate;
la traduzione translation
il trạffico traffic
la tragẹdia tragedy
il tram streetcar
la trama plot
tramontare to set (the sun, moon)
il tramonto sunset
tranquillo quiet
traslocare to move (to another place)
il trasloco moving
il trasporto transportation
trattare to treat; to deal with;
trattarsi* to have to do with;
si tratta di it has to do with
la trattoria restaurant
il treno train;
perdere il treno to miss the train
il trimestre quarter (of the year)
triste sad
il trofeo trophy
la tromba trumpet
troppo too much
la trota trout
trovare to find;
trovarsi* to find oneself; to be situated
truccarsi* to put on makeup
il trucco makeup
il (la) turista tourist
turịstico tourist;
la classe turịstica economy class
la tuta overall;
la tuta da ginnạstica sweat-suit
tutti, tutte everybody, all;
tutti e due both
tutto (*adj.*) all, every; the whole;
tutto il giorno the whole day;
tutto (*pron.*) everything;
tutti (*pron.*) everybody, all

U

ubbidire (-isc-) to obey
ubriaco drunk
l'uffịcio office;
l'uffịcio postale post office
uguale equal
ụltimo last
ụmido humid
l'umore (*m.*) humor;
essere di buon (cattivo) umore to be in a good (bad) mood
ụnico unique;
figlio ụnico only child
l'unificazione (*f.*) unification
l'uniforme (*f.*) uniform
l'unione (*f.*) union
unire (-isc-) to unite;
unito united
uno one (number);
un, uno, una (*art.*) a, an
l'università university
universitạrio (*adj.*) university
l'uomo (*pl.* **gli uọmini**) man
l'uovo (*pl.* **le uova**) egg;
le uova strapazzate scrambled eggs
usare to use, to take
l'usanza custom
usato used, secondhand
uscire* to go (come) out
l'uscita exit
l'uso use
ụtile useful
l'uva grapes

V

la vacanza vacation, holiday
la valịgia (*pl.* **valigie** *or* **valige**) suitcase;
fare le valigie to pack
la valle valley
il vantạggio advantage
vantare to boast
il vaporetto waterbus (in Venice)
variare to vary
la varietà variety
vạrio varied

variopinto many colored
la vasca (da bagno) (bath) tub
il vaso vase
vẹcchio old
vedere (*p.p.* **visto, veduto**) to see
vegetariano vegetarian
la vela sail;
barca a vela sail boat;
fare della vela sailing
veloce fast
la velocità speed;
limite di velocità speed limit
vẹndere to sell
la vẹndita sale;
in vẹndita for sale
il venerdì Friday
Venẹzia Venice
veneziano Venetian
venire* (***p.p.*** **venuto**) to come
il vento wind;
tira vento it is windy
veramente truly; really, actually
il verbo verb
verde green;
essere al verde to be broke
la verdura vegetables
la vergogna shame;
Che vergogna! What a shame!
la verità truth
vero true;
È vero! That's right!
il verso line (of poetry);
verso (*prep.*) towards
vestirsi* to get dressed
il vestito dress; suit
i vestiti clothes
il veterinạrio veterinarian
la vetrina shop window; display
la via street, way;
via (*adv.*) away, off
viaggiare to travel
il viaggiatore, la viaggiatrice traveler
il viạggio trip, voyage;
il viạggio di nozze honeymoon;
Buon viạggio! Have a nice trip!
la vicinanza vicinity
vicino (*adv.*) close, nearby;
vicino a near
il vicino, la vicina neighbor
vietato (entrare, fumare, etc.) do not (enter, smoke, etc.)
il vịgile (urbano) city police officer
la vigna vineyard
la vignetta drawing, cartoon
il villạggio village
la villeggiatura summer vacation
vịncere (*p.p.* **vinto**) to win
il vino wine
viola (*inv.*) purple
la violenza violence
il violino violin
il violoncello cello
la vịsita visit
visitare to visit, to examine
la vita life
la vitamina vitamine
il vitello veal;
arrosto di vitello roast veal
la vittọria victory
Viva! Hurrah !
vịvere (*p.p.* **vissuto**) to live
vivo alive, living
il vocabolạrio vocabulary, dictionary
la vocale vowel
la voce voice;
ad alta (bassa) voce in a loud (low) voice
la vọglia desire;
avere vọglia di to feel like
volentieri gladly; willingly
volere to want;
voler dire to mean;
volersi* bene to love each other;
ci vuole, ci vọgliono it takes
il volo flight
la volontà will
la volta time;
una volta once;
(C'era) una volta once upon a time;
due volte twice;
qualche volta sometimes
ogni volta everytime
votare to vote
il voto grade; vote;
un bel (brutto) voto a good (bad) grade
il vulcano volcano
vuoto empty; vacant

Z

lo zạino backpack
lo zero zero
lo zio, la zia uncle, aunt
zitto silent;
sta'zitto be quiet
lo zoo zoo
lo zụcchero sugar
la zuppa di verdure vegetable soup

ENGLISH–ITALIAN VOCABULARY

A

able: to be able to potere
about circa, di
above sopra, su;
above all sopratutto
abroad all'ẹstero
absent assente
abstract astratto
abundant abbondante
to accelerate accelerare
to accept accettare
accident l'incidente (*m.*)
to accompany accompagnare
according to secondo
accountant il ragioniere, la ragioniera
act l'atto; **to act** recitare
activity l'attività
actor l'attore
actress l'attrice
ad l'annụncio pubblicitạrio
address l'indirizzo
to admire ammirare
to admit ammẹttere (*p.p.* ammesso)
adult l'adulto, l'adulta
advance l'antịcipo;
in advance in antịcipo
advantage il vantạggio
adventure l'avventura
advertising la pubblicità
advice il consịglio
to advise consigliare
affection l'affetto
afraid: to be afraid avere paura
after dopo
afternoon il pomerịggio
afterwards poi
again ancora
against contro
age l'età;
Stone Age l'Età della pietra
ago fa;
How long ago? Quanto tempo fa?
to agree ẹssere d'accordo
air l'ạria
airplane l'aẹreo, l'aeroplano
alarm clock la svẹglia
alive vivo
all tutto
to allow permẹttere (*p.p.* permesso), lasciare
almost quasi
alone solo (*adj., adv.*)
along lungo;
to get along andare d'accordo
already già
also anche
although benchè
always sempre
American americano
among fra (*or* tra)

amount la dose
amusing divertente
analysis l'ạnalisi (*f.*)
ancient antico
and e
animal l'animale (*m.*)
to announce annunciare
announcer l'annunciatore, l'annunciatrice
annoyed seccato
anonymous anọnimo
another un altro
answer la risposta;
to answer rispọndere (*p.p.* risposto)
antique antico
anxiety l'ạnsia
anyway ad ogni modo
apartment l'appartamento;
studio apartment il monolocale
to apologize scusarsi*
to appear apparire* (*p.p.* apparso)
to applaud applaudire
applause l'applạuso
apple la mela
appointment l'appuntamento
to appreciate apprezzare
to approach avvicinarsi*
April aprile
arcade la galleria
architect l'architetto
architecture l'architettura
architectural architettọnico
area la superfịcie;
area code il prefisso
to argue litigare
arm il brạccio (*pl.* le brạccia)
armchair la poltrona
around intorno (a), verso
arrival l'arrivo
to arrive arrivare*
art l'arte (*f.*)
article l'artịcolo
artistic artịstico
as come
to ask domandare, chiedere (*p.p.* chiẹsto)
asleep addormentato;
to fall asleep addormentarsi*
at a, in, da (*at the house of*);
at least almeno
athlete l'atleta (*m.* or *f.*)
athletic sportivo
to attend assịstere;
to attend a course seguire, frequentare
attention l'attenzione (*f.*)
to attract attirare
attractive attraente
audience il pụbblico
August agosto
aunt la zia
author l'autore, l'autrice
autobiography l'autobiografia
automobile (*f.*) l'automọbile
autumn l'autunno
available lịbero, disponịbile
away via

B

backpack lo zạino
bad cattivo;
too bad! Peccato!
bag la borsa;
handbag la borsetta;
sleeping bag il sacco a pelo
balcony il balcone, la galleria
ball la palla; il pallone (*soccer*)
bank la banca
barman barista
basketball la pallacanestro (*f.*)
bath il bagno;
to take a bath fare il bagno;
bathroom la stanza da bagno;
bathtub la vasca da bagno
to be ẹssere* (*p.p.* stato)
to be able to potere;
to be acquainted with conoscere;
to be bad for fare male a;
to be born nạscere;
to be broke ẹssere al verde;
to be called (named) chiamarsi*;
to be careful stare attento;
to be on a diet ẹssere a dieta;
to be distant distare;
to be a doctor (a lawyer, etc.) fare il dottore (l'avvocato, ecc.);
to be enough bastare;
to be a fan fare il tifo (per);
to be in a hurry avere fretta;
to be necessary bisognare;
to be ... years old (afraid, cold, hot, hungry, thirsty, right, wrong, sleepy) avere anni (paura, freddo, caldo, fame, sete, ragione, torto, sonno)
beach la spiạggia
beard la barba
beautiful bello
beauty la bellezza
because perchè;
because of a causa di
to become diventare*;
to become ill ammalarsi*
bedroom la cạmera da letto
beer la birra
before (*prep.*) davanti (a); (*conj.*) prima (di)
to begin (in)cominciare
beginning l'inizio
behind dietro
to believe crẹdere (a)
bell tower il campanile
to belong appartenere
below sotto
besides inoltre
between tra (*or* fra)
bicycle la bicicletta
big grande; **bigger** maggiore
bill il conto

biology la biologia
birth la nạscita
birthday il compleanno;
Happy Birthday! Buon compleanno!
bitter amaro
black nero
blackboard la lavagna
blond biondo
blouse la camicetta
blue blu (*inv.*)
boat la barca
body il corpo
bone l'osso (*pl.* le ossa)
book il libro
bookstore la libreria
boot lo stivale
to border confinare
bored: to get bored annoiarsi*
boredom la nọia
boring noioso
born: to be born nạscere* (*p.p.* nato)
boss il capoufficio
to bother dare fastịdio
bottle la bottịglia
boy, boyfriend il ragazzo
boxer il pụgile
boxing il pugilato
to brake frenare
bread rọmpere (*p.p.* rotto); rompersi*
breakfast la colazione;
to have breakfast fare colazione
brick il mattone
brilliant brillante
to bring portare
broke: to be broke ẹssere al verde
brother il fratello;
brother-in-law il cognato
brown castano, marrone
to build costruire (-isc-)
building l'edifịcio; il palazzo
bus l'ạutobus (*m.*);
bus stop la fermata dell'ạutobus
business l'affare (*m.*)
busy occupato
but ma, però
butter il burro
to buy comprare
by da

C

cab il tassì (*inv.*)
cafeteria la mensa
cake la torta
calculator la calcolatrice
calendar il calendạrio
to call chiamare;
to be called chiamarsi*
calm calmo
camera la mạcchina fotogrạfica
camping il campẹggio;
to go camping fare il campẹggio
can potere
candidate il candidato
capital la capitale
car l'auto(mọbile) (*f.*), la mạcchina
careful attento;
to be careful stare attento
carpet il tappeto
to carry portare
to cash incassare
castle il castello
cat il gatto
cathedral il duomo
cause la cạusa
to celebrate festeggiare
cellar la cantina
central centrale
century il sẹcolo
certain certo
chain la catena
chair la sẹdia
chalk il gesso
champion il campione, la campionessa
change il cambiamento, la moneta;
to change cambiare;
to change one's clothes cambiarsi*;
to change one's mind cambiare idea
channel il canale
chapel la cappella;
the Sistine Chapel la Cappella Sistina
chapter il capịtolo
character il personạggio
charity la beneficenza
cheap econọmico
check il conto, l'assegno;
to check controllare
cheerful allegro
cheese il formạggio
chemistry la chịmica
chicken il pollo
child il bambino, la bambina, (*pl.*) i bambini, i figli;
only child il fịglio ụnico, la fịglia ụnica;
grandchild il (la) nipote;
as a child da bambino
Chinese cinese
chocolate il cioccolato;
chocolate candy il cioccolatino
choice la scelta
to choose scẹgliere (*p.p.* scelto)
Christmas il Natale
church la chiesa
cigarette la sigaretta
city la città
civilization la civiltà, la civilizzazione
class la classe, la lezione
classmate il compagno, la compagna di classe
clean pulito;
to clean pulire (-isc-)
clear sereno
clerk l'impiegato, l'impiegata

client il (la) cliente
climate il clima
to climb salire
clock l'orologio;
alarm clock la sveglia
to close chiudere (*p.p.* chiuso)
closet l'armadietto
clothes i vestiti
clothing l'abbigliamento
cloudy nuvoloso
clown il pagliaccio;
to clown around fare lo spiritoso
coach l'allenatore, l'allenatrice;
to coach allenare
coast la costa
coat la giacca;
winter coat il cappotto
coffee, coffee shop il caffè
cold freddo;
to be cold avere freddo;
it is cold fa freddo;
to catch a cold prendere il raffreddore
to collaborate collaborare
colleague il (la) collega
to come venire* (*p.p.* venuto);
to come back ritornare;
to come in entrare;
to come down discendere* (*p.p.* disceso);
Come on! Dai!
comedian il comico
comedy la commedia
comfort la comodità
comfortable comodo
comic comico
comment il commento
common comune
to communicate comunicare
Communist comunista
company compagnia, ditta azienda
to compare paragonare
competition la competizione, la gara
to complain lamentarsi* (di)
completely completamente
complicated complicato
to compose comporre (*p.p.* composto)
composer il compositore, la compositrice
compulsory obbligatorio
computer science l'informatica
concert il concerto
concierge il portinaio
conclusion la conclusione
condition la condizione
confusion la confusione
Congratulations! Congratulazioni!
congressman, congresswoman il deputato, la deputata
to consider considerare;
to consider one's self considerarsi*
to console consolare
to consume consumare
consultant il (la) consulente
continent il continente
to continue continuare
continually continuamente
contract il contratto
contrary il contrario;
on the contrary anzi
to control controllare
conversation la conversazione
cook il cuoco, la cuoca;
to cook cucinare;
cooking la cucina
cool fresco
corner l'angolo
to correct correggere (*p.p.* corretto)
cost il costo;
to cost costare
costume il costume
cotton il cotone
couch il divano
cough la tosse
to count contare
country il paese;
countryside la campagna
couple la coppia
courage il coraggio
courageous corraggioso
course il corso, la classe
cousin il cugino, la cugina
covered coperto
crazy pazzo;
to go crazy impazzire*
crisis la crisi
critic il critico (*m.* or *f.*)
to criticize criticare
crooked storto
to cross attraversare
crowded affollato
cruise la crociera
to cry piangere (*p.p.* pianto)
cup la tazza
to cure guarire
curious curioso
curtain la tenda, il sipario
customer il (la) cliente
customs la dogana
to cut tagliare;
to cut oneself tagliarsi*
cute carino

D

dad il papà
to damage rovinare
to dance ballare
danger il pericolo
dangerous pericoloso
dark buio;
dark-haired bruno
date la data; l'appuntamento
daughter la figlia;
daughter-in-law la nuora
day il giorno, la giornata;
the next day il giorno dopo
dear caro
death la morte
December dicembre
to decide decidere (*p.p.* deciso)

decision la decisione
deep profondo
defect il difetto
to define definire (-isc-)
degree il tịtolo di stụdio
delicious delizioso
democracy la democrazia
dentist il (la) dentista
departure la partenza
to depend dipẹndere*;
it depends (on) dipende (da)
deposit il depọsito;
to deposit depositare
depressing deprimente
to descend (di)scẹndere* (*p.p.* disceso)
to describe descrịvere (*p.p.* descritto)
description la descrizione
designer lo (la) stilista
desk la scrivania
dessert il dolce
to detest detestare
development lo sviluppo
to dial formare il nụmero
dialect il dialetto
dialogue il diạlogo
diary il diạrio
dictionary il vocabolạrio
to die morire* (*p.p.* morto)
diet la dieta;
to be on a diet stare a dieta
difference la differenza
different differente
difficult diffịcile
difficulty la difficoltà
diligent diligente
dinner il pranzo;
dining room sala da pranzo;
to have dinner pranzare
direction l'indicazione (*f.*)
directly direttamente
director il direttore, la direttrice
disadvantage lo svantạggio
disappointment la delusione
discovery la scoperta
to discuss discụtere (*p.p.* discusso)
discussion la discussione
disease la malattia
dish il piatto
dishwasher la lavastovịglie
distance la distanza
distant distante;
to be distant distare
district il quartiere
to divide divịdere (*p.p.* diviso)
divorced divorziato
to do fare (*p.p.* fatto)
doctor il dottore, la dottoressa; il mẹdico
document il documento
documentary il documentạrio
dog il cane
dollar il dọllaro
door la porta
doubt il dụbbio;
to doubt dubitare
downtown il centro; in centro
to draw disegnare
drawer il cassetto
drawing il disegno
dream il sogno
to dream sognare
dress l'ạbito, il vestito;
to dress vestire;
to get dressed vestirsi*
drink la bevanda;
to drink bere (*p.p.* bevuto)
to drive guidare
driver l'automobilista (*m.* or *f.*)
driving la guida
drunk ubriaco
dry secco
to dry asciugare;
to dry oneself asciugarsi*
during durante
duty il dovere

E

each ogni
ear l'orẹcchio (*pl.* le orẹcchie);
earache mal d'orẹcchio
early presto
to earn guadagnare;
to earn one's living guadagnarsi* il pane
earth la terra
Easter la Pasqua
eastern orientale
easy fạcile
to eat mangiare
economy l'economia
to educate istruire (-isc-)
education l'istruzione (*f.*)
egg l'uovo (*pl.* le uova)
either ... or o ... o
election l'elezione (*f.*)
electricity l'elettricità
elegant elegante
elementary elementare
elevator l'ascensore
to eliminate eliminare
to embrace abbracciare
emotion l'emozione (*f.*)
employee l'impiegato, l'impiegata
employment l'impiego;
employment agency l'agenzia di collocamento
empty vuoto
to encourage incoraggiare
end la fine;
to end finire (-isc)
engagement il fidanzamento
engineer l'ingegnere (*m.*)
engineering l'ingegneria
England l'Inghilterra
English inglese
to enjoy godere;
to enjoy oneself divertirsi*
enough abbastanza;
to be enough bastare

to enroll iscriversi* (*p.p.* iscritto)
to enter entrare* (in)
entertaining divertente
enthusiastic entusiasta
entire intero
entitled intitolato
equal uguale
error l'errore (*m.*)
especially specialmente
Europe l'Europa
even perfino;
not even neanche, nemmeno
evening la sera, la serata;
Good evening! Buon sera!;
this evening stasera
event l'avvenimento
every ogni (*inv.*);
everybody ognuno
everyone ognuno
exact esatto
exactly esattamente
exam l'esame (*m.*);
to take an exam dare un esame
example l'esempio;
for example ad esempio, per esempio
to exceed superare
excellent eccellente, ottimo
except eccetto
exception l'eccezione (*f.*)
to exchange (money) cambiare
excursion l'escursione (*f.*)
excuse la scusa;
Excuse me! Scusi! Scusa!
exercise l'esercizio
exhibition la mostra
to exist esistere* (*p.p.* esistito)
expense la spesa
expensive caro, costoso
experience l'esperienza
experienced esperto
experiment l'esperimento
expert esperto
to explain spiegare
explanation la spiegazione
to explore esplorare
to express esprimere (*p.p.* espresso)
expression l'espressione (*f.*)
eye l'occhio
eye doctor l'oculista (*m.* or *f.*)
eyeglasses gli occhiali (*pl.*)

F

fable la favola
face la faccia
fact il fatto;
in fact infatti
factory la fabbrica
fair giusto
faithful fedele
fall l'autunno;
to fall cadere*
familiar familiare
family la famiglia
famous famoso
fan tifoso;
to be a fan fare il tifo (per)
fantastic fantastico
far (from) lontano (da)
farmer il contadino, la contadina
fascinating affascinante, avvincente
fascism il fascismo
fashion la moda
fashionable di moda, alla moda
fast rapido, veloce
fat grasso
father il padre;
father-in-law il suocero;
grandfather il nonno
favor il favore
favorable favorevole
fear la paura, il timore;
to fear temere
February febbraio
to feel sentire, sentirsi*;
to feel like avere voglia di
feeling il sentimento
feminine femminile
festivity la festa
fever la febbre
few pochi(e);
a few alcuni(e)
fiancé, fincée il fidanzato, la fidanzata
field il campo
to fill riempire;
to fill it up fare il pieno
final definitivo
finally finalmente
to finance finanziare
to find trovare
fine la multa
finger il dito (*pl.* le dita)
to finish finire (-isc-)
fire il fuoco;
fireplace il caminetto;
to fire licenziare
firm la ditta
first (*adj.*) primo, (*adv.*) prima
fish il pesce;
fried fish pesce fritto;
to fish pescare
to fit andare bene
to fix (an appointment) fissare un appuntamento
flag la bandiera
flaw il difetto
floor il pavimento, il piano
Florence Firenze
flour la farina
flower il fiore
flu l'influenza
flute il flauto
fog la nebbia
to follow seguire
fond (of) appassionato (di)
food il cibo
foot il piede;
on foot a piedi
for per
to forbid proibire (-isc-)

foreign straniero
foreigner lo straniero, la straniera
to forget dimenticare
fork la forchetta
fountain la fontana
frankly francamente
free lịbero, gratụito
freeway l'autostrada
French francese
fresco l'affresco
Friday il venerdì
friend l'amico(a)
friendship l'amicịzia
from da, di
frozen surgelato
fruit la frutta;
  piece of fruit il frutto
full pieno
fun il divertimento;
  to have fun divertirsi*
to function funzionare
furious furioso
furniture i mọbili (*pl.*);
  a piece of furniture un mọbile

G

to gain guadagnare;
  to gain weight ingrassare
gallery la galleria;
  art gallery la galleria d'arte
game il gioco, la partita
garden il giardino
garlic l'ạglio
gasoline la benzina;
  gasoline pump il distributore di benzina
to gather riunirsi* (-isc-)
gender il gẹnere
general generale
generally in gẹnere
generous generoso
genius il gẹnio
gentleman il signore
geography la geografia
German tedesco
Germany la Germạnia
to get prẹndere;
  to get along andare d'accordo;
  to get bored annoiarsi*;
  to get engaged fidanzarsi*;
  to get lost pẹrdersi*;
  to get mad arrabbiarsi*;
  to get married sposarsi*;
  to get near avvicinarsi* (a);
  to get sick ammalarsi*;
  to get tired stancarsi*;
  to get up alzarsi*;
  to get used to abituarsi* (a)
gift il regalo
girl la ragazza;
  little girl la bambina;
  girlfriend la ragazza
to give dare;
  to give back restituire (-isc-);
  to give a lift dare un passạggio;
  to give a present regalare
glad contento
glass il bicchiere;
  glasses gli occhiali
gloves i guanti (*pl.*)
to go andare*;
  to go back ritornare*;
  to go camping fare il campẹggio;
  to go down scẹndere*;
  to go in entrare*;
  to go near avvicinarsi*;
  to go out uscire*;
  to go shopping fare la spesa (le spese);
  to go up salire*
gold l'oro
god buono, bravo
Good-bye Arrivederci! (*fam.*); ArrivederLa! (*form.*); Ciao!
government il governo
grade il voto
to graduate laurearsi*; diplomarsi*
grandfather il nonno;
  grandmother la nonna;
  grandparents i nonni
grapes l'uva
grass l'erba
grateful riconoscente
gray grịgio
great grande
green verde
to greet salutare
greeting il saluto;
  greetings tanti saluti
groom lo sposo
group il gruppo
to grow crẹscere*
to guess indovinare
guest l'ọspite (*m.* or *f.*), l'invitato(a)
guide la guida
guilty colpẹvole
guitar la chitarra
gulf il golfo
guy il tipo
gym la palestra

H

hair i capelli;
  dark-haired bruno
hairdresser il parrucchiere, la parrucchiera
half la metà, mezzo (*adj.*)
hand la mano (*pl.* le mani);
  to shake hands dare la mano
handkerchief il fazzoletto
handsome bello
to happen succẹdere* (*p.p.* successo)
happiness la felicità
happy felice
hard duro
to hate detestare, odiare

to have avere;
to have breakfast fare colazione;
to have dinner cenare;
to have fun divertirsi*;
to have a headache (toothache, stomachache, backache, sore throat) avere mal di testa (denti, stọmaco, schiena, gola);
to have to dovere
head il capo, la testa
health la salute
to hear sentire
heart il cuore
heavy pesante
hell l'inferno
hello ciao, pronto (*telephone*)
help l'aiuto;
to help aiutare
here qui;
Here is ...! Ecco...!
hero l'eroe (*m.*)
high alto
hill la collina
to hire assụmere (*p.p.* assunto)
historical stọrico
history la stọria
to hit colpire (-isc-)
hitchhiking l'autostop (*m.*);
to hitchhike fare l'autostop
holiday la festa, la vacanza
home la casa;
at home a casa
homeless i senzatetto
homework il cọmpito
to hope sperare
horse il cavallo
hospital l'ospedale (*m.*)
hot caldo;
to be hot avere caldo;
it is hot fa caldo
hotel l'albergo
hour l'ora;
rush hours le ore di punta
house la casa;
at the house of a casa di;
at his/her house a casa sua
housewife la casalinga
how? come?;
How much? Quanto?;
How are you? Come sta? (*form. s.*), Come stai? (*fam. s.*), Come va?;
How come? Come mai?
however comunque, però
huge grosso
humid ụmido
hundred cento (*inv.*)
hunger la fame;
to be hungry avere fame
hurry la fretta;
to be in hurry avere fretta;
in a hurry in fretta
to hurt oneself farsi* male
husband il marito

I

ice il ghiạccio; **ice cream** il gelato
idea l'idea
ideal ideale
if se
ignorant ignorante
ill (am)malato;
to become ill ammalarsi*
illness la malattia
imagination l'immaginazione (*f.*)
to imagine immaginare
immediately immediatamente
impatience l'impazienza
impatient impaziente
impolite maleducato
importance l'importanza
important importante
impossible impossịbile
to improve migliorare
in in, a; fra
included compreso
increase l'aumento;
to increase aumentare
indeed davvero, veramente
independent indipendente
industrial industriale
inexperienced inesperto
inflation l'inflazione (*f.*)
information l'informazione (*f.*)
ingredient l'ingrediente (*m.*)
inhabitant l'abitante (*m.*)
to inherit ereditare
inheritance l'eredità
injection l'iniezione (*f.*)
ink l'inchiostro
inn la pensione, l'albergo
insensitive insensịbile
inside dentro, in
instead (of) invece (di)
instructor l'istruttore, l'istruttrice
instrument lo strumento
intellectual intellettuale
intelligent intelligente
to intend avere intenzione di, pensare di
intention l'intenzione (*f.*)
interest l'interesse (*m.*);
to interest interessare;
to be interested in interessarsi* a
interesting interessante
intermission l'intermezzo
intersection l'incrọcio
interview il collọquio
to introduce presentare;
to introduce onself presentarsi*
to invent inventare
to invite invitare
Irish irlandese
island l'ịsola
Italian italiano;
Italian language l'italiano
Italy l'Itạlia
item l'artịcolo

J

jacket la giacca
January gennạio
Japan il Giappone
Japanese giapponese
job il lavoro
to joke scherzare
journalist il (la) giornalista
joy la giọia
juice il succo;
orange juice il succo d'arạncia
July lụglio
to jump saltare
June giugno
just (*adj.*) giusto; (*adv.*) appena

K

to keep tenere;
to keep up to date aggiornarsi*
key la chiave
to kill uccịdere (*p.p.* ucciso)
kilogram il chilo (chilogrammo)
kilometer il chilọmetro
kind gentile; il gẹnere
king il re
kiss il bạcio;
to kiss baciare
kitchen la cucina
knee il ginọcchio (*pl.* le ginọcchia)
knife il coltello
to know conọscere (*p.p.* conosciuto), sapere;
to know how sapere;
Who knows! Chissà!
knowledge la conoscenza

L

ladder la scala
lady la signora
lake il lago
lamp la lạmpada
land la terra
landlord, landlady il padrone (la padrona) di casa
landscape il paesạggio
language la lingua;
foreign language la lingua straniera
large largo, grande
last ụltimo, scorso;
to last durare
late tardi;
to be late ẹssere in ritardo
to laugh rịdere (*p.p.* riso)
laughter il riso
law la legge
lawyer l'avvocato, l'avvocatessa
lazy pigro
to learn imparare
leather il cuoio, la pelle
to leave lasciare, partire*
lecture la conferenza
left la sinistra, (*adj.*) sinistro;
to the left a sinistra
leg la gamba
legal legale
to lend prestare
less meno
lesson la lezione
to let lasciare
letter la lẹttera
library la biblioteca
license (driver's) la patente;
license plate la targa
lie la bugia;
to lie dire una bugia
life la vita;
still life la natura morta
lifeguard il bagnino, la bagnina
lift il passạggio;
to give a lift dare un passạggio
light la luce; (*adj.*) leggero;
traffic light il semạforo;
to light accẹndere (*p.p.* acceso)
like come;
to like piacere (*p.p.* piaciuto)
limit il lịmite;
speed limit il lịmite di velocità
line la fila;
to stand in line fare la fila
lip il labbro (*pl.* le labbra)
lira la lira (*Italian currency*)
to listen to ascoltare
literature la letteratura
little pịccolo
to live abitare, vịvere (*p.p.* vissuto)
London Londra
long lungo;
for a long time a lungo
to look (at) guardare;
to look (+ *adj.*) avere un'ạria;
to look for cercare;
to look like assomigliare a
to lose pẹrdere;
to get lost pẹrdersi*;
to lose weight dimagrire
lot (a lot) molto, un sacco (di)
love l'amore (*m.*);
to love amare;
to be in love (with) ẹssere innamorato (di);
love (*closing a letter*) con affetto
low basso
luck la fortuna;
bad luck la sfortuna;
Good luck! Buona fortuna!
luckily per fortuna
lucky fortunato

M

mad: to get mad arrabbiarsi*
magazine la rivista
magnificent stupendo
to mail spedire (-isc-)
main principal
major la specializzazione
majority la maggioranza
to make fare (*p.p.* fatto);
to make the acquaintance fare la conoscenza;
to make a movie girare un film;
to make up fare la pace
man l'uomo (*pl.* gli uọmini)
manifest il manifesto
manuscript il manoscritto
many-colored variopinto
map la carta geogrạfica
marble il marmo
March marzo
market il mercato
marriage il matrimọnio
to marry sposare;
to get married sposarsi*;
married sposato (a)
masculine maschile
mask, masked character la mạschera
mass media i mezzi di diffusione
masterpiece il capolavoro
match la partita (*sports*)
mathematics la matemạtica
mature maturo
May mạggio
may potere;
it may be that può darsi che
maybe forse
meal il pasto
mean cattivo
to mean significare, voler(e) dire
meaning il significato
means il mezzo;
by means of per mezzo di;
means of transportation i mezzi di trasporto
meat la carne
mechanic il meccạnico
medicine la medicina
to meet conọscere (*p.p.* conosciuto); incontrare
meeting la riunione
memory la memọria
message il messạggio
messy disordinato
meter il metro
midnight la mezzanotte
mild mite
mile il mịglio (*pl.* le mịglia)
milk il latte
millionaire il milionạrio
minute il minuto
misadventure la disavventura
miss signorina
mistake l'errore (*m.*)
mister signore
to mix mescolare
mixed misto
model il modello, la modella
modern moderno
modest modesto
mom la mamma
moment il momento
Monday il lunedì
money il denaro, i soldi
monologue il monọlogo
month il mese
monthly mensile (*adj.*)
monument il monumento
mood l'umore;
to be in a good (bad) mood ẹssere di buon (cattivo) umore
moon la luna
more più; ancora
morning il mattino, la mattina;
in the morning di mattina;
this morning stamattina;
Good morning! Buon giorno!
mother la madre;
mother-in-law la suọcera;
grandmother la nonna
motorcycle la motocicletta
motorist l'automobilista (*m.* or *f.*)
mountain la montagna
moustache i baffi
mouth la bocca
to move traslocare;
moving il trasloco
movie il film;
to go to the movies andare al cịnema
movie theater il cịnema
much molto;
too much troppo
museum il museo
mushroom il fungo
music la mụsica;
opera music mụsica operịstica;
folk music mụsica folclorịstica
musician il (la) musicista
must dovere

N

name il nome;
last name il cognome
napkin il tovagliolo
Naples Nạpoli
narrow stretto
nation la nazione
nationality la nazionalità
naturally naturalmente
nature la natura
Neapolitan napoletano
near vicino;
to get near avvicinarsi*

neat ordinato

necessary necessạrio;

to be necessary bisognare

neck il collo

need il bisogno;

to need avere bisogno di

neighbor il vicino, la vicina

nephew il nipote

nervous nervoso

never mai

nevertheless ciononostante

new nuovo;

What's new? Cosa c'è di nuovo?

news la notịzia

newspaper il giornale

next to vicino (a);

next week la settimana prọssima

nice simpạtico

niece la nipote

night la notte;

Good night! Buona notte!;

last night ieri sera

no no

nobody nessuno

noise il rumore

noon il mezzogiorno

Northern settentrionale

nose il naso

not non

notebook il quaderno

notes gli appunti

nothing niente

to notice notare

noun il nome

novel il romanzo

November novembre

now adesso, ora

number il nụmero;

phone number il nụmero telefọnico

nurse l'infermiere, l'infermiera

O

to obey ubbidire (-isc-)

object l'oggetto

to obtain ottenere

occasion la circostanza

to occupy occupare

ocean l'ocẹano

October ottobre

of di

to offend offẹndere (*p.p.* offeso)

offer l'offerta;

to offer offrire (*p.p.* offerto)

office l'uffịcio;

Post Office la Posta

often spesso

oil l'ọlio

O.K., very well va bene

old vẹcchio

Olympic olịmpico

on su, sopra

once una volta;

once upon a time c'era una volta

onion la cipolla

only solo (*adv.*), solamente, appena, soltanto

open aperto;

to open aprire

opera l'ọpera

opinion l'opinione (*f.*)

opportunity l'occasione (*f.*)

opposite il contrạrio

optimist ottimista

or o

orange l'arạncia;

orange juice il succo d'arạncia

order l'ọrdine (*m.*);

to order, to put in order riordinare;

in order to per;

in order that affinchè

to organize organizzare

oriental orientale

origin l'orịgine (*f.*)

original originale; l'originale (*m.*)

other altro

out fuori

outdoors all'aperto

outside fuori

outskirts la periferia

to owe dovere

owner il proprietạrio, la proprietạria

P

to pack fare le valịgie;

back pack lo zạino

package il pacco

page la pạgina

pain il dolore

to paint dipịngere (*p.p.* dipinto)

painter il pittore, la pittrice

painting la pittura, il quadro

pair il paio (*pl.* le paia)

palace il palazzo

pants il pantaloni

paper la carta

parents i genitori

park il parco;

to park parcheggiare

parking lot il parchẹggio

party la festa; il partito (*political*)

to pass passare

passenger il passeggero, la passeggera

passport il passaporto

past il passato; passato (*adj.*)

pastry il pasticcino

patience la pazienza

patient paziente
to pay pagare;
to pay attention fare attenzione;
to pay a visit fare visita
paycheck lo stipendio
peace la pace
peach la pesca
pear la pera
peas i piselli
peasant il contadino, la contadina
pedestrian il pedone
pen la penna
pencil la matita
peninsula la penisola
pension la pensione
people la gente; **some people** alcune persone
pepper il pepe
perfect perfetto
perfectly alla perfezione
to perform rappresentare, recitare
performance la rappresentazione
perfume il profumo
perhaps forse
period il periodo
person la persona
pessimist pessimista
pharmacy la farmacia
phone il telefono;
to phone telefonare;
phone call la telefonata;
phone book l'elenco telefonico
photograph la foto(grafia)
physician il medico
physics la fisica
picture la fotografia, il quadro
pie la torta
pill la pillola
pink rosa (*inv.*)
place il luogo, il posto;
to place mettere
plan il progetto;
to plan progettare, pensare (di + *inf.*)
play la commedia, il dramma;
to play (an instrument) suonare;
to play (a game) giocare;
to play (a part) recitare;
player il giocatore, la giocatrice
playwright il commediografo, la commediografa
pleasant piacevole
please per piacere, prego
pleasure il piacere;
with pleasure con piacere
plot la trama
plumber l'idraulico
plus più
pocket la tasca
poem il poema
poet il poeta
poetry la poesia
point il punto;
point of view il punto di vista
police la polizia
policeman il poliziotto
polite educato
political politico
politics la politica
pollution l'inquinamento
poor povero
popular popolare
popularity la popolarità
populated popolato
portrait il ritratto
position il posto
possible possibile;
as little as possible il meno possibile
possibility la possibilità
postcard la cartolina
poster il manifesto;
electoral poster il manifesto elettorale
post office l'ufficio postale
pot la pentola
potato la patata;
fried potatoes le patate fritte
practical pratico
to practice allenarsi*; esercitarsi*
to pray pregare
precious prezioso
precise preciso
prefer preferire (-isc-)
preferable preferibile
to prepare preparare
to prescribe prescrivere (*p.p.* prescritto)
prescription la ricetta
present il regalo
president il presidente, la presidentessa
press la stampa
pretty carino
price il prezzo
print la stampa
private privato
prize il premio
probable probabile
problem il problema
producer il produttore, la produttrice
profession la professione
professor il professore, la professoressa
program il programma
to prohibit proibire (-isc-)
project il progetto, il piano
to promise promettere (*p.p.* promesso)
prompter il suggeritore
pronoun il pronome
protest la protesta;
to protest protestare
provided purchè
proud orgoglioso
public il pubblico
publicity la pubblicità
to publish pubblicare

publisher l'editore (*m.*), l'editrice (*f.*)
to pull tirare
punctual puntuale
to punish punire (-isc-)
puppet il burattino
purple viola (*inv.*)
purpose il fine
to put mẹttere (*p.p.* messo);
  to put on mẹttersi*;
  to put make up on truccarsi*

Q

qualification la qualifica
quality la qualità
quarrel il litịgio;
  to quarrel litigare
quarter il trimestre, il quarto
question la domanda;
  to ask a question fare una domanda
quiet tranquillo;
  to be quiet stare zitto
to quit abbandonare, lasciare

R

radio la radio
rain la piọggia;
  to rain piọvere
raincoat l'impermeạbile (*m.*)
rare raro
rather piuttosto
to react reagire (-isc-)
to read lẹggere (*p.p.* letto)
reader il lettore, la lettrice
reading la lettura
ready pronto
reality la realtà
to realize rendersi* conto (*p.p.* reso)
really davvero
reason la ragione
receipt la ricevuta
to receive ricẹvere
recently recentemente
recipe la ricetta
to recite recitare
to recognize riconọscere (*p.p.* riconosciuto)
record il disco;
  record player il giradischi
to recover guarire (-isc-)
red rosso
referee l'ạrbitro
refrigerator il frigo(rịfero)
region la regione
regular regolare
relationship il rapporto, la relazione
relative il (la) parente
to remain rimanere* (*p.p.* rimasto), restare*
remarkable notẹvole
to remember ricordare, ricordarsi*
Renaissance il Rinascimento
to renounce rinunciare
renowned noto, famoso
rent l'affitto;
  to rent affittare;
  to rent (a car) noleggiare
to repair riparare
to repeat ripẹtere
to reply rispọndere
to reproach rimproverare
republic la repụbblica
research la ricerca
reservation la prenotazione
to reserve prenotare
to rest riposarsi*
restaurant il ristorante, la trattoria
result il risultato
to retire andare in pensione
return il ritorno;
  to return ritornare*, restituire (-isc-)
reunion la riunione
rice il riso
rich ricco
to ride (the bicycle) andare in bicicletta
riding l'equitazione (*f.*)
right giusto;
  to be right avere ragione;
  to the right a destra
ring l'anello
river il fiume
road la strada
role la parte;
  to play the role recitare la parte (di)
romantic romạntico
Rome Roma
roof il tetto
room la cạmera, il locale, la stanza;
  living room il soggiorno (la sala);
  bedroom la cạmera da letto
roommate il compagno, la compagna di stanza
rose la rosa
rowing il canottạggio
rug il tappeto
run la corsa;
  to run cọrrere (*p.p.* corso)

S

to sacrifice sacrificarsi*
sad triste
safety la salvezza;
  safety belt la cintura di sicurezza
sailing: to go sailing andare in barca;

sailor il marinạio
salad l'insalata
salary lo stipẹndio
salesperson il commesso, la commessa
salt il sale
same stesso
sand la sạbbia
sandwich il panino imbottito
sarcastically sarcasticamente
satisfied soddisfatto
Saturday il sạbato
sauce la salsa
sausage la salsịccia
to save risparmiare, salvare
saving il rispạrmio
to say dire (*p.p.* detto);
  to say good-bye; to say hello salutare
scene la scena
schedule l'orạrio
scholarship la borsa di stụdio
school la scuola;
  elementary school la scuola elementare;
  junior high school la scuola mẹdia;
  high school il liceo
science la scienza;
  political science le scienze polịtiche
scientist lo scienziato
to scold rimproverare
to score segnare
to scream gridare
to sculpt scolpire
sculptor lo scultore, la scultrice
sculpture la scultura
sea il mare
serious grave
season la stagione
seat il posto, la poltrona (*theater*)
seated seduto
second secondo; il secondo
secret il segreto
secretary il segretạrio, la segretạria
to see vedere (*p.p.* visto, veduto)
to seem parere, sembrare
to sell vẹndere
semester il semestre
senator il senatore, la senatrice
to send mandare
sensitive sensịbile
sentence la frase
September settembre
serious sẹrio
to serve servire
to set (*the table*) apparecchiare (la tạvola)
several diversi(e)
sex il sesso
shape la forma
to share divịdere, condivịdere (*p.p.* diviso, condiviso)
sharp in punto
to shave rạdersi* (*p.p.* raso)
sheet (of paper) il fọglio (di carta)
shelf lo scaffale
shirt la camịcia
shoe la scarpa
shop il negọzio
shopping: to go shopping fare le spese;
  to go grocery shopping fare la spesa
short basso, breve
to shout gridare
show la mostra, lo spettạcolo;
  to show (di)mostrare
shower la dọccia;
  to take a shower fare la dọccia
Sicilian siciliano
Sicily la Sicịlia
sick ammalato
sidewalk il marciapiede
sign il cartello;
  to sign firmare
signal il segnale;
  to signal segnalare
signature la firma
silence il silẹnzio
silent silenzioso
silk la seta
similar sịmile
simple sẹmplice
since siccome; da quando
sincerity la sincerità
to sing cantare
singer il (la) cantante
single nụbile (*woman*); cẹlibe, scạpolo (*man*)
sink il lavandino
sir signore
sister la sorella;
  sister-in-law la cognata
to sit (down) sẹdersi*
situation la situazione
size la tạglia
skates i pạttini
skating il pattinaggio
ski lo sci (*inv.*);
  to ski sciare;
  skier lo sciatore, la sciatrice
to skip saltare
skirt la gonna
sky il cielo
skyscraper il grattacielo
sleep il sonno;
  to sleep dormire;
  to be sleepy avere sonno
slice la fetta
slim snello
slow lento
to slow down rallentare
slowly adạgio
small pịccolo
to smile sorrịdere (*p.p.* sorriso)
to smoke fumare
snack lo spuntino;
  snack bar la tạvola calda
snow la neve;
  to snow nevicare
so così;
  so much così tanto;
  so that affinchè
soccer il cạlcio

socialist socialista
sock il calzino
sofa il divano
solitude la solitụdine
some alcuni (alcune), qualche di + *def. art.*, un po' di
someone qualcuno
something qualcosa
sometimes qualche volta
son il fịglio;
son-in-law il gẹnero
song la canzone
soon presto;
as soon as possible appena possịbile
sorry spiacente;
to be sorry dispiacere (*p.p.* dispiaciuto)
soup la minestra;
vegetable soup il minestrone
South il sud
Southern meridionale
Spanish spagnolo
to speak parlare;
to speak about parlare di
special speciale
specialist lo (la) specialista
specially specialmente
spectator lo spettatore, la spettatrice
speech il discorso
speed la velocità
to spend spẹndere (*money*) (*p.p.* speso); passare (*time*)
spendthrift spendaccione
splendid splẹndido, magnịfico
spoon il cucchịaio
sporty sportivo
spring la primavera
square la piazza
stadium lo stạdio
stage il palcoscẹnico;
to stage rappresentare
stamp il francobollo
to stand in line fare la fila
to start incominciare
state lo stato
station la stazione
statue la stạtua
to stay restare*, stare
steak la bistecca
to steal rubare
still fermo; ancora (*adv.*)
stingy avaro
stocking la calza
to stop smẹttere (*p.p.* smesso); fermare, fermarsi*
store il negọzio
story la stọria;
short story il racconto
straight diritto, dritto;
straight ahead avanti diritto
strange strano
strawberry la fragola
street la strada;
street corner l'angolo della strada
strength la forza
strict severo
strike lo sciọpero
to strike scioperare
strong forte
stubborn ostinato
student lo studente, la studentessa
studious studioso
studio il monolocale
study lo stụdio;
study room lo stụdio;
to study studiare
stuff la roba
style lo stile
subject l'argomento, il soggetto
subtitles le didascalie
subway la metropolitana
to succeed (in) riuscire* (a)
success il successo
suddenly improvvisamente
to suffer soffrire (*p.p.* sofferto)
sugar lo zụcchero
to suggest suggerire (-isc-)
suit il completo;
bathing suit il costume da bagno
suitcase la valịgia
summary il riassunto
summer l'estate (*f.*)
sumptuous lussuoso
sun il sole
Sunday la domẹnica
sunglasses gli occhiali da sole
sunny: it is sunny c'è il sole
supermarket il supermercato
supper la cena; **to have supper** cenare
sure sicuro, certo; già
surface la superfịcie
surgeon il chirurgo
surprise la sorpresa;
to surprise sorprẹndere;
surprised sorpreso
to surround circondare
sweater il maglione
sweat suit la tuta da ginnạstica
sweet dolce
to swim nuotare
swimming il nuoto;
swimming pool la piscina
system il sistema

T

table il tạvolo, la tạvola;
coffee table il tavolino
tablecloth la tovạglia
to take prẹndere (*p.p.* preso), portare;
to take a bath (a shower, a walk, a trip, a picture, a break) fare il bagno (la dọccia, una paseggiata, un viạggio, una foto, un pạusa);
to take care curare;
to take a class seguire un corso;
to take an exam dare un esame;
to take part (in) partecipare (a);

to take place avere luogo;

it takes ci vuole, ci vọgliono

to talk parlare;

to talk about parlare di

tall alto

to tan abbronzarsi*

tape recorder il registratore

taste il gusto

tax la tassa

tea il tè

to teach insegnare

teacher il maestro, la maestra

team la squadra

telegram il telegramma

telephone il telẹfono;

telephone book l'elenco telefọnico;

telephone operator il(la) centralinista;

to telephone telefonare

television la televisione;

TV set il televisore;

TV news il telegiornale

to tell dire (*p.p.* detto); raccontare

tenant l'inquilino, l'inquilina

tent la tenda

terrible terrịbile

thank you grạzie;

to thank ringraziare;

thanks to grạzie a

that che; quello;

that is cioè

theater il teatro;

movie theater il cịnema

then allora, poi;

since then da allora

theory la teoria

there là, lì;

there is c'è;

there are ci sono

therefore perciò

thief il ladro, la ladra

thin magro

thing la cosa

to think pensare;

to think of pensare a

thirsty: to be thirsty avere sete

this questo

thought il pensiero

thousand mille, (*pl.*) mila

through attraverso

Thursday il giovedì

ticket il biglietto;

round trip ticket il biglietto di andata e ritorno

tie la cravatta

tight stretto

time il tempo, la volta, l'ora;

it is time è (l')ora di;

to be on time ẹssere in orạrio

timid tịmido

tip la mạncia

tire la gomma;

a flat tire una gomma a terra

to tire stancare, stancarsi*

tired stanco

tiring faticoso

title il tịtolo

to a, in, da

today oggi

together insieme

token il gettone (*for the telephone*)

tomato il pomodoro

tomorrow domani;

the day after tomorrow dopodomani

tonight stasera

too anche;

too much troppo

Too bad! Peccato!

tooth il dente;

toothache mal di denti;

toothbrush lo spazzolino da denti;

toothpaste il dentifrịcio

topic (for a discussion) l'argomento

tour il giro, la gita;

to tour girare;

tour bus il pullman

tourist il (la) turista

towel l'asciugamano

towards verso

tower la torre

town il paese, la città

toy il giocạttolo

trade il mestiere

traffic il trạffico;

traffic light il semạforo

tragedy la tragẹdia

train il treno

to train allenarsi*

tranquil tranquillo

travel il viạggio;

to travel viaggiare;

travel agency l'agenzia di viaggi

traveler il viaggiatore, la viaggiatrice

to treat curare

treatment la cura

tree l'ạlbero

trip il viạggio;

to take a trip fare un viạggio;

Have a good trip! Buon viạggio!

trousers i pantaloni

trout la trota

true vero

truly veramente

trumpet la tromba

trunk il portabagagli

truth la verità

to try cercare di + *inf.*;

to try on provare

T-shirt la maglietta

tub la vasca

Tuesday il martedì

tuition la tassa universitạria

to turn girare;

to turn on accẹndere (*p.p.* acceso);

to turn off spẹgnere (*p.p.* spento)

to type scrịvere a mạcchina

typist il dattilọgrafo, la dattilọgrafa

typewriter la mạcchina da scrịvere

U

ugly brutto
umbrella l'ombrello
uncertain incerto
uncle lo zio
undecided indeciso
under sotto
to understand capire (-isc-)
unemployed disoccupato
unemployment la disoccupazione
unfavorable sfavorẹvole
unfortunately purtroppo
unhappy infelice, scontento
university l'università
unknown sconosciuto
unless a meno che
unlucky sfortunato
unpleasant antipạtico
until (*prep.*) fino a, (*conj.*) finchè
unwillingly malvolentieri
use l'uso;
  to use usare;
  to get used to abituarsi*
useful ụtile
useless inụtile
usual sọlito;
  usually di sọlito;
  as usual come al sọlito

V

vacant lịbero, vuoto
vacation la vacanza
valley la valle
vase il vaso
veal il vitello;
  roast veal arrosto di vitello
vegetables la verdura
Venice Venẹzia
verb il verbo
very molto
victory la vittọria
view la vista
village il villạggio
vineyard la vigna
violin il violino
visit la vịsita;
  to visit visitare, esaminare, andare a trovare
vocabulary il vocabolạrio
voice la voce;
  in a loud voice ad alta voce;
  in a low voice a bassa voce
vote il voto;
  to vote votare
vowel la vocale
voyage il viạggio

W

to wait (for) aspettare
waiter il cameriere
waitress la cameriera
to wake up svegliarsi*
walk la passeggiata;
  to walk andare a piedi, camminare;
  to take a walk fare una passeggiata
wall il muro, la parete
wallet il portafọglio
to want volere
war la guerra
wardrobe l'armạdio
warm caldo
warmly calorosamente
to wash lavare;
  to wash oneself lavarsi*
to waste (time) pẹrdere (tempo)
watch l'orolọgio;
  to watch guardare
water l'ạcqua
way il modo;
  anyway ad ogni modo
weak dẹbole
wealth la ricchezza
to wear mẹttere, mẹttersi*; portare
weather il tempo;
  weather forecast le previsioni del tempo
wedding il matrimọnio
Wednesday il mercoledì
week la settimana
weekend il fine settimana
weight il peso;
  to lose weight dimagrire (-isc-)
welcome benvenuto
well be' (bene);
  to be well stare bene
western occidentale
what? che? che cosa? cosa?
when quando
where dove
wherever dovunque
which quale
while mentre
white bianco
whom, whom che, il quale;
  who; whom? chi?
whoever chiunque
whole tutto;
  the whole day tutto il giorno
whose? di chi?
why perchè
wide largo
wife la mọglie
willingly volentieri
to win vịncere (*p.p.* vinto)
wind il vento
window la finestra, la vetrina (*shop*)
wine il vino
winter l'inverno
wish il desidẹrio, l'augụrio;
  to wish desiderare, augurare;
  I wish vorrei
with con

without senza
witty spiritoso
woman la donna
to wonder domandarsi*
wonderful meraviglioso
wonderfully meravigliosamente
wood il bosco; il legno
wool la lana
word la parola
work il lavoro, l'occupazione (*f.*);
  work of art l'ọpera d'arte;
  to work lavorare
worker l'operạio
world il mondo;
  worldwide mondiale
worry la preoccupazione
to worry preoccupare, preoccuparsi* (di);
  worried preoccupato
to write scrịvere (*p.p.* scritto)
writer lo scrittore, la scrittrice
wrong sbagliato;
  to be wrong avere torto

Y

yawn sbadigliare
year l'anno;
  to be ... years old avere... anni;
  New Year's Day il Capodanno
yellow giallo
yes sì
yesterday ieri;
  the day before yesterday l'altro ieri
yet eppure;
  not yet non ancora
young giọvane;
  young lady signorina;
  young man giovanotto

INDEX

A

E

F

G

H

I

K

L

M

N

O

P

Q

R

S

T

U

V

W

LITERARY AND PHOTO CREDITS

Page 1, Andrew Brilliant; 9, Hugh Rogers/Monkmeyer Press Photo; 10, Andrew Brilliant; 13, Macduff Everton/The Image Works; 15, Catherine Ursillo/Photo Researchers Inc.; 16, Iconos/Explorer/Photo Researchers Inc.; 30, T. Di Girolamo/Marka/Stock, Boston; 31, Stuart Cohen/COMSTOCK; 33, Marka/Stock, Boston; 34, Andrew Brilliant; 35, Margot Granitsas/The Image Works; 47, Peter Menzel/Stock, Boston; 48, C. Dogliani/Marka/Stock, Boston; 51, L. Barbazza/Marka/Stock, Boston; 52, Phyllis Greenberg/COMSTOCK; 53, Jerry Cooke/Photo Researchers Inc.; 54, Greg Meadors/Stock, Boston; 67, Sebastian Cassarino; 62, Stuart Cohen/COMSTOCK; 72, G. Simeone/Marka/Stock, Boston; 73, Adam Tanner/ COMSTOCK; 74, 76, 77, Sebastian Cassarino; 89, Peter Menzel/Stock, Boston; 93, Patrick Montagne/Photo Researchers Inc.; 94, Sebastian Cassarino; 95, Will & Deni McIntyre/Photo Researchers Inc.; 96, C. Seghers/Photo Researchers Inc.; 105, Mario Federici; 108, Hugh Rogers/Monkmeyer Press Photo; 113, Will & Deni McIntyre/Photo Researchers Inc.; 114, Margot Granitsas/The Image Works; 115, Sebastian Cassarino; 128, Akos Szilvasi; 131, Harrison/The Image Works; 132, Andrew Brilliant; 133, Stuart Cohen/COMSTOCK; 134, P. Cipelli/Marka/Stock, Boston; 150, W. Hille/Leo de Wys Inc.; 154, William Katz/Photo Researchers Inc.; 155, D. & J. Heaton/Stock, Boston; 156, P. Picciotto/Marka/Stock, Boston; 157, Gilly Safdeye/Leo de Wys Inc.; 173, T. Conti/Marka/Stock, Boston; 177L, Stuart Cohen/ COMSTOCK; 177R, M. Perelli/Marka/Stock, Boston; 179, T. Conti/Marka/Stock, Boston; 180, Catherine Ursillo/Photo Researchers Inc.; 195, G. Veggi/Photo Researchers Inc.; 198, Mario Federici; 200, Janet Wishnetsky/COMSTOCK; 201, Roberto Koch/Photo Researchers Inc.; 202, Sebastian Cassarino; 203, NEPI LaCucina Italiana, Milan; 205, Franco Galli; 218, Richard Laird/Leo de Wys Inc.; 221, F. Pizzochero/Marka/Stock, Boston; 225, G. Sosio/Marka/Stock, Boston; 226, Pascale/Explorer/Photo Researchers Inc.; 227, G. Sosio/ Marka/Stock, Boston; 233, Mario Federici; 241, Chris Caswell/Photo Researchers Inc.; 247L, Palmer & Brilliant; 247R, Andrew Brilliant; 248, Nicozzi/Gamma-Liaison; 263, "Er compagno scompagno" by Trilussa, reprinted by permission of Arnoldo Mondadori Editori; 265, G. Sosio/Marka/Stock, Boston; 270T, John Ross/Photo Researchers Inc.; 270B, F. Garufi/ Marka/Stock, Boston; 271, Sebastian Cassarino; 272, Mike Mazzaschi/Stock, Boston; 289, Mary Ann Hemphill/Photo Researchers Inc.; 290, M. Cristofori/Marka/Stock, Boston; 291, Sebastian Cassarino; 292, R. Cano/Marka/Stock, Boston; 311, Francesco Scavullo, courtesy of Doubleday Books; 312, S. Ferraris/Marka/Stock, Boston; 313, M. Cristofori/ Marka/Stock, Boston; 314, F. Giaccone/Marka/Stock, Boston; 330, Mike Mazzaschi/Stock, Boston; 332L, Sina/Leo deWys Inc.; 332R, Hartman-Dewitt/ COMSTOCK; 333,335, Jean-Paul Nacivet/Leo de Wys Inc.; 337, Fridmar Damm/Leo de Wys Inc.; 338, Mike Mazzaschi/Stock, Boston; 339, Stuart Cohen/COMSTOCK; 350, Akos Szilvasi/Stock, Boston; 352T, L. Giuliani/ Marka/Stock, Boston; 352M, David Simson/Stock, Boston; 352B, Mike Mazzaschi/Stock, Boston; 356, B. Gatti/Marka/Stock, Boston; 357, Ronny Jacques/Photo Researchers Inc.; 358, Will & Deni McIntyre/Photo Researchers Inc.; 375, Jerry Wachter/Photo Researchers Inc.; 376, Reuters/Bettmann; 377, Bonnie Rauch/Photo Researchers Inc.; 378, Andrew Brilliant; 394, Hugh Rogers/Monkmeyer Press Photo; 399, Andrew Brilliant; 400, Mario Federici; 401, A. Ramella/ Marka/Stock, Boston; 413, F. Giaccone/Marka/Stock, Boston; 419, Berliner/Gamma-Liaison; 420, S. Malli/Marka/Stock, Boston; 421, Hugh Rogers/ Monkmeyer Press Photo; 432, UPI/Bettmann; 434L, Art Resource; 434R, Alinari/Art Resource; 435, Art Resource; 437, M. Perelli/Marka/Stock, Boston.